The Evolutionary Foundations of Economics

It is widely recognized that mainstream economics has failed to translate micro- consistently into macroeconomics and to provide endogenous explanations for the continual changes in the economic system. Since the early 1980s a growing number of economists have been trying to provide answers to these two key questions by applying an evolutionary approach. This new departure has yielded a rich literature with enormous variety, but the unifying principles connecting the various ideas and views presented are, as yet, not apparent. This volume brings together fifteen original articles from scholars – each of whom has made a significant contribution to the field – in their common effort to reconstruct economics as an evolutionary science. Using mesoeconomics as an analytical entity to bridge micro- and macroeconomics as well as static and dynamic realms, a unified economic theory emerges, offering an entirely new approach to the foundations of economics.

KURT DOPFER is Professor of Economics and Director of the Institute of Economics at the University of St Gallen, Switzerland.

The Evolutionary Foundations of Economics

edited by

Kurt Dopfer

CAMBRIDGE
UNIVERSITY PRESS

PUBLISHED BY THE PRESS SYNDICATE OF THE UNIVERSITY OF CAMBRIDGE
The Pitt Building, Trumpington Street, Cambridge, United Kingdom

CAMBRIDGE UNIVERSITY PRESS
The Edinburgh Building, Cambridge, CB2 2RU, UK
40 West 20th Street, New York, NY 10011–4211, USA
477 Williamstown Road, Port Melbourne, VIC 3207, Australia
Ruiz de Alarcón 13, 28014 Madrid, Spain
Dock House, The Waterfront, Cape Town 8001, South Africa

http://www.cambridge.org

First published 2005

Printed in the United Kingdom at the University Press, Cambridge

Typeface Plantin 10/12 pt.   *System* LaTeX 2_ε [TB]

A catalogue record for this book is available from the British Library

ISBN 0 521 62199 2 hardback

Contents

Contributors

ALLEN, PETER M. – Professor of Economics at Cranfield University and Director of the International Ecotechnology Research Centre, Cranfield, United Kingdom.

CHEN, PING – Research Fellow at the Ilya Prigogine Center for Studies in Statistical Mechanics and Complex Systems, the University of Texas at Austin, Austin, Texas, United States.

DAVID, PAUL A. – Professor of Economics at Stanford University, Stanford, California, United States, and at the University of Oxford, All Souls College, Oxford, United Kingdom.

DOPFER, KURT – Professor of Economics at the University of St Gallen, Director of the Institute of Economics (FGN), St Gallen, Switzerland.

DOSI, GIOVANNI – Professor of Economics at the St Anna School of Advanced Studies, Laboratory of Economics and Management (LEM), Pisa, Italy.

FAGIOLO, GIORGIO – Professor of Economics at the St Anna School of Advanced Studies, LEM, Pisa, Italy.

FOSTER, JOHN – Professor of Economics at the University of Queensland, Brisbane, Australia.

HAKEN, HERMANN – Professor of Physics at the Institute for Theoretical Physics, Center for Synergetics, University of Stuttgart, Stuttgart, Germany.

HODGSON, GEOFFREY M. – Professor of Economics at the University of Hertfordshire Business School, Hertford, United Kingdom.

MARENGO, LUIGI – Professor of Economics at the University of Trento, Trento, Italy.

METCALFE, J. STANLEY – Professor of Economics at the University of Manchester, Director of the Centre for Research on Innovation and Competition (CRIC), Manchester, United Kingdom.

MOKYR, JOEL – Professor of Economics at Northwestern University, Evanston, Illinois, United States.

NELSON, RICHARD R. – George Blumenthal Professor of International and Public Affairs and Henry R. Luce Professor of International Political Economy at Columbia University, New York, United States.

PRIGOGINE, ILYA – Professor of Physics at the International Solvay Institutes at the Université Libre de Bruxelles, Brussels, Belgium, and Director of the Ilya Prigogine Center for Studies in Statistical Mechanics and Complex Systems, The University of Texas at Austin, Austin, Texas, United States (deceased).

SILVERBERG, GERALD – Professor of Economics at Maastricht University, Maastricht Economic Research Institute on Innovation and Technology (MERIT), Maastricht, the Netherlands.

SIMON, HERBERT A. – Professor of Economics, Carnegie Mellon University, Pittsburgh, Pennsylvania, United States (deceased).

VERSPAGEN, BART – Research Fellow at the Eindhoven Centre for Innovation Studies (ECIS), Eindhoven University of Technology, Maastricht, the Netherlands.

WINTER, SIDNEY G. – Professor of Economics at the Wharton School of the University of Pennsylvania, Philadelphia, Pennsylvania, United States.

WITT, ULRICH – Professor of Economics at the University of Jena and Director of the Max Planck Institute for Research into Economic Systems, Evolutionary Economics Group, Jena, Germany.

Figures

Tables

Prolegomenon

1   Evolutionary economics: a theoretical framework

Kurt Dopfer

1   Introduction

The last two decades have seen an explosion of research in economics inspired by evolutionary thinking. There has been an upsurge in the number of publications addressing evolutionary themes, paralleled by the foundation of new journals and new academic societies devoted to the subject matter. Heterodox contributions in themselves do not yet signal any extraordinary event; in fact, the ongoing challenge of the received view is part and parcel of the theoretical discourse of any 'normal' science. What gives the recent advances in this field – grouped loosely under the heading 'evolutionary economics' – their distinct hallmark are the rapid pace and persistent power of the underlying intellectual dynamic. The 1982 book by Richard Nelson and Sydney Winter on *An Evolutionary Theory of Economic Change* has served as an ice-breaker that arguably gave the early process its critical momentum. In their contributions to this volume, these authors address one of the core issues of evolutionary economics: the change of economic knowledge as it applies to technology and production.

What are the factors that may conceivably account for the present dynamism of evolutionary economics? We get a first hint when we consider that, in their field of study, orthodox economists encounter decreasing marginal returns with respect to new theoretical findings per additional unit of research effort or research time. Linking this with the conjecture that creative minds are attracted by new opportunities for developing their theory enables us to obtain a hypothesis that accounts for the phenomenon that outstanding neoclassical economists are increasingly turning to research areas that can be linked to evolutionary ideas.

Another explanation for this extraordinary dynamism relates to the particular meaning associated with the notion of evolution. In a nutshell, an evolutionary approach addresses foundational issues: it invites not only an exploration of new theoretical vistas but also a rethinking of the paradigmatic-ontological premises on which these are based. Other heterodox approaches differentiate themselves primarily at a less abstract theoretical level. A key aspect of the economic world is usually singled out and used to designate its subject matter. For instance, institutional economics builds its explanations around the notion of institution, and Keynes' legacy provides the hallmark of Keynesian macroeconomics. Evolutionary economics can also be stated in terms of distinct theoretical areas and, in its various theoretical extensions, is linked to specific precursors. In addition, however, the notion of evolution transcends the plane of the theoretical discourse and features criteria that, on the basis of paradigmatic-ontological distinctions, mark the boundaries of the various research areas.

As a consequence, the notional distinction between 'evolutionary' and 'non-evolutionary' runs through the various theoretical approaches and reassembles them with regard to their paradigmatic foundations. Institutional economics, for instance, is divided into an original 'old' branch, in which evolutionary ideas play a paradigmatic role, and a more recent 'new' branch, which lacks a comparable paradigmatic orientation. Analogously, a paradigmatic borderline can be drawn between the hydraulic version of Keynesianism (its neoclassical or 'new' synthesis) and post-Keynesian approaches with notions of radical uncertainty, non-equilibrium, etc. that are linked with evolutionary thinking. In fact, the paradigmatic divide also runs through the field of evolutionary economics itself; some of the theoretical works address evolutionary themes but are still rooted in mechanistic-physicalist thinking. Borderline disputes have emerged about whether the theoretical works of, for example, evolutionary game theory or of equilibrium-based endogenous growth theory satisfy the above-mentioned criteria of the field.

In the following we take the view that evolutionary economics is defined not only by a range of theoretical themes but also by distinct paradigmatic-ontological foundations. This volume brings together contributions by eighteen scholars, each of whom is a pioneer in his field, that address the issue of the nature of the *evolutionary* – as distinct from non-evolutionary – foundations of the science of economics.

2   A posteriori ontology

The view that a valid economic theory requires the explication of its paradigmatic-ontological foundations is not generally accepted. Economists whose allegiance is positivist argue that there is a direct link from empirical observation to theoretical statements and that any reference to foundational statements would blur the objectivity of the process of theory formation, or, at best, would be superfluous. We may concede that this is a reasonable view to start with, and that any alternative contention must furnish plausible arguments against it. Any theory or coherent set of hypotheses (H) represents, in its bare bones, a generalization of a designated range of particular real phenomena (R). The methodological step from the inspection of many individual cases to a general statement in its widest sense represents the process of *induction*. The inductive procedure is employed in the process of both hypothesis generation and hypothesis testing. The inductive inspection of reality thus occurs both before and after the generalization and this yields the schema R-H-R for the entire process of theory formation. A methodological battle has been waged over the issue of whether the primary inferential procedure should be from R to H or from H to R. The *Wiener Kreis* adherents of positivism advocated the inferential procedure R-H, while theoreticians of science led by Karl Popper objected to this inferential route and disapproved of its confirmatory bias. Although this *Methodenstreit* lasted a long time, it should be apparent from the suggested R-H-R schema that verificationism and falsificationism are simply two sides of the same inferential coin. Verification (as a hypothetical claim) is *ex ante* induction, falsification is *ex post* induction. What remains in limbo on this methodological plane, however, is the more basic issue of whether theoretical induction – *ex ante* or *ex post* – meets all the criteria needed to arrive at valid theoretical statements.

The positivist canon presumes that scientists have an innate ability to practise their *métier* in an objective fashion. Scientists are presumably equipped with an inherited set of rules that a priori allows them to arrive at valid scientific statements. Historians of science, however, have provided a substantial body of evidence that demonstrates that the rules scientists employ in their practice change over time and that ontological beliefs and perceptions about which problems are relevant or which methodological standards are acceptable may differ substantially from one 'scientific community' to another. There is no objective a priori base for theory formation. Thomas Kuhn has argued that members of a scientific community are united by a specific '*paradigm*' and in their scientific practice rely on a '*disciplinary matrix*' that provides '*exemplars*' that mark its nature and signal its boundaries. In an analogous vein, Imre Lakatos has argued that scientists always work within a '*scientific research program*' the '*hard core*' of which they defend with an armoury of 'positive heuristics' and 'negative heuristics'. In the positivist agenda the set of rules is constant, and its influence on the inferential procedure can, like a constant in a mathematical equation, be neglected without further consequences. Once we accept the possibility of different rules, we have to explicitly recognize the formative power of a deductive component in the inferential process. The issue subsequently is not whether we accept the notion of a paradigmatic core in the inferential procedure but rather which criteria we can furnish that suggest its validity. What are the procedures that allow us to arrive at a scientifically acceptable paradigmatic core?

There are basically two methodological routes: the a priori and the a posteriori. The former belongs to metaphysics, but, interestingly, scientists also take an a priori posture when it comes to the issue of paradigm or central research questions. In his later writing, Karl Popper explicitly acknowledged the paradigmatic significance of the idea of evolution, but he argued that it was ultimately rooted in metaphysics. Science, by its own codex, cannot, however, rely on an a priori stance; it is bound to take an a posteriori one. Deductive schemes, such as paradigms and research programmes, represent the most abstract views about the status of reality. In philosophical terms, the paradigmatic core comprises a set of *ontological* statements. Given its empirical nature, the paradigmatic core of a scientific theory must be derived with the same methodological rigour as the statements of the theory itself. Hence we suggest applying the standard channel of induction also to the inferential procedure that deals with the paradigmatic-ontological foundation of a theory. This metatheoretical inference can be called *paradigmatic induction*.

Induction builds on many observed or conjectured individual cases. In theory formation the inductive base is associated with a statistical data set of individual observations defined by a particular discipline. In its paradigmatic application the inductive range must encompass all individual cases of all scientific disciplines. Paradigmatic induction does not aim to reach generalization about a (theoretically defined) class of real phenomena. In fact, its focus is 'all' reality – the unity that all existences share: its *ontological* status. As humans we are, of course, not equipped with lenses that would allow us to inspect all statistically significant individual cases; but carrying out this Herculean task is not required to enable us to arrive at reasonable inductive conclusions. Paradigmatic induction essentially means opening up an intellectual discourse between philosophy and science and, within the boundaries of the latter, between the various disciplines. Modern early twentieth-century philosophy under the leadership of Charles Peirce, Alfred North Whitehead and Henri Bergson made a substantial effort to put ontology on a scientific basis. Similarly, scientists of various disciplines have contemplated their own scientific findings and have arrived at conclusions for a reconstructing ontology on a posteriori grounds. In their contributions to this volume Ilya Prigogine and Hermann Haken discuss some of the implications that major advances in modern physics have had on our world-view. Geoffrey Hodgson and Herbert Simon, in their contributions, explore the relationship between economics and biology, and, by so doing, discover their common onto-logical ground. The following discussion – for which the contributions of this volume have been an indispensable source of inspiration – represents a preliminary attempt to arrive at a set of ontological statements.

3   The legacy of mechanical thinking

In the age of enlightenment Isaac Newton saw the universe as a vast space in which the stars and planets – following eternal laws – moved with clock-work precision. Carolus Linnaeus charted the natural world of minerals, plants, animals and man using a taxonomy that posited all entities in ascending order of casually observed complexity. The scientific advances were paralleled by radical societal changes propelled by political and tech-nological revolutions. The European *ancien régimes*, with their autocratic rule, guild order, regulated earnings and regulated prices, broke down and gave way to freedom of trade and a dynamic market economy. Technical inventions, such as the steam engine and the mechanical loom, paved the way for economic growth and structural change unprecedented in human history.

These societal developments were partly the outcome of the advances in the natural sciences, but they themselves also called for a scientific explanation, leading in the second half of the eighteenth century to the birth of modern economics (then called political economy). From the very beginning, the natural sciences served as a paradigmatic archetype for the young science. The theoretical objectives were, on the one hand, to detect the invisible law (or 'hand') that governed the *coordination* of many individual economic actions, and, on the other hand, to establish the *laws of motion* that determined the long-run pace and distribution of the aggregate resources' magnitudes. Adam Smith's work has gener-ally been associated with the first of these two grand questions, that of David Ricardo and Thomas Robert Malthus, and later Karl Marx, with the second. The classical economists employed a broad scope and they enriched their analyses with many empirical details. In retrospect, their writings appear to us as typically interdisciplinary. This intellectual basis itself suggests that the classicals did not take a narrow mechanistic view or use reductionist modelling. This was particularly apparent in those cases where the factor of economic knowledge played a major role, as in Smith's analysis of the division of labour in the economy and in the firm. But, precisely because their scope was interdisciplinary, they also obtained major inspiration from Newtonian physics.

The birth of what in recent decades has been called 'modern eco-nomics' came with *neoclassical economics* in the second half of the nineteenth century. The economists of that period criticized their classical precursors for having worked with aggregate magnitudes and for having assumed an 'objectivity' for the economic process that, in their view, it simply could not have. They challenged the tenet of an objective law that would determine the developmental pace and the distribution between the economic aggregates. They suggested looking at the individuals and reconstructing economics on the basis of a better understanding of human cognition and behaviour. If there was a value theory that could explain market coordination and solve the *Smith problem* – the major, and for a long time the only, research interest of the neoclassicals – then it was a subjective one. It seemed that the focus on the individual would open a new, subjective (subject-related) chapter in economics, but the opposite was the case. The neoclassicals criticized the classical economists not for having used invariant laws as such but only for having looked for them in the wrong places. As for the nature of the laws, the neoclassicals wanted to outdo their precursors by introducing mathematics (basically, Newton's calculus) and called for the utmost formal rigour and precision. Mechanics became, to echo Alfred Marshall's dictum, the Mecca of economics. At that time it was probably not entirely recognized that the method also brought with it an *ontology*. To reduce the subject character of the individual to its mechanical properties was, in any case, bold. Hermann Gossen, Léon Walras, Henry Jevons, Vilfredo Pareto and others frequently used mechanical analogies and metaphors. Hodgson's contribution in this volume discusses the use of mechanical analogies and metaphors in economics from the 1880s to the present day and shows how and why biology, the other potential Mecca of economics, has still largely been ignored. In his contribution Sydney Winter describes the turn from the classical distribution theory to the neoclassical marginalist production function, and the appearance of the mechanistic paradigm in the modern works of linear programming and activity analysis.

A major contribution to the philosophical foundations of the classical paradigm was made by René Descartes. Ilya Prigogine recalls in his contribution the essence and influence of *Cartesian dualism*, stating that 'on one side there was matter, "res extensa", described by deterministic laws, while on the other there was "res cogitans", associated with the human mind. It was accepted that there was *a fundamental distinction* between the physical world and the spiritual – the world of human values.' The corporeal things – all physical and biological phenomena – were visible, definable and measurable in terms of shape, size or motion; they made up the 'hard' side of reality. The incorporeal entities – comprising conscious experience, thinking, ideas, mind, imagination, information, creativity and the soul – were invisible, unextended and incomprehensible and outside the numerical scale of time and space; these made up the 'soft' side of reality. Cartesian dualism, as Prigogine and Ping Chen both point out, went with the important implication that only the 'hard' part of reality was considered to be amenable to scientific inquiry, empirical scrutiny and theory construction. The 'soft' side lacked object character, hence 'objectivity', and consequently fell outside the domain of science; that side contained the stuff from which the *arts* were made. The classical sciences, such as physics, biology and – arguably – economics, were at their very philosophical core designed to be *hard sciences*.

What was the ontological nature of the objects that the hard sciences dealt with? One interpretation of the classical canon that was around the corner would seem to be: matter-energy. However, this interpretation is only half right, and therefore particularly misleading. Descartes had proposed mathematizing science, and, if the job of science was not merely to provide an enumeration of scaled and measured facts, this implied that there was some generality inherent in the objects. Dualism between corporeal and incorporeal things did not preclude some members of the former sharing a common property. This position was also basically that of Aristotle, who proposed that all things had two properties: an essential property and an accidental property. The essential denoted a general property of a thing, the accidental its individual concretization. In this categorization Aristotle left room for Plato's view that the essential had to be associated with some perfect idea, and the individual cases with its imperfect concretizations. Descartes rejected Plato's idealism, and endorsed the modern view that all objects follow a law. This left metaphysics behind, and was a step towards constructing modern science. Nevertheless, its fundamental ontological message was still the same: the property or the behavioural mode of matter-energy – the *essential property* expounded by a *law* – does *not change*.

The statement that an object follows a law involves the assumption that there is some *informant agency* that makes an object behave in a certain way and not in any other way. The term 'informant' here conveys the idea that a 'form' is 'in' an object. At this point this has no causal or information-theoretic significance, but simply means that there is something that occurs in a certain way and not in any other way. If there is only one informant agency for all objects of a kind in all time, we call it a *law*, as understood in the classical sciences. If the informant agency changes over time, we cannot speak accordingly of a law in the classical sense. A statement of difference between informant agencies requires that the nature of the informant agencies compared be specified. We call this specification of an informant agency *idea*. A set of ideas allows us to distinguish between objects on the basis of different informant agencies, or, in classical terms, laws. The classical sciences assume a single universal law, and we do not require the notion of 'idea' to denote a difference between informant agencies. All differences can be stated in terms of their physical actualization of the objects and can be measured exclusively in quantities. It should be noted that here we have a language for talking about change and non-change, but still do not have any causal hint or explanation for these phenomena.

In Newtonian physics the objects are composed of matter with mass that has gravitational force. Every object or body continues in its uniform motion, or its state of rest, unless it is compelled to change that state when forces act upon it. Not only is Newton's gravity law unchanging; the events the law describes also do not change endogenously unless an exogenous force is introduced into the system. The model is *universally deterministic*. Given complete information about the initial and subsidiary conditions, the law allows us to retrodict events precisely on to the past and to predict them to precisely on to the future. The law holds for all bodies, independent of the quantity of their mass, weight or size. For instance, starting from the same height (in a vacuum) a body weighing 1 kilogram will fall with the same speed as one of 10 kilograms. Small bodies can be aggregated into a large body, but aggregation will not change the informant agency of the small bodies.

The power of the Newtonian model is particularly apparent in those cases where it has served as a paradigmatic cornerstone when theoretical discussions were carried into new areas of the discipline. Prigogine and Haken discuss the case of thermodynamics in the mid-nineteenth century, and demonstrate the particular role that the Newtonian model played in its development. Practical work with steam engines and experiments have shown that initial temperature differences between ensembles of particles tend to become zero or to converge over time to a thermodynamic equilibrium. There is a general tendency of a thermodynamic ensemble (in a closed system) for its potential – i.e. its free energy – to tend towards a minimum or maximum entropy respectively. This thermodynamic property can be given an informational twist. The initial relative motions of the particles can be conceived of as a *structure*, and then the informational quality of the dynamics can be interpreted as an irreversible process *from order to chaos* (chaos here denoting simply non-order, without the predictive connotation of the chaos models). A piece of wood that is completely burned up would be an example of entropy conceived of as informational decay.

The concept of 'structure' invites the conjecture that there may be some law that appertains not to its individual particles but to the ensemble *as a whole*. We could assume, for instance, that, under certain thermodynamic conditions, the particles change their behavioural mode spontaneously and lead to a de-structuring of the whole that, in turn, feeds back to the individual particles, causing them to behave in a way that reinforces that structural decay. This is precisely the way Prigogine and Haken have developed their non-classical models of thermodynamics that explain structure and evolutionary change. In the present case the non-classical thermodynamic model would not explain the self-organization of order but rather the self-organization of chaos. There is no such theory available in thermodynamics (in fact, there is none that explains entropy rather than describing it statistically), but the essential point to get across here is that such a *non-classical* view would open up new vistas for a *macroscopic* interpretation of the laws of thermodynamics. In their contributions Prigogine and Haken show how nineteenth-century physics turned to Newtonian physics in trying to explain the behaviour of a thermodynamic ensemble on the basis of a description of the individual trajectories of the particles. The whole of the ensemble could be constructed as an aggregate of individual particles, and from that, in turn, the individual behaviour of the particles could be computed in a disaggregating fashion.

The theoretical statement about the whole in terms of its parts required assigning an invariant informant agency – the classical law – to each of them, thus precluding the introduction of ideas that would have been required for locating the position of the parts within the whole. This approach, pioneered by Ludwig Boltzmann, went a long way; but it had its limitations. Probability distributions and statistical averages, used in classical thermodynamics for computational convenience, could serve the purpose for describing structural decay (entropy), but were bound to fail when it came to a theoretical statement about the *self-organization* of structure and its *evolutionary* dynamics. Non-classical thermodynamics, as pioneered by Prigogine and Haken, shows that, under certain thermodynamic conditions, macroscopic structures – for example, dissipative and synergetic structures – emerge and that the dynamic of an ensemble is characterized by order through fluctuations, phase transitions and cascades of bifurcations, leading to the continuity of evolution. The advances in non-classical thermodynamics indicate that the *Newtonian* model denotes a *special* case rather than a general one. Irreversibility and time asymmetry play an important role, and – as Prigogine says – 'what we need are not approximations to the existing laws of nature, but an extension of these laws to include irreversibility. . . . [L]aws of nature no longer express certitudes, but "possibilities".' To the extent that a paradigm calls for *generality*, Newtonian physics and classical thermodynamics do not provide appropriate guidance for devising an empirically warranted paradigm.

At this point it seems useful to summarize the characteristics of the classical, or metaphorically, mechanical paradigm, since it shows up as a major competitor to an evolutionary one. A paradigm comprises a set of ontological statements, and the ambitious venture that goes with its construction calls for an appropriate methodological path. We propose to state the ontological essence of a paradigm in terms of *axioms*. Ontological statements refer to the status of reality, and, in this general sense, are considered to be the last deductive recourse. This in itself, however, does not warrant their acceptance. We have previously called for an inductive path to warrant ontological statements and have argued that they must be 'worth' (in Greek '*axio*') being considered as such statements. Ontological statements are, therefore, unchallenged not only because they are the last instance on a deductive ladder but also because we consider their *empirical* validity as being *worthy*. Axioms are frequently used in mathematics, but there the criterion of validity is formal-analytical adequacy. Ontological statements are – as *empirical axioms* – fallible, and by their nature tentative.

The *first axiom* of a mechanistic paradigm recognizes that reality refers to a 'hard' entity as being composed of matter-energy. Its behaviour is informed by an invariant law. There are no ideas employed to denote an essential distinction between objects. A *second axiom* recognizes that entities are mutually independent in the use of their invariant information. An individual entity does not change its behavioural mode by enriching its informant agency with ideas from other entities, nor does it offer any export of information. The law is valid in an isolated way for each particle; individual entities do not associate in a structure. Finally, a *third axiom* of a mechanistic paradigm recognizes that there is no endogenous change in the system. As axiom 2 states that there is no structure, so axiom 3 states that there is no change of structure, or, alternatively, no process defined as change of structure. In the system there is only continuity of motion (dynamics) or rest (statics); there is no self-caused spontaneous change from within the system.

4   Towards an evolutionary ontology

The publication of *On The Origin of Species* by Charles Darwin in 1859 set off a paradigmatic earthquake in the sciences, and to some degree in society at large. Classical biology had assumed species to be given and immutable, and, in fact, the Greek word *eidos* was also translated by the word 'species'. When a learned biologist talked about species, the language used meant that it would already be associated with something unchangeable. The *immutability* of species was the undisputed canon of classical biology. To use the word 'origin' in connection with the word 'species', as Darwin did in the title of his book, was in itself an enormous provocation. The doctrine of immutability was associated with the view of God as a 'watchmaker', so that Darwin was ultimately shaking the foundations of the entire creationist canon.

Darwin's theory was built, essentially, on three facts and a simple conclusion. One fact was that organisms vary, and these varied traits are inherited by their offspring. Linnaeus' *Philosophia Botanica* had already provided overwhelming evidence for the perennial variety of life. To this fact Darwin added a conjecture that signalled the possibility of an important further fact: variety changes over time. There is *variation*. The traits of organisms are mutable. The third fact was that organisms produce more offspring than can possibly survive. Any child who learned that kittens were killed because the household was unable to accommodate them all got a practical demonstration of the consequences of superfecundity operating in a finite environment. To some extent, these facts were quite obvious, and Darwin's genius was to see the significance of the obvious with regard to the formulation of an acceptable theory.

An immediate conclusion was that there had to be some 'mechanism' that brought the population of a species into balance with its habitat's space and food supply. Which variations would be inherited by the offspring of organisms or species? The hypothesis of chance was readily available, but Darwin provided a plausible explanation. To survive, organisms must be *adapted* to their environment. As organisms vary over time, the conditions of the environment – defined as a complex of relations among organisms and the nature surrounding them – alters continuously. The organisms have to adapt to the continuously altering conditions of their environment, and the term 'adaptation' had to be given a *dynamic* meaning. From here, it was only a small step to the central theoretical tenet that variations that were in any degree profitable to an individual of any species would tend to result in the *preservation* of that individual and, generally, be *inherited* by its offspring. In looking for a good name for this insight, Darwin turned to the practice of artificial selection designed to adapt organic beings to human uses through the accumulation of slight but useful variations. Applying an analogy, Darwin called the principle by which slight variations, if useful, are preserved *natural selection*.

Historians of science have drawn attention to a remark that Darwin made in one of his *Notebooks*; he said that he got his flash of inspiration for the selection principle when reading Malthus' *Essay on the Principle of Population*. Malthus argued that an extension of cultivated land, or some technical improvement, would increase the food supply, and that would consequently lead to an increase in the fertility rate and population. This would, in turn, decrease the per capita food supply and so prompt a subsequent decrease in the fertility rate and, possibly, an increase in the mortality rate of the population, bringing the system back to its original subsistence equilibrium. This cycle recurred over time, but, in view of the fact that resources are finite, it would finally collapse in a – 'dismal' – secular stabilized subsistence equilibrium. The demonstration of the inevitability of the events brought about by this mechanism may well have produced the spark in Darwin's thinking.

Malthus was probably the first to demonstrate the power of feedback, which is a further instance that suggests that any interpretation of classical economics as a simple Newtonian model would be misplaced. Having referred to its sophistication, it is all the more revealing to look at the remaining differences between the two models. Malthus had operated with aggregate magnitudes, arguing that the average rates of change of total food supply and total food demand (defined as number of population times average consumption) would determine the long-run development of an economy. Malthus did not allow for any variation in the general exposition of his work, and consequently did not pursue theoretical studies into the issues of adaptation and selection further. Selection was in Malthus' – in this sense 'mechanistic' – model 'selection in the aggregate', while for Darwin selection based on *variety and differential adaptation* was the central building block of his theory.

Darwin gave no adequate explanation for mutation and variation; his theory was pre-Mendelian. The body of Darwinian theory was, in principle, accepted in biology from the onset on, but the 'classical' questions relating to the nature of given life – or, in an Aristotelian metaphor, of the 'chain of being' – still dominated the agenda for decades. Hodgson argues in his contribution that the neo-Darwinian synthesis in biology – a synthesis between the theory of selection and Mendelian genetics – did not make its appearance as a new paradigm of biology until the 1940s, although the elements of this synthesis had been in place long before this. Turning to the more recent period, Hodgson remarks that '(t)he post-war "evolutionary synthesis" gave the Darwinian idea of natural selection a renewed vitality that has continued to this day'.

Darwin's thought challenged major ontological positions of the classical doctrine. *Variety* went with the notion that there are many individuals of a kind, where each constitutes an actualization of a distinct idea. There are, on the one hand, many individuals that are many matter-energy actualizations, and, on the other hand, many ideas that can be actualized. In biology, the former concept is considered to represent a population, the latter concept a gene pool. The notion of a distinct phenotype overthrows the classical notion of a single informant agency that yields homologous actualizations. The evolutionary concept of variety presumes a *fuzziness of ideas* with respect to the actualizations of a kind. As J. Stanley Metcalfe points out in his contribution, variety contradicts typological thinking, which is concerned with a uniform law, ideal types and the essence of existences. By contrast, variety calls for population thinking where 'the focus of attention is on the variety of characteristics within the population and, *pace* typological thinking, variety is not a nuisance that hides the underlying reality; rather, it is the distribution of variety that is the reality and that is the prerequisite for evolutionary change'.

Mutation or *variation* is change in variety. While variation contradicts the law of uniformity at a particular time, mutation contradicts its universal application over time. Newton stated the law of endogenous continuity, Darwin that of *endogenous discontinuity*.

Adaptation means that entities relate to each other in a specific, *informationally non-arbitrary* way. This contradicts the classical law for an isolated informant agency, which holds that relations among bodies are determined by invariant physical parameters of mass and force.

Selection means that not all relations can exist, and it introduces an instance that determines the future existence and future non-existence of an actualized entity. The creation and collapse of matter do not correspond at all to Newtonian laws. As a corollary of adaptation, selection is inconsistent with the demands of the classical model. Selection defines the 'relative existence' of the relations among individual entities in *non-arbitrary directions*.

Retention refers to a law that describes the continuation of something. Retention circumscribed in this unspecified way is identical with the law of continuity in classical physics. However, in contrast to Newtonian or thermodynamic notions, Darwinian retention describes a continuity that has an *endogenous origin*. Retention originates from a process of mutation and selection, and describes the powers required to maintain the selected informant variant over time. A system can be said to be *stable* if these powers are not challenged by those of renewed mutation and selection. Since in the model this possibility is explicitly assumed, the stability of the system is permanently threatened, and, using a term introduced by Prigogine, Haken and Chen in their contributions, the system can be said to be *meta-stable*.

The ontological nature of the Darwinian propositions stated in the language of classical science can be summarized as follows:
1. Variety: law of informational fuzziness;
2. Mutation: law of discontinuity;
3. Adaptation: law of relations;
4. Selection: law of direction;
5. Retention: law of meta-stability.

The non-classical laws so defined provide the essential building blocks for an evolutionary theory. Methodologically, the notion of a 'law' is usually associated with a nomological statement, which typically relies on the assumptions of invariancy and time symmetry. The non-classical laws just mentioned, however, have nothing that is inherently nomological. In fact, viewed from a non-classical stance, they turn reality upside down. Looked at through evolutionary lenses, we see a world of continuous change and creative advance that incessantly unfolds into new forms. This process is inherently *historical*. Evolutionary theory is principally a *historical theory*. By a historical (economic) theory we mean one that makes theoretical statements about the *historicity* of (economic) phenomena. A historical theory differs from historical analysis in that it generalizes and, unlike historical analysis, does not attempt to provide an exhaustive account of all details of a time- or space-specific singular case. During the process of generalization a historical theory employs criteria such as irreversibility, non-ergodicity, non-repeatability, non-periodicity or path dependence. It discusses laws (nomo-) that allow for the historicity (histor-) of real phenomena, and, to give the child a name, we can call such statements *histonomic* ones (thus avoiding the tongue-twister 'histor-o-nomic'). This neologism allows us to address the subject matter in its general nature without making inadequate references to the specific terms. It demonstrates the power of the classical canon that we do not yet have an accepted *non*-classical counterpart for the term 'nomological'. In their contributions Joel Mokyr and Paul David attempt to highlight the role economic history could play in the *histonomic reconstruction* of economics.

The succession of the above-mentioned Darwinian laws marks the 'logic of history' of an evolutionary process. Starting with variation, mutation, for instance, precedes selection, and selection precedes retention. There is a synchronicity in the operations of the various laws, but the sequential dependence of the evolutionary process is essentially *directed* and *irreversibly* 'locked in'. On various occasions in their contributions Richard Nelson, Peter Allen, Metcalfe, Ulrich Witt, and Gerald Silverberg and Bart Verspagen draw attention to the historical logic of economic evolution, and stress in particular the role that innovation plays as a necessary causal antecedent for selection and related processes.

The entire sequence from (1) to (5) can be conceived of as an *evolutionary regime*. Evolution occurs as one or more *transition*s from one regime to another. The analytical unit of change is a regime transition defined as a process that occurs from (5) to (2). The case of non-change or meta-stability is given by the link between (5) and (1). Change has as its starting point a meta-stable variety (1), and represents a transformation from this into a new variation pattern brought about by (2). This change works out along the phases of the evolutionary regime, and settles down in a new variation regime at (5).

The explanatory principles or non-classical laws stated are derived from Darwin's model. Other principles or laws are conceivable. We will later suggest a homologous schema that differs slightly in its theoretical specification; it will be constructed for the purpose of theory making in economics. Furthermore, we shall briefly discuss the criteria of validity and practicability when devising such master schemes for the explanation of change. At this juncture let us first briefly conclude with a statement about a set of empirical axioms of an evolutionary ontology.

Axiom 1 recognizes that all real phenomena are *physical actualizations of information*, or, equivalently, *information actualized as matter-energy*. It rejects the Cartesian separation of the ontic categories of matter-energy and information and its correlates. There is a necessary *bimodality* in the *actualization* of all real phenomena. Axiom 1 excludes a Platonic view. By way of an example, Darwin's phenotype is not an actualization of a pre-given 'idea' (in Plato's sense); the idea comes into being with the existence of that phenotype. The 'average idea' results from many existing phenotypes, and cannot be obtained in any other way. Furthermore, with no a priori idea in the first place, there can also be no a priori 'perfect idea'. A monistic materialistic position fails similarly, since the *variety* in the *informant agencies* call for a recognition of idea, if not for ontological reasons then for operational ones.

Axiom 2 recognizes existences as *relations* and *connections*. Relations are conceived to be between *ideas* ('idea' used in an ontological, not an epistemological, sense). *Relations* constitute *information* – more precisely (and in contradistinction to Shannon's notion) *semantic information*. The informant agency is hence not specified as a 'law' (a single idea) but as *informational relations*. Matter-energy entities – as 'carriers' of information – are seen as being *connected* with each other. Physical connections extend and can be scaled in space. Informational relations and physical connections are two aspects that, together, are viewed as constituting *associations*. We call the ensemble of associations of an entity its *structure*. The distinction between informational relations and physical connections will be important when returning to the '*deep*' and '*surface*' levels of the macro-domain of an economic system.

Axiom 3 recognizes existences as *process*. A process is conceived of as *associations* or as *structure in time*. Following axiom 2, relations constitute (semantically distinct) *information*. Actualized as *process*, information represents *knowledge*. Knowledge is, hence, information self-maintained by an entity in time. Processes can be in either of two primitive states: the states of *repeating* and *non-repeating* associations or structure. The endogeneity of the states presumes that processes are *self-caused or spontaneous*. The power of self-causation or spontaneity exists simultaneously on both levels of associations (parts) or structure (whole) – on that of *informed relations* and that of *connected matter-energy particles*.

In a nutshell, the three axioms are:

Axiom 1: **Bimodality axiom**
> Existences are bimodal actualizations of matter-energy and information;

Axiom 2: **Association axiom**
> Existences are structured in informational relations and matter-energy connections;

Axiom 3: **Process axiom**
> Existences are processes in time, structured as knowledge.

5   Analytical language

A young discipline, such as evolutionary economics, suffers from a *language deficit*. Language allows us to provide terms for the reality under investigation, and agreement on the terms enables communication. A language deficit is a handicap both for theoretical expression and for its communication. Existing language offers us an enormous pool of linguistic terms, and the general problem is not to invent new ones but, rather, to specify their semantic content in our context. In the present case, that context is defined by the theory employed – specifically, by evolutionary economic theory. Language must be adapted to express and communicate the theoretical content of this disciplinary context. We have seen that non-classical physics and, particularly, evolutionary biology offer us a rich source of terms. There is no reason why economists should reinvent the wheel rather than tap this source. The problem is that these terms designate theoretical contents that relate specifically to physics and to biology, and not to economics. It would not be permissible to transfer their theoretical content along with these terms, as if we were simply riding the same horse along a common disciplinary road. The terms must therefore undergo a process of *theoretical decontextualization*. This means that we must distinguish between a general meaning of a term and a specific meaning. The general meaning used in biology can be, for instance, evolution, selection or population, and the specific meaning can be biological evolution, biological selection or biological population, or, used in economics, can be economic evolution, economic selection or economic population. We call the general meaning of terms *analytical* terms. We arrive at analytical terms by theoretical decontextualization, and obtain theoretical terms, in turn, by the theoretical *recontextualization* of analytical terms.

In this procedure, the *validity* of the analytical terms is of paramount importance. Analytical terms are not valid by virtue of their theoretical decontextualization alone. We may wish to accept the general content of analytical terms only if it is obtained a posteriori. Validity then depends essentially on the process of paradigmatic induction (see chapter 2). In brief, analytical terms must have *ontological validity*. Therefore, appropriate analytical terms must meet these two conditions: that they are ontologically warranted, and that they are general and can be employed in all theories.

It is important to recognize that when we talk about the general meaning of a term we always associate it with some ontological content. Generality, and the ontological content it carries, may come in different guises. It may be expressed, for instance, as a set of conditions that must be met if generality is to be assumed. Metcalfe highlights the generality of the term 'evolution' in this way, arguing '(t)hat evolution is a core concept in biology does not mean that it is an inherently biological concept. Evolution can happen in other domains provided that the conditions for an evolutionary process are in place.' Similarly, in his contribution David discusses various *histonomic* terms, and we may conclude that, given its degree of generality, 'non-ergodicity' is an analytical term while 'path dependence', which refers primarily to economic phenomena, is a theoretical term. Analytical language is a theoretical working tool (while ontological language is basically for philosophers), and its appropriateness will generally depend on its satisfying the criteria of operational convenience. We shall introduce later the analytical terms 'rule' and 'carrier', since they are operationally useful and because they provide a bridge for analogies to biology – for instance, by allowing routines to be called 'genes' (see Nelson and Winter).

Theoretical *recontextualization* requires that the levels of complexity are appropriately considered and the boundaries between theories are drawn with care. By way of an example, in his contribution John Foster shows how the analytical term 'self-organization' may be applied – possibly wrongly – in theoretical domains of different levels of complexity. Self-organization in physio-chemical contexts deals with problems of structurization with an energetic focus and an emphasis on exogenously determined boundary conditions, while self-organization in biological contexts must take account of the endogenous structuring of inflowing and outflowing information, given external thermodynamic conditions. There is another 'gear change', Foster argues, in economic self-organization where '(t)he boundary limit of a developmental process is still strongly

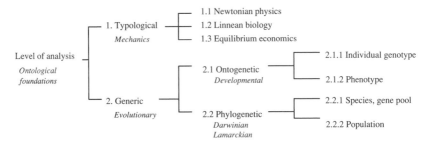

Figure 1.1 Analytical schema

influenced by history but . . . is also affected by forward-looking plans enacted through institutions entirely absent in the biological domain'.

Many analytical terms that are obtained by way of the *decontextualisation* of the theoretical language of biology are used widely in the contributions to this volume. In general, the biologically coloured language is used widely in the writings of evolutionary economists. Analogies and metaphors abound. An important distinction that also reflects differences in research interests is that between *ontogeny* and *phylogeny*. Figure 1.1 provides an overview that starts with the distinction between *typological* and *generic* approaches. The former is associated with a mechanistic paradigm, and features thinking along the lines of Newtonian physics and Linnean biology. In contradistinction the generic approach is related to the evolutionary paradigm. The analytical term 'generic' is useful, since it provides the linguistic genus for the terms 'ontogenetic' and 'phylogenetic'. The term 'gene' may be seen as referring in its roots to both the biological term 'gene' and to 'genesis'. 'Ontogenetic' has to do with the *one*, 'phylogenetic' with the *many*.

Ontogenetic analysis embraces approaches ranging from general (living) system theory to special theories of organisms. Allen discusses in his contribution various system properties, and distinguishes between different types of mechanical, self-organizing and evolving systems. Generally, ontogenetic analysis reflects *system thinking*. It deals with the analysis of structure and the development of systems given their generic 'mechanism', systemic blueprint or knowledge base. In biology, the distinction usually made is between an individual genotype and a phenotype. Taken as analytical terms, these may be recontextualized for purposes in economic theory – as, for instance, in Nelson's and Winter's contributions – by viewing the individual genotype as the organizational blueprint of a firm, and the phenotype as the *organizational routines* actually adopted, learned and selectively adapted. Analytically, the term 'phenotype' always describes an actual organism or system as it has developed in interaction with its environment. Ontogenetic analysis can also refer to a single economy, as in Hodgson's contribution.

Phylogenetic analysis refers to many of a kind. In biology, the distinction is usually made between *gene pool* and *population*. The gene pool stands for the genotype of a species. A population is the set of all members of phenotypes in a gene pool. In economics, a gene pool may comprise routines – say, technological or institutional rules selectively adapted as routines in an industry – while a population would be the firms in that industry. In the same way, a division of a firm may be expressed in terms of a pool of routines and a population in that division. Phylogenetic analysis – referring to many of one kind – features, as Metcalfe mentions, '*population thinking*'. The dynamic of phylogeny can be analysed on the basis of an evolutionary trajectory defined in terms of a succession of the regime phases or 'laws' mentioned.

The following discussion is divided into three parts: evolutionary micro-, meso- and macroeconomics. The distinction concerns the traditional division between micro- and macroeconomics. The above analytical *tableau*, simple though it may be, allows us to conclude that the step from micro to macro cannot be accomplished directly. The phylogenetic domain is neither micro nor macro. Accepting its relevance, we take this domain to be that of *meso*economics. Microeconomics is then viewed as part of mesoeconomics, and mesoeconomics as part of macroeconomics.

6   The missing link: *Homo sapiens oeconomicus*

We consider *Homo sapiens oeconomicus* (HSO) to be the basic unit of an evolutionary microeconomics. The distinction between this concept and *Homo oeconomicus* is that it expressly recognizes the traits of human nature.

A note on the methodological stance we are taking appears appropriate at this juncture. The stance usually taken by mainstream economists is *instrumental*. They argue that the empirical content of assumptions is irrelevant so long as these serve as instruments for a predictively valid (or simply consistent) theory. We believe, however, that *empirical groundwork* along *interdisciplinary* lines will indeed contribute to the reconstruction of a more valid economic theory. This position does not endorse the view that there is virtue per se in doing interdisciplinary research. The 'realist' position we take is arguably also 'instrumental' in the sense that the findings from other disciplines are considered to be useful only to the extent that they serve the purpose of *economic* theory making. Instead of dichotomizing the two positions, we take what can be called the methodological stance of *instrumental realism*.

The notion of *Homo sapiens* signifies the 'realism of assumptions' and specifically rejects the idea that the complex human nature relevant for explaining economic phenomena can be reduced to the truncated creature of *Homo oeconomicus*. As we shall see, Pareto's distinction between the logical and illogical actions of humans is, in an essential way, empirically flawed. It is not the reduction to the attribute 'oeconomicus' that is ill-conceived but rather the general underlying assumptions about human nature. A reconstruction of *Homo oeconomicus* thus starts with a reassessment of what the central traits of humans are. *Homo sapiens oeconomicus* is, however, conceived of as operating in economic contexts, and the further question is how assumptions about *Homo sapiens* can serve their instrumental purpose in the reconstruction of economic theory.

Evolutionary anthropology, biology and related sciences have made various conjectures and hypotheses about what it is that makes *Homo sapiens*. One of the most distinct faculties of the human species is tool making. *Homo sapiens* is not only a tool-using animal (other primates use tools as well) but also a tool-making animal. The human species actively changes the environment (often) in conscious anticipation of future consequences. A second faculty in which *Homo sapiens* excels over all other primates is the self-perception and use of symbolic-verbal language. Symbolic language may have been largely a consequence of tool making and using. In any case, in the course of evolution language has fed back to human cognition in a profound way. Additionally, language has opened up new efficient and efficacious forms of social communication. The members of this species have an evolved *biological predisposition* to make and use tools to solve complex problems and to communicate socially in abstract language. This biological predisposition has evolved over time and has survived because of its selective advantage in coping with problems posed by the environment. Both evolutionary biology and evolutionary psychology tell us that the human brain is a product of biological evolution, and that it is this that makes the evolution of culture both possible and probable.

How do we describe and explain theoretically the evolution of tools, communication structures or productive social organization? How does the *cortical disposition* of *Homo sapiens* coevolve with its culture? We conceive tool making, communication, social organization, etc. as processes in which *rules* are involved; for instance, tools involve tool-rules and language involves language-rules, and so on. We thus conceive of *Homo sapiens* as a rule-making and rule-using animal. *Homo sapiens oeconomicus* is, accordingly, *Homo sapiens as a rule-making and rule-using animal in economic contexts*, such as production, consumption and transaction. The subject matter of evolutionary economics is the analysis of the evolution of economic rules. We define rules as *deductive schemes that allow economic*

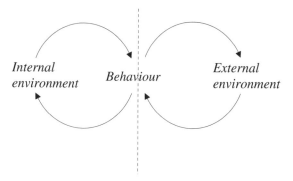

Figure 1.2 Human behaviour in internal and external environments

operations to take place. The term 'deductive' will be given a comprehensive meaning that encompasses heuristics, designs, techniques, algorithms, logico-deductive schemes, legal rules, strategies, etc.

The *coevolutionary circuit* between individual and environment is an important concept upon which fundamental theoretical statements of the subsequent analysis will be based. Figure 1.2 provides a bird's-eye view of its overall structure. The key variable is behaviour, which is linked with an environment denoted by the right-hand circular arrows. This behaviour, however, is also linked with an environment that is inside the individual. We call the latter 'internal', as distinct from the previous 'external' environment.

A model of *Homo sapiens* that can serve as an explanatory platform for economic analysis must include aspects of the neurosciences and the cognitive and behavioural sciences. One such model that integrates essential elements of the three areas is shown in figure 1.3. We now conceive the inner environment of figure 1.2 as an agent's cortical disposition for cognition and behaviour. From a neurophysiological perspective it represents the neuronal architecture of the brain. We distinguish crudely between the *arche*typical areas, which comprise automatisms and negative feedback that determine *internal behaviour* (for instance the regulation of the blood, the respiratory system, metabolism, etc.), and the *neo*cortical areas that govern *thinking and consciousness*. The cortical structure is thus linked on the one hand with internal behaviour and on the other hand with cognition. A third circular link is from *external behaviour* to the *external environment*. We consider this to be governed basically by the neo-cortical areas of the brain.

It is essential to recognize that the neocortex has evolved from, and then coevolved with, the archecortex and that both are intrinsically neuronally connected. Cognition is neuronally embedded in the overall cortical structure and extends to internal and external behaviour. The thalamic

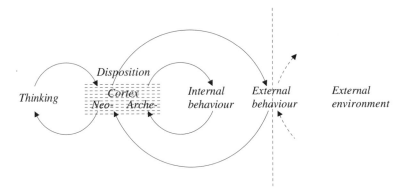

Figure 1.3 Neural-cognitive and neural-behavioural compartments of HSO

cortices and related feedback automatisms create an internal milieu that may be considered to put humans into what may be called 'bodily consciousness'. Emotions, moods and feelings influence cognition.

The cortical interdependencies are demonstrated in figure 1.3 by the two sets of reciprocal arrows, which on the one hand link the archecortical areas with internal behaviour and on the other hand link the neocortical areas with cognition. Neuronal interconnectivity between the cortical sites is denoted by the block of dashed lines, which intentionally disallows any precise cortical localization for the resulting behaviours.

An evolutionary improvement unique to humans is the hemispheric specialization of the brain. The left and right sides of the neocortex perform distinct functions. The hemispheric specialization of the human cortex can be assumed to have coevolved in response to the unique demands made by language and tool making. The increasing demand for complex problem solving could be met not only by expanding the size of the cortex but also by specializing it on the basis of some 'cortical division of labor'. The left hemisphere is specialized with respect to the analytical, sequential and propositional abilities required for verbal expression and arithmetic. It allows syntactical reasoning and computational operations such as adding, subtracting or multiplying to be made. The right hemisphere is specialized, by contrast, with respect to the geometric, synthetic, integrating, pictorial and spatial abilities. It enables elements to be combined into a whole – for example, coloured blocks to be assembled into a mosaic picture. It allows us to appose or compare singular observations, images or conceptions on the basis of a *gestalt*. While the left hemisphere is positional and breaks up the whole into its parts, the right hemisphere is able to conceive isolated entities as complementary components of a whole and to comprehend this holistic nature. The division of knowledge and labour of an economy essentially builds on the ability of this type of relational and appositional thinking.

The left and right cortical hemispheres accommodate two types of basic abilities relevant for problem solving in an economy. One, which is very much at the centre stage of neoclassical economics, is *efficiency*. The left hemisphere, with its analytical and computational abilities, provides the cognitive fundament for the solution of the varied problems of economic efficiency. We can define the measure of efficiency as a relation between two given quantifiable magnitudes – for example, the input-output ratio that measures productive efficiency. In their contribution Giovanni Dosi, Luigi Marengo and Giorgio Fagiolo look at the issue of computational problem solving from the angle of complexity theory and, in accordance with Simon's bounded rationality, argue that there is a significant range of problems the complexity of which does not allow an adequate solution to be found on the basis of the genetically available 'natural' inferential and computational machinery. The second fundamental economic problem – one that cannot be found at all in the neoclassical research agenda – is *efficacy*. The issue here is whether two or more components – say, A and B – fit together; that is, are mutually adapted to their complementary tasks or problem solutions. Component C may score better on the grounds of efficiency, but if it fails to meet the required complementary criteria the whole argument of superior efficiency performance breaks down because it lacks feasibility. Neoclassical production theory starts with the assumption of feasible production sets and thus ignores what is probably the most important and the most difficult economic problem. The nature of the criteria of complementarity is qualitative, and they thus cannot be reduced to any single-valued quantitative measure. Problems of efficacy are central to evolutionary economics, since, by their very nature, the structure and the dynamics of economic knowledge involve relational phenomena. Accordingly, the locus of the solution of problems of efficacy is to be found in the specialized abilities of the right cortical hemisphere.

The human brain as a whole can be looked at as being composed of an archecortical and a neocortical area, with the latter divided into specialized hemispheres. One or other compartment dominates the neuronal activities depending on the type of cognition or behaviour involved at a particular time. However, to suggest that there is an isolated link from a single specialized ability to a specific mode of cognition or behaviour would contradict neurophysiological evidence. The governing agency is the cortical domain, which interconnects both with the old and new areas and with the two specialized hemispheres. A feature of neuronal organization is the rich thalamocortical interconnectivity, which represents a hub from which any site of the cortex can communicate with one or more other sites. Related evidence shows that the cerebellum is not only a device for coordinating body movements, it is also a device for homologous cognitive abilities, learning and memory. The cortical levels interconnect and, in particular, allow the neocortex to control areas responsible for body-sensory functions and emotions. Individuals have a cognitive ability to identify, understand and instrumentalize emotions adaptively and to use them as some form of 'intelligence'. In his contribution Allen bridges 'emotional intelligence' with the demands of an evolving system, arguing that 'the ability to "respond" with appropriate adaptive innovations over the longer term can be defined only as "intelligent", but this is not the rational, logical form of intelligence that corresponds to the IQ but instead "evolutionary intelligence", which reflects the ability to learn and change'. Conversely, higher-order mental activities are embedded in neuronal structures of the archecortex producing cognition that is emotionally coloured. The archecortical areas, particularly the thalamic, cerebellar and hippocampic ones, that interconnect with the neocortical site equip humans with a cortical organization that provides them with intelligent emotions and emotional intelligence.

Similar interconnectivities exist with respect to the lateralization of the brain. The left hemisphere adds to the performance of the right by providing some essential verbal symbolism and syntactical assistance. The right hemisphere, in turn, supports the left with its pre-eminent properties with regard to spatial, relational and integrating abilities. One hemisphere does not unilaterally dominate the other – say, the left over the right; instead there is *complementary specialization*. The hemispheric interconnectivities generate basic 'fuzziness' in human cognition; but we may assume that it is precisely this indeterminacy in the cognitive process that constitutes a major source of human creativity. The interplay of distinct, but complementary, specialized abilities triggers the imagination that is at the root of novelty, which, in its turn, propels economic growth and development. Various contributors to this volume suggest that any economic theory designed to cope with economic change must recognize the creative and imaginative sources of novelty, discovery and new problem solving.

The interconnected sites of the human cortex accommodate specific abilities. Besides these, the cortex also has a non-specific ability to conceive its *unity*. Where we should localize the cortical self-reflection or self-recognition that can be embraced under the notion of *consciousness* still seems to be an open issue in the literature of the neurosciences and philosophy. Eccles and Popper have proposed a dualistic interaction theory where the conscious self interacts with the dominant left hemisphere of the brain. This theory contradicts – given the separation of the ideational component (self) and the physiological (neuronal machinery) – the ontological premise introduced earlier, that all real phenomena are matter-energy actualizations of idea or information. The bimodality in actualization forbids the separation of the two ontic constituencies. The proposition could also be challenged theoretically on neurophysiological grounds, given that the right hemisphere has holistic abilities that would seem to be better for coping with the phenomenon of unity. We assume that the domain of all cortical interconnectivities denoted in figure 1.3 by the dashed square is not only the locus of instrumentally specific cognitive abilities but also that of non-specific human consciousness. Consciousness is generally a state of being, physiologically supported by the entirety of cortical interconnections. It manifests itself non-specifically in well-being or various substantive states of consciousness. An empirical welfare theory can build on the recognition of a notion of consciousness defined in this way.

However, consciousness also has instrumental significance. On the one hand, it constitutes the source of *self-identity* that makes an individual a *person*. It allows an individual's self-recognition as a whole to exist and provides guidance in delineating the boundaries to the environment. Consciousness, on the other hand, allows *intentionality*. If intentionality is to have practical significance and not to remain mere fantasy, it must be supported by *willpower*. This component of instrumental consciousness provides the basis for individual decision making and individual choice. Consciousness grants the individual the *autonomy* to engage in deliberate, meaningful economic action. The neuronal pattern of the conscious state can also change depending on the dominance of the neuronal activities of the cortical sites. The strength and places of cortical dominance hence may vary, and this will give human autonomy its distinct character at a particular time. As well as bounded rationality, there is also *bounded autonomy*.

The brain of HSO has a number of characteristics that can serve as assumptions with regard to cognition and behaviour in evolving economic contexts. The preceding discussion has been guided by the methodological imperative of the 'realism of assumptions'. Nevertheless, on various occasions the sketch of the cortical architecture has also indicated the instrumental usefulness of the findings for economic theory formation. The following propositions about HSO are implications of the preceding discussion; they provide some substantive rationale for a critique of the fundamental shortcomings of neoclassical *Homo oeconomicus*, and they may serve as an interdisciplinary platform for the subsequent discussion. The propositions are:

1. *Non-separability* of cortical levels and hemispheres governing human cognition and behaviour;
2. *Non-homogeneity* or *variety* given evolutionary distinct and specialized cortical areas compounded by complex cortical double-interconnectivities;
3. *Non-periodicity* of both dominant and fuzzy interconnected neural processes.

The proposition of non-separability strikes a fatal empirical blow against the unilateral model of *Homo oeconomicus*. Computational, calculatory and analytical abilities are emotionally coloured, and at the same time they are also linked to the ongoing pattern generation of the lateral counterpart. 'Perfect rationality' based on splitting the cortical hemispheres and the exclusive activation of the left one is an abstruse concept given the findings of modern neuroscience. The neoclassical separability assumption not only results in an ill-conceived concept of rationality, its ignorance of the cross-cortical fuzziness also shuts all the doors to an investigation of the sources of creativity and ingenuity in complex economic problem solving.

Secondly, the proposition of non-homogeneity provides a departure point for the analysis of the complex variety that governs economic cognition and economic behaviour. In his contribution Metcalfe demonstrates the fundamental, ontologically rooted difference between typological thinking on the one hand and population thinking that accepts diversity and variety on the other hand. The neoclassical 'representative agent' appears again as a *machine à l'homme* that is entirely at odds with neurophysiological evidence.

Thirdly, the proposition of the non-periodicity of cortical activities and, concomitantly, a low probability that any particular rationally designed economic action can be repeated in a precise way have both theoretical and methodological implications for economics. Theoretically, the varying differences in repeated rationally designed economic actions are not anomalies but constitute the normal case. Furthermore, the intercortical fuzziness supports the view that any external pressure exerted on an agent may generate novelty and change in problem solutions. In their contributions Foster, Chen and Allen discuss the role of positive feedback that is self-generated during the course of economic action where there are increasing environmental constraints, and that precludes – given the novel problem solutions – this action's repeatability. Methodologically, the validity test for the model cannot rely on the conventional repeatability criteria but must instead allow for non-repeatability that accepts heterogeneity and change as standards of normality.

Finally, intentionality and will constitute essential assumptions for cognition and behaviour that are relevant in most economic contexts.

Neoclassical economists of the second half of the nineteenth century made a major contribution to economics and social philosophy by recognizing and specifying the autonomy of individuals in making their choices. This important discovery falls short of a scientific breakthrough since it fails to recognize the internal (as distinct from external) constraints that cortical interconnectivities impose on all human expression, including consciousness and economic freedom. Recent experimental evidence at a physiological-sensory level has demonstrated that unconscious cognitive flashes precede conscious acts of cognition. This challenges the traditional positions with respect to the nature of both rationality and the intentionality that directs it.

7   Microeconomics: generic and operant levels

Homo sapiens oeconomicus is, like any living being, embedded in an environment. In figure 1.3 the circularity between external behaviour (as governed by the internal environment of the cortical disposition) and the external environment is indicated by the reciprocal loops. The environment poses problems that individuals are able to tackle on the basis of problem-solving mechanisms. The preceding discussion suggested that humans are equipped with a highly developed cognitive machinery that allows them to adapt to complex problem settings. This is a remarkable evolutionary achievement, but it is not unique to humans. Various experiments have shown that other primates, too, demonstrate surprising abilities when exposed to problems with solutions that call for cognitive skills. Apparently they have innate mechanisms that generate adequate problem-solving responses in a spontaneous way. These primates even exhibit some form of learning – for instance, when transmitting behavioural patterns, such as using sticks for hunting or washing fruit in the ocean; but they do not develop anything like a culture from these single instances of rule adoption. The 'culture' of these primates is innate and basically unchanging. In an early developmental stage human infants have homologous cognitive responses in comparable problem situations. There is apparently no previous learning or previous rule adoption involved in this type of problem solving. These problem-solving agents are, like *Homo oeconomicus*, genuinely perfect. The agents at their disposal have a sort of *original cognition* and *original behaviour*.

Problem solving by humans embedded in culture is distinctively different. The individuals basically rely on a problem-solving mechanism that is composed of *acquired rules*. Solving a problem depends critically on the previous creation and the selective adoption of adequate rules. As in Austrian capital theory, there must be a 'cognitive roundabout' process nurtured by rule-investment. At this juncture, it seems important to grasp the significance of the distinction between the *generic* and the *operant* levels of cognition and behaviour. Generic cognition and generic behaviour refer to the creation, selective adoption, adaptation and retention of problem-solving rules. Operant cognition and operant behaviour, in contrast, relate to economic operations – production, consumption and transaction – that are performed on the basis of a mechanism composed of acquired rules. Hence, there is a fundamental distinction here that sets the stage for an evolutionary analysis of economic phenomena. It is between the

1. **Generic level** – generic cognition and generic behaviour; and
2. **Operant level** – operant cognition and operant behaviour.

In its very essence, evolutionary economics deals with the generic level: the dynamic of generic cognition and generic behaviour as it coevolves with, and continuously restructures and changes, an economy.

In conventional economics the analytical unit of a model dealing with the evolution of rules is not an issue. The individual agent moves in an environmental problem space that is furnished with opportunity sets, indifference curves, isoquant cost curves and relative market prices, and the solution to a problem is a rational choice based on cognitive and informational omniscience. The individual typically reacts to an environmental situation but does not take the initiative by changing the initial and secondary environmental conditions. The agent is not proactive; and the initial and secondary environmental conditions remain *exogenous*. The trajectory of the economic process has a distinct direction: it starts with an environmental stimulus, which is followed by a rational response. The individual participates only at an *operant* level in this behavioural reaction scheme. The initial rule mechanism is given by the assumption of rationality, and the external rule environment is part of the *ceteris paribus* clause. There is no explanatory hint concerning the rules that govern economic operations.

Turning to reality, it can be said that an evolutionary model starts when one or more of the agents use initiative and imagination to generate an option – say, to produce and introduce into the market a new consumer item or new production technique. There is spontaneity and an element of self-causation in this process. Economic agents adjust to the magnitudes of their individual demands and supplies within a given environment but they also initiate generic change by altering the environment's structure by infusing it with novelty. The trajectory of the economic process once again has a distinct direction: it starts with *human action,* is followed by *reaction,* and finally settles down into a *meta-stable* state. The evolutionary model attempts to explain all three phases of the generic trajectory.

The first phase can be conceived of as the *origination* of a generic process. It refers to rule creation – the creative ability and imagination to generate novelty. The locus of this generic process is the human cortex, and, although the research and development (R&D) departments of firms may lend substantial support to human ingenuity, the ultimate production of knowledge takes place in the cortex of the individual. The second phase has to do with the *adoption* of a novel rule. There are two environmental domains in which adoption takes place. One is internal, and refers to the adoption of a rule by an individual agent that is based on a process of learning and adaptive accommodation. The other environmental domain is external. In addition to the original adopter, the external adoption process also involves other individuals as potential and actual adopters. The third phase deals with *retention*. It refers to rule stabilization and the ability to use the adopted rule recurrently. Again, the retention process can take place in the cortical domain of a single individual and in the external environment inhabited by many individuals.

The unit of the evolutionary dynamics is thus composed of a *microscopic* trajectory that relates to the generic process of the individual and a *macroscopic* trajectory that relates to the rule dynamics of an external, multi-agent environment. The general logic of the trajectory phases applied to the microscopic processes can be summarized as follows:

Phase 1: **Rule origination**
> *Micro*: exploration, informed by creativity and imagination, leads to novel rules;

Phase 2: **Rule adoption**
> *Micro*: internal selection, learning and adaptation of rule in a given generic knowledge base;

Phase 3: **Rule retention**
> *Micro*: memory, information retrieval and recurrent rule activation manifest themselves behaviourally in habits and routines.

Dosi et al., Witt, Nelson and Winter all discuss the various cognitive abilities of economic agents that are needed to solve generic tasks that relate to the three trajectory phases. Dosi et al. discuss models that allow for various cognitive rule categories, such as heuristics, frames, mental schemes and complex problem-solving algorithms. In their contribution they refer to the nature of complexity inherent in all generic problem solving. Drawing on computability theory, the authors introduce a 'dividing line between problems that are solvable by means of general recursive procedures in non-exponential times and problems that are not', and conclude that there is 'an upper bound of complexity of the problems for which the theory is allowed to assume that the agents "naturally" possess the appropriate problem-solving algorithm . . . and that it happens . . . . that many decision tasks within . . . . the economic domain fall outside this category'. Computational and complexity theories pull the contextual carpet out from under the feet of the omniscient *Homo oeconomicus*.

The macroscopic trajectory unfolds in an environment populated by many agents. To grasp the intricacies of the relationship between the microscopic and macroscopic trajectories, it will be helpful to clarify the notions of 'carrier', 'information' and 'knowledge'. An agent is seen as representing a *carrier of information*; any information thus 'carried' is called *knowledge*. The concept of information relates to its semantic properties – as an idea applied in conceptual or perceptional rules. Looking for opportunities to purchase or sell lemons, or to buy cheaper microelectronic equipment, means gathering operant information and gaining operant knowledge. As previously argued, evolutionary economics involves analysing the generic characteristics of economic processes, and thus entails *generic information* and *generic knowledge*.

A microscopic trajectory turns into a macroscopic one whenever generic information crosses the boundaries of a micro-unit and extends into the external environment. As a producer of novelty the micro-unit is the exporter of a rule; the other agents are rule importers. From an economic point of view, the distiction between tradable and non-tradable information is critical. In the case of marketable information, crossing the boundary goes along with the transfer of property rights and is at the root of market transactions and the exchange of resources.

From an evolutionary view point, the domain of relevant generic information is wider than the market. There is a broad range of cultural knowledge and language rules, and a rich body of knowledge produced by the arts and sciences, all of which have a substantial impact on the dynamics of economic growth and development. Silverberg and Verspagen discuss the 'deep level' of culturally 'embodied capital' as an engine of economic growth in their contribution. Nelson discusses adjacent aspects of the 'body of understanding' as a source of successful practice in technological and economic communities in firms and industries.

The theoretical aspect of boundary crossing is essential for grasping the logic of the evolution of rules. Reducing the issue to its bare bones, there is a problem with respect to the coding of generic information and a problem of a deeper human quality associated with this process. The generic knowledge carried by agents serves the instrumental purpose of *encoding and decoding rules*. In terms of adoption, created rules are feasible only if they are encoded in a message. The actualization of the potential of a feasible rule depends, in turn, on the ability of the agents to decode the information contained in that rule. The feasibility constraints apply both to the inventor of the rule and to those who follow it.

The other issue relates to what may be conceived of as *rule ethics*. In the course of their evolution humans, as rule-producing and rule-adopting animals, have acquired not only cognitive abilities but also 'normative' abilities when dealing with rules. In his contribution Simon suggests that humans are biologically predisposed to providing the general public with rules generously and without claiming any material or non-material rewards. They have an innate propensity for *non-reciprocal altruism*. At the generic level, individuals therefore tacitly contribute in important ways to the evolution of their economic environment. Simon rejects the idea advocated in some strands of 'neo-institutional economics' that reduces human altruism to its myopic operant reciprocal form.

On the other side of the generic borderline, there must be agents who trust the information conveyed. A second predisposition enters the stage here. Simon argues that economic agents are equipped with '*docility*', which enables them to communicate and adopt rules with unbounded trust. In a similar vein, Mokyr argues that causal relations are often hard to observe directly, and that mostly we simply have to trust what others say. The hub that connects non-reciprocal altruism and docility is *trust*. Various cherished economic concepts or assumptions appear in a new light when looked at against this background. Simon thus emphasizes that his seminal concept of 'bounded rationality' makes sense only if it is linked to the concepts of non-reciprocal altruism and docility.

8   The evolutionary theory of the firm

The micro-unit of neoclassical economics is *Homo oeconomicus*. We have contrasted this conception with *Homo sapiens oeconomicus*, and have defended it methodologically on the grounds of instrumental realism. The quest for realism, however, does not end with *HSO*. This construction constitutes an elementary unit and not the micro-unit itself. In economic reality, a micro-unit can be an individual, as assumed in the neoclassical model. But in many cases a micro-unit will be a *socially organized entity*: the production unit will be a socially organized productive unit, the *firm*; the consumption unit a socially organized consumption unit, the *household*.

The neoclassical model does talk about firms and housholds, but it actually assumes that individuals and socially organized entities are identical. The cortical and the social organization govern homologously microeconomic operations. Human cortex and social body are indistinguishable with respect to their rational course of action, their determining variables and their consequences.

The microeconomic position was reached basically by following two research strategies. One is the *black box* strategy that proposes considering any micro-unit as a maximizing agency and does not bother about the operational determinants. The problem has been solved by using a mathematical equation in which an *in*equality can be transformed into an equality. The left side of the individual and the right side of the socially organized entity were multiplied by the zero value of the black box. This procedure is inadmissible in mathematics and is meaningless in economics.

The second research strategy, alluded to in Winter's contribution, is more sophisticated, but its results boil down to a microeconomic view that also lacks empirical meaning. The upshot of this procedure is the reduction of productive knowledge to a physical entity that can be measured on a numerical scale. Winter discusses the case of linear activity analysis, where 'ways of doing things' that naturally involve the human factor are translated into 'basic activities' that are formally presented by vectors of technical coefficients. In this model each of the productive components can be scaled up and down at will, and the results made additive. The relations among the productive components represent a physical pattern, and this pattern can be changed by altering the coefficients of the components proportionally. There is a coordinating idea – a plan – behind the relations, but in this model, as Winter says, 'the sum of feasible production plans is itself feasible'. In his contribution Chen mentions David Ricardo's *Gedankenexperiment* of cash doubling that applies the same logic of additivity in the macroeconomic domain. The nature of human knowledge that resides in the productive components is reduced to a machine, and the task of coordinating these components is assumed to be performed by a super-machine the rationale of which is masterminded by smart engineers – or, arguably, by neoclassical economists.

In following an evolutionary course, we view the firm as a *productive socially organized unit*. The firm is, as Metcalfe calls it, an 'organizational-cum-technological complex', where the notion of 'organizational' is associated with human activities 'defined as set of routines . . . which collectively constitute the knowledge base'. Structurally, the firm exibits the features of the division of knowledge and labour in a small-scale form. The components are individuals or groups of individuals who are the carriers of productive knowledge. More generally, a firm constitutes a domain of *relations* between components that perform *special* tasks. An individual component must meet two basic functional requirements. It must have the special knowledge appropriate for carrying out a specific productive task, and it must be capable of relating its operations to those of other individual components.

Carrying out a specific task is closely associated with the notion of *efficiency*. Positive economies of scale and capital deepening, as discussed in the chapters by Silverberg and Verspagen, Metcalfe, David and Winter, are factors that contribute to increasing efficiency. At any level of efficiency, the operations performed by a productive unit must relate appropriately to those of others. The issue here is *efficacy*, as defined in the previous section. In the market, the price mechanism provides guidance for allocating complementary items efficaciously. What is the mechanism that coordinates the divided productive operations in the firm? Specifically, what is it that is coordinated? And then, what are the specific instances of the coordination mechanism? The process of coordination, on the one hand, can be seen as referring to resources. At productive site A a resource is being transformed and subsequently transported to productive site B, where the resource is further transformed, to produce a sequence of partial transformations and – finally – its end result. The instrument that brings about the relation between productive components is locomotion. The paradigmatic nature of 'locomotional relation' can be captured by the example of an assembly line. At the resources level, information enters in the form of technical coefficients, and coordination corresponds to the art of 'administering' these resources. The traditional term 'business administration' echoes fittingly this physicalist view.

If productive activities involve humans, the various components cannot be related to each other in this mechanistic fashion. Productive relations come about in important ways through *communication*. The efficacy of the relations depends in essential ways on the character of the rules adopted to govern the processes of encoding and decoding the information that is exchanged by the agents involved in a productive relation. Nelson's contribution highlights the relevance of '*communities*' in the firm, and distinguishes between 'technological communities' and 'economic communities' as important players in the domain of productive relations. The various communities have their own shared rules, which are differentially crystallized in a '*body of understanding*' and a '*body of practice*'. Simon explores the role of non-reciprocal altruism and docility, which are at work in the cooperative processes that govern productive relations in the human realm of a firm. In his contribution Witt refers to the 'cognitive coherence among firm members', and argues that a firm organization 'usually forms an intensely interacting group' the members of which 'may share some common standards of conduct exemplified by socially shared models of behaviour'.

The coordination of physical resources and the coordination of human activities thus differ substantially. At the level of physical resources, a plan may indeed be implemented by applying a rationale similar to the coordinating device that underlies a fully automated assembly line or conveyer belt. If feasible at all, the planned coordination is much more intricate when it relates to messages that the various productive units exchange and that, essentially, bring about the coordination. The management – or, generally, the centralized authority – can set down a scheme of paths and rules of communication plus desiderata, or an objective or 'success function', but generally it will simply lack the information needed to order the coordination of the productive activities in any detail. It is, as Winter points out, a 'matter of *distributed* knowledge; i.e. complementary parts of the same functional unit of knowledge being held by several individuals and applied in a coordinated way – the coordination itself being a crucial aspect of the knowledge'.

If we recognize that the old industrial paradigm had its heyday in the first half of the last century and that it has been withering away in recent decades at an accelerating rate, thus making way for a new industrial paradigm promoted by dramatic advances in the new information and communication technology, then an evolutionary theory of the firm seems imperative if the theory of production and microeconomics are to achieve any solid empirical basis. In their contributions Simon and Dosi et al. raise objections to the misplaced 'strong empirical assumptions' that characterize neoclassical economics, and suggest reconstructing economics by rethinking its basic cognitive and behavioural assumptions.

The productive knowledge base of the firm involves an ongoing process. Knowledge must be created, selectively adopted, learned, adapted and retained for repeated use in economic operations. In the preceding section we have sketched the generic trajectory of *Homo sapiens oeconomicus*. This trajectory now extends into the context of the firm: what evolves here is the *knowledge of the firm*. It is the growth of the specialized knowledge of the various productive agencies and their capacity to connect with each other and effectively coordinate their activities. In this vein, Winter argues that any approach that confines knowledge to the locus of a single brain is likely to misstate the nature of knowledge in the firm.

The *first* phase of the knowledge trajectory of the firm deals with the exploration of economic opportunities or the path of profitable actions. By looking inside the firm, the entrepreneur or management will explore the opportunities for bringing about and eventually initiating organizational change (Witt). Technological ingenuity that is based on a technological 'body of understanding' will come from a firm's R&D department, but this activity will connect with the 'economic community' that uses its own selective criteria to filter the technically feasible projects and to determine the probability that the productive end results will withstand the pressures of a selective market environment (Nelson). In the exploration phase, the firm will generally face 'hazy frontiers' (Winter), exposing it to radical uncertainty in its decision making and productive operations. The 'fuzziness' generated by the neuronal interconnectivities of the human brain mentioned earlier will often be the origin of a course that exibits the characteristics of environmental haziness.

The *second* phase deals with the social processes of selective knowledge adoption. Dosi et al. point out that all cognitive categories are ultimately 'grounded in the collective experience of the actors and in the history of the institutions in which an agency is nested'. The authors discuss various cognitive and behavioural models of learning that may have a bearing on the way in which an evolutionary theory of the firm is conceptually sketched, and call for a 'unified approach' that marries cognitive and behavioural economics. Dosi et al. and Nelson show in their contributions how individuals or communities employ different selection criteria when operating within the boundaries of the firm and when coping with the challenges of an external selective environment. David takes up the role that path dependence can play in selective rule adoption and learning processes in economic contexts, such as the firm. Witt emphasizes, from the point of view of integration, the role of the entrepreneur in marshalling productive social knowledge and in winning the struggle for 'cognitive leadership' in an environment of competing X-inefficient knowledge demands.

The *third* phase of the knowledge trajectory of the firm refers to the stabilization and retention of the knowledge base. Rules are memorized and activated repeatedly in their operant use. We call rules that are stabilized and retained for repeated operant use '*routines*'. Individual routines can be associated with the notion of *habit*. Hodgson discusses in his contribution the role of habits in Veblen's seminal institutional economics. Routines of socially organized units, like those of the firm, represent – following Nelson and Winter's pioneering footsteps – '*organizational routines*'. Individual routines are cortically stabilized and retained patterns of individual cognition and individual behaviour. Organizational routines represent a complex of socially organized individual routines or habits that are *co*-stabilized and *co*-retained.

In the previous presentation of the firm as a dynamic division and coordination of knowledge and labour the boundaries of the firm were left undetermined. These boundaries are often dictated by criteria of technical feasibility. For instance, to assemble the complementary parts of a car the production line in the automobile industry must be a certain size and have a certain scope. While it is difficult to sell only half a car, the frequent case of outsourcing shows that the technical criterion is not the only or – possibly increasingly less frequently – the most important one. This hints at a host of factors that all may determine the boundaries of the firm to various extents and in various ways.

The firm in its daily routine makes ongoing decisions about economic operations. For instance, it may decide either to carry out a productive activity within its own domain or to purchase an equivalent productive item in the market. A useful analytical standard unit at the operant level is the *transaction*, and a distinction can be made between internal and external transactions. The outcome of a (bounded) rational transaction choice as dealt with in transaction cost economics will determine, in a precise (stochastic) way, the *operant boundaries* of the firm. Further along the operant level, the firm has been viewed as a 'nexus of contracts'. The management decides on the level and coordination of the resources transactions within the firm, and between the firm and its customers and suppliers, on the basis of contractual arrangements. The contractual arrangements empower the management to demand the cognitive and behavioural activities required of the agents employed. For realism, bounded loyalty and bounded honesty are assumed for the individual agents. The resources coordination scheme is therefore supplemented by an incentive- and sanction-loaded monitoring scheme. *Operant governance* means bringing the demands for resources coordination into accordance with those for attendant productive social behaviour. Given bounded rational governance, a second (bounded first) best coordination of a firm's resources is feasible. The firm defined as transaction-cum-nexus-of-contracts – in what is called the *new institutional economics* – represents an analytical unit that fits in well with the demands of the received neoclassical model of partial and general equilibrium. Its 'boundedness' is arguably a methodological nuisance, but its core is still nomological, and further advances in the neighbouring province of equilibrium economics may make the 'new institutional unit' a candidate if the 'microfoundation' discussion has a renaissance.

A firm's ongoing operations are based on its knowledge base. Efficiency and effectiveness are achieved not only at the operant level but also at the generic level. Governance that is preoccupied with the operant level, and therefore fails to recognize the demands of the generic level, will sooner or later kill the goose that lays the golden eggs. In order to survive in the medium or long run, a firm requires *generic governance*. This type of governance is designed to control the generic knowledge base and to give attention to the creation, learning and continous adaptation and stabilization of the firm's socially organized productive knowledge. Coordination is an important aspect, but, unlike in a traditional theory of the firm, in an evolutionary theory of the firm coordination involves an extremely dynamic process along the generic knowledge trajectory mentioned earlier. Generic governance calls on the entrepreneur or the management to provide, in Witt's words, 'entrepreneurial vision'. The development of a firm's productive performance may depend crucially as he points out, on the kind of organizational changes introduced by the entrepreneur or the management, and a change in the organization that includes a transition from entrepreneur-ruled to management-ruled governance may be among those changes at a generic level.

In a firm, knowledge is coordinated in complex socially *structured networks*. Any success in planning the coordination of generic knowledge will depend crucially on the recognition of the largely informal and tacit character of that knowledge. Winter and Dosi et al. discuss various aspects of the intangible, informal and tacit nature of the firm's generic knowledge base. A major problem of knowledge control, besides the intra-firm coordination, is to keep the knowledge within the boundaries of the firm. The domain of knowledge networks in which knowledge is created, exchanged and retained often crosses the legal or operational boundaries of the firm. Generic governance then means evaluating gains and losses from shifting and controlling the generic boundaries of the firm with respect to the internal and external domains of the entire knowledge network. The generic boundaries of the firm may be blurred and continuously shifting. This phenomenon has been well recognized by contemporary entrepreneurs and managers, and has led to an explicit recognition of the cooperation with respect to knowledge within contexts that include firms crossing the operational boundaries of individual firms. These developments, prompted by the dynamic nature of knowledge, are increasingly recognized in evolutionary economics and have stimulated a growing body of research in areas such as industrial districts, regional knowledge clusters, learning regions, inter-firm industrial organization, technical or local milieux, national innovation systems, networks with weak or strong ties, and cognitive support communities of the Linux/open-source type.

This research is neither micro nor macro, but typically occupies a domain between these that is sometimes referred to as *meso*. It is an appropriate term to denote the analysis of complex knowledge structures that often have fuzzy and shifting boundaries of control, benefits and claims. The term 'meso' is used in various ways in the literature, and, both in its richness and its ambiguity, it reflects the nature of the reality it refers to. With a view to meeting the operational demands, in the following section the term will be given a more general meaning, but also, in its theoretical application, a more precisely defined meaning.

9   Bridging micro and macro: mesoeconomics

The connection between micro and macro is traditionally accomplished by aggregation. A standard price serves as a numerical scale that allows not only the quantities of the various heterogeneous commodities to be added but also their values. The aggregation procedure has been the source of numerous difficulties, and there is some consent in the scientific community that the task of transforming micro into macro has not been accomplished in any satisfactory way. Any attempt to derive aggregate consumption from individual consumer behaviour has been plagued by the impossibility theorem, and any analogous attempts to derive aggregate production from individual firm behaviour have encountered difficulties that stem from the mathematical properties of a production function. Relatedly, the monetary and the real sides are still waiting for adequate answers with regard to a theoretical synthesis. In his contribution Chen discusses some of the ontological fallacies of the 'rational expectations' and related approaches that have emerged from a monetarist perspective and represent contemporary 'new classical macroeconomics'. From an evolutionary perspective, the major problem is the *collapse of structure* in the aggregation procedure. If we look at a lump of gold, our imagination can be relied on to help us find an infinite number of uses for it. Economists who rely on conventional macroeconomics have developed various criteria for disaggregating an economy's 'lump of gold'. In drawing up these criteria, their imagination has been animated by statistical convenience and policy-guided theoretical 'ad-hocery'. Any *ex post* structure imposed on the aggregate magnitudes is both possible and consistent with the rationale of conventional macroeconomics.

Evolutionary economists attempt to define the micro-unit in a way that makes aggregation possible but does not require them to pay the theoretical costs of eliminating structure when applying it. Assuming bimodality (axiom 1 of the evolutionary ontology), any real phenomenon represents a matter-energy actualization of an idea. The microeconomic application of the ontological bimodal premise has led to the view that a microeconomic unit represents a physical actualization of an idea and therefore can be referred to as a 'carrier' of rules in an analytical context. The ontological premise imposes restrictions on the course of economic theory formation. It forbids the formulation of a micro theory in terms of an agency that is composed of a single operational rule and is thus isolated and incapable of promoting economic change. The recognition of the ontic category

Generic categories / Domains	Rule(s) 'Deep'	Carrier(s) 'Surface'
Micro	rule g_j^i	carrier $a_i = a_i(g_j^i)$
Meso	rule pool species g_j, where $g_j^i \in g_j : g_j(g_j^1,....,g_j^n)$	population $a^* = a^*(g_j)$
Macro	many rule pools $g_1,....,g_k$	many populations $a_1^*, ..., a_k^*$

Figure 1.4 Rules and carriers in several domains

of 'idea' brings variety and change into the model. A single individual agent is now not governed by a single, invariant rule; it is able to choose, and adopt from, a range of rules the efficiency and efficacy of which differ. Each rule – as idea – is distinct, and thus introduces variety in its synchronic and diachronic dimensions. As a universal single-rule carrier, *Homo oeconomicus* is always and everywhere the same. In paying tribute to 'realism', the personality traits of real agents are flattened out to the statistical average of the 'representative agent' – and are part, as Metcalfe points out, of the traditional *typological* research programme.

A bimodal rule allows multiple actualizations. Each rule, in concomitance with its multiple actualizations, will be called a *meso-unit*. The micro-unit is a single carrier that actualizes the rule of a meso-unit. It is a member of a *population* of all agents adopting a meso-rule.

A synoptic view based on a taxonomy that comprises the categories of rule and carrier (row) on the one hand and those of micro, meso and macro (column) on the other hand is provided in figure 1.4. A rule based on an idea can be adopted by a single carrier, g_j^i. The micro-unit constitutes an individual carrier a_i that has adopted a rule g_j. A micro-unit may be conceived as a phenotype $a_i = a_i(g_j^i)$. 'Phenotype' means that the rule g_j could have been actualized differently if a carrier in a different environment had adopted that rule.

The meso-domain constitutes a *rule pool* g_j. Whether we define a meso-rule as homologous or as a pool composed of different rules with the same genus – i.e. fundamental content – is an empirical matter. In biology, the empirical evidence has led to the application of the concept of a gene pool. In cultural evolution, it is conceivable that a rule is distinct and satisfies itself uniquely in some form of perfection.

Does zero variety in a rule of a particular kind exclude selection? To deal with this question, it is useful to distinguish between selection due to differentials in *efficiency* and selection due to differentials in *efficacy*. The former presumes that there is variety in the rules adopted by the members of a rule pool. Selection feeds on the variety in differential rule efficiency. To work, selection that operates on efficacy does not require a variety in efficiency. Variant A must fit into the structured complementarities of an environment, and if it were not adapted to, say, B in terms of its complementarity it would not be selected. A and B are selected by meeting the conditions of adapted co-variation. To work, selection by efficacy does not require a population. It always works, but in much of reality a single variant is a very special case.

In many cases, cultural rules explain variety in the generic unity. This holds for both technical and social rules, which often come in various guises. The distinction between a single rule and a pool of rules is exceedingly difficult to make (onto-) logically because it is a distinction between ideas. There is a 'distance' between ideas but the measuring rod employed is qualitative. Methodological ingenuity is required for devising criteria that can determine what a 'big' rule is and what a 'small' one is; for instance, what distinguishes a big technological invention from a small one. The common distinction between technical improvements and radical technical invention would call exactly for this kind of criterion of distinction. One criterion sometimes mentioned relates to the developmental consequences that accompany technological or other rule inventions. Various strands in technology and innovation research mentioned in the contributions by Silverberg and Verspagen, Nelson, Allen, David and Mokyr deal with this conceptual problem. Generally, a meso-rule $g_j : g_j(g_j^1, \ldots, g_j^n)$ is subject to actualization by a population of carriers. These carriers are the members of a population who are the current adopters of a rule.

The macro-domain is composed of many rule pools $g_1, \ldots, g_k$, structured according to their complementary functions and their corresponding rule populations $a_1^*, \ldots, a_k^*$. In the next section we shall return to the static and dynamic 'deep' and 'surface' aspects of the economic macro-structure.

The above taxonomic scheme is composed of analytical terms. The notion of 'rule' can be theoretically specified – for instance, like a gene, as in biology, or like technical, cognitive and behavioural rules, as in economics. Analogies, such as the term 'economic genes', are permissible, since the notion of 'rule' is ontologically warranted. There are still distinct differences between biology and economics at a theoretical level. A major one is that biological rules relate to an entire organism, while economic or cultural rules may be partitioned and need not necessarily refer to the whole corpus. In evolutionary biology, 'heritage' means the replication of an entire organism, and the partial adoption of single genes is an impossible route for rule transmission. The Darwinian variation-selection-retention scheme is meaningful as a *universal* benchmark only to the extent to which it comprises both forms of rule transmission. The suggested scheme of *origination-adoption-retention* is tailored conceptually to serve as a tool for theoretical inquiry in economics. Whether it describes general features that allow the biological and non-biological schemes of the evolutionary dynamic to be included will need further assessment by the proponents of other theoretical disciplines. The present analysis does not claim cross-disciplinary generality. In proceeding along such a line, the touchstone would be the concept of adoption; the further general usefulness of this concept will depend on future developments with respect to a generalized information theory that is conducive to substantiating the concept of adoption.

The meso-trajectory has the same analytical skeleton as the micro-trajectory, but its multiplicity of actualizations means that it extends to the macroscopic domain. The term 'macroscopic' must not be confused with the term 'macro'; 'microscopic' refers to one actualization, and 'macroscopic' to many. Both microeconomics and macroeconomics include the two analytical terms.

Phase 1 of the meso-trajectory is, again, rule *origination*. Micro-analysis has brought into focus the determinants, or rule creation, such as creativity, imagination, trial and error or R&D activities. In meso-analysis, the factor of primacy is again the essential aspect of phase 1, but the emphasis in the analysis is now given to the *primacy of adoption*. The primacy of rule creation is associated with invention, the primacy of rule adoption with innovation. These represent the two sides of the coin of rule origination. An important issue in rule primacy concerns the boundary crossing of a rule from the inventor to the innovator. In the cognitive case, the crossing is from the brain of an individual to the social context. Taking a further step, it is from a socially organized unit – say, a firm – to the social context or environment of that unit. The rule creator does not necessarily have to be the first rule adopter. In fact, human knowledge in a firm is rarely translated into direct individual adoption. Similarly, firms can sell patents, and do not necessarily have to – and often will not – use new knowledge within their own production sites.

Phase 2 deals with macroscopic rule adoption. In its archetypal form, macroscopic adoption represents a *replicator* model. Metcalfe's, Chen's, and Silverberg and Verspagen's contributions discuss the salient features of the Lotka-Volterra type and the copying aspects of the replicator model.

Chen and Foster discuss the statistical patterns of macroscopic adoption processes, referring to various forms of the logistic curve.

Meso-models are usually structured as paths of macroscopic adoption that involve two or more rules. Variety is, as Nelson and Metcalfe note, at the root of the selection process. Metcalfe states, 'Clearly, the members must share some attributes in common, but they must also be different enough for selection to be possible. Evolutionary populations cannot be based on identical entities.'

The selection dynamic relevant for a large class of economic phenomena can be described using a *path dependence model*. By the term 'path-dependent', David means 'that the process is *non-ergodic*: a dynamical system possessing this property cannot shake off the effects of past events, and its asymptotic distribution . . . therefore evolves as a function of its own history'. The adoption probability of an individual decision maker is dependent, and it will change in the course of the macroscopic adoption frequency of the population of which that individual is a member. Decision making in the present depends on the macroscopically cumulated decisions in the past, and, when that decision is made, it is going to influence the future course of the meso-trajectory. Under many conditions, as David says, 'small events of a random character, especially those occurring early on the path, are likely to figure significantly in "selecting" one or another among the set of stable equilibria, or "attractors", for the system'. In their contributions Allen and Mokyr refer similarly to the significance of the positive feedback that drives the macroscopic adoption dynamic.

Phase 3 of the meso-trajectory concerns the exhaustion of the adoption process. The adoption frequency has reached its maximum, as described by the upper bound of the logistic curve. The third phase describes the stabilized and retained collective cognition, knowledge or behaviour. The recurrent macroscopic adoption pattern can be associated with the notion of *institution*. We have encountered institutional behaviour when discussing organizational routines. The term 'organizational' refers to the semantic aspect of the rule adopted; the term 'routine' refers to its temporarily stabilized *adoption frequency* and recurrent use. Generally, the notion of *institution* combines a *semantic* aspect of its use or application context with the aspect of *adoption frequency*. Nelson-Winter routines represent the productive rules of the firm that are used recurrently for its operations on the basis of a meta-stable frequency pattern.

The meso-dynamic does not end with the third phase. In fact, the factors that support a stable state of the system in turn constitute a source of a regenerative dynamic. An increase, or maximum, in the adoption frequency of a rule – for instance, of a technology – not only leads

Micro-trajectories   *a*   *b*   *c*

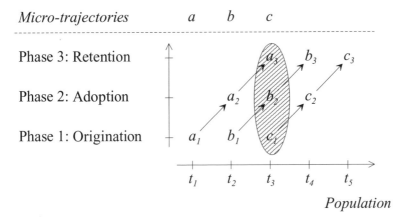

Figure 1.5 Meso-trajectory composed of micro-trajectories: time scale and time scope

to a confirmatory bias with respect to decision making or increasing returns accruing from positive scales, it also transforms the environment of the individual adopters into one where market opportunities and profits have a tendency to become exhausted. A system at maximum adoption frequency is therefore not stable, but rather, as Prigogine and Chen point out in their contributions, *meta-stable*. In his logistic model Chen integrates aspects of price competition and market share competition under conditions where profit margins tend to zero, thus connecting the conventional equilibrium with the 'biological' relative frequency approach of market shares. In the same vein, John Foster explains that 'if a system moves into the saturation phase of the logistic, the likelihood of instability and discontinuous structural transformation will increase'. Just as the cognitive pressure on creative minds will increase as a pool of interesting puzzles and opportunities for discovery becomes exhausted, so entrepreneurial unrest will increase as market opportunities and profit rates fall. Capitalism, as Metcalfe contends, is inherently 'restless'.

The interplay between microscopic and macroscopic adoption processes yields a picture of the meso-trajectory that shows both a *scale* and a *scope* dimension. The total dynamic can be captured by the replicator model, the three trajectory phases and the descriptive account of the logistic curve. In figure 1.5 the time scale of macroscopic adoption is shown on the horizontal line. At t_1 the adoption frequency is at x_1 and at t_2 it is at x_2, where x stands for a carrier – say, a, or b or . . . – and its subscript for one of the three trajectory phases actualized at time t_j on the time scale that relates to the adoption frequency of the population. The adoption process may refer to the introduction of a new technology or a new consumer product into the market or the introduction of a new institutional rule. The origination of the meso-trajectory is at t_1, with a carrier – say, firm a_1 – adopting the rule of the meso-regime for the first time. The agents b_1 and c_1 follow in the adoption of that rule. Looking inside the boundaries of a rule adopter, we know that the time that has passed from the first individual adoption by a carrier to the present macroscopic adoption will differ with the various carriers. When carrier b adopts the rule in phase 1, carrier a is already in phase 2. We thus have a time structure for the macroscopic adoption process at t_2 that is defined by the phase differential phase 1 / phase 2. Each of the carriers lives through its own history, and at a specific time of macroscopic adoption has a specific adoption 'depth'. The macroscopic scale hence obtains some sort of 'scope'. A scope pattern that involves all three phases of microscopic adoption is shown by the dashed area in figure 1.5. Carrier c is in the first phase, b in the second phase and a in the third phase of their individual adoption of the macroscopic adoption process at time t_3. The scope structure at t_3 is different from the structures before and after it; in historical time, the present adoption scope is different from those in the past and the future. Given this structural dynamic, and the response behaviour and positive feedback at work in macroscopic adoption processes, its genuine *historicity* is apparent. In their contributions David, Mokyr and Foster highlight in various ways the historicity inherent in economic processes, including seemingly simple diffusion and adoption processes.

The integrated model of a 'scaled' and 'scoped' meso-trajectory offers a conceptual basis for the attempt Witt makes to marry the ontogenetic and the phylogenetic approaches with a view to constructing a fully-fledged evolutionary theory of the firm. The integrated core model can be refined in various ways by allowing for factors that are either internal or external to the meso-adoption process. Internally, various specific assumptions can be made with regard to agent learning. Dosi et al. highlight the issue of population-level versus agent-level learning by introducing a range of models that distinguish between macroscopic adoption with and without agent learning. The population models differ with respect to their 'depth' depending on the assumed cognitive and behavioural characteristics of the learning agents. Models constructed on the assumption of rational Bayesian decision makers are substituted with a range of alternative models that rely on imaginative, future-open, rationally bounded and variously adapting learning agents. Externally, Foster enriches the logistic curve by making b and K functions of other variables, thus opening the door to an endogenous explanation of the non-constancy of the diffusion coefficient and the factors determining the capacity limits.

Foster's model thus gains a quality that is germane to the synergy model that Haken discusses in his contribution.

The general *dynamic of the trajectory phases*, now applied to the *meso-*domain, can again be summarized:

Phase 1: **Rule origination**
> *Meso*: primacy of adoption, decision to innovate, first rule adoption in carrier founding new rule population;

Phase 2: **Rule adoption**
> *Meso*: macroscopic adoption in population, replication, environmental selection, path dependence, population learning;

Phase 3: **Rule retention**
> *Meso*: adoption dynamics is exhausted, macroscopic retention and stabilization of rule in population, adopted rule as institution – e.g. organizational routine of firm.

The *meso-regime*, defined by a rule, a population of adopters and the respective meso-trajectory, represents the *component of macroeconomics*. It substitutes for what comprises the individual and its aggregate units in conventional macroeconomics – for instance, aggregate consumption or aggregate production. The meso-unit as a component of macroeconomics can naturally be combined and further developed in various ways. In all theoretical variants, however, it will be essential for both the qualitative ideational – *semantic* – nature of rules and the quantitative aspect of *statistical adoption frequency* to play their constituent roles. Evolutionary macroeconomics is the integral analysis of the deep structure and the surface structure of an economy. The following analysis provides some suggestions about what this means specifically.

10   Evolutionary macroeconomics

Interrelated *rules* and interconnected *populations* that exhibit features of *structure* denote the *macro*-domain. Each of the rule components constitutes an idea, a semantic aspect, of the macro-structure. The interrelated rules describe the logic of the complementary relations of the macro-structure. Rules, being ideas, are invisible, and we can call the invisible structure of interrelated rules the '*deep structure*' of an economic system. This structure embodies the *qualitative* attributes of an economic structure. The other level is concerned with the structure of interconnected populations of rule carriers. As sets of visible agents, these can be observed empirically and described statistically. We call this visible macro-structure of an economic system its '*surface structure*'. It has *quantitative* attributes and can be measured statistically in terms of the relative frequencies of rule-adopting populations. Summarizing we have:

1. **Deep structure:** invisible interrelated rules;
2. **Surface structure:** visible interconnected populations.

It should be noted that both the deep structure and the surface structure are integral to the generic level of an economic system. That level has been distinguished from the operant level. Economic operations take place on the basis of an evolved generic level. So, the focus in evolutionary macro-analysis is on how the system changes and not on how it operates.

The structure of the macro-domain defines a specific process state of complementary relations. When all complementary relations are completed, we say that the structure is *coordinated*. The dynamic of the coordination process can be stated in terms of the *three generic trajectory phases* introduced previously. A new structural relation comes into being with the origination of a rule. In the *first* phase, the new rule disturbs the prevailing coordinate relations, and constitutes a potential source of structural *de-coordination*. In the second phase, the novel rule is adopted in the population, and a process of a *continuous breaking up* of the structural relations takes place. This process of de-coordination, however, runs parallel with a continuous process of *re-coordination*. Because the agents adopt the new rules, new structural relations are established. The process of the second macro-phase is one of re-coordination converging towards the third phase. Although we could emphasize the aspect of de-coordination, it is one of the peculiarities of an evolutionary approach that only the survivors are interesting. Our analysis draws attention to the dynamic of the *selected* structural components and to that of the *selected* structural relations. In the *third* macro-phase, the process of re-coordination is completed, and the new structure is coordinated; that is, the coordinated adopted rules are retained in a meta-stable state.

The dynamic of the trajectory phases applied to the macro-domain can again be summarized as follows:

Phase 1: **Rule origination**
    Macro: de-coordination
Phase 2: **Rule adoption**
    Macro: re-coordination
Phase 3: **Rule retention**
    Macro: coordination

The dynamics of the coordination process takes place within both the deep and the surface structures. The deep coordination refers to the ideational content of rules. It constitutes the relational or, in its narrower sense (using the term 'gene'), the *generic coordination*. The coordination of the surface structure relates to the connections between the carriers of rules. The surface coordination describes the interconnectivities between populations or between relative population adoption frequencies. We denote this, in turn, as *connective coordination*.

The three phases of the coordination process correspond to various regimes of the generic and connective coordination. The *third* phase can serve as the *benchmark* with respect to *coordination adequacy* or *coordination failure*. The generic coordination secures the macro-*efficacy* of economic operations. A 'generic gap' leads to a *generic coordination failure*. Small generic gaps that concern required complementarities may have large consequences for economic operations, particularly productive operations. Connective coordination refers to the connectivities between relative adoption frequencies, and a '*connectivity gap*' shows up as *connective coordination failure*. Generic coordination failure means that new technologies or other rules have to be introduced in order to close the coordination gap, while connective coordination failure can be redressed by adjusting the quantitative measures of the relative rule adoption frequencies.

Quantitative change in the economic system can be defined as the change of macroscopically structured relative rule adoption frequencies. An increase in the interconnected rule adoption frequencies constitutes an increase in the generic *capacity* of the system. Various scale economies can occur because the connective surface structure of the system changes. A change in the adoption frequency may lead to increasing efficiency in cases of coordinated positive scale economies, or, in cases of uncoordinated scale development, there may be a loss in efficacy, and as a result efficiency declines.

Assuming the generic coordination level as given, both coordination adequacy and coordination failure can occur at the *operant* level. At given investment or technology levels, productive capacities can be used at different scales. An operant coordination failure results from a lack of complementarities between the available capacities of ongoing economic operations. Operant coordination failures can be seen as market failures, as described in neoclassical theory.

Evolutionary macroeconomics (which may influence policy) can be designed so as to distinguish between three types of *coordination failures*:

1. *Generic coordination failure*
   Disproportionate generic relations, lacking rule complementarity;
2. *Connective coordination failure*
   Disproportionate connectivities between relative rule adoption frequencies, lacking adoption adjustment;
3. *Operant coordination failure*
   Disproportionate relative magnitudes of ongoing economic operations, lacking capacity adjustment.

The economic *macro*-structure is composed of *meso*-components that, in turn, are composed of *micro*-components. The macro-structure thus has various levels of analytical depth, and, depending on the theoretical issue dealt with, the theoretical inquiry will investigate one or more of these depth levels. A full-blown theoretical explication of the *dynamic* of the economic *macro-structure* involves *all three levels*. It starts with exploration and rule creation at the micro-level, it proceeds with its macroscopic rule adoption in a population at the meso-level, and finally, at the macro-level, it copes with the issue of the de-coordination of a given stabilized structure. In this way, the overall complexity of the various processes can be brought into theoretical focus. A reference scheme for macroeconomic analysis that integrates the three trajectory phases with the micro-, meso- and macro-levels can be as follows:

Phase 1: **Rule origination**
> *Micro*: creative exploration generates novel rule
> *Meso*: primacy of adoption in population
> *Macro*: de-coordination of macro-structure;

Phase 2: **Rule adoption**
> *Micro*: individual adoption, learning and adaptation of rule to individual or socially organized knowledge base
> *Meso*: population adoption, selection and path dependence
> *Macro*: re-coordination of macro-structure;

Phase 3: **Rule retention**
> *Micro*: neural-cognitive disposition, manifest behaviourally in habits and routines
> *Meso*: retention and stabilization of rule in population, rule as institution – e.g. organizational routines
> *Macro*: coordination of macro-structure.

The overall analytical schema represents an integration of the various partial domains of theoretical inquiry discussed in the previous sections. The various contributions to this volume deal with one or more aspects of evolutionary macroeconomics. Generally, this can be divided into a macro-static domain and a macro-dynamic domain. The two domains are closely interrelated. As Chen and Foster demonstrate in their contributions, the 'statics' of self-organization and the 'dynamics' of processes are simply two sides of the same coin of evolutionary economics. Recognizing this, a *unified self-organization approach* is suggested that works out the genuine *historicity* of the dynamic, as highlighted in the contributions by David and Mokyr. Given their historicity, there can be no predictive account of these processes. As David explains, 'non-ergodic systems can settle into "basins of attraction" that are suboptimal; . . . perturbations and shifts in the underlying parameters can push such systems into the neighbourhood of other, quite different attractors'. The economic macro-structure receives its dynamics from all three phases of the micro-economically embedded meso-trajectory. Allen's contribution addresses the multidynamic of the interchanging microscopic and macroscopic domains, highlighting the non-linearity of their relations and the endogenous feedback at work. Specifically, as Allen says, 'the multiple scales of non-linear interactions lie at the heart of the emerging structures of an evolving economic system, as exploratory changes tap into unexpected loops of positive feedback, leading to amplification and structural evolution'. Prevailing coordination patterns impose constraints on the ongoing operations of the agents, and their exploratory drive changes these patterns and constraints continuously and provides the economic process with its evolutionary, potentially welfare-enhancing, engine.

How do self-organization and self-generation lead to *long-run economic change*? We have stated that the meso-regime is the analytical unit of an evolutionary economic macro-theory. With respect to its static properties, the regime relates rules and connects populations to form a macro-structure. With respect to their complementary tasks or functions, meso-units are coordinated in a macro-structure. In its dynamic properties, a meso-unit represents a *regime transition*. A sequence of transitions represents a long-run meso-change or *meso-growth trajectory*. A regime R_{j-1} is followed by a regime R_j, and that is followed by R_{j+1}, and so forth, where j stands for the present time and the negative and positive signs for the past and future time respectively. The two-dimensional properties of a meso-regime as an analytical unit of macroeconomics make up a *transition-cum-complementarity unit*.

Two general sets of models that build on this unit can be distinguished: one focuses on structure, the other on transitional features. Both constitute integral elements of a *general eveolutionary theory of economic growth*. Exploring issues of population dynamics and relative frequencies, Metcalfe brings the structural features of economic growth into perspective, contending that 'structural transformation is the central fact about economic growth'. Given the different evolutionary paths of the various meso-regimes, economic growth is bound to be a *discontinous* process. Various evolutionary meso-models and adjacent micro-models provide specific explanations of the structural dynamic of economic growth. Silverberg and Verspagen discuss a number of models that address one or more characteristics of a meso-trajectory and connect them with various behavioural assumptions at the micro-level. Depending on the theoretical emphasis, at the meso-level the models highlight issues of innovation, learning and routines, and at the micro-level they consider various assumptions about the cognition and behaviour of individuals or firms. Silverberg and Verspagen emphasize the diversity of the models, and look at scientific progress along a theoretical line that integrates a large number of aspects with a view to increasing explanatory power, but that also retains properties that satisfy the operational demands of mathematical tractability and quantification.

Applying Ockham's razor, the quest is not to integrate as many explanatory variables as possible but, instead, to detect that set of critical variables that explains a large part of the growth process. Turning to the entire range of models discussed, Silverberg and Verspagen conclude that '[t]hey do not provide insight into exactly which factors play which role in the growth process'. This leaves evolutionary growth models at a disadvantage compared with neoclassical growth models, but, as the authors argue, 'it is indeed one aim of evolutionary models to demonstrate that the sense of precision offered by the mainstream models is to some extent illusionary'. This statement clearly exemplifies the general case: evolutionary theory copes imperfectly with a complex reality, while neoclassical theory decribes with precision and rigour a simple world that apparently does not exist. If we accept the methodological stance of instrumental realism (section 5), and demand that the requirements for a minimum of realism and a minimum of formal rigour are met (whatever this may mean in a practical case), we may get a scientifically 'good' theory; but it should be also quite clear that, depending on the viewpoint of the scientists at work, we must expect to arrive at different standards of judgement and thus different 'good' theories.

Evolutionary economists who deal with the theory of economic growth generally share the view not only that the neoclassical model has integrated an inadequate number of determining growth factors – an increasing number is endogenized in the 'new economic growth theory' – but that the model stucture, with its production-function-cum-equilibrium-based resources mechanics, is itself ill-equipped to integrate the essential variables that would enable the dynamic of the micro- and meso-trajectories to be portrayed. As long as the 'representative agent' continues to be honoured, providing an improved micro-foundation for an economic growth theory will be like building a castle on the sand. An innovative entrepreneur or an innovative business leader just is not an average agent, and a population with zero-variety and homogenous traits cannot drive the dynamic of selection and learning new rules, and thus the dynamic of structural change that has been considered to be the central fact of economic growth.

What are the building blocks for a general evolutionary theory of economic growth? First of all, the *carriers* of rules and the *rules* themselves must be specified. Figure 1.2 provides us with a scheme of analysis. Behaviour connected to an external environment, represented by the right-hand circular loop, takes the central place. Stated in terms of carriers, the human represents *one* carrier, and the environment represents *many* carriers. The latter can be many of one kind – that is, a population of carriers that actualizes one rule (or, as assumed, a rule complex). This represents the *meso*-unit of carriers, the recognition of which is essential for explaining structure (as a unit of structure) and change (locally as phases of a trajectory, globally as a sequence of transitions). Furthermore, the term 'many' represents many of various rules, each of which may have many actualizations. Many rules and many populations are the constituencies of a macro-structure, defined – at its deep level – as related rules and – at its surface level – as connected populations.

Drawing on the agent-environment distinction, behaviour can be seen as individual or socially shared behaviour. Individuals employ rules that govern cognition and individual behaviour. External behaviour is co-determined by the internal behaviour of cognition, shown in figure 1.2 by the left-hand circular loop. Cognition calls for the adoption of *cognitive rules*. Cognitive rules adopted by an individual are employed, on the one hand, for tool making and tool using, and, on the other hand, for social communication. The individual behaviour is thus interpreted as *social behaviour* and as *technical behaviour*. Tools – say, machines, instruments or technical equipment – are actualizations of tool rules. When they refer to objects they constitute *object rules*, which must be distinguished from *subject rules*, which refer to one or many subjects. The *environment* is composed of *many structured object rules* and *many structured subject rules*. The former constitute all forms of technical organization, including firm organization and the division of labour, and the latter constitute the social domain or social rules that in their meta-stable state represent institutions.

A tool or technology is conceived of as an instrument for serving economic purposes. It is mostly used in a productive context to perform complex productive tasks. In growth theory, the distinction is usually made, as discussed in the contribution by Silverberg and Verspagen, between capital-embodied technology and capital-disembodied technology. Accepting the bimodality axiom (2), there is – strictly speaking – no such thing as disembodied technology, as there is always a physical carrier of any idea, such as technology. The physical carrier could be a paper that contains a technical blueprint, the carrier in this case being an *information medium*. The carrier would be humans in the case where the model refers traditionally to disembodied technology. Translated into the language of growth theory, *capital-disembodied technology* corresponds to *labour-embodied technology*. At this point, a brief look into the history of ideas is revealing. In the 1930s and 1940s John Dewey and other

American pragmatists used the term *embodied cognition* to emphasize the
bodily and neurophysiological nature of human cognition. Conceivably,
the proponents of early economic growth theory were inspired by the
idea of the human body when using it as an analogue for physical capital.
Physical capital, however, is an object, while the human body must be
associated with a subject. Analogies are valid, we have argued, if they are
ontologically warranted (section 4). The expression used in traditional
growth theory conveys an empirically invalid message, and the choice of
the analogy reflects a realism of words, not a realism of assumptions. Over
the last few decades conventional growth models have focused on the
factor of capital-embodied technology and employed vintage and related
approaches. Capital-disembodied technology was introduced only gradually from the 1980s onwards. In modern growth theory the disembodied
side of technological change is, as Silverberg and Verspagen state, 'still
even more of a black box than the embodied side'. What is recognized as
a black box in the received models is the very cornerstone of an evolutionary theory of economic growth. The carriers of economic growth are
both subjects and objects. However, the origination of all rules resides in
the domain of the *subject*, and thus the growth-generating 'engine' resides
in the subject. Subjects are usually socially organized into a unit that is
an element of a structured macro-system. The origination of economic
growth therefore lies, macroscopically, in *social and technical institutions*
that support human action.

   In following the course of evolutionary economics, the emphasis of the
future research agenda of economic growth theory – or any related theory
of (more narrowly or more broadly defined) economic change – will shift
from a capital-focused approach to a *human-focused* approach that deals
with human cognition and human behaviour. *Homo sapiens oeconomicus*
will be a concept relevant for future evolutionary economists. Conventional concepts, such as embodiment and vintages, may provide an instrumental service when reconstructing growth theory, but the shift from
object rules to subject rules, and from resource objects to humans as carriers of rules, will be essential for their theoretical application. The concept
of vintages may, for instance, be applied in association with the pragmatist concept of 'embodied cognition' and with the concept of 'embodied
behaviour', and we may employ the notions of *'cognitive vintages'* and
'behavioral vintages'. Equally, and perhaps less radically, the concept of
object rules could be extended beyond capital-embodied technology to
include *various types* of resource objects, particularly *consumer* products.
The endogenization of explanatory factors into a theory of economic
change or growth will, arguably, be easier to accomplish with respect
to object rules and their physical carriers than with respect to subject

rules and individual and socially organized humans. However, if the endogenous explanation of the major determinants of economic change or growth are to be part of a future research agenda, it will not be possible to circumvent this theoretical challenge.

Acknowledgements

This introductory chapter includes references only to the various contributors to this volume. Reference sections, containing – in total – around a thousand titles, are provided at the end of each chapter. I gratefully acknowledge insightful comments and criticism from numerous people, among them Stefania Bandini, Georg D. Blind, Hans-Jörg Brunner, Uwe Cantner, John L. Casti, Ping Chen, John Foster, Cornelia Friedrich, Simon Grand, Gerhard Hanappi, Stefan Hauptmann, Carsten Herrmann-Pillath, Geoffrey M. Hodgson, Elias Khalil, Matthias Klaes, Mauro Lombardi, Sara Manzoni, J. Stanley Metcalfe, Rainer Metz, Mark Perlman, Andreas Pyka, Klaus Rathe, Winfried Ruigrok, Jan Schnellenbach, Markus Schwaninger, Flaminio Squazzoni, Jean-Robert Tyran, Jack J. Vromen, Ulrich Witt and Kiichiro Yagi. A source of continued inspiration has been Jason Potts, with whom I am currently working on a textbook and related ventures. Special thanks are due to Patrick Baur for his editorial assistance and to Juli Lessmann and Mike Richardson for their proof editing. All errors are mine.

I

Ontological foundations

A

Evolutionary physics: a non-Cartesian
bridge to economics

2   The rediscovery of value and the opening of economics[1]

Ilya Prigogine

1   The open universe

It is only in the nineteenth century that we find a discipline called 'economic science'. At this time, the Western world was dominated by Cartesian dualism. On one side there was matter, 'res extensa', described by deterministic laws, while on the other there was 'res cogitans', associated with the human mind. It was accepted that there was a *fundamental distinction* between the physical world and the spiritual – the world of human values. When Thomas Hooke drew up the statutes of the Royal Society in 1663, he inscribed as the objective 'to improve the knowledge of natural things, and all useful Arts, Manufactures', adding the phrase 'not meddling with Divinity, Metaphysics, Moralls, Politicks, Grammar, Rhetoricks, or Logick'. These statutes incarnated already the division of the ways of knowing into what C. P. Snow would later call the 'two cultures'. This separation of the two cultures rapidly assumed the flavour of a hierarchy, at least in the eyes of scientists. On one side, we had the laws of nature, of which Newton's second law (acceleration proportional to force) was the foremost example. These laws (including today quantum mechanics and relativity) have two general aspects. They are deterministic (if you know the initial conditions, both future and past are determined) and time-reversible. Past and future play the same role. Therefore, science was associated with *certainty*.

Many historians believe that an essential role in this vision of nature was played by the Christian God, as conceived in the seventeenth century as an omnipotent legislator. Theology and science agreed. As Leibniz wrote, 'in the least of substances, eyes as piercing as those of God could read the whole course of the things in the universe, *quae sint, quae fuerint, quae mox futura trahantur* [those which are, which have been and which will happen in the future]'. The discovery of nature's deterministic laws was thus bringing human knowledge closer to the divine, atemporal point of view. The other forms of knowledge, associated to economy or social

[1] Section titles inserted by editor.

science, had a lower status. They were dealing with events, with *possibilities* instead of *certitudes*.

It is not astonishing that John Stuart Mill wrote: 'The Science (of human nature) falls far short of the standards of exactness now realized in Astronomy; but there is no reason that it should not be as much a science as Tidology is, or as Astronomy . . .'

But, curiously, recent decades show the opposite trend. Classical science emphasized stability and equilibrium; now we see instabilities, fluctuations and evolutionary trends on all levels of science, from cosmology to chemistry and biology.

Whitehead has stated that there are two goals that have shaped the history of the Western world: the *intelligibility of nature*, 'to frame a coherent, logical, necessary system of general ideas in terms of which every element of our experience can be interpreted'; and then the concept of *humanism*, closely associated to the idea of *democracy*, which emphasizes human freedom, creativity and responsibility. The idea of humanism implies choice and, therefore, the concept of value.

But for a long time it seemed that these goals were incompatible. As far back as the third century BC Epicurus felt that we were confronted by a dilemma. As a follower of Democritus, he believed that the world was composed of atoms and the void. Moreover, he concluded that atoms had to fall with the same speed on parallel paths through the void. How, then, could they collide? How, then, could the novelty associated with new combinations of atoms ever appear? For Epicurus, the problem of science, the problem of the intelligibility of nature and the destiny of men, could not be separated. What could be the meaning of human freedom in the deterministic world of atoms? Epicurus wrote to Meneceus: 'Our will is autonomous and independent and to it we can attribute praise or disapproval. Thus, in order to keep our freedom, it would have been better to remain attached to the belief in gods rather than being slaves to the fate of the physicists[2]. The first gives us the hope of winning the benevolence of deities through promise and sacrifices; the latter, on the contrary, brings with it an inviolable necessity.'

Epicurus thought that he had found a solution to this dilemma: the 'clinamen'. As expressed by Lucretius, 'while the first bodies are being carried downward by their own weight in straight lines through the void, *at times quite uncertain and at uncertain places, they swerve a little from their course*, just so much as you might call a change of direction'. But no mechanism was given for this clinamen. No wonder it has been considered as a foreign, arbitrary element.

---

[2] Epicurus probably had in mind the Stoics, who believed in a kind of universal determinism.

With the triumph of the Newtonian world view, it seemed that there would be no place for choice or, therefore, for values. In a message to the great Indian poet Tagore, Einstein wrote (translation from German by A. Robinson):

If the moon, in the act of completing its eternal way round the earth, were gifted with self-consciousness, it would feel thoroughly convinced that it would travel its way of its own accord on the strength of a resolution taken once for all.

So would a Being, endowed with higher insight and more perfect intelligence, watching man and his doings, smile about the illusion of his that he was acting according to his own free will.

This is my belief, although I know well that it is not fully demonstrable. If one thinks out to the very last consequence what one exactly knows and understands, there would hardly be any human being who could be impervious to this view, provided his self-love did not ruffle up against it. Man defends himself from being regarded as an impotent object in the course of the Universe. But should the lawfulness of happenings, such as unveils itself more or less clearly in inorganic nature, cease to function in front of the activities in our brain?

This seemed to Einstein the only position compatible with the achievements of science. But this conclusion is as difficult to accept to the modern mind as it was to Epicurus.

It is not astonishing that the great historian Alexander Koyré wrote:

Yet there is something for which Newton – or better to say not Newton alone, but modern science in general – can still be made responsible: it is the splitting of our world in two. I have been saying that modern science broke down the barriers that separated the heavens and the earth, and that it united and unified the universe. And that is true. But, as I have said, too, it did this by substituting for our world of quality and sense perception, the world in which we live, and love, and die, another world – the world of quantity, of reified geometry, a world in which, though there is a place for everything, there is no place for man. Thus the world of science – the real world – became estranged and utterly divorced from the world of life, which science has been unable to explain – not even to explain away by calling it 'subjective.'

True, these words are everyday and – even more and more – connected by the *practice*. Yet for *theory* they are divided by an abyss.

Two worlds: this means two truths. Or no truth at all.

This is the tragedy of the modern mind which 'solved the riddle of the universe,' but only to replace it by another riddle: the riddle of itself. (Koyré, 1968, pp. 128–39)

An amusing point is that *Newton was not Newtonian*. He, on the contrary, believed in an evolving world. The world would go into 'confusion' and the 'agent' (God?) would have to repair it.

What I would like to emphasize is that, thanks to recent developments in physics and mathematics, we can now overcome the Cartesian duality and reach a reunified picture encompassing the two goals of the Western world as described by Whitehead. This has important consequences, as it *restores the idea of value and opens economics, bringing it closer to natural sciences.*

2   Self-organization and 'laws of possibilities'

The nineteenth century left us a conflicting legacy: on one side, the idea of deterministic, time-reversible laws; on the other, the notion of entropy associated with the unidirectionality of time, with irreversibility. How to reconcile these two conflicting views? That is the time paradox. It is interesting that the time paradox was identified only in the second half of the nineteenth century. It was then that the Viennese physicist Ludwig Boltzmann tried to emulate what Charles Darwin had done in biology and to formulate an evolutionary approach to physics. But, at that time, the laws of Newtonian physics had for long been accepted as expressing the ideal of objective knowledge. As they imply equivalence between the past and the future, any attempt to confer to the arrow of time a fundamental meaning was resisted as a threat to the ideal of objective knowledge. Newton's laws were considered final in their domain of application, somewhat as quantum mechanics is considered today to be final by many physicists. How, then, to introduce unidirectional time without destroying these amazing achievements of the human mind?

A popular interpretation is that it would be us, through our approximations, who would be responsible for the 'apparent' observation of irreversible processes. To make such an argument plausible the first step is to present the consequences of the second law as trivial, as self-evident. For a 'well-informed' observer, such as the demon imagined by Maxwell, the world would appear as perfectly time-reversible. We would be the father of evolution, not the children. But recent developments in non-equilibrium physics and chemistry point in the opposite direction.

Let us briefly summarize the present situation. At equilibrium, one of the thermodynamic potentials (i.e. the free energy) is minimum. As a result, fluctuations of external or internal origin are damped as they are followed by processes which bring the system back to the minimum of the potential. Near equilibrium, it is the entropy production per unit time which is minimum. This again implies stability, but there is a new factor: irreversibility may become a source of order. This is already clear in classical experiments, such as thermal diffusion. We heat one wall of a box containing two components and cool the other. The system evolves to a steady state in which one component is enriched in the hot part and the other in the cold part. We have an *ordering process*[3] that

---

[3] It was in 1945 that the author pointed out the constructive role of irreversibility (Prigogine, 1945).

would be impossible in equilibrium. As has been shown by P. Glansdorff and the author, far from equilibrium being attained there is no longer in general any extremum of any potential, and stability is not assured. Fluctuations may then be amplified and lead to new spatio-temporal structures, which I named 'dissipative structures' as they are conditioned by a critical value of the distance from equilibrium. Dissipative structures are characterized by a new coherence associated with long-range interactions and symmetry breaking (well-known examples are chemical clocks and the so-called Turing structures). The appearance of dissipative structures occurs at 'bifurcation points', where new solutions of the non-linear equations of evolution become stable. We have, in general, a succession of bifurcations, which leads to an historical dimension. At bifurcations, there are generally many possibilities open to the system, out of which one is randomly realized. As a result, determinism breaks down, even on the macroscopic scale. It is worthwhile to quote the basic conditions we derived in the 1960s for the appearance of dissipative structures. They are:

1) non-linear evolution equations
2) feedback (or catalytic) effects; if substance X produces Y, Y also may produce X
3) the distance from equilibrium

These remain the basic conditions. Many examples are known today. The non-linearity implies the existence of multiple solutions. At the bifurcation points the system 'chooses' between various possibilities. That is the meaning of 'self-organization' – a basic concept in non-equilibrium physics. Of course, the term 'self-organization' has been used before, but here it acquires a new and precise meaning.

I would like to quote a report to the European Communities, in which C. K. Biebracher, G. Nicolis and P. Schuster wrote:

The maintenance of the organisation in nature is not – and can not be – achieved by central management; order can only be maintained by self-organisation. Self-organising systems allow to adapt to the prevailing environment, i.e. they react to changes in the environment with a thermodynamic response which makes the systems extraordinarily flexible and robust against perturbations of the outer conditions. We want to point out the superiority of self-organising systems over conventional human technology, which carefully avoids complexity and hierarchically manages nearly all technical processes. For instance, in synthetic chemistry, different reaction steps are usually carefully separated from each other and contributions from the diffusion of the reactants are avoided by stirring reactors. An entirely new technology will have to be developed to tap the high guidance and regulation potential of self-organising systems for technical processes. The superiority of self-organising systems is illustrated by biological systems, where complex products can be formed with unsurpassed accuracy, efficiency and speed.

In conclusion, we see that irreversibility has an important constructive role; therefore, what we need are not approximations to the existing laws of nature, but an extension of these laws to include irreversibility. In this new formulation, laws of nature no longer express certitudes, but 'possibilities'. The main aim of this article is to give a short introduction to these new ideas. A first remark is that we need an extension of dynamics only for classes of systems where we expect irreversible processes to arise. A well-documented example is 'deterministic chaos'. These are unstable systems. Trajectories corresponding to different initial conditions diverge exponentially in time (this leads to the 'butterfly effect'). The rate of divergence is known as the 'Lyapunov exponent'.

It has been well known since the pioneering work of Gibbs and Einstein that we can describe dynamics from two points of view. On the one hand, we have the individual description in terms of trajectories in classical dynamics, or of wave functions in quantum theory. On the other hand, we have the description in terms of ensembles described by a probability distribution, ρ (called the 'density matrix' in quantum theory). For Gibbs and Einstein, the founders of ensemble theory, this point of view was merely a convenient computational tool when exact initial conditions were not available. In their view, probabilities expressed ignorance, a lack of information. Moreover, it has always been admitted that, from the dynamical point of view, the consideration of individual trajectories and of probability distributions constituted equivalent problems. We can start with individual trajectories and then derive the evolution of probability functions, or vice versa. The probability distribution, ρ, corresponds indeed to a superposition of trajectories. It is, therefore, natural to assume that the two levels of description – the 'individual' level (corresponding to single trajectories) and the 'statistical' level (corresponding to ensembles) – would be equivalent.

Is this always so? For stable systems where we do not expect any irreversibility, this is indeed true. Gibbs and Einstein were right. The individual point of view (in terms of trajectories) and the statistical point of view (in terms of possibilities) are indeed equivalent. But for unstable dynamical systems, such as those associated with deterministic chaos, this is no longer so. At the level of distribution functions we obtain a new dynamical description that permits us to predict the future evolution of the ensemble including characteristic timescales. This is impossible at the level of individual trajectories or wave functions. The equivalence between the individual level and the statistical level is then broken. We obtain new solutions for the probability distribution that are 'irreducible', as they do not apply to single trajectories. In this new formulation, the symmetry between the past and the future is broken.

We shall consider in this article chaotic maps because they are the simplest systems to illustrate how irreversibility emerges from unstable dynamics. A map, which is a discrete-time dynamical process, may arise from a continuous-time system or it may describe a process that acts at certain time intervals with free motion in between. One may also consider a map simply as a model which can be used to illustrate essential features of dynamics.

The simplest chaotic system is known as the 'Bernoulli map'. We have a variable, x, defined on the interval from 0 to 1. This interval is the 'phase space' of the system. The map is given by the rule that the value of x, at some given time step, is twice the value at the previous time step. In order to stay in the interval from 0 to 1, though, if the new value exceeds 1 only the fractional part is kept. The rule for the map is thus concisely written as $x_{n+1} = 2x_n$ (mod 1), where n represents time, which takes integer values.

This very simple system has the remarkable property that, even though successive values of x are completely determined, they also have quite random properites. If x is written in binary notation, then successive values are obtained simply by removing the first digit in the expansion and shifting over the remaining digits. This means that, after m time steps, information about the initial value to an accuracy of 2^{-m} is now amplified to give whether the value of x is between 0 and $1/2$ or $1/2$ and 1. This amplification in any initial uncertainty of the value of x makes following trajectories for more than a few time steps a practical impossibility.

These facts suggest that a much more natural way to consider the time evolution in chaotic systems is in terms of ensembles of trajectories defined by probability distributions. The evolution of an ensemble, determined by a probability distribution, is given by superposing trajectories. Then the probability distribution evolves through the application of an operator, usually denoted by U, known as the 'Frobenius–Perron operator'. To obtain the distribution $\rho(x, n)$, at some time n, we apply the operator n times successively to the initial distribution, $\rho(x, 0)$. Thus, $\rho(x, n) = U^n \rho(x, 0)$. In contrast to the unpredictable trajectories behaviour, that of the probability distribution is completely predictable and, furthermore, for all 'smooth' initial distributions, approaches an equilibrium state. By a smooth distribution, we mean one that does not just represent a trajectory, which would be a distribution localized at a single point. Then we would get back just to the problem with trajectories.

Operator calculus has become an essential part of physics since quantum mechanics. In quantum mechanics, physical quantities are represented by operators. An operator acting as a function is just a mathematical operation, such as derivation, or integration made on a function.

In general, it transforms a function into another. But there is a class of functions called 'eigenfunctions' that remains intact. You just get back the eigenfunction times a numerical constant, which is the 'eigenvalue'. The set of eigenfunctions and eigenvalues of an operator is known as its 'spectrum'.

The spectrum of an operator depends upon not just how the operator acts on a function, but on the type of functions the operator is considered to act on. In quantum-mechanical problems, the operators are considered to act on 'nice' normalizable functions that are members of a collection of functions known as a 'Hilbert space'. (The Hilbert space is a generalization of the usual vector space dealing with vectors of finite length.) Time evolution operators, even in classical mechanics, have traditionally been analysed in Hilbert space. A class of operators known as 'Hermitian operators' plays a special role. These operators have real eigenvalues only in Hilbert space. The time evolution is then expressed as $e^{i\omega t}$, which is a purely oscillating function because ω is a real number. In order to have an explicit approach to equilibrium expressed by decay modes as $e^{-\gamma t}$ it is necessary to go outside the Hilbert space, *where Hermitian operators may have complex eigenvalues.*

After this excursion into operator theory, let us go back to the chaotic system. The important point is that the eigenfunctions of the evolution operator do not belong to the Hilbert space; they are 'fractals', to use the terminology of Mandelbrot (for more details see, e.g., Prigogine and Stengers, 1993). This is the reason why we obtain, for chaotic maps, new solutions irreducible to trajectories.

All this can be generalized to *unstable* dynamical systems both in classical and quantum mechanics. The basic quantity is then the statistical distribution function, and no longer Newtonian trajectories or Schrödinger's wave function. Of course, for *stable* systems, we receive the usual results. Irreversiblity appears as an emergent property. We can define only at the level of ensembles, somewhat as states of matter. An isolated molecule is neither solid nor liquid. States of matter are also emerging properties.

3   Historical time: where physics meets economics

It seems to me remarkable that the main conclusions we obtained remain meaningful for the complex systems studied by economics. Today, we overcome the artificial divisions between the supposedly autonomous realms of the political, the economic and the social. Now social systems are trivially *non-linear* and also trivially (as all living systems) *far from equilibrium*. Each action leads to negative or positive feedback. The conditions for the appearance of dissipative structures and self-organization are obviously satisfied. Economic systems are also unstable, 'chaotic' systems. While chaos realized in dynamics is indeed an unexpected phenomenon (the individual equations of motion are deterministic while the outcome is random), we have to expect instability in social systems as decisions are no longer associated with some deterministic rule. Each decision implies the remembrance of the past and an anticipation of the future. We can now make models applicable to economic systems which incorporate these elements. I shall not go into details here; examples will be provided in the chapters by my colleagues in this volume.

The decision-making process introduces an essential difference between physical and social systems. We can only hope for a statistical description of economic or social evolution. But this evolution appears now as rooted in the basic laws of nature. No longer is there a gap between the 'hard' sciences speaking of certitudes and the 'soft' sciences dealing with possibilities. Of course, the existence of a common arrow of time is only a necessary condition of consistency. The arrow of time appears on all levels, from cosmology to human cultures, although it takes different forms. The universe appears somewhat as akin to *The Arabian Nights*, in which Scheherazade tells stories embedded one in the other: there is cosmology, the history of nature embedded in cosmology, life embedded in matter, and human societies as part of the history of life.

The statistical element which appears on each level means that the universe is ruled both by laws and by events, such as events associated with bifurcations. Therefore we have choices, we have values. It goes far beyond the competence of a physicist to describe the origin and variety of human values. My more modest role has been to emphasize that the existence of values, and therefore also of economic values, is in line with our present description of the physical universe. To describe nature, including our position in nature, we are looking for a narrow path – somewhere between the deterministic description which leads to alienation and a random world in which there would be no place for human rationality.

In all fields, whether physics, cosmology or economics, we come from a past of conflicting certitudes to a period of questioning, of new openings. This is perhaps one of the characteristics of the period of transistion we face at the beginning of this new century.

REFERENCES

Koyré, A. (1968), *Newtonian Studies*, Chicago: University of Chicago Press.
Prigogine, I. (1945), 'Etude thermodynamique des phénomènes irreversibles', *Bull. Acad. Roy. Belg.* **31**: 600.
Prigogine, I., and I. Stengers (1993), *Das Paradox der Zeit*, Munich: Piper.

3 Synergetics: from physics to economics

Hermann Haken

1   Introduction

Why should a physicist such as the present author write about economics? Indeed, at first sight, there seem to be fundamental differences between physics and economics. Let us briefly discuss some typical differences. Physics deals with comparatively simple objects, which are studied under well-controlled conditions so that the experiments can be repeated again and again under the same conditions. The change of one or a few parameters allows the experimenter to study their influence on the experimental outcome in detail. In physics, it is rather generally believed that its laws are eternally valid and applicable to the whole universe. One of the outstanding features of the physical laws seems to be their capability to predict the future. This is clearly demonstrated, for instance, when a rocket is sent to the moon. Below we shall see that some of these statements are no longer valid, as has been shown by more recent developments.

Let us now turn to economics. It deals with systems that are far more complex than any physical system. In it, psychological aspects play an important role, and a number of important economic processes are governed by expectations about future events, hopes and fears. On the other hand, scientific prediction of the future of any economic system seems to be extremely difficult. In addition, practically no experiments under well-defined circumstances are possible. In other words, economics is characterized by its historicity.

In spite of these differences between physics and economics, and a number of further differences, in the past – occasionally – physical laws have been applied to economics. For instance, thermodynamics – especially the concept of entropy – were used to describe a number of phenomena connected with the increase of disorder. Or, to mention another example, the gravitational force was invoked as a metaphor for the formation of settlements or cities. In retrospect, these applications seem to be rather superficial, and it thus appears understandable that a number of sociologists and economists are reluctant to consider such translations of physical laws into those of economics.

What, then, is the purpose of writing an article such as this one? In fact, there have been new developments in physics that bring physics and economics closer together. In contrast to thermodynamics, the new areas in physics deal with open systems, which are driven by a continuous influx of energy or raw materials into states that exhibit qualitatively new features, in particular the formation of specific macroscopic structures. In addition, physics has to deal with systems that are increasingly complex. Furthermore, it has become apparent that in physical systems as well there are fundamental limitations to predictability. One such limitation was discovered in the first quarter of the last century at the atomic or microscopic level. But, nevertheless, it was still believed that these laws did not curb the predictability of macroscopic events in physics. This situation has now changed, in particular since the advent of synergetics and chaos theory, as we shall discuss below. Physical systems are still comparatively simple compared to those of economics, but probably complex enough to be used as paradigms, metaphors or models. As I shall show below, the emerging new field of synergetics allows the development of strategies for coping with complex systems. This is made possible by methods that, at least in a number of cases, permit a reduction in complexity and the establishment of general laws, concepts, and principles governing the behavior of complex systems.

This chapter is organized as follows. In section 2 I shall give a brief historical account of how I was led into the study of complex systems, and in section 3 I shall generalize the concepts encountered in section 2. In section 4 I shall deal with the phenomenon of evolution in biology, but also in other systems. Section 5 will be devoted to some sociological and economic implications arising from a synergetic approach. Section 6 will briefly discuss the concept of synergy, while section 7 will be devoted to learning, where I shall deal with the synergetic computer. In section 8 I shall look at chaos theory, and section 9 will discuss different kinds of concepts of self-organization, which are playing an increasingly important role in the discussion of economic processes and management theories.

2   Two paradigms of synergetics: lasers and fluids

First, I wish to discuss why the physical effects shown by lasers and fluids under specific conditions came as a big surprise to many physicists. According to the laws of thermodynamics and statistical mechanics, any physical system should tend to a structureless state at the macroscopic level, while at the microscopic level the system tends to a maximum

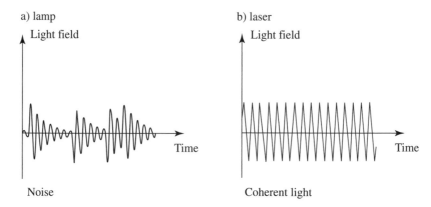

a) lamp

Light field

Time

Noise

b) laser

Light field

Time

Coherent light

Figure 3.1 The amplitude of the light wave versus time.
a) In the case of the lamp, the light wave is entirely irregular.
b) In the case of the laser, the light wave is highly coherent.

degree of disorder – or, in other words, to a maximum entropy. This can be exemplified most easily by looking at a gas that consists of very many individual atoms or molecules. If at a given instant we succeeded in bringing all the atoms into a line and letting them all move in the same direction at the same velocity, then after a very short time the velocities, directions and position would become randomly distributed – i.e. a microscopically chaotic motion would appear and the disorder of the atomic motion would become a maximum under the constraint that the total energy of the system is fixed. Thus, the gas would fill the whole space practically homogeneously – i.e. there would be no macroscopic structure visible.

Let us now consider the light source or lamp called a *laser*. An example is provided by a glass tube that is filled with a gas. At its end faces two mirrors are mounted. A current sent through the gas may excite the individual atoms, which thereupon emit light waves. It is as if we are throwing a handful of pebbles into water: a wild, excited water surface will result. Similarly, in the present case of the lamp, the light field will be microscopically chaotic, consisting of very many uncoupled wave trains (figure 3.1a). When we increase the electric current through the gas, suddenly the microscopically chaotic light waves may become entirely ordered. A giant, highly regulated light wave emerges (figure 3.1b). This can be understood only when the individual atoms that emit the light waves become highly coordinated in their light emission process. Since the individual atoms of the gas are not controlled from the outside in order to force them into this highly cooperative process, we may speak of

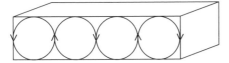

Figure 3.2 In a fluid heated from below a rolling pattern can emerge

an act of self-organization. Interestingly enough, the transition from the lamp state to the laser state is connected with a pronounced increase in efficiency. Since this article is not addressed to physicists, I shall not dwell here on the physical mechanism that leads to this self-organization process; rather, I wish to present the underlying concepts. Before the laser light wave is generated, a competition between various kinds of waves occurs. One of these waves wins the competition and survives. This wave is like a water wave on a lake on which boats are floating. The boats are, of course, pulled up and down according to the motion of that water wave. Similarly, in the laser, the laser light wave forces the electrons in the atoms to move in a highly ordered fashion according to the oscillations of the laser light wave. In this way, the motion of the electrons within the gas atoms becomes ordered. In the parlance of synergetics, we call the laser light wave the *order parameter* and say that the order parameter enslaves the individual parts of the system. On the other hand, the electrons of the atoms act like little radio antennae that, in the present case, emit light so that the light wave is maintained. Thus, in a self-organizing system, the order parameter determines the behaviour of the individual parts, but, in turn, the individual parts of the system maintain the order parameter.

Quite a similar relationship may be found in fluids that are heated from below. For instance, when a fluid in a square vessel is heated from below and the temperature difference between the lower and upper surfaces of the vessel exceeds a critical value, a rolling pattern consisting of up- and down-welling currents can suddenly be formed (figure 3.2). We thus observe the spontaneous formation of a macroscopic structure. In the case of the laser as well as in fluids, new patterns – i.e. the laser light wave or the rolling pattern – are formed when a critical value of an external control parameter is reached. In the case of the laser this control parameter is the electric current; in the case of the fluid it is the temperature difference mentioned above. In contrast to thermodynamics, in both cases macroscopic patterns may be formed – patterns that are connected with an ordering at a microscopic level. The conflict between thermodynamics and these phenomena is solved by the fact that thermodynamics deals with energetically closed systems, whereas here we are dealing with systems into which energy is being pumped continuously.

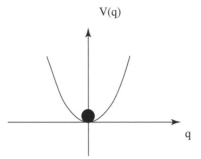

Figure 3.3 Visualization of the behaviour of an order parameter of size q by means of a ball that moves in a landscape; below the threshold there is only one valley

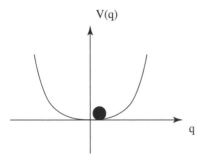

Figure 3.4 As in figure 3.3, except that the system is at the instability point: the valley has become very flat

For applications to be dealt with later I shall mention some important features of the order parameter. The size of the order parameter – i.e. the amplitude of the light wave in the laser case – obeys specific mathematical equations, the meaning of which can easily be visualized by comparing the pictures in figures 3.3 to 3.5. We plot to the right-hand side the size of the order parameter, and visualize the behaviour of that order parameter by identifying it with a ball that slides down the slope of a mountainous landscape. If the electric current in the laser is small, the landscape has the form shown in figure 3.3. Quite evidently, the ball slides down to the bottom of the valley, which corresponds to a vanishing order parameter. In the case of the lamp, the individual light waves are, occasionally, emitted, spontaneously which would correspond to gentle pushes being exerted on the ball (which stays close to the bottom of the valley). When the electric current is increased, the landscape suffers a deformation; its bottom becomes very flat. This leads to two interesting

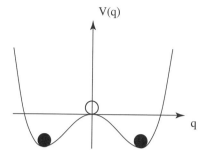

Figure 3.5 As in figure 3.3, but above the instability point: instead of one valley, two valleys are now formed

phenomena. Because the restoring force is very small, under the action of the pushes the ball can move far away from its equilibrium point at $q = 0$. We speak of *critical fluctuations*. At the same time, quite evidently, because of the flatness of the bottom, the ball rolls to its equilibrium value only very slowly. We speak of *critical slowing down*. Later on, I shall argue that such phenomena can also be observed in quite different systems, such as those in economics, under specific conditions.

When the control parameter (the electric current) is further increased, suddenly the landscape is again deformed, and it acquires – for instance – two valleys. Now the system has two states that its order parameter can occupy, but a *decision* has to be made as to which valley will be taken. In physics, the effect we are dealing with here is called *symmetry breaking*. To study this process, consider that first the ball lies at $q = 0$ – i.e. at the top of the mountain in between the two valleys. Then it has to experience a gentle push in one direction or the other so that it can roll down to the corresponding valley. As it turns out, this push is of a stochastic nature – i.e. a small fluctuation in the system decides which macroscopic state the system will later on acquire. A microscopic chance event decides the macroscopic fate of the system.

3   General concepts of synergetics

In the preceding section I tried to introduce some of the basic concepts of synergetics (Haken, 1983, 1984, 1993) by means of simple physical examples. It must be stressed, however, that these concepts – as well as the conclusions – can be formulated in a far more general manner, because they can be derived from general mathematical relationships. It will, of course, be far beyond the scope of the present chapter to give these mathematical theorems; rather, I wish to present a survey of the corresponding results. Quite generally, I consider systems that are composed of many individual parts or components. These parts interact among each other, thus mutually influencing their individual behaviour. In addition, a system is subject to one or several control parameters, which act in a rather unspecific manner on the system. In the foregoing section, in the laser case the individual parts were the electrons of the individual atoms, in the case of a fluid the individual molecules. When external control parameters are given, the system possesses a certain state – for instance, a resting spatially homogeneous state. Then, when a control parameter is changed, this old state may become unstable – i.e. the system tends to leave this old state. Close to this instability point, the collective motion of the individual parts of a system is governed by one or several order parameters (an example for the behaviour of a single order parameter has already been discussed). Close to the instability point, critical fluctuations and critical slowing down will occur. Order parameters may compete, coexist or cooperate. It becomes possible to classify the behaviour of a complex system by its order parameters. For instance, when there is one order parameter, the system will tend to an equilibrium state. In this way, the order parameter may be interpreted as the 'invisible hand' that occurs in Adam Smith's theory of economics. When there are two order parameters, either a stable equilibrium point, which is also called a fixed point, may be reached, or regular oscillations may occur. In the case of three order parameters, either of the two above-mentioned cases may be realized, or a third one, namely so-called *deterministic chaos*. In this case, the system may show quite irregular behaviour at its macroscopic scale, though microscopically many individual parts operate in the same way.

Quite evidently, the enslavement of the individual parts of the system by the order parameters – in short, the slaving principle – implies an enormous reduction of information. Instead of describing the behaviour of the individual parts, it is sufficient to describe the behaviour of the few order parameters. An important characteristic of order parameters and enslaved parts results from timescales, which may be explained in the following fashion: when we disturb the order parameters, they react slowly compared to the reaction of the individual parts upon a perturbation of the latter. I shall illustrate this relationship later by explicit examples from sociology.

These results have a direct influence on the question of how to control a system, which, incidentally, establishes a fundamental difference between cybernetics and synergetics. In cybernetics (Wiener, 1953) the idea is to control a system by a feedback mechanism. A well-known example is that of controlling the room temperature, where the actual temperature is measured and communicated to the control device, which opens or closes the corresponding valves so that the prescribed temperature may be reached. In synergetic systems there is no direct control mechanism steering the behaviour of the individual parts of the system; rather, the system is controlled indirectly via the setting of control parameters that tend to be unspecific. Note that, in the laser, the electric current acts on the individual electrons of the atoms in a quite unspecific way, or that the heating of the fluid acts on the molecules entirely homogeneously. Nevertheless, in both cases the systems find their specific structures by self-organization. Quite evidently, similar control parameters exist in economics – for instance, in the form of taxes.

These remarks of mine may elucidate the fact that the application of synergetic principles to processes in economics is based not on analogies to physics but on results from mathematical relationships. In the following, I wish to show by a few examples how these general concepts of synergetics may be applied to a number of processes in the context of the present volume.

4   Evolution

The concept of evolution plays an important role in biology and is connected with the names of Darwin and Wallace. It should be remembered, however, that Darwin, in turn, had been influenced by sociological and economic theories. Let us start, in the present context, with biological evolution. The order parameters may be identified with the number of individuals of a species. Each order parameter corresponds to one such number. These order parameters may compete with each other, which, under specific circumstances, may lead to the survival of one order parameter – i.e. we observe the effect of selection. It may be amusing to note that there is a strong analogy between the behaviour of lasers and species, which is based on a one-to-one correspondence between laser equations (Haken and Sauermann, 1963a, 1963b) and those for the evolution of biomolecules (Eigen, 1971). In section 2 I mentioned the effect of chance events. In this instance they correspond to mutations, in which new species are spontaneously generated by the mutation of genes. We may also observe a number of cooperative effects between order parameters, such as in symbiosis. Order parameters may coexist because of ecological niches, as do species.

The growth rate or size of order parameters may show local or global optima. The general results of synergetics shed new light on different theories of evolution. While one kind of theory assumes that evolution occurs under constant environmental conditions – under constant values of control parameters, so to speak – other theories assume that there are specific changes of, say, climate or of other conditions that influence biological evolution, in the same way that control parameters influence the self-organization of, say, physical systems.

In the context of the present book it may be interesting to establish analogies between economic and biological systems. For instance, control parameters may be taxes, order parameters may be the number of companies of a specific kind, and mutations, fluctuations or chance events may be identified with inventions or innovations. An interesting case study in an automobile factory has recently been performed by Ruth Beisel (1994), who studied the way in which the concepts of synergetics come into play when a company is restructured.

5   Sociological and economic implications

In this section I wish to elucidate the relationship between order parameters and individual parts by means of examples taken from sociology and management. I am fully aware that my remarks will not find favour with all sociologists because of the term '*slaving principle*', but nevertheless I think this relationship discussed below is worth a closer consideration.

Let me start with a relatively innocent example, namely language. The language of a nation is, of course, far longer-lived than any individual member of that nation. When a baby is born, he or she is subjected to the language of his or her parents, learns the language and, eventually, carries the language further to the next generation. It is evident that language plays the role of the order parameter and the individual humans play that of the enslaved parts. Quite clearly, the timescale of lifetimes plays the fundamental role here. A similar remark may apply to the relationship between rituals and the members of a specific group exhibiting these rituals.

When we speak of fashion, we may think that fashion is far shorter-lived than any individual. That is certainly true in most cases, but when speaking of short-lived and long-lived systems we must be aware of the aspect to which we apply these terms; the opinion of people may change rapidly, whereas a fashion may survive for longer compared to these rapid changes of an individual's opinion. In this case, individuals are again subjected to fashion, which acts as an order parameter. The same holds true for the formation of public opinion. Another example of the relationship between order parameters and individuals is the company ethos or corporate identity.

I would even go so far as to claim that ethics plays the role of an order parameter that is subject to evolutionary processes. This point of view was clearly spelled out by the famous economist Friedrich August von Hayek

(1949), who stated that ethics is the result of an evolutionary process in which the economic system that survives has the most appropriate ethics. So he clearly predicted the breakdown of the Soviet Union, for instance, because it entirely ignored private property.

Once the order parameters (some of which have been listed above) are established, it becomes very difficult to change them. In the line of thought of synergetics, changes in practically all cases, become possible only as a result of a change in external control parameters. For instance, the ethos of a company cannot be changed by ordering the individual members to be friendly to each other, but rather by changing conditions, for example with regard to cooperation between the individual members. Changes in economic systems can, of course, be caused by a change in the underlying political system – something which is, at present, clearly exhibited by events in the former Soviet Union. It may be worthwhile recalling figures 3.3 to 3.5 at this moment, in which during the transition period critical fluctuations and a critical slowing down occur – phenomena that are quite obvious in the former Soviet Union. At the present moment, I think it is worthwhile taking into account the effect of symmetry breaking; that means a self-organizing system does not necessarily tend to a unique new state, but there is a possibility of different solutions that, once realized, can not easily be replaced later on by the other solution. In the case of figure 3.5 this would amount to surmounting the mountain in between the two valleys, which would require the application of a very strong external push. Another example of the impact of control parameters on the economic system is provided by the sharp increase in the oil price that happened a number of years ago. Some people believed that the oil price hike would force economies into a self-organization process in order to develop alternative energy sources – an endeavour that, clearly, has enjoyed only limited success.

6   Synergy

The concept of synergy plays a considerable role when company mergers are performed. The underlying idea is, of course, that by bringing two companies together, or even amalgamating them, it will increase the efficiency of the resulting entity. More than fifteen years ago I studied models in which systems were coupled to each other and their efficiency was studied. To my surprise it turned out that both eventualities may occur for the same unified system: in one case the efficiency increases, in the other case the efficiency – or, in other words, the synergy – decreases. This was independent of the form of the merger, but depended, rather, on the initial state of the two systems at the time they were brought together.

As a general conclusion I would suggest that the merging of companies does not necessarily imply an increase of efficiency – i.e. a synergy effect need not be there. Rather, the combining of companies requires a very detailed knowledge of the kind of information exchanged between the companies, and relies on many other decisions.

7   Learning

Since sociologists occasionally make the statement that synergetic systems cannot learn, I wish to present an example where learning plays a crucial role in a synergetic system. Incidentally, I shall be concerned with the following question: how far do the concepts of order parameters and the slaving principle reach when we are dealing with complicated patterns? Remember that the slaving principle leads to a considerable compression of information in complex systems, because it allows one to express the behaviour of the numerous components of a system by means of just a few quantities – namely the order parameters. To demonstrate the power of the order parameter concept, we constructed the *synergetic computer*, which is based on the principles of synergetics and allows for pattern recognition. Since this computer has been described elsewhere in great detail (Haken, 2004), I shall not dwell here on the details but instead stress its salient features. The basic idea is as follows: a specific pattern is described by its order parameter and the slaving principle by which the system is brought into the state prescribed by the order parameter. Once a set of features – e.g. the eyes and the nose – are given, the system generates its order parameter, which competes with the other order parameters to which other noses or eyes, etc., belong. This competition is eventually won by the order parameter that is connected with the presented nose and eyes. Once this order parameter has won the competition, it is able to restore the whole pattern. The original relationship between each order parameter and its pattern is determined by a learning procedure. To this end, the faces (or other patterns) to be learned are shown again and again to the computer, which then establishes the prototypes and their order parameters. Figure 3.6 shows some examples of the learning of faces by the synergetic computer. Figure 3.7 shows how it can restore the full face, if necessary including the family name. It is clear, therefore, that the computer can recognize faces by means of individual features.

The order parameter concept is thus a highly powerful tool in constructing a new type of computer, which can, moreover, be fully parallelized and therefore act as a competitor to the neural computers discussed at present. It may be worthwhile here to elucidate the similar features and, in particular, the differences between neural and synergetic

Figure 3.6 Development of the prototype patterns during the learning process

Figure 3.7 An example of the recognition of a face that was learned by the computer, including its family name encoded by a letter
Note. The recognition process takes place in the presence of all the other learned patterns.

computers. Both concepts aim at realizations of computers by architectures in which computations are carried out in specific basic cells in parallel. In neural computers these cells have just two internal states, namely on and off. A switch from the off state to the on state occurs if the input signals from the other cells exceed a certain threshold. The cells of the synergetic computer may occupy a continuum of states and their activity depends, smoothly and in a non-linear fashion, on the input from the other cells. In contrast to neural computers there exists a complete learning theory with synergetic computers and their performance leads to unique results, whereas in neural computers there are still difficulties to be overcome – for instance, the appearance of so-called 'spurious states'.

The results reported in this section demonstrate that synergetic systems can, indeed, learn, and that the patterns governed by order parameters can be arbitrarily complicated.

8   Chaos

Since chaos theory plays an increasingly important role in theoretical studies of economic processes, I shall add a few remarks on this field (see, for instance, Schuster, 1988). First of all, and most importantly, we have to distinguish between microscopic and macroscopic or deterministic chaos. Microscopic chaos occurs when many individual parts of a system act in a random – i.e. unorganized – fashion. An example from physics would be the motion of the individual parts of a gas, or the entirely independent movements of people in a street. This is certainly not the kind of chaos that is described in more recent literature; rather, these references are to deterministic chaos, in which the behaviour of just a very few variables is studied. But how can complex systems with very many variables be described by just a few variables? This is made possible by means of the slaving principle, according to which, close to instability points at least, the behaviour – even of complex systems – may be governed by a few variables, namely the order parameters. Thus the slaving principle of synergetics allows – under well-defined conditions – the results of chaos theory to be applied to complex systems.

The most fundamental property of chaotic processes is their so-called *sensitivity* with respect to initial conditions. This sensitivity is somewhat counter-intuitive, but it can easily be visualized. It is counter-intuitive because it contradicts our conception of the laws which we are familiar with – for instance, those of mechanics. When we drop a stone so that it falls to earth, it will hit a certain point. When we drop the stone from a slightly different initial position, it will hit the earth at a different point, but close to the former point. Thus, a small change in the initial condition causes only a small change in the final position. Thus, for instance, when we make a change to an investment, it may seem later on that the results differ little from what they would otherwise have been. But look at the following example. Consider a razor blade in an upright position, on which we drop a small steel ball. If the steel ball hits the edge of the razor blade somewhat to the left, it will follow a trajectory that goes far to the left; in the other case, a trajectory that goes far to the right. A tiny change in the initial position may cause a considerable change in the subsequent macroscopic motion. This has led to the idea that the future course of events cannot be predicted, because we never know the initial conditions exactly enough. For a number of years I have been advocating the view, however, that even under these new conditions the course of events of a system can again be regulated by small controlling operations that are exerted more or less continuously, but gently, on the system. My expectations were fully substantiated by more recent results (Ott et al., 1994), in which it was shown both theoretically and experimentally that a number of systems in physics and chemistry can be controlled that would otherwise show chaotic motion. It is to be expected that at least some of these control mechanisms may also work in the field of economics though we must not forget that for some people economics has the characteristics of a game.

9   Different kinds of self-organization

Self-organization is by no means a modern concept. It can even be traced back to ancient Greece (Paslack, 1991). It should, perhaps, be stressed that there are different concepts of self-organization in modern science (for a discussion of self-organization phenomena in management compare Ulrich and Probst, 1984, p. 2, with further references). I want to elucidate two kinds of them in particular. These considerations are still incomplete and serve to show that we have to be careful when we use the term 'self-organization', because different scientists may understand different processes by this term. Here I wish to contrast the opinion of Von Förster with that of the present author. Von Förster (1984) pioneered the concept of self-organization, particularly in the sociological context, and an example of his – which I remember well – is that of the Battle of Midway during the Second World War, which was fought by the fleets of the United States and Japan. In that battle the American admiral's ship was hit and he was unable to give commands to the other ships of the fleet. As a result each ship had to develop its own strategy for fighting the enemy's ships. In this case self-organization took place because of the initiative shown by the individual members of a group. In the case of synergetics, the concept of self-organization seems to be rather different: here the individuals of a group establish one or several order parameters, which, in turn, determine the collective behaviour. It could well be that these concepts are closer together than appears to be the case at present, but the study of their relationship may be a task left to be completed in the future.

The concepts of self-organization in synergetics have a number of consequences for management (Haken, 1991). They advocate a horizontal rather than a hierarchical structure. They stress the important role of indirect control via adequate control parameters. But they also point to the fact that self-organization contains some pitfalls, for instance because of symmetry breaking. A system that has been destabilized by a change of control parameters may run into several possible states, among which may be the desired one, but also other, non-desirable states. Thus, for instance, at the outset of self-organization, some steering may be very important.

10   Concluding remarks

In this chapter I have tried to give an outline of the basic concepts of synergetics and to provide the reader with an idea on how these concepts may find applications in economics and management theory. Some of these concepts have been adopted in some relatively recent books (Zhang, 1991; Beisel, 1994), or have had some influence on others (Arthur, 1994).

REFERENCES

Arthur, W. B. (1994), *Increasing Returns and Path Dependence In the Economy*, Ann Arbor, MI: University of Michigan Press.
Beisel, R. (1994), *Synergetik und Organisationsentwicklung*, Munich and Mering: Rainer Hampp Verlag.
Eigen, M. (1971), 'Molekulare selbstorganisation and evolution', *Die Naturwissenschaften* 58(10): 465–523.
Förster, H. von (1984), 'Principles of self-organization – in a socio-managerial context', in H. Ulrich and G. J. B. Probst (eds.), *Self-Organization and Management of Social Systems: Insights, Promises, Doubts, and Questions*, Berlin: Springer-Verlag, 2–24.
Haken, H. (1983), *Synergetics, An Introduction*, 3rd edn., Berlin: Springer-Verlag.
    (1984), *Synergetics, The Science of Structure*, Boston: Van Nostrand-Reinhold.
    (1991), 'Synergetik im management', in H. Balck and R. Kreibich (eds.), *Evolutionäre Wege in die Zukunft*, Weinheim: Beltz-Verlag.
    (1993), *Advanced Synergetics*, 3rd edn., Berlin: Springer.
    (2004). *Synergetic Computers and Cognition*, 2nd edn., Berlin: Springer.
Haken, H., and H. Sauermann (1963a), *Z. Physik* 173: 261–75.
    (1963b), *Z. Physik* 176: 47.
Hayek, F. A. (1949), *Individualism and Economic Order*, London: Routledge and Kegan Paul.
Ott, E., T. Sauer and J. A. Yorke (1994), *Coping with Chaos*, New York: Wiley.
Paslack, R. (1991), *Urgeschichte der Selbstorganisation*, Braunschweig and Wiesbaden: Vieweg und Sohn.

Schuster, H. G. (1988), *Deterministic Chaos: An Introduction*, 2nd rev. edn., Weinheim: VCH.

Ulrich, H., and G. J. B. Probst (eds.) (1984), *Self-Organization and Management of Social Systems: Insights, Promises, Doubts, and Questions*, Berlin: Springer-Verlag.

Wiener, N. (1953), *Cybernetics*, New York: The Technology Press of MIT and Wiley.

Zhang, W.-B. (1991), *Synergetic Economics*, Springer Series in Synergetics, vol. 53, Berlin: Springer.

B

Evolutionary biology: the Mecca
of economics

4   Darwinism, altruism and economics

Herbert A. Simon

1   Introduction

Most of the chapters in this volume are concerned with the application of the Darwinian evolutionary metaphor to the development and changes that take place over time in economic systems, or in components of economic systems such as business firms and industries. An entire economy may be viewed as an evolving system, with Schumpeterian innovations serving as one of its mutational mechanisms (Schumpeter, 1934); or the competition among firms in an industry may be described in terms of mechanisms for the 'survival of the most profitable' and their implications and consequences (Nelson and Winter, 1982). These and related ways of applying the ideas of evolution to economic theory are well represented among the authors of other chapters.

The goal of this chapter is quite different. It is not concerned with the extension of an evolutionary metaphor to economics but with the direct influence of the processes of neo-Darwinian biological evolution upon the characteristics of the individual human actors in the economy, and, through these characteristics, the influence of biological evolution upon the operation of the economy. The focus will be on motivation: first, I will ask whether we can find any strong implications of evolutionary mechanisms, and – in particular – selection for fitness, for the motivational systems of economic actors; then, I will try to trace out the effects on economic behaviour of the motivational systems that evolutionary theory predicts will be selected.

The centre of our attention will be altruism and its role in economic behaviour. The first task, one not without difficulties, is to clarify the meaning or meanings of 'altruism'; the second is to determine what neo-Darwinism has to say about the evolution of altruistic traits in human societies; the third is to draw out the consequences for economics, and especially the theory of the firm, of the conclusions reached about altruism.

2   The meaning of altruism

Altruism has a distinctly different meaning in biological theory from the meanings that are usually attached to it in discussions of economic matters and human affairs generally. We need to sort these meanings out.

2.1   *Altruism in Darwinian evolution*

In neo-Darwinian theory the units of evolutionary selection are genes, and the basis for selection is *fitness* (Dawkins, 1989). Different members of the same species are not identical, but may have distinct versions (alleles) of corresponding genes. The differences originate in mutation and are preserved in reproduction. Which of the alleles of a particular gene ultimately dominates and drives the others toward extinction is determined by its fitness – that is, the number of progeny that it and its descendants have. Even small differences in fitness lead in a few generations to large differences in the relative numbers of the different alleles of a gene.

The increased fitness of a species as a whole is brought about through the gradual selection of fitter alleles for the genes of its members; and this, in turn, is reflected in the size and range of niches it will succeed in occupying in competition with other species.

2.2   *Altruism in human affairs and economics*

In most discussions of human affairs, altruistic behaviour is contrasted with selfish or egoistic behaviour, but from that point on matters become less clear. If we start with neoclassical utility theory, it seems natural to identify selfishness with behaviour that seeks to maximize the self's expected utility – a definition that, unfortunately, does not leave room for altruistic behaviour, at least for rational actors.

Let us leave irrationality aside, and agree that people have reasons for what they do. Then, to introduce a concept of altruism, we must make distinctions among reasons for actions: specifically, between actions that are undertaken on behalf of the self and actions that are undertaken on behalf of others. We can, if it pleases us and if we are willing to assume the requisite consistency in human behaviour, embed the reasons for these actions in a utility function, which then yields utility, in various amounts, for both selfish and altruistic behaviour. If we take this approach, our economic theory will predict absolutely nothing about how selfish or altruistic people will be: that will depend entirely on the contents and shape of the utility function, and, in particular, on the relative importance of its selfish and altruistic components.

In practice, research and writing in economics does not take this neutral stance. First, it generally assumes that utility, whether its selfish or altruistic component, has specific content – namely that it derives primarily from the self's or others' income or wealth. (Occasionally, especially in the economics of public choice, power is assumed also to yield utility.) Thus, economic argument typically rests on the assumption that people will mainly seek selfishly to maximize income or wealth, but, in the altruistic segment of their lives, will try to maximize the income or wealth of others. Second, in most neoclassical economic writing, the altruistic segment is treated as of trivial extent or non-existent, and the only 'altruism' that is admitted into the analysis is so-called 'reciprocal altruism', which is in fact not altruism at all (as I have defined it) but a form of far-sighted selfishness. It is easy to verify by examining the journal and textbook literature that this is an accurate characterization of the treatment of altruism in economics.

As an aside, I might observe that there is little discussion in the economic literature of what we might call 'religious altruism' – i.e. acting for others with the expectation of reward in the hereafter (the predominant form of altruism advocated in the Judaic/Christian/Islamic scriptures). The existence of any considerable amount of religious altruism would, of course, be quite as corrosive to contemporary economic analysis as the existence of substantial amounts of wholly unrewarded altruism.

Economic theory, then, as actually applied to economic problems, contains some very strong empirical assumptions about the content of the utility function which amount, very nearly, to the assertion that people single-mindedly seek to maximize their wealth, and that firms consequently seek to maximize profits. Occasionally, attempts are made to support these strong empirical assumptions with fitness arguments of a sort. At the level of the firm, it is argued that only firms that maximize profits will survive; at the level of individuals, it is argued (but less often) that wealth contributes to numbers of progeny. The empirical evidence for either claim is slight, if any such evidence exists at all. In particular, there is no evidence in today's world of a correlation between biological fitness, in terms of numbers of progeny, and success in amassing economic wealth. Of course, barring revolutions, things might turn out differently in some bleak Malthusian future.

The so-called 'new institutional economics' does not depart from neoclassical theory in any significant way in its assumptions about the motives of managers or employees of business firms (Williamson, 1975, 1985). It assumes that the relations among participants in organizations are governed by express or implied contracts, and that contract obligations will be discharged to the extent that they either coincide with long-term advantage ('reciprocal altruism') or are enforceable. Hence, there is no more room for altruism in the new institutional economics, as it is actually developed and applied, than in other parts of economics.

The description of the economy and of the behaviour of its actors that we find in economics depends critically on this set of very strong empirical assumptions about the motives that drive human behaviour. It is rather astonishing that so little effort has been made either to support or refute these assumptions, which are at the very heart of almost every descriptive or prescriptive statement that economics makes about our society.

Alas, I also am unable to supply such evidence in any systematic way; but everyday observation makes me quite sceptical about the assumptions, for, while I observe a preponderance of selfish behaviour in human societies, I frequently also observe behaviour that must be regarded as altruistic in terms of the definition just offered. These observations are, moreover, not wholly unsupported by more systematic objective evidence. By way of example, I would mention data on the substantial level of charitable contributions in the United States, or the data that have been gathered from time to time on risk-taking heroism (including the behaviour of soldiers in wartime). In addition, it has often been observed that even voting behaviour, and a great deal of other behaviour relating to public goods, is hard to explain without invoking altruistic motives.

In the course of this chapter, I hope to show that altruistic behaviour is substantially more common and significant for understanding economic and social behaviour than these examples would indicate. To do so, I must re-examine the present views of neo-Darwinism about the relation between altruism and fitness.

2.3   Altruism in neo-Darwinian evolution

It has been rather cogently argued in the evolutionary literature that altruistic behaviour, except altruism toward very close relatives (direct progeny and siblings), is not viable. The basic formal argument is quite simple. We start with a set of individuals, all possessing the same fitness, F. Altruists then engage in behaviour that is helpful to others at a cost, c, to their own fitness. All individuals benefit from the altruistic behaviour of the altruists by an amount pa, where p is the fraction of the population that has the altruistic allele. Then the net fitness of an altruist will be $F - c + pa$, while the net fitness of a non-altruist will be $F + pa$, the latter exceeding the former by c. Over time, the percentage of altruists in the population will approach zero (Simon, 1990).

The argument is very general, requiring only that the benefits of altruism are shared by altruists and non-altruists alike, and that there is some cost associated with altruism (that is, some fitness forgone that could otherwise be attained). Nevertheless, the argument is not conclusive, because it leaves out of consideration two crucial facts about the human condition: that individual human beings have 'bounded rationality', and that human beings can learn, partly from experience, but especially from social interaction. Let us consider, in turn, the implications of each of these two facts.

3   Bounded rationality

The global rationality of neoclassical theory bears almost no relation to the way in which human beings actually make choices. The reason is that, to exercise the rationality postulated by the theory, people would have to possess unthinkable levels of information and exhibit unthinkable levels of intelligence and computational skill in utilizing that information (Simon, 1955). The point has been made many times before, and is hardly contested.

Nor is it possible to argue that neoclassical theory, if not an exact description of human behaviour, offers at least a good approximation. In making our choices, we human beings do not come remotely close to taking into consideration all the components in our utility function (if we have one), all the potential and actual alternatives for choice, or all the consequences of each alternative and the associated probabilities of their occurring.

On the contrary, we approach choice within specific, quite narrow frames of reference that continually shift with the circumstances in which we find ourselves and with the thoughts that are evoked in our minds by these particular circumstances. Thus, in any given choice situation, we evoke and make use of only a small part even of the limited information, knowledge and reasoning skills that we have stored in our memory, and these memory contents, even if fully evoked, would give us only a pale and highly inexact picture of the world in which we live.

In a choice situation, we usually look at a few alternatives, sometimes including a small number that we generate for the purpose but more often limiting ourselves to those that are already known and available. These alternatives are generated or evoked in response to specific goals or drives (i.e. specific components of the utility function), so that different alternatives are generated when we are hungry from when we are thirsty; when we are thinking about our science from when we are thinking about our children. The evaluation of consequences is similarly selective, and limited to those more or less directly relevant to the goals that are evoked during the choice process. Finally, because of our ignorance about the world, we can make only the roughest, highly fallible, estimates of the probabilities of those consequences that we happen to consider. Indirect consequences unrelated to conscious goals – side effects – are frequently neglected because they are not even evoked during the decision process.

My present purpose in rehearsing these severe bounds on human rationality is not to argue again the general case that they must be taken into account in economic theory if we are to claim any close relation between that theory and what goes on in the real world. That is true enough; but the point of this chapter is very specific and much narrower: that bounded rationality has strong implications for the amounts and kinds of altruism that will be exhibited in economic behaviour, and that altruism has strong implications for the role and operation of organizations, especially business firms, in the economy.

4   Learning: experiential and social

The human species is distinguished from all other species by the extent of its ability to modify its behaviour through learning. Many, if not most, other species in the animal kingdom have capabilities for learning, but fall far short of the flexibility and power of human learning.

Learning requires some kind of feedback from the environment so that successful behaviour can be distinguished from unsuccessful behaviour, and the former gradually substituted for the latter. What especially characterizes human learning, greatly magnifies its effectiveness and distinguishes it radically from the learning of almost all other species is our ability to learn not only from individual experience but also from inputs provided by the social environment. We humans are social animals, and by far the greatest part of what we come to know and believe has been transmitted to us by social sources that we regard as trustworthy. Most important, we learners are usually in no position to test in any serious way, and thus to confirm or disconfirm, this information received through social channels.

Most of us believe that the earth is round, and that it revolves about the sun, but how many of us can give a reasoned argument that this is actually the case – and, especially, how many could have given such an argument at the time we first began to believe the statement? Many of us believe that the consumption of cholesterol tends to raise blood pressure, and accordingly we try to limit our cholesterol intake. But how many of us have ever tested empirically the relation of cholesterol to blood pressure or its consequences for health? We accept and act upon the relation, if we do, because we have learned of it through 'legitimate' channels (e.g. physicians or newspaper articles that cite reputable medical sources).

Very little of our knowledge, the ultimate legitimization of which is supposed to derive from the observation of empirical phenomena, has, in fact, been personally thus verified. Our acceptance of our knowledge has been based on the fact that it was acquired from social sources that we believe to be trustworthy – family, peers, experts, socially legitimized channels. Social learning is by far the predominant component of human learning, and the fitness of persons who are incapable of learning from social sources, or who are inordinately resistant to such learning, is dramatically lower than the fitness of their fellows.

Not all social learning, of course, transmits correct knowledge. People learn all kinds of myths (for example, world-creation legends that vary widely from one society to another, hence cannot all be true) as well as facts. However that may be, and whatever effects a belief in such myths may have upon our fitness, most of what we know that we use for daily survival and achievement is knowledge, information and skill we acquired through social channels.

I will employ the term '*docility*' to refer to the human propensity for accepting information and advice that comes through appropriate social channels – without carrying along the pejorative aura of passivity that sometimes is associated with that term. The docile are not passive; they are simply receptive to social influence, and what constitutes appropriate social influence for them is itself defined by their social environment.

Moreover, docile individuals may (or sometimes may not) use relatively sophisticated criteria to determine what information channels are to be trusted. An assessment of the self-interest of the informant is one example of such a criterion. My father gave me excellent advice when he said: 'Never sign in the presence of the salesman.' But, however sophisticated the criteria, the fact remains that most of our knowledge is a product of our docility rather than our personal experiences. Most of us learned not to touch hot stoves without the actual experience of touching one.

Although nothing is known, biologically, about how docility is transmitted, there is every reason to suppose – in the light of the strong advantage for survival that it bestows – that docility has a genetic base. I will allow myself the convenience of speaking of the 'docility gene', although a number of genes may be involved, and docility may be reinforced by such mechanisms – also having a genetic base – as guilt and shame.

5   Bounded rationality with docility produces altruism

I can now state my central thesis:

A species having only bounded rationality and endowed with a generous measure of docility, as the human species is, will exhibit substantial amounts of altruism in its behaviour. That is, members of the species will frequently engage in behaviour that sacrifices some of their own fitness but contributes to the fitness of others.

How can we reconcile this thesis with the neo-Darwinian axiom that only fitness counts? The argument will be carried out in two stages: first, I will show how altruism is compatible with fitness at the level of the individual; second, I will show how the selection of groups will reinforce the selection for altruism at the individual level.

First, I will elaborate slightly the equations for the algebra of fitness that were provided earlier, by adding a 'docility' term. Now the fitness of individuals is enhanced by the quantity d through the possession of docility, thereby becoming $F + d$. But, because docile people are receptive to social influence, their docility can be 'taxed' by sometimes giving them information and advice that, in fact, is harmful to their fitness but contributes substantially to the fitness of others. Perhaps they are told that honesty is the best policy, even when they can't be caught, or that they should risk their lives to save the lives of others.

People who are not sufficiently docile may see through such advice, and not accept it, thereby enhancing their fitness to that extent. But what is the net effect on fitness of rejecting docility? We now compare the fitness of a docile person with one who is non-docile. The fitness of the docile person, with the tax t, is now $F + d - t + pa$, where, as before, pa is the percentage $- p -$ of the population that is docile (and therefore altruistic) times a, the contribution of an altruist to the fitness of others. The fitness of the non-docile person, who avoids the tax at the expense of not receiving the benefits from what can be learned through docility, is now $F + pa$. We see immediately that, if d, the contribution of docility to fitness, is greater than t, the social 'tax' on docility, then the fitness of the docile will be greater than that of the non-docile, and the society will evolve toward a greater and greater percentage of docile (and consequently altruistic) members.

But what mechanism brings it about that the social system will 'tax' docility by urging certain kinds of altruistic behaviour on docile people? Consider two societies that are identical, except that one taxes docility and the other does not. Then altruism will be found in the first society but not in the second. The mean fitness in the first society will be $F + d - t + pa$, while in the second it will be $F + d$. Hence, provided that pa

is greater than t (the fitness contributed to others by altruism is greater than the cost in fitness to altruists), the society that taxes docility will out-compete the society that does not tax it. If there is an initial value of p for which this inequality holds, then p in the altruistic society will grow toward unity, thus increasing the initial fitness advantage.

An objection sometimes raised to this argument concerns the role of intelligence. Presumably, a docile person will sometimes be able to recognize that certain information or advice he or she receives is not really 'for your own good', but represents an attempt to induce altruistic behaviour. In these cases, the docile person can dismiss the information or advice and avoid that part of the social tax. This would give more intelligent people, who would be better able to recognize 'tax' items, a fitness advantage over less intelligent people, and would consequently produce a gradual increase in intelligence but a corresponding decrease in altruism.

The fallacy in this objection is that it assumes an independent, additive relation between intelligence and docility in the fitness equation. In fact, what we call 'intelligence' is overwhelmingly a product of the learning produced by docility. Intelligent people will be more, not less, docile than others, compensating, or perhaps more than compensating (by way of the bonus to fitness provided by docility), for an ability to detect the 'tax'. This greater docility may take the form, for example, of greater susceptibility to guilt or shame, or – to put it in more acceptable terms – a greater feeling of responsibility for playing according to the social rules.

6   Altruism and economics

Having shown that altruistic behaviour is quite compatible with neo-Darwinism, and that altruistic peoples and societies can be quite competitive with non-altruistic peoples and societies, we are led to the question of what forms altruism is likely to take in social systems, and what the consequences are of various forms of altruism for the operation of the systems. On casual observation, one particular form of altruism – loyalty to groups and group goals – appears to be especially prevalent in human behaviour, and to have direct and significant consequences for the operation of an economy. We will therefore first fix our attention on group loyalties.

Another question of interest is why selfishness, which presumably has its roots in fitness, so often takes the form of the desire to acquire wealth and/or power. Why do the usual economic motives have as much centrality in human behaviour as they appear to have? I will propose a (rather speculative) explanation of this phenomenon, again connecting it with altruism.

6.1   The mechanism of group loyalties

Human beings give frequent evidence of sacrificing personal advantage to the goals of groups to which they belong: the family, peer groups, business or other organizations that employ them, ethnic, religious or national groups – the list is almost endless. In terms of our previous analysis it is clear that, on Darwinian grounds, the altruism tax in any society would be aimed especially at enhancing the fitness of the group or groups that impose the tax (proffer the information or advice). In this way, group loyalty follows as an immediate consequence of the altruism theory. In simple societies, there is little ambiguity about what group's fitness is at issue; in a more complex society, this may itself become an important question. For the moment, we will set it aside.

Group loyalty has both a motivational and a cognitive component, the former being the more obvious. Social channels of communication will seek to induce in the individual a desire to behave so as to enhance the group's fitness – that is, its prospects for survival, prosperity and growth. At the same time, an individual immersed in group affairs will be exposed to information selectively and will pay special attention to those events and those parts of the environment that affect the group. Bounded rationality, which makes it necessary to select out of the actual situation only a limited number of variables for attention, will produce a context for decision that is highly biased toward the group's concerns. The individual's framework and representation of the situation will be cast in terms of variables relating to the group.

As a result of these workings of selective attention, it will seem 'natural' for the group participant to see the world in terms of the group, and consequently to identify with both the group's goals and the group world-view. The bias induced by selective attention and the cognitive processes it steers will reinforce the initial motivational bias.

6.2   Motivation in economic organizations

The modern industrialized societies we live in are often referred to as 'market economies'. This is really a misnomer, for only a small part of behaviour – even economic behaviour – in our societies involves individuals interacting through discrete market transactions. Much of the behaviour is employee behaviour or managerial behaviour, and most of the behaviour of consumers is best interpreted as family, rather than individual, behaviour. The salesman and the purchasing agent operate within the respective contexts of their firms and the goals of those firms. In all of this behaviour, including market behaviour in the strict sense, group goals (goals of business firm, firm department, family) and the representation of situations in terms of groups play a central role.

The operation of a modern industrial society is best described in terms of activities occurring within organizations, activities occurring within markets, and the influences of each of these kinds of activities upon the other (Simon, 1991). Now the new institutional economics has made a valiant attempt to treat activities within organizations as just special instances of contractual activities, like those that occur in markets (Williamson, 1985). But the instances become so 'special' that they are best analysed in a quite different way. Let us look at the employment relation – perhaps the most critical example for our purposes.

6.2.1   The employment relation

It has long been noticed that the employment relation, viewed as a contract, has a peculiar characteristic: it does not specify, except in the broadest and vaguest terms, the precise services an employee is expected to provide, but instead provides that the employee will perform 'within reason' those activities that the constituted authorities (managers) of the organization order or instruct him or her to perform (Simon, 1951). It is a nearly blank cheque, with, however, a few explicit constraints and many implicit ones. One of the implicit understandings is that the employees will use their knowledge and skills to carry out orders in such a way as to advance the organization's goals as effectively as possible in coordination with the activities of fellow participants.

The new institutional economics has been very much concerned with the enforcement of the employment contract (Williamson, 1975). In trying to determine the conditions under which markets will be preferred to organizations or organizations to markets, it has argued that the use of employment rather than other forms of contract may reduce or remove certain 'transaction costs'. It has also argued that employment contracts will govern behaviour only to the extent that employees' behaviour can be observed and evaluated, so that 'correct' behaviour (i.e. behaviour that advances the organization's goals) can be rewarded and 'incorrect' behaviour penalized.

Viewing the situation in this way would make the line between organizations and markets a very thin and subtle one, and would make it correspondingly difficult to explain the predominance of organizations, and especially very large organizations, in modern societies. It would come close to obliterating the distinction between an employee and an independent contractor.

The whole situation becomes much clearer when we take into account the organizational identifications, cognitive and motivational, that are induced when workers and managers accept employment in a business firm or other organization. The employment contract is not simply a contract for sale and purchase by another name. It is a relation, often one of long duration, that drastically alters the way in which people represent decision situations, the information they take into account in the process of deciding, and the methods and techniques they use in that process. The process of organizational identification, itself rooted in altruism in the form of group loyalty, is at the core of it.

Of course, establishing an employment relation does not extinguish selfishness or loyalties to competing groups (e.g. the family versus the firm). What it does do is to create a new loyalty, with both cognitive and motivational components, that under some conditions almost dominates behaviour (as, if we are to believe many accounts, it does in some Japanese work groups). Under other conditions it produces few motivational (as distinguished from cognitive) influences on behaviour beyond those that can be enforced and rewarded or punished. The term 'high morale' is usually applied to situations where organizational identification is strong, and an enormous literature has developed, especially since the Second World War, on the conditions that produce high or low morale, and the effects of the level of morale upon the level of productivity.

6.2.2   *Organizational boundaries*

Many other aspects of organizational behaviour, in addition to the nature of the employment contract, can be dealt with realistically only if the effects of organizational loyalty are taken into account. For example, it is well known that the goals of subdivisions of organizations are frequently in partial conflict with the goals of the whole organization – departments with divisions and sections with departments. Then the levels of the organization at which the primary identifications of managers and employees will attach become a matter of importance. We cannot make the simplistic assumption that, if two organizations are joined (say, through a merger), they will begin to behave as a single organization. The extent to which a merger will affect behaviour will depend on the extent to which it brings about changes in organizational identifications – itself a process involving many variables.

As another example, there are many situations where two organizations are linked by contractual relations of such complexity that they may behave, in many respects, as a single organization, and it may be almost essential for success that members identify with the joint effort rather than its parts. Such situations arise, for instance, when one organization manufactures complex components for the products of another, so that a great deal of coordination is called for throughout the design and manufacturing processes.

6.2.3   Forms of ownership

Periodically, one hears the argument that the profit motive is essential if organizations are to operate efficiently. A number of attempts have been made to compare the efficiencies of firms in industries where there is some private and some public ownership, with results that must be described as inconclusive. The evidence suggests that the form of ownership makes little difference. Everyday observation suggests the same conclusion. There is no apparent indication, much less solid evidence, that private non-profit universities are run more or less efficiently than proprietary schools, or – for that matter – than public universities.

These findings are also consistent with the observation, which goes back at least to Berle and Means (1932), that, applying a strict economic calculus and leaving organizational identifications out of account, executives in modern corporations who own only small amounts of stock have little selfish motive for aiming at the maximization of profit for the benefit of stockholders. Similar questions about motivation are raised when high executive salaries are brought to public attention.

6.2.4   Organizational survival and growth

When we add organizational identification to the theory, we see that there are good reasons why the form of ownership will not be a major determinant of the efficiency of enterprises. Whatever the goals of an organization, it can reach these goals only if it survives, and usually only if it grows. The survival, or fitness, requirement for any organization demands that sufficient revenues be brought in to cover expenses, and executive life becomes difficult if the net flow is only barely positive.

The 'good of the organization' is much the same thing independent of the form of ownership. In the case of the non-profit organization, surpluses are commonly used to expand operations or assume new functions. They are, and are regarded as, evidence of success in reaching the organization's goals. In the case of private corporations, profits are frequently reinvested to produce growth instead of being distributed to stockholders. Perhaps the motivations are different, but there is no clear evidence that they are. For those participants in both kinds of organizations who are identified with the organizational goals, survival through balanced budgets is a 'must' for the organization, and growth through the reinvestment of surpluses an important 'good'.

These considerations help to explain why income and wealth (now applied to organizations rather than individuals) are commonly perceived to be the goals of economic activity. Money is the common and wholly fungible commodity that must be obtained by the organization in order to command the resources needed to accomplish its goals (Simon, 1952–53). A positive balance of income over expense is the necessary and sufficient condition for survival and success.

Perhaps this is seen most poignantly (and even pathetically) in charitable organizations, which often have to spend a large part of their income in fund-raising activities. Here we observe the 'selfish' activity of acquiring income and wealth enlisted for the purpose of accomplishing the altruistic goals of the organization and its donors. This example illustrates the care that is required in relating the selfish/altruistic distinction, in the everyday use of these terms, to the selfish/altruistic distinction that is made in evolutionary theory.

Parenthetically, the same considerations apply to government agencies. Notwithstanding contrary popular opinion, I have encountered no empirical evidence showing that government organizations are less efficient in their use of resources than private organizations with similar goals. (We must hold goals constant in the comparison because the measurability or non-measurability of goal attainment can have an important influence on efficiency.)

The recent Eastern European experience, usually hailed (at least until very recently) as decisive evidence for the superiority of profit-oriented activity, is not very informative for at least two reasons. First, in most of the countries involved there was no history of an extensive development of effective management for large-scale organizations. Second, markets had not been used effectively, or at all, to impose budget discipline upon organizations or to coordinate relations among them.

7   Conclusions

The arguments that have been developed in this chapter can be summarized in five simple propositions:

1. Altruism in human behaviour (the sacrifice of own's fitness for the fitness of others) is wholly consistent with the assumptions of neo-Darwinian evolutionary theory that evolution is driven by natural selection – i.e. fitness.
2. Altruism will be found in an evolutionary system in species characterized by both bounded rationality and strong capabilities for learning from social inputs (the human species). The gains to fitness from the

acceptance of social influence will more than balance the 'tax' on fitness paid in the form of altruistic behaviour.

3. Altruism in human societies commonly takes the form of organizational identification and loyalty, for this form of altruism contributes directly to the fitness of the group that is seeking to exert social influence on behaviour.

4. Organizational identification, by securing behaviour in support of organization goals far beyond what could be obtained by enforcement and reward and punishment, is a major basis for the effectiveness of large organizations in carrying out economic activities.

5. The employment relation is a contract of a very special sort, which depends for its effectiveness on the human propensity to identify with organizational goals. It works well to the degree that such identification is created and maintained. The altruism mechanism provides the basic mechanism for creating and maintaining identification.

A theory of the business firm and of the evolution of firms must incorporate, if it is to be viable, a genuine theory of human motivations in organizations. An important component of that theory will be the proposition that employees and executives are usually rather strongly motivated, by the identifications they acquire, to advance the goals – hence the fitness – of the organizations to which they belong.

Organizations, especially governmental organizations but also large business organizations, have a bad press in our society today, possibly because they are frequently compared with a Utopian ideal of perfect efficiency. We should be interested in the conditions under which our organizations can be made more efficient, but there is no evidence that market mechanisms, deprived of the kinds of organization structures that exist in market economies, can produce anything like the levels of productivity that contemporary industrial societies have achieved. Nor is there evidence that the profit motive is required for organizations to operate at efficient levels. Being subjected to the discipline of a balanced budget appears to achieve the same result for non-profit organizations, at least in those cases where productivity can be measured.

REFERENCES

Berle, A. A., and G. C. Means (1932), *The Modern Corporation and Private Property*, New York: Macmillan.
Dawkins, R. (1989), *The Selfish Gene*, Oxford: Oxford University Press.
Nelson, R. R., and S. G. Winter (1982), *An Evolutionary Theory of Economic Change*, Cambridge, MA: Harvard University Press.
Schumpeter, J. A. (1934), *The Theory of Economic Development: An Inquiry into Profits, Capital, Credit, Interest, and the Business Cycle* (translated by R. Opie

from the German edition of 1912), Cambridge, MA: Harvard University Press. [Reprinted in 1989 with a new introduction by J. E. Elliott, New Brunswick, NJ: Transaction.]

Simon, H. A. (1951), 'A formal theory of the employment relationship', *Econometrica* **19**(3): 293–305.

(1952–53), 'A comparison of organization theories', *Review of Economic Studies* **20**(1): 40–48.

(1955), 'A behavioral model of rational choice', *Quarterly Journal of Economics* **69**: 99–118.

(1990), 'A mechanism for social selection and successful altruism', *Science* **250**: 1665–68.

(1991), 'Organizations and markets', *Journal of Economic Perspectives* **5**: 25–44.

Williamson, O. E. (1975), *Markets and Hierarchies: Analysis and Antitrust Implications*, New York: Free Press.

(1985), *The Economic Institutions of Capitalism*, New York: Free Press.

5 Decomposition and growth: biological metaphors in economics from the 1880s to the 1980s[1]

Geoffrey M. Hodgson

1 Introduction

In economics, the word 'evolutionary' is currently in fashion. Since the 1980s the number of economics books and articles with 'evolution' in their title has increased rapidly[2]. This revolution is not confined to heterodoxy. Leading neoclassical economists such as Kenneth Arrow and Frank Hahn have turned away from mechanics, seeing biology as the possible inspiration for the economics of the future (Anderson, 1995; Arrow 1995; Hahn, 1991, p. 48).

The relationship between biology and economics has waxed and waned over the centuries and has worked in both directions. The influence of the economists Adam Smith and Thomas Robert Malthus on Charles Darwin is widely known, even if some of the details remain controversial (Hodgson, 1993b, 1995). Ideas of competition and struggle in the writings of Smith and Malthus simultaneously inspired economics and biology. Accordingly, to some degree, biological metaphors have always been present in the foreground or background of modern economic theory. What is striking, however, is the temporal variation in the degree of their explicit popularity and use.

With the emergence of neoclassical economics in the 1870s, its principal inspiration was not biology but physics (Mirowski, 1989; Ingrao and Israel, 1990). Yet by the end of the nineteenth century the picture in economics was again modified. Alfred Marshall wrote that 'the Mecca of the economist lies in economic biology' (Marshall, 1890, p. xiv). Furthermore, leading heterodox economists such as Thorstein Veblen enthusiastically embraced biology. Overall, the biological metaphor was widely

---

[1] An earlier version of this essay was published in Hodgson (1999). The author is very grateful to Royall Brandis, Paul Dale Bush, Bruce Caldwell, Kurt Dopfer, John Foster, Uskali Mäki, Richard Nelson and Malcolm Rutherford for discussions and helpful remarks on previous drafts.

[2] For discussions of the evolution of evolutionary economics and the varied and competing claims to the 'evolutionary' epithet, see Hodgson (1995, 1999).

invoked in economics and in social science as a whole in the 1890–1914 period[3].

Yet by the end of the 1920s the use of biological and evolutionary analogies had fallen out of favour in economics and social science. From then on evolutionary ideas remained largely unexplored in economics, until the publication of a famous article by Armen Alchian in 1950. Given the recent resurgence of 'evolutionary' ideas – especially since the publication of Richard Nelson and Sidney Winter's classic 1982 work – the neglect of the biological metaphor for much of the middle of the twentieth century requires an explanation.

There is an important sub-plot here. By focusing on the inter-war decay of the biological metaphor in American economic thought, some further reasons are given for the precipitous decline of institutional economics in the United States. It was virtually the dominant paradigm in American economics in the 1920s, but by 1950 it began to be marginalized by mathematical versions of neoclassical theory. Furthermore, institutional economics was never prominent in Britain, but the turn away from biology had enormous effects on the development of Marshall's legacy.

It is the purpose of this chapter to address these issues, particularly through an examination of the scientific and ideological context in the period. The main focus is on Anglo-American economics, but other significant influences – particularly from Germany – will also be considered.

Clearly, the typical use of the biological metaphor by modern economists such as Nelson and Winter is a far cry from the biological determinism, and even racism and sexism, of many late nineteenth-century writers. Using the biological metaphor in a socio-economic context is not the same thing as believing that our behaviour is largely or wholly determined by what is in our genes.

Nevertheless, studies of the 1880–1990 period strongly suggest that the degree of acceptance of biological analogies in social science is closely correlated both with the general prestige accorded to the biological sciences and with the degree of academic acceptance of a biotic foundation for human nature. Accordingly, the popularity of organic and biological analogies throughout the Western world at the end of the nineteenth century was intimately related to the prominence of largely biological explanations of human behaviour[4]. Carl Degler (1991) shows that the idea

---

[3] See the more detailed discussions of Marshall, Veblen, Spencer, Schumpeter, Menger, Hayek and others in Hodgson (1992, 1993a, 1993b).

[4] As Bowler (1983) shows, Darwin's ideas were actually out of vogue in the 1880–1914 period. They were to be revived in the post-1930 synthesis with genetics. It is now widely recognized that most of those accused of 'social Darwinism' were much closer in their ideas to Spencer or Sumner than to Darwin himself.

of a biological root to human nature was widely accepted by social scientists by the end of the Victorian era.

Further, as social scientists began to reject biological explanations of human attributes and behaviour in the early decades of the twentieth century, their revulsion against biological thinking was such that biological and evolutionary metaphors were likewise rejected. This revulsion lasted for several decades, and persists in some quarters even today. What has helped to open up more space for a more liberal use of biological metaphors in social science since the 1970s has been the emergence of more pluralistic, multi-causal or non-reductionist discourses in biology and anthropology. Accordingly, biological metaphors have again become legitimate in economics and other social sciences. The adoption of such metaphors does not necessarily involve a return to biological reductionism.

However, it must be emphasized that, with metaphor in science, much more is at stake than the choice of analogy or mode of literary expression. Several philosophers have argued that metaphor plays a constitutive role in science, rather than being a mere 'literary frill' (Black, 1962; Hesse, 1966; Maasen, 1995). Accordingly, the development of economic theory is likely to be affected profoundly by the nature of its chosen metaphor and by the character of the field of discourse to which it is thus connected. The close parallels between the history of modern biology and of modern economics suggest that metaphor works at a deep level in science, affecting its progress in ways that its practitioners are not always aware of (Hodgson, 1997, 1999).

The question of the use of biological metaphors relates to three key philosophical issues. The first concerns ontology. For some, the use of the metaphor of an *organism* has been tied up with the incorporation of an *organicist* ontology. In an organicist ontology, relations between entities are seen as internal rather than external: the essential characteristics of an element are regarded as the outcomes of relations with other entities. Accordingly, in the context of social science, the individual is seen as being moulded by relations with other individuals. In contrast, in an *atomist* ontology – as pictured by the Greek atomists or in Newtonian physics – entities possess qualities independently of their relations with other entities. Therefore, the individual is taken as given, as in neoclassical economics and classic liberal political thought. Organicism rejects the atomistic starting point of the given individual, and sometimes chooses the cell or organism interacting with its environment as its metaphor[5].

---

[5] For a useful discussion of organicism in economics see Winslow (1989).

Second, there is the methodological problem of reductionism. Reductionism sometimes involves the notion that wholes must be explained entirely in terms of their elemental, constituent parts. More generally, reductionism can be defined as the idea that all aspects of a complex phenomenon must be explained in terms of one level, or type of unit. According to this view there are no autonomous levels of analysis other than this elemental foundation, and no such thing as emergent properties upon which other levels of analysis can be based. In social science in the 1870–1920 period reductionism was prominent, and it typically took a biological form. Accordingly, attempts were made to explain the behaviour of individuals and groups in terms of their alleged biological characteristics. In social science today reductionism is still prevalent, but it typically takes the form of methodological individualism, by which it is asserted that explanations of social structures and institutions must be couched entirely in terms of individuals. Allied to this is the sustained attempt since the 1960s to found macroeconomics on 'sound microfoundations'. There are other versions of reductionism, however, including versions of 'holism' that suggest that parts should be explained in terms of wholes. Reductionism is countered by the notion that complex systems display emergent properties at different levels that cannot be completely reduced to or explained wholly in terms of another level[6].

Third, there is the question of the use and prestige of mathematical models in economics and social science. Since the 1930s there has been a dramatic rise in the status accorded to mathematical modelling in economics. Yet sixty years of effort by thousands of economists in many countries has yielded patchy results. Even with fixed preference functions, matters are extremely complicated. It would seemingly make things even more complicated to challenge such fundamental and established assumptions. Accordingly, one reason why individuals are treated as social atoms with given preference functions is to increase the possibility of mathematical tractability. Although biology has engendered its own practices of formal and mathematical modelling, the wider acceptance of the openness and complexity of biological systems has protected the more discursive approaches.

Organic and evolutionary metaphors in social science have a very long history. Our period of concern, however, begins in the closing years of the nineteenth century. The century-long story is complex and multi-faceted; the sketchiest of accounts must be given here. What may absolve

---

[6] The possibility of emergent properties is emphasized by Bhaskar (1975, 1979). On the question of methodological individualism see Hodgson (1988, 1993b). On the failure of the microfoundations project see Kirman (1989, 1992) and Rizvi (1994).

this rudimentary overview of a complex tale is that this essay is one of the first works to address specifically the question of the decline of evolutionary and biological analogies in economics in the 1920s and their post-1945 rebirth[7].

2 The biological metaphor in German social science before 1914

Prior to the rise of Charles Darwin and Herbert Spencer in England, organic analogies were prominent in social science in the German-speaking world. Michael Hutter (1994) shows that the German roots of such organic metaphors go back to the eighteenth century and earlier. A number of German social scientists made extensive comparisons between biological and social organisms. With the rise of the German historical school, a strong dependence on the organic metaphor was manifest. It was particularly evident in the works of writers such as Karl Knies (1853), Wilhelm Roscher (1854), Paul von Lilienfeld (1873–81) and Albert Schäffle (1881).

In the German-speaking world the organic analogy took a number of forms and linked up with a variety of propositions, from the assertion of an organicist ontology, to the recognition of social influences on individuals, to the assertion of the systemic interdependence of the whole socio-economic system and to a 'stages' theory of history compared explicitly with the growth of an organism. It was also widely associated with the proposition that the socio-economic system could be analysed as if it had a will and mind of its own, surmounting those of the individuals comprising it, just as the brain and nervous system of an organism transcend its individual organs and cells[8].

The historical school was at its high point of influence in Germany and Austria when, in 1883, Carl Menger fired the opening shots of the *Methodenstreit* with the publication of his *Untersuchungen*. We need not go into the details of this famous intellectual battle here. It is sufficient to note that Menger did not target the use of the organic or biological analogy as such but the idea that independent will or purpose could be attributed to

---

[7] Partial exceptions are Degler (1991) and Persons (1950). Both devote relatively little space to economics.

[8] Notably, while Lilienfeld had argued between 1873 and 1881 that society is *actually* an organism, Schäffle in his writings from 1875 to 1881 differed, seeing the organism analogy as appropriate but not literal. For Schäffle, society was not an organism in a biological or physiological sense, but its symbolic and technological unity gave it organism-like qualities. On this basis Schäffle applied quasi-Darwinian principles to the socio-economic system, and, like others, he saw collectivities rather than individuals as the units of selection.

the 'social organism'. This idea attracted Menger's devastatingly critical pen. Although the biological analogy was not Menger's main focus, the effect of his critique was to diminish greatly its usage in German social science.

Menger pointed out that some institutions were deliberately created by individuals, but many others were not. He emphasized that social institutions often evolve unintentionally out of the purposeful actions of many interacting individuals. What had to be discarded were explanations of the emergence of social institutions that relied on a 'social will' that could not, in turn, itself be explained in terms of the purposeful behaviour of individuals. Menger is thus remembered as a critic of 'holism' and as an early architect of methodological individualism.

The *Methodenstreit* was so devastating in the two decades it lasted that the use of the organic analogy had become unpopular in Germany and Austria by the beginning of the twentieth century. Instead, there was the ascendancy of methodological individualists such as Joseph Schumpeter. The historical school itself survived the trauma but its use of biological analogies became more qualified. More formalistic and mechanistic models triumphed. As Hutter (1994, p. 306) observes, in Germany and Austria after the First World War 'the mechanistic paradigm prevailed in economic thought'. The tide of opinion against evolutionary ideas in German-speaking countries was such that even Schumpeter (1934, p. 57) accepted in 1912 that 'the evolutionary idea is now discredited in our field'[9].

3   Herbert Spencer, Alfred Marshall, John Hobson and the biological metaphor in Britain

In Britain in the 1870–1920 period biological reductionism was commonplace. It was widely believed that social progress ultimately depended on the human genetic legacy. Such ideas were common amongst both liberals and reactionaries. The first International Congress of Eugenics was held in London in 1912, and English liberal thinkers such as John Maynard Keynes, Harold Laski and Sidney and Beatrice Webb counted themselves as followers of the eugenic movement. Eugenics also had a wide following amongst American social scientists in the second and third decades of the twentieth century.

---

[9] Schumpeter did not embrace biological metaphors. He wrote that 'no appeal to biology would be of the slightest use' (Schumpeter, 1954, p. 789). Nevertheless, Schumpeter's work remains rich in insight and has had a major influence on modern evolutionary economists such as Nelson and Winter. For a detailed discussion of Schumpeter's so-called 'evolutionary economics', see Hodgson (1993b).

The towering influence over both the social and the biological sciences in the last three decades of the nineteenth century was Herbert Spencer. He attempted to build a complete system of thought that would embrace both the natural and social sciences. His popular and intellectual influence was enormous. At least in the last decade of the nineteenth century his prestige was probably even greater than that of Darwin.

Spencer developed a theory of social evolution that was strongly influenced by the German theorists. In turn he had a strong influence upon some of them, notably Schäffle (Bellomy, 1984, p. 41). The details of Spencer's view of socio-economic evolution cannot concern us here. It is sufficient to note that it was in key respects different from Darwin's theory of natural selection (La Vergata, 1995). Spencer was much closer to Jean Baptiste Lamarck than to Darwin, stressing the organism's adaptation to the environment rather that the environmental selection of the organism.

Spencer frequently compared society to a living organism. Strictly, however, his ontology was not organicist. The use of an analogy between society and a living thing is not sufficient to qualify as organicism. An individualistic and atomist outlook does not necessarily involve the rejection of the concept of society or the denial of significant human interaction. Spencer started from the individual and drew individualistic conclusions. He saw in society only a limited kind of unity. Society was still addressed in mechanistic terms. It was regarded as no more than the interplay of self-contained individuals pursuing their own ends, plus the social arrangements connecting them[10].

In sum, Spencer's view of socio-economic evolution was individualistic, deterministic and reductionist (Burrow, 1966; La Vergata, 1995). There is no discussion of emergent properties, or higher and irreducible levels of analysis. His work belongs to the nineteenth century and Victorian industrialization, where scientific prestige belonged to the mechanistic kind of thought and, as Alfred North Whitehead (1926, p. 128) puts it, even biology aped 'the manners of physics'.

Marshall was influenced by a number of theorists, but first and foremost was Spencer (Hodgson, 1993a; Thomas, 1991). In addition Marshall visited Germany several times, and the general influence of German-speaking economists upon him was extensive (Streissler, 1990; Hodgson, 2001b). Influences from Germany included Hegel, the biologist Ernst Haeckel and the aforementioned Schäffle. In front of this

---

[10] It was this aspect of his thinking that prompted Emile Durkheim's classic critique of Spencer in 1893 in *The Division of Labour in Society*. On Durkheim's use of the organic analogy, see Hejl (1995).

acquired intellectual tapestry Marshall built his own version of neoclassical economics.

The first edition of Marshall's *Principles* was published in 1890, at the height of Spencer's prestige. Marshall saw the relevance of biological analogies for economics, yet he was unable to develop them to the full. As Thomas (1991, p. 11) regretfully concludes, for Marshall economic biology 'remained promise rather than substance'.

Marshall repeated his famous sentence on 'the Mecca of the economist' in every preface to the *Principles* from the fifth edition on. However, he delayed and procrastinated over the planned second volume on economic dynamics. Spencer died in 1903 and in a few years his ideas had fallen out of favour. Marshall lost a guiding star. In fact, the Spencerian influence had thwarted the development of an adequate evolutionary analysis. The Spencerian character of Marshall's biology meant that after his death his followers were able, with relative ease, to replace these elements by notions more akin to Newtonian mechanics. Most of his disciples did not share his reservations concerning mechanistic modelling, or his concern to journey to the biological Mecca for inspiration and guidance.

Far from instigating an interdisciplinary research programme on economic dynamics, Marshall's insights from biology were subsequently ignored. As Nicolai Foss (1991, 1994b) and Neil Niman (1991, p. 32) have pointed out, later Marshallians neglected the biological aspects of Marshall's thinking and abandoned any attempt to recast economics along such lines. Hence Marshall's influential successor Arthur Pigou (1922) turned instead to physics for inspiration, and in his hands the representative firm became the firm in mechanical equilibrium (Pigou, 1928). As Scott Moss (1984) shows, equilibrium concepts were developed that were inconsistent with the existence of heterogeneous economic agents. The ease with which biology was later purged from the Marshallian system, to be replaced by a fortified metaphor from mechanics, suggests the limited extent and deficient nature of the biological ideas that had been implanted by Marshall in his *Principles*.

Unlike Marshall, John Hobson was excluded from the mainstream of British academia and never held a university post. Like Marshall, Hobson was strongly influenced by German economists and their use of the organic analogy. But Hobson's organicism is stronger and more sustained. Unlike Marshall, he was influenced by Thorstein Veblen. He drew strong methodological and anti-reductionist conclusions from his own version of organicism, writing: 'An organized unity, or whole, cannot be explained adequately by an analysis of its constituent parts: its wholeness is a new product, with attributes not ascertainable in its parts, though in a sense derived from them' (Hobson, 1929, p. 32). Hobson thus expressed the idea of emergent properties and higher, irreducible levels of analysis.

Hobson forcefully rejected mechanical metaphors, seeing them as 'squeezing out humanity' and denying human novelty and creativity (Freeden, 1988, pp. 89, 173). Recklessly ignoring Menger's arguments in the *Methodenstreit*, he regarded institutions such as the state as analogous to organisms. Hobson explicitly defended the notion that such institutions could be depicted like organisms, with wills of their own. Apart from a belated and extensive recognition by Keynes (1936, pp. 19, 364–71) of Hobson's importance, he has since been largely ignored by economists.

By the time of Marshall's death in 1924 the dialogue between economics and biology had virtually ceased, at least within the portals of British universities. In his famous article on Marshall on the centenary of his birth, Gerald Shove (1942, p. 323) noted 'a return to the mechanical as against the biological approach' in mainstream economics. As elaborated below, the Keynesian theoretical revolution did not reverse this trend.

The cause of the decline in use of biological metaphors does not lie within Marshall's work alone. Crucial developments in social science in the first three decades of the twentieth century, particularly in the United States, have to be considered to provide an adequate explanation.

4   The biological analogy and the rise of institutionalism in the United States

The influence of the German universities upon American academia prior to 1914 should not be underestimated (Herbst, 1965). Around the turn of the century 'most of the younger American economists went to Germany for their postgraduate education, where they were taught by members of the German historical school' (Morgan, 1995, p. 315). Spencer's influence in the United States was also enormous, and explicitly recognized by the founding fathers of American economics, such as Richard Ely (1903, pp. 6–7). Like many of his colleagues, Ely had also visited Germany to study.

In addition, rising American social scientists such as William Graham Sumner, Lester Frank Ward and Franz Boas had a strong influence on this generation. Sumner, Ward and Boas all embraced evolutionism and organic analogies, despite the differences in their theories and policy conclusions. The American neoclassical economist John Bates Clark followed the fashion and laced his *Philosophy of Wealth* (1885) with organic metaphors and images taken from Spencerian biology. As in Britain and Germany, organic analogies were widely adopted. Like Hobson, leading American social theorists such as Ward (1893), Franklin Giddings (1896) and Henry Jones Ford (1915) conceived of the state or society as an organism, sometimes even capable of a will of its own.

Pragmatist philosophers such as Charles Sanders Peirce and William James were also influenced by developments in biology (Scheffler, 1974). In 1890 James published his influential *Principles of Psychology* (James, 1893), which argued that much of human behaviour was dependent upon inherited instincts. For several crucial years instinct theory was prominent in both Britain and the United States. Instinct psychology was further developed by William McDougall (1908)[11].

It was in this context that Veblen published in 1898 his evolutionary manifesto in the *Quarterly Journal of Economics*, asking: 'Why is economics not an evolutionary science?' This essay embraced Darwinism and founded American institutionalism. In his subsequent *Theory of the Leisure Class* (1899) Veblen proposed that the Darwinian principles of variation, inheritance and selection should be applied to economics, with institutions – grounded on human instincts and habits – as units of selection. He favoured a complete reconstruction of economics in which mechanistic analogies would be replaced by Darwinian evolutionary metaphors. As Richard Hofstadter (1959, pp. 152–55) has remarked:

> Where other economists had found in Darwinian science merely a source of plausible analogies or a fresh rhetoric to substantiate traditional postulates and precepts, Veblen saw it as a loom upon which the whole fabric of economic thinking could be rewoven.

Notably, and in contrast to many of his contemporaries, Veblen's approach was both interactionist and anti-reductionist[12]. His interactionist perspective stressed the notion of 'both the agent and his environment being at any point the outcome of the last process' (Veblen, 1898, p. 391). Although Veblen acknowledged the biotic foundations of social life, he resisted the view that human behaviour could be explained purely and simply in terms of genetic inheritance (Veblen, 1909, p. 300).

---

[11] McDougall taught at Cambridge and Oxford and subsequently became a professor at Harvard.

[12] Two versions of interactionism are addressed in this chapter. The first suggests that actor and structure interact and mutually condition each other to the degree that explanations based on either actor or structure alone are unwarranted. The second proposes that socio-economic systems interact with their biotic foundation to the degree that (a) explanations based on biology alone are unsuitable and that (b) full explanations of some socio-economic phenomena may involve biological factors (Hirst and Woolley, 1982). These two versions of interactionism are mutually consistent and jointly opposed to reductionism.

If . . . men universally acted not on the conventional grounds and values afforded by the fabric of institutions, but solely and directly on the grounds and values afforded by the unconventionalised propensities and aptitudes of hereditary human nature, then there would be no institutions and no culture.

This and other passages suggest that Veblen acknowledged different and irreducible levels of analysis and rejected biological reductionism.

Although Veblen inspired a new school of economic thought, his theoretical research programme to build an evolutionary economics was advanced only slightly by his followers. John Commons (1934) toyed with the metaphors of quantum physics as well as evolution but saw only a limited role for such analogies. In particular, for Commons (pp. 99, 119), the comparison of society with an organism was a 'false analogy'. A difficulty for Commons and other institutionalists was the limited development of evolutionary biology at the time. Biology was going through a crisis. Darwin had failed to explain the mechanisms of heredity and the source of variation in organisms. This gap was not filled until the triumph of the neo-Darwinian synthesis of Mendelian genetics with Darwinian biology after 1940.

5   The reaction against biology in American social science

Internal problems in biology were not the only issue. The ideological abuse of science was also a matter of concern. For instance, the establishment of genetics at the beginning of the twentieth century had given a boost to racist and sexist explanations of human character and behaviour in the United States. Variations in aptitude and behaviour were regarded by some scientists and ideologists as rooted largely or wholly in the genes. In reaction against this, liberal American academia became increasing disturbed by the racist and sexist conclusions that were being drawn from a biologically grounded social science[13].

Boas, an anthropologist and a Jewish immigrant from Germany, was motivated by liberal views and strong anti-racism. He saw culture and social environment as the major influence on human character and intelligence, and as having a significant effect on some physical characteristics. Notably, Boas was one of the first to use the word 'culture' in its modern academic and anthropological sense[14].

---

[13] Much of the information and arguments in this section are derived from Degler (1991).
[14] Earlier the concept had been developed, in particular, by Sir Edward Tylor (1871) and Lewis Morgan (1877). However, both these authors embraced a teleological and unilinear notion of cultural development. Morgan fell back on psychological and biological explanations of cultural development, and Tylor hinted vaguely at an unfolding or epigenetic dynamic within culture itself.

Largely under the influence of Boas' research, a number of leading American sociologists converted from the view of the primacy of nature over nurture to the reverse. During the 1900–14 period, leading sociologists such as Charles Ellwood, Carl Kelsey and Howard Odum moved away from the opinion that innate biological factors accounted for human behaviour to the notion that human characteristics were malleable and that the environment was the most important influence. By the end of the First World War, a number of sociological and anthropological textbooks were in existence promoting Boasian views.

Boas did not deny the influence of biology on both physical and mental characteristics. He just saw social culture as far more important. However, Alfred Kroeber, a student of Boas, went further. In a number of articles published in the *American Anthropologist* between 1910 and 1917 he declared that social science should be separated, in both method and substance, from biology. For Kroeber, biological inheritance had no part in the history of humankind. Independence from biology was indispensable for understanding the meaning and use of the concept of 'culture'.

In the 1890s the biologist August Weismann had struck a blow against Lamarckism and Spencerism by giving strong arguments for the non-inheritance of acquired characteristics. In 1916 Kroeber made use of Weismann's assertion to defend his concept of culture. Weismann's idea of a barrier between an organism and its genetic inheritance suggested to Kroeber that biology could not explain social and cultural achievements.

However, Lamarckism did not necessarily lead to racist conclusions. For nineteenth-century thinkers such as Lester Ward, the Lamarckian belief in the possibility of the inheritance of acquired characters had earlier been the basis for anti-racism (Degler, 1991, p. 22). The Lamarckian view of the plasticity of organisms suggested that the environment moulded human nature. In contrast, Kroeber used the *refutation* of Lamarckism as an argument against racism and for the malleability of mankind. Ironically, the validity or otherwise of Lamarckism thus made no difference to this ideological dispute.

The underlying theoretical change was, nevertheless, dramatic. For Ward both the human organism and human society could change. But with Kroeber it was culture, not the human organism, that was malleable. This conclusion was reached by the assertion of the primacy of culture over genetic inheritance and – more controversially – by a complete separation of biology from social science. This contention was of enduring significance.

Another of Boas' students, Margaret Mead, continued Kroeber's line of argument. In 1928 she published the classic case for the supremacy of culture over biology in her *Coming of Age in Samoa*. By the 1920s the views of Boas' intellectual progeny had become widely accepted by American social scientists. Ruth Benedict, also a former student of Boas, later consolidated the victory with the publication in 1934 of the equally influential work *Patterns of Culture* (Degler, 1991, p. 206).

Biology and social science had parted company. The effects of this intellectual shift were felt through the Western academic world. Those who continued to assert that biology could explain some differences in human behaviour had lost the academic argument and become tainted by accusations of racism and sexism. With fascism rampant in Europe and in East Asia, such a position became increasingly difficult in liberal Western academia[15].

Related to this, the same period saw important changes in the prevailing conceptions of method and approach in social science. It was increasingly argued that the social sciences had to gain 'scientific' credentials, and that this should be done by imitating the empiricist and deductivist methods that were believed to be in operation in the natural sciences. The ideological abuses of biology in 'social Darwinism' were seen as a grave warning. For many, such as Max Weber, they were an impetus to render social science 'value free' (Hennis, 1988). In this climate the positivist philosophy founded by Auguste Comte grew in favour. Comtean positivism was later superseded by the logical positivism of the influential 'Vienna Circle' in the late 1920s.

Connected and parallel developments in psychology were also significant. While William James had appealed to Darwinism, and argued in the 1890s that much of human behaviour was dependent upon instinct, the aforementioned movements in anthropology and sociology undermined this notion. The president of the American Psychological Association, Charles Judd, attacked the works of James and McDougall and the very idea of instinct as early as 1909. Leading psychologists argued that instinct provided no explanation that could be verified by experiment. In an increasingly positivistic intellectual climate, the flimsiness of the empirical evidence and the manifest difficulties of experimental verification provided seemingly damning accusations against instinct-based theories of human nature (Degler, 1991, p. 157).

By the early 1920s even the existence of a sexual instinct in humans and other organisms had come under attack. The Berkeley psychologist Zing Yand Kuo asserted that all sexual appetite is the result of social conditioning. In an extreme statement of the environmentalist position,

---

[15] The metaphor that the individual is like a cell serving the organism of the nation, suggesting that the welfare of the nation has priority over the individual, was used in the 1930s in the service of fascism. However, it would be untenable to argue against all biological metaphors simply on the basis that they can be abused. Spencer, for example, used similar metaphors to sustain an individualistic political philosophy.

Kuo argued that all behaviour was not a manifestation of heredity factors but a direct result of environmental stimulation (Degler, 1991, pp. 158–59).

John Watson established behaviourist psychology in 1913, arguing on the basis of animal experiments that conditioning was primary and instinct a secondary concept. He had a radical belief in the possibilities of environmental influence over behaviour. Behaviourists attacked allegedly 'unscientific' notions such as consciousness and introspection. Such ideas could not be grounded experimentally; accordingly it was argued that they had to be dismissed from science. Considerations of intent, consciousness and cognition were scornfully dismissed as 'metaphysical': 'Merely to mention these pariah words in scientific discourse is to risk immediate loss of attention and audience' (Matson, 1964, p. 174). Behaviourists concentrated instead on empirically manifest behaviour. This tied in with a growing general adherence to positivism amongst scientists. The reliance upon measurement and experiment in behaviourism gave it an aura of dispassionate objectivity (Lewin, 1996).

The rise of behaviourism did not mean an immediate schism between psychology and biology. Indeed, drawing inspiration from the mental materialism and anti-dualism of Darwin and others, the early behaviourists argued that the difference between the mental capacities of humans and other animals was merely one of degree. This was different from the instinct psychology of James and McDougall, who saw the mind as a collection of functionally specialized faculties and instincts. In contrast, the 'doctrine of mental continuity' in evolution encouraged the imputation of human characteristics from experiments on pigeons and rats. Eventually, however, the fissure between psychology and biology widened, when the behaviourist emphasis on environmental conditioning reached the point where the specifically evolved capacities of each organism were disregarded. Learning was treated as a matter solely of environmental stimulation, ignoring those varied mental capacities bestowed by evolution. Biology and psychology went their separate ways.

Lone and ageing voices cried out in protest. McDougall (1921, p. 333) pleaded that if human instincts were successfully removed from psychological theory there would be 'a return to the social philosophy of the mid-nineteenth century, hedonistic utilitarianism'. Whitehead (1926) argued in vain that science had taken the wrong turn by treating the individual as a machine, without genuine purposefulness or creativity. But, with the rise of behaviourism in the 1920s, the idea of instinctive behaviour in human beings was sidelined. Just thirty years after the heyday of William James, the concept of instinct had virtually disappeared from American psychology.

Another aspect that changed substantially from about 1880 to 1920 was the prevailing conception of science. By the 1920s Watson's followers were embracing positivism and disregarding everything as unscientific that could not be directly measured and tested by experiment. Science had seemingly eschewed metaphysics and entered a positivistic and technocratic age.

It is impossible here to discuss all the forces behind these shifts in thinking. Former studies have identified a strong ideological element, however. For example, in seeking to explain the triumph of behaviourism in psychology, Lauren Wispé and James Thompson (1976) argued that it had much to do with the ideological commitment of Americans to individualism, democracy and personal liberty. Such values suggest to Americans that they can shape their own individual destiny. On the other hand, Darwinian evolutionary theory seemed to suggest that the individual is programmed by genes or instincts over which he or she has no control. Degler, after an extensive review of the evidence, also argues that the shift in the United States was much to do with the individualistic and aspiring ideological context of American society (1991, p. viii).

What the available evidence does seem to show is that ideology or a philosophical belief that the world could be a freer and more just place played a large part in the shift from biology to culture. Science, or at least certain scientific principles or innovative scholarship, also played a role in the transformation, but only a limited one. The main impetus came from the wish to establish a social order in which innate and immutable forces of biology played no role in accounting for the behaviour of social groups.

Furthermore, the rejection of biological and evolutionary thinking in social science was often given an impetus by the fear of giving quarter to racism and other reactionary ideas. Thus Donald Campbell (1965, p. 21) suggests that the reason why evolutionary theory was avoided in the social sciences for many years was 'the early contamination of the evolutionary perspective with the reactionary political viewpoints of the privileged classes and racial supremacist apologists for colonialism'.

In the context of racism and the growing fascism in the first four decades of the twentieth century, such developments were understandable[16]. It has to be admitted, however, that they were motivated by ideology rather than clear scientific evidence. No one decisively refuted the idea that genetic inheritance might influence human characteristics and

---

[16] Biological determinism grated with left and liberal thought in both the United States and Europe. Repulsion against it in the inter-war period explained both the rise of behaviourism in the United States and Stalin's rejection in the Soviet Union of Darwinism in favour of the Lamarckian theories of Lysenko (Joravsky, 1970; Medvedev, 1969).

behaviour, and no one has done so to this day. It may be the case that the principal constraints on our achievements are social rather than genetic, as Steven Rose et al. (1984) have forcefully argued. But that does not mean that genetic influences on our nature and behaviour do not exist. It would mean, rather, that biological determinism and *exclusively* biological explanations of human phenomena are unwarranted.

6   The eclipse of biology and the decline of American institutionalism

Following the 'golden age' of the late nineteenth century, the twentieth slipped progressively into what Stephen Sanderson (1990, p. 2) has called the 'dark age' for evolutionism in social science.

During this time evolutionism was severely criticized and came to be regarded as an outmoded approach that self-respecting scholars should no longer take seriously . . . even the word 'evolution' came to be uttered at serious risk to one's intellectual reputation.

Although nineteenth-century evolutionism in the social sciences had not always based itself on biology, it was nevertheless a victim of the times. Another casualty of the broad reaction against biology in social science was Marshall's 'economic biology'. Even more dramatically, within American economics this general move against biology and evolutionism helped the marginalization of institutionalism and the triumph of neoclassicism. It has been noted already that Veblen's project to build an evolutionary economics was hindered by problems in the development of Darwinian biology from 1900 to 1940. Having failed to develop a theoretical system to rival neoclassicism or Marxism, institutionalism was insecure.

Institutionalism was also vulnerable to shifts in the prevailing conception of scientific methodology. From the turn of the century, and in the name of science, strong American voices argued for reductionism and methodological individualism in social analysis. In 1907 the sociologist Albion Small was attacked for his 'social forces error'. As Dorothy Ross (1991, p. 347) points out, critics such as

Edward C. Hayes . . . wanted sociology to adopt 'strictly scientific methods' and study observable behaviour rather than mental states. To refer to motives as 'social forces' was to resort to a metaphysical explanation, much like resort to 'vital force' in biology. By 1910, when he issued a full-blown attack at the sociological meetings against the 'social forces error,' one commentator thought he was kicking a dead horse.

This was an American *Methodenstreit*. The shift in thinking towards reductionism was facilitated by the reduction in popularity of organic analogies. This movement in thinking gathered strength, albeit against the resistance of the so-called 'social interactionists'. Thus, in 1927, the sociologist Floyd Allport decreed 'that "the methodology of natural science" required that sociology drop the concepts of "group" and "institution" altogether' (Ross, 1991, p. 433). The response of the social interactionists was that the individual was no more a fixed unit than the group and that intersocial stimulation and social relationships affected social behaviour. Despite this resistance, reductionist notions – claiming the spurious authority of 'scientific methodology' – did much damage to the institutionalists. John Commons seemed especially vulnerable with his concept of 'collective action'.

In the United States in the 1920s both the triumph of positivism and the unpopularity of instinct psychology struck at the pragmatist foundations of institutional economics. The pragmatist ideas of Peirce and James were formative for institutionalism. Yet the rise of positivism meant that the Peircian methodological project to transcend both deduction and induction was pushed to one side. Peircian and other metaphysical and ontological speculations became unfashionable, to be replaced by a naïve faith in the unaided authority of evidence and experiment. The precipitous decline of instinct psychology also created severe difficulties for institutionalism. Deprived of such psychological foundations the institutionalist critique of the rational actor paradigm was traumatized and arguably weakened. Considering this onslaught against its deepest core ideas it is amazing that the institutionalism of Veblen and Commons survived as long as it did.

Outside institutionalism, the concept of habit followed that of instinct into exile. After occupying pride of place in the writings of Durkheim and Weber, and in sociology generally around the beginning of the twentieth century, the concept of habit was purposefully excised from the discipline (Camic, 1986). This excision was a defensive response to the conceptual homogenization of action by the behaviourist psychologists and the general emphasis that was put on environmental conditioning, even to the point of denying any space for human agency. Economics followed sociology by likewise relegating the concept (Waller, 1988). The concept of habit was seen as too closely related to that of instinct. Both were regarded as being part of the earlier and unacceptable biological baggage. The complete separation of the social sciences from biology involved the establishment of concepts of the human agent that were unrooted in physiology and biology. Seemingly alone among social scientists, the institutionalists retained the notion of habit[17].

Institutionalism survived the inter-war period by downplaying part of its legacy. This is best illustrated by considering the later generation of institutionalists, educated in the inter-war years and rising to prominence after the Second World War. The leading and by far the most influential American institutionalist in this category was Clarence Ayres[18]. As early as 1921, and unlike other institutionalists at that time, Ayres (1921, p. 561) saw the literature on instinct to be 'largely self-refuting'. His hostility to instinct psychology continued throughout his life. Hence Ayres (1958, p. 25) later declared that the very notion of instincts was 'scientifically obsolete'.

The whole mood at the time was for institutionalism to be 'scientific' – in the sense that it should be grounded on empirical methods of inquiry similar to those in the natural sciences (Rutherford, 1997, 1999, 2000). However, the positivistic climate of the 1920s pushed the institutionalists towards a naïve and untenable empiricism. For a time they were able to exploit the positivist mood, insisting on the need for an empirical foundation for the postulates of economic theory. One of the most influential living exponents of institutionalism, Wesley Mitchell, became increasingly engrossed in statistical studies. About that time he argued for the statistical salvation of institutionalism in the following terms (quoted in Ross, 1991, p. 321):

I want to *prove* things as nearly as may be and proof means usually an appeal to the facts – facts recorded in the best cases in statistical form. To write books of assertion or shrewd observation, won't convince people who have been in the habit of asserting other things or seeing things in a different perspective. . . . I often find that the only real answer lies in doing a lot of work with statistics.

Others resisted the statistical turn but Mitchell was resolute in his support of the primacy of empirical work, emphasizing this point in his 1925 presidential address to the American Economic Association. Pressed by Jacob Viner and other critics, Mitchell had some difficulty in promoting a clear and consistent defence of his empiricist view of the development of

---

[17] It was retained, however, without further significant development of the critique of and alternative to the rational actor paradigm of neoclassical theory. As in the work of Ayres (see below) an alternative, institutionalist theory of individual human agency was neglected in favour of a version of cultural determinism (Rutherford, 1994, pp. 40–1). Ayres went so far as to say (1961, p. 175): 'In a very real sense . . . there is no such thing as an individual.' Habit became simply the corporeal expression and repository of mysterious cultural forces supposedly driving all economic and technological change (Ayres, 1944).

[18] Tool (1994, p. 16) noted: 'Ayres and his students have been among the most significant contributors to the development of institutional economics in the last half-century.'

knowledge (Seckler, 1975, pp. 110–16). In 1927 an American Economic Association round-table meeting of 'eight eminent economists and statisticians, including Mitchell, debated the role of statistics in economics and all seven of Mitchell's colleagues attacked his position, arguing that statistics offered a useful empirical and analytical tool but could not remake a theory' (Ross, 1991, p. 415). Ross sees this event as the 'turning point' in the fortunes of institutionalism, evincing a gathering impatience of the critics with the failure of that school to develop a systematic theory. Seemingly having gained an initial advantage over the more aprioristic economists by embracing positivism in the new intellectual climate, institutionalism was ultimately to lose out. The positivist turn gave institutionalism no impetus to develop its own theoretical system. In any case, this task was more difficult because institutionalism had abandoned much of its philosophical and psychological legacy.

Significantly, institutionalism also adapted to the greater anthropological emphasis on the concept of culture. Such a turn was far from alien to institutionalism, as Veblen himself had pioneered an analysis of culture in his *Theory of the Leisure Class* (1899). Indeed, culture was a crucial concept within institutionalism from the beginning (Mayhew, 1987, 1989). But there is also early evidence of a shift in its explanatory status, as Malcolm Rutherford (1984) elaborates.

Although Veblen never entirely abandoned a genetically transmitted view of instinct, 'his use of instinct theory declined markedly in his later work' (Rutherford, 1984, p. 333)[19]. After Veblen, and contrary to the founder's views, leading American institutionalists began to propose that human nature and behaviour were *exclusively* determined by culture. Accordingly, although Mitchell (1910) had earlier seen instinct as central to the explanation of human behaviour, he later 'concluded that Veblen's instinct of workmanship could not be a single heritable trait, but at most a stable disposition shaped and passed on by cultural experience' (Ross, 1991, p. 384). As the institutional economist Allan Gruchy (1972, p. 43) explained approvingly, and with an apparent genuflection to positivism: 'Mitchell did not follow Veblen in emphasizing the instinctive basis of human behavior, because instincts cannot be objectively analyzed'. In the coming years it became clear that institutionalism had abandoned what had been seen as an embarrassing part of its Veblenian legacy. Mitchell (1937, p. 312) seemed to lose confidence in both Darwinism and instinct psychology as foundations for institutionalism, writing that

---

[19] In Hodgson (1992, 1993b) I mistakenly suggested that Veblen moved away from the view that instincts are biologically inherited. I am grateful to Malcolm Rutherford for correcting me on this point.

'the Darwinian viewpoint is due to be superseded in men's minds: the instinct-habit psychology will yield to some other conception of human nature'. Later on, Ayres (1958, p. 29) underlined his complete break with any notions of a biological determination of human nature. 'It is now quite conclusively established that no such complex behavior patterns are in a literal sense "inborn". We now know that such patterns are wholly cultural.' The human mind was seen as an empty vessel, or *tabula rasa*, to be filled by the culture and environment in which it was situated. This removed the question – which had much concerned Veblen, among others – of the evolved biological faculties of the mind and their relation to culture and institutions. However, in the circumstances, rather than being compromised by the increasing emphasis on a biologically untainted concept of culture, the institutionalists became its most enthusiastic devotees[20].

While the increasing emphasis on the role of culture did not seem to embarrass or undermine institutionalism, this school of thought was affected by the concomitant separation of biology and social science. Accordingly, the Veblenian research programme of building a 'post-Darwinian' and 'evolutionary' economics was compromised, if not abandoned. Although the general concept of 'culture' was not itself a problem, the intellectual context in which the shift to culture took place made the further development of a systematic institutional theory much more difficult[21].

---

[20] In contrast, Veblen held the view that culture could be moulded in part by the genetic inheritance of a group. Ayres (1952, p. 25) went so far as to describe this notion of Veblen's as racism. 'Worst of all, perhaps, was his tentative addiction to racism. He was somehow persuaded that "the dolicho-blond race" was possessed of certain peculiar propensities which shaped its culture – an idea which present-day anthropologists most decisively reject.' As Tilman (1992, p. 161) points out, this allegation ignores both the ideological and scientific context of Veblen's own time and, more importantly, the fact that Veblen never expressed animosity towards any race in his writings. The supposition of racial differences in Veblen's writings was never seen by him as grounds for racial discrimination or repression. Indeed, such a deduction would be illegitimate, as normative statements about human rights are not logically deducible from empirical statements about human differences, nor from theoretical statements about the causes of human attributes or behaviour. A similarly inappropriate accusation of 'racism' against Veblen is made by Samuels in his 1990 introduction to Veblen (1919, p. ix). It is thus suggested that propositions concerning differing attributes of different ethnic groups are racist, and that anti-racism is dependent upon the denial of such differences. On the contrary, an unconditional anti-racism, independent of the denial or assertion of any empirical or theoretical proposition, is stronger than a conditional anti-racist stance.

[21] Despite the shift away from biology, the institutionalists retained the alternative description of themselves as 'evolutionary' as well as 'institutional' economists. However, this was more to do with Ayres' (1944, p. 155) influential view that the term 'institutional economics' was 'singularly unfortunate'. He complained of 'the misnomer of "Institutionalism"' (Ayres, 1935, p. 197) because he saw institutions never as enabling

The crunch came with the Great Crash of 1929. The personal rec-
ollections of Gunnar Myrdal are particularly apposite. When he went to
the United States at the end of the 1920s institutional economics was still
seen by many as the 'wind of the future'. However, at that time Myrdal
was at the 'theoretical' stage of his own development, and he was 'utterly
critical' of this orientation in economics. He 'even had something to do
with the initiation of the Econometric Society, which was planned as
a defense organization against the advancing institutionalists' (Myrdal,
1972, p. 6). Myrdal goes on to explain a key event in the decline of the
popularity of institutionalism in the United States (p. 7)[22].

What I believe nipped it in the bud was the world-wide economic depression.
Faced with this great calamity, we economists of the 'theoretical' school, accus-
tomed to reason in terms of simplified macro-models, felt we were on top of the
situation, while the institutionalists were left in a muddle. It was at this stage that
economists in the stream of the Keynesian revolution adjusted their theoretical
models to the needs of the time, which gave victory much more broadly to our
'theoretical' approach.

It seems that the institutionalists, while emphasizing the complexity of
economic phenomena and the need for careful empirical research, were
out-theorized by the mathematical Keynesians. This group of young and
mathematically minded converts to Keynesianism, led by Paul Samuelson

but typically as a negative constraint on progress, as 'a bad thing from which we are
bound to try perpetually to redeem ourselves' (letter from Ayres to Dewey, 29 January
1930; quoted in Tilman, 1990, p. 966; see also McFarland, 1985, 1986). For Ayres, it
was 'technology', not institutions, that served human progress. Ayres' view of institutions
contrasted with that of Veblen and Commons, who saw institutions as both constitutive
and enabling of action, and even in some cases as marks of evolving civilization, as well as
accepting their possible conservative and constraining effects. The adoption of the alternative 'evolutionary' label stressed dynamic notions of economic change, in contrast to
the equilibrium thinking of neoclassical economics. As in the case of Schumpeter, it did
not necessarily connote any reference to biology. Uneasiness with both alternate labels
persisted within American institutionalism. Royall Brandis has remarked to the author
that, when the institutionalist Association for Evolutionary Economics came to establish
its journal in the late 1960s, deadlock between adherents of the 'institutional' versus
'evolutionary' labels led to the adoption of the very prosaic *Journal of Economic Issues*
title.

[22] What makes this personal testimony particularly striking is the fact that years later – in
the 1940s – Myrdal converted to institutionalism, and subsequently won the Nobel Prize
in Economics. The institutionalist Ayres (1935, p. 173) seems partially to corroborate
Myrdal's analysis by his contemporary report that the 'cutting edge of the issue between
[the neoclassical economists] and the "Institutionalists" would seem to be the incapacity
of the latter to demonstrate the failure of the present economic order which they propose
controlling'. A hostile critic of institutionalism took a remarkably similar view when he
noted that 'the greatest slump in history finds them sterile and incapable of helpful
comment – their trends gone awry and their dispersions distorted' (Robbins, 1932,
p. 115).

and others, developed what now seem in retrospect to be extraordinarily simple macroeconomic models. The attraction of this approach was partly its technocratic lure, and partly because it proposed very simple apparent solutions to the urgent problem of the day. It appeared that the problem of unemployment could be alleviated simply by increasing a variable called G. The 'solution' was plain and transparent, dressed up in mathematical and 'scientific' garb, and given all the reverence customarily accorded to such presentations in a technocratic culture[23]. Notably, without referring to Myrdal, Ross (1991, p. 419) corroborates the argument.

> Institutionalism as a movement . . . fell victim to the Great Depression and its Keynesian remedy. For self-proclaimed experts in historical change, their inability to come to any better understanding of the Depression than their neoclassical colleagues was a considerable deficit. Mitchell in particular, who predicted like everyone else that the downturn would right itself within a year or two, was driven deeper into his programme of empirical research by this proof of ignorance. Whether a more powerful and genuinely historical institutional economics would have done better is impossible to say. Like the left-liberal economists generally, the institutionalists were drawn into the Keynesian revision of neoclassicism.

Frank Knight, who regarded himself as an institutionalist – albeit a maverick one – and who was in the strategic location of Chicago in the 1930s, came to a similar verdict. He asserted that institutionalism was 'largely drowned by discussion of the depression, or perhaps boom and depression, and especially by the literature of the Keynesian revolution' (Knight, 1952, p. 45)[24].

Of course, the rising 'Keynesianism' of the 1930s was different in several key respects from the economics of Keynes. Key contributions in the 1930s and 1940s, notably from Alvin Hansen, John Hicks, Samuelson and Jan Tinbergen, helped to transform Keynesian ideas and make them mathematically tractable. As noted by Benjamin Ward (1972) and Terence Hutchison (1992), this became as much a 'formalistic revolution' as a Keynesian one. The evidence suggests, however, that Keynes himself was at best sceptical of econometrics and mathematical modelling in economics. What did emerge in the 1930s were the foundations

---

[23] Ironically, this reigning view ignored the fact that any practical implementation of a policy to increase government expenditure depended precisely on a detailed knowledge of the workings of government, financial and other *institutions*. For their concern with such details the institutionalists were much maligned by the mathematical technocrats. Their expert knowledge in this area, however, partly explains the fact that they were, in government bodies, at the forefront of the implementation of the semi-Keynesian economic policies of the Roosevelt era.

[24] Biddle (1996, p. 144) notes that citations to works by Mitchell – the leading institutionalist of the time – suffered a substantial decline as early as the mid-1930s.

of the neoclassical-Keynesian synthesis, based on key developments in neoclassical microeconomics and a mechanistic system of macroeconomic modelling with some Keynesian affinities[25].

Institutional economists were not hostile to the Keynesian revolution. Indeed, as Rutledge Vining (1939, pp. 692–3) argued, 'Much of Keynes' theory of employment can be dug from Veblen's intuitions', particularly in the *Theory of Business Enterprise* (1904). Further, the rise of Keynesianism coincided with a drift of Anglo-American opinion towards state intervention and planning, and in the 1930s American institutionalists were active in the inspiration, development and promotion of President Franklin Roosevelt's New Deal (Barber, 1994; Stoneman, 1979; Wunderlin, 1992). Sympathetic economists such as William Jaffé and Ely perceived parallels between the works of Veblen and Keynes, and their joint consummation in Roosevelt's policies (Tilman, 1992, pp. 111–12). On the theoretical side, institutionalism formed its own synthesis with Keynesianism, giving less emphasis to mathematical modelling and interpreting Keynes in terms of an organicist ontology (Dillard, 1948; Gruchy, 1948).

Biology is not necessarily an antidote to mechanistic modelling, nor would it have been reliably so in the 1920s and 1930s. Biology itself has long exhibited internal tensions between formal and discursive analysis. The decline of biology in social science did not itself directly cause the turn to mechanistic modelling. Rather, the failure of biology to deliver the theoretical goods for institutionalism in the first third of the twentieth century disabled its core theoretical research programme. As a term, 'evolutionary economics' became both unpopular and evacuated of substantive and distinctive theoretical meaning. The theoretical lacuna within institutionalism became a breach into which the voguish econometricians, modellers and mathematicians could storm.

Even in microeconomic theory the battle was lost. While in the early decades of the twentieth century the institutionalists seemed on strong empirical ground, suggesting the neoclassical postulate of maximizing behaviour was incompatible with contemporary psychology, Samuelson (1938) and others began to insist that economics could base itself on the claims of 'revealed preference' alone, and did not need to invoke any psychological theory of human behaviour (Lewin, 1996). Sociology had broken with psychology, and mainstream economics

---

[25] Keynes' own views on mathematical modelling are clear in a letter to Roy Harrod of 16 July 1938. 'In economics . . . to convert a model into a quantitative formula is to destroy its usefulness as an instrument of thought' (Keynes, 1973, p. 299). For more on Keynes' critical views of econometrics and mathematical modelling, see Moggridge (1992, pp. 621–23).

rapidly followed suit. The institutionalist objection that the assumption of maximizing behaviour was psychologically unrealistic was thus rendered largely ineffective. Mainstream economics saw itself as newly independent of any psychological postulates. The earlier separation between biology and social science had made such a stance possible.

American institutionalism had lost some of the crucial theoretical battles even before Hitler's seizure of power in Germany in 1933 and the spread of fascism in Europe diverted all eyes. Subsequently, the Nazi holocaust extinguished all varieties of biologistic social science in Anglo-American academia. Eugenic and other ideas that were common amongst liberals as well as conservatives in the pre-1914 period were seen as dangerously allied with fascism and ethnic repression. All references to biology had to be removed from social science. Anyone who argued to the contrary was in severe danger of being labelled as a racist or a fascist. Such cataclysmic political developments finally terminated the long, post-1880 flirtation of social science with biology. In 1940 such ideas were at their nadir in the Anglo-American academic world.

7   **The sporadic return of biology and the reinvention of evolutionary economics**

After the Second World War a partial return to biology occurred in the social sciences. The transition was given impetus by two separate developments in the science of life, in the 1940s and the 1970s respectively. Their effects on the social sciences were significant. In economics, two notable episodes of 'biological' thinking occurred immediately after each of these developments in biology, in 1950 and in the 1970s. This is more than mere coincidence. Indeed, in the case of developments in the 1970s, the references to the contemporary developments in biology were direct and explicit.

The first impulse was the emergence of the neo-Darwinian synthesis in biology. The elements of this synthesis had been in place long beforehand, but the new paradigm did not become fully established until the 1940s. A group of Darwinians working in Britain and the United States (principally Theodosius Dobzhansky, Ronald Fisher, John B. S. Haldane, Julian Huxley, Ernst Mayr, George Gaylord Simpson, G. Ledyard Stebbins, Bernhard Rensch and Sewall Wright) accomplished a synthesis between the theory of natural selection and Mendelian genetics. Only then did the Mendelian gene become fully incorporated into the theory of evolution, giving a plausible explanation of the presumed variation of offspring and the selection of species. Darwin or any other nineteenth-century biologist had not achieved this. As Mayr (1980, pp. 39–40) points out, 'what happened between 1937 and 1947 was . . . a synthesis between research traditions that had previously been unable to communicate'. The post-war 'evolutionary synthesis' gave the Darwinian idea of natural selection a renewed vitality, which has continued to this day.

The timing of Alchian's famous article of 1950 is, therefore, apposite. Capitalizing on the triumph of a new Darwinian biology, he made an explicit appeal to the metaphor of natural selection. However, he made no reference to the earlier work of Veblen: the memory of the earlier evolutionary foray had been lost. Alchian proposed that the assumption of overt maximizing behaviour by business firms is not necessary for the scientific purposes of explanation and prediction. Selective success, Alchian argued, depends on behaviour and results, not motivations. If firms never actually attempt to maximize profits, 'evolutionary' processes of selection and imitation would ensure the survival of the more profitable enterprises.

This evolutionary idea was taken up and modified by Stephen Enke (1951) who argued that, with sufficient intensity of competition and 'in the long run', conditions of intense competition would mean that only the optimizers remain viable. Milton Friedman (1953) developed this further, by seeing 'natural selection' as grounds for assuming that agents act 'as if' they maximize, whether or not firms and individuals actually do so. Going further than Alchian, he used 'natural selection' as a defence of the maximization hypothesis.

About the same time the inventive heterodox economist Kenneth Boulding published his *Reconstruction of Economics* (1950). In it he bor-rowed 'population thinking' and associated models from ecology. Capital goods were represented as a population with different vintages, entering the capital fund like the births and deaths of organisms in a species[26]. Further, in this work Boulding was one of the first to emphasize that the economy was part of, and depended upon, the ecosystem.

It is very likely that this flurry of evolutionary theorizing was prompted by the major developments in biology in the 1940s. Compared with that in the 1970s, the first post-war impulse from biology was much more significant from the biological point of view but it had the lesser effect on economics and social science. The much-diminished effect on social science of the first and greater impulse from biology is explicable, given its immediacy after the Nazi holocaust, and considering the prior degree of reaction against biological thinking in the social sciences in the 1920s and 1930s.

---

[26] On the nature and relevance of 'population thinking' – taken from Darwinian biology – to economics, see Foss (1994a) and Metcalfe (1988).

There were also theoretical reasons for the diminished effect of this wave of evolutionary thinking on economics. Arguing that biological analogies were inappropriate for economics, Edith Penrose (1952) responded to Alchian and Enke. Ironically, she founded her critique on a more accurate understanding of neo-Darwinian biology. Contemporary neo-Darwinian theories of evolution seemed to exclude both purposeful behaviour and the inheritance of acquired characteristics. Yet both these features are highly relevant in the socio-economic sphere. Furthermore, in economic evolution there was no heritable unit nearly as durable as the gene. At least in strict terms, the analogy with prominent versions of biological theory did not work. She was right. It took subsequent developments in biology to make a closer theoretical correspondence possible in some respects[27].

For economists, Friedman's intervention in 1953 was especially influential. It became a classic defence of the neoclassical maximization hypothesis. It used the new authority of evolutionary biology to rebut lingering institutionalist and behaviouralist doubts about that core idea. Beyond that, however, the biological analogy was little used in economics for the subsequent twenty years.

Ironically, again, Friedman's use of the metaphor of natural selection bolstered a key element in the mechanistic paradigm and rebutted the 'evolutionary' economists in the institutional camp. In an article published in the same fateful year of 1953, Gregor Sebba (1953) traced the derivation of the ideas of rationality and equilibria – the core concepts of neoclassical economics – from the inheritance of Newtonian and mechanistic thought. In fact, Friedman had applied simplistically a half-assimilated idea from Darwinian biology to reinforce the mechanistic paradigm of neoclassical economics. Eleven years later, Winter (1964) showed that Friedman's argument had a highly limited applicability, even in evolutionary terms[28].

In other social sciences the post-war re-emergence of biology was more pronounced. Immediately after the end of the Second World War the nature/nurture controversy was renewed in psychology, and in 1948 the anthropologist Clyde Kluckhohn declared that biology as well as culture had a part in the explanation of human behaviour. In the 1950s even Kroeber shifted his view and was ready to acknowledge the biological roots of human nature (Degler, 1991, pp. 218–21).

The concept of 'instinct' also enjoyed a slow rehabilitation. Much of the original impetus behind this development came from Europe. In the

[27] For discussions of the conceptual issues involved here see Khalil (1993), Depew and Weber (1995) and Hodgson (2001a).
[28] See also Boyd and Richerson (1980), Schaffer (1989) and Hodgson (1994).

1930s the Austrian ethologist Konrad Lorenz had published scholarly articles on instinctive behaviour. In 1951 the Oxford ethologist Nikolaus Tinbergen published his *Study of Instinct*, in which he argued that much of human behaviour is instinctive. By the 1960s the concept of instinct had re-emerged in American psychology. In 1973 Lorenz and Tinbergen were awarded, with Karl von Frisch, the Nobel Prize for their work on instinctive behaviour (Degler, 1991, pp. 223–4).

Furthermore, behaviourist psychology came under attack. In the 1950s Harry Harlow performed a set of famous experiments on rhesus monkeys that suggested there was more to monkey behaviour than stimulus and response. An infant monkey would cling to a soft artificial mother in preference to a wire-framed surrogate which dispensed milk. Some instinctive drive must have accounted for this apparently self-destructive behaviour. Another set of experiments, by J. Garcia and R. A. Koelling in 1966, showed that rats could not be conditioned to avoid flavoured water when deterred by electric shocks, but that the animals would readily learn to do so when drinking the water was followed by induced nausea. This suggested a functionally specific instinct to avoid nausea-inciting substances, and again undermined the notion of a generally conditioned response. Behaviourism was thus hoist by its own experimentalist petard. In addition, the critiques of behaviourism by Noam Chomsky (1959) and Cyril Burt (1962) announced a return of the concept of consciousness to psychology, thus undermining the hegemony of positivism in that subject[29].

Leading biologists themselves argued that the social sciences could not ignore the biotic foundations of human life. For instance, Dobzhansky (1955, p. 20) stated: 'Human evolution is wholly intelligible only as an outcome of the interaction of biological and social facts.' A related point was endorsed by the anthropologist Alexander Alland (1967, p. 10).

Biologists now agree that the argument over the primacy of environment or heredity in the development of organism is a dead issue. It is now generally accepted that the function and form of organisms can be understood only as the result of a highly complicated process of interaction.

By the early 1970s some sociologists, such as Bruce Eckland, and political scientists, such as Albert Somit, had argued that the ties between the

[29] More generally, although positivism greatly increased in popularity in American scientific circles in the first half of the twentieth century, the publication in 1951 of Quine's essay 'Two dogmas of empiricism' (reprinted in Quine, 1953) helped to check and reverse the movement. Quine effectively undermined the distinction between science and non-science in logical positivism and denied that statements could be judged true or false purely on the basis of sense experience. 'The publication of this essay in 1951 was one of the key events in the collapse of logical positivism' (Hoover, 1995, p. 721).

132   *Geoffrey M. Hodgson*

biology and the social sciences should be re-established. In 1970 the political scientist Thomas Thorson argued that Darwinian evolutionary theory would be useful in developing a theory of social and political change. Human affairs, he argued, would be better understood from the perspective of biology rather than physics. The dialogue between biology and politics was encouraged by an international conference in Paris in 1975, in which a number of American social scientists participated (Degler, 1991, pp. 224–26).

In several key respects, the post-war return to biology took a distinctive form. In particular, the triumph of the neo-Darwinian synthesis in the 1940s and the discovery of the structure of DNA by Crick and Watson in 1953 brought forth a renewed faith in the possibilities of reductionism. It was believed that, if the behaviour of organisms could be explained by the genetic code, all sciences should emulate this achievement and explain the whole in terms of the parts. Of course, not all biologists held such views, and many saw organisms as outcomes of interactions between genes and environment. Nevertheless, prestige had gone to those who had seemingly broken the whole into its constituent parts.

Thus, in 1972, echoing Menger in 1883, Hayes in 1910 and Allport in 1927, anthropologist George Murdock repudiated the idea of 'the social aggregate as the preferable unit for study' instead of the individual. The concept of culture was seriously flawed, he argued. It was the individual who made culture, not the other way round. A focus on the individual as the unit would bring anthropology in line with biology (Degler, 1991, p. 235). For some, the return to biology became a rejection of culture as a determinant of behaviour, and a celebration of reductionism in science. For them, it was as if the clock had been turned back to 1890. Fortunately, this stance was not universal.

It is noted below that the year 1975 marked a turning point in the influence of biology on economics. References by economists to biology were rare in the preceding twenty years. There are a few notable exceptions from 1955–74. Coming from the institutionalist tradition, Morris Copeland (1958) attempted to revive interest in Veblen's evolutionary project. Jack Downie (1958) covertly renovated the biological analogy in Marshallian economics by bringing diversity and 'population thinking' into the picture of competition between firms (Nightingale, 1993). Heralding a significant turn in his own thinking, Friedrich Hayek (1960, 1967a) began to make a number of references to evolutionary biology[30]. Michael Farrell (1970) made an isolated mathematical contribution.

[30] The philosophical basis of Hayek's turn is analysed in Lawson (1994) and Fleetwood (1995).

In economics in the 1954–74 period by far the most important work inspired by biology was by Nicholas Georgescu-Roegen: *The Entropy Law and the Economic Process* (1971). He asserted the value of biological as well as thermodynamic analogies and founded a distinctive version of 'bio-economics'. Subsequently – but apparently quite independently of institutionalism, Hayek and Georgescu-Roegen – the basis of a new theory of economic evolution was outlined by Nelson and Winter (1973, 1974)[31].

The bombshell was *Sociobiology: The New Synthesis*, published in 1975 by Edward Wilson. Even before the appearance of this book the return to biology was well under way. But its appearance stimulated a protracted interest in the alleged biotic foundations of human behaviour. The book was greeted with a great deal of criticism, from both social scientists and biologists. It nevertheless brought biology back onto the social science agenda.

The impact of the new sociobiology on economics was rapid. Gary Becker (1976) published an article suggesting a genetic determination of human behaviour modelled along neoclassical lines. Jack Hirshleifer (1977, 1978) and Gordon Tullock (1979) quickly followed with similar calls for the joining of economics with sociobiology[32]. Notably, these presentations were individualist and reductionist, and emphasized self-interest and individual competition in the biotic as well as the economic world (Gowdy, 1987).

Although their original evolutionary prospectus had appeared as early as 1973, Nelson and Winter (1982, pp. 42–43) also recognized the importance of Wilson's work. Although the genesis of their *Evolutionary Theory of Economic Change* had much to do with the growing prestige of biology and the reintroduction of biological metaphors into social science, their work is quite different from that of the Becker–Hirshleifer–Tullock school. Nelson and Winter reject the notion that genes wholly or largely determine human behaviour. Their perspective is complex and interactionist, involving different levels and units of selection, and ongoing interaction between individuals, institutions and their socio-economic environment.

---

[31] Nelson (1994) dates his own transformation into a 'full-blown evolutionary theorist' to the 1964–68 period.

[32] These calls did not go unheeded. The biologist M. T. Ghiselin (1974) had already imported the mainstream economist's notion of 'methodological individualism', and had echoed the old metaphor of 'nature's economy' in the biotic sphere. The biologists D. J. Rapport and J. E. Turner (1977) analysed food selection, 'predator switching' and other biological phenomena using indifference curves and other analytical tools taken from economics. Note also that the biologist J. Maynard Smith (1982) imported game theory – originally developed in economics by von Neumann and Morgenstern (1944) – into biology. After Maynard Smith had developed the concept of an 'evolutionary stable strategy', this idea was then transferred back to economics by Sugden (1986).

At about this time Boulding (1978, 1981) also developed an evolutionary approach. This built on his earlier work on biological analogies (Boulding, 1950), but it is significant that his fully-fledged evolutionary theory did not emerge in its developed form until the late 1970s. This is later than in other social sciences, particularly anthropology, where the word 'evolution' became quite common in the 1960s. The number of relevant works encountered in economics from 1915 to 1964 inclusive with 'evolution' or 'evolutionary' in their title or subtitle is only fourteen. A further thirteen appear in the ten years 1965–74, and twenty-nine in the 1975–84 period[33]. The number since 1984 is well into three figures.

With the revival of usage of 'evolutionary' terminology the economists of the Austrian school picked up on the trend. As in economics in general, references to biology are minimal in Austrian school writings prior to the 1960s[34]. It was Hayek who began to bring evolutionary metaphors into Austrian school economics in the last thirty years of his life. But this writer was restrained by his earlier rejection of 'scientism' in social theory and his denunciation of social theory for a 'slavish imitation of the method and language of science' (Hayek, 1952b, p. 15). Subsequently, however, Hayek (1967b, p. viii) noted a change in 'tone' in his attitude to 'scientism', attributed to the influence of Karl Popper. This is not, needless to say, a matter of mere 'tone', and the door is progressively opened for the entry of the biological analogues.

Although there were earlier hints at what was to come, the first suggestions of a more prominent 'evolutionary' approach in Hayek's work are found in works published in the 1960s (1960, pp. 40, 42, 58–62; 1967b, pp. 31–34, 66–81, 103–4, 111, 119). Patchy references to evolutionary theory are also found in a major work produced in the 1970s (1982, vol. 1, pp. 9, 23–24, 152–53; vol. 3, pp. 154–59, 199–202). But we have to

---

[33] Notably, even the use of the word 'evolution' does not necessarily indicate the adoption of a biological metaphor. Some of the appearances of such a word between 1915 and 1980 are in Alchian (1950), Boulding (1978), Edgell (1975), Haavelmo (1954), Harris (1934), Hayek (1975), Hunt (1975), von Mises (1957), Nelson and Winter (1973, 1974), Robbins (1970), Sowell (1967) and Tang et al. (1976). Three of these have Veblenian origins and two are by prominent Austrian economists. The remainder have varied intellectual pedigrees. A full list is available from the author, who would be interested to hear of any others that have been omitted. It should be emphasized that the criterion of 'evolution' in the title is relatively rough and loose, particularly as it allows Georgescu-Roegen (1971) to pass through the net.

[34] An analysis of Menger's limited notion of 'evolution' is found in Hodgson (1993b). It should be noted that Hayek's *Sensory Order* (1952a), an important critique of behaviourist psychology, made reference to biology, although it is not strictly a work in economics.

wait until the late 1980s to receive the fullest explicit statement of Hayek's evolutionary conception (1988, pp. 9, 11–28). It could not be claimed, therefore, that the Austrian school had consistently embraced the evolutionary metaphor in economics. Hayek's statements of the 1960s in this genre were notable, along with other rare voices from the 1955–74 period. But they also marked a shift in his own thinking and a reversal of his earlier opposition to 'scientism'. In part, Hayek was being carried by the tide[35].

It is too early to judge what kind of 'evolutionary economics' or 'economic biology' will triumph as the influence of biology upon social science becomes even stronger. In comparison, however, there are important differences with the type of evolutionary theorizing that was prevalent in the 1890s. For instance, due to the work of W. Brian Arthur (1989), Paul David (1985) and many others there is now a widespread recognition of the importance of path dependence, undermining the view that evolution generally leads to optimal or even near-optimal outcomes. This parallels a similar stance taken by biologists such as Stephen Jay Gould (1989).

8   Summary and conclusion

It is freely admitted that this chapter covers a vast canvas and that it has not done justice to the details. But it is a largely unseen picture, and it needs to be shown first as a whole. A number of general suggestions and observations have been made concerning the relationship between biology and economics. A summary of some of them is appropriate at this stage.

During the twentieth century biology influenced economics in a number of quite different ways. A first mode of interaction involved the suggestion that explanations of socio-economic phenomena can be reduced entirely to, and ultimately explained by, phenomena at the biotic level. Before the First World War such a position was accepted by theorists such as Spencer but rejected by others such as Veblen. In the inter-war period the influence of biotic phenomena on society was widely denied. The return of biological thinking in economics and the social sciences in the post-1945 period was marked both by views suggesting and emphasizing a genetic foundation for human behaviour (Becker, Hirshleifer and Tullock) and others that, in contrast, eschew biological reductionism (Nelson and Winter).

---

[35] See the discussion of Hayek's notion of evolution in Hodgson (1993b).

A second mode of interaction was at the level of metaphor[36]. Ideas were imported from biology to recast economics on a quite different pattern. It was at least partly in this sense that Veblen argued for a 'post-Darwinian' economics in 1898, Alchian adopted the evolutionary analogy in 1950, and Nelson and Winter subsequently constructed their theoretical system. This metaphorical mode of interaction is compatible with the view of an autonomous level of socio-economic analysis and a rejection of biological reductionism. It can involve the scrutiny, modification or rejection of particular conceptual transfers from one discipline to another, as well as their acceptance. The open and self-conscious use of metaphor may involve critical comparison rather than slavish imitation (Hodgson, 1997, 1999).

However, the move away from biological thinking in economics and other social sciences in the inter-war period meant the abandonment of *both* modes of analytical interaction: the metaphorical as well as the reductive. In particular, the elaboration of an evolutionary economics inspired by biology became extremely difficult.

Degler (1991) and others argue that ideology rather than scientific evidence largely inspired the declining influence of biology on American social science in the first four decades of the twentieth century. The rise of US economic and political prowess was associated with the rise of a relatively liberal and individualistic ideology. In intellectual circles in the early twentieth century this ideology developed some anti-racist attributes. It emphasized individual achievement, seeing it as unconstrained by biological inheritance.

Liberal and leftist ideological associations helped to raise the popularity of American institutional economics in such intellectual circles, but in addition the move away from biology weakened it at a crucial stage of its theoretical development[37]. The Veblenian project to build a post-Darwinian evolutionary economics was thwarted both by the move away from biology in the social sciences and by apparent theoretical difficulties within biology, which were not resolved until the emergence of the

---

[36] On the role of metaphor in economics see Hodgson (1993b) and Klamer and Leonard (1994).

[37] The writings of Copeland (1931, 1958) represent an atypical and consistent attempt to remind fellow American institutionalists of their original links with biology. Thus, during the crisis of institutionalism in the early 1930s, he wrote: '[E]conomics is a biological science – it studies group relationships among living organisms of the genus *Homo sapiens*. As such its generalizations must somehow make peace with the general theory of biological evolution' (1931, p. 68). However, fifty years later Copeland (1981, p. 2) wrote: '[T]here seems to be nothing in the socioeconomic evolutionary process that corresponds to natural selection.' Ironically, he seemed to have abandoned the natural selection metaphor just one year before its successful revival by Nelson and Winter.

neo-Darwinian synthesis in the 1940s. By then, American institutionalism had been severely mauled. Neoclassical and 'Keynesian' modelling had triumphed.

Furthermore, the failure of institutionalism to develop a systematic theory meant that, by 1929, it seemed muddled and impotent in the face of the Great Crash and the subsequent economic depression. Mathematical modellers offering clear remedies based on relatively simple models with few equations seemed a much more attractive counsel, especially for those concerned to put their economics to practical and humane uses. There is nowadays less faith in the benefits of such modelling (Ormerod, 1994; Lawson, 1997), but in a supremely technocratic era they seemed to be the scientific solution to the economic malaise.

So began the 'peacock's tail' process of increasing formalization in economics[38]. The timings are again apposite, with the 1930s marking the turning point. The failure of institutionalism was not the only impetus, but the loss of strategic initiative was crucial[39]. Long-term evidence of the shift comes from a study of mathematical content in five leading and long-standing economics journals (George Stigler et al., 1995, p. 342). From the 1890s to the 1920s verbal expositions continuously dominated more than 90 per cent of the published articles. After 1940 the use of mathematics began to rise spectacularly, with exclusively verbal expositions falling steadily and being confined to around 33 per cent of articles in the 1962–63 period. By 1989–90 no less than 94 per cent of articles in the five journals were dominated by algebra, calculus and econometrics. An exclusively verbal exposition was confined to a small minority.

---

[38] I owe this wonderful analogy to Allen and Lesser (1991, p. 166). They wittily suggest that the evolution of economics is a case of lock-in comparable to the evolution of the peacock's tail. Two sets of genes – producing the beautiful tail in the male, and making it sexually attractive to the female – are mutually reinforcing, and both become selected because of the greater progeny involved. However, there is no useful function formed, whether in the sense of enhancing fitness, or finding food or escaping predators. Likewise, in economics, formal models and mathematical presentations are selected in competitions over academic publications and appointments, incurring a further bias towards mathematics in subsequent generations.

[39] Some additional factors shifting US economics towards mathematical formalism may be mentioned. First, academic refugees from Continental Europe in the 1930s and 1940s often had a mathematical aptitude of superior quality to their use of English, while American scholars were often deficient in foreign language skills. Mathematical communication was thus advantaged. In addition, after the Second World War the US National Science Foundation seemingly favoured mathematical economics, deeming it to be more scientific. (The author owes these observations to Royall Brandis.) As the relative prestige of Britain as a world centre of learning in economics declined, it began more and more to ape developments in the United States. Furthermore, Continental Europe was too devastated to regain its academic standing in the crucial years immediately after 1945.

It has also been suggested that the shifting relationship between economics and biology throughout the twentieth century was closely connected to changing conceptions of science itself. The rise of positivism in the 1920s also helped to marginalize the self-conscious use of metaphor. In addition, the growing popularity of reductionism has had varying and complex effects on that relationship.

Several conclusions can be drawn. Two, however, are selected for special mention. The first is to emphasize the dangers of conflating ideology with science. The investigation of human nature and the causes of human behaviour – be they biotic or social or an interaction of both – is a matter for science and not for ideology. In general, theories should not be selected on the basis of the ideologies they appear to support. Often the same theory can be used to sustain different ideologies. Just as neoclassical general equilibrium theory was frequently deployed to support pro-market policies in the 1970s and 1980s, the very same kind of theory was used by Oskar Lange in the 1930s to support a version of socialist central planning. Obversely, different and even contradictory theories can be used to support the same ideology. For instance, it has been shown above that both Lamarckian and anti-Lamarckian biology have been used to oppose racism.

Ideology and science are inextricably bound together, but they are not the same thing. To conflate the two – to judge science in purely ideological terms – is to devalue and to endanger science itself. Scientists cannot avoid ideology. Indeed, they should be committed to a better world. Scientists have ideological responsibilities but they are not simply ideologists. To choose or reject a theory primarily on the basis of its apparent policy outcomes is to neglect the critical and evaluative requirements of science. Dogma is reinforced at both the scientific and the ideological level. The conflation of science with ideology thus degrades them both.

The second conclusion is that, just as science and ideology are related but operate on different levels, so too should biology and the social sciences. The complete separation of biology and the social sciences is untenable because, in reality, human beings are not entirely separable from their foundation in nature. The obverse error, to conflate social science and biology so that they become one and the same, carries many dangers, some of which have been explored above. Neither hermetic separation nor complete integration is desirable. A more sophisticated relationship between the disciplines has to be established[40].

---

[40] See, for example, the 'critical naturalism' discussed in Bhaskar (1979) and Jackson (1995).

The re-establishment of the links between biology and the social sciences does not mean that the latter are dissolved into the former. Arguably, it is possible to articulate a relationship between economics and biology in which each plays its part but the domination of one by the other is excluded. Such a relationship should provide a rich source of metaphorical inspiration. It remains to be seen whether these methodological and ontological insights can be deployed to develop a new evolutionary economics – to continue and consummate the project started by Veblen more than a century ago.

REFERENCES

Alchian, A. A. (1950), 'Uncertainty, evolution and economic theory', *Journal of Political Economy* **58**(3): 211–21. [Reprinted in Witt (1993).]

Alland, A., Jr. (1967), *Evolution and Human Behavior*, New York: Natural History Press.

Allen, P. M., and M. Lesser (1991), 'Evolutionary human systems: learning, ignorance and subjectivity', in P. P. Saviotti and J. S. Metcalfe (eds.), *Evolutionary Theories of Economic and Technological Change: Present Status and Future Prospects*, Reading: Harwood, 160–71.

Anderson, P. W. (1995), 'Viewpoint: the future', *Science* **267**, 17 March, 1617–18.

Arrow, K. J. (1995), 'Viewpoint: the future', *Science* **267**, 17 March, 1617.

Arthur, W. B. (1989), 'Competing technologies, increasing returns and lock-in by historical events', *Economic Journal* **394**: 116–31.

Ayres, C. E. (1921), 'Instinct and capacity – I: the instinct of belief-in-instincts', *Journal of Philosophy* **18**(21): 561–65.

(1935), 'Moral confusion in economics', *International Journal of Ethics* **45**: 170–99. [Reprinted in W. Samuels (ed.) (1988), *Institutional Economics*, Aldershot: Edward Elgar, vol. 2.]

(1944), *The Theory of Economic Progress*, Chapel Hill, NC: University of North Carolina Press.

(1952), *The Industrial Economy*, Cambridge, MA: Houghton Mifflin.

(1958), 'Veblen's theory of instincts reconsidered', in D. F. Dowd (ed.), *Thorstein Veblen: A Critical Appraisal*, Ithaca, NY: Cornell University Press, 25–37.

(1961), *Toward a Reasonable Society: The Values of Industrial Civilization*, Austin, TX: University of Texas Press.

Barber, W. J. (1994), 'The divergent fates of two strands of "Institutionalist" doctrine during the New Deal years', *History of Political Economy* **26**(4): 569–87.

Becker, G. S. (1976), 'Altruism, egoism, and genetic fitness: economics and sociobiology', *Journal of Economic Literature* **14**(2): 817–26. [Reprinted in Hodgson (1995).]

Bellomy, D. C. (1984), 'Social Darwinism revisited', *Perspectives in American History*, New Series, **1**: 1–129.

Bhaskar, R. (1975), *A Realist Theory of Science*, Leeds: Leeds Books. [2nd edn., 1978, Brighton: Harvester.]

(1979), *The Possibility of Naturalism: A Philosophic Critique of the Contemporary Human Sciences*, Brighton: Harvester.

Biddle, J. E. (1996), 'A citation analysis of the sources and extent of Wesley Mitchell's reputation', *History of Political Economy* 28(2): 137–69.

Black, M. (1962), *Models and Metaphors: Studies in Language and Philosophy*, Ithaca, NY: Cornell University Press.

Boulding, K. E. (1950), *A Reconstruction of Economics*, New York: Wiley.

(1978), *Ecodynamics: A New Theory of Societal Evolution*, Beverly Hills and London: Sage.

(1981), *Evolutionary Economics*, Beverly Hills and London: Sage.

Bowler, P. J. (1983), *The Eclipse of Darwinism: Anti-Darwinian Evolution Theories in the Decades around 1900*, Baltimore: Johns Hopkins University Press.

Boyd, R., and P. J. Richerson (1980), 'Sociobiology, culture and economic theory', *Journal of Economic Behaviour and Organization* 1(1): 97–121. [Reprinted in Witt (1993).]

Burrow, J. W. (1966), *Evolution and Society: A Study of Victorian Social Theory*, Cambridge: Cambridge University Press.

Burt, C. (1962), 'The concept of consciousness', *British Journal of Psychology* 53: 229–42.

Camic, Charles (1986), 'The matter of habit', *American Journal of Sociology*, 91(5): 1039–87.

Campbell, D. T. (1965), 'Variation and selective retention in socio-cultural evolution', in H. Barringer, G. I. Blanksten and R. W. Mack (eds.), *Social Change in Developing Areas: a Reinterpreation of Evolutionary Theory*, Cambridge, MA: Schenkman Publishing Co., 19–47.

Chomsky, N. (1959), 'Review of *Verbal Behavior* by B. F. Skinner', *Language* 35: 26–58.

Clark, J. B. (1885), *The Philosophy of Wealth: Economic Principles Newly Formulated*, London and New York: Macmillan.

Commons, J. R. (1934), *Institutional Economics – Its Place in Political Economy*, New York: Macmillan. [Reprinted in 1990 with a new introduction by M. Rutherford, New Brunswick, NJ: Transaction.]

Copeland, M. A. (1931), 'Economic theory and the natural science point of view', *American Economic Review* 21(1): 67–79. [Reprinted in W. Samuels (ed.) (1988), *Institutional Economics*, vol. 2, Aldershot: Edward Elgar.]

(1958), 'On the scope and method of economics', in D. F. Dowd (ed.), *Thorstein Veblen: A Critical Appraisal*, Ithaca, NY: Cornell University Press, 57–75. [Reprinted in Hodgson (1995).]

(1981), *Essays in Socioeconomic Evolution*, New York: Vantage Press.

David, P. A. (1985), 'Clio and the economics of QWERTY', *American Economic Review* 75(2): 332–37.

Degler, C. N. (1991), *In Search of Human Nature: The Decline and Revival of Darwinism in American Social Thought*, Oxford: Oxford University Press.

Depew, D. J., and B. H. Weber (1995), *Darwinism Evolving: Systems Dynamics and the Genealogy of Natural Selection*, Cambridge, MA: MIT Press.

Dillard, D. (1948), *The Economics of John Maynard Keynes: The Theory of a Monetary Economy*, London: Crosby Lockwood.

Dobzhansky, T. (1955), *Evolution, Genetics and Man*, London: Wiley.

Downie, J. (1958), *The Competitive Process*, London: Duckworth.

Durkheim, E. (1984), *The Division of Labour in Society*, translated from the French edition of 1893 by W. D. Halls with an introduction by L. Coser, London: Macmillan.

Edgell, S. (1975), 'Thorstein Veblen's theory of evolutionary change', *American Journal of Economics and Sociology* 34(July): 267–80.

Ely, R. T. (1903), *Studies in the Evolution of Industrial Society*, New York: Macmillan.

Enke, S. (1951), 'On maximizing profits: a distinction between Chamberlin and Robinson', *American Economic Review* 41(3): 566–78.

Farrell, M. J. (1970), 'Some elementary selection processes in economics', *Review of Economic Studies* 37: 305–19.

Fleetwood, S. (1995), *Hayek's Political Economy: The Socio-Economics of Order*, London: Routledge.

Ford, H. J. (1915), *The Natural History of the State*, Princeton, NJ: Princeton University Press.

Foss, N. J. (1991), 'The suppression of evolutionary approaches in economics: the case of Marshall and monopolistic competition', *Methodus* 3(2): 65–72. [Reprinted in Hodgson (1995).]

(1994a) 'Realism and evolutionary economics', *Journal of Social and Evolutionary Systems* 17(1): 21–40.

(1994b) 'The biological analogy and the theory of the firm: Marshall and monopolistic competition', *Journal of Economic Issues* 28(4): 1115–36.

Freeden, M. (ed.) (1988), *J. A. Hobson: A Reader*, London and Boston: Unwin Hyman.

Freeman, C. (ed.) (1990), *The Economics of Innovation*, Aldershot: Edward Elgar.

Friedman, M. (1953), 'The methodology of positive economics', in M. Friedman, *Essays in Positive Economics*, Chicago: University of Chicago Press, 3–43.

Georgescu-Roegen, N. (1971), *The Entropy Law and the Economic Process*, Cambridge, MA: Harvard University Press.

Ghiselin, M. T. (1974), *The Economy of Nature and the Evolution of Sex*, Berkeley: University of California Press.

Giddings, F. A. (1896), *The Principles of Sociology*, New York: Macmillan.

Gould, S. J. (1989), *Wonderful Life: The Burgess Shale and the Nature of History*, New York: Norton.

Gowdy, J. M. (1987), 'Bio-economics: social economy versus the Chicago school', *International Journal of Social Economics* 14(1): 32–42. [Reprinted in Hodgson (1995).]

Gruchy, A. G. (1948), 'The philosophical basis of the new Keynesian economics', *International Journal of Ethics* 58(4): 235–44.

(1972), *Contemporary Economic Thought: The Contribution of Neo-Institutional Economics*, London and New York: Macmillan.

142   *Geoffrey M. Hodgson*

Haavelmo, T. (1954), *A Study in the Theory of Economic Evolution*, Amsterdam: North-Holland.

Hahn, F. (1991), 'The next hundred years', *Economic Journal* **404**: 47–50.

Harris, A. L. (1934), 'Economic evolution: dialectical and Darwinian', *Journal of Political Economy* **42**(1): 34–79.

Hayek, F. A. (1952a), *The Sensory Order: An Inquiry into the Foundations of Theoretical Psychology*, London: Routledge and Kegan Paul.

(1952b), *The Counter-Revolution of Science: Studies on the Abuse of Reason*, Glencoe, IL: Free Press.

(1960), *The Constitution of Liberty*, London and Chicago: Routledge and Kegan Paul, and University of Chicago Press.

(1967a), 'Notes on the evolution of systems of rules of conduct', in F. A. Hayek, *Studies on Philosophy, Politics and Economics*, London: Routledge and Kegan Paul, 66–81. [Reprinted in Witt (1993).]

(1967b), *Studies on Philosophy, Politics and Economics*, London: Routledge and Kegan Paul.

(1982), *Law, Legislation and Liberty*, 3-volume combined edition, London: Routledge and Kegan Paul.

(1988), *The Fatal Conceit: The Errors of Socialism, the Collected Works of Friedrich August Hayek*, vol. 1, edited by W. W. Bartley III, London: Routledge.

Hejl, P. (1995), 'The importance of the concepts of "organism" and "evolution" in Emile Durkheim's *Division of Social Labor* and the influence of Herbert Spencer', in S. Maasen, E. Mendelsohn and P. Weingart (eds.), *Biology as Society, Society as Biology: Metaphors*, Sociology of the Sciences Yearbook, vol. 18, Boston: Kluwer Academic Publishers, 155–91.

Hennis, W. (1988), *Max Weber: Essays in Reconstruction*, London: Allen and Unwin.

Herbst, J. (1965), *The German Historical School in American Scholarship: A Study in the Transfer of Culture*, Ithaca, NY: Cornell University Press.

Hesse, M. B. (1966), *Models and Analogies in Science*, Paris: University of Notre Dame Press.

Hirshleifer, J. (1977), 'Economics from a biological viewpoint', *Journal of Law and Economics* **20**(1): 1–52. [Reprinted in Hodgson (1995).]

(1978), 'Natural economy versus political economy', *Journal of Social and Biological Structures* **1**: 319–37.

Hirst, P. Q., and P. Woolley (1982), *Social Relations and Human Attributes*, London: Tavistock.

Hobson, J. A. (1929), *Wealth and Life: A Study in Values*, London: Macmillan.

Hodgson, G. M. (1988), *Economics and Institutions: A Manifesto for a Modern Institutional Economics*, Cambridge: Polity Press.

(1992), 'Thorstein Veblen and post-Darwinian economics', *Cambridge Journal of Economics* **16**(3): 285–301.

(1993a), 'The Mecca of Alfred Marshall', *Economic Journal* **417**: 406–15.

(1993b), *Economics and Evolution: Bringing Life Back Into Economics*, Cambridge and Ann Arbor, MI: Polity Press and University of Michigan Press.

(1994), 'Optimization and evolution: Winter's critique of Friedman revisited', *Cambridge Journal of Economics*, **18**(4): 413–30.

(ed.) (1995), *Economics and Biology*, Aldershot: Edward Elgar.

(1997), 'Metaphor and pluralism in economics: mechanics and biology', in A. Salanti and E. Screpanti (eds.), *Pluralism in Economics: New Perspectives in History and Methodology*, Aldershot: Edward Elgar, 131–54.

(1999), *Evolution and Institutions: On Evolutionary Economics and the Evolution of Economics*, Cheltenham: Edward Elgar.

(2001a), 'Is social evolution Lamarckian or Darwinian?', in J. Laurent and J. Nightingale (eds.), *Darwinism and Evolutionary Economics*, Cheltenham, Edward Elgar, 87–118.

(2001b), *How Economics Forgot History: The Problem of Historical Specificity in Social Science*, London and New York: Routledge.

Hofstadter, R. (1959), *Social Darwinism in American Thought*, rev. edn., New York: Braziller.

Hoover, K. D. (1995), 'Why does methodology matter for economics?', *Economic Journal* 430: 715–34.

Hunt, E. K. (1975), *Property and Prophets: The Evolution of Economic Institutions*, New York: M. E. Sharpe.

Hutchison, T. W. (1992), *Changing Aims in Economics*, Oxford: Basil Blackwell.

Hutter, M. (1994), 'Organism as a metaphor in German economic thought', in P. Mirowski (ed.), *Natural Images in Economic Thought: Markets Read in Tooth and Claw*, Cambridge: Cambridge University Press, 289–321.

Ingrao, B., and G. Israel (1990), *The Invisible Hand: Economic Equilibrium in the History of Science*, Cambridge, MA: MIT Press.

Jackson, W. A. (1995), 'Naturalism in economics', *Journal of Economic Issues* 29(3): 761–80.

James, W. (1893), *The Principles of Psychology*, 2nd edn. New York: Holt.

Joravsky, D. (1970), *The Lysenko Affair*, Cambridge, MA: Harvard University Press.

Keynes, J. M. (1936), *The General Theory of Employment, Interest and Money*, London: Macmillan.

(1973), *The Collected Writings of John Maynard Keynes*, vol. XIV, *The General Theory and After: Defence and Development*, London: Macmillan.

Khalil, E. L. (1993), 'Neoclassical economics and neo-Darwinism: clearing the way for historical thinking', in R. Blackwell, J. Chatha and E. J. Nell (eds.), *Economics as Worldly Philosophy: Essays in Political and Historical Economics in Honour of Robert L. Heilbroner*, London: Macmillan, 22–72. [Reprinted in Hodgson (1995).]

Kirman, A. P. (1989), 'The intrinsic limits of modern economic theory: the emperor has no clothes', *Economic Journal* 395: 126–39.

(1992), 'Whom or what does the representative individual represent?', *Journal of Economic Perspectives* 6(2): 117–36.

Klamer, A., and T. C. Leonard (1994), 'So what's an economic metaphor?', in P. Mirowski (ed.), *Natural Images in Economic Thought: Markets Read in Tooth and Claw*, Cambridge: Cambridge University Press, 20–51.

Knies, K. (1853), *Politische Ökonomie vom Standpunkt der geschichtlichen Methode* [*Political Economy from the Perspective of the Historical Method*], Braunschweig: Schwetschke.

144   *Geoffrey M. Hodgson*

Knight, F. H. (1952), 'Institutionalism and empiricism in economics', *American Economic Review* 42(2): 45–55.

La Vergata, A. (1995), 'Herbert Spencer: biology, sociology, and cosmic evolution', in S. Maasen, E. Mendelsohn and P. Weingart (eds.), *Biology as Society, Society as Biology: Metaphors*, Sociology of the Sciences Yearbook, vol. 18, Boston: Kluwer Academic Publishers, 193–229.

Lawson, T. (1994), 'Hayek and realism: a case of continuous transformation', in M. Colunna, H. Haggemann and O. Hamouda (eds.), *Capitalism, Socialism and Knowledge: The Economics of F. A. Hayek*, Aldershot: Edward Elgar.

(1997), *Economics and Reality*, London: Routledge.

Lewin, S. B. (1996), 'Economics and psychology: lessons for our own day from the early twentieth century', *Journal of Economic Literature* 34(3): 1293–323.

Lilienfeld, P. von (1873–81), *Gedanken über zur Sozialwissenshaft der Zukunft* [*Thoughts on the Social Science of the Future*], Hamburg.

Maasen, S. (1995), 'Who is afraid of metaphors?', in S. Maasen, E. Mendelsohn and P. Weingart (eds.), *Biology as Society, Society as Biology: Metaphors*, Sociology of the Sciences Yearbook, vol. 18, Boston: Kluwer Academic Publishers, 11–35.

Marshall, A. (1890), *Principles of Economics*, London: Macmillan. [8th edn., 1920, London: Macmillan. 9th variorum edn., 1961, London: Macmillan.]

Matson, F. W. (1964), *The Broken Image*, New York: Doubleday.

Mayhew, A. (1987), 'The beginnings of institutionalism', *Journal of Economic Issues* 21(3): 971–98.

(1989), 'Contrasting origins of the two institutionalisms: the social science context', *Review of Political Economy* 1(3): 319–33.

Maynard Smith, J. (1982), *Evolution and the Theory of Games*, Cambridge: Cambridge University Press.

Mayr, E. (1980), 'Prologue: some thoughts on the history of the evolutionary synthesis', in E. Mayr and W. B. Provine (eds.), *The Evolutionary Synthesis: Perspectives on the Unification of Biology*, Cambridge, MA: Harvard University Press, 1–48.

McDougall, W. (1908), *An Introduction to Social Psychology*, London: Methuen.

(1921), 'The use and abuse of instinct in social psychology', *Journal of Abnormal Psychology and Social Psychology* 16: 331–43.

McFarland, F. B. (1985), 'Thorstein Veblen versus the institutionalists', *Review of Radical Political Economics* 17(4): 95–105.

(1986), 'Clarence Ayres and his gospel of technology', *History of Political Economy* 18(4): 593–613.

Medvedev, Z. (1969), *The Rise and Fall of T. D. Lysenko*, New York: Columbia University Press.

Menger, C. (1883), *Untersuchungen über die Methode der Sozialwissenschaften und der politischen Ökonomie insbesondere*, Tübingen: Mohr. [Translated by F. J. Nock (1963), *Problems of Economics and Sociology*, Urbana, IL: University of Illinois Press.]

Metcalfe, J. S. (1988), 'Evolution and economic change', in A. Silberston (ed.), *Technology and Economic Progress*, Basingstoke: Macmillan, 54–85. [Reprinted in Witt (1993).]

Mirowski, P. (1989), *More Heat Than Light: Economics as Social Physics, Physics as Nature's Economics*, Cambridge: Cambridge University Press.

Mises, L. von (1957), *Theory and History: An Interpretation of Social and Economic Evolution*, New Haven, CT: Yale University Press.

Mitchell, W. C. (1910), 'The rationality of economic activity', *Journal of Political Economy* 18(2–3), parts I and II, 97–113 and 197–216.

(1937), *The Backward Art of Spending Money and Other Essays*, New York: McGraw-Hill.

Moggridge, D. E. (1992), *Maynard Keynes: An Economist's Biography*, London: Routledge.

Morgan, L. H. (1877), *Ancient Society*, Chicago: Charles Kerr. [Reprinted in 1964 with an introduction by L. A. White, Cambridge, MA: Harvard University Press.]

Morgan, M. (1995), 'Evolutionary metaphors in explanations of American industrial competition', in S. Maasen, E. Mendelsohn and P. Weingart (eds.), *Biology as Society, Society as Biology: Metaphors*, Sociology of the Sciences Yearbook, vol. 18, Boston: Kluwer Academic Publishers, 311–37.

Moss, S. J. (1984), 'The history of the theory of the firm from Marshall to Robinson and Chamberlin: the source of positivism in economics', *Economica* 51(August): 307–18.

Myrdal, G. (1972), *Against the Stream: Critical Essays in Economics*, New York: Pantheon Books.

Nelson, R. R. (1994), personal communication to G. M. Hodgson, 21 September.

Nelson, R. R., and S. G. Winter (1973), 'Towards an evolutionary theory of economic capabilities', *American Economic Review* 63(2): 440–49.

(1974), 'Neoclassical vs. evolutionary theories of economic growth: critique and prospectus', *Economic Journal* 336: 886–905. [Reprinted in Freeman (1990).]

(1982), *An Evolutionary Theory of Economic Change*, Cambridge, MA: Harvard University Press.

Neumann, J. von, and O. Morgenstern (1944), *Theory of Games and Economic Behaviour*, Princeton, NJ: Princeton University Press.

Nightingale, J. (1993), 'Solving Marshall's problem with the biological analogy: Jack Downie's competitive process', *History of Economics Review* 20 (Summer): 75–94. [Reprinted in Hodgson (1995).]

Niman, N. B. (1991), 'Biological analogies in Marshall's work', *Journal of the History of Economic Thought* 13(1): 19–36. [Reprinted in Hodgson (1995).]

Ormerod, P. (1994), *The Death of Economics*, London: Faber and Faber.

Penrose, E. T. (1952), 'Biological analogies in the theory of the firm', *American Economic Review* 42(4): 804–19.

Persons, S. (ed.) (1950), *Evolutionary Thought in America*, New Haven, CT: Yale University Press.

Pigou, A. C. (1922), 'Empty economic boxes: a reply', *Economic Journal* 128: 458–65.

(1928), 'An analysis of supply', *Economic Journal* 150: 238–57.

Quine, W. van O. (1953), *From a Logical Point of View*, Cambridge, MA: Harvard University Press.

Rapport, D. J., and J. E. Turner (1977), 'Economic models in ecology', *Science* 195: 367–73. [Reprinted in Hodgson (1995).]

Rizvi, S. A. T. (1994), 'The microfoundations project in general equilibrium theory', *Cambridge Journal of Economics* 18(4): 357–77.

Robbins, L. (1932), *An Essay on the Nature and Significance of Economic Science*, London: Macmillan.

(1970), *Evolution of Modern Economic Theory*, London: Macmillan.

Roscher, W. (1854), *Das System der Volkswirtschaft* [*The System of the Folk-Economy*], Stuttgart: Cotta.

Rose, S., L. J. Kamin and R. C. Lewontin (1984), *Not in Our Genes: Biology, Ideology and Human Nature*, Harmondsworth: Penguin.

Ross, D. (1991), *The Origins of American Social Science*, Cambridge: Cambridge University Press.

Rutherford, M. H. (1984), 'Thorstein Veblen and the processes of institutional change', *History of Political Economy* 16(3): 331–48. [Reprinted in M. Blaug (ed.) (1992), *Thorstein Veblen (1857–1929)*, Aldershot: Edward Elgar.]

(1994), *Institutions in Economics: The Old and the New Institutionalism*, Cambridge: Cambridge University Press.

(1997), 'American institutionalism and the history of economics', *Journal of the History of Economic Thought* 19(2): 178–95.

(1999), 'Institutionalism as "scientific economics"', in R. E. Backhouse and J. Creedy (eds.), *From Classical Economics to the Theory of the Firm: Essays in Honour of D. P. O'Brien*, Cheltenham: Edward Elgar, 223–42.

(2000), 'Institutionalism between the wars', *Journal of Economic Issues* 34(2): 291–303.

Samuelson, P. A. (1938), 'A note on the pure theory of consumer's behaviour', *Economica*, New Series, 5(17): 61–71.

Sanderson, S. K. (1990), *Social Evolutionism: A Critical History*, Oxford: Blackwell.

Schaffer, M. E. (1989), 'Are profit-maximisers the best survivors? A Darwinian model of economic natural selection', *Journal of Economic Behaviour and Organization* 12(1): 29–45. [Reprinted in Hodgson (1995).]

Schäffle, A. (1881), *Bau und Leben des socialen Körpers* [*Anatomy and Life of the Social Body*], Tübingen: Lapp.

Scheffler, I. (1974), *Four Pragmatists: A Critical Introduction to Peirce, James, Mead, and Dewey*, London: Routledge and Kegan Paul.

Schumpeter, J. A. (1934), *The Theory of Economic Development: An Inquiry into Profits, Capital, Credit, Interest, and the Business Cycle* [translated by R. Opie from the German edition of 1912], Cambridge, MA: Harvard University Press. [Reprinted 1989 with a new introduction by J. E. Elliott, New Brunswick, NJ: Transaction.]

(1954), *History of Economic Analysis*, Oxford: Oxford University Press.

Sebba, G. (1953), 'The development of the concepts of mechanism and model in physical science and economic thought', *American Economic Review* 43(2): 259–68. [Reprinted in Hodgson (1995).]

Seckler, D. (1975), *Thorstein Veblen and the Institutionalists: A Study in the Social Philosophy of Economics*, London: Macmillan.

Shove, G. F. (1942), 'The place of Marshall's *Principles* in the development of economic theory', *Economic Journal* 208: 294–329.

Sowell, T. (1967), 'The "evolutionary" economics of Thorstein Veblen', *Oxford Economic Papers* 19(2): 177–98. [Reprinted in M. Blaug (ed.) (1992), *Thorstein Veblen (1857–1929)*, Aldershot: Edward Elgar.]

Stigler, G. J., S. M. Stigler and C. Friedland (1995), 'The journals of economics', *Journal of Political Economy* 105(2): 331–59.

Stoneman, W. (1979), *A History of the Economic Analysis of the Great Depression*, New York: Garland.

Streissler, E. W. (1990), 'The influence of German economics on the work of Menger and Marshall', *History of Political Economy* 22, Annual Supplement, 31–68.

Sugden, R. (1986), *The Economics of Rights, Co-operation and Welfare*, Oxford: Blackwell.

Tang, A. M., F. M. Westfield and J. S. Worley (eds.) (1976), *Evolution, Welfare and Time in Economics: Essays in Honor of Nicholas Georgescu-Roegen*, Lexington, MA: Lexington Books.

Thomas, B. (1991), 'Alfred Marshall on economic biology', *Review of Political Economy* 3(1): 1–14. [Reprinted in Hodgson (1995).]

Tilman, R. (1990), 'New light on John Dewey, Clarence Ayres, and the development of evolutionary economics', *Journal of Economic Issues* 24(4): 963–79.

(1992), *Thorstein Veblen and His Critics, 1891–1963: Conservative, Liberal, and Radical*, Princeton, NJ: Princeton University Press.

Tool, M. R. (1994), 'Ayres, Clarence E.', in G. M. Hodgson, W. J. Samuels and M. R. Tool (eds.), *The Elgar Companion to Institutional and Evolutionary Economics*, Aldershot: Edward Elgar, vol. 1, 16–22.

Tullock, G. (1979), 'Sociobiology and economics', *Atlantic Economic Journal*, September, 1–10. [Reprinted in Hodgson (1995).]

Tylor, E. B. (1871), *Primitive Culture*, 2 volumes, London. [Reprinted in 1958, New York: Harper.]

Veblen, T. B. (1898), 'Why is economics not an evolutionary science?', *Quarterly Journal of Economics* 12(3): 373–97. [Reprinted in Veblen (1919).]

(1899), *The Theory of the Leisure Class: An Economic Study in the Evolution of Institutions*, New York: Macmillan.

(1904), *The Theory of Business Enterprise*, New York: Charles Scribner's. [Reprinted in 1975 by Augustus Kelley.]

(1909), 'Fisher's rate of interest', *Political Science Quarterly* 24(June): 296–303. [Reprinted in T. B. Veblen (1934), *Essays on Our Changing Order*, edited by L. Ardzrooni, New York: The Viking Press.]

(1919), *The Place of Science in Modern Civilisation and Other Essays*, New York: Huebsch. [Reprinted in 1990 with a new introduction by W. J. Samuels, New Brunswick, NJ: Transaction.]

Vining, R. (1939), 'Suggestions of Keynes in the writings of Veblen', *Journal of Political Economy* 47(5): 692–704.

148   *Geoffrey M. Hodgson*

Waller, W. J., Jr. (1988), 'Habit in economic analysis', *Journal of Economic Issues* **22**(1): 113–26. [Reprinted in G. M. Hodgson (ed.) (1993), *The Economics of Institutions*, Aldershot: Edward Elgar.]

Ward, B. (1972), *What's Wrong With Economics?* London: Macmillan.

Ward, L. F. (1893), *The Psychic Factors of Civilization*, Boston: Ginn.

Whitehead, A. N. (1926), *Science and the Modern World*, Cambridge: Cambridge University Press.

Wilson, E. O. (1975), *Sociobiology: The New Synthesis*, Cambridge, MA: Harvard University Press.

Winslow, E. A. (1989), 'Organic interdependence, uncertainty and economic analysis', *Economic Journal* **398**: 1173–82.

Winter, S. G. (1964), 'Economic "natural selection" and the theory of the firm', *Yale Economic Essays* **4**(1): 225–72.

Wispé, L. G., and J. N. Thompson (1976), 'The war between the words: biological versus social evolution and some related issues', *American Psychologist* **31**(5): 341–51.

Witt, U. (ed.) (1993), *Evolutionary Economics*, Aldershot: Edward Elgar.

Wunderlin, C. E., Jr. (1992), *Visions of a New Industrial Order: Social Science and Labor Theory in America's Progressive Era*, New York: Columbia University Press.

C

Evolutionary history: reconciling economic reality with theory

6 Path dependence in economic processes: implications for policy analysis in dynamical system contexts

Paul A. David

1 Introduction: credo and context

I believe that the future of economics as an intellectually exciting discipline lies in its becoming an *historical* social science. Much of my work as an economic historian has sought to convey a strong sense of how 'history matters' in economic affairs by undertaking applied studies, focused on the behaviour of stochastic processes at either the micro- or the macro-economic level, in which the proximate and eventual outcomes could be said to be *path-dependent*. By the term 'path-dependent' I mean that the process is *non-ergodic*: a dynamical system possessing this property cannot shake off the effects of past events, and, consequently, its asymptotic distribution (describing the limiting outcomes towards which it tends) evolves as a function of its own history.

Although path dependence will be found where a dynamic resource allocation process is not described by a first-order Markov chain, it can be encountered also in some stochastic systems where the transition probabilities are strictly state-dependent (first-order Markovian) – namely, in those systems where a multiplicity of absorbing states exists. Under such conditions, small events of a random character – especially those occurring early on the path – are likely to figure significantly in 'selecting' one or other among the set of stable equilibria, or 'attractors', for the system. Although the nature of the specific selecting events themselves may elude prediction, it does not follow that the particular equilibrium configuration – among the multiplicity that are available *ex ante* – remain unpredictable. It will be seen that there are a variety of non-ergodic stochastic processes, some admitting of predictably and others that do not. Being able to identify the critical structural characteristics in that respect, while the system's history is still evolving, therefore has interesting implications for economic policy analysis.

On some earlier, more methodologically self-conscious, occasions[1] I have pointed out that those economists who shared my beliefs about the importance of history could find some encouraging signs for the future of our discipline in the fact that the existence of *local positive feedback* mechanisms – and consequent *multiple equilibria*, arising from a variety of sources – was becoming more widely acknowledged in current economic analysis. Rather than shunning models with multiple equilibria on account of their indeterminacy, economists increasingly are content to leave open a door through which aleatory and seemingly transient influences, including minor perturbations specific to an historical context, can play an essential role in shaping the eventual outcomes. As the implications of mechanisms of self-reinforcing change in economics come to be more thoroughly and extensively investigated in the context of stochastic processes, using available methods from probability theory, economic theorists and economic historians should begin cooperating on useful programmes of research.

My main purpose in this chapter is to continue attempting to promote cooperation between theorists and economists of an historical persuasion, so that the beliefs of the latter will become more widely shared. I therefore wish to emphasize the variety and richness of the dynamic problems in economics that possess a common structure arising from the interdependence of individual choices under conditions of positive local feedback, and which would thus lend themselves to a research approach that allowed for historical contingency. For reasons to be indicated shortly, in section 2 I will forgo the attempt to instruct by presenting detailed historical examples in favour of making my argument in more a more abstract, heuristic style. Section 3 presents one very simple, illustrative path-dependent equilibrium system that could lend itself to a number of quite different economic interpretations, and section 4 examines some of its formal properties. The potential topical applications cited in the chapter's following two sections (5 and 6) include macroeconomic phenomena, arising from exchange and investment coordination problems created by supply-side externalities, as well as 'bandwagons' in public opinion formation and the emergence of collusive oligopoly behaviour (cartel cooperation). However, as there is some virtue to specialization within scientific disciplines, I shall concentrate my more detailed

[1] See, for example, David (1988). This technical report is a revision of my presentation to the seminar series held at the Institute for Mathematical Studies in the Social Sciences (IMSSS) Summer Workshop (August 1988) on the subject of path-dependent historical processes in economic resource allocation. See also David (1989b), a paper presented at the Second Meeting of the International Cliometrics Society (ICS), Santander, Spain, 27 June 1989, and reproduced in the *Proceedings of the Second ICS Meetings*.

comments on the application of this type of model to problems of technological change (section 5) and the emergence of institutions (section 6), which must be central and perennial preoccupations of economic historians – indeed, of all those concerned with long-term processes of economic development.

The question of what shift, if any, the reorientation towards 'historical economics' implies for the way our discipline approaches policy analyses is one that is just beginning to be considered. It is obviously important, and so the large magnitude attaching to the significance of the question may excuse the far smaller one attached to the preliminary ruminations on the subject that I offer in section 7. Although the latter is quite specific, and concretely grounded upon the preceding discussion of path dependence in the emergence of technological standards in network industries, it is suggested as a potentially useful paradigm of a more general approach emphasizing the importance of *timing* in decisions about whether or not to intervene in market allocation processes. A concluding section (8) offers some rather broader considerations of the implications of path dependence for the future of economic analysis.

2   Concreteness, abstraction and the appreciation of historical contingency

On past occasions, as a rule, I have sought to convey my vision of the importance of remote historical events in shaping the course of subsequent economic changes by giving it a very concrete form, in one practical demonstration or another of the economic historian's craft. The idea was to spread the faith through specific 'good works' – by explicitly postulating non-ergodic models that could be applied to concrete problems in economic history, and actually applying them.

To delve deeply into some set of realistic historical contexts is, of course, essential for any convincing demonstration of the way that what we might want to call 'path-dependent equilibrium analysis' would look and feel in practical applications. The amount of specialized knowledge of technologies and institutions required to appreciate the details of this style of empirical inquiry, however, soon strains the patience of even the most tolerant general audience of economists. For better or worse, ours is an intellectual environment in which it is slow and tedious work making sparks with brass tacks.

That is why, eventually, I came to wonder whether it would it do any further good here to recapitulate the results of previous such efforts, either those on my part or similar historical research by others. Indeed,

I doubt that it would be generally edifying to wheel out that hoary model of localized technical changes generated by stochastic 'learning by doing' in industrial production[2], which I found useful in explaining nineteenth-century Anglo-American contrasts in the rate and direction of techno-logical progress. It is true that the model to which I have just alluded contained all the essential ingredients for strong (non-ergodic) history; that it showed how myopic localized learning in a fluctuating factor input price environment could allow particular events remotely situated in the factor price history of a particular economy to cause the region's manu-facturing industries to become 'locked in' to one or another of several available technological trajectories. But the pitch of that model was tuned to accompany one particular song, and those especially interested in the non-neoclassical reformulation of the 'Rothbard–Habakkuk thesis' have probably heard it already, or can locate it without too much difficulty[3].

The same framework of analysis, while attempting to synthesize Atkin-son and Stiglitz's 1969 model of localized technological progress with Rosenberg's 1969 ideas about the way existing production techniques acted as 'focusing devices' for further technical improvements[4], allowed also for changes in fundamental scientific or engineering knowledge to occasion radical innovations. These could initiate new trajectories that held out prospects for faster 'learning', and wider adoption, and so would threaten to disrupt long-established environments for localized learning – namely those complex systems that previously had been built up incre-mentally, through the sequential generation and adoption of many small and technically interrelated subsystems. Nevertheless, the usefulness of this way of looking at the process of technological change remains hard to assess in the abstract; and, again, those prepared to get into specifics will, most probably, have found their way to my various applications of it in studies of agricultural mechanization, and the parallels between con-temporary industrial experience with the application of robotic technolo-gies and historical experience in the development and adoption of farm machinery[5].

Much the same could be said of my more recent brief account of a familiar but striking piece of technological and economic history: an *his-toire raisonnée* of the standardization of typewriter keyboards that occurred around the beginning of the twentieth century[6]. Although my version of

[2] See David, 1975, chapter 1.
[3] See also James and Skinner, 1985, for a more recent discussion, and (happily) econometric evidence supporting the argument I advanced in 1975.
[4] See Atkinson and Stiglitz (1969), which has been elaborated upon more recently in Stiglitz (1987) and Rosenberg (1969).
[5] See David, 1975, chapters 4 and 5, 1986a, 1944c.
[6] See David, 1985, 1986b. Another case study focused on the early rivalry between alternat-ing and direct current electricity supply systems: see David, 1991, and – relatedly – David

the story of QWERTY invoked some powerful theoretical results from Brian Arthur, Yuri Ermoliev and Yuri Kaniovski[7] about the properties of a certain class of path-dependent stochastic processes (namely, generalized Polya urn processes), at heart it was a tale of how, when historical contingency rules, 'one damn thing follows another'. I meant it to be read by the many as a kind of allegory – and actually concluded it with a moral-like 'message'. I thought that a careful investigation of just how we collectively came to be stuck using the suboptimal QWERTY keyboard layout would provide an effective medium for transmitting my main methodological point about the necessity of taking an historical approach to certain classes of economic phenomena. This received considerably more notice, if only because its brevity increased the odds that people would read all the way to the conclusion.

But there was another 'hook' to catch the non-specialist's interest: telling modern economists that a dynamic market process has everyone 'locked in' to using an inefficient technology is a reliable way at least to get their momentary attention[8]. Fortunately, however, with the appearance subsequently of other case studies from which the generic features of 'lock-in' phenomena are also evident[9], the initial sceptical view of the story of QWERTY as being (at best) a *curiosum* has begun to give way to its acceptance as a metaphor for a class of multiple equilibrium processes – dynamic coordination games – that may yield Pareto inferior outcomes. There was, however, a 'downside', in the unintended identification of QWERTY as emblematic (as well as illustrative) of the phenomenon of path dependence. This fostered a mistaken supposition on the part of some economists and economic historians that a defining property of path dependence in economic processes is the sub-optimality of resulting market equilibria[10].

---

and Bunn. For more formal extensions and broader applications to problems concerning the emergence of de facto technical interface standards, see David, 1987.

[7] See Arthur et al., 1986.

[8] In due course I did receive in the mail a charming luncheon invitation from the president of the International Dvorak (Keyboard) Society. As was to be expected, not everyone was persuaded: S. J. Liebowitz and S. E. Margolis (1990) dispute the claim that the Dvorak Simplified Keyboard developed in the mid-1930s was an ergonomically superior alternative; and, presumably, also that the Ideal Keyboard (a late nineteenth-century contemporary of QWERTY) would also have been preferable. In Liebowitz and Margolis' view, this casts doubt on my 1985 characterization of the historical episode. But their discussion begins from the premise that, if there were a more cost-effective keyboard than QWERTY, some firm would find it possible to make a profit by introducing it – a position that fails to distinguish between efficiency *ex ante* and *ex post*, and denies that network externality considerations and 'installed base effects' could have a bearing on an innovating firm's profitability in this context.

[9] See, for example, Cowan (1990, 1991) and Cusumano et al. (1990).

[10] Worse still, that error has been compounded and reinforced by Liebowitz and Margolis' sustained campaign to dismiss the story of QWERTY as the founding 'myth' of

Despite the flurry of interest among applied microeconomists in industrial organization issues raised by problems of technological compatibility and standardization[11], no great rush has yet been seen among economists to generalize broadly from the analysis of 'excess momentum' and 'lock-in' mechanisms in that specific technological context. Perhaps it is overspecialization that inhibits wider recognition of the deeper connections that should be made, say, with Thomas Schelling's path-breaking work on static models of 'tipping behaviour' (see Schelling, 1978); and which keeps many economists from leaping ahead to see what bearing QWERTY-like dynamics might have for our understanding of other kinds of decentralized decision situations – where individual agents embedded in social and informational networks are subjected to analogous positive feedback forces that can cause collective choice processes to tip towards one extreme or another.

Whatever the cause for it, smart people continue to take these detailed stories so literally that they ask: 'Are you suggesting that historical influences upon present-day economic life come only through the path-dependent nature of technological change, and not via institutions, or the formation of tastes?' Quite the opposite is the case, of course: I meant to suggest the fundamental homomorphism of the dynamic processes that are at work in all of these domains. Evidently, the problem is how to convey my main analytical points simply and effectively, so that others can be enlisted in considering the larger implications of this different way to doing economics. The following section attempts the alternative, quite abstract, expositional style that is favoured by a theory-driven discipline.

3   Networks, interdependence and history: a heuristic model

I remain persuaded that, by examining problems of individual choice and decentralized decision making in 'network contexts', economists can

a new assault on market capitalism based upon the concepts of path dependence and hysteresis. This travesty, and other confusions and misapprehensions in the writings of Liebowitz and Margolis on the subject of path dependence, are sorted out and – hopefully – dispelled in David (2001). Correcting the distortions in these authors' (1990) historical account of QWERTY is the too long-deferred task of a forthcoming paper *History Matters, QWERTY Matters*, presented as the Tawney Lecture to the Meetings of the Economic History Society, in Glasgow, 1 April 2001.

[11] Among the influential recent theoretical publications in this genre, see Farrell and Saloner, 1986, and Katz and Shapiro, 1986. More extensive references will be found in David and Greenstein, 1990.

arrive at a deeper understanding of the role of such structures in propagating the influence of historical events, or what I call 'strong history'[12]. The network contexts I have in mind are not restricted to those created by the interrelatedness of production technologies; real economic actors function within many varieties of networks – social, and kinship-related, as well as commercially transactional and technological. Each of these potential webs of interaction and positive reinforcement into which individual agents may be drawn provides a theatre for the unfolding of historical dramas.

So, I shall make another effort at getting that general idea across, by resorting to an entirely hypothetical example. Given my technical limitations, any economic model that I might design to have others take home to play with is going to be a very simple toy indeed. But perhaps this will be an advantage, in that its structure (the starker for having fewer lifelike complications) will be more immediately grasped as one that can be adapted and elaborated by others more adept at rigorous model building – and eventually put to some good use in studying a wide array of empirical questions. The history of economic analysis surely offers much support for gambling on the lure of artificiality: those models that have succeeded best in becoming paradigms for thinking about everything are precisely the ones with specifications making it plain that they are not meant to apply directly to any actual situation.

The illustrative problem I have chosen for this purpose is one that (I'm almost sure) must have been thought through thoroughly by Schelling while he was writing *Micromotives and Macrobehavior*. But I haven't yet located the place where he, or anyone else of similar bent, has fully worked it out[13]. I call it 'the snow shovelling problem', and will sketch it here in the following way.

3.1   The 'snow shovelling problem'

(1) There is a city block lined with stores, and there is a snowstorm in progress: the snow is falling continuously but gently.

---

[12] See David, 1988, section 2, for a taxonomy of models differing in the strength of the role played by history.

[13] In *Micromotives and Macrobehavior* (p. 214) 'shoveling the sidewalk in front of your house' is mentioned among a large collection of decision problems involving a binary choice, the influence of which is external to the agent-actor's own accounting of benefits and costs but is internal to some other agent's accounting, purview or interest. The other examples given included: getting vaccinated; carrying a gun, or liability insurance; and wearing hockey helmets. Schelling's essentially static formal analysis of these problems emphasized positive feedback from the macro-state to the micro-decision, although, as noted below, his discussion recognizes the implications of local positive interaction effects (externalities).

(2) The pavement in front of each shop can be kept passable if the shop-keeper goes out from time to time and shovels off the snow. In other words, given the available shovel technology, it is quite possible for each of them to keep pace with this moderate storm – in removing snow from his/her own portion of the pavement.

(3) A typical shopkeeper rightly believes there will be a net benefit from shovelling his/her own bit of pavement *if and only if* the pavement outside at least one of the shops immediately adjoining is also being kept passable, as customers then would be able to get through to his/her doorway. To keep things simple, consider only shops with neighbours on both sides; if you like, picture the stores being arranged around a four-sided city block[14].

(4) However, the merchant's private net gain isn't big enough to make it worthwhile for him/her to hire someone to shovel off the next-door pavement if and when it becomes obstructed, or to put up with the hassle (transactions costs) of persuading the neighbour to do so.

(5) Being busy with customers and other tasks, the shopkeepers do not continuously monitor the state of the pavement. Instead, each follows a strategy of checking on conditions outside when they have a randomly timed free moment. But things are so arranged that the interval between these moments is short enough for him/her to expect to be able to keep up with the snowfall should he/she want to maintain a clear stretch of pavement throughout the storm's entire (long) duration[15].

When a shopkeeper happens to peer outside his/her door, here's what his/her response pattern is going to be.

---

[14] The condition given for there to be a private net benefit from shovelling one's own part of the pavement could hold true for every shop in the system if one supposes there were potential customers already inside the shops when the storm began, as well as others who could reach the pavement from the street. Note that the physical arrangement of the shops can also make a difference. If there are boundaries to the system, conditions at the boundaries may exercise a special influence. This point is made by Schelling (1978, p. 214), who gives an example of people who are able to read if they and both their neighbours keep their lights on, and will turn their own light off if either neighbor does so. There will be two equilibria when the group is arranged in a circle; if they are in a line, however, the people at the ends will not keep their light on under any condition and the whole system will go dark.

[15] We may assume some special conditions to ensure that this sampling procedure is compatible with a sensible individual decision strategy. For example, suppose there is – relative to the rate and variability of snowfall – a powerful shovelling technology at each shop's disposal (a large gang of children?) that imposes a fixed cost per 'job', irrespective of the actual volume of snow that has to be removed per job. So, no matter how long a time has elapsed since the last shovelling, the cost (and anticipated net benefit to the owner) of clearing would be the same on every occasion.

(a) First, suppose that his/her own pavement is clear because his/her decision at the previous point was to have it shovelled. If he/she finds the pavements on either side are similarly clear, he/she will decide to keep his/her pavement clear. And if both his/her neighbours' pavements are piled high with snow, he/she will decide to let the snow accumulate on his/hers. But if he/she finds the pavement is clear on one side and not on the other, he/she flips a (fair) coin to decide whether or not to continue a policy of shovelling – on the reasonable supposition of there being equal probability that potential customers could be trying to reach his/her shopfront by coming from either direction, right or left.

(b) Alternatively, suppose that the time before he/she had decided not to shovel. The pay-offs from instantly clearing his/her pavement will be the same as those that apply under the condition already considered: they depend upon what his/her neighbours have done. So, again, he/she will stick to his/her previous policy (no shovelling, in this instance) if he/she finds that is what both neighbours are doing; and his/her policy will switch (therefore opting to shovel) if it is found to be out of line with the neighbours'. When he/she receives a 'mixed signal' from the condition of the neighbouring sections of the pavement, there is a 50 per cent chance he/she will switch from (or continue) the previous policy.

An obvious problem-cum-question has by now formed in your mind. What can we expect to happen on this block as the storm goes on? Will there be sections of pavement that are being kept clear, whereas in front of other rows of shops the snow has been allowed to pile high? Will the entire length of the pavement turn out eventually to be impassable, or can the system find its way to the opposite, far happier macro-condition – with the entire pavement being kept clear, and business humming? Is there any way to predict successfully which of these configurations will eventually emerge? What does economic intuition tell you?

3.2   Snow shovelling, Markov random fields and the wider world

Before proceeding towards answers, there are four remarks to be made about the foregoing set-up. Three of these are technical observations, and the fourth concerns the generality of the basic structure – and hence the applicability of the methods suitable for its analysis to a wider class of economic phenomena. I shall take up these points, briefly, in turn.

The first thing to notice is that at each random ('sample and decide') point in time, the individual shopkeepers' transition probabilities are strictly state-dependent and not path-dependent; they are described completely when the current 'state' is characterized by a triplet indicating the prevailing snow condition (previously shovelled or not) on his/her own length of pavement, and on the right- and left-adjoining pavements. Thus the evolution of his/her snow shovelling policy can be said to follow a *first-order Markov chain*. Notice that many microeconomic decision-problems involve binary (or discrete multinomial) choices, and where these are subject to revisions conditional on changes in the agent's environment (current state) it is quite conventional for economists to model the micro-behaviour as a first-order Markov chain.

A second point is that the course of action just described is exactly equivalent to another, even simpler strategy. It wouldn't take one of these shopkeepers long to realize that, instead of checking both neighbours and flipping a coin on occasions when they do not agree, he/she could flip the same (fair) coin in order to decide which one of the adjoining pavements to look at exclusively. When his/her past policy choice was found to be out of line with the prevailing policy of the selected neighbour, he/she would switch to match what that neighbour was doing; and if the two of them were found to coincide he/she would continue with his/her previous policy. But, either way, his/her strategy can be reduced to this: at a random moment adopt whichever policy a neighbour selected at random has been following most recently.

The third point is now immediately apparent. When we move to the macro-level and ask about the properties of a system composed of all the shopkeepers on the block, their collective behaviour can be viewed as a stochastic process formed from *additively interacting Markov processes*, or – as we might say – 'interdependent Markov chains with locally positive feedbacks'. This last observation is quite a help, because there already exists a substantial literature in probability theory for economists to consult on the subject of interacting Markov processes and *Markov random fields*[16].

Some formal definitions may be supplied at this point to make clearer just why the latter measures are of relevance. So, let $G = G(A, E)$ be a graph with $A = (a_1, a_2, \ldots, a_n)$ the vertices or nodes, and $E = (e_1, e_2, \ldots, e_n)$ the edges or shortest line connections between nodes. A (spatial) configuration x is an assignment of an element of the finite set S to each point of A. In our example we can denote the policies of 'shovelling' and 'not shovelling' by + and − respectively, and define $S = (+, -)$; a

[16] See, for example, Spitzer (1970) and Griffeath (1979), which are technically rather beyond me. Liggett (1985) provides a comprehensive recent treatise. Less formidable recent surveys containing numerous references to earlier work are also available; see Liggett (1980) and Kindermann and Snell (1980a, 1980b).

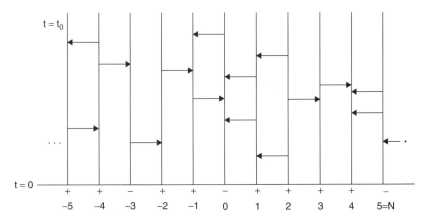

Figure 6.1 A schematic representation of the 'snow shovelling model'.
Note: It uses a Harris-type diagram (adapted from Kindermann and
Snell, 1980b) to show how each store will revise its policy in exponential time – adopting the policy that was being followed by a randomly
selected neighbour.

configuration is then an assignment of a + or – to every shop location
(node) of the graph (the horizontal baseline of figure 6.1) describing our
city block. The neighbours N(a) of shop a are the set of all points b of A,
such that (ab) is an 'edge'. (My notation follows Kindermann and Snell,
1980b.)

Now we can say that a random field p is a probability measure $p(x)$
assigned to the set X of all configurations x such that $p(x) > 0$ for all x.
Random field p is called a Markov random field if

$$p[x_a = s | x_{A-a}] = p[x_a = s | x_{N(a)}]$$

That is that, – in order to predict the value obtaining at node a (policy
state + or – at shop location a), given the entire configuration of A – we
need only know the values (the prevailing policy states) assigned to the
neighbours of a.

There is more than the satisfaction of intellectual curiosity to be gained
from exercising one's intuition on the particular mental jungle-gym I set
up in section 3.1. Although artificial and deliberately simplistic, the 'snow
shovelling' construct is meant to bear a resemblance to core features
of many natural, and more complicated, dynamic processes involving
coordination equilibria. These appear in macroeconomics, industrial organization economics pertaining to oligopoly behaviour, the microeconomics of technological competition and standardization, and the

economic analysis of social conventions and institutions[17]. Recognition of this wider sphere of relevance should be sufficient motivation for the moment. It will be easier to grasp some details of those connections after working through the simple illustrative model.

4   Interacting Markov processes: properties of the model

The structure of the particular interacting Markov process that we have been looking at is one that has been introduced in different contexts[18], by Clifford and Sudbury in 1973 and Holley and Liggett in 1975, and has since been very thoroughly investigated. In briefly presenting its dynamic properties I can borrow from the work of Ross Kindermann and J. Laurie Snell, who have, in turn, made use of a neat graphical representation by Harris.

A linear graph of the location of stores (points) situated contiguously around the perimeter of the city block appears in figure 6.1 – along the horizontal axis. Eleven locations are indicated, five on each side of store zero. (In general one can consider the regular graph consisting of the points $-N, -N+1, \ldots, 0, 1, \ldots, N$, but the figure shows the case $N = 5$.) The reference set (neighbours) of a shop at point i consists of neighbouring points (shops) $i - 1$ and $i + 1$ for $-N < i < N$ – i.e. except for the points at the extreme left and right ends of the graph. Since we have laid out the block's surrounding pavement on a line, the neighbours of N are actually points $N - 1$ and $-N$, and the neighbours of $-N$ are $-N + 1$ and N.

Time is indicated in figure 6.1 by distance along the vertical lines constructed at each point from the base line (corresponding to $t = 0$). The times *between* a shopkeeper's reassessments of the snow conditions on the adjoining pavements is assumed to be distributed exponentially with a mean 1. To represent this, along each time-line one can randomly draw horizonal arrows pointing to the right neighbour, letting the distance separating these arrows be exponentially distributed with a mean 2, and then do the same for arrows pointing in the other direction.

[17] An early and important connection between games involving both coordination equilibria and social conventions and the role of expectations grounded on historical precedent in supporting conventions was made by D. K. Lewis. In his book (1969, p. 42) 'convention' is defined as a regularity in the behaviour of agents faced with a recurrent coordination problem, about which it was a matter of 'common knowledge' (in the technical sense of something known to be known, and known to be known to be known, ad infinitum) that every agent would conform, and was expected by every other agent to conform, because no one would be better not conforming given that the others conformed. For a recent discussion of these and related ideas, see Sugden, 1989, and Elster, 1989.
[18] See Clifford and Sudbury, 1973, and Holley and Liggett, 1975. See also Harris, 1978, and Kindermann and Snell, 1980b.

The dynamic evolution of a shopkeeper's snow shovelling policy from the initial assignment is now readily determined: move up the shop's time-line until you come to an arrow pointing towards it, at which time the shop adopts the policy of the neighbour from which that arrow comes. The whole process can therefore be described as a finite-state continuous-time Markov chain, with states being configurations of the form $x = (+ + - + \cdots + + 1)$, where $x(i)$ is the policy of the i-th shopkeeper. The configurations x^+ and x^-, where everyone is in agreement on shovelling or not shovelling, represent the *absorbing states* of this process. It is self-evident that when either of those states is reached no further policy changes can occur.

So now we have a pretty good intuition of what we should expect to find if the snowstorm is extended infinitely: complete standardization on either a positive or a negative policy in regard to snow shovelling represents the stable attractors into the domain of which the dynamics of the system will be pushed. In fact, a quite simple proof will be given shortly for the proposition that for any starting state (initial configuration) x the chain will, with certainty, eventually end up in one or the other of these two absorbing states, x^+ or x^-. Notice that the existence of a multiplicity of absorbing states means that this process is plainly non-ergodic, inasmuch as it cannot invariably shake loose from all initial configurations. If the block started off with everyone out shovelling the pavement, things would stay that way; and, likewise, if everyone started off by not shovelling until they saw what their neighbour(s) did. Which of these extreme outcomes will emerge when this game is actually played cannot be indicated with certainty at its outset. Quite obviously, if the process remains undisturbed, the identity of the eventual equilibrium will be determined by the initial configuration of policy assignments *and* the subsequent random timing of the visits the shopkeepers make to check on conditions in the immediate neighbourhood.

4.1   The predictability of the limiting macro-state

Even more interesting than the certainty that the outcome will be one of these extremal solutions is the predictability of the asymptotic state of the system for more general initial configurations – that is, when the initial condition is not a trivial case involving the complete unanimity of policy assignments. It turns out that for this continuous-time finite-state Markov chain prediction *ex ante* is possible, and the following intuitively plausible proposition can be shown to hold: starting in configuration x, the probability that the chain will end in absorbing state x^+ is equal to the proportion of + policies in that initial configuration.

164   *Paul A. David*

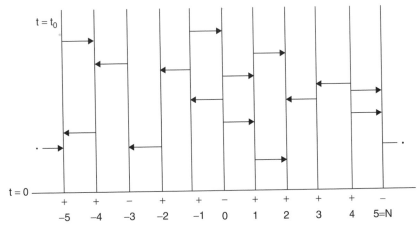

Figure 6.2 A dual representation for the snow shovelling process.
Note: This reverses the arrows in figure 6.1. By tracing a random walk
backwards through time for store 0, it is seen that the probability of
the + policy being followed by that store at (large) time $t = t_0$ in the
actual process will approach the proportion of +'s in the original policy
assignment.

A simple graphical device due to Harris has been applied by Kindermann and Snell in a way that makes this proposition quite easy to
confirm: figure 6.2 introduces what is called a *dual graph* for the percolation substructure represented by the 'snow shovelling process'. The
dual graph is constructed simply by reversing the direction of each of the
arrows in figure 6.1, and the directionality of the time axis.

To determine the probability that store 0 in figure 6.1 starting with
policy assignment x will arrive at policy + after time t_0, one can go to
the dual graph and trace events back in time from t_0 towards $t = 0$. So,
starting on the store 0 line at time t_0, follow the path *downwards* in the
direction of the arrows until $t = 0$. By construction, store 0 eventually
acquires the policy (+) of the store at the end of the path indicated in
figure 6.2.

This random path is the outcome of a continuous-time random walk
with states defined (in general) as the integers $-N$ to N; it moves downwards an exponential time the mean of which is 1, and then with probability 1/2 leftward one step, and with probability 1/2 rightward one step. It
is known that the limiting distribution for this (symmetric) random walk,
as t becomes infinitely large, assigns uniform probabilities over all the
attainable states $-N$ to N. Therefore, the probability that the downward

path for store 0 in the dual graph will end at a (location with) + policy is just the proportion of +'s in the configuration at $t = 0$. But this represents, in the original process, the probability that, after a long time, storekeeper 0 will be following a + policy.

Now consider shops at two different locations, and ask: 'what is the probability that at some time t both will have the same policy – say, +?' Going to the dual graph in figure 6.2, two random walks can be traced downwards, starting from those locations at time t_0. Clearly, these will not be independent; if they ever intersect they will continue together as a single random walk. But it is known (from a theorem due to Polya[19]) that, in infinite time, two symmetric random walks performed in one dimension – and also random walks in two dimensions – will meet with probability 1. The answer to the question now before us, therefore, can be given directly from the preceding one: the probability that after some long time both shopkeepers will be following the + policy approaches the proportion of +'s in the initial configuration.

This argument can be generalized directly to arrive at the result that the probability of the shops at all (the finite numbered) locations after some long time having a + policy – i.e. the probability of x^+ being the limiting configuration – is just the proportion of + assignments in the initial configuration. By analogy, the probability of x^- being the limiting configuration is the proportion of the initial assignments that are *not* +. Together, these results establish that there is zero probability of the limiting configuration containing both +'s and −'s.

The fact that random walks in two dimensions, like those in one dimension, will intersect with probability 1 in infinite time means that these asymptotic properties will hold also for Markov random fields defined on two-dimensional graphs. The square lattice (or the chequerboard array) is perhaps the most easily visualized two-dimensional network design: the decision units located in such arrays are represented by the nodes (or cells), each of which has four nearest neighbours – east and west, and north and south[20]. Sequential binary choices made under the influence of additive local interactions with these near neighbours will, in the limit, converge to one or the other uniform configuration; and the outcome will be predictable, as has been seen, simply from the proportions in which the alternative policy assignments were made in the initial configuration.

[19] See Feller, 1969, pp. 360–62, for alternative formulations and a proof of Polya's theorem.
[20] In the one-dimensional array of figure 6.1, each shop belongs to three three-party local networks; in the square lattice arrangement just described, each actor would be a member of five 'local networks' – the one in which he/she occupies the central position, and those in which his/her four near neighbours, respectively, are centrally positioned. In a hexagonal arrangement on the two-dimensional lattice, with agents positioned at the vertices, every agent participates in seven overlapping local networks.

4.2   *Limitations on generalizations of the model*

Intuitively, one would not expect these results to be robust to further generalizations of the model in this direction. The reason is that there is no certainty of meetings between random walks performed in three-dimensional, or still higher-dimensional, spaces. When agents' decisions are subject to 'network externality effects' of such complexity that they cannot be reduced to a two-dimensional representation, there is no guarantee of their policies becoming *perfectly* correlated in the long run; all possible assignments of policies for any particular finite set of agents will have positive probability in the limit. But, at the level of three dimensions, some strong correlation still can be expected to emerge[21].

There is another direction in which the foregoing model cannot be generalized without losing the qualitative properties of eventually locking in to an extremal solution, and of having that outcome be predictable on the basis of some 'initial' or 'intermediate' configuration. These properties will hold strictly only for finite populations of agents. The behaviour of very large finite systems, however, may well be better indicated by that of an infinite population – a continuum of shopkeepers. For the case of a continuum, a random walk being performed on all the real integers, it is found that there will not be a time after which the system remains in an absorbing state[22]; in the limit of the snowstorm the process oscillates between the extreme of perfectly correlated policies – with all pavements shovelled clear at one moment, and all the shops being snowbound at another moment[23].

What may we surmise, if the evolution of collective behaviour in extremely large networks with positive local externalities is likely to resemble that of the infinite population case? Even under stationary structural conditions, such populations should not be expected to become

---

[21] Although there is thus no certainty in the three-dimensional case that the system eventually will 'lock in' to one of the extremal (uniform) configurations, in the limit there will be strong correlation among the policy assignments arrived at by members of the network. See Kindermann and Snell (1980b, pp. 79–80) and Bramson and Griffeath (1979) for further discussion.

[22] See Kindermann and Snell, 1980, p. 11.

[23] Qualitative results of this sort are familiar in the framework of general dynamic models of systems in which particles are subject to spontaneous random reorientations (policy switches, in the present metaphor), which are influenced by additive local interaction effects. This framework has been studied extensively in connection with dynamic two-dimensional 'Ising models' of magnetization (following Ising, 1924, Peierls, 1936, and Griffiths, 1964). Durlauf (1990, 1993) pioneered in using the stochastic Ising model framework to characterise the linkage between micro-level investment coordination and macroeconomic growth. For an analysis of metastability in this class of probabilistic reversible spin systems, applied to a model of technology choices in spatial systems with imperfect factor market integration, see David, Foray and Dalle (1998).

inextricably 'locked in' to one of a number of locally stable equilibria. But, as noted below, they may linger for many periods of time in these neighbourhoods.

What, then, can be said with regard to the qualitative macro-behaviour of smaller ensembles of interacting decision agents, when these remain isolated from external interference and their internal structural relations remain undisturbed? If there is no inherent tendency for the behavioural orientation of the individual agents to undergo 'spontaneous' changes (that is, changes not prompted by interactions or signals received from the macro-state of the system) these systems will be most prone to exhibiting the workings of history in its strongest form: convergence to an indefinitely persisting equilibrium (i.e. 'lock-in') characterized by perfectly correlated individual policy choices. Moreover, the prevailing collective policy, or behavioural norm arrived at, will have been 'selected' adventitiously, as a result of some particular concatenation of small events on the historical path. Inasmuch as the policy thus settled upon may well be one that is globally inefficient – indeed, collectively disastrous – this may be a reason why small systems of social and economic interaction appear historically to have a greater tendency to become extinct or absorbed into larger systems.

In dynamic models where the orientation (say, $+$ or $-$) of the individual particles are subject to continuous *spontaneous* random perturbations, as well as to the influence of positive feedback from the macro-state of the system (say, the difference between the global proportions of $+$ and $-$ particles), the expected time interval separating the transitions the system makes between the neighbourhoods of its local equilibria will lengthen rapidly if the number of particles in the (finite) system is increased[24]. An intuitive explanation can be given for this size effect: it is the spontaneous random perturbations of the system's micro-units that serve to push it out of the neighbourhood of one potential minimum and beyond the point of instability, whence it can move towards the other point of locally minimum potential. In a larger population it is a lower probability event that enough independently distributed random perturbations will be positively correlated to produce such a 'shock'. This is the same principle that prevents a large herd of horses that are tethered together from moving any great distance in finite time, whereas, as any cowboy knew, a small band of horses tied together for the night could easily be out of sight by sunrise.

---

[24] Weidlich and Haag (1983, pp. 37–50) examine explicit solutions for such a model, which exhibits such 'fluctuation-dominated motions' between two points of minimum potential, and show that the transition time is an *exponentially* increasing function of the number of units in the system.

5   Reinterpretations and immediate applications

The foregoing model lends itself readily enough to several loose reinter-
pretations that show the general bearing these methods and results can
have on the programmes of applied research currently being pursued by
a wide assortment of economists. Among these I would include some of
the following people:

(i) macroeconomists concerned with the implications of so-called 'trad-
     ing externalities', 'investment spillovers' and 'Keynesian coordina-
     tion problems'[25];

(ii) microeconomists working on the range of classic problems relevant to
     the 'organic' or spontaneous emergence of social customs and social
     institutions affecting resource allocation[26]; included with these here
     is the important historical process of the institutionalization of non-
     obligatory contractual and organizational forms governing long-term
     trading and employment relations[27];

(iii) those interested in endogenous aspects of consumer taste formation
      and in the interplay between narrowly economic psycho-social forces
      in the formation of public opinion on matters of political economy,
      particularly processes through which emerge a public consensus in
      'collective conservatism'[28];

(iv) industrial organization economists working on oligopoly dynam-
     ics and strategic behaviours sustaining implicit collusion or cartel

[25] See, for example, Diamond (1982, 1984), Howitt (1985) and Heller (1986). Durlauf
(1990, 1993) goes far beyond earlier work in this vein by examining the time-series
properties of a fully specified dynamic stochastic process.

[26] My reference to these as 'classic' alludes to the following famous passage from Carl
Menger's *Problems of Economics and Sociology* (p. 130 in the 1963 translation by F. J.
Nock):

The normal function and development of the unit of an organism are thus conditioned
by those of its parts; the latter in turn are conditioned by the connection of the parts to
form a higher unit.... We can make an observation similar in many respects in reference
to a series of social phenomena in general and human economy in particular.... Similarly
we can observe in numerous social institutions a strikingly apparent functionality with
respect to the whole. But with closer consideration they still do not prove to be the result
of an *intention aimed at this purpose*, i.e., the result of an agreement of members of society
or of positive legislation. They, too, present themselves to us rather as 'natural' products
(in a certain sense), as *unintended results of historical development*.

For further discussion of the relevance of information network paradigms to the development of social organization and cultural institutions, see David, 1994a.

[27] See, for example, Wright (1988), Murrell (1983) and Sundstrom (1988). See also Romer
(1984) for a different but somewhat related analysis of the macro-consequences and
reinforcement of micro-beliefs affecting adherence to 'social custom' in employment
relations.

[28] See, for example, Granovetter (1978, 1985) and Kuran (1987). A critical survey of the
literature, with many references, will be found in Kuran (1988).

cooperation – particularly where the monitoring of cartel adherence is imperfect[29]; and

(v) applied economists worrying about standards for technological compatibility in 'network' industries, especially the competitive diffusion of alternative technologies characterized by 'increasing returns to adoption' and the emergence of de facto standardization[30].

The seeming diversity of this collection notwithstanding, an area of common ground remains clear. It lies in the interdependence of choices made sequentially by agents pursuing their private interest within contexts where substantial benefits arise from coordinated or synergetic actions, and where individual decision-agents are all limited (for various reasons) to considering only the actions of the members of a particular reference group, or subset of 'significant others', within the collectivity. As in the snow shovelling problem, however, the reference groups of agents in question generally are not disjoint; because the 'neighbours' of one agent are also 'neighbours' of some other agents, individual units' decisions become linked indirectly by the intersecting networks of local relationships, which transmit and communicate their effects.

Rather than attempting to elaborate all these contexts of application explicitly, I prefer to invite those more deeply involved in each of the various specialized areas to take up the task. In that spirit I will direct the main thrust of my remaining comments to the microeconomics of competitions among alternative technologies, and among alternative organizational and institutional forms. Having elsewhere avoided dwelling on the applicability of this particular model for analyses of the economics of compatibility standards and the emergence of de facto standardization, I feel freer to do so here without inviting the surmise that I regard path

---

[29] See, for example, Kreps et al. (1982), Kreps and Spence (1985), Green and Porter (1984) and Abreu et al. (1986). Kreps and Spence (p. 364) remark that the technique of setting up games of incomplete information, and seeking a noncooperative equilibrium of the cartel game where each participant is assumed to condition its actions on the private information it has received, 'captures the idea that history matters. At intermediate points in the game, participants use the actions of their rivals to make inferences concerning those things about which they were initially uncertain. . . . Since rivals tomorrow will be looking back [if they are able] to see what you did today, today you should look forward to gauge the consequences of your actions on tomorrow's competition.' The snow shovelling process makes history *really* matter, by restricting the informational capabilities of the agents to what they can discover just by observing their neighbours. This is brought out explicitly in David (1988, section 5).

[30] The sample of works cited here all give formal and explicitly dynamical treatments of these subjects: Arthur (1989); Farrell and Saloner (1986); Katz and Shapiro (1986); David (1987); and Puffert (1991, especially chaps. 2–4).

dependence solely as a feature of the gradual evolution of technological systems and social institutions[31].

When we consider what application the preceding model might have to analysis of the dynamics of technology adoption under conditions of positive network externality, the correspondence between a binary policy choice and a binary technology choice is immediately transparent. The relevance of the analysis of the preceding section – based as it is on the structure described by Holley and Liggett (1975) as a 'voter model' – to Kuran's (1987) theory of the formation of public policy consensuses should also be sufficiently self-evident to require no further comment here. Only slightly less self-evident, in my view, is its relevance to the dynamics of the institutionalization of certain organizational practices, such as the granting of procedural rights to university professors under the tenure system, in which the significance of withholding the right is affected by how many other organizations aspiring to the same status (i.e. the neighbourhood set for comparisons) have done so.

Equally transparent is the representation of the 'locally bounded' nature of the technological network externalities that impinge upon users' choices. Telephone service subscribers may care only about the ease of communicating directly with their family, friends and business associates, not with someone drawn at random from the entire community; and computer users may give weight only to the advantages of being able to share specialized software applications and technical information with identified co-workers. This form of local, or neighbourhood, 'boundedness' was not explicitly considered – to my knowledge anyway – in the early theoretical literature devoted to the dynamics of technological competition under conditions of positive feedback due to network externalities. Arthur (1989) discusses the properties of a generalized Polya urn process featuring a different kind of 'bounded' increasing returns: the probability of adding a ball of one colour rather than another to an urn at each moment is assumed to improve as a function of the *global* proportion of the balls in the urn that currently are of that colour, with the improvement function's slope decreasing to zero within the domain of the probability distribution's support. Although Arthur has shown that such processes can reach limiting states in which more than one colour will be represented by a finite share of the urn's population, this result

---

[31] Aspects of similarity and of differentiation between path-dependent processes affecting technological development, on the one hand, and the formation and evolution of social organizations and institutions, on the other hand, are treated in David (1994b). That analysis draws on the important but generally overlooked insights that appear in Kenneth Arrow's Fels Lectures (see Arrow, 1974) regarding the role of history in the internal functioning of firms and other multi-agent organizations.

implies nothing about the behaviour of the one- and two-dimensional systems of locally interacting particles considered here. It does have a rough analogue, however, in the behaviour of three-dimensional finite particle systems – where the random perturbations impinging upon each particle are capable of overwhelming the local positive feedback effects. Extension of the model to two dimensions offers a quite natural representation of a spatial context within which choice-of-technique decisions arise affecting compatibility and 'connectivity'. This has been applied, for example, by Puffert (2002) in a dynamic stochastic simulation model of the process through which extended railway networks of a standardized gauge may emerge from decentralized gauge choices by local lines[32]. By contrast, most entries in the recent spate of studies dealing with the dynamics of the competitive diffusion of alternative technologies subject to network externalities of one kind or another assume that micro-decisions are directly influenced by positive feedback from the macro-state of the system; they suppose that individual equipment buyers of VCRs, for example, select between Sony Betamax and VHS formats by balancing their intrinsic preferences against considerations that depend upon the relative share of the installed base that each of the competing technologies holds in the *global* market. The same simplification is typically made in constructing analogous models of 'tipping dynamics' and 'bandwagon momentum' in public voting and crowd behaviour – in which individuals' private preferences are seen as being first subjugated in favour of deriving the approbation of the majority, and ultimately modified (to minimize cognitive dissonance) by perceiving virtue in the state that prevails[33].

Because the snow shovelling model is focused upon the macro-dynamics that emerges from the micro-level process of policy revision, it lends itself immediately to the analysis of technology choices that can be revised when equipment wears out[34]. Most theoretical treatments of competitive diffusion abstract from such complications by

[32] Puffert (2002) tackles the problem in a spatial network model that is far more complex than the one suggested here – which he studies using stochastic simulation methods.
[33] Like Stephen R. G. Jones (1984), Kuran (1988) invokes Leon Festinger's *Theory of Cognitive Dissonance* (1957) in suggesting a micro-level (taste formation) mechanism that would serve to 'lock in' rapidly a social (or, in Jones' context, a work group) consensus reached by bandwagon dynamics. Taking a longer real-time perspective, Kuran (1988, pp. 32–33) also suggests that the educational and informal socialization of new cohorts may serve as mechanisms strengthening the tenacity of the past's hold. But, as one so often observes in revolutionary regimes, re-education and 're-socialization' are, equally, instruments employed in freeing societies from their history – for better or worse.
[34] The assumption that the previously installed technology wears out – and so must be completely replaced – abstracts from 'switching costs' or 'conversion costs' that arise from the technical interrelatedness among the producer's portfolio of real assets. The necessity of rewriting code for specialized applications software, for example, creates substantial 'switching costs' for mainframe computer users who are considering changing

assuming that the alternatives come embodied in infinitely durable capital goods. In such models the only way the share of each variant in the total installed base can change is if there are additions made to the stock, and such additions have a different distribution from that of the stock itself. This is the set-up of Arthur's 1989 model of sequential commitments to rival technological systems, for example. But assuming infinite durability is not realistic and suppresses important aspects of the way that de facto standardization has been achieved historically.

Nor are the strict irreversibility of technology commitments at the micro-level or physical durability conditions necessary to produce the result that a decentralized choice process with positive local externalities will eventually 'lock' to one or another of its extremal solutions – complete standardization on one or other version of the technology. Such 'lock-in' has been shown to be a property of the foregoing model, in which the exponential time process of policy revision can be immediately reinterpreted as an exponential process of replacing a randomly depreciating durable (embodying one or other version of the technology) the expected service life of which is unitary[35].

How the global 'replacement market' first comes into existence is not part of the story described by the snow shovelling model. A more complete if stylized account would describe some process generating an initial, possibly jumbled configuration of users of incompatible versions – say, the P(lus)-variant and the M(inus)-variant, which could represent PC and Macintosh computers – of the new technology. By a simple modification, for example, we could add a phase at the outset during which additional discrete points (store owners, or computer owners) were being inserted on the horizontal line in figure 6.1, each of whom came with an initial policy assignment reflecting the owner's inherent preferences.

Imagine, then, such a 'birth' or 'entry' process in which new P's and M's (+'s and −'s) take up positions randomly in the circular graph – doing so in exponential time with a mean interval shorter than the unitary mean of the policy revision (or technology replacement) process. So long as this rapid entry phase lasts, the population will be tending to increase without limit, and, correspondingly, the proportion of P's and M's in the growing total will be tending towards random fluctuations between the extrema.

to equipment using an operating system different from that already installed. See, for example, Greenstein, 1988.

[35] Such a good would resemble the 'one-horse shay', famously recollected by Oliver Wendell Holmes: an item of transport equipment that had served perfectly well until the day it fell apart.

But, if the mean interval between the arrival of new entrants was increased with the passage of time, eventually it would exceed the unit mean interval of the exponential replacement process and cause the dynamic properties of the system to alter so that they asymptotically approached the model already described. When a critical point was reached at which the (finite) population had become sufficiently large and the entry rate had become sufficiently slow so that only the stochastic replacement process was driving further changes in the share of the total assignments that were P's (or M's), the latter proportion would accurately predict which of these two variant technologies would ultimately emerge as the universal standard. Naturally, as the perturbation of the existing proportions of P's (or M's) by entry died away and that critical point was approached, the accuracy of the predictions about the eventual outcome of the competition based upon observations of the existing distribution of installed base would be raised.

At that stage the formation of expectations would become a potent additional positive feedback mechanism, particularly if there was a gain to be achieved by individual agents joining the emerging consensus sooner rather than later[36]. Were the individual agents able to benefit by aligning themselves sooner with the emerging consensus, and were they to possess the knowledge that the identity of the limiting correlated configuration was predictable from the currently observable configuration, monitoring of the sufficient statistic describing the macro-state of the system (namely, the proportion of P's [or M's]) would become a worthwhile activity. Moreover, the formation of expectations on that basis would, under many plausible suppositions regarding individuals' behaviour, drive the system more rapidly towards the 'selection' of the probability-favoured equilibrium[37].

6   Towards further expansion of the historical framework

It is evident that, in the finite population situation, some a priori beliefs about what the neighbours are going to do (when the snowstorm is just starting) can govern the eventual outcome. David Lewis (1969, pp. 33 ff.)

---

[36] In the illustrative example of the shopkeepers, since the intervals between policy reconsiderations are exponentially distributed it is quite possible that a given shopfront would remain blockaded by snow for some extended period of time (thereby missing opportunities for business) even though the pavements for some distance to either side had all been cleared. An ability to assign probabilities to the alternative consensuses that could emerge would thus permit the development of a superior choice strategy to the one based on the myopic consideration of randomly arriving information about the state of the neighbourhood.

[37] On the role of self-fulfilling expectations in dynamic stochastic systems of this kind, see David (1987) and Arthur (1988).

has made the more general point that the creation of a consistent structure of mutual expectations about the preferences, rationality and actions of agents can help in achieving rational (non-arbitrary) solutions to coordination problems. Shared historical experiences, and conscious perceptions of a shared past, provide one of the principal means by which groups of people may justifiably form a system of consistent mutual expectations when they are not readily able to arrive at a common course of action by directly discussing the problem that currently faces them. When individuals who cannot communicate are confronted with a pure coordination problem, according to the classic observations of Schelling (1960), they try for a coordination equilibrium that is in some way 'salient' – one that distinguishes itself from the other candidates by possessing some unique and remarkable feature, which need not be held to have any intrinsic value[38]. So, precedent is an important source of salience in such contexts: a solution to a coordination game can acquire 'conspicuous uniqueness' simply by having been part of the players' shared history – because they remember having reached it on a previous, similar occasion.

Thus, through the reinforcement of mutual expectations, 'accidents of history' may acquire a status of surprising durability in human social arrangements. As Lewis (1969, pp. 39, 41–42) puts it,

It does not matter *why* coordination was achieved at analogous equilibria in the previous cases. Even if it had happened by luck, we could still follow the precedent set [. . .] Each new action in conformity to the regularity adds to our experience of general conformity. Our experience of general conformity in the past leads us, by force of precedent, to expect a like conformity in the future. And our expectation of future conformity is a reason to go on conforming, since to conform if others do is to achieve a coordination equilibrium and to satisfy one's own preferences. And so it goes – we're here because we're here because we're here because we're here. Once the process gets started, we have a metastable self-perpetuating system of preferences, expectations, and actions capable of persisting indefinitely.

In the hypothetical coordination problem that we have been examining, there would be an obvious functional role for a pervasive ideology of civic-mindedness – 'block pride', or whatever – if that created expectations which sufficed to induce every shopkeeper at least to begin by adopting a positive policy on the question of whether or not to shovel his/her bit of pavement. And, of course, such community spirit would be reinforced by the happy material outcome: merchants located on blocks that embraced that ideology unanimously would be rewarded, individually and collectively, by staying in business with certainty throughout the storm season, whereas other communities lacking their unanimity

---

[38] See Schelling, 1960, pp. 83–118, 291–303.

could become snowbound. But ad hoc appeal to *universal* ideologies as a source of consistent mutual expectations is a rather unsatisfying device for historians to employ in explaining (predicting) the outcome of collective behaviour in such situations. How would such ideologies come to have been formed in the first place? Moreover, in keeping with the spirit of economic imperialism, economists surely should be attempting to analyse and explain the dynamics of collective opinion formation (see Kuran, 1987, 1988, for examples). Why should we want to place the origins (and decay) of ideologies firmly outside the system, safely beyond the reach of being reinforced or undermined by the microeconomic and macroeconomic results of dynamic resource allocation processes such as the one we have been considering? If there are ways thus to represent the coevolution of microeconomic behaviour with regard to technology choices (technical standardization), or conformance with social norms (custom and convention) and correlated patterns of ideology or beliefs carrying normative force (subjective conformism), the explanatory apparatus available to economists studying long-term trends in technology and social institutions will surely be much more powerful[39].

The beauty of a system such as the one that has been set out above is that it lends itself neatly to being nested, or 'embedded', in a larger historical model, in which the macrocosmic outcome or distribution of microcosmic outcomes from one extended, storm-like epoch might be supposed to influence the initial policy assignments adopted by players in a subsequent epoch. We would have a choice, of course, between modelling such linkages between successive 'epochs' in a way that made the transition strictly Markovian (state-dependent) or entertaining a richer historical vision in which societies' evolving common knowledge of their past channelled the course of change.

7   Policy intervention quandaries: the paradigm of network technology standards

Three generic problem areas for policy makers concerned with network technology industries are highlighted by the foregoing heuristic exercises. The presence of network externalities plays a dual role in this context. Firstly, such externalities are a source of non-convexities that have the potential to result in the emergence of inefficient outcomes where resource allocation is left to the workings of competitive markets. That

---

[39] On the importance of taking account of induced and self-reinforcing normative messages, rationalizing and sanctioning behavioural trends among some segments of a population, see Fuchs (1985). The coevolution of contraceptive technologies and sexual ideologies during the nineteenth century is examined by David and Sanderson (1986).

176   Paul A. David

this may create a rationale for public intervention is well known. Secondly, the self-reinforcing dynamics that such externalities set in motion is a source of path dependence in the system, which makes it essential to consider questions that may hinge on the detailed timing of events and policy actions.

This latter consideration has tended to pass without much notice in general economic analyses of microeconomic policy interventions. Certainly, a number of the difficult problems to which they give rise continue to be overlooked by the prevailing, essentially static treatment of the welfare economics of technology standards and standardization in the context of network industries. In the hope of making three of those problems at least more memorable, the following brief review affixes somewhat colourful labels to them.

7.1 Management quandries in the world of narrow windows, blind giants and angry orphans

First in logical order comes the problem that I refer to as the 'narrow policy window paradox'[40]. The existence of positive feedback in adoption processes makes available 'windows' for effective public policy intervention at modest resource costs. Such interventions may involve the manipulation – with high leverage effects – of private sector technology adoption decisions by means of taxes and/or subsidies, or informational programmes and announcements designed to shape expectations about the future adoption decisions of other agents. Publicity about government procurement decisions may also be a potent and relatively inexpensive instrument to use in this connection.

But for public agents to take advantage of these 'windows' while they remain open is not easy. The point at which such interventions can have maximum leverage over the course of the diffusion and development of network technologies tends, under natural conditions, to be confined towards the very beginnings of the dynamic process, and to have an uncertain but generally brief temporal duration. The brevity of the phase that leaves the widest latitude for policy interventions aimed at altering decentralized technology adoption decisions is, of course, a relative matter – the comparison indicated here being that with the course of the market competition that may ensue as one system or another progresses towards de facto emergence as the industry's universal standard. The actual temporal durations would depend upon the real-time rate at which system users were becoming sequentially committed to one network

---

[40] The discussion in this section draws heavily on that in David, 1987.

formulation or another, in the fashion depicted by the model presented in section 6.

What is it, exactly, that defines these policy action 'windows' and causes them to narrow? Essentially, it is the growing weight attached to considerations of network externalities (as determined by the distribution of installed base) among the range of factors influencing the system choices of new users. Simulation experiments of the kind first carried out by Arthur (1988, 1989) for Polya urn models of sequential, infinitely durable adoption decisions generate striking stochastic time-paths for the proportions of users who become connected to each of the alternative technological systems. These show, of course, that under positive feedback from the global state of the system one or other variant technology contending to become the universal standard will become 'locked in' – in the sense of approaching complete market dominance with probability 1. This happens as the number of users becomes sufficiently large for changes in the relative size of the system use benefits to depend upon changes in the distribution of users between the two networks rather than upon the absolute enlargement of the entire user community. At the outset of the diffusion process, when there are few members of either network, the network externality benefit effects play a less dominant role in sequential decisions by new entrants to the user population, and there is a wider range through which the global market shares can fluctuate without reaching the boundary values that cause 'lock-in' and 'lock-out' among competing standards.

If the rate of flow of new customers into the market is variable and not known precisely, it can be hard to predict the rate at which the 'window' defined by these boundaries will be closing. But it is no less true that new windows may pop open quite suddenly, as a result of the unanticipated appearance of a technologically superior or economically more attractive formulation of the system. An obvious implication for those charged with making technology policy is that instead of being preoccupied with trying to figure out how to mop up after the previous 'battle between systems', or manage competitive struggles that are well advanced, they would find it better to spend more time studying nascent network technologies in order to plan ahead for the dynamic systems rivalries that are most likely to emerge.

This brings me directly to what I have called the 'blind giant's quandary'. The phrase is meant to encapsulate the dilemma posed by the fact that public agencies are likely to be at their most powerful in exercising influence upon the future trajectory of a network technology precisely when they know least about what should be done. The important information they need to acquire concerns aspects such as identifying the characteristics of the particular technology that users eventually will come to value most highly, and discovering if differences might exist between the potentialities that the available variants have for undergoing future technical enhancement as a result of cumulative, incremental innovation. Prescribing action guidelines for 'blind giants' is a dubious business at best.

One strategy worth considering, however, is that of 'counteraction'. A suitable objective for an inadequately informed public agent may be to prevent the 'policy window' from slamming shut before the policy makers are better able to perceive the shape of their relevant future options. This requires positive actions to maintain leverage over the systems rivalry, preventing any of the currently available variants from becoming too deeply entrenched as a standard, and so gathering more information about technological opportunities even at the cost of immediate losses in operations efficiency. A passive 'wait and see' attitude on the part of public agencies is not necessarily what is called for by the prevailing state of uncertainty, profound though these uncertainties may be. Private sector commitments to specific technologies will surely be made in the face of ignorance. In circumstances where positive network externalities are strong and, consequently, markets beg for technical standards, governmental passivity leaves a vacuum into which will be drawn profit-seeking sponsors of contending standards, and private standard-writing organizations that are dominated (typically) by industry constituencies.

Regarded from this vantage point, the prevailing US public policy stance, which seeks to avoid mandatory standards but which encourages the formation of widely representative committees to write voluntary technical standards, would be misguided were it to lead more often to the early promulgation of technical interface standards. Voluntary standard-writing exercises, however, do not converge quickly – especially in areas of technology where scientific and engineering fundamentals are perceived to be changing rapidly. This is not necessarily a failing that should be laid entirely at the door of committee politics and strategic behaviour by self-interested sponsors of contending standards. As an engineering task, the writing of technical standards involves a continual interplay between efforts to be currently cost-effective and ambitions to 'push the state of the art', in which it is quite natural for new designs to be proposed even when they are not meant to serve as place holders for nascent competitors. Thus, inventive and innovative responses to the opportunities perceived in such circumstances have a side effect, in contributing to delaying the work of voluntary standard-writing organizations[41].

---

[41] For further discussion of the political economy of organizations developing standards in the telecommunications technology area, see, for example, David and Shurmer, 1996.

The present perspective suggests, however, that something more may be needed than so unreliable a device for postponing the establishment of a standard until more information has been gathered. Quite possibly, government agencies should be urged to pursue purchasing and other policies that, in effect, handicap the leader and favour variant systems that remain behind in 'the race for installed base'. A particular form for such counteractive policies would involve subsidizing only the system in second place: it addresses some part of the moral hazard problem created when leaders are saddled with handicaps, since one has to make an effort to avoid being left in third place, or even farther behind. What would be the effect upon the rate of adoption of the system that was in first place were such a policy to be announced? It is not self-evident that the adoption of the leader technology would be delayed. Instead, one can imagine conditions under which knowledge that government intervention would eventually be directed towards building momentum for a second-system bandwagon might lead to strategies that sought to accelerate the speed of the bandwagon carrying the first-place system. The matter is complicated and deserves more detailed examination than it can be given here.

In addition to whatever effects a public programme of second-system subsidization might be found to have upon the dynamic competition among existing system variants, attempting to keep the policy window from closing would be likely to encourage continuation of private R&D devoted to creating new variants, or fundamentally enhancing the older ones. The very fact that the identity of the victor in an ongoing rivalry remains more uncertain, rather than less, may be seen to reflect the persistence of conditions that hold out stronger – as opposed to weaker – incentives for profit-seeking firms to invest in more basic exploration of the technological opportunity space.

This may seem a rather paradoxical assertion, since it is nowadays commonplace to be told that private investment in basic R&D is much inhibited by the great margins of uncertainty surrounding its economic pay-offs. But the paradox is resolved when it is recognized that the market situation envisaged must be evaluated not only from the viewpoint of the existing rivals but from that of potential entrants; a would-be entrant – say, the sponsor of a newly developed network technology that enjoyed a specified margin of superiority (in cost or performance dimensions) – will have a greater expectation of being able eventually to capture the market when there is no incumbent holding so large a share of the installed base that the 'lock-in' of an inferior technology must be considered a high-probability outcome. In markets characterized by increasing returns that remain substantially unrealized, system sponsors and would-be sponsors confront a situation having a pay-off structure resembling a tournament. The certainty of market dominance by one system or another implies that a firm having exclusive property rights – in at least one, strictly complementary component of the winning system – could count on collecting some monopoly rents as a tournament prize. It is socially costly, however, to continue trying to offset the advantages conferred by installed base in order to induce a high rate of learning about the potential trajectories along which a network technology might be developed. There are, *ex hypothesi*, some positive network externalities that remain unexhausted, and which might be gained through a movement towards standardization and complete system integration. We therefore cannot ignore the realistic prospect that, even if no one system variant eventually managed to gain a clear technological superiority, any rationally conducted public policy course would call for an end to handicapping the leader in the competition for market dominance. Yet, when suppliers and sponsors of vanquished rival systems are left to fend for themselves – and possibly to perish – in what Schumpeter referred to as the 'competitive gale', their withdrawal or demise is likely to make 'orphans' of the users of the now unsupported network technologies.

'Angry technological orphans', who are likely to complain publicly that their technological expectations were falsely nourished by governmental programmes, pose both a political problem and an economic problem. The economic difficulty is that the existence of the proposed technology management policy tends to induce the allocation of resources to non-market activities, by firms seeking to protect the value of sunk investments. The political trouble is that they may find it somewhat easier to form lobbies and pressure groups to protect themselves from injury by perpetuating the governmental programmes that were originally designed only to prevent 'premature' standardization (de facto and de jure). Bygones are just bygones when one is concerned with economic efficiency (as I am at this point), rather than with considerations of equity – unless, of course, memory draws the past into the present and makes it a basis for actions affecting efficiency in the future.

So, a third policy dilemma cannot be evaded. How to cope with the 'angry orphans' who may be left in the wake of the passing competitive storm? The goal here is not one of equity but, rather, the maintaining of the credibility of the government's announced technology policies for the future. To achieve it, one must also strive for a solution that will not encourage behaviours on the part of future network sponsors that simply add moral hazard to the already appreciable risks that adopters face in choosing from alternative technologies.

As this is likely to be a politically delicate as well as difficult task, one reasonable approach is for public agencies to anticipate the 'orphans' problem and render it less serious, by reducing at least the costs to society that result when otherwise functional hardware or software is discarded because it has become incompatible with the emergent standard for the industry. Governmental support for R&D can be focused upon the development of 'gateway technologies', such as physical adapters, power transformers, code translators and electronic gateway devices, that will permit the *ex post facto* integration of distinct system variants into larger networks.

Profit-seeking firms, without any public interventions, may find their own incentives to develop what I have referred to as 'gateway innovations' and converter technologies. In recalling the constructive resolution of the late nineteenth-century 'battle of the systems' between AC and DC, one may point to the role played by the 'rotary converter', an invention from 1888 attributed in the United States to Charles S. Bradley, a former Edison Co. employee, who soon afterwards set up his own company to manufacture the device[42]. Rotary converters allowed existing DC electric motors to be supplied with current from AC generation plants and transmission lines, and so they were soon recognized by General Electric and Westinghouse as an important area for further technological innovation, as well as a profitable line of manufacturing activity. The periodic appearance of new converter technologies in the computer software field, more recently, as well as universal file servers for personal computer networks, stands as testimony to the fact that markets still do work. The question, however, is whether they can be trusted to work sufficiently well to generate the right amount of 'gateway' innovations.

There is still room for doubts on this score, and consequent grounds for considering the previously suggested modes of public intervention. Private systems sponsors may be justifiably wary about supplying customers with cheap 'gateways' to other systems. Public management of the preceding phase of open dynamic rivalry, in accordance with the principle of second-system subsidization (as previously proposed), may carry side benefits in this regard. It may provide additional market incentives for new entrants to supply missing gateways, *ex post facto*; by concentrating the population of users in a relatively small number of variant systems, the costs of engineering gateways among them can be reduced, and the potential number of customers for any specific type of gateway device may be enlarged.

---

[42] See David and Bunn, 1988, and further references therein.

But, equally, public policy makers seeking to mitigate the costs of inheritance in compatibilities must recognize that even in this regard there can be such a thing as 'too much, too soon'. The achievement of *ex post* compatibility in respect to some part of an interrelated system may render it vulnerable to 'takeovers' that will allow the tastes of a minority of users to impose losses upon the majority, who do not share those tastes but may nonetheless be obliged to share the costs. Moreover, providing easy connections between existing variant systems that cater to somewhat different user needs is likely to promote the technological specialization of these variants rather than the further development of a broader range of capabilities within each. It is arguable that the advent of the rotary converter resolved the battle between AC and DC in a way that suspended fundamental research on the possibilities of an integrated electricity system utilizing direct current, delaying the development of high-voltage DC transmission (see David and Bunn, 1988). The trade-off between immediate cost savings and 'pushing the state of the art' thus remains an ineluctable one for the makers of technology policy in this connection, as in others: premature reductions of gateway costs may exact unforeseen economic penalties by discouraging investment in R&D programmes aimed at establishing the technological dominance of one system over its rivals.

The special set of technology standards policies within the focus of the foregoing discussion has not been concerned with the reliability of 'labels' or the guaranteeing of minimum quality. The policies belong, instead, to the class concerned with the ways in which levels of economic welfare in the present and future may be raised through the manipulation of products' 'interface' characteristics – those affecting the compatibility of sub-components of existing and potential 'network technologies'. Public policy interventions of this kind can indirectly channel market-guided microeconomic resource allocation processes that otherwise would determine the development and diffusion trajectories of emerging technologies.

This initial delimitation of the discussion has simply set aside what is probably the greater portion of the range of policy interests that occasion governmental actions having intended or unintended consequences for the generation and diffusion of technological innovations. Into the 'excluded' category went ethical and political considerations raised by the potential redistributive effects of technical 'progress'; so also did the hardy perennial question of new technology's impact on job creation and job displacement, and such bearing as it may have upon short-run dimensions of macroeconomic performance, such as unemployment and price stability. Issues of military defence, national power and the maintenance of sovereignty have been ignored, even though they may be affected crucially by interface standards in the telecommunications field. Yet, even with these blinkers held firmly in place, the subject matter immediately in view remains so complex – especially in relation to my analytical powers – that the foregoing treatment has fallen far short of being comprehensive, much less conclusive. Most of it remains on a frankly speculative plane. One cannot fail to recognize that the public policy choice problems surrounding technological standards have been presented here in a drastically oversimplified and, possibly, misleading form. For this, however, I will make no apologies but claim justification for the effort by reference to the obvious importance of the issues at stake and the consequent value of directing to the subject the attention of others more capable of pursuing it successfully[43].

8   Path dependence and 'historical economics': some broader implications

Depending upon how you feel about path dependence, the foregoing digression into the history of economic thought and policy analysis could be either heartening or horribly discouraging. It certainly will have suggested to some, in a paradoxically self-referential manner, that analyses of 'lock-in' phenomena associated with path dependence might be taken as warning us to remain sceptical – or, at least, only guardedly optimistic – about the surface signs that a fundamental reconsideration of economics is now under way. Admitting that much does not say that the intellectual path we have (collectively) trod must have been 'the best way' for economic knowledge to advance. We know that, although path dependence is neither a necessary nor a sufficient condition for market failure, non-ergodic systems can settle into 'basins of attraction' that are suboptimal. Yet we know also that perturbations and shifts in the underlying parameters can push such systems into the neighbourhood of other, quite different attractors. Therefore, I believe it is thoroughly justifiable to insist that understanding the kind of self-reinforcing dynamics that generates a multiplicity of stable equilibrium configurations in physical and social systems also points to reasons for entertaining the possibility that we are, indeed, witnessing a significant intellectual 'regime change' that is raising the likelihood of an escape from ahistorical economics. A number of considerations can be briefly cited in support of this hopeful contention.

First, over the past two decades physicists and philosophers of physics have come to accord more and more emphasis to causation in physical theories, and to the importance of distinguishing the mathematical

---

[43] See, however, further discussion of the political economy of technology standards in David, 1987, David and Steinmueller, 1990, and David, 1994a.

derivation of an effect from the causal process that generates the effect[44]. Physicists today seem to want to know at some level of generality not only what happens but *why* it happens. Now, even a complete and 'realistic' derivation of equilibrium relationships does not, in itself, provide an account of the process by which an effect is generated. It may indicate those factors that figure importantly in any such process, but the need to describe a causal sequence remains. Thus, a sophisticated appreciation of the role of historical narrative has supplanted the older conception of explanation in physics, which simply subsumed a particular event under a 'covering law', or general regularity.

Economic theorists, too, have begun to worry more than they used to about causation – a condition that became particularly evident in the disaffection with the artificiality of the 'tatonnement' process imagined in the theory of competitive general equilibrium[45]. Causes are 'events' or changes in the pre-existing state that produce other changes, which we label 'effects'. If there is no perceptible change in a system, then, *ipso facto*, there can be no perceptible causation. Robin Cowan and Mario Rizzo (1991, pp. 9–10) have called attention to one of the profound consequences of the mainstream theoreticians' view that one could proceed as if there never have been 'events' in the history of the economic systems. They write:

The elimination of change and, consequently, of causation is characteristic of much current neo-classical thinking. Part of the implicit research program is to 'demonstrate' that what appears to be internal change really is not. Both actual change and the potential for change are illusory, because the economic system is always in equilibrium. [. . .] The neo-classical response to a putative disequilibrium phenomenon (which would have agents encountering unpredicted changes and so altering their beliefs) is to show that by including a formerly ignored market (often the market for information) in the analysis, the phenomenon is in equilibrium after all.

This inattention to causal explanation involving sequential actions, and to the disequilibrium foundations that must underlie any predictively useful theories of economic equilibrium (see Fisher, 1983), has impoverished modern economic theory and contributed to the disjunction between theoretical and empirical programmes of research. Efforts within the profession, finding external encouragement if such is needed, must move us towards acknowledging the possible path dependence of outcomes. For example, in the standard Edgeworth box analysis, it is trivial to show in general that, if one permits Pareto improving trades

---

[44] See Cowan and Rizzo, 1991, for a discussion of related work in the philosphy of science.
[45] See, for example, Arrow and Hahn (1971) and Fisher (1983).

to occur at non-equilibrium prices, exactly where on the contract curve one will end up is not completely determined by the preferences of the agents and their initial commodity endowments. The actual equilibrium configuration of prices and quantities that is eventually attained will have been be determined also by the details of the intervening sequence of (non-equilibrium) transactions[46].

Second, there has been a great weakening in the reinforcement that economists who pay attention to the natural sciences can derive for persisting in focusing on the investigation of linear – or linearized – systems, in which equilibria, when they exist, typically will be unique. During the past decade natural scientists and engineers have been turning increasingly to problems in the analysis of complex dynamical systems of the 'self-reinforcing' or 'autocatalytic' type – notably in chemical kinetics, in statistical mechanics and associated branches of physics, in theoretical biology and in ecology[47].

Fascinating as these phenomena are, economists should not count upon finding perfect paradigms, ready-made for their use in dynamic Ising models of ferromagnetism, or in the oscillating chemical reaction model of Belousov-Zhabotinskii, or in the theory of 'solitons' (non-dissipative wave phenomena), or the 'strange attractor' models that generate the Lorenz 'butterfly' paths that have become emblematic of deterministic chaos. Our positive feedback systems, unlike these physical systems, contain volitional agents the actions of which reflect intentions based upon expectations, and we therefore will have to fashion our own paradigms. But, undoubtedly, there will continue to be 'spillovers' from the natural sciences, especially in conceptual approaches and research techniques. Therefore, a third favourable external consideration to be noted is simply one of the impacts of 'the computer revolution' on quantitative research. Advances in computational power and programmes available for studying and displaying graphically the properties of complex, non-linear dynamical systems – advances that are being induced in large measure by developments in other sciences – are steadily reducing the attractiveness of striving to formulate mathematical economic models with unique real roots the qualitative properties of which can be uncovered by purely analytical methods.

In short, there has been an alteration in the general climate of thought, which is according new significance to details of historical sequence – a

---

[46] One should perhaps underline the point that all the equilibria (in the negotiation set) that can be reached from the initial allocation in this path-dependent fashion are Pareto efficient. See David (2001) for further discussion.

[47] For surveys, see – for example – Haken, 1983, Prigogine, 1980, Prigogine and Stengers, 1984, and Stein, 1989.

development associated with the growth of interest in non-linear dynamics across many disciplines and the consequent emergence of the so-called 'sciences of complexity'[48]. This intellectual ferment may be eroding the basis of the former stability of the ahistorical path on which our particular discipline has remained trapped (all too self-contentedly, it should be said) for well over a century. But, of equal importance, if not more decisively so, will be the attainment of 'critical mass' among the subset working on problems of positive feedback within the discipline of economics.

In the enthusiasm for the novel it is all too easy often to lose perspective and the appreciation of the familiar. Therefore, I must make it clear that I believe that any satisfactory development of 'historical economics' eventually will have to integrate heterodox insights with the knowledge previously gained about (linear) systems in which random disturbances are always 'averaged away', and convergence to the unique equilibrium solution is ensured. After all, there are many aspects of economic life where the interactions among agents (through markets and via other channels of social exchange) do not seem to be dominated by perceptible positive feedback effects. Decreasing and constant returns activities, like situations too fleeting to permit the acquisition of habit, or too thoroughly explored and disclosed to offer significant scope for experiential learning, are *not* likely to generate the multiplicity of equilibria required for such strong forms of history as system bifurcations and 'lock-ins' by adventitious occurrences.

So, it will continue to be important work empirically identifying those resource allocation processes that are well explained in terms of linear models informed by conventional 'convergence' theories, leading to historical narratives of a simpler form in which the influence of initial conditions – arising from sunk costs of a non-durable sort – is quite transient, and thus compatible with long-run *ergodic* behaviour. Eventually, in such circumstances, the system in question will shake itself free from the grip of its past, and the relevant empirical question concerning the influence of history becomes: 'Just how long is the long run?'

I come at last to the promised point of describing what conditions would be like on the new path, towards which that imagined critical mass

---

[48] See, for example, Stein, 1989. The term 'complex system' has no standard meaning and is used in many different ways. Some writers use it to signify deterministic systems with chaotic dynamics; others refer to cullular automata, disordered many-body systems, 'neural' networks, adaptive algorithms, pattern-forming systems, and still others. Daniel Stein (1989, p. xiv) observes that complex systems share the property of exhibiting surprising and unexpected behaviour that somehow seems to be a property of the system as a whole. So, a common characteristic of 'complexity research' is a synthetic approach, as opposed to reductionism.

of 'historically oriented economists' will be attracting their colleagues. We can proceed by reviewing some of the more general implications that flow from the adoption of the path dependence approach to the study of economic phenomena.

(1) Because transient situations and 'events' leave a persisting influence (hysteresis), the details of timing and circumstance, which are the very stuff of narrative history, cannot be ignored or treated simply as rhetorical devices; economic models that failed to specify what happens away from the equilibrium position(s) would not be taken seriously. Consequently, a great deal more empirical attention would have to be devoted to characterizing the reactions of agents to unpredicted changes in their environment.

(2) At certain junctures individual human actors of unheroic stature can indeed affect the long-run course of history, and so, under conditions of positive feedback, the personality of 'inner-directed' entrepreneurs and the ideological convictions of public policy makers turn out to possess far stronger potential leverage affecting ultimate outcomes than they otherwise might be presumed to hold; greater attention would therefore be paid to the heterogeneity of beliefs, and the degree to which agents were 'inner-directed' – rather than 'other-directed' – in their expressed preferences. In systems where positive feedback dominates, it is the inner-directed agents who exercise a disproportionate influence upon the motion of the system, because those who are other-directed tend eventually to adapt to the views of those around them (see Haltiwanger and Waldman, 1985, 1988).

(3) Sudden shifts in structure, corresponding to the new evolutionary biologists' notions of 'punctuated equilibria', can be explained analytically in non-linear positive feedback systems. This may open a way for the formulation of dynamic models that are compatible with 'stage theories' of development, whereas stage theories formerly have had a bad name in economics because they merely offered a choice between simple taxonomies and tautologies.

(4) Analysis of stochastic processes that are non-ergodic and display the property of converging to one out of a multiplicity of stable attractors shows that comparatively weak 'shocks' occurring early in the dynamic path can effectively 'select' the final outcome (see, e.g., Arthur, 1989). Later on, however, when the system has slipped into one or other 'basin of attraction', it acquires sufficient momentum that economically costly actions are required to redirect its motion. This implies that effective public intervention in social and economic affairs is more a matter of achieving optimal timing than has been

admitted by ahistorical modern welfare analysis (see David, 1987). 'Windows' for taking fiscally and administratively feasible actions that could tip the system's evolution in one direction rather than another tend to open only briefly. The study of history, along with that of the underlying structural conditions that define the location of 'basins of attraction' and the 'watershed lines' (separatrixes) between them, would therefore be an integral part of policy analysis, inasmuch as it would help to anticipate and identify such propitious moments for action.

(5) Another implication to add to the list I have just adumbrated concerns predictability. 'Complexity', as a property of dynamic stochastic systems, implies that the domain of empirical relevance for the theory of rational expectations is quite severely circumscribed, as a suitably complicated statistical formulation by Mordecai Kurz has shown.[49] The nub of the problem is that there are some dynamic structures that can never generate a time series long enough for the agents involved to be able to use it to form consistent probability estimates about possible future states of the world. If we wish to understand the behaviour of historical actors who are obliged to make choices in conditions of Knightian uncertainty, more attention will have to be devoted to learning about the cognitive models they call upon when interpreting their society's visions of its past and forming expectations about its future. Even for economists, then, '*mentalité* matters'.

(6) Finally, perhaps the most heretical implication of all is that the central task allotted to economic theorists would need to be redefined. Acceptance of the idea that mechanisms of resource allocation, and the structures of material life, resemble biological mechanisms – in that they have evolved historically through a sequence of discrete adaptations – would seem to warrant this. Francis Crick (1988, pp. 109–11, 138–41) argues that it is virtually impossible for a theorist, 'by thought alone, to arrive at the correct solution to a set of biological problems', because the mechanisms that constitute 'nature's solution to the problem', having evolved by natural selection, are usually too accidental and too intricate. 'If one has little hope of arriving, unaided, at the correct theory,' suggests Crick, 'then it is more useful to suggest which class of theories are *un*likely to be true, using some general argument about what is known of the nature of the system.'

---

[49] For a collection of interrelated papers challenging 'rational expectations equilibrium' theories, and showing these to be the degenerate case of the more general concept of 'rational belief equilibria,' see Kurz, 1996, 1997.

This is one respect in which economics (many of the most profound contributions to which can be, and in some instances already have been, formulated as 'impossibility' propositions) might well model itself on biology rather than physics. To underline this point I can do no better than to conclude here by repeating Crick's further observations on the matter, with some suitable editorial interpolations (1988, p. 139).

Physicists [and economic theorists who mimic them] are all too apt to look for the wrong sorts of generalizations, to concoct theoretical models that are too neat, too powerful, and too clean. Not surprisingly, these seldom fit well with the data. To produce a really good biological [or economic] theory one must try to see through the clutter produced by evolution to the basic mechanisms lying beneath them, realizing that they are likely to be overlaid by other, secondary mechanisms. What seems to physicists to be a hopelessly complicated process may have been what nature [another historical evolution of technologies, institutions, and cultures] found simplest, because nature [these evolutionary processes] could only [or largely] build upon what was already there.

REFERENCES

Abreu, D., D. Pearce and E. Stacchetti (1986), 'Optimal cartel equilibria with imperfect monitoring', *Journal of Economic Theory* **39**(1): 251–69.
Arrow, K. J. (1974), *The Limits of Organization*, New York: Norton.
Arrow, K. J., and F. Hahn (1971), *General Competitive Analysis*, Edinburgh: Oliver & Boyd.
Arthur, W. B. (1988), 'Self-reinforcing mechanisms in economics', in P. W. Anderson, K. J. Arrow and D. Pines (eds.), *The Economy as an Evolving Complex System*, Santa Fe Institute Studies in the Sciences of Complexity, Reading, MA: Addison-Wesley.
 (1989), 'Competing technologies, increasing returns and lock-in by historical events', *Economic Journal* **394**: 116–31.
Arthur, W. B., Y. M. Ermoliev and Y. M. Kaniovski (1987), 'Strong laws for a class of path-dependent urn processes', in V. Arkin, A. Shiryayev and R. Wets (eds.), *Proceedings of the International Conference on Stochastic Optimization, Kiev, 1984*, Lecture Notes in Control and Information Sciences no. 81, Berlin: Springer-Verlag, 287–300.
Atkinson, A. B., and J. E. Stiglitz (1969), 'A new view of technical change', *Economic Journal* **315**: 573–78.
Bramson, M., and D. Griffeath (1979), 'Renormalizing the 3-dimensional voter model', *Annals of Probability* **7**: 418–32.
Clifford, P., and A. Sudbury (1973), 'A model for spatial conflict', *Biometrika* **60**: 581–88.
Cowan, R. W. (1990), 'Nuclear power reactors: a study in technological lock-in', *Journal of Economic History* **50**(September): 541–68.

(1991), *Sprayed to Death: On the Lock-in of an Inferior Pest Control Strategy*, Research Report no. 91-23, C. V. Starr Center for Applied Economics Research.

Cowan, R. W., and M. J. Rizzo (1991), *The Genetic-Causal Moment in Economic Theory*, Research Report no. 91-13, C. V. Starr Center for Applied Economics Research.

Crick, F. (1988), *What Mad Pursuit: A Personal View of Scientific Discovery*, New York: Basic Books.

Cusumano, M. A., Y. Mylonadis and R. S. Rosenbloom (1990), *Strategic Maneuvering and Mass-Market Dynamics: The Triumph of VHS over Beta*, Consortium on Competitiveness and Cooperation Working Paper no. 90-5, Center for Research in Management, University of California, Berkeley.

David, P. A. (1975), *Technical Choice, Innovation and Economic Growth: Essays on American and British Experience in the Nineteenth Century*, Cambridge: Cambridge University Press.

  (1985), 'Clio and the economics of QWERTY', *American Economic Review* 75(2): 332–37.

  (1986a), 'La moissonneuse et le robot: la diffusion des innovations fondées sur la micro-électronique', in J.-J. Salomon and G. Schmeder (eds.), *Les Enjeux du Changement Technologique*, Paris: Economica, chap. 5.

  (1986b), 'Understanding the economics of QWERTY: the necessity of history', in W. N. Parker (ed.), *Economic History and the Modern Economist*, Oxford: Basil Blackwell, chap. 4.

  (1987), 'Some new standards for the economics of standardization in the information age', in P. Dasgupta and P. L. Stoneman (eds.), *Economic Policy and Technology Performance*, Cambridge: Cambridge University Press, chap. 8.

  (1988), *Path-Dependence: Putting the Past into the Future of Economics*, Technical Report no. 533, Institute for Mathematical Studies in the Social Sciences, Stanford University.

  (1989a), *Information Technology, Social Communication Norms and the State: A Public Goods Conundrum*, paper presented at the Centre de Recherche en Epistémologie Appliquée conference on standards, norms and conventions, 27–29 March, Ecole Polytechnique, Paris.

  (1989b), *A Paradigm for Historical Economics: Path-Dependence and Predictability in Dynamic Systems with Local Network Externalities*, paper presented at the second meeting of the International Cliometrics Society, 27–29 June, Santander, Spain [reproduced in the *Proceedings of the Second ICS Meetings*].

  (1991), 'The hero and the herd in technological history: reflections on Thomas Edison and the battle of the systems', in P. Higgonet, D. S. Landes and H. Rosovsky (eds.), *Favorites of Fortune: Technology, Growth, and Economic Development Since the Industrial Revolution*, Cambridge, MA: Harvard University Press, chap. 2.

  (1994a), 'Les standards des technologies de l'information, les normes de communication et l'Etat: un problème de biens publics', in A. Orléan (ed.), *L'Analyse Economique des Conventions*, Paris: Presses Universitaires de France, 219–48.

(1994b), 'Why are institutions the "carriers of history"? Path dependence and the evolution of conventions, organizations and institutions', *Structural Change and Economic Dynamics* 5(2): 205–20.

(1994c), 'The reaper and the robot: the adoption of labour-saving machinery in the past and future', in F. M. L. Thompson (ed.), *Landowners, Capitalists and Entrepreneurs: Essays for Sir John Habakkuk*, Oxford: Clarendon Press, 275–305.

(2001), 'Path dependence, its critics and the quest for historical economics', in P. Garrouste and S. Ioannides (eds.), *Evolution and Path Dependence in Economic Ideas: Past and Present*, Cheltenham: Edward Elgar, 15–40. [Also available as Working Paper 00-011 from http: www.econ.stanford.edu/faculty/workp/.]

David, P. A., and J. A. Bunn (1988), 'The economics of gateway technologies and network evolution: lessons from electricity supply history', *Information Economics and Policy* 3: 165–202.

David, P. A., D. Foray and J.-M. Dalle (1998), 'Marshallian externalities and the emergence and spatial stability of technological enclaves', *Economics of Innovation and New Technology* (Special Issue on Economics of Localized Technical Change, ed. C. Antonelli), 6(2–3): 147–82.

David, P. A., and S. Greenstein (1990), 'The economics of compatibility standards: an introduction to recent research', *Economics of Innovation and New Technologies*, 1(1–2): 3–41.

David, P. A., and W. C. Sanderson (1986), 'Rudimentary contraceptive methods and the American transition to marital fertility control', in S. L. Engerman and R. E. Gallman (eds.), *Long-Term Factors in American Economic Growth*, Chicago: University of Chicago Press (for the National Bureau of Economic Research), 307–90.

David, P. A., and M. Shurmer (1996), 'Formal standards-setting for global telecommunications and information services', *Telecommunications Policy* 20(10): 789–815.

David, P. A., and W. E. Steinmueller (1990), 'The ISDN bandwagon is coming – but who will be there to climb aboard? Quandaries in the economics of data communication networks', *Economics of Innovation and New Technology*, 1(1–2): 43–62.

Diamond, P. A. (1982), 'Aggregate demand management in search equilibrium', *Journal of Political Economy* 90(5): 881–89.

(1984), *A Search-Equilibrium Approach to the Micro Foundations of Macroeconomics: The Wicksell Lectures 1982*, Cambridge, MA: MIT Press.

Durlauf, S. N. (1990), *Locally Interacting Systems, Coordination Failure, and the Behavior of Aggregate Activity*, Technical Paper no. 194, Center for Economic Policy Research, Stanford University.

(1993), 'Nonergodic economic growth', *Review of Economic Studies*, **60**: 349–66.

Elster, J. (1989), 'Social norms and economic theory', *Journal of Economic Perspectives*, 3(4): 99–118.

Farrell, J., and G. Saloner (1986), 'Installed base and compatibility: innovation, product preannouncements, and predation', *American Economic Review* 76(5): 940–55.

Feller, W. (1969), *An Introduction to Probability Theory and Its Applications*, 3rd edn., New York: Wiley.

Festinger, L. (1957), *A Theory of Cognitive Dissonance*, Stanford, CA: Stanford University Press.

Fisher, F. M. (1983), *The Disequilibrium Foundations of Equilibrium Economics*, New York: Cambridge University Press.

Fuchs, V. R. (1985), *A Note on Prices, Preferences, and Behavior*, Memorandum, National Bureau of Economic Research, Stanford, CA.

Granovetter, M. (1978), 'Threshold models of collective behavior', *American Journal of Sociology* **83**: 1420–43.

(1985), 'Economic action and social structure: the problem of embeddedness', *American Journal of Sociology* **51**: 481–510.

Green, E. J., and R. H. Porter (1984), 'Noncooperative collusion under imperfect price information', *Econometrica* **52**(1): 87–100.

Greenstein, S. (1988), *Computer Systems, Switching Costs and Organization Responses: The Federal Government Experience*, Technology and Productivity Workshop paper, Economics Department, Stanford University, CA.

Griffeath, D. (1979), *Additive and Cancellative Interacting Particle Systems*, Lecture Notes in Mathematics no. 24, New York: Springer-Verlag.

Griffiths, R. B. (1964), 'Peierls' proof of spontaneous magnetization in a two-dimensional Ising ferromagnet', *Physics Review* **136**: A437–A439.

Haken, H. (1983), *Synergetics, An Introduction*, 3rd edn., Berlin: Springer-Verlag.

Haltiwanger, J., and M. Waldman (1985), 'Rational expectations and the limits of rationality: an analysis of heterogeneity', *American Economic Review* **75**(6): 326–40.

(1988), *Responders vs. Nonresponders: A New Perspective on Heterogeneity*, working paper, Department of Economics, University of California – Los Angeles.

Harris, T. E. (1978), 'Additive set-valued Markov processes and percolation methods', *Annals of Probability* **6**: 355–78.

Heller, W. (1986), *Coordination Failure with Complete Markets in a Simple Model of Effective Demand*, Discussion Paper no. 84-16, Department of Economics, University of California, San Diego.

Holley, R., and T. M. Liggett (1975), 'Ergodic theorems for weakly interacting systems and the voter model', *Annals of Probability* **3**: 643–63.

Howitt, P. (1985), 'Transactions costs in the theory of unemployment', *American Economic Review* **75**: 88–100.

Ising, E. (1924), 'Beitrag zur Theories des Ferrogmagnetismus', *Z. Phys.* **31**: 253–58.

James, J. A., and J. S. Skinner (1985), 'The resolution of the labor-scarcity paradox', *Journal of Economic History* **45**(3): 513–40.

Jones, S. R. G. (1984), *The Economics of Conformism*, Oxford: Basil Blackwell.

Katz, M. L., and C. Shapiro (1986), 'Technology adoption in the presence of network externalities', *Journal of Political Economy* **94**(4): 822–41.

Kinderman, R. P., and J. L. Snell (1980a), *Markov Random Fields and their Applications*, Contemporary Mathematics, vol. 1, Providence, RI: American Mathematical Society.

(1980b), 'On the relation between Markov random fields and social networks', *Journal of Mathematical Sociology* 7: 1–13.

Kreps, D. M., P. Milgrom, J. Roberts and R. Wilson (1982), 'Rational cooperation in the finitely repeated prisoners' dilemma', *Journal of Economic Theory* 27: 245–52.

Kreps, D. M., and A. M. Spence (1985), 'Modelling the role of history in industrial organization and competition', in G. R. Feiwel (ed.), *Issues in Contemporary Microeconomics and Welfare*, London: Macmillan, chap. 10.

Kuran, T. (1987), 'Preference falsification, policy continuity and collective conservatism', *Economic Journal* 387: 642–55.

(1988), 'The tenacious past: theories of personal and collective conservatism', *Journal of Economic Behavior and Organization* 10(2): 143–71.

Kurz, M. (ed.) (1996), 'Rational beliefs and endogenous uncertainty: a symposium', *Economic Theory* 8(3).

(1997), *Endogenous Economic Fluctuations: Studies in the Theory of Rational Beliefs*, Berlin: Springer-Verlag.

Lewis, D. K. (1969), *Convention: A Philosophical Study*, Cambridge, MA: Harvard University Press.

Liebowitz, S. J., and S. E. Margolis (1990), 'The fable of the keys', *Journal of Law and Economics* 33: 1–25.

Liggett, T. M. (1980), 'Interacting Markov processes', in W. Jager, H. Rost and P. Tautu (eds.), *Biological Growth and Spread*, Lecture Notes in Biomathematics, vol. 38, New York: Springer-Verlag, 145–56.

(1985), *Interacting Particle Systems*, New York: Springer-Verlag.

Menger, C. (1883), *Untersuchungen über die Methode der Sozialwissenschaften und der politischen Ökonomie insbesondere*, Tübingen: Mohr. [Translated by F. J. Nock (1963), *Problems of Economics and Sociology*, Urbana, IL: University of Illinois Press.]

Murrell, P. (1983), 'The economics of sharing: a transactions cost analysis of contractual choice in farming', *Bell Journal* 14: 283–93.

Peierls, R. E. (1936), 'On Ising's ferromagnet model', *Proceedings of the Cambridge Philosophical Society* 32: 477–81.

Prigogine, I. (1980), *From Being to Becoming: Time and Complexity in the Physical Sciences*, New York: Freeman.

Prigogine, I., and I. Stengers (1984), *Order Out of Chaos: Man's New Dialogue with Nature*, Boulder, CO: New Science Library.

Puffert, D. J. (1991), *The Economics of Spatial Network Externalities and the Dynamics of Railway Gauge Standardization*, Ph.D. dissertation, Department of Economics, Stanford University.

(2002), 'Path dependence in spatial networks: the standardization of railway track gauge', *Explorations in Economic History* 39: 282–314.

Romer, D. (1984), 'The theory of social custom: a modification and some extensions', *Quarterly Journal of Economics* 98: 717–27.

Rosenberg, N. (1969), 'The direction of technological change: inducement mechanisms and focusing devices', *Economic Development and Cultural Change*, 18(1). [Reprinted as chapter 6 of Rosenberg (1976).]

(1976), *Perspectives on Technology*, Cambridge: Cambridge University Press.

Schelling, T. C. (1960), *The Strategy of Conflict*, Cambridge, MA: Harvard University Press.

(1978), *Micromotives and Macrobehavior*, New York: Norton.

Spitzer, F. (1970), 'Interaction of Markov processes', *Advances in Mathematics* 5: 246–90.

Stein, D. (ed.) (1989), *Lectures in the Sciences of Complexity*, vol. 1, Santa Fe Institute Studies in the Sciences of Complexity, Redwood City, CA: Addison-Wesley.

Stiglitz, J. E. (1987), 'Learning to learn, localized learning and technological progress', in P. Dasgupta and P. L. Stoneman (eds.), *Economic Policy and Technological Performance*, Cambridge: Cambridge University Press, chap. 5.

Sugden, R. (1989), 'Spontaneous order', *Journal of Economic Perspectives* 3(4): 85–98.

Sundstrom, W. A. (1988), *Institutional Isomorphism: The Standardization of Rules and Contracts in Business Firms and other Institutions*, working paper, Economics Department, Santa Clara University.

Weidlich, W., and G. Haag (1983), *Concepts and Models of a Quantitative Sociology*, New York: Springer-Verlag.

Wright, G. (1988), *Historical Processes in Land Tenure and Labor Market Development*, Summer Workshop paper, Institute for Mathematical Studies in the Social Sciences, Stanford University, CA.

7   Is there a theory of economic history?[1]

Joel Mokyr

1   Theory and history

Is there a theory of economic history? More than thirty years ago this
question was posed in John Hicks' *Theory of Economic History* (1969).
Hicks noted that very few scholars have even ventured to answer the
question. Looking at those who have since the heady days of Karl Marx
and Oswald Spengler, we get an idea why. It is, quite simply, hard to
do, and Hicks, who was widely read in general history (to say nothing
of economic theory), paid little heed to what was already at that time a
huge body of literature in economic history. He could not be bothered
with details, because he was interested exclusively in general tendencies,
trends and moments. A few observations that did not lie on his curve did
not bother him, he said, because he was not dealing with 'theory' as it
would be understood in our time: tight logical propositions formulated
as theorems, which are refuted by a single counter-example. That kind
of theory did not and will not exist in economic history. But Hicks was
looking elsewhere.

What Hicks meant by a theory of economic history is something close
to what Marx meant: namely to take from economics some general ideas,
which he then applied to history so that the pattern he saw in history had
some extra-historical support. A rereading of his book suggests that he
was – at best – only partially successful in this undertaking. While it is rich
with insights and neat stories, it is not easy to find in it a great deal that
could not have been worked out by a level-headed historian who had not
written such seminal pieces in economics as *Value and Capital* and 'Mr
Keynes and the "Classics"'. It is a sequence of clever essays on the emergence of the market, the finances of the sovereign, the importance of city
states and so on, and while they are – of course – informed and enriched
by the economic insights of one of the greatest minds of our profession,
there is little evidence in these essays of *formal* theory. There is plenty of

[1] This chapter is in part based on Mokyr, 2002.

informal theory in his book, but perhaps informal economic theory these days is a contradiction in terms. Unlike Marx, who really did construct a theory that encompasses all, Hicks' book does not deliver on its promise.

In the thirty years since the publication of his book, thousands of economic history papers have been written that have applied some sort of formal economic theory to problems of economic history. Yet there have been few attempts to write a general theory of economic history (as distinct from ambitious syntheses on the 'European miracle'), and the few who have tried have been either regarded as crackpots in love with their own tautologies[2] or focusing too much on one particular aspect to the exclusion of others to qualify as a comprehensive 'theory of economic history'[3]. If the project of finding such a theory rooted in modern economic analysis has been disappointing, it is, above all, because economic history is bigger than economic theory – vastly bigger.

The fundamental reason for this discrepancy is that economic history is anchored in facts, not in logical constructs of 'stylized' social processes. This proposition has come under fire in recent decades in the humanities[4]. While economic historians have always maintained a healthy suspicion of what the data told them and how contemporaries interpreted them, they seem immune to the extreme postmodern notion that the facts did not exist. To pick an example, we may not know precisely who first made a mechanical clock in late twelfth-century Europe, but we do know that *somebody* did. Economic historians may disagree about England's GDP in 1688, but we agree that a finite and countable number of goods and services was produced in that year, and that if only we could measure that number and attach market prices to those goods and services we could compute it. As things are, of course, the task of economic history is to compute these numbers as accurately as possible, and – failing that – to provide some reasonable approximations or bounds within which such numbers can lie. The body of such 'approximate' historical facts included in economic history is vast, and growing every day.

The task of 'theory' is to make sense of these facts and to help us pick and choose among them. Economic historians are overwhelmed by

---

[2] Examples include Snooks (1996, 1998).
[3] For recent contributions, see especially Diamond (1997) and Landes (1998).
[4] Facts and narratives, we have been told by some extremists in the postmodernist reaction, are themselves social constructs; records are written by people who have a particular notion of what they are describing and reporting, and then read and interpreted by people who are themselves conditioned by their social environment. What we kid ourselves as being 'facts' are really 'representations' – reflecting power structures, prejudices, ignorance, greed and so on. This historical nihilism has, fortunately, made little inroad into economic history. For an excellent survey and for a critique, see Kitcher (1993), and, for a critique specifically aimed at history, see Appleby et al. (1995, chap. 6).

data and facts, surrounded by important questions of 'how?' and 'why?' Theory builds the connections. But there is no single theory that can possibly do that for us in all matters of interest. The best we can do is to choose a particular issue, and then search for a theory that seems most applicable to help us sort through the evidence and build a model. By a 'model' I mean a logical construct that captures some subset of historical reality and connects endogenous with exogenous variables. In history, however, very little – some would say nothing at all – is truly exogenous. Hence we inevitably chop history up into manageable pieces, so that for the analysis of an event at time t we assume that whatever was at t–1 needs no further explanation. This way of going about things is inevitable, but it makes a truly *general* theory of economic history hard to construct. For instance, if we are to follow David Landes (1998) in arguing that the economic success of the West was due to a different *culture*, we have to presume the exogeneity of culture. If we then try to explain the acquisitive and aggressive culture of the West – say, by linking it to the Judaeo-Christian religion in the traditions of Max Weber and Lynn White – we have to explain those. The problem of infinite regression was termed 'the colligation problem' by my late colleague Jonathan Hughes (1970) a year after the publication of Hicks' book. Perhaps something resembling the ubiquity of Marx's historical materialism or Arnold Toynbee's challenge and response will eventually resolve to provide a general set of tools applicable to all situation, but it seems unlikely. Hicks was the pre-eminent theorist of his generation. If he could not find in the formal models of theory much that would serve as a building block for a general theory of economic history, can we do any better?

If anything, the ability of standard economic theory to help the historian in the thirty years since Hicks' book has diminished. In 1969 most of economics was still based on a world that had some reassuring properties. These properties – really assumptions made on an a priori basis – were that the rationality of individual decision makers together with the characteristics of the technological environments in which they operated promised, in most cases, that there was an equilibrium, that it was stable and unique, and that it would usually be a 'good' (i.e. efficient) outcome. Economic historians of the cliometric school, nursed on these traditions, chose and interpreted their facts accordingly. Hence, if they observed that British entrepreneurs were slow to adopt the basic steelmaking process or that American farmers were slow in adopting the mechanical reaper, this could be explained by some hitherto unobserved constraint. Economic historians took special pleasure in uncovering these constraints, and persuaded each other and their students that economic history

had confirmed what economists had believed all along. As Alexander
Pope exclaimed, whatever was, was good, and the forces of competition
ensured that inefficiency could not survive in the very long run. Hence,
the analysis tended to be focused heavily on markets and market-like
phenomena.

In the generation that has passed since 1969, economics has become
more flexible and in many ways more realistic. Yet, precisely for that
reason, I think that it has become a less hopeful discipline from which
historians can draw the extra-historical support Hicks was looking for.
From a variety of directions we are learning that observed outcomes –
even if they are equilibria – are not necessarily Pareto optimal or even
desirable at all, and that there are a multitude of realistic conditions that
lead to multiple equilibria of which only one – at best – can be viewed as
efficient. There is a growing realization that very similar initial conditions
can lead to vastly different outcomes, and hence we can no longer justify historical outcomes as 'logical', let alone 'inevitable'. The changing
emphasis in economics has been away from market-driven processes, in
which large numbers of competitors eventually drove the system into an
efficiency of sorts, to game-theoretical or information-theoretical models of strategic behaviour and coordination problems in which multiple
equilibria are the norm (e.g. Bohn and Gorton, 1993). The same is true
for a variety of new macro-growth models with increasing returns, various forms of learning, strong complementarities, externalities and other
forms of positive feedback[5]. Theory has gained in realism but lost in neat-
ness. Economic history still looks at theoretical work for guidance, but
the help we get from theory today seems less neat, less clear-cut, more
equivocal. Many different historical outcomes can be rationalized as a
coordination failure, or a principal agent problem or a Nash equilibrium
in some kind of game.

2   Beyond economics

It is perhaps for this reason that economic history is turning outside economic theory to look for its theoretical support. Let me illustrate this with
three examples. One is the difficult question of the standard of living. How
do we compare economic welfare between two societies that are separated
by time, technology, culture and institutions? Dasgupta (1993, chaps. 4
and 5) and Sen (1987) both point to variables outside economics as theoretically appropriate: physical health, life expectancy, political freedom,
civil rights and economic security are all obvious variables that ought to

[5] The literature here is vast. Much of it is summarized in Aoki (1996) and Cooper (1999).

be included. Attempts to gauge changes in long-term living standards by looking at GDP, real wages, consumption per capita, or even some partial measure such as sugar consumption per capita all run into serious theoretical and measurement problems[6]. Hence the growing interest economic historians have recently displayed in anthropometric proxies of nutritional status, the decline in infectious diseases, changes in fertility control and infant mortality, and suchlike[7]. But the theoretical issues involved in that literature soon reach far beyond economics. Height as a measure of economic well-being is intriguing, but how much do economic historians know about the pituitary gland, which regulates the growth hormone, and how sensitive it is to nutritional deprivation as opposed to the insults of infectious disease? Economic theory will be no help here; the economic historian needs to talk to an endocrinologist. Or consider infant mortality, widely regarded a good measure of living standards: its precipitous decline in the twentieth century is by now universally viewed as proof of how much better life is today than a hundred years ago, and even before that it was regarded as a good proxy for the quality of life (Williamson, 1982). Yet it turns out that the single most important determinant of infant mortality in the nineteenth century was breastfeeding practices (Imhof, 1984). Why did some women nurse babies for longer periods? How were they persuaded to change their minds? Economic historians will get part of the answer from economics, particularly from a Beckerian analysis of the opportunity costs of women's time and possibly from the kind of intra-household bargaining models that have been proposed by Shelly Lundberg and Robert Pollak (1996). Formal models of social learning, analysed by Glenn Ellison and Drew Fudenberg (1993), can also be helpful in examining how women were persuaded of the advantages of breastfeeding. But, once we get into the social role of women in society and households, other kinds of theory must be accessed or invented (see, for instance, Fildes, 1986).

A second example of economic history reaching beyond economics is institutional change. Most economic historians today would agree that most economic growth before the Industrial Revolution, and much of it afterwards, depended crucially on the kinds of rules by which the economic game was played. Two pioneers, Douglass North and the late Mancur Olson, have tirelessly advocated and preached for a more explicit

[6] This literature is particularly rich in the context of the historiography of the British Industrial Revolution. For a brief survey, see Mokyr, 1998. For a sample of papers on the standard of living in the United States, see Gallman and Wallis, 1992.

[7] The literature on anthropometric history has blossomed in recent years. For surveys and a few representative collections, see especially Steckel (1995), Komlos (1994) and Steckel and Floud (1997).

inclusion of institutional change in economic history[8]. The historical significance is clear. In all past societies resources were allocated very inefficiently. Market arrangements before the modern era worked fairly well when they existed, but in most cases they were either woefully incomplete or constrained and circumvented by political processes and violence, not to mention informational limitations. Hence, there were opportunities for enormous profits to be made from the gains from trade and even minor changes in the mobility of factors and improvements in the allocation of land. By 1650, say, the riches of the Netherlands or England compared to the poverty of Andalusia or Poland were almost entirely explicable in terms of better institutions and superior markets, made possible by the existence of better property rights, enforceable contracts and a reduction in uncertainty.

But that takes us back to the colligation problem. Do we have a theory of institutions that explains why in some areas institutions evolved one way and in others in another? The idea of using the notion of an equilibrium in a repeated game as the definition of an institution is not new, but it was applied for the first time to a specific historical situation by Avner Greif (1993, 1994, 1997, 2004). Greif adds to the idea of using strategic behaviour in a repeated game set-up the idea of consistency analysis – that is, how feedback from the game itself and its manifestations reinforce the set-up. This is a big step forward in solving the colligation problem, but to do so Greif has to rely on insights from sociology and social psychology, and use concepts such as 'trust', 'values' and 'cultural beliefs'. In other words, he, too, has to look beyond economic theory to make his theory rich enough to work for the historical issues he is interested in. After all, Greif's institutional analysis tells us why a particular historical outcome can be sustained once it is achieved, but not why a particular one is chosen from all the possible ones except as a logical consequence of previous outcomes. It remains an *inductive* analysis, with some extra-historical support for the way the analysis is set up – much like what Hicks had in mind.

Despite the depth with which Greif has analysed the issues he is concerned with and the deserved impact his work has had on economic history (as well as on political science and sociology), the range of institutions he has been able to deal with is narrow, and a general theory of economic institutions is still very far away. How, for instance, do we apply Greif's 'historical and comparative institutional analysis' to such issues as corruption, despotism, representative political institutions,

---

[8] The two most important works are Olson (1982) and North (1990). An excellent collection of articles in this tradition is that by Drobak and Nye, 1997.

altruism and poor relief, trade associations, marriage contracts, families as allocation mechanism, intergenerational contracting, personal feudal relations, the emergence of universal banking and so on? Much exciting work is being done by economic historians, but so far no single set of multi-purpose tools that fits all cases of institutional change has emerged similar to the universal suitability of supply and demand curves to all market analyses. It is interesting to note that the prophet of institutional analysis in economic change, North, is now reaching to cognitive science in order to understand institutions[9].

A third example has to do with technological progress and its unique function in modern economic history. It may not have been the driving force behind economic growth until the Industrial Revolution, but it was always a catalyst for change. For the last two centuries, the connection between economic growth and 'useful knowledge' (which includes not just 'science' but also a great deal of practical engineering and purely empirical facts and regularities) has been central to *modern* growth, as Simon Kuznets (1965, pp. 85–87) has pointed out[10]. Yet, as economic historians have long understood, technology is knowledge: something that exists in people's minds. It is *not*, in the final analysis, a social construction, although it does often get intricately mixed up in all kind of societal arrangements and institutions. Technology *au fond* exists only in people's minds. It involves an awareness and understanding of natural phenomena and regularities and their manipulation for the material advantage of people. It is the outcome of a game against nature. The rest is commentary.

Formal, deductive economics does not help us a lot with theories of knowledge, which are quite distinct from information theory. This is not the place to get into the much-debated distinction between information and knowledge, but clearly the consensus is that *information* can exist anywhere, such as in DNA molecules, whereas *knowledge* somehow has to do with us and our minds. What counts for the economic historian interested in the impact of new technology on growth and living standards

---

[9] North (2004) points out that institutions set up the incentive structure of society but that people make choices on the basis of pay-offs. The way they perceive these pay-offs is a function of the way their minds interpret the information they receive. 'Hence the focus of our attention must be on human learning . . . and on the incremental process by which beliefs and preferences change over time' (p. 6).

[10] Kuznets wrote categorically that modern economic growth was based on an acceleration in the stock of useful or 'tested' knowledge. He argued that 'one might define modern economic growth as the spread of a system of production . . . based on the increased application of science'. This seemed obvious to Kuznets because, after all, 'science is controlled observation of the world around us [whereas] economic production is manipulation of observable reality for the special purpose of providing commodities and services desired by human beings'.

is how new knowledge came into being, how it spread, how it came to be believed and how it persuaded households and firms to alter their behaviour and to use new technology in some form. Economists have focused on the dilemmas and trade-offs of new technological knowledge: such knowledge is a pure public good yet it is not costless to produce. Knowledge is a pure public good, in that it does not cost me anything to give it to someone else but is not always costless to acquire. No single individual can know everything, but the precise marginal cost of acquiring another piece of knowledge is not easy to specify. But, even if we could, how do we specify a selection mechanism by which decision makers decide which knowledge to acquire and which to forgo, which knowledge to act upon and which to discard?

Modelling the emergence of useful knowledge in economic history is, therefore, a difficult problem (Mokyr, 2002, 2004). Again, the theoretical building blocks come mostly from *outside* economics proper. To be sure, here and there ingenious economists are trying to tackle this issue, such as Gary Becker and Kevin Murphy (1992), who point out that such a constraint is precisely what is behind specialization and the division of labour in modern manufacturing. But much can also be learned here from the formal analysis carried out by philosophers such as Philip Kitcher (1993), who tries to model the costs and benefits of adopting a particular piece of knowledge in a social setting and in the presence of imperfect testing procedures.

3   Evolution and economic history

A very different approach is suggested by the work of evolutionary epistemologists in the traditions of Donald Campbell (1960) and David Hull (1988) and by theories of cultural evolution, such as those of Boyd and Richerson (1985) and Luigi Cavalli-Sforza (1986). These models suggest an evolutionary modelling of the growth of new knowledge, in which new knowledge is produced by some kind of stochastic process and then subjected to a host of 'filters', which decide what will be adopted right away, what will be 'stored away' for possible future reference, and what will be rejected and forgotten. Instead of worrying about 'exogenous' variables 'causing' knowledge to grow, we have a logical structure in which time-specific filters work on an available supply of new ideas. Selection, of course, is the defining Darwinian characteristic and it provides an essential ingredient of a theory of how useful knowledge evolved over time. It will not explain *all* economic history, but it may help us understand something about the historical growth of useful knowledge in economic history – and that is quite a lot.

Using biological analogies mindlessly – or, worse, using the terms 'evolution' in a vague and poorly defined way – will, of course, hardly constitute a theory of economic history[11]. What I will describe below, however, is not really a biological analogy but what I believe to be a more generalized theory of evolution. Darwin and the biologists were there first, but this work is no more a slavish adaptation of biology than, say, *Value and Capital* is of classical physics.

Applying a paradigm from one science to another is a risky venture. Using the theory of evolution for the purpose of analysing economic history presupposes a certain uniformitarianism. It must be shown that the dynamics inherent in systems of the kind that Darwinism is concerned with is inherently similar even if the systems obey quite different rules and follow dramatically different time scales. *Mutatis mutandis*, some of the basic principles that are true in natural systems must be assumed to hold in social systems or systems of knowledge. If such isomorphisms are taken too literally and too much is claimed for them, they are likely to be abandoned when the differences become obvious. The argument here is not so much that technology is in some ways 'similar' to living beings but that Darwinian models transcend biology, and that, indeed, evolutionary biology is just a special case of a much wider and broader set of models that try to explain how certain kinds of systems evolve over time[12]. Darwinian models are more than just models of how *Homo sapiens* descended from apes or how and why dinosaurs disappeared: they are theories about history and about how certain observable 'outcomes' came about and others did not. Cultural features such as table manners or musical styles, though not quite the same as technology, share the same feature.

---

[11] Although many biologists (such as Stebbins, 1982, p. 432, Vermeij, 1995, p. 144, Mayr, 1988, p. 259, and Vogel, 1998, pp. 298 ff.) as well as system theorists (such as Cohen and Stewart, 1994, p. 330, and Kauffman, 1995, p. 202) have been sympathetic to an analogy between natural history and technological history, some have remained quite skeptical (e.g. Gould, 1987). A powerful criticism on such analogies has recently been launched by Foster (2000), mirroring much earlier doubts voiced by Penrose (1952). Yet much of this criticism seems to be aimed at an analogy in which selection occurs at the level of the *firm*, as proposed in the 1950s by Alchian and Friedman, and not the selection of epistemological units in the more recent Nelson and Winter tradition. The attraction of evolutionary reasoning to historians of technology (especially Vincenti, 1990, Basalla, 1988, Petroski, 1993, and Constant, 1980) has been evident. For a set of papers that provide a variety of perspectives on the use of evolutionary models in the analysis of technology, see Ziman (2000).

[12] In doing so I follow the argument made by Campbell (1965, p. 26), who made a similar argument that his model of 'cultural cumulations' was not based on an analogy with organic evolution per se, 'but rather from a general model of adaptive fit or quasi-teleological processes for which organic evolution was but one instance'.

Economically interesting ('useful') knowledge comes in two forms. One is the concept of technique or 'routine' pioneered by Richard Nelson and Sidney Winter. This *prescriptive knowledge* comes in algorithmic form – that is, a set of implicit or explicit instructions that, if followed, yields output. The monstrous meta-set of all feasible techniques in a society will be denoted as λ. A technique is 'selected' if someone actually chooses that technique from this menu and carries out the instructions, which could be regarded as similar to an organism being 'alive'. The other is the *underlying knowledge* on which techniques are based – a catalogue of natural phenomena and the formulation of predictable and exploitable relations between them. I will refer to this as the propositional knowledge set Ω, though this term might be a bit confusing[13]. A moment of reflection yields the realization that 'science' is a subset of this knowledge, but arguably a fairly small (if growing) subset through most of history[14]. The set should not just be seen as 'understanding' nature or be identified with a reductionist approach that looks at the modus operandi of natural phenomena in terms of their constituent components. Much of what accounts for 'useful knowledge' is just observation, cataloguing and measurement. Such compendia may not make 'good science' (Francis Bacon notwithstanding) but they can be quite useful in supporting techniques. Ω is the union of all pieces of knowledge in society that reside in people's minds or in storage devices.

This distinction has a lineage in epistemology[15]. A simplistic analogy with biology might equate useful knowledge with the genotype and instructional knowledge with the phenotype, but this seems less than

[13] See Mokyr, 2002, for details. Arora and Gambardella (1994), who make a similar distinction, refer to Ω-knowledge as 'abstract and general knowledge'.

[14] Much of modern technology relies on basic insights into mechanics, heat, the behaviour of animals and plants, and geography that would not really qualify as 'science'. Before 1800, it is safe to say, production of chemicals proceeded without chemistry, as iron and steel did without metallurgy and energy without thermodynamics. The historical record shows, without any question, that a great deal of progress can be made with little or no science.

[15] Both reflect some form of knowledge and thus are subject to the same kinds of difficulties that economics of knowledge and technology encounters. But the knowledge set is partitioned by kinds of knowledge. Polanyi (1962, p. 175) points out that the difference boils down to observing that Ω can be 'right or wrong', whereas 'action can only be successful or unsuccessful'. He also notes that the distinction is recognized by patent law, which will patent inventions (additions to λ) but not discoveries (additions to Ω), though some new techniques, of course, are not patentable. In some way, the dichotomy between Ω and λ is symmetric to the distinction made by Ryle (1949; see also Loasby, 1996) between knowledge 'that' and knowledge 'how'. It could be argued that λ is just one more subset of Ω and that there is no justification for including a technique as a separate form of knowledge.

helpful. All the same, it is obvious that any working technique needs to have some minimum of basis in useful knowledge to exist[16].

Selection is a critical part of this model[17]. There is no selection without variation, and no variation without innovation. Hence, focusing on selection abstracts from other elements of an evolutionary theory of history. But why is there variation and what is being selected? Darwin believed that selection was inevitable because species reproduced more rapidly than nature could accommodate them – a concept known as superfecundity[18]. Whether superfecundity has an obvious equivalent in knowledge systems or not, it is clear that there are far more ways to skin a cat than their are cats, and that picking one technique over another involves real opportunity costs. History, geography, culture and contingency have conspired to create a great deal of technological variability in the set of techniques λ. So have human creativity and human folly. For instance, there are many ways to drive from Cincinnati to Kansas City, and among those certain specific routes are selected and others are not. One would conjecture that drivers would settle on the shortest, fastest or cheapest route, but this will depend on what the agent knows and likes, as well as on road conditions, which could change. We can be reasonably sure, all the same, that the chosen route does not lead through Philadelphia. The outcome is then evaluated by a set of selection criteria that determine whether this particular technique will actually be used again or not, in a way comparable to the fashion in which natural selection criteria pick living specimens and decide which technique will be selected for survival and reproduction, and thus continue to exist in the gene pool.

It is hard to deny that economic historians really can learn something from the similarities in the problems faced in biology. If the environment is changing, selection is the tool that brings about adaptation. In a constant environment, however, the availability of selection in the system depends on a continuous emergence of new techniques. If the supply of innovation dries up, every selector ends up picking a technique that satisfies

---

[16] In the limiting case, when a discovery is truly serendipitous and nothing is known about a technique except that 'it works', this basis is degenerate and such techniques could be called 'singleton' techniques.

[17] It has been pointed out many times that in evolutionary biology selection is a 'metaphor' and that there is no conscious process of actual choice. In technological systems this is, of course, not the case: firms and households purposefully choose techniques based on well-understood criteria.

[18] There is some dispute on how necessary superfecundity is to the logical coherence of a Darwinian system. Darwin himself clearly thought so, hence his famous acknowledgment to Malthus. In a classic paper outlining the characteristics of an evolutionary system, Lewontin (1970) explicitly denies the importance of superfecundity.

his/her criteria, and apart from random noise there will no further effective selection, though there may still be variability simply because not all environments are the same. Variability, in the words of Lewontin: 'Selection is like a fire that consumes its own fuel . . . unless variation is renewed periodically, evolution would have come to a stop almost at its inception' (Lewontin, 1982, p. 151; see also Sober, 1984, p. 159). Selection and innovation are complementary parts of the historical process. Without innovation, selection occurs on existing entities only, and whatever variation exists at any time will eventually either disappear or congeal into non-competing niches. Without selection, innovation either disappears entirely (if a new technique never has a chance of being chosen – that is, implemented – new ideas will dry up) or becomes completely chaotic (if any new technique proposed is automatically adopted).

Note that in technological systems – as in systems of living beings – variability migrates from one area to another, supplying new options to societies even if within those societies themselves there has been little by way of innovation. Historically, the selection of techniques invented elsewhere has been one of the main forces driving towards historical changes. Societies were and are exposed to options made by other societies. Their ability and willingness to select such novelty provides the main reason for the difference in economic performance between, say, Afghanistan and South Korea. Different trajectories of past evolution mean that there will be global variability even if there was not much local variability. Globalization in recent decades means that worldwide variability is diminishing, and in the limit, if the entire system converges to a single technique, all differences between the local and global will disappear and such migration effects will be lost. Migration also takes place in living systems, but long-distance mobility is less easy, and natural barriers such as oceans and mountain ranges may in many cases have been insuperable[19].

This selection process is what provides the entire system with much of its historical direction by determining the likelihood that a certain technique will actually be used. As Nelson has pointed out (1995, p. 55), the theory's power depends on its ability to specify what precisely these selection criteria are. The general answer must be that they are historically contingent. It would be nice if all selection criteria could be collapsed into a profit maximization motive, but this would be silly. For instance, some societies – such as the nineteenth-century United

---

[19] The intervention of *Homo sapiens* in that process has been far-reaching, to the point where, in many previously sheltered niches, indigenous flora and fauna have been replaced by more aggressive (or better fitted) species from other places (Crosby, 1986).

States – emphasized price and production efficiency above all, whereas others – such as France – selected against mass production and large factories and preferred techniques based on individually manufactured custom-made products wherever possible.

Selection depends as much on persuasion as on preferences. At times, of course, the superiority of a new technique is easily demonstrable: Watt's double-acting steam engine was so much more efficient than its atmospheric predecessor that it required probably no more persuasion than it took in our own time to get people to switch from dot matrix to laser printers. But, in many technical choices, the results are not easy to verify, especially if they take the form of expected values. From the adoption of nuclear power to the growing and consumption of genetically modified crops, persuasion is at the heart of the matter. In medical technology this is particularly the case. It took many years to persuade people to change their household technology and domestic habits in response to the discovery of the germ theory (Mokyr and Stein, 1997). Persuasion, of course, is one form in which technological outcomes *are* determined by social processes.

So far, I have only discussed *technical choice* – that is, assume that (given some epistemic base and its mapping into instructional knowledge) a menu of techniques is presented from which selectors make selections. Is there, however, also selection at the level of Ω? Techniques are 'selected' when they are being 'used' by someone. It is more ambiguous as to what it means for a unit of Ω to be 'selected'. To be included in Ω at all, a piece of knowledge must be in existence either in someone's mind or in a storage device from which it can be retrieved. Unlike in biological systems, Ω has an exosomatic existence – that is, in knowledge systems storage of information does not have to be carried exclusively by the techniques that embody them. It is therefore unclear what precisely would be meant by 'superfecundity'. Selection becomes necessary only if there is some physical constraint about the amount of knowledge that society can carry as a whole. Only if there is some form of congestion of knowledge or storage cost will society shed some pieces of knowledge as it acquires and selects better ones. Whereas this is surely true for an individual with a finite memory, it is less obvious for society's knowledge, which is the *union* of all knowledge stored in memory banks, libraries, hard disks and so on.

To be sure, through most of human history before the age of the gigabyte such congestion was a reality; books were hugely expensive before the invention of printing, and while their price fell with the advent of printing they were still quite costly by the time of the Industrial Revolution. Other forms of storage outside human memory banks, such as drawings, models and artefacts in museums, were all hugely expensive. Some selection may, therefore, even have occurred at that level. But, when storage costs fell to negligible levels, physical congestion disappeared, and thus the issue of selection became less pressing. Libraries are full of old science and engineering books, as well as books on alchemy, astrology, and other forms of knowledge about the regularities of the natural world, and the knowledge in them can be retrieved. Yet the growth in the ability to store knowledge is matched by the ability to generate new knowledge, and even now we must dispose of some knowledge that seems redundant, so selections are made. What matters, perhaps, as much as selection is *accessibility* – the costs of finding and retrieving knowledge that has been preserved.

Evolutionary epistemology has suggested a different answer to the question of what we mean by the selection of knowledge. Selection may be viewed as the process by which some people choose to *believe* certain theories and regularities about natural phenomena and reject others[20]. While, of course, certain views of nature are incompatible with each other, meaning that some theories must be rejected if others are accepted, they do not necessarily become extinct in the technical sense of being inaccessible. Thus the humoral theory of disease is still 'understood' today, but it no longer serves as a source for prescriptive techniques in modern medicine. Scientific theories that are 'accepted' will normally be the ones that are mapped onto the techniques in use, whereas the ones that are rejected will become dormant, known only to historians of knowledge or stored in library books. Accepting the work of Antoine Lavoisier meant that one had to abandon phlogiston theory, but not destroy all traces of it. Copernican and Ptolemaic views of the universe reside together in Ω, though, of course, not in the same position.

Such a definition, however, is not entirely satisfactory either. Insofar as there are such incompatibilities between different subsets of Ω, people have to choose between them, and to do so they will if they can, in some sense, rank them (Durlauf, 1997). For many purposes, we may want to distinguish between knowledge that is 'widely accepted' (consensus) and knowledge widely believed to be false. In that sense, as most of the proponents of evolutionary epistemology (such as Campbell, 1960, and Hull, 1988) have argued, Ω-knowledge – or, in their interpretation, that subset of Ω we call 'science' – lends itself admirably to Darwinian analysis.

---

[20] Hull (1988, p. 445) points out that Copernican astronomy grew out of Ptolemaic astronomy, and only much later did it become a competing theory, with one eventually prevailing over the other. Selection of this kind, he points out, occurs at a number of hierarchical levels of organization.

But, from the point of view of techniques in use, a distinction between acceptance and rejection is consequential only if it leads to differences in the rate at which these different pieces are being mapped onto the techniques in use. Perhaps no steel ingots are being made today on the basis of insights gained from phlogiston theory, but medical practices on the basis of the Chinese dualistic approach to universal truth known as *yin-yang*, or Christian Science, and the prediction of the future on the basis of the stars are still common technological practices, and their bases in Ω are 'valid' even if most readers of this book reject them[21]. Epistemological absolutes such as 'truth' or 'falsehood' are useless here, since 'truth' is at best a consensus among experts. Some discredited or fringe views of nature may still serve as epistemic bases for techniques that are actually in use[22]. Those who believe that mosquitoes can transmit HIV will take any precaution possible to avoid being bitten. Many beliefs about nature remain 'in dispute' or 'in doubt' at each point of time, and clearly those who adhere to a particular subset of Ω will be the ones who map this knowledge onto techniques and select those techniques.

To put it differently: knowing is not the same as believing. And beliefs can themselves vary a great deal over the population. Rejection and acceptance of parts of Ω are, of course, intensely *social* phenomena. The *tightness* of a piece of knowledge, defined as the ease with which others can be persuaded to accept it, depends on the consensus-forming mechanisms and rhetorical tools that are admissible in distinguishing between it and its alternatives. What is interesting, in addition to its practical importance, is the extent to which the rhetorical conventions accepted in society persuade people that something is 'true', or at least 'tested'. 'Tightness' measures the degree of consensus and the confidence that people have in the knowledge, and – what counts most for a historian of technology – their willingness to act upon it. Such rhetorical conventions vary from 'Aristotle said' to 'the experiment demonstrates' to 'the estimated coefficient is 2.3 times its standard error'. These standards are invariably set socially within paradigms. What constitutes logical 'proof'? What is an acceptable power of a statistical test? Must we always insist on double-blindness when testing a new compound? How many times need

---

[21] Chinese science, which developed independently from Western science, did produce a completely different way of looking at the world. But, by the kind of evolutionary standard described here, it did not do as well: the West has not adopted any of the main propositions of Chinese science, such as the organic world of two primary forces (*yang* and *yin*) and the five basic elements *wu hsing*, representing metal, wood, earth, water and fire. By contrast, Western science, engineering and medicine are taught and practised all over China.

[22] An example is the computer programs used by satellites that use a Ptolemaic paradigm of the sun revolving around the earth (Constant, 2000, p. 227).

an experiment be replicated before the consensus deems it sound? Much of the tightness of knowledge is a function of social relations, such as 'who is an authority' on a subject, who appoints those authorities, and how often non-experts can question authority. If a piece of knowledge is not very tight, as Steven Durlauf shows, choosing between competing pieces of knowledge may well become a function of imitation, persuasion and fashion[23].

How and why such choices take place is, of course, one half of the central issue in the history of science, with emphasis varying between scholars as to the extent to which evolutionary success is correlated with some measure of 'progress' or 'truth' (see Hull, 1988, and Kitcher, 1993). The other half is how the menu from which selectors choose techniques came into being in the first place and why certain things are on it and others are not[24].

Since much of Ω is irrelevant to application at any given time (even if it may become relevant subsequently), selection at that level is not necessary unless statements are patently inconsistent. The earth cannot be flat and spherical at the same time, but diseases *can* have multiple causes, and statements such as 'there exists' can be accommodated ad infinitum[25]. Even when there is a necessary choice to make, it may not matter. If a new theory regarding the structure of black holes or the great Permian extinction wins the day over another, such a change is not likely to map onto different techniques and is thus inconsequential for our purpose. 'I don't know and I don't care' is a valid and costless statement that selectors can make for much of what is in Ω. When application to techniques and routines is at stake, however, selection on Ω matters a

---

[23] One example to illustrate this principle. A Scottish physician by the name of John Brown (1735–88) revolutionized the medicine of his age with 'Brownianism', a system that postulated that all diseases were the result of over- or underexcitement of the neuromuscular system by the environment. Brown was no enthusiast for bleeding, and instead treated all his patients with mixtures of opium, alcohol and highly seasoned foods. His popularity was international: Benjamin Rush brought his system to the United States, and in 1802 his controversial views elicited a riot among medical students in Göttingen, requiring troops to quell it. A medical revolutionary in an age of radical changes, his influence is a good example of the difficulty that contemporaries had in selecting amongst alternative techniques and the enormous possibilities for failure in this area; Brown was asserted to have killed more people than the French Revolution and the Napoleonic Wars combined.

[24] For some speculation on this matter and on the use of counterfactual analysis in evolutionary models of economic history, see Mokyr (2000b).

[25] The notion that the earth cannot be flat and spherical at the same time, so natural to us, may itself be a social construct. Non-Western societies had completely different notions as to what is meant by a true statement. An example is the Jain belief of *syadvada*, which can be summarized to say that 'the world of appearances may or may not be real, or both may and may not be real, or may be indescribable, or may be real and indescribable, or unreal and indescribable, or in the end may be real *and* unreal *and* indescribable'. Cited by Kaplan, 1999, p. 45 (emphasis added).

great deal. When choosing between two techniques, all other things being equal, we would prefer a technique based on knowledge that we believed to be correct. One of the interesting characteristics of selectionist models of knowledge is that they imply that the tightness of Ω and that of λ are mutually reinforcing. Knowledge in Ω will become tighter if it maps into techniques that can actually be shown to work. Thus, once biologists in the 1890s discovered that insects could be the vectors of pathogenic microparasites, insect-fighting techniques gained wide acceptance. The success of these techniques in eradicating yellow fever and malaria was the best confirmation of the hypotheses about the transmission mechanisms of the disease, and helped gain them wide support. Another example is the relationship between aeronautics and the techniques of building machines that would actually fly[26]. To put it crudely, the way we are persuaded that science is true is that its recommendations work visibly (Cohen and Stewart, 1994, p. 54). Chemistry works: it makes nylon tights and polyethylene sheets. Physics works: aeroplanes fly and pressure cookers cook rice. Every time. Strictly speaking, this is not a correct inference, because a functional technique could be mapped from knowledge that turns out to be false (though that would be unusual). At the same time, techniques may be 'selected' because they are implied by a set of knowledge that is gaining acceptance. This is especially true if the efficacy of a technique is hard to observe directly and we have to trust the insights that suggest its use, as would be the case in psychoanalysis. No smoker can observe directly with any accuracy the causal relation between smoking and disease; trust in the knowledge of others is essential.

4   Conclusions

Applying a Darwinian theoretical framework does not answer all the questions one may want to ask in economic history. It may be true, as Theodosius Dobzhansky once famously wrote, that in biology *nothing* makes sense except in the light of the theory of evolution; this surely is not true in economic history, where the application of models

---

[26] The fundamentals were laid out early by George Cayley in the early nineteenth century. Much of the knowledge in this branch of engineering was experimental rather than theoretical, namely attempts to tabulate coefficients of lift and drag for each wing shape at each angle. The Wright brothers relied on the published work (especially of Otto Lilienthal) of the time to work out their own formulas, but also ended up working closely with the leading aeronautical engineer of the time, Octave Chanute, who supplied them continuously with advice right up to Kitty Hawk (Crouch, 1989). Their ultimate success lent support to the rather crude understanding of aeronautics of the time, and stimulated its further development by Ludwig Prandtl (Constant, 1980, pp. 104–6).

from price theory, finance, international trade and macroeconomics has had considerable success. But in the long-run development of technology, material culture and the way we cope with our environment, such approaches will be of little use. A Darwinian outlook is enlightening, but it is also sobering: it is at least as good in making clear what we can *not* know[27].

On what issues can an evolutionary perspective provide insights to the economic historian? One issue that has been at the forefront of the agenda in economic history for over a century is the Industrial Revolution. In a number of papers, I have attempted to re-examine the questions of why the Industrial Revolution occurred when and why it did, using some of the terminology and concepts above (Mokyr, 1998, 2000a, 2002, 2005). The debates on whether there was an Industrial Revolution at all, and the extent to which economic history follows a *natura non facit saltum* dynamic or not, mirror in an interesting way similar debates between biologists. An even bigger issue is why the Industrial Revolution and subsequent events occurred in the West and not, say, in China. An evolutionary analysis of the interactions between useful and instructional analysis, and the kind of environment that enhances not only the emergence of novelty but also the willingness of society to adopt it, can help tell a coherent tale of technological development. It needs to be added that such an analysis cannot draw directly on the tool kits of the evolutionary biologist but has to develop its own tools. Selectionist models are not specific to biology, and even if they were first applied successfully there this is no reason to dismiss them, any more than it would be to dismiss the concept of equilibrium in economic theory *just because* it derives from an analogy with classical physics.

The main conclusion that an evolutionary history comes up with is that history is not inexorable; what happened did not have to happen. Neither the forces of omnipotent 'invisible hands' nor those of the material relations of production are able to remove contingency from history. There is strong path dependence in both the evolution of living beings and that of technology, and the outcomes we observe are indeterminate *ex ante*

---

[27] Lewontin (2000, p. 213) has written: 'We come back to the original problem of explanation in evolutionary genetics . . . we are trying to explain a unique historical sequence, filled with historical contingency, by reference to a set of weak, interacting, causal forces whose operation is best inferred by making a historical assumption. Under these circumstances the best to which population geneticists can aspire is a formal structure that sets the limits of allowable explanation and a set of existentially modified claims about what has actually happened in the real history of organisms. To demand more is to misunderstand both the nature of the phenomena and the limits of observation.' This statement could be adapted to much of long-term economic history simply by replacing the word 'genetics'.

and depend a great deal on accidental events. There are at least three different levels at which contingency can take place in the kind of model described above. First, there is contingency in the knowledge embodied in Ω[28]. Second, even given that the underlying knowledge exists, there is no necessity that this knowledge be mapped into λ – that is, that the inventions be made[29]. Third, even if the inventions are made, it is still indeterminate whether they will be selected, depending a great deal on what the preferences and beliefs of society are[30]. Such contingency is part and parcel of modern evolutionary thinking, even if few people are willing to go as far as Stephen Jay Gould, whose belief in indeterminacy is rather extreme[31].

Evolutionary theory as a historical tool explains the form of creatures not in terms of their constituent parts ('DNA') but in terms of their historical development within a changing environment. An entity is what it is because this is what happened over time. Whether we are looking at something major, such as the development of nuclear reactors (Cowan, 1990), or something minor, such as the invention of the zip (Petroski, 1993, chap. 6), the story is always one in which a menu of choices is written, and then firms and households select. There is a historical order, although there is often substantial feedback from the selection to the writing of menus in the future. Evolutionary models tend to be open, time-variant systems that are continuously interacting with their environment,

[28] The issue can be well illustrated by the following example. The discovery of America by Europeans was one of the greatest additions to the set of useful knowledge in Western society in its history. It is hard to believe that the discovery itself – as opposed to the timing – was contingent; had Columbus not made the journey, sooner or later someone else would have done so, given the European navigational and shipbuilding technology of 1490, and America would still have been there in exactly the same location. Is the same true, say, for the laws of physics and chemistry, for our understanding of infectious disease – indeed, for the theory of evolution itself? Are most natural laws and regularities 'facts' that just sit out there, or are they, as many modern scholars in the humanities assert, social constructs? Had another society other than Western Europe discovered 'modern science', the dominant Ω set in the world (assuming there was one) might have looked closer to Chinese science, or perhaps something quite different from either.

[29] The conditions leading to such 'technological creativity' are widely discussed, among others, in Rosenberg and Birdzell (1986) and Mokyr (1990).

[30] A special topic in economic history suggested by this approach is the political economy of technological progress, which examines the rational resistance by small interest groups to socially beneficial innovations. See Mokyr, 1998.

[31] Gould (1989, p. 283) states that contingency is a central principle of history. A historical explanation does not rest on direct deductions from laws of nature, but on an unpredictable sequence of antecedent states, where any major change in any step of the sequence would have altered the final result. This is a more extreme version of Paul David's notion of path dependence, which attributes outcomes to the trajectory taken in some identifiable circumstances (which may be very common but by no means universal).

and do not necessarily converge[32]. They do not lend themselves to precise formulations that predict accurately, given only sufficient boundary conditions. Moreover, as Ziman (2000) points out, whereas closed systems, such as physics, tend to be statistical in that they reflect expected values, selectionist systems – of any kind – tend to amplify *rare* events (such as successful mutations or brilliant ideas). Because these 'rare' events are themselves not inexorable, and because it is unknown which of them will actually be amplified – as opposed to being rejected – by the selection process for one reason or another, they infuse an irrepressible element of indeterminacy into the system. A counterfactual analysis can then proceed under the assumption that a 'rare event' that did in fact occur did not happen.

To sum up, then, economic history is too big to be amenable for *one* single theory. Its subject matter is all the material culture of the past. To write down a unified set of propositions that can help us sort all of that out without absurd assumptions and simplifications seems beyond reach. Some kind of impossibility theorem, in the spirit of Gödel's Theorem, may well be formulated, if not proven. Oddly enough, I find that reassuring. Apart from Marx, nobody has had much success in persuading many readers that he had all the answers, and given the track record of *his* theory and its adherents perhaps nobody should try. History should be analysed in units of manageable size, and no larger.

REFERENCES

Aoki, M. (1996), *New Approaches to Macroeconomic Modeling: Evolutionary Stochastic Dynamics, Multiple Equilibria, and Externalities as Field Effects*, Cambridge: Cambridge University Press.
Appleby, J., L. Hunt and M. Jacob (1995), *Telling the Truth About History*, New York: Norton.
Arora, A., and A. Gambardella (1994), 'The changing technology of technological change: general and abstract knowledge and the division of innovative labor', *Research Policy* 23(5): 523–32.
Basalla, B. (1988), *The Evolution of Technology*, Cambridge: Cambridge University Press.
Becker, G. S., and K. M. Murphy (1992), 'The division of labor, coordination costs, and knowledge', *Quarterly Journal of Economics* 107(4): 1137–60.

---

[32] One possibility, raised by Nelson (1995) and developed further in Murmann (2003), is that technical knowledge *coevolves* with its institutional environment, and even if either one of those on its own might reach some kind of attractor their continued interaction means that outcomes become completely unpredictable. Again, biologists and systems analysts have made precisely the same point: compare Vermeij (1994) and Kauffman (1995, pp. 215–24).

Bohn, H., and G. Gorton (1993), 'Coordination failure, multiple equilibria and economic institutions', *Economica* **60**(239): 257–80.

Boyd, R., and P. J. Richerson (1985), *Culture and the Evolutionary Process*, Chicago: University of Chicago Press.

Campbell, D. T. (1960), 'Blind variation and selective retention in creative thought as in other knowledge processes', *Psychological Review* **67**: 380–400. [Reprinted in G. Radnitzky and W. W. Bartley III (eds.) (1987), *Evolutionary Epistemology, Rationality, and the Sociology of Knowledge*, La Salle, IL: Open Court, 91–114.]

——— (1965), 'Variation and selective retention in socio-cultural evolution', in H. Barringer, G. I. Blanksten and R. W. Mack (eds.), *Social Change in Developing Areas: A Reinterpretation of Evolutionary Theory*, Cambridge, MA: Schenkman Publishing Co., 19–47.

Cavalli-Sforza, L. L. (1986), 'Cultural evolution', *American Zoologist* **26**: 845–55.

Cohen, J., and I. Stewart (1994), *The Collapse of Chaos*, New York: Penguin.

Constant, E. W. (1980), *The Origins of the Turbojet Revolution*, Baltimore: Johns Hopkins University Press.

——— (2000), 'Recursive practices and the evolution of technological knowledge', in J. Ziman (ed.), *Technological Innovation as an Evolutionary Process*, Cambridge: Cambridge University Press, 219–33.

Cooper, R. W. (1999), *Coordination Games: Complementarities and Macroeconomics*, Cambridge: Cambridge University Press.

Cowan, R. (1990), 'Nuclear power reactors: a study in technological lock-in', *Journal of Economic History* **50**(3): 541–68.

Crosby, A. (1986), *Ecological Imperialism: The Biological Expansion of Europe, 900–1900*, Cambridge: Cambridge University Press.

Crouch, T. (1989), *The Bishop's Boys: A Life of Wilbur and Orville Wright*, New York: Norton.

Dasgupta, P. (1993), *An Inquiry into Well-being and Destitution*, Oxford: Oxford University Press.

Diamond, J. (1997), *Guns, Germs and Steel: The Fates of Human Societies*, New York: Norton.

Drobak, J. N., and J. V. C. Nye (eds.) (1997), *The Frontiers of the New Institutional Economics*, San Diego: Academic Press.

Durlauf, S. N. (1997), *Reflections on How Economic Reasoning can Contribute to the Study of Science*, Working Paper 97-05-043, Santa Fe Institute, Santa Fe.

Ellison, G., and D. Fudenberg (1993), 'Rules of thumb for social learning', *Journal of Political Economy* **101**(4): 612–43.

Fildes, V. (1986), *Breasts, Bottles and Babies: A History of Infant Feeding*, Edinburgh: Edinburgh University Press.

Foster, J. (2000), 'Competitive selection, self-organization and Joseph A. Schumpeter', *Journal of Evolutionary Economics* **10**(3): 311–28.

Gallman, R. E., and J. J. Wallis (eds.) (1992), *American Economic Growth and Standards of Living before the Civil War*, Chicago: University of Chicago Press.

Gould, S. J. (1987), 'The panda's thumb of technology', *Natural History*, **1**, 14–23.

(1989), *Wonderful Life: The Burgess Shale and the Nature of History*, New York: Norton.

Greif, A. (1993), 'Contract enforceability and economic institutions in early trade: the Maghribi Traders' Coalition', *American Economic Review* 83(3): 525–48.

(1994), 'Cultural beliefs and the organization of society: a historical and theoretical reflection on collectivist and individualist societies', *Journal of Political Economy* 102(5): 912–50.

(1997), 'On the interrelations and economic implications of economic, social, political, and normative factors: reflections from two late medieval societies', in J. N. Drobak and J. V. C. Nye (eds.), *The Frontiers of the New Institutional Economics*, San Diego: Academic Press, 57–94.

(2004), *Institutions Theory and History*, New York: Cambridge University Press.

Hicks, J. R. (1969), *A Theory of Economic History*, Oxford: Oxford University Press.

Hughes, J. R. T. (1970), *Industrialization and Economic History*, New York: McGraw-Hill.

Hull, D. (1988), *Science as a Process*, Chicago: University of Chicago Press.

Imhof, A. E. (1984), 'The amazing simultaneousness of the big differences and the boom in the 19th century – some facts and hypotheses about infant and maternal mortality in Germany, 18th to 20th century', in T. Bengtsson, G. Fridlizius and R. Ohlsson (eds.), *Pre-Industrial Population Change*, Stockholm: Almqvist and Wiksell, 191–222.

Kaplan, R. (1999), *The Nothing That Is*, Oxford: Oxford University Press.

Kauffman, S. A. (1995), *At Home in the Universe: The Search for the Laws of Self-Organization and Complexity*, Oxford: Oxford University Press.

Kitcher, P. (1993), *The Advancement of Science: Science without Legend, Objectivity without Illusions*, Oxford: Oxford University Press.

Komlos, J. (ed.) (1994), *Stature, Living Standards, and Economic Development: Essays in Anthropometric History*, Chicago: University of Chicago Press.

Kuznets, S. (1965), *Economic Growth and Structure*, New York: Norton.

Landes, D. S. (1998), *The Wealth and Poverty of Nations: Why Some are so Rich and Some so Poor*, New York: Norton.

Lewontin, R. C. (1970), 'The units of selection', *Annual Review of Ecology and Systematics* 1: 1–18.

(1982), *Human Diversity*, New York: Scientific American Books.

(2000), 'What do population geneticists know and how do they know it?', in R. Creath and J. Maienschein (eds.), *Biology and Epistemology*, Cambridge: Cambridge University Press, 191–214.

Loasby, B. (1996), *The Organization of Industry and the Growth of Knowledge*, Lectiones Jenenses no. 7, Max-Planck-Institute for Research into Economic Systems, Jena, Germany.

Lundberg, S., and R. A. Pollak (1996), 'Bargaining and distribution in marriage', *Journal of Economic Perspectives* 10: 139–59.

Mayr, E. (1988), *Toward a New Philosophy of Biology*, Cambridge, MA: The Belknap Press.

Mokyr, J. (1990), *The Lever of Riches: Technological Creativity and Economic Progress*, Oxford: Oxford University Press.

(1998), 'Editor's introduction: the New Economic History and the Industrial Revolution', in J. Mokyr (ed.), *The British Industrial Revolution: An Economic Perspective*, Boulder, CO: Westview Press, 1–127.

(2000a), 'Knowledge, technology, and economic growth during the Industrial Revolution', in B. Van Ark, S. K. Kuipers and G. Kuper (eds.), *Productivity, Technology and Economic Growth*, The Hague: Kluwer Academic Press, 253–92.

(2000b), *King Kong and Cold Fusion: Counterfactual Analysis and the History of Technology*, unpublished manuscript.

(2002), *The Gifts of Athena: Historical Origins of the Knowledge Economy*, Princeton, NJ: Princeton University Press.

(2004), 'Long-term economic growth and the history of technology', in P. Aghion and S. Durlauf (eds.), *Handbook of Economic Growth*, Amsterdam: North-Holland.

(2005), 'The intellectual origins of modern economic growth' [presidential address], *Journal of Economic History*, forthcoming.

Mokyr, J., and R. Stein (1997), 'Science, health and household technology: the effect of the Pasteur revolution on consumer demand', in R. J. Gordon and T. Bresnahan (eds.), *The Economics of New Products*, Chicago: University of Chicago Press for the National Bureau of Economic Research, 143–205.

Murmann, J. P. (2003), *Knowledge and Competitive Advantage*, Cambridge: Cambridge University Press.

Nelson, R. R. (1995), 'Recent evolutionary theorizing about economic change', *Journal of Economic Literature* **33**: 48–90.

North, D. C. (1990), *Institutions, Institutional Change and Economic Performance*, Cambridge: Cambridge University Press.

(2004), *Understanding the Process of Economic Change*, Princeton, NJ: Princeton University Press.

Olson, M. (1982), *The Rise and Decline of Nations*, New Haven, CT: Yale University Press.

Penrose, E. T. (1952), 'Biological analogies in the theory of the firm', *American Economic Review* **42**(4): 804–19.

Petroski, H. (1993), *The Evolution of Useful Things*, New York: A. Alfred Knopf.

Polanyi, M. (1962), *Personal Knowledge: Towards a Post-Critical Philosphy*, Chicago: University of Chicago Press.

Rosenberg, N., and L. E. Birdzell (1986), *How the West Grew Rich: The Economic Transformation of the Industrial World*, New York: Basic Books.

Ryle, G. (1949), *The Concept of Mind*, Chicago: Chicago University Press.

Sen, A. (1987), *The Standard of Living*, Cambridge: Cambridge University Press.

Sober, E. (1984), *The Nature of Selection*, Cambridge, MA: MIT Press.

Snooks, G. D. (1996), *The Dynamic Society: Exploring the Sources of Global Change*, London: Routledge.

(1998), *Long-run Dynamic: A General Economic and Political Theory*, New York: St Martin's Press.

Stebbins, G. L. (1982), *Darwin to DNA, Molecules to Humanity*, San Francisco: W. H. Freeman.

Steckel, R. H. (1995), 'Stature and the standard of living', *Journal of Economic Literature* **33**(4): 1903–40.

Steckel, R. H., and R. Floud (eds.) (1997), *Health and Welfare during Industrialization*, Chicago: Chicago University Press.

Vermeij, G. J. (1994), 'The evolutionary interaction among species: selection, escalation, and coevolution', *Annual Review of Ecological Systems* **25**: 219–36.

(1995), 'Economics, volcanoes, and phanerozoic revolutions', *Paleobiology* **21**(3): 125–52.

Vincenti, W. (1990), *What Engineers Know and How They Know It*, Baltimore: Johns Hopkins University Press.

Vogel, S. (1998), *Cats' Paws and Catapults: Mechanical Worlds of Nature and People*, New York: Norton.

Williamson, J. G. (1982), 'Was the Industrial Revolution worth it? Disamenities and death in 19th-century British towns', *Explorations in Economic History* **19**: 221–45.

Ziman, J. (ed.) (2000), *Technological Innovation as an Evolutionary Process*, Cambridge: Cambridge University Press.

II

A framework for evolutionary analysis

A

Evolutionary microeconomics

8   Towards an evolutionary theory of production[1]

Sidney G. Winter

1   Introduction

Since the time of Adam Smith, Francois Quesnay and David Ricardo economists have sought to ground their theoretical analyses of economic organization in an appreciation of the nature of real production activity. Any such effort must balance two competing concerns. On the one hand, the obviously fundamental role of productive activity in economic life seems to demand a highly accurate appraisal, presumably based on detailed scrutiny. On the other hand, the objectives of economic science often seem best served by a broad-brush characterization carried out from a considerable distance. These scientific objectives are, after all, quite different from those of engineering or operations management.

In mainstream neoclassical theory, the second of these considerations clearly seems dominant. Production theory as it has developed in that tradition is strong on abstract generality and treats production in a way that is convenient for the neoclassical analyst. In that tradition, production theory is partly for answering questions about production and its place in economic organization, but it is at least equally concerned with sealing off questions that are not considered fruitful for economists. It places a boundary marker that serves to identify the limits of the specifically economic concern with production, beyond which lie areas of concern to engineers, managers and technologists.

It should be obvious that evolutionary economics needs to strike quite a different balance. Evolutionary thinking sees questions of production as tightly and reciprocally connected with questions of coordination, organization and incentives. Also, production activity is embedded – now more than ever – in a variety of processes of knowledge creation; theory needs to

---

[1] Particularly in its history of thought aspects, this chapter draws extensively from my 1982 paper 'An essay on the theory of production' (Winter, 1982). It also draws on more recent joint work with Gabriel Szulanski, some reported in Winter and Szulanski (2001) and Szulanski and Winter (2002), and some still in progress. I am indebted to Giovanni Dosi and Kurt Dopfer for the encouragement and guidance they have provided for this undertaking.

make room for those links. A major deficiency of the mainstream theory is its isolation from the realities of organizational knowledge. Above all, the evolutionary economist is concerned mainly with change, not with the principles of resource allocation in a hypothetical static world.

As is discussed below, a review of the historical development of production theory shows conclusively the shaping role of the analytical objectives held at each stage by the economists who made the contributions. On the contemporary scene, production function formulations now dominate, because they provide a convenient basis for applied econometrics and because the sorts of questions that require more general apparatus are no longer as salient for the discipline as they were a few decades back.

The dominance of the production function apparatus in contemporary mainstream treatments of technological change is also a 'panda's thumb' phenomenon; it reflects the logic of path-dependent evolution (Gould, 1980). The apparatus was created and developed for various other reasons, and when questions of technological change came to be confronted it was conveniently available. The basic apparatus was extended and supplemented by a variety of formal treatments of technological change, the simplest being the introduction of the multiplicative factor A in the relation $Q = A f(x)$. Negligible attention was paid to the question of whether plausible real-world mechanisms might actually produce knowledge changes with effects that correspond to these formalisms; the formalisms are convenient and hence chosen for reasons other than micro-level verisimilitude[2]. The major investment in building a truly knowledge-based production theory, well suited to close analysis of the problems of change, was never made. Recently, however, some beginnings have at least been made.

This chapter sketches some of these beginnings, and attempts to establish their links both to parts of mainstream production theory and to the actual phenomena. Section 2 reviews the historical development of production theory and substantiates the claims made above. Section 3 argues that the sort of 'knowledge' that is applied in productive activity – henceforth, *productive knowledge* – has specific attributes that make it quite different from the things termed 'knowledge' in other contexts. Section 4 examines some deep issues surrounding the seemingly straightforward notion of 'spatial replication' – i.e. the idea that the same knowledge can be used in more than one location. Section 5 discusses the place of production theory in the evolutionary economics framework and identifies some of the research tasks on the agenda.

---

[2] One example of such attention is Atkinson and Stiglitz, 1969. Their analysis, however, tends to reduce further one's confidence in the idea that the standard array of neutrality concepts for technological change corresponds to something real.

2   Origins and varieties of production theory

The topics that we now count as part of the theory of production were, over much of the history of the subject, addressed primarily in the context of the problem of distribution, which was itself viewed as the problem of explaining the division of the social product among the classic 'factors of production' – land, labour and capital. The major uses that we now find for the theory of production – in analysis of the role of production possibilities in the determination of relative prices, and in the efficient allocation of resources – began to acquire something like their present importance only with the advent of neoclassical economics late in the nineteenth century. In classical economics it was the marginal productivity schedule, and not the production function or the cost function, that was the focus of attention. The question was not 'how much output can be obtained, at a maximum, from this list of inputs?' but rather 'by how much will output increase if the amount of this particular input is increased some, with all other inputs held constant?'

From our present-day theoretical standpoint, we recognize that the latter question is not well posed unless there is some understanding about how the increment of the variable input is to be used. Our standard resolution of this problem is to understand both the original input list and the augmented list to be used in such a way as to produce a maximum output given the 'state of the art' – i.e. to refer back to the first of the two questions just posed. In the classical treatments, however, the discussion of the 'laws of returns' is not so clearly founded on the concept of technical efficiency. Rather, the propositions are advanced more as observational laws characterizing the results of experiments – actual or imagined, natural or planned. These experiments involve simple incremental modifications of familiar methods for producing output. The increments of input are apparently conceived as being applied in a reasonable way, but there is little suggestion that the matter requires or receives careful consideration. The important point is that the quasi-empirical marginal productivity schedule involved in the classical conception does not raise any troubling questions of how it is known that the methods involved actually yield maximum output for given inputs. To put it another way, the conception does not challenge the theorist to develop the idea of a 'state of the art' with the care appropriate to the importance bestowed on that concept by the modern interpretation of the production function.

The primacy of the distribution problem and of the quasi-empirical conception of the marginal productivity schedule persists in early neoclassical discussion of production. Particularly significant here is Philip Wicksteed's *Essay on the Coordination of the Laws of Distribution* (1894).

His title names his task, which was to show that separate laws of distribution, involving a classical application of marginal productivity principles to each factor in turn, are mutually consistent in the sense that the resulting factor shares exhaust the product. It was in introducing this problem that he made the notion of the production function explicit in economic analysis for the first time, in the following terms (p. 4):

The Product being a function of the factors of production we have $P = f(a, b, c \ldots)$.

Neither in this statement nor in Wicksteed's subsequent analysis is there any hint that there is anything conceptually problematic about the idea of such a function; it is merely a mathematically explicit expression of the long-familiar idea that, if the input quantities vary, the output quantity will vary as well, and in certain characteristic ways.

Even today, introductory treatments of the production function and of factor substitution in textbooks and lectures often follow much the same Ricardian path, with the same agricultural examples. The strength of the approach lies in the plausibility of variable-proportions production in the agricultural context, and in the simple, commonsense arguments that establish the general character of the response of output to variation in a single input. A casual acquaintance with a relatively simple and commonly encountered production technology is the only prerequisite for understanding. But this strength is also a source of weakness of the sort suggested above; the loose way in which the technology is discussed tends to leave obscure the conceptual connections among productive knowledge, the production function and technical efficiency.

No sooner had the production function made its explicit appearance in economic analysis than it was straightaway – in the lines immediately following the above-quoted line from Wicksteed – specialized to being homogeneous to the first degree. This was the basis of Wicksteed's coordination of the laws of distribution – i.e. his demonstration that the product is precisely exhausted when inputs are paid according to their marginal products. In beginning his examination of the validity of the constant returns to scale assumption, Wicksteed stated (p. 33):

Now it must of course be admitted that if the physical conditions under which a certain amount of wheat, or anything else, is produced were exactly repeated the result would be exactly repeated also, and a proportional increase of the one would yield a proportional increase of the other.

Elaborating this statement, Wicksteed made clear that the replication had to be understood to involve a replication of the inputs in exact detail; otherwise one would not be exactly repeating the original condition. He then went on to deal, in a somewhat confused way, with the fact that the economic laws of distribution had to involve something more than the physical conditions of producing the 'mere material product'. What he did not pause to explain – but presumably had in mind – was that the 'physical conditions' that are 'exactly repeated' include not merely an identity of context but an identity of production method. This supposition does make the result obvious, in the sense that a replication of a given physical experiment, hypothetically perfectly controlled, necessarily yields the same result. What is noteworthy in the present context is a) that this interpretation is inappropriate given the modern understanding of the production function, which presumes that there is a choice of method, and b) that Wicksteed's discussion manages to slide past the problem of characterizing the set of available methods, or 'state of the art'.

At some point, the connection between the production function concept and technical efficiency began to be emphasized. A clear statement may be found in Sune Carlson's book, first published in 1939, *A Study on the Pure Theory of Production* (1956, pp. 14–16; emphasis in original)[3].

If we want the production function to give only one value for the output from a given service combination, the function must be so defined that it expresses the *maximum product* obtainable from the combination at the existing state of technical knowledge. Therefore, the purely *technical* maximization problem may be said to be solved by the very definition of our production function.

To whatever historical depth some awareness of this point might be traced, it seems clear that its salience was vastly enhanced by the advent of new approaches to production theory that gave explicit consideration to production methods *not* 'on the production function'. These new approaches comprised the members of the family of linear models of production, including linear activity analysis, linear programming and input-output analysis, and also such descendants and relatives of this family as process analysis, non-linear programming and game theory. They made their appearance in the work of von Neumann, Leontief, Koopmans, Kantorovich, Dantzig and others over the period 1936 to 1951[4].

The linear activity analysis framework, as developed by Koopmans, is most relevant here. This contribution introduced into economics a workable abstract representation of what the classics called the 'state of the art' – what Carlson calls 'the existing state of technical knowledge' in the passage cited above. Productive knowledge was described first of all

---

[3] Carlson attributes the idea to Francis Edgeworth, but the cited passage in Edgeworth is rather unclear.
[4] For citations and discussion, see Koopmans, 1977.

by 'basic activities', formally represented by vectors of technical coefficients, but conceived as corresponding to identifiable, concrete 'ways of doing things'. Further, the theory adduced a set of principles that described how the productive knowledge represented by the basic activities could be extended in scope, combined and modified. Central to these principles were the assumptions that activities could be scaled up or down at will while maintaining the same proportional relations among inputs and outputs, and that the results of activities performed simultaneously would be additive. If these assumptions held true, then the whole scope of technological possibilities could be characterized in relation to the basic activities involved. This would mean, in particular, that in the case of a single output production process the numerical specification of all basic activities would make it possible, in principle, to determine the maximum output that could be produced from a particular input combination. If the data were available and the problem not too large relative to the computation budget, linear programming solution algorithms would make such a determination possible not merely in principle but in practice.

Still another mode of abstract representation of technological possibilities became common in economic theory with the development of modern general equilibrium theory by Arrow, Debreu, and others (Arrow and Debreu, 1954, and Debreu, 1959). This approach generalizes the earlier ones by going simply and directly to the abstract heart of the matter. Commodity outputs in amounts represented by the list $q = (q_1, \ldots, q_M)$ may or may not be producible from input commodities in amounts represented by the list $x = (x_1, \ldots, x_N)$. If q is producible from x, then the input-output pair (x, q) is 'in the production set' (or 'production possibilities set'). Whatever is known or considered plausible as a property of the structure of technological knowledge is, in this representation, treated as a postulate about the properties of the production set. For example, the linear activity analysis model is recovered as a special case if it is postulated that the production set comprises a finite set of basic activities, plus the combinations and modifications permitted under the activity analysis assumptions.

It is useful to note what is gained and what is lost in going from linear activity analysis to a general production set. What is gained is generality; there is a simple abstract representation for states of knowledge the structure of which may not conform to that postulated by activity analysis. What is lost, naturally enough, is specificity – and potential empirical content. No longer is there the suggestion that it might be possible to characterize fully an actual state of technological knowledge by looking in the world for 'basic activities'. In particular, there is no guidance as to how one would test the claim that a specific input-output pair not actually observed in the world is 'not possible given the existing state of technical knowledge'. Thus, to refer back to earlier discussion, the concept of a production function that expresses the 'maximum product obtainable' from each input combination is once again left without any direct empirical interpretation. This is not to say that its status as a purely logical construct is impaired; given additional mathematical restrictions, which are commonly imposed, it is logically possible to define such a function on the basis of an underlying production set representation of the state of technical knowledge. The construct thus defined may be employed in further theoretical development, and may perhaps in that way be related, ultimately, to empirical data.

The situation may be summed up in the following terms. It is the production set concept that stands, in contemporary formal theory, for the classical idea of a 'state of the art' or for an 'existing state of technical knowledge'. Arrow and Hahn concisely say (1971, p. 53):

Thus the production possibility set is a description of the state of the firm's knowledge about the possibilities of transforming commodities.

To assume that the production set has certain properties – for example, those that correspond to the linear activity analysis model – is thus an indirect way of imputing analogous properties to the 'state of knowledge' that the production set describes. I have proposed here that this indirect approach may be understood as a reflection of the historical development of the theory. In the modern synthesis of the subject, production sets are a fundamental concept, production functions are a derived construct, and marginal productivity schedules are an implied attribute of production functions. Historically, however, it happened in the opposite order. Marginal productivity came first (Ricardo), then production functions (Wicksteed), then production sets (Koopmans, Arrow and Debreu). In the 'finished' structure of modern theory, the concepts that developed later are logically antecedent to those that appeared earlier. The development of the more recent arrivals has been strongly influenced by their logical role in an already extant theoretical structure; they did not have much chance to develop a life of their own.

Thus it happened that it became much easier for the theorist to describe the logical connection between the production set and the production function than to explain the substance of what the production set supposedly represents – a state of knowledge. This neglect of the independent conceptual anchoring of the production set idea has inhibited both the recognition of its limitations and the development of alternative and complementary theoretical treatments of productive knowledge. The following section initiates the discussion of such treatments by exploring the central concept itself.

3   The nature of productive knowledge

It may be helpful to begin by pointing out that the word 'productive' is here serving as something other than a simple modifier in the term 'productive knowledge'. In fact, while it is certain that this discussion is about production, whether it is exclusively about 'knowledge' is a semantic issue that may be open to dispute. To many people, 'knowledge' and 'knowing' denote concepts the characteristic locus of which is the individual human mind. Books, manuals, computer files and other symbolic records supplement and augment human memories, but do not actually engage in 'knowing'. Neither are groups or organizations conceived as 'knowing'. However, an important implication of the discussion to follow is that a narrow focus on what goes on in human minds can seriously impede understanding what goes on when organizations produce things. That sort of understanding is the true objective here, and the scope of the term 'productive knowledge' is therefore deemed to be expandable as necessary to cover whatever needs to be understood.

There are several important differences that separate the subject of productive knowledge from other knowledge domains. These will be discussed in turn.

3.1   *Pragmatic validity*

Over the span of human history, a quest for knowledge has been a shared concern of philosophers, mystics, scientists, engineers, captains of ships and captains of industry. What these different sorts of seekers have meant by knowledge, and the uses they made of it, have been quite different. All have been aware, however, of the question of validity. It has long been recognized that, in every realm of knowledge, there is some false coin in circulation, and it can be a problem to distinguish it from the real thing. When it comes to the level of concern with validity, and the sorts of tests used to establish it, the different sorts of knowledge seekers part company again. The philosophers have generally been the most concerned with the quest for certainty and the critical scrutiny of claims to validity, asking whether and how we can know, and how we can *know* that we know. Overall, their conclusions have not been reassuring. Meanwhile, the specific concerns of the other seekers have generally led them to make lesser demands for certainty, and to employ tests of validity that the philosophers would scorn. Again, the differences of view among the other seekers are notable; experimental scientists see the validity issue in quite different terms from mystics.

For engineers, production managers and corporate strategists, the visible face of the validity problem is the question of transferability across time and space. The process worked well today; will it also work well tomorrow? If we build a similar facility in a remote location, can we confidently expect that one to work as well? The salience of these questions depends critically on the degree to which the answers seem to be in doubt. When experience seems to confirm the temporal and spatial transferability of the knowledge in use, it quickly acquires a 'taken for granted' character. When problems arise, attention is directed to them until they are solved 'for practical purposes'. Under both conditions, the judgements made are not those of philosophers or scientists, who care about the validity question for its own sake, but of practical people, who need to get a job done and have other urgent demands on their attention.

In some areas, production activity is indeed akin (as Wicksteed implied) to the repetition of a well-controlled scientific experiment, and the validity of productive knowledge is there akin to the validity of knowledge based on experimental science. The domain of productive activity is broad, however, and within that broad domain the question of validity plays out in diverse ways. In some areas, the metaphor of the scientific experiment is very wide of the mark[5]. Consider agriculture: from before the dawn of history, the unpredictability and variability of results achieved in agricultural production has been an important, often central, fact of human existence. That uncertainty has been dealt with in diverse ways, and methods of production have reflected those diverse understandings. Is it important to appease the local gods with appropriate rituals? To choose the best time to plant with the aid of an accurate calendar? To burn the stubble after the crop is harvested? To attempt to produce plant hybrids or control how domestic animals pair up in mating? To choose which crop to plant on the basis of the meteorological office's long-range weather forecast, or of the predictions in the *Farmer's Almanac*?

While modern thinking may dismiss some beliefs and related practices as plainly superstitious and others as ill-founded, the line between superstition and practical knowledge is often difficult to draw. The traditions of folk medicine have contributed some valid treatment approaches, such

---

[5] In using experimental science to anchor the high-validity end of a notional continuum, I am oversimplifying the situation in the interests of brevity. There is a substantial literature in the sociology of science that documents the fact that the validity issues that I here associate with (parts of) the productive knowledge domain also arise in (parts of) the domain of experimental science (see, e.g., Collins, 1985). The contrast between the domains is real, but not as sharp as I here pretend.

as quinine for malaria symptoms, along with much mystical obfuscation and harmful error. Similarly, a specific folk practice in agriculture may reflect genuine empirical regularities that, *at least in its actual context*, lend it practical value. For example, a primitive understanding of the phenomena of genetic inheritance has shaped the way humans have used plants and animals for many millennia. The actual contribution of a folk practice may or may not take the form contemplated in the culturally approved rationale of the practice. Contrarily, the fact that modern scientific and engineering understanding have been applied in the creation of a new pesticide does not provide a guarantee against adverse effects arising, for example, from unintended consequences for the local ecology.

The unifying generalization here is that agricultural production is highly exposed to contextual influences arising in imperfectly understood natural systems of great dynamic complexity. Because of that exposure, the character of productive knowledge in agriculture has traditionally been remote from the model of repeated scientific experiments, and modern agricultural research has not entirely eliminated that gap[6]. Beliefs about sound practice have at best a contingent validity that depends on the context being constant in ways that certainly cannot be assured by the available tools of 'experimental control', and may in varying degrees be unidentified, unanalysed and unobservable. At worst, these beliefs may entail significant misunderstandings and perpetuate ways of doing things that are significantly counter-productive.

Although agricultural production is unusual in its obvious exposure to vigorous environmental influences, the issue of context dependence is actually pervasive. Semiconductor production, for example, is at least superficially at an opposite extreme from agriculture in its exposure to context. A semiconductor factory (a 'fab') and its operating procedures can be viewed as an enormous and costly effort to achieve strong 'experimental control' on the production process for semiconductor devices, made in the interests of attaining consistently high yields. But that extraordinary effort is made because it is economically reasonable to make it, and it is reasonable because of the extraordinary sensitivity of semiconductor production processes. Extreme efforts at control notwithstanding, that sensitivity continues to present serious challenges to production engineers (Flaherty, 2000). Thus, while one might plausibly suppose that

---

[6] Of course, outcome variability per se is not necessarily inconsistent with valid and reliable productive knowledge. It could be the case that the variability takes the form of an additive random disturbance, complicating the problem of determining the best method without being causally intertwined with it. This is the sort of assumption statisticians like to make, but it is not the way that 'randomness' actually appears in the sorts of deterministic but complex dynamical systems that constitute so much of our familiar reality.

such a tightly controlled context would be one in which the physical principles underlying production were fully understood and 'recipes' were
highly reliable, in fact the opposite is the case. Occasionally, the struggle to increase and sustain yields has invited characterization in terms of
superstitious belief rather than scientific practice[7]. Elements that might
(superficially) appear to be superstitious even appear in codified organizational practice, as in Intel's 'Copy EXACTLY!' technology transfer
policy (McDonald, 1998; emphasis in original).

Everything which might affect the process or how it is run is to be copied down
to the finest detail, unless it is either *physically impossible* to do so, or there is an
overwhelming competitive benefit to introducing a change.

This policy establishes a burden-of-proof context for transfer decisions
that could easily lead to careful 'ritualistic' copying of details that don't
matter. Of course, its true basis is not superstition but a very rational
adaptation to the reality that understanding of what *does* matter is limited.
As in the case of folk practices in medicine or agriculture, the absence
of a coherent scientific rationale for the details of the practice does not
suffice to establish the absence of pragmatic validity.

Of course, common sense finds the grounds of confidence not in science but in experience. This, however, is the kind of confidence that is
placed in what is 'taken for granted'. As David Hume (1999, originally
published in 1748) classically observed, natural experience by itself cannot resolve causal ambiguity; and quantity of experience does nothing by
itself to remedy its qualitative incapacity to speak to causation. Although
overstated as a conclusion on induction in general, this point has special force regarding the knowledge displayed in complex production processes. The knowledge invoked in such productive performances resides
for the most part in individual skills and in organizational routines that
are, at the multi-person level, the counterpart of individual skills. Skills
are formed in individuals, and routines in organizations, largely through
'learning by doing'. They are developed in particular environments and
meet standards of pragmatic validity that are characteristic of those environments. As is discussed below, the validity of a skill or routine shaped
by such a learning process is typically dependent in a variety of ways
on features of the environment in which it developed. Many of these

[7] For example: 'Despite the fact that the semiconductor silicon is likely the most intensively
studied and well-understood solid material on earth, when it comes to making integrated
circuits in large quantities, the pure white gowns and caps of production line workers
might as well be covered with moons and stars of the type that bedeck the robes of the
conjuror . . . the causes of defects are not always understood, nor are they easy to control
when they are understood' (Robinson, 1980).

dependences may not be obvious and may go unremarked in the learning process – particularly in the case of dependence on conditions that are constant over time in the environment of learning but may vary over the environment of application. Because skills and routines reflect learning processes that are context dependent and in part unconscious, they are inevitably ambiguous in their temporal and spatial scope. Whether the new circumstances of a new site – or simply a new morning – are different enough to be disruptive is a matter that is hard to be confident about *ex ante*.

Finally, there is one major obstacle to the validity of productive knowledge that the examples of agriculture and semiconductor production may not adequately suggest: people are involved. The work done by human beings in productive roles involves not only the physical manipulation of tools and work in process but also human information processing of both simple and complex kinds. The specific physical effects the actors can produce depend on physical attributes such as their strength and stature; the information processing they do depends on their sense organs and their minds. Needless to say, human beings are quite heterogeneous with respect to these attributes, and in many cases the attributes are quite difficult to observe. These considerations limit very seriously the relevance of the validity model provided by repeated, perfectly controlled scientific experiments. Further, 'people are involved' in production in other ways besides their roles as sources of input services. People are also involved as the customers, the consumers and the ultimate arbiters of productive achievement. When the product is corn or computer chips, it may be reasonable to consider that the 'experiment' ends when the product appears, and set the customer response aside as a separate problem. But what if the product is education, business consulting, health care, elder care or day care, entertainment or just 'the dining experience'? Certainly, the arrangements and processes that yield these products ought to be within the scope of a useful theory of productive knowledge: not only do the national income statisticians regard them as production, they account collectively for a substantial fraction of GDP! Yet, if the true definition of the outcome of the productive 'experiment' lies somewhere within the being of the customer, it is clear that another broad range of contextual influences is potentially relevant – and that the prospects for high validity are dimmed accordingly.

By way of conclusion to this discussion of pragmatic validity, it is important to underline the fundamentally important difference in the operative incentives that distinguishes the economic production context from experimental science. In the former, the direct pay-off is to output, not to depth of understanding. Of course, the process of scientific inference from experimental results is itself subject to well-known hazards, even when a strong theory of what might affect the result guides a diligent effort at control. The hazards of inference from 'this has worked up to now' are notably larger in the context of productive knowledge, where the dominant motivational focus from the very start is on *whether* something works, and not why. Quite rational satisficing principles dictate that investment in the quest for understanding be deferred until there is a symptom of trouble to deal with. When the pace is fast and the competitive pressure intense, such deferral may even involve the suppression of ordinary scepticism about the rationale for the prevailing ways of doing things. Paradoxically, 'practical men' are constrained to be gullible, while high standards of proof are a luxury reserved to certain cliques among the inhabitants of the ivory tower.

3.2   Hazy frontiers[8]

The operational aspect of validity was identified above as the transferability of existing knowledge across time and space. When the activity attempted is of a novel kind in itself, judgements about feasibility are subject to hazards and uncertainties well beyond those that attend such transfer. The part of the knowledge territory that is near the advancing frontiers has special importance and a special character, and requires separate attention.

The special importance of this area arises from its place in the linked realities of economic competition and historical change. Competition, for gain and for survival, pushes organizations to seek out new and better ways of doing things. Even for similarly situated business firms that are doing the same thing in roughly the same way, competitive success or failure often rides on the small differences among them, and those differences often reflect efforts at incremental innovation. In other contexts, innovation competition is the central competitive fact. Attempting major advances, firms necessarily find themselves operating at the fringe areas of known technology. In these areas, in the nexus of economic motivation and advancing knowledge, lie the sources of economic growth. It is in these areas that the vision offered by mainstream production theory, with its image of a static 'state' of valid knowledge represented by sharply defined production sets, is most distorted and misleading. As economists always emphasize, 'incentives matter' – but in this area they matter in ways that cannot be cleanly separated from the ongoing, path-dependent evolution of the technological opportunities.

---

[8] Or perhaps it should be 'fuzzy frontiers'. 'Hazy' provides a better metaphor, but 'fuzzy' would evoke – quite properly – the concept of a 'fuzzy (production) set'.

The resource allocation decisions that shape the path of advancing knowledge are necessarily made, at each point of the path, on the basis of the limited knowledge then available. Surveying available knowledge from such a vantage point is like surveying a landscape on a hazy day. Some things are sufficiently close to be seen clearly, others sufficiently remote to be totally invisible. The intermediate conditions cover a broad range and are complex to describe. To define the limits of visibility at a particular vantage point, or the visibility status of a particular feature, requires reference either to an arbitrary standard or to a precise statement of the objectives of observation. It depends on what definition of 'visible' is chosen from the range of plausible available alternatives. Similarly, whether something is to be regarded as 'known' or not will often depend on what one chooses to mean by 'known', and why one cares; ultimately, it depends on the degree of indefiniteness concerning details that is regarded as consistent with the thing being 'known'.

Visibility across the landscape of productive knowledge is, arguably, an even more complex phenomenon than ordinary visibility. The idea of a sharply defined state of knowledge has as an obvious implication the proposition that the universe of production problems divides sharply into those that can clearly be seen *ex ante* to have solutions and those that equally clearly cannot be solved. In fact, however, practical knowledge in all spheres consists in large measure of knowledge of how to *try* to find solutions to previously unencountered problems, including techniques for patching together solutions of old problems to solve new ones. Knowledge of this sort cannot yield any clear *ex ante* distinction between problems that can be solved and those that cannot, such as would exist if the knowledge consisted merely of an easily accessible file of achieved solutions. Rather, it permits a range of judgements of widely varying reliability as to the likelihood that the available problem-solving techniques will prove effective in the various cases posed.

Thus, decisions near the knowledge boundary are made in the face of a lot of haziness about the details and significant uncertainty about how the general picture will develop down the road. Decision makers are generally aware that the best, and often the only, way to get a clearer picture of what lies ahead is to move further down the road. Effort devoted to assessing the possibilities for progress from a given vantage point has an opportunity cost in terms of progress itself – if for no other reason than that attention and cognitive powers are scarce. Thus, decisions are made in a haze that arises partly from exogenous constraints but is partly a chosen response to a recognized trade-off between thinking and doing, between analysing prospects and making progress.

A closely related issue here is the relationship between knowledge of possibility and of impossibility. In standard theory, where production sets have sharply defined boundaries, the absence of the affirmative knowledge required to produce q from x is logically equivalent to '(x, q) is not in the production set' and hence to '(x, q) is technically impossible'. Change the sharp boundary to a hazy frontier and some new issues appear. A high-confidence claim of possibility is one thing, a high-confidence claim of impossibility is quite another, and there can be a lot of room in between. The distinction is significant because some economic propositions depend on affirmative assumptions of possibility, while others rest on assumptions of *im*possibility. For example, using arbitrage arguments to show that some price relationships will not be observed is a familiar exercise that depends only on the availability (to numerous actors) of the arbitrage actions referred to – e.g. buy here, ship from here to there, sell there. Consider, by contrast, the prediction that cost increases will result from a regulatory intervention that requires products to be modified in ways that buyers generally desire. Confidence about this conclusion rests on confidence about what firms *cannot do*. The claim is that, if firms could achieve these modifications at zero incremental cost, 'they would have done it already' – since buyers attach positive value to the change. If one cares about the level of confidence that predictions deserve, and also acknowledges that the frontiers are hazy, one notices that quite different approaches are involved in assessing the confidence to be placed in the two different sorts of propositions. In particular, the regulatory example demands some assessment of how the change affects the incentives to explore previously untried approaches that lie in the hazy zone. This question falls under the important heading of 'induced innovation'. The topic has sometimes been addressed, in a more or less mainstream fashion. The influence of standard production theory has been, on the one hand, to induce a severe discount on the pervasiveness and importance of the topic and, on the other, to suggest a framework for the problem that largely duplicates the limitations of production theory itself[9].

3.3   Distributed character

A third distinctive attribute of productive knowledge is that it frequently resides in work groups or organizations rather than in individuals. This is not simply a matter of the same knowledge being held by several individuals, although such common knowledge may play an important role. Neither is it adequately captured by the image of complementary specialized skills being coordinated in the execution of a 'recipe', because the recipe – or, at least, much of the knowledge required in its execution – often exists

---

[9] See the exchange between Vernon Ruttan (1997) and Dosi (1997). Dosi upholds the evolutionary approach to induced innovation and summarizes it effectively.

only as it is evoked in the actual activity of the group. It is crucially a matter of *distributed* knowledge – i.e. of complementary parts of the same functional unit of knowledge being held by several individuals and applied in a coordinated way, the coordination itself being a crucial aspect of the knowledge. Such a 'functional unit' might comprise, for example, the ability of a cockpit crew to get an airliner safely to its destination[10], of a surgical team to perform an open-heart operation, or of a string quartet and a piano player to perform Schubert's 'Trout' Quintet. It is the obvious significance of these sorts of functional units of organizational knowledge and performance that makes the idea of distributed knowledge inescapable. We would find little use for a theory that was either inapplicable to such performances or pretended that they involved no knowledge, or admitted the knowledge content of the performance but offered no answer to the question of where the knowledge resides, or obstinately pretended that in such cases all the knowledge is held in the mind of a single individual. Accepting the view that knowledge can reside in a group is, in this sense, a 'forced move'.

There is nothing either novel or mysterious about the notion of productive knowledge residing in a group rather than in individual minds. Primitive peoples have long used collective hunting methods involving specialized individual roles. The question of how such distributed knowledge can arise in a group has multiple answers, but one is particularly clear and straightforward: such knowledge is the product of shared experiential learning. Just as practice allows an individual to improve in the performance of a complex skill through improved coordination, so the shared practice of a group permits patterns of multi-person coordinated action to arise, improve and stabilize. In both cases, 'procedural memory' – in which micro-responses are evoked sequentially by cues arising in large part from the emerging action itself – is a key mechanism of learning (see Squire, 1987, and Cohen and Bacdayan, 1994). In the individual case, these cues move intrapersonally as nerve impulses from sensory systems, including the kinaesthetic sense, to the brain. In the group case, cues move interpersonally and include verbal messages as well as mutual observation. Although individual minds are a principal locus of storage for distributed knowledge, the coherent enactment of the functional unit of knowledge is a phenomenon that occurs at the level of the group. The more sharply differentiated the individual roles in the group performance, the more obvious it is that there is no individual who knows what

---

[10] See the ethnographic study of a cockpit crew by Hutchins and Klausen (1996). Among other helpful studies in the same volume, see particularly Shaiken (1996) on the 'collective nature of skill'.

the group knows. Whatever standing a group of diverse specialists may have achieved in the development and retention of a functional unit of some type of knowledge, it cannot be contested by any individual mind but only by another group encompassing the same specialities.

The reality of distributed knowledge, and of the shared experiential learning that typically produces it, seems obvious and incontrovertible. The aesthetic appreciation of high levels of interpersonal coordination is, for example, part of the enjoyment of watching a great team play soccer or basketball. Yet this obvious and important point about productive knowledge is often resisted. Intellectual inclinations towards reductionism are no doubt part of the reason. Strongly amplifying these philosophical dispositions is the practical reality that distributed knowledge is a phenomenon that is very awkward to capture in a simple analytical framework. It brings history into the picture and implies that an adequate representation of individual actors would have to record not only what they have done in the past but with whom they have done it. This complexity contrasts sharply with the standard economic theory of production, which adopts the very convenient fiction of homogeneous input categories, but is thereby forced to adopt the awkward complementary fiction that the distributed productive knowledge in an experienced team of input suppliers resides somewhere outside the team.

In recent years, however, the fact that productive knowledge often resides in groups rather than in individuals has received increasing attention both from business firms and from scholars outside the economics discipline. There has been a striking degree of mutual reinforcement between the interest in these issues on the business side, driven by the practical concerns of an increasingly knowledge-based economy, and the academic scholarship.

As is true of knowledge held by individuals, the productive knowledge distributed in groups is of a variety of types. There is a spectrum ranging from the highly 'automatic' performance of organizational routines, analogous to the exercise of tacit psycho-motor skills in an individual, through coordinated attacks on well-posed problems, and on to the solution of ill-posed problems and attempts at high creativity. Verbal communication among group members plays an increasing role as the attributes of the situation call increasingly for highly deliberate and/or creative response; it may play no role at all when response is automatic. In the latter case, the reality of knowledge at the group level is manifested in the quality of the coordination visible in action, but at the more creative end of the spectrum the efficacy of verbal communication is an important key to both the enactment and the assessment of group knowledge. Groups that communicate well tend to make better choices of action; the reality of group knowledge is manifest in the communications that precede the choices as well as in the choices themselves.

A simple schematic model of this point might run as follows. Suppose Group I, consisting of individuals A_1, B_1, C_1, . . . , must arrive at a course of action with respect to problem Z_N, and a lot of what they observably do consists of 'talking it over'. Group II, consisting of individuals A_2, B_2, C_2, . . . , confronts Z_N as well. Neither group has ever encountered Z_N before. Group I, however, has a long history of engaging broadly similar problems Z_1, Z_2, . . . , etc., not to speak of less similar problems X_1, X_2, . . . , and Y_1, Y_2, ... Group II's members are similar to those of Group I, and have – in particular – the same native language, the same levels of the non-verbal skills required for action, the same experience at the individual level of the issues presented in Z_N, the same term of mutual acquaintance and the same quality of interpersonal relations – but not the shared problem-solving history. It seems clear that Group I is likely to be more efficacious in addressing Z_N than Group II. The shared experience of its members should leave them with a shared vocabulary and conceptual orientation to the problem – or, having much the same effect, a shared and precise understanding of how everyday language maps onto the situation. Although they have never encountered precisely the Z_N problem before, they have encountered the challenge of communicating with each other about similar problems, and presumably worked out many of the snags in that communication process. Because that 'working out' takes place among specific individuals in the course of encountering a sequence of specific problems, its details may well be idiosyncratic in various ways that reflect the attributes of the problems and the actors involved.

Ethnographic research has produced significant evidence supportive of this schematic proposition, although, by their nature, ethnographic studies do not benefit from the experimental control suggested by the careful statement. A particularly influential contribution was Julian Orr's detailed ethnographic study of the work of service representatives for Xerox Corporation (Orr, 1996). Triggered largely by the urgent need for repairs to malfunctioning photocopiers, the work of the service representatives is highly unpredictable in timing and content. At that level of analysis, it is not governed by routine. A majority of the individual repair tasks are, however, non-problematic in that they are covered by the company's directive documentation, are within the 'high-frequency' domain of the technicians' skills, or both[11]. The knowledge applied in addressing

---

[11] Consistent with a point about frequency made by Zollo and Winter (2002), Orr notes (p. 109) that experienced technicians do not refer to the documentation when solving the most common problems.

the less common failure modes is of a different character. Orr recounts how the technicians use stories to organize and deepen their collective understanding of the ambiguous behaviour of the complex photocopier machines they deal with. The totality of that specialized knowledge resides in the community of technicians, and is mobilized by the individual technician or a small group when attacking difficult problems. Status in the community depends in part on contributions to the common knowledge pool and awareness of what it contains.

This image of knowledge residing in a 'community of practice' has been highly influential, in part because of its extension and effective explication to a broader audience by the work of Brown and Duguid (1991, 2000)[12]. Its significance derives partly from its relation to a particularly important segment of the knowledge problems that organizations encounter, and partly from its rich psychological, sociological and organizational aspects. An important open issue is whether an effective community of practice can be created deliberately by management – as many companies have tried to do – or whether they are necessarily spontaneous and informal, open at most to acceptance and some facilitation by management. In any case, communities of practice represent only a subset, albeit an important one, of the broader phenomenon of distributed knowledge.

Apart from displaying the phenomenon of organizational knowledge distributed in a community of practice, Orr's study documented several other points consistent with the general view of productive knowledge presented here. The work of the technicians is not understood at higher levels in the organization, or, in particular, by the creators of the repair documentation. In effect, the organization's functioning depends on productive knowledge of which management is unaware and on practices that contravene management's counter-productive efforts to control behaviour. Particularly striking is the fact that management seems not to recognize that keeping the customers happy is an important and challenging part of the job of a technician, which Orr observed to be quite distinguishable from the challenge of repairing machines. In line with the discussion above, the conclusion is that the true end point of the service production process is not in the state of the machine but in the customer's head. Perhaps if managers thought about it carefully, they would agree that keeping the customers happy warrants a lot of attention and even a page or two in the documentation; in practice, though, they appear not to think about the technician's job in that light.

---

[12] The term 'community of practice' is usually associated with Lave and Wenger (1991); see also Maanen and Barley (1984) on 'occupational communities'. In his introduction to Orr's book (p. xiii), Stephen Barley comments that 'Orr puts the flesh of everyday life on Lave and Wenger's idea of a community of practice'.

4   Replication

As noted above, the question of the pragmatic validity of productive knowledge is, at its most basic level, a question of whether the use of a functional unit of knowledge can be extended in time and in space – that is, whether a productive performance can be repeated, or whether a functionally equivalent performance can be accomplished at a different site. It is tempting to jump to an affirmative conclusion; standard production theory certainly suppresses doubt about this, and perhaps 'common sense' does as well. There is, however, much to be learned by letting the doubts resurface.

The 'obvious' feasibility of temporal and spatial replication is a conclusion that is derived, first, by abstracting away complications that are often significant in real production situations. The standard theory dispatches many of these complications by the assumption that inputs are conveniently sorted into categories that are both homogeneous and readily recognized, others by the assumption that productive knowledge has a central (though unspecified) locus that is somehow inherently associated with the firm itself, and then by simply ignoring the remaining issues. In the background is, perhaps, an implicit reliance on the 'repeated scientific experiments' view of the nature of productive knowledge, and/or on the unmentioned problem-solving capabilities that fill the knowledge gaps when conditions change. As for the 'common sense' appraisal, it is probably dominated by the familiar experience of seeing similar operations in different places – without looking too closely and without, of course, any real assessment of whether it is 'the same knowledge' that is being used. More careful scrutiny of the way knowledge figures in these 'simple' issues of temporal and spatial replication deserves a prominent place on the initial agenda of an evolutionary approach to production.

4.1   Standard theory

In standard production theory, something akin to the explicit discussion of replication arises in the context of the formal axiomatic treatment of production set properties. More specifically, it appears in statements that seek to motivate the assumption of *additivity*, and a review of this standard analysis provides both a starting point and a contrast for an evolutionary approach.

Additivity says that the sum of feasible production plans is itself feasible. If it is known how to produce output vector q^a from input vector x^a, and also how to produce q^b from x^b, then it is known how to produce $(q^a + q^b)$ from $(x^a + x^b)$. In the special case when $x^a = x^b$ and $q^a = q^b$, the conclusion is that $2q^a$ is producible from $2x^a$ – the doubling of a feasible plan yields a feasible plan. It is this form of the proposition that has often been advanced in less formal discussion, as in, for example, the Wicksteed passage about exactly repeating a particular production plan for wheat, or in the following statement by Frank Hahn (1949).

The common sense proposition that the duplication of a given industrial process (together incidentally with a duplication of entrepreneurs or entrepreneurial function) will lead to a doubling of the output is unassailable. . . .
    If two identical entrepreneurs set up two identical plants, with an identical labor force, to produce an identical commodity x, then the two together will produce twice the amount of x that could be produced by one alone.

In a similarly confident vein, Kenneth Arrow and Hahn (1971, p. 61) said more recently that 'the assumption of additivity . . . can always be defended and indeed made essentially tautologous'.
    Lurking well beneath the surface here are some significant issues involving the relationship of additivity to knowledge and to the spatial distribution of productive activity. Note first that the image suggested by Hahn's two identical plants or Wicksteed's notion of conditions 'exactly repeated' is an image of *spatially distinct* but otherwise identical production activities. Since production is understood to involve input and output flows, or amounts over a designated time interval, the doubling of production must be understood as a concurrent replication of activity – not, for example, doing the same thing over again. It is then plain enough that a second manufacturing plant or a second wheat field cannot be in precisely the same location as the first, and also that nothing resembling a replication of the original activity could be accomplished by trying to squeeze twice the activity into the same physical space. In short, the additivity axiom must be understood as relating to the aggregation of the results of activity occurring in different places. Hahn's example of the two plants makes it particularly clear that this is the correct interpretation. In this sense, the additivity axiom seems to say little more than 'addition works', and perhaps that is why Arrow and Hahn said that it can be 'made essentially tautologous'.
    There is, however, a limit on how 'different' the places can be, which Hahn does not emphasize. Since location generally matters, the spatial distinction between the sites is potentially of economic significance, in which case it might not be meaningful to add quantities across sites. Adding California lemons and Italian lemons is as erroneous as the proverbial adding of 'apples and oranges', so far as economics is concerned. If transportation costs are small relative to the input and output values, because distances are short or for other reasons, the addition is

justified[13]. Yet, if the distances are very short, it seems possible that the validity of the conclusion might be undercut because of physical interference between the sites. Does production do something to the local environment in terms of air quality, noise, vibration or other considerations that might matter to similar activity nearby? So, in addition to its implicit relationship to location economics (implying that distances are short), the additivity axiom turns out also to have an implicit relationship to the topic of 'externalities' (implying, perhaps, that distances can't be *too* short).

This is a lot of implicit theorizing to pack into one little axiom. The hidden complexities are, however, aspects of a more basic point: the usual production set formalism is simply not a very helpful tool for probing the relationship between 'states of knowledge' and production possibilities. (The historical discussion above argues that this is an understandable consequence of the developmental trajectory of standard production theory.) The proposition that is really at issue is that the use of existing productive knowledge can be extended geographically. This is a proposition with great plausibility on the face of it, such that it is often taken for granted, and one that seems crucially important to understanding the historical development and current functioning of the economy. It is, therefore, the sort of proposition that is worth deep and careful examination. The additivity axiom is a shallow and imperfect abstraction that does more to obscure the issues relevant to this proposition than to illuminate them.

4.2   The challenges of replication

To explore the issues more carefully, it is best to face the central issue directly. Abandoning the grandiose ambition of trying to characterize the structure of everything that is feasible (regardless of whether it is happening), begin with the supposition that some productive activity corresponding to (x, q) is *actually being conducted successfully* at site A. What does that imply about the possibility that a similar success can be achieved at site B? More specifically, the question is whether the cost of achieving similar success at B is significantly reduced by the fact that (in some

---

[13] Awareness of this point is reflected in Gérard Debreu's classic *Theory of Value* in his reference to 'elementary regions' within which transportation costs are negligible (1959, p. 29). When they offer data on, for example, national production of Portland cement, economic statisticians are, in effect, treating the nation as such a region. Debreu would probably be sceptical about this.

sense) the requisite knowledge has apparently been developed and is in actual use at A.

The possibility of such cost reduction seems to be implicit in the most basic teaching about information (or knowledge), which is its property of being 'non-rivalrous in use'. The knowledge required to produce at A is not used up or degraded by also being used at B. The question is what this proposition has to do with the concrete task of making success at B happen, and with the cost of accomplishing this task. To isolate analytically the specific issues of extending the use of knowledge, the assumption here is that, perhaps after some initial period, the specific resources involved in production at B are entirely different from those at A. (It is not a case, for example, of having key workers at A work a second shift at B.) Also set aside for this discussion is the issue of temporal replication; in general, temporal replication presents attenuated versions of the same issues that arise in spatial replication. Finally, recognize that such replication will not happen without some organized managerial effort; the relevant actor will be called 'top management'. The word 'top' serves only to flag the point that there are, typically, other management layers below the level from which the replication effort is initiated, and these generally attenuate the top's knowledge of operational details.

As the above discussion of pragmatic validity suggests, the premise that productive activity is going forward successfully at A actually has only limited implications for the state of productive knowledge at A, particularly as regards the depth of causal understanding. It has still less implication for the feasibility of successful transfer from A to B, given the distributed character of productive knowledge. Much of organizational knowledge is largely tacit, in a sense analogous to the tacit nature of individual skill; a great deal gets done without the 'conscious awareness' of top management, even if the knowledge at lower levels is quite explicit. Even if systematic and sophisticated attempts at codification are made, there is inevitably a limit to the coverage of details. Many of these may be known to individual workers, and be describable by them, but not known to fellow workers, supervisors or managers. Others may be known but tacit – impossible to describe in a way that is helpful to a learner. Some may be secrets, cherished for their contribution to making work easier, and some may be contrary to the prevailing formal rules. Finally, it is well established in the psychology literature that there can be 'learning without awareness'; people can learn to adapt their behaviour effectively to varying stimuli without ever being consciously aware either of the stimulus conditions to which they are responding or of the fact of their adaptation (Stadler and Frensch, 1997). There is little reason to doubt that this type of learning goes on in the natural settings of business activity, as it does in the psychology labs.

Thus, if management wishes to replicate at B the success it is having at A, a first challenge it faces is to devise methods to evoke the transfer of details of which it is unaware, including some of which nobody is aware, and some that represent information that is in various ways 'impacted'. This is a tall order, which can never be filled completely; the gaps in the transfer will be filled by independent reinvention.

The literature of situated cognition points to the fact that the productive knowledge exercised at A exists in an intimate interconnection with the context of activity at A, in both its designed and coincidental features. Of particular importance here is the equipment used in the work. In contemporary work settings, crucially important knowledge is often embedded in the equipment, and the local understanding of its functioning is narrowly instrumental. Computers and software are the most ubiquitous and familiar examples of this issue, but there are 'low-tech' examples as well. The spatial organization of activity at the micro-level affects patterns of interaction and communication, and this can affect outcomes in ways that are not fully recognized or understood.

Here, then, is a second challenge. While top management can attempt to establish a local context at B identical to that at A, a variety of obstacles can arise. The site layout may have to be different, perhaps because of its position relative to transportation corridors. Perhaps new generations of computers and software have succeeded those installed at A. The latter may represent progress and ultimately be economically advantageous overall, but it is not advantageous in the specific terms of achieving economies by reusing the productive knowledge that exists at A. Again, a need for reinvention, relearning and – perhaps – creativity is implied.

Next, as discussed in relation to validity, there are the various relationships of the activity to its external physical environment. Depending on the character of the specific activity, there may be significant effects from the weather, from air quality and atmospheric pressure, from noise and vibration levels, the electromagnetic radiation environment and so forth[14]. To the extent that these influences remain constant at A, their causal significance is likely to have gone unrecognized. If the environment at B is significantly different, the relevance of productive knowledge

---

[14] Alfred Marshall's characterization of 'land' as a factor of production is one point here. He recognized that it is not just the soil but the whole bundle of physical attributes specific to a location that is involved: 'the space relations of the plot in question, and the annuity that nature has given it of sunlight and air and rain' (Marshall, 1890, p. 147). Evoking the potential relevance of environmental influence to non-agricultural production requires a substantially longer attribute list.

imported from A can be undercut in ways that are mysterious, at least initially. Learning and problem solving are called for.

Finally, the success of the activity at A depends on the attributes and behaviours of exchange partners encountered there – customers, employees and suppliers. While these may be influenced through the prices (wages), specifications and monitoring arrangements put forward, the specific responses to these influences are ultimately up to the exchange partners and not to the focal enterprise. Some of the causal principles governing such responses may be understood at a crude level, and careful monitoring may be effective in limiting variability. Nevertheless, important details often remain quite obscure, notwithstanding the substantial research efforts devoted to such questions, both in business firms and academe. Do customers read the warning labels on hazardous chemicals and behave accordingly? Do they use products only in recommended ways? Do assemblers follow the drawings? Can they? (See Bechky, 2003.) How serious is the adverse selection that inevitably occurs when the organization is in some distress and employees with good alternatives quit? To the extent that operations at B entail interactions with different exchange partners (which they necessarily do, at least so far as employees are concerned), differences in the populations of partners encountered constitute another reason why things may not function at B the way they do at A. Once again, the ability to operate successfully at A clearly does not entail possession of the sort of knowledge required to cope with the different circumstances at B. And, once again, there is an implied requirement for new learning.

In some cases, top management may be totally unaware of the fact that considerations in these various categories are relevant to success. For example, this is inevitably so for procedural details that have been learned without awareness. In many cases, however, it is fairly obvious that the success of an activity depends in various ways on features of its context. Management may understand very well, for example, that the skills and personalities of employees have considerable bearing on the results achieved. What is unlikely to be known, however, are the size and interrelations of the tolerance intervals – how slow or fractious can the employees become before success is actually undermined? An abstract statement of the general issue here is this: there is a region in the multidimensional space of contextual variables in which success can be achieved, but operations at the initial site neither entail nor reveal more than a little knowledge of where the boundaries of that region lie. From a performance point of view, it is, of course, a good thing if contextual variables stay – with high reliability – well within the region where success is possible. But the reliability that sustains successful performance also sustains causal ambiguity. If understanding were the goal, it would actually be better to experience the response to wider variation in the variables.

Frequently, new sites are chosen that are highly dissimilar from the original in some dimensions, because they are expected to be highly advantageous in other dimensions – e.g. locations that look good in terms of customer flows and income levels may be ones where it is hard to attract employees at acceptable wage levels. This means that the shallowness of causal understanding, which remains latent in the successful operations at site A, can easily frustrate the necessary efforts to adapt to the circumstances of the new site.

4.3   Replication in practice

The above discussion suggests that replication is potentially quite challenging. It is not necessarily viewed as such, however. Often, managements seem to take quite a relaxed attitude towards such challenges. While the relaxed attitude may be justified in some cases, it is arguable that many managers still have a good deal to learn about the subject[15]. Where special circumstances force the issue to management attention, such as the technological peculiarities of semiconductor production (Intel), or McDonald's strategic devotion to a uniform customer experience, we do see managerial practices that are consistent with the general picture offered above.

The example of Intel's Copy EXACTLY! policy is particularly valuable because it rests precisely on the recognition that there is more productive knowledge implied in achieved high yields than the organization can capture in the form of comprehensive causal understanding of the method in use. It exemplifies almost perfectly the notion of reliance on the knowledge embedded in the 'template' of an existing achievement, as put forward by Richard Nelson and me (Nelson and Winter, 1982, pp. 119–20). Since it eschews adaptation and improvement as a matter of policy, this approach might be considered to be at odds with the above emphasis on the inevitable role of new learning and problem solving in achieving successful replication. This is not the case at all; the point is to control the *amount* of new learning and problem solving required. Every decision to create a difference between the sites is an addition to a list of unintended and hidden differences that will occur in spite of the policy. Interaction effects tend to make complexity rise exponentially with the number of discrepancies to be dealt with; it is better to keep the list as short as possible. There will be no shortage of problems to solve.

---

[15] See Winter and Szulanski, 2001. A further statement on this, with a stronger prescriptive message, is in Szulanski and Winter, 2002.

There are several reasons why the problematic aspects of replication often go unnoticed. A basic one, surely, is that exploiting existing knowledge from the original site is rarely an end in itself. The objective is successful operation at the new site, regardless of the mix of replication and new problem solving, and it is the time and cost of the combination that matters. The opportunity to exploit newer technology at the new site often tips the balance away from replication – or seems to. Further, the very fact that there are differences between the sites softens expectations concerning the level of performance achievable at the new one, so the occasion to question the success of the replication may not arise.

The empirical information on replication processes is relatively sparse and scattered, but it speaks quite uniformly on the point that significant costs and managerial challenges are involved. Szulanski's study of Banc One (Szulanski, 2000) provides specifics concerning time, costs and challenges. More importantly, it provides a uniquely systematic and comprehensive view of the specific processes involved in the development and application of a strategy of spatial replication in US banking – in this case, via the conversion of newly affiliated banks to the common systems and products of the bank holding company. In the relevant time period, Banc One was an industry leader both in its ability to carry out conversions successfully and to improve earnings by the application of its common systems. The overall conversion process for a new affiliate took about six months, but culminated in a single frenetic weekend that separated the 'before' and 'after' identities of the affiliate from the customers' point of view. A successful conversion is one that is a 'non-event' from the perspective of all but those concerned with carrying it out, but particularly from the viewpoint of customers. Banc One had many successes, but a few traumatic conversions were key learning episodes. Szulanski observed that Banc One became increasingly ambitious as it learned and routinized its conversion process, taking on conversions of increasing scope while failing to address fully the implied scheduling problems for its conversion capabilities. A major conversion effort ultimately hit multiple snags, triggering new learning efforts directed at scope and scheduling issues.

5   Production theory evolving

That knowledge and information are not exhausted by use is a kind of economic magic, a cheerful exception to the manifold scarcities that give the 'dismal science' its name. The insight that accords this magic a central role in the processes of economic development is fundamentally on target – but the magic is not simple magic. To extend the use of existing knowledge in time and space is not at all the trivial matter it is often made out to be. A first point illustrated by the above account of replication is the way that words such as 'learning', 'problem solving', 'creativity' and 'management' inevitably come into play in a realistic discussion – even in relation to this, perhaps the simplest of all major issues in the economics of productive knowledge. Those words signal, in turn, the presence of costs and organizational capabilities that are typically overlooked by economists, and hence of potentials for competitive superiority and inferiority that are also neglected.

To recognize the scope for new learning, problem solving and creativity implicit in the 'simple' idea of spatial replication is to recognize the magnitude of the conceptual gap that separates the evolutionary formulation of these issues from the standard apparatus, with its sharp distinction between the 'known' and 'unknown' techniques. There is a very basic contrast between, on the one hand, behaviour that is learned and practised and, on the other, behaviour that may be improvised or planned – but in either case is not practised. This contrast is fundamental to evolutionary economics in general and to evolutionary production theory in particular. Representing it, reflecting on it and exploring its many intricacies is a large part of what the evolutionary programme is about.

A second point that is highlighted by the replication discussion is the role of the individual, functioning productive unit – the 'establishment', in statistical parlance – as a locus and repository of productive knowledge. Near the beginning of their discussion of organizational capabilities, Nelson and Winter (1982, p. 97) suggest in a cautionary footnote that the concepts presented there may be more relevant at the establishment level than they are at the level of the multi-unit business firm. In other contexts, however, evolutionary theory is (quite appropriately) associated with the idea that '*business firms* are repositories of productive knowledge', or that '*business firms* are organizations that know how to do things' (Winter, 1982, 1991 respectively, emphasis added). There is an issue here, and an important agenda, on which only limited progress has been made. On balance, that progress tends to support the validity of the footnote warning, and suggests that the relative importance of the establishment and firm levels as repositories of knowledge is something that evolutionary economics badly needs to address. Intra-firm homogeneity of method across establishments is definitely not something that just happens; it happens only when managements work hard to achieve it and devote substantial resources to the task. This is the lesson equally from Intel and McDonald's, and it is the lesson in the recent enthusiasm for the 'internal transfer of best practices'. Regarding the latter, the starting point is the observation that valuable intra-organizational variety arises naturally; the experience is that it is often possible, but rarely easy, to exploit that variety and improve the average by transferring practices (Szulanski, 1996). Giving the establishment level its appropriate place in the productive knowledge picture does not deny the importance of the firm level, but it certainly implies that there is a major challenge in creating a picture that is appropriately balanced and indicative of the great diversity of situations. The fact that there is an active market in establishments, sometimes grouped into business units or whole firms, only enhances the interest and difficulty of that challenge.

The overall agenda facing evolutionary production theory is, of course, much larger than the territory explored in this chapter. A plausible next step, much in the spirit of the discussion here, would be to examine the issue of returns to scale in production – meaning, in substance, the issue of *increasing* returns in production. These phenomena are excluded in axiomatic treatments of 'well-behaved' production situations by the assumption of divisibility (or, more directly, 'non-increasing returns to scale'). From the same analytical attitude at which one can observe that the additivity axiom has a certain common-sense plausibility to it, one can observe also that the divisibility axiom does basic violence to the truth – but, like additivity, divisibility can be viewed as an approximation, better in some cases than others. The counterpart to the above replication discussion would take as its starting point an ongoing activity successfully producing q from x, and ask how capacity can be increased to $3q$ from $3x$. One answer would be: by creating two replicas of the original – an undertaking subject to the various hazards and qualifications noted above. The crucial point is that there is additional design freedom conferred when scale is increased. In particular, there is the possibility that equipment units of greater physical size might be more efficient. If replication or partial replication is also possible, the additional design freedom should tip the balance to increasing returns – subject, no doubt, to a long list of qualifications potentially relevant to an individual case. That there is substantial empirical reality to this picture is hardly contestable (see Levin, 1977, and Scherer, 1975). A major part of the analysis that is needed here involves exploring the sources and nature of the design freedom, and the way its exploitation is complemented by replication. The major objectives include better understanding of the contribution of increasing returns to rising productivity, its relation to technical change, and the reasons for the diversity in its role across activities.

Skipping forward across a wide range of subjects of intermediate size and complexity, I conclude by sketching one very large problem that builders of evolutionary production theory ought to have in view. Environmental concerns, and particularly the problem of global climate change, raise the related problems of designing regulatory interventions and estimating the economic response to such interventions. The relevant time horizons for most of these concerns are (we hope) quite long – though not so long as to warrant complacency. The problem posed involves 'induced innovation' on a grand scale, operating at many levels and loci in the economic, technological and scientific systems, and posing challenges of policy, management and institutional design. The capacity to analyse complex problems that lie in the domain of the 'hazy frontiers', where evolving technological prospects mix with uncertain and changing economic incentives, would be very valuable in dealing with this problem. Perhaps it is indispensable. Economics has thus far done little to help build this sort of capacity; the way standard economics defends its boundaries and seals out alien problems has been a factor limiting its contribution. By contrast, evolutionary theory has few, if any, commitments that are put seriously at risk by ideas or facts from other disciplines. As this chapter has attempted to illustrate, it has open frontiers, lives with other disciplines in what is recognizably the same world, and has much to gain from trade. The evolutionary approach offers the kind of economics, and should provide the kind of production theory, needed to address the problems that progress brings to the planet.

REFERENCES

Arrow, K. J., and G. Debreu (1954), 'Existence of equilibrium for a competitive economy', *Econometrica* 22(3): 265–90.
Arrow, K. J., and F. Hahn (1971), *General Competitive Analysis*, Edinburgh: Oliver & Boyd.
Atkinson, A., and J. Stiglitz (1969), 'A new view of technical change', *Economic Journal* 315: 573–78.
Bechky, B. A. (2003), 'Sharing meaning across occupational communities: the transformation of knowledge on a production floor', *Organization Science* 14: 312–30.
Brown, J. S., and P. Duguid (1991), 'Organizational learning and communities-of-practice: toward a unified view of working, learning and innovation', *Organization Science* 2: 40–57.
  (2000), *The Social Life of Information*, Boston: Harvard Business School Press.
Carlson, S. (1956), *A Study on the Pure Theory of Production*, New York: Kelley and Millman.
Cohen, M., and P. Bacdayan (1994), 'Organizational routines are stored as procedural memory: evidence from a laboratory study', *Organizational Science* 5: 554–68.
Collins, H. M. (1985), *Changing Order: Replication and Induction in Scientific Practice*, London: Sage.
Debreu, G. (1959), *Theory of Value*, New York: Wiley.
Dosi, G. (1997), 'Opportunities, incentives and the collective patterns of technological change', *Economic Journal* 444: 1530–47.

Flaherty, M. T. (2000), 'Limited inquiry and intelligent adaptation in semicon-
    ductor manufacturing', in G. Dosi, R. R. Nelson and S. G. Winter (eds.),
    The Nature and Dynamics of Organizational Capabilities, Oxford: Oxford
    University Press, 99–123.
Gould, S. J. (1980), *The Panda's Thumb: More Reflections in Natural History*, New
    York: Norton.
Hahn, F. H. (1949), 'Proportionality, divisibility and economies of scale: com-
    ment', *Quarterly Journal of Economics* **63**: 131–37.
Hume, D. (1999), *An Enquiry Concerning Human Understanding*, Oxford Philo-
    sophical Texts series, T. L. Beauchamp (ed.), Oxford: Oxford University
    Press.
Hutchins, E., and T. Klausen (1996), 'Distributed cognition in an airline cockpit',
    in Y. Engestrom and D. Middleton (eds.), *Cognition and Communication at
    Work*, Cambridge: Cambridge University Press, 15–34.
Koopmans, T. C. (1977), 'Concepts of optimality and their uses', *American Eco-
    nomic Review*, **67**(3): 261–74.
Lave, J., and E. Wenger (1991), *Situated Learning: Legitimate Peripheral Participa-
    tion*, Cambridge: Cambridge University Press.
Levin, R. C. (1977), 'Technical change and optimal scale: some implications',
    Southern Economic Journal **2**: 208–21.
Maanen, J. v., and S. R. Barley (1984), 'Occupational communities: culture and
    control in organizations', in B. M. Staw and L. L. Cummings (eds.), *Research
    in Organizational Behavior*, Greenwich, CT: JAI Press.
Marshall, A. (1890), *Principles of Economics*, London: Macmillan (8th edn., 1920,
    London: Macmillan; 9th variorum edn., 1961, London: Macmillan).
McDonald, C. J. (1998), 'The evolution of Intel's Copy EXACTLY! technol-
    ogy transfer method', *Intel Technology Journal* (4th quarter), http://www.intel.
    com/technology/itj/941998/articles/art_2.htm.
Nelson, R. R., and S. G. Winter (1982), *An Evolutionary Theory of Economic
    Change*, Cambridge, MA: Harvard University Press.
Orr, J. E. (1996), *Talking About Machines: An Ethnography of a Modern Job*, Ithaca,
    NY: ILR Press/Cornell University Press.
Robinson, A. L. (1980), 'New ways to make microcircuits smaller', *Science*
    208(May): 1019–26.
Ruttan V. W. (1997), 'Induced innovation, evolutionary theory and path
    dependence: sources of technical change', *Economic Journal* **107**: 1520–
    29.
Scherer, F. M. (1975), *The Economics of Multi-plant Operations: An International
    Comparisons Study*, Cambridge, MA: Harvard University Press.
Shaiken, H. (1996), 'Experience and the collective nature of skill', in
    Y. Engestrom and D. Middleton (eds.), *Cognition and Communication at Work*,
    Cambridge: Cambridge University Press, 279–95.
Squire, L. R. (1987), *Memory and Brain*, Oxford: Oxford University Press.
Stadler, M. A., and P. A. Frensch (1997), *Handbook of Implicit Learning*, Thou-
    sand Oaks, CA: Sage Publications.
Szulanski, G. (1996), 'Exploring internal stickiness: impediments to the transfer
    of best practice within the firm', *Strategic Management Journal* **17**(winter
    special issue): 27–43.

(2000), 'Appropriability and the challenge of scope: Banc One routinizes replication', in G. Dosi, R. R. Nelson and S. G. Winter (eds.), *The Nature and Dynamics of Organizational Capabilities*, Oxford: Oxford University Press, 69–98.

Szulanski, G., and S. G. Winter (2002), 'Getting it right the second time', *Harvard Business Review* **80**: 62–69.

Wicksteed, P. (1894), *An Essay on the Coordination of the Laws of Distribution*, London: Macmillan.

Winter, S. G. (1982), 'An essay on the theory of production', in S. Hymans (ed.), *Economics and the World Around It*, Ann Arbor, MI: University of Michigan Press, 55–91.

(1991), 'On Coase, competence and the corporation', in O. E. Williamson and S. G. Winter (eds.), *The Nature of the Firm: Origins, Evolution, and Development*, Oxford: Oxford University Press: 179–95.

Winter, S. G., and G. Szulanski (2001), 'Replication as strategy', *Organization Science* **12**: 730–43.

Zollo, M., and S. G. Winter (2002), 'Deliberate learning and the evolution of dynamic capabilities', *Organization Science* **13**: 339–51.

9   Learning in evolutionary environments[1]

Giovanni Dosi
Luigi Marengo
Giorgio Fagiolo

1   Introduction

In the most generic terms, learning may occur in all circumstances when agents have an imperfect understanding of the world in which they operate – either due to lack of information about it, or, more fundamentally, because of an imprecise knowledge of its structure; or when they master only a limited repertoire of actions in order to cope with whatever problem they face – as compared to the set of actions that an omniscient observer would be able to conceive of; or, finally, when they have only a blurred and changing understanding of what their goals and preferences are.

It is straightforward that learning, so defined, is a ubiquitous characteristic of most economic and – generally – social environments, with the remarkable exception of those postulated by the most extreme forms of economic modelling, such as those assuming rational expectations (RE) or canonical game-theoretic equilibria. But, even in the latter cases (and neglecting any issues about the empirical realism of the underlying assumptions), it is natural to ask how agents learned in the first place about – for example – the 'true model' of the world in an RE set-up, or the extensive form of a particular game. And, moreover, in the widespread case of multiple equilibria, how do agents select among them (i.e. how do they learn how to converge onto one of them)?

Of course, learning acquires even greater importance in explicitly *evolutionary* environments (which we believe are indeed the general case), where a) heterogeneous agents systematically display various forms of 'bounded rationality'; b) there is a repeated appearance of novelties, both as exogenous shocks and, more importantly, as the result of technological,

[1] Support for this research from the International Institute of Applied Systems Analysis (IIASA – Laxenburg, Austria), the Italian National Research Council (CNR) and the Italian Ministry of Research ('MURST, Progetti 40%') is gratefully acknowledged. The authors benefited from comments on earlier drafts by Giovanna Devetag, Daniel Friedman, Luigi Orsenigo, Oliver Williamson and the participants in the Schumpeter Society conference, Stockholm, 2–5 June 1996, and from the lectures given by one of them at the University of Paris I in May 1996.

behavioural and organizational innovations by the agents themselves; c) markets (and other interaction arrangements) perform as selection mechanisms; d) aggregate regularities are primarily emergent properties stemming from out-of-equilibrium interactions (more detailed discussions are in Dosi and Nelson, 1994, Nelson, 1995, and Coriat and Dosi, 1998).

The purpose of this chapter is to present a sort of selective guide to an enormous and diverse literature on learning processes in economics insofar as they capture at least some of the foregoing evolutionary aspects. Clearly, this cannot be a thorough survey. Rather, we shall just refer to some examples of each *genre*, trying to show their links and differences, setting them against a hypothetical ideal framework of 'what one would like to understand about learning'. This will also permit easier mapping of a wide and largely unexplored research agenda. A significant emphasis will be put on learning *models*, in their bare-bone formal structure, but we shall always refer to the (generally richer) non-formal theorizing about the same objects.

Needless to say, we are exclusively concerned here with *positive* (i.e. descriptive) theories of learning: standard 'rational choice' models might well go a longer way as *normative* tools.

In section 2 we set the scene for the discussion that follows by reference to the usual decision-theoretic archetype, briefly outlining many compelling reasons why one needs to go well beyond it in order to account for most learning processes. Once we do that, however, a pertinent and unified – albeit probably irrelevant – paradigm is lost. Learning happens in different cognitive and behavioural domains, has different objects, and most likely occurs through somewhat different processes. Relatedly, we propose that a few basic empirical regularities on cognition, decision making and learning stemming from disciplines outside economics – ranging from cognitive psychology to sociology – should be among the 'building blocks' of an emerging theory of agency (section 3). Some taxonomic exercises are a useful introductory device; these we present in section 4. A taxonomy of learning dynamics, and the restrictions on its domain, helps in grouping and assessing various classes of learning models. In particular, a useful distinction appears to be whether one retains some elements of Savage's original 'small world assumption' (Savage, 1954) – in essence, the idea of a finite list of objects exhaustively present from the start in the 'heads' of learning agents. This is the case of learning representations through 'evolutionary games' and other mechanisms of adaptation via environmental reinforcement. Conversely, lower restrictions on the domain of learning and on the dimensionality of the state space may well entail *open-ended* evolutionary dynamics involving not only adaptation but also the discovery and emergence of novelty; in section 5 we compare different formal approaches in these various veins.

The general thrust of the argument, there and throughout this work, is that learning crucially entails cognitive activities of construction and the modification of mental models and behavioural patterns hardly reducible to well-defined problems of choice under imperfect information and probabilizable risk.

Some achievements and limitations of current learning models within this perspective and a few other broad topics of investigation – such as the relationship between learning and selection in evolutionary models, the possible tension between individual and collective learning, and the specificity of organizational learning – are outlined in section 6.

2   Beyond 'rational choice' and Bayesian learning: some preliminaries

As is well known, the standard decision-theoretic model depicts agency (and, *in primis*, economic agency) as a problem of choice where rational actors select, among a set of alternative courses of action, the one that will produce (in their expectation) the maximum outcome as measured against some utility yardstick. In that, agents are postulated to know the entire set of possible events of 'nature', all possible actions that are open to them, and all notional outcomes of the mapping between actions and events – or, at least, come to know them after some learning process. Clearly, these are quite demanding assumptions on knowledge embodied in or accessible to the agents – which hardly apply to complex and changing environments. In fact, they *cannot* apply, almost by definition, in all environments where innovations of some kind are allowed to occur – irrespective of whether they relate to technologies, behavioural repertoires or organizational arrangements; as Kenneth Arrow has been reminding us for some time, if an innovation is truly an innovation it could not have been in the set of events that all agents were able to contemplate before the innovation actually occurred . . .

Moreover, equally demanding are the implicit assumptions concerning the *procedural rationality* involved in the decision process. As a paradigmatic illustration, take the usual decision-theoretic sequence leading from 1) representation/'understanding' of the environment (conditional on whatever 'information' is available) to 2) evaluation/judgement, 3) choice, 4) actions and – ultimately – 5) consequences – determined, for example, by the stochastic pairing of actions and 'events of nature' and/or actions by other agents.

We argue at some greater length elsewhere (Dosi et al., 1999) that, in order for this 'rationalist' view to hold, at least two assumptions are crucial.

First, the linearity of that sequence must strictly hold. That is, one must rule out the possibility of reversing, so to speak, the procedural sequence. For example, one cannot have preferences and representations that adapt to an action that has already been undertaken, and, likewise, one must assume that consequences do not influence preferences (i.e. preferences are not endogenous).

Second, at each step of the process agents must be endowed with, or be able to build, the appropriate algorithm in order to tackle the task at hand – be it representing the environment, evaluating alternatives, choosing courses of action, or whatever.

There are some rather compelling reasons why these assumptions may, in fact, be a misleading starting point for any *positive* theory of learning and choice.

2.1   Complexity and procedural rationality

On purely theoretical grounds, computability theory provides some sort of dividing line between problems that are solvable by means of general recursive procedures in non-exponential times and problems that are not (for discussions and some results, see Lewis, 1985a, 1985b, Casti, 1992, Andersen, 1994, Dosi and Egidi, 1991, and Dosi et al., 1999). It is plausible to use such criteria to establish the *upper bound* of the complexity of the problems, for which the theory is allowed to assume that the agents 'naturally' possess the appropriate problem-solving algorithm (or are able to access it in finite time). It happens, however, that many decision tasks within and outside the economic domain fall outside this category (Lewis, 1986, Dosi et al., 1999).

We do not mean to overemphasize this point. After all, human agents tackle every day, with varying degrees of success, highly complex and 'hard' problems (in the sense of computability theory). However, we do claim that the understanding of how and when they happen to do it is a major challenge for any theory of cognition and learning, which cannot be written out by assuming that agents embody from the start a notionally unbounded procedural rationality[2]. Note that all this equally applies to the 'procedural rationality' of both decision processes and of

---

[2] In this respect, the reader might notice that the view suggested here tends to imply a somewhat more radical departure from fully 'rational' theories of decision than Herbert Simon's ground-breaking works on 'bounded rationality' (Simon, 1976, 1981, 1988), in that it does not only demand a constructive theory of the procedures themselves by

learning. The 'rationality' of the latter implies the availability of some inferential machinery able to extract the 'correct' information from environmental signals (Bayes' rule being one of them, and possibly also the most demanding, in terms of what the agents must know from the start about alternative hypotheses on what the world 'really is'). But, again, our foregoing argument implies that such an inferential machinery cannot be postulated innocently. Indeed, outside the rather special domain of 'small worlds' the structure of which is known *ex ante* to the agents, a few impossibility theorems from computation theory tell us that a generic inferential procedure does not and cannot exit (more on this point in Dosi and Egidi, 1991, Dosi et al., 1999, and Binmore, 1990).

What has been said so far mainly implies restrictions on the applicability of the canonical 'rational' account of learning and decision making. The bottom line is that the demands it makes in terms of the a priori knowledge of the environment and 'algorithmic endowments' of the agents cannot be met, *even in principle*, except for the simplest decision problems.

But, then, how do we theoretically depict agency and learning?

2.2   'As . . . if' interpretations of rational behaviour

One possible strategy basically involves a continuing commitment to 'rational' micro-foundations of economic interactions, together with a radical redefinition of the status of rationality assumptions themselves.

'Rationality' (however defined), rather than being an approximation to the empirical behaviour of purposeful and cognitively quite sophisticated agents, is assumed to be – so to speak – an 'objective' property of behaviours in equilibrium. Add the presumption that (most) observed behaviours are indeed *equilibrium* ones. And, finally, postulate some dynamics of individual adaptation or intra-population selection leading there. What one gets is some version of the famous 'as . . . if' hypothesis, suggested by Milton Friedman (1953) and rejuvenated in different fashions by more recent efforts to formalize learning/adaptation processes the outcome of which is precisely the 'rationality' assumed from the start (archetypical examples of this faith can be found in Sargent, 1993, and Marimon, 1997).

A thorough and critical discussion of the 'as . . . if' epistemology has been put forward by Sidney Winter in various essays (e.g. Winter, 1971), to which we refer the interested reader (see also Silverberg, 1988, Andersen, 1994, and Hodgson, 1988).

---

which agents develop their representations and action rules but it allows the possibility of persistently incoherent procedures. There is more on this later.

For our purposes here let us just note the following.

(i) Any 'as . . . if' hypothesis on rationality, taken seriously, is bound to involve quite a few restrictions similar to those briefly overviewed earlier with reference to more 'constructive' notions of rational behaviours, simply transposed into a more 'ecological' dimension – be it the 'ecology' of minds, ideas, organizations, populations, or whatever. That is, canonical rationality, *stricto sensu*, postulates that one decides and acts by purposefully using the appropriate procedures, or by learning them in purposeful, procedurally coherent ways. 'As . . . if' hypotheses of any kind apparently relax the demands on what agents must consciously know about the environment, their goals and the process of achieving them, but at the same time must assume some background mechanism that generates the available alternatives – *which must include the 'correct' ones*. However, without any further knowledge of the specific mechanisms, such a possibility remains a very dubious short cut, and it is utterly unlikely when there are infinite alternatives that ought to be scanned.

(ii) While 'realistic' interpretations of rationality put most of the burden of explanation upon the power of inbuilt cognition, 'as . . . if' accounts shift it to selection dynamics – no matter whether driven by behavioural reinforcements, like salivating Pavlovian dogs, or by differential reproduction of traits within populations[3]. But, then, supporters of the view ought to show, at the very least, that robust convergence properties are demonstrated by some *empirically justifiable* selection dynamics. In our view, as it stands, nothing like that is in sight. On the contrary, except for very special set-ups, negative results are abundant in, for example, evolutionary games or other forms of decentralized interactions. No matter whether applied to biology or economics, path dependency cannot easily be disposed of; cyclical limit behaviours might occur (see Posch, 1994, and Kaniovski et al., 1996), etc. And all this appears even before accounting for environments that are genuinely evolutionary in the sense that novelties can emerge over time.

---

[3] Note incidentally that the outcomes of purely 'Pavlovian' – i.e. reinforcement-driven, consciously blind – and 'Bayesian' – apparently sophisticated and rational – dynamics can be shown to be sometimes asymptotically equivalent (the reviews in Suppes, 1995a and 1995b, develop much older intuitions from behaviourist psychology – e.g. Bush and Mosteller, 1955). However, in order for that equivalence to hold, reinforcements must operate in the same direction as the Bayesian inferential machinery – which is a hard demand to make indeed. The so-called condition of 'weak monotonicity' in the dynamics of adjustment that one generally finds in evolutionary games is a necessary, albeit not sufficient, condition to this effect. Moreover, it is a subtle question with regard to the interpretative value that one should attribute to asymptotic results: what do they tell us about finite time properties of empirical observations? We come back briefly to this issue later.

Of course, the 'as . . . if' theoretical enterprise in its wildest formulation does not set any falsification challenge for itself. Any kind of observation-based discipline on behavioural assumptions tends to be contemptuously dismissed as 'ad hoc'. Thus, the question 'what do people do and how do they learn' is generally transformed into another one, namely 'given whatever behaviour, and knowing that, *of course* (?!), such a behaviour is an equilibrium one, how can I – the theorist – rationalize it as the outcome of some adaptive process?' (Dr Pangloss, theologians and Marxist-Leninists would not have any problem with such an exercise . . .)

2.3   Bounded rationality

Another major perspective maintains that cognitive and behavioural assumptions have to keep some empirical foundations, and thus, when needed, account for constraints on memory, on the maximum levels of complexity of problem-solving algorithms and on computational time. It is, in a broad sense, the *bounded rationality* approach, pioneered by the work of Simon (best encapsulated, perhaps, in Simon, 1986) and developed in quite different fashions in, for example, organizational studies (starting with March and Simon, 1958, and Cyert and March, 1992); evolutionary theories (building on Nelson and Winter, 1982; see also Dosi et al., 1988, Andersen, 1994, and Hodgson, 1993); and 'evolutionary games' (for a rather technical overview, see Weibull, 1995). For insightful remarks on bounded rationality and games in general, see Kreps (1996), and also in otherwise quite orthodox macroeconomics see, for example, Sargent (1993)[4]. Again, this is not the place to undertake any review of this vast literature. However, a few comments are required.

Necessarily, the very idea of 'bounds' on rationality implies that, at least in finite time, agents so represented fall short of full *substantively rational* behaviour, the latter involving – among other things – a) a full knowledge of all possible contingencies; b) an exhaustive exploration of the entire decision tree; and c) a correct appreciation of the utility evaluations of all mappings between actions, events and outcomes (Simon, 1986, 1988).

Given that, a first issue concerns the characterization of the origins and nature of the 'boundedness' itself. It is not at all irrelevant whether it relates mainly to limitations on the memory that agents carry over from the past, or to algorithmic complexity, or to a limited ability of defining preferences over (expected) outcomes, or whatever. Alternatively, and

---

[4] Note, however, that in some interpretations – including Sargent's and others discussed in section 4 – boundedly rational behaviours are considered mainly insofar as they entail convergence to some pre-defined equilibrium outcomes. Hence, they turn out in the end to be primarily instrumental building blocks of some dynamics vindicating, in the intentions of the proponents, an 'as . . . if' story.

more radically, couldn't it be due to the fact that agents get it basically wrong (in terms of representation of the environment, etc.)?

Here the theory faces a subtle but crucial crossroads. One alternative (unfortunately found all too often in economic models, and especially – but not only – in game theory) is to select the bounded rationality assumptions with extreme casualness, suspiciously well fitted both to the mathematics the author knows and to the results he wants to obtain. We have no problem in aligning ourselves with those who denounce the 'adhockery' of this procedure. The other alternative entails the acknowledgement of an *empirical discipline* on the restrictions one puts upon the purported rationality of the agents. No doubt we want to advocate here the scientific soundness of this procedure, notwithstanding the inevitable 'phenomenological' diversity of cognitive and behavioural representations that one is likely to get. That is, whether and how 'rationality is bounded' is likely to depend on the nature of the decision problem at hand, the context in which the decision maker is placed, the pre-existing learning skills of the agents, etc. Taxonomical exercises are inevitable, with their seemingly clumsy reputation. But, in a metaphor inspired by Keith Pavitt, this is a bit like the comparison of Greek to modern chemistry. The former, based on the symmetry of just four elements, was very elegant, but grounded in underlying philosophical principles that were utterly irrelevant and, from what we know nowadays, essentially wrong. The latter is clumsy, taxonomic and for a long time (until the advent of quantum mechanics) lacking in underlying foundations, but it is undeniably descriptively and operationally more robust.

A second major issue is with regard to *procedural* rationality. Granted the bounds on 'substantive' rational agency, as defined above, when and to what extent should one maintain any assumption of coherent purposefulness and logical algorithmic consistency on the part of the agents[5]? In a first approximation, Simon's approach suggests such a theoretical commitment (associated as it is with major contributions to the identification of *constructive* procedures for learning and problem solving in this vein; see Newell and Simon, 1972, and Simon, 1976). However, even procedural consistency might not be a generic property of empirical agents at all (including, of course, us!). A lot of evidence from most social disciplines also seems to point in this direction (this discussion is picked up again later).

---

[5] Note that procedural rationality requires all the 'linearity assumptions' mentioned above (ruling out, for example, state-dependent preferences) and also consistent search heuristics (allowing, for example, assessment rules along any decision tree that, at least in probability, lead in the 'right' direction).

Third, and relatedly, the very notion of 'bounded rationality' commits from the start to an implicit idea that 'full rationality' is the underlying yardstick for comparison. In turn, this implies the possibility of identifying some metrics upon which 'boundedness' and, dynamically, learning efforts can be measured and assessed. In quite a few circumstances this can be achieved fruitfully[6], but in others it might not be possible either in practice or even in principle. In particular, this applies to search and learning in complex functional spaces (as many problems within and outside the economic arena commonly do)[7]. And, of course, this is also the case of most problems involving the discovery of and/or adaptation to novelty.

Since these features are highly typical of evolutionary environments, an implication is that one might need to go well beyond a restricted notion of 'bounded rationality', characterized simply as an imperfect approximation to a supposedly 'full' one – which, in these circumstances, one is even unable to define precisely.

But then, again, how *does* one represent learning agents in these circumstances?

3   'Stylized facts' from cognitive and social sciences as building blocks of evolutionary theories of learning

Our somewhat radical suggestion is that evolutionary theories ought to make a much greater and more systematic use of the evidence from other cognitive and social sciences as sort of 'building blocks' for the hypotheses on cognition, learning and behaviours that one adopts. We fully realize that such a perspective almost inevitably entails the abandonment of any invariant axiomatics of decision and choice. But, to paraphrase R. Thaler (1992), this boils down again to the alternative between being 'vaguely right' or 'precisely wrong': we certainly advocate the former (however, compare Marimon, 1997, for a sophisticated contrary view).

In this respect, the discussion of *routines* as foundational behavioural assumptions of evolutionary models in Nelson and Winter (1982) is an excellent example of the methodology we have in mind, unfortunately not pursued enough in subsequent evolutionary studies (for a discussion of the state of the art in this field, see Cohen et al., 1996).

---

[6] Promising results stem from a better understanding of the formal structure of problem-solving heuristics (see, for example, Pearl, 1984, and Vassilakis, 1995, and – in a suggestive, experimentally based instance – Cohen and Bacdayan, 1994, and Egidi, 1996). See also below.

[7] For example, in Dosi et al., 1994, we consider quantity and price setting as cases in point.

There are, however, many other fields that a positive theory of learning in economics can draw on, ranging from cognitive and social psychology all the way to anthropology and the sociology of knowledge.

3.1   Cognitive categories and problem solving

A crucial aspect of learning is with regard to *cognition* – that is, the process by which decision makers form and modify representations in order to make some sense of a reality that is generally too complex and uncertain to be fully understood. Hence the necessity to acknowledge the existence (and persistence) of a systematic gap between the agent's cognitive abilities and 'reality' (were there an omniscient observer able to grasp it fully). Such a gap can take at least two, often interrelated, forms[8]: first, a *knowledge gap*, involving incomplete, fuzzy or simply wrong representations of the environment; and, second, a *problem-solving* gap between the complexity of the tasks agents face and their capabilities with respect to accomplishing them.

Regarding both, evolutionary theories of learning might significantly benefit from that branch of cognitive studies concerned with the nature and changes of *categories and mental models* (for different perspectives, see Johnson-Laird, 1983, 1993, Lakoff, 1987, Holland et al., 1986, and Margolis, 1987, and for the presentation of a few alternative theories see Mayer, 1992). It is crucial to notice that, if one accepts any 'mental model' view, learning cannot be reduced to information acquisition (possibly including Bayesian processing of it) but rather is centred around the construction of new cognitive categories and 'models of the world'. Few studies in economics have explicitly taken this road: one of them is the promising attempt in Tordjman (1996) to interpret the dynamics of financial markets in this framework (see also Marengo and Tordjman, 1996, and Palmer et al., 1994).

In turn, robust evidence shows that cognitive categories are not clearcut constructions with sharp boundaries, put together in fully consistent interpretative models. Rather, they seem to display (in all our minds!) blurred contours, shaded by an intrinsic fuzziness, held around some cognitively guiding 'prototypes', and organized together in ill-structured systems kept operational only via a lot of default hierarchies (on all those points, see Lakoff, 1987, Holland et al., 1986, Tversky and

---

[8] Heiner (1983) introduces a similar concept, which he calls the 'C-D (competence-difficulty) gap'. In his definition, such a gap reflects the agent's imperfect ability to process correctly the available information and act reliably. Heiner's C-D gap does not properly belong to the realm of cognitive gaps, but, rather, it captures their behavioural consequences.

Kahneman, 1982, Kahneman and Tversky, 1986, Griffin and Tversky, 1992, Marengo, 1996, Margolis, 1987, Marengo and Tordjman, 1996, and Einhorn and Hogarth, 1985)[9].

3.2   Framing and social embeddedness

Cognitive categories, it has been repeatedly shown, go together with various mechanisms of *framing*, by which information is interpreted and also rendered operationally meaningful to the decision makers (see Kahneman et al., 1982, Borcherding et al., 1990, and March, 1994).

Indeed, frames appear to be a ubiquitous feature of both decision making and learning. What one understands is filtered by the cognitive categories that one holds, and the repertoires of elicited problem-solving skills depend on the ways the problem itself is framed. That is, framing effects occur along all stages of the decision-making process – affecting representations, judgements and the selection of behaviours (see Kahneman et al., 1982, and, concerning the patterns of activation of experts' skills, Ericsson and Smith, 1991).

As James March (1994, p. 14) puts it,

[d]ecisions are framed by beliefs that define the problem to be addressed, the information that must be collected, and the dimensions that must be evaluated. Decision makers adopt paradigms to tell themselves what perspective to take on a problem, what questions should be asked, and what technologies should be used to ask the questions. Such frames focus attention and simplify analysis. They direct attention to different options and different preferences. A decision will be made in one way if it is framed as a problem of maintaining profits and in a different way if it is framed as a problem of maintaining market share. A situation will lead to different decisions if it is seen as being about 'the value of innovation' rather than 'the importance of not losing face'.

Note that, in this view, 'frames' include a set of (not necessarily consistent) beliefs over 'what the problem is' and the goals that should be achieved in that case; cognitive categories deemed to be appropriate to the problem; and a related menu of behavioural repertoires.

Moreover, framing mechanisms appear at different levels of cognitive and behavioural observation: they do so in rather elementary acts of judgement and choice, but are also a general organizing principle of

---

[9] 'Prototypization' is easy to understand intuitively: you would give a sparrow rather than a penguin as an example of what a bird is . . . But, with that, it is also easier to understand the basic ambiguity of borderlines, fuzziness and categorical attributions by default. How should one treat a duck-billed platypus? As a mammal? Or should one create a separate category – that of ovoviviparous? A discussion of these issues bearing on economic judgements and behaviours is in Tordjman (1996).

social experience and collective interactions (Bateson, 1972, Goffman, 1974).

One can also intuitively appreciate the links between framing processes and the *social embeddedness* of both cognition and action[10].

Frames – in the broad definition given above – have long been recognized in the sociological and anthropological literature (whatever name is used to refer to them) as being grounded in the collective experience of the actors and in the history of the institutions in which the agency is nested[11].

Indeed, embeddedness seems to go a strikingly long way and affect even the understanding and use of cognitively basic categories, such as that of causality and the very processes by which humans undertake basic operations such as inferences, generalizations, deductions, etc. (Lakoff, 1987, Luria, 1976).

3.3   Heuristics in judgement and learning

We mentioned above the issue of *procedural coherence* in decision making and learning (which, to repeat, is a quite separate one from the sophistication – in terms of memory and computing power – of the procedures themselves). An overwhelming body of evidence points to the widespread use by empirical agents of *heuristics*, which may well lead to systematic biases in judgements and action choices compared to the predictions of 'rational' decision-theoretic models (see Kahneman et al., 1982, and also Kahneman and Tversky, 1986, Slovic et al., 1989, Borcherding et al., 1990, Thaler, 1992, and Shafir and Tversky, 1992).

Broadly defined, heuristics are methods, rules or criteria guiding – for example – representation, judgement or action, and they include simple rules of thumb but also much more sophisticated methods explicitly evoking the use of mental categories.

It is impossible to provide here any thorough account of the findings in this area (the classic reference is Kahneman et al., 1982). Let us just recall heuristics such as *representativeness* (i.e. evaluating whatever observation in terms of distance from some prototype or modal case)[12], *availability*

---

[10] On the notion of 'social embeddedness' from contemporary economic sociology, see Granovetter (1985) and several contributions in Smelser and Swedberg (1994). There is also a discussion quite germane to the argument developed here in Tordjman (1996).

[11] Within an enormous volume of literature, a good deal of the sociological tradition has been influenced by the works of Talcott Parson or of the classic Pierre Bourdieu (1977); in anthropology, among others, see the discussions of 'embeddedness' by Karl Polanyi (1944, 1957) and Clifford Geertz (1963); see also Robert Edgerton (1985).

[12] Tordjman (1996) discusses speculative expectations in this light.

(i.e. 'what is primarily in your mind is what is in your sight'), and *anchoring* (the initial conditions, related either to the way the problem is posed or to how the experience of the agent influences the final judgement). Other observed phenomena – touching, togetherness, representations, choices and the perceived utility of the latter – include *status quo biases* (entailing, for choice under risk, risk aversion for gains and risk seeking for losses – as formalized by Kahneman and Tversky through 'prospect theory'); *overconfidence* and the *illusion of control* (associated with the overestimation of one's own capabilities and the neglect of potentially relevant outside information[13]); and, more generally, systematic 'incoherence' vis-à-vis any canonical model of utility-based decision under uncertainty.

Note that all these cognitive and behavioural regularities apply both to decisions (taken once and for all) *and learning processes* (for example, representativeness heuristics leads to learning patterns at odds with Bayesian predictions; and illusion of control is likely to entail information censuring and escalating commitments in the face of unfavourable outcomes).

It is straightforward that those cognitive and behavioural patterns openly conflict with 'procedural rationality' – which, as mentioned earlier, is a fundamental and necessary condition for a standard decision-theoretic account of agency.

It is also remarkable that the foregoing evidence has been drawn to a considerable extent from experiments that are simple enough to provide a corresponding 'correct' decision-theoretic answer (i.e. procedurally coherent, making the best use of the available information and in accordance with some supposedly basic preference axioms)[14]. And, in fact, much emphasis has been placed on the *biases* that all this entails, as measured against the canonical normative yardstick. However, together with such (crucial) exercises of empirical falsification, our impression is that not enough has been done in terms of the development of *alternative theories of cognition and action* (Kahneman and Tversky's 'prospect theory'

---

[13] See Kahneman and Lovallo (1993) and Dosi and Lovallo (1997).

[14] Incidentally, an issue that is seldom raised, and that – unfortunately – we shall not be able to discuss here either, is whether the 'rationality' of decision and learning is assessed *procedurally* at each elicited step of the process or whether it is 'black-boxed' and just evaluated in terms of the coherence of final (expected utilities/revealed preferences) outcomes. It is a matter bearing some resemblance both to the 'as . . . if' discussion and also to entrenched debates in psychology between 'behaviourist' and 'cognitivist' views (whether 'strong', *à la* Chomsky, or much weaker ones, *à la* Johnson-Laird or Lakoff). We do not profess the arrogant casualness by which some practitioners of economics switch from one to the other. However, just note that the experimental results on heuristics etc. are equally damaging for the defences of standard rationality in *both* views. So, for example, one finds that not only 'cognitive incoherence' but also revealed behaviours might well display the 'pessimization' (!) as opposed to the 'maximization' of utility (Herrnstein and Prelec, 1991).

being one of the few exceptions in the wider picture). More than that: it might well be that so-called 'biases' emerging in relatively simple decision set-ups could be revealing clues about cognition and behaviour in all other genuinely evolutionary circumstances that are common to human decision makers (whether individuals or organizations). After all, pushing it to the extreme, the collective evolution of human cultures has not been drawn from repeated trials on lotteries but on quite diverse experiences that have in common, nonetheless, *uniqueness* features, out of which our cognition and beliefs had to make some precarious sense – ranging from the various threats in the forest to the deaths of the relatives, from unexpected violence by kinsfolk to the discovery of fire[15].

3.4   Endogenous preferences

The separation here from the previous point is somewhat arbitrary; indeed, the aforementioned heuristics and behavioural patterns often entail preferences that are state-dependent. *Status quo* biases are a case to the point: the reference is not some invariant utility – however defined – but '. . . where I was, what I had, etc., at time t minus one . . .'[16]. Moreover, as has been shown, the framing of the problem shapes revealed preferences (a vast amount of literature in the field of marketing points in this direction, but particularly relevant experiments are to be found in Kahneman et al. (1990) and, in connection with authority relations, in Milgram (1974).

Endogenous preference may often be driven by attempts to reduce regret and cognitive dissonance (see Festinger, 1957): that is, as it is put jokingly in Dosi and Metcalfe (1991), citing a pop song from the 1960s, 'if you can't be with the one you love, love the one you're with!' Finally, of course, endogeneity of preference is likely to stem from social imitation and other forms of social interactions (such as Veblenian 'conspicuous consumption' and 'snob effects', etc.; an early discussion is in Leibenstein, 1950)[17].

---

[15] To the best of our (limited) knowledge, one of the few exploratory attempts to account positively for 'rational biases' as crucial clues to cognitive patterns is to be found in Margolis, 1987. Sharing the idea that they should not simply be dismissed as pathologies (see Tordjman, 1996), in another work (Dosi and Lovallo, 1997) it is suggested that they could indeed provide a crucial *collective* evolutionary role, at least with regard to a particular bias – i.e. overconfidence and illusion of control. See also below.

[16] Which, of course, is in open violation of any standard, utility-based decision-theoretic approach, whereby preferences are supposed to be defined on levels and not history-dependent variations and, moreover, are supposed to change on a time scale that is significantly longer than the decisions and random occurrences of 'nature'.

[17] In economics, empirical studies of preference formation were a lively field of investigation in the 1950s and 1960s (see Katona, 1951, 1968), but they were pushed aside

3.5   Collective beliefs, behaviours and learning

What has been said so far about cognition, judgement, etc. applies in principle also to all set-ups where individual agents may be assumed, in a first approximation, to act as insulated entities (notwithstanding, of course, the whole experience of socialization that they carry with them). Other circumstances, however, are explicitly and immediately social; decision making by multiple actors, such as that required by 'teams', economic organizations and other institutions, belong to this group (for a thorough discussion, see March, 1988a, 1988b and 1994).

Once more, it would be futile to try to review the enormous quantity of publications in the field. Let us just offer a few comments.

First, the evidence suggests that, if anything, collective decision making rather than curbing the judgemental 'biases' mentioned earlier (say, via some equivalent of a 'law of large numbers') tends, on the contrary, to reinforce them (Lovallo, 1996; March, 1994).

Second, the 'opaqueness' of the relationship between beliefs, behaviours and outcomes undermines the usefulness of representing multi-actor choice in terms of the canonical, linear, sequence outlined at the beginning of section 2. Rather, the general case seems to fit quite well the observation of Purkitt and Dyson (1990, p. 363), who – describing the decision process during the Cuban missile crisis – note the general lack of 'explicit linkages between information, a sense of the problem and problem responses' (!). On the contrary, the archetypical decision process – and, dynamically, the archetypical learning process – might fit quite well the *garbage can* model (Cohen et al., 1972). That is (p. 200),

in a garbage can process, it is assumed that there are no exogenous, time-dependent arrivals of choice opportunities, problems, solutions, and decision-makers. Problems and solutions are attached to choices, and thus to each other, not because of any means-ends linkage but because of their temporal proximity. At the limit, for example, almost any solution can be associated to almost any problem – provided they are evoked at the same time.

Third, multiple (and possibly conflicting) beliefs, goals and identities are likely to entail systematic decision inconsistencies, while learning and adaptation in these circumstances may well 'path-dependently' strengthen these inconsistencies themselves (March, 1988a, 1994).

by a new generation of believers in expected utility theory. Among the few contemporary discussions and formal models dealing with these issues in economics see March (1988a, 1988b), Akerlof and Dickens (1982), Kuran (1991) and Brock and Durlauf (1995).

All this applies, only even more so, in the presence of multiple objectives of individual organizational members and of the organization as a whole. (A related and more detailed discussion is in Dosi, 1995a.)

3.6   *Rules, organizational routines and competencies*

More generally, the issue of *organizational learning* involves the understanding of the processes by which organizational *rules* and *action patterns*[18] change over time. Here, the relevant evidence coming from organizational studies – albeit far from 'clean' and unequivocal – points to organizations as being rather inertial behavioural entities, which are, nonetheless, able to change (path-dependently), either under the pressures of external adversities or internal conflicts (see, from an immense range of published material, March and Simon, 1958, March, 1988a, Nelson and Winter, 1982, and Levinthal, 1996b, 1996a). A particularly important analytical task, in this respect, concerns the identification of the nature of *organizational routines* (i.e. recurring, often complex, rather automatic action patterns, set in an organizational context) and their changes; in our view, the discovery, establishment and modification of routines are indeed an essential part of organizational learning (on all these issues, see Cohen et al., 1996). Routines, in this perspective, store and reproduce a good deal of the problem-solving competencies of the organization and, together, its acquired patterns of governance of potentially conflicting interests among its members (Nelson and Winter, 1982; Coriat and Dosi, 1995).

3.7   *Towards an 'evolutionary' view of agency and learning?*

There are deep linkages among the findings, conjectures and 'stylized facts' that we have telegraphically mentioned so far. In fact, we would dare to suggest that eventually they may fit well together into an 'evolutionary' view of agency and learning, still to come. Some basic features, however, can be appreciated already[19].

---

[18] Note that the two might not correspond at all, if by 'rules' one means the explicitly stated operating procedures of organization, and 'action patterns' are what members of the organization actually do in practice.

[19] We call it an 'evolutionary view' because it is consistent with the evolutionary research programme as it is emerging in economics. Similar views, defined from the perspective of other disciplines, might well take different labels. For example, what we label here as 'evolutionary' has considerable overlap with the research programmes on 'adaptive learning' and 'mental models' in cognitive psychology and artificial sciences. See also below.

As we see it, such a view is going to embody the following 'building blocks':

- Cognitive foundations focused on the dynamics of *categories* and *mental models*;
- *Heuristics* as quite general processes for decision and learning;
- *Context dependence*, and, relatedly, *social embeddedness* with regard both to interpretative models and decision rules;
- *Endogeneity* with respect to (possibly inconsistent) *goals* and *preferences*;
- *Organizations as behavioural entities* in their own right (the persistence and learning patterns of which undoubtedly also depend on what the members of the organization do and learn, but cannot at all be reduced to the latter)[20]; and
- Processes of *learning, adaptation* and *discovery* apt to guide representations and behaviours (imperfectly), including (or primarily?) in *ever-changing environments* (so that, even if one 'cannot bathe twice in the same river', one still tries to develop some robust representations of the river itself and some swimming heuristics).

It is easy to understand the radical divergence that this view entails vis-à-vis the canonical decision-theoretic one.

First, it abandons any 'small world' assumption; in fact, it is centred on a sort of *open world* postulate (one tries to make sense and survive in a world where there are many more things between heaven and earth than in anybody's philosophy – and, thus, one always has to face surprises). The clear downside of this perspective is that, *in practice and in principle*, neither the agents we want to describe nor the theorist (if not a god with an *infinitely* accurate knowledge of all possible histories[21]) might be able even to define what a 'rational' decision procedure is. The experimental evidence recalled above suggests, in fact, that most of us also depart from it when such procedures exist and are rather simple. To reiterate, however, these 'biases' might be precious symptoms of the ways we develop tentatively robust cognitive categories, search heuristics and decision rules in environments intrinsically characterized by knowledge gaps and problem-solving gaps. The upside is that one is also able to recombine cognitive categories in unlikely, highly conjectural *thought*

---

[20] In fact, in Dosi (1995a) we push the argument further and suggest that, for many purposes, *institutions rather than individual 'rationality' and preferences* ought to be considered as the *fundamentals* of the analysis.

[21] Note that this condition on infinitely perfect knowledge does not apply only to the case of genuinely evolutionary worlds; it holds also in all environments where the basic laws of motion are given and understood but exhibit non-linearities and sensitive dependence on initial conditions – such as chaotic dynamics (a few further remarks are in Dosi and Metcalfe, 1991, and the references therein).

experiments and, paraphrasing March et al. (1991), 'learn from samples of one or fewer'!

Second, the evolutionary view, as we see it, is not committed to any procedural consistency; rather than black-boxing the algorithms for cognition and action, it considers the understanding of their mistake-ridden development as a crucial analytical task.

Third, it implicitly acknowledges the failure – as a general *descriptive* theory – of the axiomatic route and undertakes the less elegant path of a *constructive theory*, almost inevitably tinted by phenomenological specifications and restrictions.

The challenges and enormous difficulties involved in this research programme on the 'evolutionary micro-foundations' of socio-economic change should be quite obvious to every reader. And these difficulties are compounded by the too frequent lack of robust taxonomies, models and generalizable 'process stories' from the social disciplines where one should find them (e.g. psychology, sociology, etc.). In fact, in an ideal perspective, an economist with evolutionary/institutionalist inclinations ought to be able to get there some 'level zero' first-approximation properties – concerning, for example, cognition, social adaptation, collective learning, etc. – in order to build his microeconomic assumptions[22]. Unfortunately, this too is rarely the case. Worse still, one has witnessed significant inroads by the canonical decision-theoretic axiomatics into the soft underbelly of many other social sciences (with the result that one finds childbearing, voting behaviour, drug addiction and – coming soon, no doubt – infibulation as the equilibrium results of forward-looking rational choices . . .)[23].

---

[22] A bit like, say, the relationship between physics and chemistry, whereby quantum physics provides – so to speak – the 'micro-foundations' of chemical laws; or, probably more pertinently, the relationship between chemistry and biology. While it is impossible to derive the notion of what a cow is just from the laws of chemistry, at the very least the description of a cow should be consistent with the latter, and, at best, the laws ought to provide 'level zero' bricks in a constructive theory of cows' development. For a fascinating discussion of the generative processes of different levels of biological organization, with some possible bearings on the issues of concern here, see Fontana and Buss (1994).

[23] It is impossible to discuss here the reasons for this phenomenon, which have to do, jointly, with the incumbent epistemological looseness of those disciplines; the apparent rigour, parsimoniousness on assumptions and generality of 'economic imperialism' (going back again to the strength of being rigorously wrong); and, last but not least, a social Zeitgeist that makes today 'intuitively obvious' an account of behaviours in terms of utility maximization in the way that it was grace/temptation/Divine Providence up to three centuries ago. (On the latter, Hirschman, 1965, presents a broad fresco on modern cultural history, which helps in putting Gary Becker and disciples into perspective; nearer to the disciplinary topics of this paper is Hodgson, 1988; more specifically, on the current interchanges between economic and sociology, see Barron and Hannan, 1994; a less concise outline of the views on these themes of one of the authors is in Dosi, 1995a.)

However it may be arrived at, the evolutionary research programme on agency and learning in economics cannot remain just as a user of 'stylized facts' and workable generalizations from other disciplines. Rather, it seems to us, it has become an urgent matter to put to the practitioners of other disciplines the backlog of puzzling questions that one faces when dealing with the micro-foundations of evolutionary processes, and possibly also acquire some of their investigative skills[24].

Rather than developing any comprehensive synthesis, it is useful to start, more modestly, from some basic taxonomical exercises.

4 Learning processes: some taxonomies and appreciative theories

It is tautological to say that learning has the precondition of knowing less than one notionally could. And, of course, the simplest representation of a learning process – familiar from anyone's economic training – is in terms of refinements of information partitions, or the updating of probability distributions, or estimations of parameters of some model, or statistically coherent comparisons among competing models, etc.

However, if one accepts the view of cognition and problem solving sketched above, one needs also to open up the 'procedural black box' and map different learning procedures into diverse types of problems and learning contexts. Let us consider them from a few, complementary, perspectives.

4.1 Substantive and procedural uncertainty

One angle from which to look at learning processes focuses on the levels of *cognitive* and *problem-solving complexity*, and the causes of this complexity.

It is useful to distinguish between two different, albeit interrelated, sets of causes that make problems 'hard' and that match our earlier distinction between knowledge gaps and problem-solving gaps. In general, knowledge gaps arise from the lack of isomorphism between the environment and the agent's model of it. This is what is called – in Dosi and Egidi (1991), paraphrasing Herbert Simon – *substantive uncertainty*. In turn, one may further distinguish between *weak* uncertainty (i.e. probabilizable

---

[24] The list of such questions is, obviously, very long: it includes, for example, possible invariance in individual and organizational learning processes, the nature and evolution of 'rules' for both cognition and action, and better specifications of the social embeddedness of individual behaviours. Regarding the interdisciplinary efforts we have in mind, the works by Cohen and Bacdayan (1994) and Egidi (1996) on routines and learning are good examples.

risk) and *strong* uncertainty, involving genuine ignorance and the intrinsic inadequacy of the mental models of the agents to capture fully the structure of the environment.

Conversely, problem-solving gaps entail different degrees of *procedural uncertainty*, with or without substantive uncertainty (an impressionistic taxonomy is presented in figure 9.1). The distinction is clear, for example, with reference to puzzles such as the Rubik cube. Here the structure of the problem is rather simple, the rules are known, and there is no substantive uncertainty: rather, solving the problem itself is the difficult task, involving relatively complex skills of sub-problem decomposition and sophisticated logical skills (Dosi and Egidi, 1991). Similar considerations apply to activities such as theorem proving, and – nearer to the economist's concerns – to many tasks associated with technological innovation, such as the design and implementation of new products and processes.

The distinction also helps to illuminate the somewhat different nature of the related learning processes. In the case of procedural uncertainty they concern primarily the development of problem-solving skills and heuristics.

Conversely, when the latter can be reduced to rather simple and well-understood algorithms, but uncertainty is primarily substantive, learning essentially concerns the representation and framing of the problem[25].

4.2   Learning and the 'logic of appropriateness'

We have already mentioned that, in most circumstances, knowledge gaps and problem-solving gaps are related.

First of all, they are likely to appear together in evolutionary environments; it is a logical assumption that the possibility that innovations will arrive continually implies 'strong' substantive uncertainty, but, relatedly, this implies a symmetric procedural uncertainty. (How can I cope with a changed environment? How can I, myself, innovate?)

Moreover, the psychological evidence shows that knowledge of the 'structure' of the problem and our problem-solving capabilities strongly influence each other: the way we perceive the structure of the problem depends largely on the kind of problem-solving skills we possess, and, conversely, the problem-solving skills we develop are shaped by the ways we frame the problem. (A germane discussion of the intertwining between a particular representation and a particular expertise is in Lane et al., 1996.)

---

[25] Note incidentally that the standard decision-theoretic tool kit handles essentially substantive uncertainty (in its 'weak' form) but is much less appropriate for dealing with learning in the case of problem-solving procedures.

Substantive uncertainty / Procedural uncertainty		Certainty	'Weak' uncertainty (risk)	'Strong' uncertainty
Certainty		Trivial maximization problems (e.g. choosing between winning or losing $1 with certainty!)	Lotteries and most other set-ups considered by standard theory of decision under uncertainty	
Procedural uncertainty	With finite decision trees	Puzzles such as the Rubik cube	Quite a few game-theoretic problems; relatively simple economic decisions in stationary environments	
	With infinite decision trees	Proving theorems; developing technological innovations on the grounds of known physical/chemical principles, etc.	Non-recursively computable games	Adaptation and innovation in an evolutionary environment

Figure 9.1 Substantive and procedural uncertainty: a taxonomy of problems

The phenomenon hints at a more general property of decision making and learning, which March has named the *logic of appropriateness*. As opposed to the archetypical decision process, based on the evaluation of alternatives in terms of the consequences for utilities (i.e. the 'logic of consequences'), in the appropriateness logic (March, 1994, pp. 57–58)

individuals and organizations fulfill identities, they follow rules or procedures that they see as appropriate to the situation . . . [while] neither preferences as they are normally conceived nor expectations of future consequences enter directly into the calculus . . .

Decision makers are imagined to ask (explicitly or implicitly) three questions:
1 – The question of *recognition:* what kind of situation is this?
2 – The question of *identity:* what kind of person am I? Or what kind of organization is this?
3 – The question of *rules:* what does a person such as I, or an organization such as this, do in a situation such as this?

Note that under the logic of appropriateness, so defined, an important part of learning is about the understanding and implementation of the appropriate rules, and – in a broader perspective – entails the coevolution of identities, representations and rules.

It is our belief that the logic of appropriateness does indeed inform a good deal of individual and organizational behaviour, and, to anticipate one of our conclusions, an urgent task ahead is to incorporate it formally into evolutionary theorizing.

4.3   Information, knowledge and learning[26]

Many contributors to contemporary evolutionary theory have drawn a fundamental distinction between *information* and *knowledge*. The former entails *well-stated and codified* propositions about a) the state of the world (e.g. 'it is raining'), b) properties of nature (e.g. 'A causes B'); c) the identities of the other agents ('I know Mr X and he is a crook') and d) explicit algorithms on how to do things[27]. Conversely, knowledge, in the definition we propose here, includes a) cognitive categories; b) the codes of interpretation of the information itself; c) tacit skills; and d) search and problem-solving heuristics that are irreducible to well-defined algorithms.

So, for example, the few hundred pages of demonstration for Fermat's last theorem would come under the heading of 'information'. Having said that, only some dozen mathematicians in the world have adequate *knowledge* to understand and evaluate it. On the other hand, a chimpanzee,

---

[26] This section is drawn largely from Dosi, 1995b.
[27] These four sets correspond quite closely to the codified aspects of Lundvall's taxonomy, distinguishing *know-what, know-why, know-who* and *know-how* (Lundvall, 1995).

facing those same pages of information, might just feel like eating them; and the vast majority of human beings would fall somewhere in between these two extremes[28]. . . Similarly, a manual on 'how to produce micro-processors' is 'information', while knowledge concerns the pre-existing ability of the reader to understand and implement the instructions contained therein. Moreover, in this definition knowledge includes tacit and rather automatic skills, such as operating a particular machine or correctly driving a car to overtake another one (without stopping first in order to solve the appropriate system of differential equations!).

Finally, it also includes 'visions' and ill-defined rules of search, such as those involved in most activities of scientific discovery, and in technological and organizational innovation (e.g. proving a *new* theorem, designing a *new* kind of car or figuring out the behavioural patterns of a *new* kind of crook who has appeared on the financial markets).

In this definition, knowledge is to varying degrees tacit, at the very least in the sense that the agent itself, and even a very sophisticated observer, would find it very hard to state explicitly the sequence of procedures by which information is coded, behavioural patterns are formed, problems are solved, etc.

In fact, as Winter (1987) suggests, varying degrees of tacitness together with other dimensions (see figure 9.2) provide a sort of interpretative grid by which to classify different types of knowledge.

In this perspective, learning has three interrelated meanings.

First, rather obviously, it might involve – as in the conventional view – the acquisition of more information (conditional on the ability of correctly interpreting it).

Second, it entails various forms of augmentation of knowledge *stricto sensu* (which might well be independent of any arrival of new pieces of information).

Third, it might concern the articulation and codification of previously tacit knowledge (learning here involves, so to speak, 'knowing better what you know').

---

[28] This argument largely overlaps with the so-called (post-Keynesian) Shackle-Vickers view, for which ignorance is a fact of economic life and is determined by the inability to know and fully understand the past and the present as well as the impossibility of foreseeing the future (see Shackle, 1955, 1969, and Vickers, 1986). The unexpected can – and most often does – occur, if anything because some aspects of the future are created by human action today (Davidson, 1996). This idea is at the core of Shackle's crucial experiment analysis: a crucial decision is one that changes the economic environment for ever so that identical conditions are never repeated. Such 'uniqueness' of a course of action is also stressed by Katzner (1990) with reference to firms' behaviour, and is strictly related to the notion of the irreversibility of decisions (see Lesourne, 1991).

| Tacit ----------- Articulable |
| Not teachable ---------- Teachable |
| Not articulated ---------- Articulated |

| Not observable in use ---------- Observable in use |

| Complex ---------- Simple |

| An element of a system ---------- Independent |

Figure 9.2 Taxonomic dimensions of knowledge assets
Source: Winter, 1987, p. 170.

In particular, this third aspect has recently sparked a lively debate about whether new information technologies accelerate the pace of codification and fundamentally upset the relative importance in contemporary economies between 'information' and 'tacit knowledge' (for different views on this point, see, for example, Foray and Lundvall, 1996, and several contributions therein, and Hicks, 1936).

4.4   *Appreciative theories of knowledge accumulation and innovation*

The levels of generality of most of what has been said so far – on decisions, knowledge, learning processes, etc. – place the argument very near major foundational issues on cognition and agency in evolutionary environments. However, a good deal of (highly complementary) efforts by evolution-inclined scholars has recently been devoted to empirically grounded 'appreciative' theories (to use the definition of Nelson and Winter, 1982), in particular in the fields of technological and organizational learning. As a result, within the broad field of the 'economics of innovation', one knows much more than, say, thirty years ago about the variety of processes by which knowledge is augmented and diffused in the economy; major contributions in this area include those of Christopher Freeman (1982, 1994), Nathan Rosenberg (1976, 1982, 1994), Keith Pavitt (1984), Richard Nelson (1987, 1993) and Paul David (1975, 1985).

A first broad property (which is probably not surprising for non-economists, though it has far-reaching analytical implications) is the diversity of learning modes and sources of knowledge across technologies and across sectors. For example, in some activities knowledge is accumulated primarily via informal mechanisms of 'learning by doing' and 'learning by interacting' with customers, suppliers, etc. In others it involves much more formalized search activities (such as those undertaken in

R&D laboratories). In some fields knowledge is mostly generated internally and is specific to particular applications. In others it draws much more directly upon academic research and scientific advances. Recent research suggests that this diversity of learning modes may be a major determinant of the diverse patterns of evolution in industrial structures (e.g. in terms of the distribution of firm sizes, the natality and mortality of firms, and corporate diversification).

An important step in the understanding of the 'anatomy' of contemporary systems of production and knowledge accumulation has involved taxonomic exercises (e.g. Pavitt, 1984) trying to map families of technologies and sectors according to their sources of innovative knowledge and their typical innovative procedures. At the same time, one has tried to identify possible invariance that holds across technologies, in the patterns of learning (notions such as 'technological paradigms', 'regimes' and 'technological trajectories' belong to this domain of analysis), and descriptive indicators for these same patterns (e.g. Dosi, 1984). Relatedly, variables such as the levels of 'innovative opportunity' associated with each technological paradigm, the degrees of 'cumulativeness' displayed by technical advances, etc. have turned out to be quite useful in interpreting the determinants of the particular 'trajectories' of innovation that one observes (Malerba and Orsenigo, 1996).

Second, in modern economies firms are major, albeit by no means unique, *repositories of knowledge*. Individual organizations embody specific ways of solving problems that are often very difficult to replicate in other organizations or even within the organization itself. In turn, organizational knowledge – as mentioned earlier – is stored to a considerable extent within the operating procedures ('the routines') and the higher-level rules (concerning, for example, 'what to do when something goes wrong', or 'how to change lower-level routines') that firms enact while handling their problem-solving tasks in the domains of production, research, marketing, etc.

Dynamically, technological knowledge is modified and augmented partly within individual firms and partly through the interaction with other firms (competitors, users, suppliers, etc.) and other institutions (universities, technical societies, etc.). In these domains, a growing body of literature on organizational capabilities and competencies has begun to explore the links between specific ensembles of organizational routines, types of organizational knowledge and corporate strategies (see Teece and Pisano, 1994, introducing a special issue of *Industrial and Corporate Change* on these topics; Lundvall, 1996; Winter, 1987, 1988; Montgomery, 1995; and also the somewhat more theoretical considerations in Dosi and Marengo, 1994).

Third, building upon the foregoing properties of the nature of technological learning and of the ways that organizations incorporate knowledge, a few scholars have started to explore an explicit coevolutionary view, whereby the accumulation of technological knowledge is shaped and constrained by the nature of the organizations and institutions where this knowledge demand originates, possibly triggering changes in corporate organizations and broader institutions (Nelson, 1994, Kogut, 1993, and Coriat and Dosi, 1995).

4.5   *From appreciative theories to formal models*

To what extent have formal theories been able to capture the foregoing 'stylized facts', taxonomies and historically grounded generalizations on collective learning?

In order to offer some answers, let us rephrase the earlier taxonomic intuitions into a language nearer to possible modelling translations.

Recall the canonical steps of decision processes mentioned at the beginning of this work (i.e. representation; judgement; choice; action; consequences). When accounting for learning, each of these steps defines some *state-space* of exploration. Accordingly, different classes of learning models can be distinguished with respect to the dimensions of the state-space in which learning occurs.

4.6   *Objects and state-spaces of learning processes*

What is learning about?

There are basically four classes of *objects of learning*: a) the 'state of the world' (as in games against nature); b) other agents' behaviours (as in strategic games); c) how to solve problems (where the object of learning is not forecasting but designing algorithms); and d) one's own preferences (i.e. agents learn, so to speak, about their own characteristics and identity).

Note, first, that a full-fledged evolutionary model (yet to come) ought to be able to account for all four classes, and – even better – generate empirically testable conjectures on the coupled dynamics among the different learning processes.

Second, it may well be that different objects of learning may also imply *different mechanisms of search and learning* (as far as we know, no robust generalization appears to be available on this issue; this is yet another question that needs to be sorted out with cognitive psychologists, sociologists, etc.).

This categorization of learning objects partially maps into a different formal representation of the dimensions of the state-space in which learning is generally assumed to occur, namely a) the space of representations or models of the world, b) the space of parameters within a given model, c) the space of actions, and d) the space of realized performance outcomes[29].

In the former case, learning is modelled as a search for *better* representations of the environment in which the agent is operating. Agents are supposed to hold models of the environment either explicitly (as, within psychology and artificial sciences, in rule-based models) or implicitly (as in connectionist models), and learning is defined as a structural modification (and not just the tuning of parameters) of the models themselves. Note that, in the expression 'better representation', *better* can have two very different meanings: it can either indicate better performing models – that is, yielding more effective action – or more knowledgeable models – that is, producing better predictions of the state of the environment. In the case where 'better' means 'better performing', the agent is assumed to adjust behaviours according only to the pay-offs he receives, and a completely wrong representation that by chance produces effective action in relation to the actually experienced states of the world has to be preferred to an 'almost' correct representation that, though being 'close' to the real model, produces less effective actions in some of the same states of the world. But a similar question also arises when 'better' means 'better predicting', both because – in a similar fashion – bad representations that produce good predictions are preferred to good representations that produce worse predictions, and also because the very perception of what a good prediction is depends on the model itself. For instance, a change in the state of the world form s_i to s_j might not be perceived as such by the agent whose information partition has s_i and s_j in the same equivalence class, and thus the agent is led to think that his model has not decreased his predictive power (see also below).

Learning in the space of parameters assumes that the model of the world is given in its functional structure and is equal or at least isomorphic to the 'real' one, and learning is just a refinement of the estimation of some unknown parameters. A typical example is Bayesian learning, where the learning agent updates his probability estimates within a given and immutable set of categories that constitute a partition of the real world.

Learning in the space of actions assumes, instead, that either the representation is constant or that it does not exist at all. As we shall see, this

---

is typically the case with simple stimulus-response models of learning and most of the evolutionary games models, where the learning is simply modelled as a selection process in the space of alternative actions.

Finally, learning can be modelled as a dynamic process in the space of realized performance outcomes, whereby the actual process of learning is not modelled at all but the model considers only its results in terms of dynamics in the space of some performance parameters. Typical examples can be found in models of technological learning, where learning is a stochastic process in the space of productivity coefficients.

It is clear that a) implies b) implies c) implies d): learning in the space of representations involves also the possibility of parameter estimates within a given structural form and a selection process among possible actions[30], and – of course – results in some movement in the space of performance outcome. Thus, modelling strategies that remain at the higher level of description and do not explicitly address the 'deeper' cognitive search and behavioural adaptation either assume that the latter has been 'solved' (for instance, the 'right' information partition has been found) or – acknowledging the relevance of these lower levels – only model, more parsimoniously, a 'reduced form'.

4.7   *Domains and constraints of learning processes*

Given the underlying object of learning, or, more formally, the dimensions of state-space of learning dynamics, what constraints does one assume on the domains of learning processes themselves?

Here the most important distinction is between search/adaptation over a *fixed menu* of possibilities that are all accessible from the start to all agents and an *open-ended dynamics* where the discovery of genuine novelties is always possible. As we shall illustrate below, this distinction marks an important cleavage between alternative modelling frameworks.

If all the notional elements of the learning set are known from the start, agents might be assumed to attach probabilities to each of them and to their consequences, thus possibly using some inferential procedure to adjust their behaviours (here the basic paradigm is the Bayesian model). Or, often with the same effect, the sheer availability of all possible behaviours in a population, given a stationary environment, establishes an environmental landscape in which it might be too difficult to define the adaptation drive at work and the related equilibria (the philosophy of 'evolutionary games' is near to this spirit). Conversely, whenever novelties

---

[30] Note that actions might be considered part of the representation, as is the case, for instance, when representations are modelled as condition-action rules.

happen to appear persistently, probability updating is likely to turn out to be a rather clumsy learning procedure, since the state-space can no longer be usefully partitioned due to the emergence of surprises and unforeseen (indeed, unforeseeable) events[31].

Rather symmetrically, in population-based adaptive frameworks the systematic appearance of novelties also implies an ever-expanding pay-off matrix, continuously deformed by the interaction with new events and strategies[32].

4.8   Mechanisms of learning

The very notion of 'learning', as in common usage, implies a sort of reference yardstick, measuring some 'improvement' – however defined – in terms of, for example, cognition, forecasting abilities, collectively assessed performances, inwardly evaluated utilities, etc.

Assume, in a first approximation, that those same criteria are what drive the learning process. Even then, one may well find quite different mechanisms at work (and correspondingly different formal 'laws of motion'). For example, 'learning' could be simply a shorthand characterization of a population-level selection mechanism involving the differential reproduction of entities (e.g., in economics, business firms) carrying different behavioural, organizational or technological traits. Or, it may mean an adaptation process driven by stimulus-response adjustments, without any explicit underlying cognitive process. Or, again, it could be based on agent-specific mechanisms involving expectations, the internal involvement of credit, etc. While in the simplest specifications of the object of learning the three types of dynamics may well turn out to be (asymptotically) equivalent, they may also make a major difference in terms of *finite-time* properties even for simple learning processes, and, *a fortiori*, in terms of the long-term outcomes of discovery and adaptation in more complex evolutionary environments.

With respect to the modelling frameworks, at one extreme stimulus-response adaptation (with or without environmental selection) implies

---

[31] It is true that probabilistic decision making allows for the introduction of a 'complement to the universe' category (i.e. 'all other events') in the information partition in order to close it, but in the presence of genuine novelty (that is, 'strong' substantive uncertainty, as defined above) it is unreasonably far-fetched to assume that a probability could be attached to an unbounded set of events not even conceivable to the decision maker. On the debate between the advocates of non-probabilistic approaches to uncertainty and supporters of the probability paradigm, see also Dubois and Prade (1988) and the references therein.

[32] In biological models, this corresponds to endogenous landscapes with no *ex ante* definable fitness maxima.

Learning spaces

		Action/strategies	Representation/ 'models of the world'	Realized performances	Preferences
Domains and constraints on learning processes	'Fixed menus'	■ Learning in game-theoretic set-ups ■ 'Evolutionary' games ■ Adaptive learning in multi-arm bandit problems (e.g. Arthur, 1993) ■ Self-organization models *à la* Lesourne (1991) ■ Urn models and other types of innovation adoption models (see Arthur et al., 1987, Arthur and Lane, 1993, Kirman, 1992, etc.) ■ Special cases of evolutionary models (see Winter, 1971) (Implicitly) adaptive models in stationary environments (e.g. Arifovic, 1994, Marimon et al., 1990)	■ Bayesian reduction of information incompleteness in games	■ Learning by doing and by using for given best-practice technologies (e.g. Silverberg et al., 1988, Eliasson, 1985)	■ Socially shaped preferences (e.g. Kuran, 1987, Brock and Durlauf, 1995, Akerlof and Dickens, 1982)
	'Open-ended' sets of learning objects	Behavioural search, in Lindgren, 1991, Silverberg and Verspagen, 1995b, Andersen, 1994 ■ Marengo and Tordjman (1996) and Dosi et al. (1999)		■ Open-ended technological search, such as in Nelson and Winter, 1982, Silverberg and Verspagen, 1994, Chiaromonte et al., 1993, Dosi et al., 1995	

Figure 9.3 Dimensions of learning and constraints on the learning process: a guide to the (modelling) literature

agents without any explicit 'reasoning', memory or inferential algorithms leading from the outcomes of their actions to the revision of their future decision rules. At another extreme agents may be modelled as forward-looking users of the best available information (at least in terms of what their bounded competencies allow).

In some peculiarly simple circumstances, the two apparently opposite mechanisms of learning can be shown to lead to identical limit outcomes (which all too often look like those cases whereby electrical shocks to rats lead them to converge to those equilibrium behaviours predicted by 'rational expectation' rats facing the same environment)[33].

However, in most other set-ups the specification of the mechanisms of learning does make a difference: this is an area where, unfortunately, to our knowledge, one does not yet have empirically robust generalizations that can be translated easily into formal modelling assumptions.

On the basis of the foregoing distinctions, figure 9.3 presents an impressionistic classification of examples of each *genre* in the current modelling literature. These differences in learning processes can also be formally accounted as variations and restrictions on the basis of a unified basic representation. This is what we attempt to do in the next section.

5   A basic model and various specifications

Let us consider a standard decision problem whereby an agent faces an environment that can have one out of an enumerable set of elementary outcomes:

$$S = \{s_1, s_2, \ldots, s_i, \ldots\}$$

In most relevant economic problems, the agent will not know the whole set of states of the world S (and even less so their causal links), but he will possess only an imprecise and partial representation thereof:

$$\Theta^t = \left\{\vartheta_1^t, \vartheta_2^t, \ldots, \vartheta_j^t, \ldots\right\}$$

where $\vartheta_j^t \subseteq S$ and $\Theta^t \subseteq 2^S$.

Each ϑ_j includes all the states of the world that the agent considers to be possible, or cannot discriminate, when one or more elementary outcomes contained in ϑ_j occur. (Note that in most economic models it is assumed that $\Theta^t = S$, meaning that the agent 'knows' the structure of the world; or, at least, Θ^t is assumed to be a partition of S.) Assuming

---

[33] This is precisely the amusing behavioural support that Lucas (1986) proposes for the rational expectation hypothesis.

instead that, more generally, $\Theta^t \subseteq 2^S$, we have a representation that can account for

1. complete ignorance:

$$\vartheta_i^t = S$$

for every $i = 1, 2 \ldots n$;

2. partial ignorance of some states of the world, if

$$U_i \vartheta_i^t \subset S$$

(i.e. the agent may be 'surprised' by some events that he did not even think of);

3. hierarchies of hypotheses and/or partially overlapping hypotheses:

$$\vartheta_i \subset \vartheta_j$$

or, more generally,

$$\vartheta_i \cap \vartheta_j \neq \oslash \quad \text{and} \quad \vartheta_i \neq \vartheta_j;$$

4. systematic mistakes, when an outcome is believed to occur when it does not, and is not thought to be possible when it actually does occur.

Let us, then, assume that the agent is notionally endowed with an innumerable set of possible actions:

$$A = \{a_1, a_2, \ldots a_j, \ldots\}$$

At any point in time the agent holds a finite behavioural repertoire constructed from the basic 'atomic' actions contained in A, subject to revision, modification and recombination. Note that, in general, one ought to allow the agent to know only a subset of the complete notional repertoire derivable from A. Let us call the known repertoire at time t

$$\Xi^t = \{\xi_1^t, \xi_2^t, \ldots \ldots, \xi_j^t, \ldots \}$$

where $\xi_j^t \subseteq A$ and $\Xi^t \subseteq 2^A$.

It must be pointed out that Θ^t and Ξ^t not only reflect the agent's sharpness at interpreting the information coming from the environment, by defining how sharp or coarse his categories are ('information-processing capabilities', in the standard decision-theoretic jargon), but also embed much of the 'cognitive order' that the agent imposes on the world. Θ^t, in particular, contains the variables and categories that the agent perceives as relevant to the representation problem in the undifferentiated flow of signals coming from the environment.

Hence, beyond very simple and special cases, Θ^t and Ξ^t entail some sort of *grammar* determining the legal cognitive and behavioural structures that can be notionally generated. Genuinely constructive models of cognition and problem solving ought to tackle the processes of search in some functional space of which some ϑ's are themselves the outcome. So, for example, the proposition 'we are in the state ϑ_i' is generated through cognitive operations attributing a semantic value to the signals received in the environmental state interpreted by the agent under ϑ_i. As we shall see, we are, unfortunately, still very far from the fulfilment of this research task (see, however, Fontana and Buss, 1996, for a fascinating framework that may possibly also be applicable to these problems).

The set of 'perceived' histories at time t contains some finite-length histories of perceived states of the world and perceived actions that have occurred up to time t:

$$H^t = \{h_k^t\}, \quad k = 1, 2, \ldots, t$$

where $h_k^t \in \Theta^k \times \Theta^{k+1} \ldots \times \Theta^t \times \Xi^k \times \Xi^{k+1} \ldots \times \Xi^t$.

We have repeatedly emphasized that a satisfactory understanding of learning processes entails an account of cognitive categories and 'mental models' that attribute a causal structure (an 'interpretation') to perceived histories. In this formal setting, an interpretation or model can be seen as an algorithm that attributes a causal sense to perceived histories or a subset of them. Call such 'models'

$$\Phi^t = \{\varphi^t(h), h \in H\}$$

There are three points to note. First, particular cases include those whereby agents retain only a dissipating memory of their representations and actions. Second, a single agent may well hold multiple (and contradictory) models at each t. Third, in terms of most current models, a sort of naive 'transparency assumption' rules out an interpretation stage ('everyone knows what really happened').

A decision rule is a mapping between interpretations, so defined, and action repertoires:

$$r_i^t \colon \Phi^t \to \Xi^t$$

A special case, which is commonly considered in the models discussed below, is when the mappings r_i^t define a probability distribution over the set of action repertoires.

An agent's decision-making capabilities at time t can, therefore, be represented by the (finite) set of decision rules it holds:

$$\mathfrak{R}^t = \{r_1^t, r_2^t, \ldots, r_q^t\}$$

When the agent acts upon the environment, it receives a 'response' (or an outcome) out of a set P of possible responses:

$$p^t: S \times A \to P$$

However, in general, the agent will know only an imprecise and partial representation of such outcomes. Moreover, over time it might well change its evaluation criteria (i.e., in standard language, its 'preferences'). Call such evaluations *pay-offs* in terms of some desirability criterion (be it utility, peace of mind, a problem-solving achievement, morality, pleasure and pain, minimum regret, etc.):

$$U^t = \Psi^t\ (p^t)$$

Hence, let us define a pay-off function as:

$$\pi^t: \Theta^t \times \Xi^t \to U^t$$

On the strength of this very general sketch of a decision-making model, we can re-examine the different *loci* of learning discussed earlier in a more qualitative fashion. However, it might be useful to begin with some extreme examples in order to flag some basic points of this exercise.

First, note that the most familiar economic models of decision making assume that:

a) Θ's are strictly partitions of S;

b) there is a known and often trivial set of action repertoires Ξ and, hence, the distinction between Ξ and A is redundant (witness the fact that economists and decision theorists are generally more comfortable in dealing with metaphors such as lotteries, where the very action – putting a finger on the object of the set – could be performed by any chimpanzee, rather than building computers, proving theorems, etc.);

c) 'interpretations' are always identical to 'true' stories, and, again, the Φ algorithm is redundant;

d) evaluation criteria on outcomes are time invariant, so that one can also innocently assume invariant pay-off functions that drive learning.

All in all, under this scenario it turns out that some well-specified dynamics on learning about the mapping $S \times A \to R$ include everything one needs to know.

Second, at the opposite extreme, a caricatural 'sociological' individual might well claim that:

a) as a first approximation, Ξ's are invariant in t (i.e. 'you do what you are supposed to do');

b) outcomes are always 'good' (Dr Pangloss' rule: we live in the best of all possible worlds; for simplicity, U^t is always in the neighbourhood of some $\overline{U}$, irrespectively of p^t – 'like what you get no matter what');

c) learning is basically about the endogenous development of representations, interpretations and 'utilities' that fulfil the invariance in the Ξ's and U's.

No doubt, the former caricatural model has been taken formally more seriously than the latter. However, as a first *descriptive* approximation, we tend to bet on the worth of the latter.

5.1   Learning about the states of the world[34]

This obviously implies changing the representation Θ^t. Moreover, these changing representations can simply involve a search in the parameter space or, more fundamentally, the very structure of the model of the world itself.

Suppose, for instance, that S is governed by a stochastic process. The agent might know which kind of stochastic process generates the sequence of states of the world (e.g., for sake of illustration, a Markov process) and have only to 'learn' the correct estimate of the parameters (e.g. Markov transition probabilities). Or he might ignore the nature of the stochastic process itself, or even deny that there is a stochastic process at all[35].

Note also that the possibility for the decision maker to learn about the stochastic process in S depends on the representation Θ^t he holds: only if the latter discriminates among the states in the sequence $s_1, s_2, \ldots ,$ $s_t, \ldots$ in separate categories will the agent have a chance of correctly learning the underlying stochastic process. But the converse might also be true: having chunks of states held together might make it easier to find deterministic patterns out of what might look like a random sequence.

The nature and degree of uncertainty about the stochastic process depends also on the general causal structure of the environment. In particular, we can distinguish among:

• interactions with nature without feedback;
• interactions with nature with feedback;
• multi-agent strategic interactions (including standard game-theoretic ones)[36].

---

[34] Here and throughout we shall hint at some basic and proximate structure of a few models, with inevitable gross approximations on both the detailed formalisms and the assumption refinements. Apologies to misinterpreted authors are due.

[35] There exists ample experimental evidence that probability matching, which amounts to ignoring that data are generated by a stochastic process, is a typical judgemental bias that appears even in the behaviour of expert decision makers.

[36] A similar distinction is made in Marimon (1997).

A fundamental case for our purposes arises when the actions of the agent himself generate new states of the world that did not exist in the original notional set S. Innovative behaviours are a typical case in point: new environmental opportunities are endogenously created, thus also making any sharp distinction between exploration over S and exploration over A only a first-cut approximation[37]. As argued in Dosi and Egidi (1991), it may well be the case that in such an innovative environment a) the set S loses the enumerability property and b) even an agent who has a perfect knowledge of S to start with will be bound to revise his representation.

5.2   *Learning about the actions space (changing the repertoires Ξ^t)*

The set of action repertoires Ξ^t can be modified through time, reflecting the 'technology' of the agent. New actions can be discovered that were not in the agent's repertoire beforehand, or existing actions can be combined in new ways: both circumstances are isomorphic to the search in the problem-solving space (and the related procedural uncertainty) discussed earlier.

5.3   *Learning about the pay-off function (changing the mapping π^t)*

If the agent does not know S and A but holds only imprecise and partial representations thereof, *a fortiori* he will have an imprecise and partial knowledge of how the pay-off function – as earlier defined – maps into 'objective' outcomes. It is worth pointing out that most learning algorithms model learning as a modification of representation of the world, and action repertoires where the learning agent adaptively develops *quasi-pay-off-equivalent* categories of events and actions – i.e. categories that tend to reflect the regularities of the pay-off function rather than the regularities of the underlying sets of states and actions. Thus, under some conditions, adaptive learning algorithms tend to produce better knowledge of the pay-off function than of the sets S and A.

Note also that endogenous preferences *and* a reduction of cognitive dissonance etc. (see above) involve a dynamics in both π^t and Θ^t conditional

---

[37] Notwithstanding this, we maintain that it is a useful first approximation, and in this we take issue with the radical proponents of 'social constructivism' (which, in the formal framework presented here, would also mean collapsing representations into actions). Putting it in a rather caricatural way, while we claim that a world with the atomic bomb entails a set of events different from (and greater than) a world without it, we also maintain that any exploration in the problem-solving space, no matter how well 'socially constructed', will hardly allow violation of the law of gravitation or the time reversibility of actions. Several issues concerning the 'social construction' of technological knowledge are discussed in Rip et al. (1995). From a different angle, collective learning processes are discussed in Lane et al. (1996).

on past realizations – something that one hardly finds in any current model, evolutionary or not.

5.4   Learning about the decision rules (changing the set of rules $\mathfrak{R}^t$)

A basic (and again largely unresolved) issue concerns the dimension of the state-space of rule search. In the spirit of the foregoing discussion, it ought to concern some (metaphoric) representation, internal to the agent, of the mappings on $\Theta^t \times \Xi^t \times \pi^t$. However, the general run of existing models is stuck to a much simpler view (a reduced form – or, rather, a trivialization?) with a fixed menu of rules to begin with and three, possibly overlapping, learning mechanisms. These are, first, some selection mechanism that modifies the weights attributed to each rule, and therefore its probability of being selected for action; second, mechanisms for modifying the domain of applicability of a rule – that is, the subset of the set of perceived histories that fires the rule; and, third (often not easily distinguishable from the above), a process for generating new rules that did not exist previously, possibly by modifying or recombining in some way already existing ones.

What kind of formal modelling and results does one currently find? In the rest of this section we will discuss briefly some of the main classes of models. Departing from a sketch of the classical Bayesian learning models, we will then consider a class of models that is evolutionary in the sense that they explicitly take on board learning and adjustment dynamics of some kind, although they primarily tackle adaptation rather than evolution *stricto sensu*. In other words, they still keep some 'small world' assumption on S, A, etc., and, moreover, they generally tend to rule out (with some noticeable exceptions) any endogeneity of the environmental (or cognitive) landscapes over which representations, actions and decision rules are selected. (Most of the work in this field comes under the heading of 'evolutionary games'.)

5.4.1   Bayesian learning: single- and multi-agent situations without feedback

As a starting point, consider Bayesian learning in the single- and multi-agent situations without feedback from the environment. A typical case is based on the assumptions that the state of the world is determined by some stochastic process and the agent has to select at each time t a proper action. Hence, the agent has to produce an estimate of the stochastic process and compute the expected utility of a course of action. A 'subjectively rational' agent holds a prior distribution μ, which he updates through a Bayesian rule by computing a posterior distribution after observing the realizations of the stochastic process and the pay-off received.

In the multi-agent case (Kalai and Lehrer, 1993), the prior distribution concerns the actions of the other players (their 'types'). Contrary to the hypotheses that are made in the literature on, for example, rationalizable strategies, such a prior distribution does not require knowledge of the other agents' pay-off matrices, but only of one's own; however, S and A must be common knowledge.

Bayesian updating processes in this case strongly converge ('strongly merge') if the sequence of posterior distributions converge, in the limit, to the real distribution on S (Blackwell and Dubins, 1962). But this can happen only if prior distributions attach positive probability to all, and only the subsets of S that have positive probability for the underlying stochastic process. This amounts to postulating perfect *ex ante* knowledge of all possible events. Kalai and Lehrer (1993) show this result in an $n \times n$ game without feedback, in which they assume that agents do not have complete knowledge of the space or strategies of the other players, and that they do not have to share homogeneous priors, but their prior must be 'compatible with the truth' – that is, they have to attach positive probability to all, and only the events that can occur with positive probability (the so-called 'grain of truth' condition).

Moreover, Feldman (1991) has shown that, if the set A is non-enumerable, convergence of posterior distributions to the true one cannot be guaranteed.

5.4.2   Stochastic learning models

Of course, Bayesian learning is highly demanding on the prior knowledge agents are assumed to have from the start (a point also acknowledged nowadays by scholars otherwise inclined to some 'rationalist' axiomatics of learning processes).

A much less demanding way to introduce learning, common in the contemporary literature, is to suppose some form of selection process among a finite set of possible actions. Two modelling strategies are possible in this respect. On the one hand, models might assume the existence of a population of agents, each identified with one action[38], and consider the learning/selection process taking place entirely at the population level. On the other hand, each agent could be modelled by a set of actions, with the selection process being a metaphor of its search capabilities (see Fudenberg and Kreps, 1993, and Kaniovski and Young, 1994). This distinction goes beyond the interpretation of the metaphor itself, but – as will shall see – has some substantial consequences on the modelling strategy.

---

[38] Coherently with the terminology introduced in the basic model, we use the term 'action' rather than the more common 'strategy' for this kind of model.

First, consider a face-value interpretation of standard evolutionary games. Indeed, evolutionary games assume away any problem of representation, both on states of the world and on actions, and – so to speak – collapse the learning of decision rules into selecting among a set of given behavioural repertoires (further assuming that such a selection process is exogenously driven by the environment). Agents carry no cognitive capability, but have basically two roles: that of carrying the 'memory' of the system (e.g. that of being 'replicators' of some kind), and that of introducing some exploration (via random mutation).

In one standard formulation, evolutionary game models (see the pioneering work of Maynard Smith, 1982, and later, with regard to economics, examples such as the work by Friedman, 1991, Kandori et al., 1993, Young, 1993, and Weibull, 1995) assume that there exists a population of N agents and a finite set of actions $a_1, a_2, \ldots, a_k$. If we denote by $n_i(t)$ the number of agents adopting strategy a_i, the basic selection principle states that

$$\frac{n_i(t+1) - n_i(t)}{n_i(t)} > \frac{n_j(t+1) - n_j(t)}{n_j(t)}$$
if and only if $\pi^t(a_i, s_t) > \pi^t(a_j, s_t)$ \hfill (1)

The fundamental selection principle therefore implies that actions that have a higher pay-off are increasingly sampled in the population. It is often (though not always) the case that this selection principle takes the special form of replicator dynamics equation, originally suggested by biological arguments (see Maynard Smith, 1982, and – earlier – Fisher, 1930) but also widely used in economic models – though with less convincing arguments[39]

$$n_i(t+1) = g\left(\pi^t(a_i, s_t) - \overline{\pi}^t\right) n_i(t) \hfill (2)$$

where $\overline{\pi}^t$ is the average pay-off across the population.

Learning is driven by the joint action of a selection principle and a variation mechanism – i.e. the constant introduction of search by means of random mutation, whereby some agents mutate their strategy with some given (small) probability.

Originally, mutation was conceived as a pointedly and isolated phenomenon (Maynard Smith, 1982), introduced as a device for studying the evolutionary stability of equilibria. An equilibrium was said to be

[39] Many recent models have worked with a more general setting, where broader classes of selection rules are considered, rather than strict replicator dynamics (see, for instance, Kandori et al., 1993, and Kaniovski and Young, 1994).

evolutionarily stable if, once achieved, it could not be disrupted if a small proportion of mutants appeared in the population. More recent developments (see, for instance, Kandori et al., 1993, Foster and Young, 1990, and Fudenberg and Harris, 1992) of stochastic evolutionary games have incorporated mutation as a continuous process; hence, the equilibria generally emerge as limit distributions of some dynamic process (in some cases, however, ergodicity is lost – as in Fudenberg and Harris, 1992, and Kaniovski and Young, 1994).

Further developments concern the nature of the selection process in (2). The dynamics can, in fact, be made dependent upon the past history of interactions, as summarized by the relative frequencies of actions within the population and/or by some sample of past pay-offs. Along these lines, Young (1993) considers a stochastic version of a replication mechanism whereby an action diffuses across the population according to a sample of the pay-off obtained in the last few periods. Along similar lines, a class of models (see especially Milgrom and Roberts, 1991, Fudenberg and Kreps, 1993, and Kaniovski and Young, 1994) considers more sophisticated agents by endowing them with some form of memory that keeps track of the consequences of actions and of the other players' replies in the past. Learning becomes a process of selection of a sequence of actions that constitute the best reply to sampled strategies (Kaniovski and Young, 1994) and might induce the emergence of 'conventions' – i.e. stable patterns of behaviour (which are, at least, locally stable Nash equilibria; Young, 1993, shows this in the cases of very simple memory endowments).

5.4.3   Stochastic models with self-reinforcement

In evolutionary games it is customary to assume that actions that have performed better in the past tend to diffuse more rapidly across the population of players, while the selection mechanism itself is either a replicator equation or is constructed via adaptation driven by infinitely frequent interactions among agents at each iteration (as in Kandori et al., 1993). Other kinds of models consider different mechanisms of diffusion, where agents choose an action according to some simple algorithm, such as a majority rule – that is, choosing the action that is adopted by the majority of some observed sample of the population.

First, if one considers a finite population of players, the number of agents who select action a_k at time t defines a Markov chain where transition probabilities depend on actual frequencies of actions in the population. For instance, assume a population of N individuals and $A = \{a_1, a_2\}$. Agent i, who has selected action a_1 at time $t-1$, switches at time t to action

a_2 with probability

$$P_i^t(a_1 \rightarrow a_2) = \alpha \frac{n_2(t)}{N} + \varepsilon \qquad (3)$$

where $n_2(t) = N - n_1(t)$ is the number of agents selecting action a_2. The α parameter measures the weight of the self-reinforcing component of the selection process, while ε captures components that are independent from the choice of the other agents[40]. It is possible to show the existence of a limit distribution: see Kirman, 1992, 1993, Orléan, 1992, and Topol, 1991. Depending on the values of α, the population may oscillate between the two states, with the limit distribution itself determining the average frequencies at which the system is observed in each state in the limit.

A second modelling strategy considers infinitely growing populations, where at each time step t a new agent makes a 'once and for all' choice of action a_k, with probability depending on the relative frequencies of past choices. In these models (see, among others, Arthur et al., 1987, Dosi and Kaniovski, 1994, Kaniovski and Young, 1994, and Fudenberg and Kreps, 1993) learning takes place primarily at the population level (agents cannot change their decision), and this occurs in a typical 'incremental' fashion.

The population dynamics can be described by an equation of the type

$$x_k(t+1) = x_k(t) + \frac{1}{N_t}\{[f_k(x_k(t+1)) - x_k(t)] + \varepsilon(x(t), t)\} \qquad (4)$$

where N_t is the size of the population after t arrivals of 'new agents', $x_k(t)$ is the share of the population that has chosen action a_k, and $\varepsilon(x(t), t)$ is a stochastic term with zero mean, independent in t.

The function f_k embeds possible self-reinforcing mechanisms, and its functional form determines the number and the stability properties of fixed points. In case of multiple equilibria, the process is generally non-ergodic (i.e. it displays path dependency), and convergence to one or other equilibrium depends on the initial conditions and sequences of 'early' choices (see Arthur et al., 1987, and Glaziev and Kaniovski, 1991).

It is worth pointing out that in the former class of models with finite population, in the limit the population might also keep oscillating between states and spend some fraction of time on each of them. Models can predict only the limit distribution and – possibly – the average time the population spends on each of the states that have, in the limit, positive

---

[40] As mentioned above, we skip any technical details here – such as, for example, the not so minor difficulty of keeping such dynamics as those represented in (3) consistently on the unit simplex.

probability measure[41]. In the latter class of models with infinitely increasing population, the size of the population instead goes to infinity in the limit and the system will almost surely be found in one of the absorbing states. But, if such absorbing states are multiple, which one is selected depends on the initial conditions and on the path followed by the system in finite time[42].

Moreover, in both classes of models it is assumed that agents base their decisions on observed frequencies. Thus, if these models are to be taken as representations of distributed, agent-based learning, such information must somehow be available to them. For example, a plausible interpretation of Arthur et al., 1987, is that frequencies are free public information (possibly with noisy disturbance), while Dosi, Ermoliev et al., 1994, assume that agents estimate frequencies by observing a sample of the population.

Finally, note that in the models with infinite population no learning takes place at the level of a single agent, as the latter cannot modify its once and for all decision, while in finite population models some primitive form of individual learning does occur, as agents modify their actions in line with some observation of the behaviour of other agents.

In fact, all this hints at a more general issue, namely the interaction between – so to speak – the 'weight of history' and agents' abilities to extract information from it. For example, Arthur and Lane, 1993, consider a model of choice between two technologies A and B, with a feedback between past adoptions and choice criteria. The states of the world represent the properties of such technologies $S = \{s_A, s_B\}$; these

---

[41] It is true that, after determining the limit distribution as $t \to \infty$, one might collapse it to a measure-one mass corresponding to one of the equilibria by further assuming that $\varepsilon \to 0$ (i.e. that the 'error' or 'search' term vanishes). However, it seems to us that this is primarily a display of technical *virtuosity*, with not much interpretative value added. Note also, in this respect, that if one takes the assumption of $\varepsilon \to 0$ as realistic one must, symmetrically, allow a speed of convergence to the 'good' equilibrium that goes to zero.

[42] Note also that the infinite population case, most often formalized through generalized Polya urns (for a survey and applications, see Dosi and Kaniovski, 1994), allows a much easier account of dynamic increasing returns. Formally, the latter imply some equivalent to a possibly unboundedly increasing *potential function*. Conversely, all the finite population cases we are aware of are driven by some equivalent to an invariant *conservation principle*. As we see it, learning most often does imply dynamic increasing returns; for example, even in the most trivial cases, efforts in search, when successful, yield relatively easy replication (and thus near-zero marginal costs). A straightforward implication is that history matters, and increasingly so as the process goes on. The fact that, so far, in the finite population cases one must rely formally upon time-invariant Markov processes most often leads – due to the formal properties of the model itself – to the conclusion that the system may also fluctuate in the limit across action patterns (or systems of collective representations). We do not have any problem with accepting the heuristic value of the conclusion under bounded increasing returns (such as those stemming from informational interdependencies on, for example, financial markets), but we have great reservations in the cases where returns to knowledge are in principle unbounded.

are unknown to agents, who only hold prior distributions $N(\mu_A, \sigma_A)$ and $N(\mu_B, \sigma_B)$. At each time t one agent adopts one of the two technologies by maximizing his expected utility:

$$E[U(c_i)] = \int U(c_i)\pi(c_i|X)dc_i \qquad (5)$$

where U is the utility function (with constant risk aversion) and $\pi(c_i|X)$ is the posterior distribution computed as follows. When an agent makes its choice, it samples τ agents among those who have already chosen. X is thus a vector of dimension τ, the components of which are each a single observation in the sample, which is supposed to be drawn from a normal distribution with finite variance

$$x_j = c_i + \varepsilon \quad \varepsilon \approx N(0, \sigma^2)$$

By applying Bayesian updating, agents can compute posterior distributions and choose the technology with higher expected utility.

Interestingly, it can be shown that in these circumstances, notwithstanding the procedural 'rationality' of the agents, the dynamics might lead to collective lock-in into the 'inferior' option (but, remarkably, in Lane and Vescovini, 1996, it appears that less 'rational' decision rules turn out to be dynamically more efficient from a collective point of view).

Note that this model is equivalent to a learning model with single agent and environmental feedback: at each time t the agent observes τ realizations of the states of the world, where the probability that each observation is generated by A or B is initially identical and is then modified through Bayesian updating. But this very learning process will change the distribution from which the agent samples the following time step by producing feedback on the states of the world. (In this respect, notice incidentally that, empirically, agents tend to display much less procedural rationality than that postulated here, leading to systematic misperception even in simple deterministic environments: see Sterman, 1989a, 1989b).

5.4.4 Models with local learning

The class of models illustrated above assumes that agents base their actions on some global observation of (or feedback with) the population or a sample thereof. Another perspective describes instead set-ups where agents respond to some *local* observation of the characteristic of a given subset of the population. Agents observe only their 'neighbours' (see, for instance, Kirman, 1997, David, 1992, and Dalle, 1993, 1994a, 1994b), defined according to some spatial or socio-economic measure of distance. Let $d(i, j)$ be the distance between agents i and j and d^* be a given threshold; the set of agents who are neighbours of agent i is defined as

$$V_i = \{j \in I : d(i, j) \le d^*\}$$

If the set V_i is not mutually disjoint, it is possible that local phenomena of learning and adaptation (i.e. inside a given neighbourhood) spread to the entire population.

One way of modelling this kind of process is based on Markov fields (see, for example, Allen, 1982a, 1982b, An and Kiefer, 1995, Dalle, 1994a, 1994b, Durlauf, 1994, and Orléan, 1990), assuming that agents stochastically select their actions depending on the actions or 'states' of their neighbours. Suppose, for instance, that pay-offs increase in the degrees of coordination with neighbours. Collective outcomes will depend upon the strength of the incentives (as compared to some 'internal' motivation of each agent): when incentives are not strong enough, high levels of heterogeneity will persist; conversely, if the premium on coordination is high enough, the system will spend most of its time in states of maximal coordination (though it might keep oscillating between them – see Kirman, 1993)[43].

Another class of models assumes that agents choose their action deterministically (see Blume, 1993, 1995, Berninghaus and Schwalbe, 1992, 1996, Anderlini and Ianni, 1996, Herz, 1994, and Nowak and May, 1992, 1993), in ways that are basically isomorphic to simple cellular automata, whereby the state of each agent depends – according to some deterministic rule – on the states of its neighbours.

Certainly, having some space that specifies learning mechanisms, conditional (in principle) on 'where a particular agent belongs', is a fruitful development in accounting for heterogeneity and path dependency in processes of adaptive learning[44]. However, note also that, in terms of how learning occurs, a fixed 'spatial' structure implies in fact a 'structure' – be it on metaphorically geographical, technological or cultural spaces – that ought to be phenomenologically justified; on the contrary, it is lamentable to find very often a two-dimensional lattice, or a torus, or something else being introduced with careless casualness.

In the perspective discussed so far, both stochastic and deterministic models of local learning consider learning as a selection over a fixed menu of *actions*. However, an alternative interpretation suggests that they could somehow also model processes of learning in the (fixed) space of *representations*.

Consider N agents on a bidimensional graph who select among k possible actions, and assume further that:

---

[43] Such results do not seem to show much robustness, however, with respect to both the algorithm that agents use to choose actions and the size of the population; see Föllmer (1974) and Hors and Lordon (1997).

[44] An important limitation of these models is the rigidity with which the structure of the neighbourhood is defined. However, Kirman et al. (1986), Ioannides (1990) and Bala and Goyal (1998) have given a more general formulation, in which the very structure of the graph is modified stochastically.

- the set of states of the world is given by all the Nk possible configurations of the graph (assuming that the action taken by the corresponding agent characterizes the state of a node); and
- agents hold a partial representation of such a set S, so that they observe only a part of the state of the world – i.e. that given by the state of their neighbours.

An agent's neighbourhood represent a sort of window through which it can observe only a part of the world; thus the agents try to infer adaptively the state of the entire graph from such window observation.

But, given this interpretation, we should expect that learning would involve a progressive 'enlargement of the window', so that agents can achieve an ever more complete picture of the world. Some results show that, above a threshold of interconnection in the graph, all agents globally converge to a state where they implicitly have access to all the information available in the system (see Bala and Goyal, 1998, Hammersley and Welsh, 1980, and Grimmett, 1989). However, there seems to be no monotonicity in the relation between the 'width of the window' and the asymptotic quality of the learning process (holding the nature of interconnections constant, between agents and between the past and the present).

5.4.5   Population-level versus agent-level learning

We have already remarked that one way of interpreting standard evolutionary games is in terms of agents who are simple replicators and who, individually, do not actually learn anything: only the population does. More sophisticated models (see, for instance, the already mentioned contribution by Young, 1993) take a different route, and are also meant to explore some (boundedly rational) cognitive capability of agents, such as some memory of previous events and some simple decision-making algorithms[45].

But it is clear that, with some modification, these kinds of selection-based models also have an immediate appeal as models of individual learning, once the population of individuals – each characterized by a single action – has been replaced by a single individual who adaptively learns to select among a set of possible actions at his disposal. Stochastic approximation models of adaptive beliefs try to move in this direction. The basic idea behind these models can be cast in the following way. Suppose that the learning agent has a set of actions $A = \{a_1, a_2, \ldots, a_n\}$; he does not know the realization of the state of the world s^t, but perceives only a realized pay-off π^t. In this case, a rational Bayesian decision maker

---

[45] A further step towards models of agent-level learning could be introduced by labelling agents (see the models with local learning presented below).

should form prior beliefs on all the possible pay-off matrices. An adaptive learner, instead, randomly chooses among actions according to some strength that he attaches to actions. Let us call F_k^t the strength assigned to action a_k at time t. The strength is updated according, say, to the rule

$$F_k^{t+1} = F_k^t \frac{f^k(\pi^t(s^t, a_k))}{\sum\limits_h f^h(\pi^t(s^t, a_h))} \tag{6}$$

Actions are randomly selected at t with probabilities given by

$$P^t(a_k) = \frac{F_k^t}{\sum\limits_i F_i^t} \tag{7}$$

This selection mechanism induces a stochastic process on the strengths assigned to competing rules, the asymptotic behaviour of which can be studied.

This and similar selection mechanisms can be found, for instance, in Arthur (1993), Posch (1994), Easley and Rustichini (1995), Fudenberg and Levine (1995) and Marimon et al. (1990). Easley and Rustichini's model, in particular, provides a neat connection between population-level and individual-level evolutionary arguments. In their model, Easley and Rustichini consider an individual decision maker facing an unknown environment, represented by a stochastic variable. Instead of forming beliefs on the set of possible processes and updating them according to the Bayesian approach, he adaptively selects among a set of behavioural rules $\Re$ (of the same kind as our basic model) according to a strength-updating rule of the kind of expression (6) and a random selection rule of the kind of expression (7). This enables them to study the stochastic process induced on the strengths of rule r_i, which is given by the expression

$$F_k^{t+1} = \prod_{z=0}^t F_k^z \frac{f^k(\pi^z(s^t, a_k^t))}{\sum\limits_h f^h(\pi^z(s^t, a_h^t))} \tag{8}$$

With some further assumptions on the characteristics of the underlying stochastic process on the states of the world (stationarity and ergodicity) and on the selection dynamics (monotonicity, symmetry and independence), they are able to prove that an individual who uses this kind of adaptive selection dynamics eventually acts as if it were an objective expected utility maximizer, and, moreover, that the set of rules selected by such dynamics corresponds to the set of rules that would be selected by a replicator dynamics.

Some considerations on the importance and limitations of these kinds of model are in order. First of all, note that these approaches end up being pure adaptation/selection models. It is an encouraging result indeed that such simple selection mechanisms are sometimes (but not always) able to select behavioural rules that mimic the optimizing behaviour prescribed by normative theories, but, of course, a necessary (and highly demanding) condition for such behaviour to be selected is that it is there in the first place. Populations must contain optimizing individuals in order to have them selected by replication mechanisms of selection. By the same token, rules that mimic the expected utility-maximizing behaviour must be in the decision maker's endowment of behavioural rules in order to have them asymptotically selected by the strength-updating process. One could say that, by moving from standard models of optimizing behaviour to stochastic models of adaptive learning, one moves from a world where agents are assumed to be naturally endowed with the correct model of the world to a world where agents are endowed with the correct behavioural rules (which define an implicit model of the world), but that these are mixed together with incorrect ones and have to emerge adaptively. It is clear that the latter assumption amounts to assuming away the cognitive problem of how such rules are formed and modified. In complex and changing environments in particular, it seems a rather far-fetched assumption to start with. In fact, stationarity in the underlying selection environment is a fair approximation whenever one can reasonably assume that the speed of convergence to given fundamentals is an order of magnitude faster than the rate of change in the fundamentals themselves. Ergodicity comes here as a handy auxiliary property: if it does not hold, much more detail is needed on initial conditions and adjustment processes.

Relatedly, an important question concerns how long the selection process takes to select good rules[46].

Second, and again related to the previous points (as in Easley and Rustichini, 1995), suppose that, at each stage of the adaptive learning process, the strength of all rules is updated according to the pay-off they would have received in the realized state of the world. This assumption is justified if, and only if, the learning agent's actions do not determine any feedback on the environment and if, and only if, the agent knows it. When this is not the case, only the strength of the rule actually employed can be updated, and therefore lock-in phenomena and non-ergodicity may well

---

[46] Some considerations on this problem can be found in Arthur (1993), who argues that the speed of convergence is highly sensitive to the variance of the pay-offs associated with different actions. Of course, the longer the convergence process the more implausible appears the assumption of the stationarity of the environment.

emerge: exploitation versus exploration and 'multi armed bandit'-type dilemmas are unavoidable.

These quite fundamental questions in fact hints at some general issues, *a fortiori* emerging in fully-fledged evolutionary environments. And, indeed, a theoretical in order to explore them is based on so-called 'artificially adaptive agents' (AAAs), which are briefly examined in the next section.

5.4.6   *Artificially adaptive agents*

If we drop the assumption that agents are naturally endowed with the correct model of the environment in which they operate, the fundamental topic of inquiry shifts to how models and representations of the world are generated, stored and modified by economic agents. On the one hand, as we have already argued, this consideration carries the requirement for some form of cognitive and psychological grounding. On the other hand, it opens new possibilities for applications to the economics of families of models developed in artificial intelligence (AI), and especially in that branch of AI that considers selection and variation mechanisms as a basic driving force for learning.

The main point of interest in these kinds of model is that the dynamics involved is essentially open-ended, both when the object of the modelling exercise is the dynamics of multi-agent interactions and when, instead, modelling concerns individual learning[47]. For a general overview on the AAA perspective in economics, see, for instance, Arthur (1993) and Lane (1993a, 1993b).

Open-ended dynamics is a consequence of two strong theoretical commitments of the AAA perspective. First, AAA models are not restricted to pure selection dynamics, but consider the introduction of novelty, innovation and the generation of new patterns of behaviour as a basic force for learning and adaptation. Thus, the dynamics never really settles into equilibrium states.

Second, the AAA perspective considers heterogeneity among agents and the complexity of interaction patterns (among agents in models of collective interaction and among behavioural rules in models of individual learning) as crucial aspects of the modelling exercise. In fact, in the

---

[47] All this notwithstanding the spreading practice of using AAA models to show adaptive convergence to conventional equilibria (often characterized by seemingly 'rational' forward-looking behaviours at the equilibrium itself). Of course, we do not deny that adaptive AAA learning might lead there sometimes. However, we consider the epistemological commitment to the search for those adaptive processes displaying such limit properties (often also at the cost of ad hoc rigging of the learning assumptions) as a somewhat perverse use of AAA modelling techniques.

AAA approach heterogeneity among agents (in terms of representations, expectations and learning paths) is the norm and homogeneity the exception; therefore, seemingly persistent equilibria tend in fact to be transient states of temporary 'ecological' stability, where small variations can trigger non-linear self-reinforcing effects.

An interesting prototypical example of AAAs can be found in Lindgren (1991). He considers a classical repeated prisoner's dilemma played by a given population of players. Each agent is defined by a strategy, which deterministically maps finite-length histories of the game (here represented by sequences of 'defeat' or 'cooperate' actions performed by the player itself and his opponent) into an action (defeat or cooperate). This population is then processed via an extended genetic algorithm that allows for variable-length genomes. Simply allowing for strategies based on variable-length histories makes the number of possible species in the population practically infinite and the search space unlimited. Hence, evolution is no longer a selection path in a finite and closed space of alternatives, but 'can then be viewed as a transient phenomenon in a potentially infinite-dimensional dynamical system. If the transients continue for ever, we have *open-ended evolution*' (Lindgren, 1991, p. 296; emphasis in original).

The dimension and complexity of strategies themselves become two of the elements subject to evolutionary selection and variation. This perspective enriches the concept of strategy implicit in the standard evolutionary game framework. While, in the latter, 'strategy' is most often squeezed down to an action taken from a given set of possibilities, in AAA models it is easy to account for evolving 'strategies' made up by changing combinations of a set of basic operators, categories and variables. (However, what is still missing in AAA models is the possibility of modelling learning as a modification of this set of basic operators, variables and detectors of environmental states, unless they originate from some combination of the elementary ones with which the system is initially endowed.) In terms of our earlier basic model, this difference amounts to an explicit search process regarding the algorithm mapping 'internal' representations to action patterns (in the case of AAA models), as compared to its 'black-boxing' into the adaptive selection of actions themselves (in the case of most evolutionary games).

This distinction is even clearer in more explicitly rule-based AAA models. Rule-based AAA models differ from the stochastic models outlined in the previous section in at least two fundamental respects. First, they consider learning as the joint outcome of the processes of the generation, replication, selection and modification of behavioural rules. As the space of behavioural rules is potentially unlimited – even in relatively simple problems – and the search space itself is ill-defined and subject to change, the generation of new rules, new representations and new actions is an essential mechanism for learning and adaptation.

The second aspect, related to the previous one, is that – except in very simple problems nested in stationary environments – the outcome of the learning process cannot be constrained to be a single behavioural rule but may be a whole 'ecological' system of rules, which together form a representation of the environment (on the so-called 'computational ecologies', see also Huberman and Hogg, 1995). Behavioural patterns that emerge in AAA models may, therefore, be much richer than those predicted by pure selection models. Here, learning takes place explicitly in both spaces of representations/models of the world and action repertoires[48].

A prototypical example of rule-based learning models is represented by the so-called 'classifier systems' (see Holland et al., 1986; for an overview of actual and possible applications to economics, see Arthur, 1991, 1993, and Lane, 1993b; for some specific applications, see Marimon et al., 1990, Marengo, 1992, and Marengo and Tordjman, 1996; for a survey, see also Hoffmeister and Bäck, 1991).

Learning in classifier systems presents the following general features.

(i) Learning takes place in the space of *representations*. In a complex and ever-changing world, agents must define sets of states that they consider to be equivalent for the purpose of action. In other words, they have to build representations of the world in order to discover regularities that can be exploited by their actions. These representations have a pragmatic nature and are contingent upon the particular purpose the routine is serving.

(ii) Learning must be driven by the search for better performance. Learning agents must therefore use some system of *performance assessment*.

(iii) If rules of behaviour have to be selected, added, modified and discarded, there must exist a procedure for the *evaluation of the usefulness* of rules. This problem may not have a clear solution when the performance of the system is assessed only as a result of a long and complex sequence of interdependent rules (such as in the game of chess, for instance).

---

[48] In this respect, a particularly interesting question concerns the circumstances under which simple behavioural patterns do emerge notwithstanding the potential cognitive complexity that these models entail. In Dosi et al. (1995) it is shown that this is often the case in the presence of competence gaps of the agent vis-à-vis the complexity of the changing environment (see also below).

Let us consider again the basic model of decision making introduced above and suppose that it is faced repeatedly by the same agent. The decision maker, by using his/her experience of the previous stages of the game, makes a forecast of the state of the world that will occur next and chooses an action that he/she considers as appropriate. At the outset the player has no knowledge either of the pay-off matrix or of the 'laws' that determine the changes in the environment. The decision process consists therefore of two elements: the state of knowledge about the environment, represented by the agent's forecasting capabilities; and the rules for choosing an action, given this forecast.

In its most basic formulation, a classifier system is a set of condition-action rules that are processed in parallel. Each rules makes the execution of a certain action conditional upon the agent's perception of a certain state of the world.

A first element that characterizes a classifier system is the message (signal) the learning agent receives from the environment. Such a message has to be interpreted and connected to a consequent action according to a model of the world that is subject to revisions. The signal is usually encoded as a binary string of given length:

$$m_1 \, m_2 \, \ldots \, m_n \quad \text{with } m_i \in \{0,1\}$$

Learning is modelled as a set of condition-action rules that are processed in a parallel fashion. Each rule makes a particular action conditional upon the fulfilment of a condition concerning the present state of the world. The condition part is, therefore, actually made up of a string of the same length as the message's, which encodes a subset of the states of nature and is activated when the last detected state of the world falls into such a subset:

$$c_1 \, c_2 \, \ldots \, c_n \quad \text{with } c_i \in \{0,1,\#\}$$

The condition is satisfied when either $c_i = m_i$ or $c_i = \#$. That is, the symbol # acts as a 'don't care' symbol that does not pose any constraint on the corresponding part of the environmental message.

Thus, consistently with the framework discussed in the previous section, a set of conditions defines a subset of the power set of S. It is important to notice that each condition defines one subjective state of the world, as perceived by the agent, and defines its relationship with the objective states of the world. This relationship always remains unknown to the decision maker, who 'knows' only the subjective states.

The action part is, instead, a string of length p (the number of the agent's possible actions) over some alphabet (usually a binary one) that encodes possible actions:

$$a_1 \, a_2 \, \ldots \, a_p \quad \text{with } a_i \in \{0,1\}$$

The decision maker can therefore be represented by a set of such condition-action rules

$$R = \{R_1, R_2, \ldots, R_q\}$$

where

$$R_i : c_1 \, c_2 \, \ldots \, c_n \rightarrow a_1 \, a_2 \, \ldots \, a_p \quad \text{with } c_i \in \{0,1,\#\}$$

$$\text{and } a_i \in \{0,1\}$$

In addition, each rule is assigned a 'strength' and a 'specificity' (or its reciprocal 'generality') measure. The *strength* basically measures the past usefulness of the rule – that is, the pay-offs cumulated every time the rule has been applied (minus other quantities, which will be specified later). The *specificity* measures the strictness of the condition; the highest specificity (or lowest generality) value is given to a rule where the condition does not have any symbol '#' and is therefore satisfied only when that particular state of the world occurs, whereas the lowest specificity (or the highest generality) is given to a rule where the condition is formed entirely by '#'s' and is therefore always satisfied by the occurrence of any state of the world.

At the beginning of each simulation the decision maker is usually supposed to be absolutely ignorant about the characteristics of the environment; initially, therefore, all the rules are randomly generated. The decision maker is also assumed to have limited computational capabilities; as a result, the number of rules stored in the system at each moment is kept constant and relatively 'small' in comparison to the complexity of the problem that is being tackled.

This set of rules is processed in the following steps throughout the simulation process.

(i) *Condition matching*: a message is received from the environment that informs the system about the last state of the world. The message is compared with the condition of all the rules, and the rules that are matched – i.e. those that apply to such a state of the world – enter the following step.

(ii) *Competition among matched rules*: all the rules where the condition is satisfied compete in order to designate the one that is allowed to execute its action. To enter this competition each rule makes a bid based on its strength and on its specificity. In other words, the bid of each matched rule is proportional to its past usefulness (strength) and its relevance to the present situation (specificity).

$$\text{Bid}(R_i,t) = k_1(k_2 + k_3 \text{ Specificity}(R_i)) \text{ Strength}(R_i,t)$$

where k_1, k_2 and k_3 are constant coefficients. The winning rule is chosen randomly, with probabilities proportional to such bids.

(iii) *Action and strength updating*: the winning rule executes the action indicated by its action part and has its own strength reduced by the amount of the bid and increased by the pay-off that the action receives, given the occurrence of the 'real' state of the world. If the j-th rule is the winner of the competition, we have

$$\text{Strength}(R_j,t+1) = \text{Strength}(R_j,t) + \text{Payoff}(t) - \text{Bid}(R_j,t)$$

(iv) *The generation of new rules*: the system must be able not only to select the most successful rules but also to discover new ones. This is ensured by applying 'genetic operators', which, by recombining and mutating elements of the already existing and most successful rules, introduce new ones that may improve the performance of the system. In this way new rules are constantly injected into the system, and scope for new search is continually made available.

Genetic operators generate new rules that both recombine the 'building blocks' of and explore other possibilities in the proximity of the currently most successful ones, in order to discover the elements determining their success and exploit them more thoroughly; the search is not completely random but influenced by the system's past history. New rules so generated substitute the weakest ones, so that the total number of rules is kept constant.

Three types of genetic operators are normally employed. The first two types are forms of simple mutation that operate in opposite directions:

a) *specification*: a new condition is created that increases the specificity of the parent one; wherever the parent condition presents a '#', this is mutated into a '0' or a '1' (randomly chosen) with a given (small) probability;

b) *generalization*: the new condition decreases the specificity of the parent one; wherever the latter presents a '0' or a '1', this is mutated into a '#' with a given (small) probability.

The third operator is a standard *crossover*, which reflects the idea of generating new conditions by recombining the useful elements ('building blocks') of the conditions of successful rules. Two parent rules are probabilistically selected among the ones with higher strength, then a random crossover point is selected for each condition part and strings are exchanged across such crossover points.

If, for instance, the conditions of the two parent rules are

aaaaaa

AAAAAA

with a, A $\in \{0,1,\#\}$, if 2 is randomly drawn as the crossover point the two following offspring are generated

aaAAAA

AAaaaa

The above-mentioned economic models, which employ classifier systems for the analysis of multi-agent interaction problem, basically study the emergence of 'ecologies of representations'. Heterogeneous agents adaptively modify their models of the world in order to achieve better performance, and stationary environments tend to generate relatively stable ecological equilibria, but – in general – agents will not converge to homogeneous models, but only to models that are somehow 'compatible' for the particular states of the world that actually occur. The same environment can in fact support very diverse non-partitional representations: stochastic elements in the learning process, combined with the high degree of path dependency of the systems, will very likely produce a high degree of diversity of representations even when we begin with perfectly homogeneous agents. Moreover, learning never actually stops, and the application of the genetic algorithm always introduces an element of exploring new possibilities, which might disrupt the temporary ecological equilibrium.

Marengo (1992, 1996), applies this model to the emergence of a commonly shared knowledge basis in team decision-making processes, and shows that different types of environment can generate very different balances between the homogeneity and heterogeneity of knowledge. Palmer et al. (1994), Vriend (1995) and Marengo and Tordjman (1996) examine a population of rule-based AAAs operating in an artificial market and show that the market can sustain a persistently high degree of diversity between agents' models of the world and, at the same time, generate a price dynamics that has many features in common with real speculation market phenomena.

A slightly different modelling strategy, albeit very much in the same spirit, employs 'genetic programming' (Koza, 1993); unlike standard genetic algorithms and classifier systems, search does not take place in the space of fixed-length binary string representations but in the space of all variable-length *functions* that can be generated with a given, primitive set of operators and operands. Representations here are no longer mere sets of subsets of subjective states of the world but are more complex functional relationships, linking variables to actions by means of mathematical and logical operators. Dosi et al. (1994) show an application of this methodology to pricing decisions by firms in oligopolistic markets[49].

In general, these models produce simulations of 'artificial economies', in parallel with the 'artificial life' approach; see Langton (1989) and Langton et al. (1991), in which the analysis is no longer based on equilibrium concepts and on the search for convergence and stability conditions but on the investigation of collective emergent properties – i.e. aggregate regularities that are relatively robust and persistent (see also Lane, 1993a, 1993b).

An interesting family of 'artificial economy' models analyses local learning phenomena. For instance, Epstein and Axtell (1996) consider a population of agents located on a bidimensional space where some resources (e.g. food) are also (unevenly) distributed. Agents are endowed with a set of simple algorithms that control their movements, their use of available resources and their behaviour towards other agents they can meet. Adaptation takes place at two different levels: a) with respect to the environment, agents move towards sites where they more easily fulfil their objectives; b) with respect to their neighbours, they generate a local organization of exchange (i.e. markets where they can exchange goods and achieve a Pareto superior distribution of resources). Take all this as a preliminary metaphor of a set of models – still to come – where propositions of economic theory (e.g. downward-sloping demand curves, laws of one price, etc.) can be derived as emergent properties of decentralized interaction processes.

5.5   Learning as dynamics in the space of outcomes

The typologies of learning models reviewed so far attempt, to different degrees, to provide some account of the dynamics of, for example, what agents know about the world, or the ways people select among different actions.

Alternative modelling strategies involve, on the contrary, an explicit 'black-boxing' of the learning/decision processes, folding them together into some dynamics on the possible states in which the agents might happen to be. In turn, this 'black-boxing' in some approaches has to be considered as just a *reduced form* of an underlying richer dynamics on

---

[49] In particular, what was demonstrated was the endogenous emergence of pricing routines as an evolutionary robust form of adaptation to non-stationary environments.

cognition, problem solving, etc., while in others almost all that can be said about learning tends to be considered.

The latter perspective certainly applies to a long tradition of formal models in psychology building on stimulus-response processes, dating back at least to Estes (1950), and Bush and Mosteller (1955). (Note that, insofar as the 'states' – through which the agents are driven by reinforcement – are behavioural responses, this modelling philosophy largely overlaps with that of 'evolutionary games', briefly discussed earlier.)

A good summary of the basic ideas is from Suppes (1995a, p. 5).

> The organism is presented with a sequence of trials, on each of which he makes a response, that is one of several possible choices. In any particular experiment it is assumed that there is a set of stimuli from which the organism draws a sample at the beginning of each trial. It is also assumed that on each trial each stimulus is conditioned to at most one response. The probability of making a given response on any trial is postulated to be simply the proportion of sampled stimuli conditioned on that response, unless there is no conditioned stimuli in the sample, in which case there is a 'guessing' probability for each response. Learning takes place in the following way. At the end of the trial a reinforcement event occurs that identifies which one of the possible responses was correct. With some fixed probabilities the sample stimuli become conditioned to this response, if they are not already, and the organism begins another trial in a new state of conditioning . . .

Notice that here all the dynamics on Θ, Ξ, R, and π that one was trying to disentangle above are black-boxed into the distribution of stimuli and the conditional probabilities of transition across responses.

A simple illustration (Suppes, 1995a) with two states, one conditioned to the correct response (C) and the other unconditioned (U), is a Markov process of the type

	C	U
C	1	0
U	C	1–C

with the elements of the matrix being the transition probabilities. Not too surprisingly, 'learning is the convergence to the absorbing state'.

Moreover, notice that the basic methodology requires an underlying 'small'/stationary world assumption (all states must have from the start a positive probability measure) and is essentially looking for asymptotic properties of the models[50].

---

[50] It is true that, in some simple experimental set-ups, stimulus-response models also generate predictions on the convergence paths. But this is not the case in general, especially outside the domains where stimulus sampling and conditioning can be given a straightforward psychological interpretation (representation building and problem solving are

5.6   Technological learning

Nearer to the spirit of a good deal of contemporary evolutionary theories, a quite different type of 'black-boxing' is common to a lot of models of growth and industrial change driven by technological advances. Here the learning dynamics is typically represented in terms of changes in the space of some technological coefficients.

Possibly the simplest formalization is the early account by Arrow (1962), of learning by doing, subsequently corroborated by a few empirical studies, showing a 'quasi-law' of falling costs (or increasing productivity) as a function of cumulated production[51].

In Silverberg et al. (1988), learning how to use a new capital-embodied technology efficiently (i.e. a new 'paradigm'; see above) is formalized via a logistic-type dynamics on firm-specific skills (s_i), dependent on current and cumulated production using the new technology (x_i and X_i, respectively).

$$s_i' = B_1 \frac{x_i}{X_i + C} s_i(1 - s_i) \quad \text{if } s_i \geq s_p$$
$$s_i = s_p \qquad\qquad\qquad \text{otherwise}$$

where s_i' is the time derivative, C is a constant proportional to the capital stock and s_p is the level of skills generally available in the industry, which is a sort of dynamic, industry-wide externality changing as

$$s_p' = B_2(\bar{s} - s_p)$$

with $\bar{s}$ a weighted average of firm-specific skills[52].

Further, many evolutionary models, starting with the seminal work of Nelson and Winter (1982), account explicitly for the uncertainty associated with technical search, and often also for the dependence of future discoveries upon the knowledge already achieved in the past. In the last

two cases in point). So, for example, one is left to wonder what the empirical content is of the 'main theorem' from Suppes, 1969 (see also Suppes, 1995a), according to which 'given any finite automaton, there is a stimulus-response model that under appropriate learning conditions asymptotically becomes isomorphic to the finite automaton'. One is very far indeed from any constructive, empirically disciplined notion of learning . . .

[51] Something like $c_t = c_0 X_t^\beta$, where X_t is cumulated production, $-1 < \beta < 0$, and c_0 is unit production costs.

[52] Of course, $\bar{s}$ and s_p are bound to be less than or equal to one (i.e. the 'perfect' ability to exploit fully the technical specifications of use on any one given vintage of capital). Somewhat more complicated learning patterns, modelled in a similar spirit, are in Eliasson (1985). A 'Verdoorn-Kaldor' law, with learning driven by learning by doing and economies of scale, underpins the model by Verspagen (1993). And system-level deterministic learning dynamics is presented in Granstrand (1994).

resort, modelling learning in the technology space comes down to spec-ification of the stochastic process driving agents from one technique to the next.

For example, in one of the models presented in Nelson and Winter (1982) learning occurs in the space of two variable input coefficients a_1 and a_2. After some renormalization[53], assume that the technique of each firm at time t is the random pair U_t, V_t, and the search outcome is represented by the random pair (G_t, H_t), which captures the number of steps that the firm takes in the U and V dimensions[54], with (G_t, H_t) – in the simplest formulation, independent of $(U_{t,1}, V_{t,1})$ – distributed on a finite support (Nelson and Winter, 1982, pp. 177–79). The time-independent random process, together with a selection criterion simply comparing $(U_{t,1}, V_{t,1})$ and (U_t, V_t) at prevailing input prices, implies that the sequence of techniques is a Markov chain[55]. The distribution of innovative outcomes is centred on the prevailing productivity of a firm, and, in the more general formulation, there is no exogenous constraint on technological possibilities (Nelson and Winter, 1982, p. 285), although there is one related to internal capabilities: what one knows limits what one can achieve within a given number of search periods.

Other representations in a similar spirit include Silverberg and Lehnert, (1994), whereby innovations arrive according to a Poisson distribution, adding to the productivity of new technological vintages of equipment; Chiaromonte and Dosi (1993) and Chiaromonte et al. (1993), which have the support of the probability distributions on (labour) coefficients for 'machine' production and machine use dependent on time T real-izations for each firm; Dosi et al. (1994) and Dosi et al. (1995), who model the dynamics of (proportional) increments in firm 'competitive-ness' drawn from different variants of a Poisson process; and Kwasnicki (1996), who presents more complex dynamics of search driving as well as recombination and mutation on incumbent knowledge bases (see also below).

In other versions of evolutionary models, one assumes an exogenously determined drift in learning opportunities (a metaphor for scientific advances, etc.). For example, in another model presented in Nelson and

---

[53] So that the refined dimensions are $U = \log (a_2/a_1)$ and $V = \log (a_1\, a_2)$.

[54] Subject to the constraint that $u_1 \leq U \leq u_n$. Conversely, V, itself a proxy for input productivity (in the spirit of evolutionary models), is allowed to range on $-\infty < V < +\infty$.

[55] See Nelson and Winter, 1982, pp. 179–92. Note also that in this Nelson–Winter model, while in terms of relative input intensities the process defines a finite, time-invariant Markov process, in the V-dimension the number of states is notionally infinite and the system is allowed, so to speak, to climb to ever greater levels of productivity (although only finite levels of them are accessible from a given state).

Winter (1982), firms sample from a log-normal distribution of values of capital productivities the increasing mean of which follows a time-dependent trend. And, somewhat similarly, Conlisk (1989) postulates productivity growth driven by draws from a normal distribution (with positive mean).

Finally, a few evolutionary models also account for learning via *imitation* – that is, by the stochastic access of each firm to the best practice available at each time or to the set of combinations between best practice and the technique currently known by any generic incumbent (see Nelson and Winter, 1982, Chiaromonte et al., 1993, Silverberg and Verspagen, 1994, 1995b, and Kwasnicki, 1996, among others).

The first point to note is that the spirit of most formalizations of learning processes in a technology space, however defined, has an essentially 'phenomenological' flavour; formal representations are meant to capture stylized facts, basic dynamic regularities, etc. generally placed at a much 'higher' (and more aggregate) level of description than the 'foundational' processes of cognition, problem solving, etc. discussed earlier (we shall come back in a moment to the relationships between the two levels). Given this more phenomenological level, however, a requirement far from fulfilled in the current state of the art concerns the *empirical robustness* of the purported dynamics[56]: for example, on what empirical grounds does one justify the assumption of Poisson arrival processes? Why not another random process? On what criteria does one choose the specification of the Markov processes driving search? The questions could go on . . .

This is an area where evolutionary modellers would certainly benefit from more precise insights coming from 'inductive' statistical exercises concerning, for example, microeconomic processes of innovation, productivity growth, etc.

The second point is that, even when considering learning over an upper-bounded set of 'knowledge states' (such as in Silverberg et al., 1988), and – obviously so – in open-ended knowledge dynamics, the analytical focus is upon *transient* rather than limit properties.

An example in the set-up concerning innovation diffusion and learning by using on two technologies is presented in Silverberg et al., 1988. The properties of limit states could, in principle, be found – given the initial conditions, etc. However, the attention is mainly devoted to the *finite-time* properties of the system and the finite-time learning profile of individual agents.

---

[56] Indeed, this should be a self-criticism of all of us who have worked on evolutionary modelling . . .

A fortiori, all this applies to learning dynamics that is *open-ended* in the sense that there is an infinite number of states that agents can take as time goes to infinity, even if, most likely (conditional on the given knowledge level), only a finite number of states can be reached with positive probability in a finite time[57]. The third point is that it seems to us rather obvious that any representation of learning as a dynamics across technological (or, for that matter, 'organizational') states in low-dimensional spaces is just an inevitable (indeed, very useful) *reduced form* of underlying learning process in spaces of explosively high dimensionality (like those entailed in the earlier, more 'constructive' discussion of exploration on cognitive and problem-solving categories)[58]. But then the question of the compatibility and mappings across different levels of description becomes crucial (let alone a direct derivation of 'higher' from 'lower' levels, which might well turn out to be an impossible task without a lot of further phenomenological details and constraints).

5.7   Behavioural and cognitive foundations of technological learning

Of course, the easiest way to provide cognitive/behavioural foundations to learning in the technology space is by assuming that it is the direct outcome of the choices of fully rational (and forward-looking) agents. This is, indeed, the path followed by 'new growth' theories – if their microfoundations are to be taken at face value (see Romer, 1990, Grossman and Helpman, 1991, or – in a stochastic version – Aghion and Howitt, 1992)[59].

However, if one accepts the foregoing argument, fully 'rational' decision models fall well short of applicability to technological search and innovation: on the contrary, this is the domain where one is most likely to find strong substantive and procedural uncertainty, surprises, delusions

---

[57] A major analytical challenge ahead regards the possibility of characterizing in the limit some expected (average) properties of these open-ended processes (an ongoing research involving Sidney Winter, Yuri Kaniovski and the authors at the International Institute of Applied Systems Analysis, Austria, is currently beginning to address the problem painstakingly).
[58] Collective learning entities such as 'firms' further explore the space of search/adaptation.
[59] This applies equally to, for example, game-theoretic models of innovation and diffusion, 'patent races', etc. (thorough surveys are in Stoneman, 1995). Whether such microfoundations ought to be taken seriously is a debatable question. The more sophisticated view suggests that they should not, forward-looking representative agents etc. being only a sort of theoretical short cut in order to get to some some aggregate dynamic properties that *a fortiori* hold under less restrictive behavioural assumptions; a lot of contributions by, for example, Paul Romer and, in other perspectives, Joseph Stiglitz (among others) are interpretable in this way. On the contrary, the conclusions of too many other models seem to be sensitively dependent upon the fine specifications of 'rational behaviours' themselves.

and unexpected successes (for a review of the empirical evidence in this area, see Dosi, 1988). But then one is back to the relationships between a phenomenological account of learning processes and the underlying cognitive and behavioural procedures . . .

In this respect, Nelson and Winter (1982) suggest a promising appreciative theory, nesting technological learning (and some of its properties, such as the possible cumulativeness of technological advances, the 'locality' of search, etc.) into a theory of organizational learning based – in good part – on the establishment, reproduction and change of organizational routines.

Moreover, Nelson and Winter – as well as, earlier, the inspiring work of Cyert and March (1992, but first published in 1963), and later, many models in this evolutionary tradition – formally model the 'access' to change as being triggered or driven by some stylized decision rule. A way of capturing this bridge between the behavioural domain and an apparently 'agent-free' learning dynamics is by assuming some sort of rather simple 'allocation to search' rule (such as 'invest X per cent of turnover in R&D') – which is indeed robustly corroborated by the managerial evidence – and then formalize a probability of access to innovative (or imitative) learning dependent on these search efforts. A binomial distribution of the kind

$$P(\text{inn} = 1) = a \cdot \exp(b \cdot \text{R\&D})$$

is a first approximation to the general idea (with a and b being parameters that implicitly account for both 'objective' opportunities and firm-specific competencies; see, for example, Nelson and Winter, 1982, and Chiaromonte et al., 1993)[60].

Hence, the learning dynamics is modelled as the outcome of a two-stage stochastic process, separating a first ('behavioural') process depending, in principle, on beliefs, expectations and action patterns (that is, the ϑ and ξ variables in our earlier formulation) from a second one trying to capture some modal properties of the learning process itself[61].

Other formalizations of the interactions between behaviours and learning modes stylize 'triggering effects', so that, for example, change and search is undertaken only if actual performance falls below a certain threshold level[62].

---

[60] The same goes for imitation as well.

[61] Which, putting it into our earlier formalization, would be a synthetic account of externally evaluated (or 'market-evaluated') performances of the combinations between menus of actions and 'states of the world'. It is also important to notice that the general assumption here is that agents do not and cannot know that mapping algorithm.

[62] See Nelson and Winter (1982) and also, outside the technological domain, Cyert and March (1992).

For many analytical purposes, the assumption that behavioural rules (such as R&D rules) are given and invariant throughout the history of each agent is a perfectly legitimate approximation (which also captures the relative inertia of organizational routines). And this is what one finds in many evolutionary models up to now.

In fact, invariant search rules (or invariant 'meta-rules' for change) can be understood in two ways, namely a) as empirically grounded 'stylized facts', or b) as useful first-approximation assumptions the precise status of which has also to be understood in terms of complementary processes of behavioural learning. They certainly capture a bit of both; in order to move further at the former level, though, it is vital to achieve more robust micro-behavioural evidence[63], and, at the latter level, it is essential to show if and how endogenous processes of adaptation lead to relatively persistent (meta-stable) search rules. This latter analysis is what Silverberg and Verspagen (1995a) have begun to do, assuming rules that are invariant as such but with parameters that may adaptively change via a stochastic search process (with different modelling tools based on genetic algorithms, Kwasnicki, 1996, explores a similar path).

Alternatively, one might want to take a more constructive route to behavioural search and adaptation, but, so far, only at the cost of further simplifying the environment in which agents operate (an example is Dosi et al., 1994, where 'routines' such as mark-up pricing are indeed shown – as already mentioned – to be endogenous emergent properties but one totally neglects learning in the technology/problem-solving domain).

More generally, technological learning is possibly one of the most revealing points of observation in order to assess the state of the art in theories of learning in evolutionary environments. Hopefully, there should be little doubt that technologies (together with organizational forms and institutions) are major domains of economic evolution. Technical change is also one of the few fields where explicitly inspired evolutionary thinking has a widely acknowledged lead in the methodology of empirical reseach and appreciative theories, not to mention formal models. And it also continues to be a major challenge for all those scholars who want to take micro-foundations seriously. As it stands now, it is probably a crucial test for any foundations of cognition, decision and learning (at least in economics) that are robust enough to account for what people and organizations do when they inevitably know little about what the future might

---

[63] The collection of this evidence, interestingly enough, has nearly stopped since the 1960s, partly as a result of the conflict between what researchers were finding and the axiomatic boldness of the theory (see, for example, the neglect on mark-up findings with regard to pricing behaviours; a short but pertinent discussion is in Winter, 1975).

deliver to them. In this respect, 'rational' formalizations sometimes sound hopelessly silly (suppose, for example, that Stone Age men had rational expectations about helicopters, or that IBM's first senior executives knew what a PC was and had some prior probability distribution on its impact . . .). But competing interpretations face the equally formidable challenge of developing 'level zero' theories consistent with 'higher-level' models of the empirical patterns of learning in, for example, companies, industries, communities or whole countries.

For the purposes of this work, let us just notice that a major step forward would result from constructive theories of entities that, at higher levels of observation, one calls 'knowledge bases', 'organizational competencies', 'heuristics', etc. – that is, theories showing how elementary 'pieces of knowledge', or routines or elementary actions, coherently combine in higher-level entities that self-maintain over time. But, in turn, as convincingly argued by Fontana and Buss (1994, 1996) in the domain of biology, this demands a constructive theory of organizations, the existence of which, on the contrary, is usually postulated rather than explained[64].

6   Many open questions by way of a conclusion

It was one of the purposes of this chapter to provide a broad map of diverse lines of enquiry that, in different ways, take the analysis of cognition, action and learning beyond the boundaries of the canonical model of rational decision and rational learning. The underlying perspective – as we have tried to argue – is that a positive theory of agency in evolutionary environment will have to rely upon quite different building blocks compared to the standard model.

Notwithstanding the length of this essay, we have been obliged to leave out a few pertinent issues. Let us conclude by flagging them, and by suggesting some further research questions that we consider to be very high on the evolutionary research agenda.

---

[64] In economics, principal/agent models as well as transaction cost theories, of course, try to do that. In the former case, though, they do it by reducing them to a sort of epiphenomenological 'veil', which is just a collective name for an ensemble of contracts among rational agents. Conversely, transaction cost models do fully acknowledge organizations as entities in their own right, but, in our view, they still fall short of providing a 'physiology' of organizations themselves, whereby governance procedures and problem-solving knowledge are reproduced and modified over time. For remarks in a similar spirit, see Padgett (1997), who also presents a simple 'hypercycle model' of the emergence of an 'ecology' of mutually consistent skills. See also Warglien (1995) on the evolution of organizational learning as a hierarchically nested process of selection among 'projects'.

6.1   Learning and selection

Coupled with learning, the other major tenet of evolutionary theory is, of course, selection; that is, some collective mechanism providing differential rewards and penalties (also involving differential diffusion and survival probabilities) for different traits (be they behaviours, routines, technologies or whatever), of which the agents are – so to speak – 'carriers'[65].

More generally, we suggest that almost all dynamics of socio-economic change fall somewhere in between the two extreme archetypes of 'pure learning' and 'pure selection'. The former corresponds to the extremist decision-theoretic or game-theoretic models: all agents make the best use of the available information, are endowed with identical information-processing algorithms, etc. (representative-agent rational expectation models are the most striking example). Clearly, selection plays no role here since every agent has the same access to the available opportunities (i.e., in some loose sense, has the same 'environmental fitness'). Conversely, in the opposing 'Darwinian' archetype, nobody learns, and system dynamics is driven by selection operating upon blindly generated variants of, for example, behaviours, technologies, etc. (taken literally, this is also the 'as . . . if' interpretation of rational behaviour). As briefly discussed earlier, the outcomes of the two dynamics, for whatever given environment, are equivalent only in some rather special cases. In general, the balance and interaction between learning and selection matters in terms of both the finite-time properties of the process and the long-term outcomes.

An implication of this is that the nature and intensity of selective mechanisms are not orthogonal to learning patterns. There might be subtle trade-offs here. Weak selective pressures most likely allow the persistence of 'slack' and 'inefficient' behaviours (no matter how 'efficiency' is defined in a particular context). On the other hand, excessively strong selective pressure might hinder learning insofar as the latter involves trial-and-error processes that are probably destined to be, on average, failures. It is a dilemma that March has phrased in terms of 'exploitation versus exploration' (March, 1991).

It can also be seen as a timescale issue: learning and selection may well proceed at different paces. So, for example, even the tightest selection environment can leave room for individual learning provided that

---

[65] General discussions about selection processes in socio-economic evolution can be found in Nelson and Winter (1982), Hodgson (1988), Dosi and Nelson (1994), Witt (1992), Metcalfe (1994), Nelson (1995), Silverberg (1988) and Winter (1988), among others.

selection is a low-frequency event compared to the rates of search/ learning. In biology, selection takes place at a generational time scale. Hence the trade-off is very clear: individual learning is favoured by having long-living organisms, while collective evolution takes advantage of short-living organisms and frequent generational renewal. Conversely, in the social domain the picture is more complicated: environments such as markets are not only fundamental selection mechanisms but also an essential source for feedback that stimulates learning processes.

Low-frequency feedback can slow down and render 'opaque' individual learning, but a frequent and tight application of selective forces might leave little room for experimentation and innovation. Moreover, note that the cultural reproduction of knowledge and behaviours within economic institutions introduces strong 'Lamarckian' features into the relationships between learning and selection.

Another, related, issue concerns the possible tension between individual and collective learning; for example, it might well happen that persistent individual mistakes (e.g. decision biases) turn out to have a positive collective role (an interpretation along these lines of the process of entry of business firms is in Dosi and Lovallo, 1997, but a lot more needs to be done in order to explore the value of this conjecture).

6.2   Learning, path dependency and coevolution

A quite general property of learning processes is often their path-dependent nature. This sometimes holds even under quite conventional learning mechanisms[66], and even more so in evolutionary environments. Of course, path dependency implies that initial conditions and/or early fluctuations along the learning path shape long-term outcomes. Furthermore, if learning entails the development of rather inertial cognitive frames and routinized action rules, one should indeed expect inertia and 'lock-in' to be one of the corollaries of the very fact that 'agents have learned'.

Above, we have surveyed a few models of, for example, technological learning that do generate path dependency, lock-in, etc. even in rather simple environments, driven by some form of dynamic increasing returns or social adaptation. A more complicated and fascinating question

---

[66] For example, this is true for Bayesian learning if the set of events upon which agents form their priors is different, and also in finite time if agents hold the same priors but are exposed to different sample paths. It also appears as a limit property of environments where Bayesian agents sample across other Bayesian agents in order to decide among alternative options (see Arthur and Lane, 1993).

concerns those path-dependent outcomes that are driven by the correlation across cognitive, behavioural or organizational traits, which in biology comes under the heading of *epistatic correlation* (see Levinthal, 1996a, for a suggestive exploratory application to the analysis of organizational 'inertia')[67]. The basic intuition is simple. Suppose that, say, cognitive and behavioural repertoires come as rather folded packages – due either to some proximate internal coherence or simply to the fact that originally they randomly happened to come together. For example, in the above formal framework, suppose that the set of representations/actions that turned out to be 'learned' involves the rule r_p mapping an 'understanding' of the world in terms of $(\vartheta_1, \vartheta_2, \ldots)$ into procedures $(\xi_1, \xi_2, \ldots)$. Suppose also that that rule happened to 'win' because, in an environment with 'true' states that are cognitively coded under ϑ_i, procedure ξ_i was reinforced by the obtained pay-offs. However, under some other states (which, say, are coded in ϑ_j, triggering ξ_j), the decision rule is strikingly bad. Of course, with no trait correlation, agents would hold on to that part of the original rule that links ϑ_i to ξ_i and change the rest of the repertoire by merging it with, for example, representation ϑ_k and intended action ξ_k. However, suppose that the first 'package' can hardly be unbundled, and that the same applies to the other one, where, say, ϑ_k and also ξ_k come correlated within another 'model', yielding 'bad' responses under the states coded under ϑ_i. One can intuitively see here how some system interrelatedness can easily produce inertia and lock-in (see David, 1992, who also discusses the appealing analogy between technological and institutional systems).

It is important to note that interrelatedness and trait correlation are far from being theoretical *curiosa*. Rather, it is almost as if they are intrinsic properties of all entities embodying relatively coherent inner structures. This applies to knowledge systems, as well as business organizations and all other institutions. (A deeper understanding of this correlation leads back to the challenge of developing constructive theories of these entities themselves, as mentioned earlier.)

The ramifications of this point are even broader, linking with the idea of *learning as a coevolutionary process*. It is a straightforward conclusion from our earlier discussion that the general view of learning that we propose rests on coevolution between cognitive representations, behavioural repertoires and preferences. In a nutshell, this implies a notion of mutual adaptation not only, of course, along the canonical sequence from what one believes to know to what one does (judged according to what one

---

[67] Kauffman's model of biological evolution is an acknowledged source of inspiration (Kauffman, 1993).

deems to be better for himself) but also the other way round, from what
one does to what one has to believe in order to justify what has been done,
and from what one gets to what one likes.

6.3   Preference and expectation

We have presented above some tentative insights towards the formalization of coevolution between mental models and action repertoires. Two
other domains, however, have been largely neglected so far, namely expectation formation and endogenous preferences. With regard to expectations, the rather unfortunate state of the art is that one is largely stuck
between a rational expectation paradigm (which basically assumes agents
who already know what they are supposed to learn) and various extrapola-
tive expectation mechanisms. Between the two, evolutionary modellers
tend – and rightly so – to choose the latter as a first approximation (see,
for example, Chiaromonte et al., 1993), but sooner or later one should
try to model agents that elaborate conjectures about the 'structure of the
world' and its parametrization and test them against experience. More
precisely, this is indeed what adaptive learning models do (e.g. Holland
et al., 1986, and Marengo and Tordjman, 1996), but the drawback is that
one either has 'pure forecast' models (whereby the triggered 'action' is the
forecast itself) or models where forecast and action selection (concerning, for example, price levels, selling or buying, etc.) are folded together.
A major step forward, in our view, would be the development of models whereby search in the space of expectations on the states of the world
and search in the space of actions is partly decoupled[68]. One consequence
would be the possibility of handling the coexistence of partly conflicting
systems of belief and action patterns[69], and it would also allow an explicit
account of phenomena such as cognitive dissonance (see Festinger, 1957,
Hirschman, 1965, and Akerlof and Dickens, 1982, for some economic
applications)[70].

This leads directly to the issue of endogenous preferences. Some
progress has recently been made towards modelling preferences as

---

[68] See a preliminary attempt in Riolo (1990).
[69] Think, for example, of action patterns that continue to be implemented because they
'work' even if they conflict with agent-held theories. Speculative behaviour involving
both a rule ('buy as long as the market is bullish') and an expectation ('the market is
going to collapse') belongs to this class (we owe this observation to Tordjman).
[70] The fact that the belief system and the action system remain partly coupled generally
entails imperfect attempts to reduce cognitive dissonance by modifying the system of
beliefs in order to accommodate the action patterns. Every smoker, for example, is
familiar with such exercises! In a similar vein, we plan to call a model of this kind (which
we are beginning to build) 'the spirit is strong, but the flesh is weak . . .'(!?).

influenced by social interactions (see, for example, Kuran, 1987, and Brock and Durlauf, 1995). The time is perhaps ripe to take the issue further, right into the foundational model of agency, and account for the endogeneity of the criteria by which representations, actions and 'payoffs' are evaluated, certainly as a result of social imitation but also driven by attempts to adjust 'desires' to realized outcomes. (A probably apocryphal saying attributed to Joseph Stalin mentions his definition of 'pure happiness as the perfect correspondence between expectations and reality' [!]; certainly, he was trying hard to work on the former . . .) So far, these phenomena have been neglected by adaptive learning models; indeed, an aspect that we consider rather unsatisfactory is the general assumption of an invariant pay-off function, which also drives the learning process by providing the yardstick against which the outcomes of cognition/action are judged. Our proposal, on the contrary, in our earlier language, is to render the π function endogenous – some implications being that one disposes of any notion of 'utility' as one of the primitives of the theory and operationalizes an idea of the adaptive identities of agents much nearer a lot of sociological intuitions.

6.4   *Coevolutionary determinants of routines and other organizational traits*

Isomorphic issues appear also at higher levels of description. Consider, for example, the coevolution of technologies, business organizations and related institutions, raised in an appreciative and theorizing mode by Nelson, 1994); or the multiple nature of routines as procedures for both problem solving and the governance of conflict (Coriat and Dosi, 1995). In both these cases organizational learning is driven by multiple, and possibly contradictory, selection mechanisms (for example, success in innovative search but also control over the possibility of opportunistic or conflictual behaviours, and the political 'coherence' of the organization, etc.)[71]. There is a wealth of empirical evidence supporting all this, and one starts forming some appreciative theories; it might be worth also beginning to explore some simple formal models whereby organizational learning concerns the development of collectively shared cognitive models and action repertoires that, so to speak, 'make sense' according to multiple dimensions (suggesting also that what members of the organization 'know', do and believe to be their interests all coevolve).

A major implication of all this is that evolutionary theories of learning might head towards the hierarchically nested levels of description

---

[71] A few more comments are in Dosi (1995a).

of learning processes[72], possibly related to different learning entities. At one extreme, one is only beginning to explore the dynamics of, so to speak, 'agentless' organizations where learning is driven by evolution under some selective pressure upon bundles of routines, skills, etc. (preliminary efforts are to be found in Marengo, 1996, and Padgett, 1997). At the other extreme, it seems equally promising to explore explicitly agent-based models where collective knowledge emerges from endogenous networking among entities embodying diverse pieces of knowledge[73].

Somewhere in between, as discussed at greater length in Coriat and Dosi (1995) a major challenge ahead is modelling agents that imperfectly learn how to adapt (in terms of skills, behaviours and goals) to existing institutions while the imperfection of adaptation is itself a fundamental source of institutional change[74].

There is much food for thought here. It seems to us that one faces nowadays the possibility of an interdisciplinary construction of a positive theory of agency and learning the scope of which goes well beyond the limits of applicability of the usual (rational) decision-theoretic model. And, for the first time, one is beginning to develop the instruments to make it 'harder' – able also to generate formal 'toy models' that, moreover, have a positive interaction with models based on more orthodox notions of rationality. (In our view, though, it will never be able to present the axiomatic 'hardness' of the latter, notwithstanding its measure-zero empirical content, whenever stripped of any phenomenological restrictions.)

As economists, we are tempted to mark this emerging approach with the label of 'evolutionary' or 'institutionalist'. But, in other disciplines similar approaches come under quite different headings. Moreover, even within the economists' arena, a few 'revisionist' developments building on 'bounded rationality', 'far-from-equilibrium learning', etc. promise challenging dialogues. At the present moment it is certainly far too early to know whether it will turn out to be scientifically more fruitful to pursue some equivalent of a 'new Ptolemaic synthesis' or, conversely, some more radical views, still largely to be developed. Where our inclinations are should be clear from this chapter. In any case, whether one

---

[72] An exploratory attempt is in Warglien (1995).

[73] This would certainly put on a more rigorous footing the Hayekian proposition about capitalist institutions (including markets) as mechanisms for the coordination of distributed knowledge (see also Egidi, 1996, and Lane et al., 1996).

[74] One can easily see how this could also represent a major bridge between evolutionary theories and institutionalist analyses of the mechanism holding together and changing the social fabric (a thorough discussion of many related issues is to be found in Hodgson, 1988). Enormously difficult but fascinating issues such as, for example, the dynamic coupling between institutions and economic behaviours, and the role of trust and power, come under this broad heading.

succeeds or not, it remains important to establish some sort of equivalence classes, partly mapping problems and formal instruments across different approaches. This kind of bridge is also part of what we have tried to achieve in this chapter.

7   A post-scriptum (October 2001)

Even though the bulk of this chapter was written in 1996, we have decided to keep it – with the exception of some bibliographical updating – largely unaltered. It has, hopefully, its own internal consistence and, conversely, it would be futile to try to follow up on the fast-expanding literature of the last few years; a brand new article would be required.

Here, let us just flag for the convenience of the reader some promising directions of enquiry that overlap, complement or improve upon those discussed so far.

First, growing attention has been focused on learning processes in general and experimental games in particular; see, among others, Erev and Roth (1998, 1999), Camerer (1997) and Camerer and Ho (1998, 1999).

Second, empirical regularities in decisions and behaviour – concerning systematic deviations from the predictions of canonical 'rational' theories in particular – are at least adding up into an emerging 'behavioural' perspective concerning, for example, intertemporal choices, financial investments and consumption; after the early contributions in Loewenstein and Elster (1992), see the discussions in Browning and Lusardi (1996) and Rabin (1998), among many others.

A big and controversial issue, of course, concerns how the observed patterns of decision and behaviour ought to be interpreted. One way involves the 're-axiomatization' of choice, twisting it just enough so as to make theoretical postulates not conflict too much with the evidence (for example, rationalization of the evidence on intertemporal choice just in terms of hyperbolic rather than exponential discounts is a paramount illustration of this genre).

An alternative way of tackling observed 'biases' is by arguing that, in fact, they are not biases after all, but rather relatively smart forms of evolutionary adaptation (e.g. Gigerenzer et al., 1999, and Gigerenzer, 2000, and some of the contributions to Gigerenzer and Selten, 2001).

Third, yet another approach, in tune with some of the conjectures discussed in the preceding section, painstakingly proceeds with the exploration of the very foundations of reasoning and 'mental models' underlying cognition, motivations and behaviours; see Girotto et al. (2000), Goldvarg and Johnson-Laird (2000), Johnson-Laird (2000) and Johnson-Laird and Byrne (2000).

The alternative interpretation of purported 'biases', as well as of seemingly 'unbiased' behaviours, hints in fact at deeper conjectures on 'human nature' itself (whatever that means). Being unable to discuss here the many controversies concerning the tangled relations between learning and environmental selection, let us just mention three critical issues.

(i) What is the extent of the 'hard-wiring' of human cognition and behaviours into some underlying 'genetic' predisposition?

(ii) Does such evidence, if any, regard primarily syntactic and inferential rules (such as our relative ability of performing syllogism, *modus ponens* versus *modus tollens*, deduction versus induction, etc.)? Or does it impinge on the very content of behavioural patterns (such as our deepest inclinations to selfishness, obedience, altruism, etc.)?

(iii) Can one impute some optimality properties to whatever 'mankind-invariant' regularities these may be, if any?

Given the preceding section, our deep scepticism about 'strong hard-wiring' *à la* Dawkins (1986) should come as no surprise. And, even more so, it comes together with deeply rooted presumptions on the evolutionary optimality of the revealed outcomes (the arguments in Cosmides and Tooby, 1994, 1996, being an appealing but, in our view, also misleading template).

Instead, our discussion above is quite agnostic as to 'hard-wired' inclinations, leaving the possibility of this existence very much open, but, all in all, we conjecture: a) a very long leash between genes and utterly diverse cultural expressions; and b) the general lack of evidence supporting Panglossian attitudes ('whatever exists, it must be optimal, at least in a local sense, otherwise it would not exist').

Indeed we are rather worried about the increasingly frequent encounters between Dr Pangloss and rudimentary versions of evolutionary theories, yielding rather unfounded but often sinister apologies for a status quo the optimality of which is supposedly grounded in our very genes.

One way of supporting such a theoretical perspective has been through what we consider an improper use of *evolutionary games*. As hinted above and argued at some length in Dosi and Winter (2002) in the socio-economic domain such games are important instruments to explore 'reduced form' evolutionary processes essentially driven by collective adaptation. We are adamant, though, in considering rather far-fetched any application grounded on daring equivalencies between 'genes' and 'cultural memes', and on doubtful simplifications of the selection landscapes over which socio-economic adaptation occurs.

Fourth, today, compared to just a few years ago, one finds a much richer discussion about *endogenous preferences*. They can indeed be studied from many different angles. In some quarters, tentative beginnings to the exploration of the coupled dynamics of preferences, behaviours and mental models are being made (see, for example, Aversi et al., 1999, and the critical discussion of the evidence in Devetag, 1999). Along different lines of research, others ingeniously attempt to unveil the 'rationality' hidden behind preference dynamics (see Elster, 1998).

Fifth, over the last few years a lot of work has gone into the understanding of *organizational* capabilities and learning; see, among others, Dosi et al. (2000). At the same time, a few researchers have attempted to formalize the problem-solving dynamics of organizations themselves, in ways certainly rooted in the pioneering lessons of Herbert Simon but possibly further relaxing even the Simonesque requirements of procedural rationality and the quasi-decomposability of problems; see Levinthal (1996), Levinthal and Warglien (1999) and Marengo and Lazaric (2000).

Nonetheless, it remains the case that many of the issues raised in this chapter concerning a would-be positive theory of agency are obviously still far from settled. However, the comparison between the state of the art even half a decade ago and nowadays highlights a genuinely encouraging picture. To be sure, there are still many neoclassical 'Talibans' at large, and there is still a lot of fuzziness regarding alternative perspectives on cognition, behaviours and learning. But, encouragingly, there are also many and various signs of progress towards the micro-foundations of economic behaviours that do less and less violence to the increasingly rich micro-evidence.

REFERENCES

Aghion, P., and P. Howitt (1992), 'A model of growth through creative destruction', *Econometrica* **60**(2): 323–51.
Akerlof, G. A., and W. T. Dickens (1982), 'The economic consequences of cognitive dissonance', *American Economic Review* **72**(3): 307–19.
Allen, B. (1982a), 'A stochastic interactive model for the diffusion of information', *Journal of Mathematical Sociology* **8**: 265–81.
  (1982b), 'Some stochastic processes of interdependent demand and technological diffusion of an innovation exhibiting externalities among adopters', *International Economic Review* **23**: 595–608.
An, M., and N. Kiefer (1995), 'Local externalities and societal adoption of technologies', *Journal of Evolutionary Economics* **5**(2): 103–17.
Anderlini, L., and A. Ianni (1996), 'Path dependence and learning from neighbours', *Games and Economic Behavior* **13**: 141–78.
Andersen, E. S (1994), *Evolutionary Economics: Post-Schumpeterian Contributions*, London: Pinter.
Arifovic, J. (1994), 'Genetic algorithm learning and the cobweb model', *Journal of Economic Dynamics and Control* **18**: 3–28.

Arrow, K. J. (1962), 'The economic implications of learning by doing', *Review of Economic Studies* **29**: 155–73.

Arthur, W. B. (1991), 'On designing economic agents that behave like human agents: a behavioural approach to bounded rationality', *American Economic Review* **81**: 353–70.

——— (1993), 'On designing artificial agents that behave like human agents', *Journal of Evolutionary Economics* **3**(1): 1–22.

Arthur, W. B., Y. M. Ermoliev and Y. M. Kaniovski (1987), 'Strong laws for a class of path-dependent urn processes', in V. Arkin, A. Shiryayev and R. Wets (eds.), *Proceedings of the International Conference on Stochastic Optimization*, Kiev, 1984, Lecture Notes in Control and Information Sciences no. 81, Berlin: Springer-Verlag, 287–300.

Arthur, W. B., and D. Lane (1993), 'Information contagion', *Structural Change and Economic Dynamics* **4**: 81–104.

Aversi, R., G. Dosi, G. Fagiolo, M. Meacci and C. Olivetti (1999), 'Demand dynamics with socially evolving preferences', *Industrial and Corporate Change* **8**: 353–408.

Bala, V., and S. Goyal (1998), 'Learning from neighbors', *Review of Economic Studies* **65**: 595–621.

Barron, J. N., and M. T. Hannan (1994), 'The impact of economics on contemporary sociology', *Journal of Economic Literature* **32**: 1111–46.

Bateson, G. (1972), *Steps to an Ecology of Mind*, New York: Ballantine Books.

Berninghaus, S. K., and U. G. Schwalbe (1992), *Learning and Adaptation Processes in Games with a Local Interaction Structure*, Mimeo, University of Bonn.

——— (1996), 'Evolution, interaction and Nash equilibria', *Journal of Economic Behavior and Organization* **29**: 57–85.

Binmore, K. (1990), *Essays on the Foundations of Game Theory*, Oxford: Blackwell.

Blackwell, D., and L. Dubins (1962), 'Merging of opinions with increasing information', *Annals of Mathematical Statistics* **33**: 882–86.

Blume, L. E. (1993), 'The statistical mechanics of strategic interaction', *Games and Economic Behaviour* **5**: 387–424.

——— (1995), 'The statistical mechanics of best-response strategy revision', *Games and Economic Behavior* **11**: 111–45.

Borcherding, K., D. L. Larichev and D. M. Messick (eds.) (1990), *Contemporary Issues in Decision Making*, New York: North-Holland.

Bourdieu, P. (1977), *Outline of a Theory of Practice*, Cambridge: Cambridge University Press.

Brock, W. A., and S. N. Durlauf (1995), *Discrete Choice with Social Interactions I: Theory*, Working Paper 9521, Social Systems Research Institute, University of Wisconsin, Madison.

Browning, M., and A. M. Lusardi (1996), 'Household saving: micro theories and micro facts', *Journal of Economic Literature* **34**: 1797–855.

Bush, R. R., and F. Mosteller (1955), *Stochastic Models for Learning*, New York: Wiley.

Camerer, C. F. (1997), 'Progress in behavioral game theory', *Journal of Economic Perspectives* **11**: 167–88.

Camerer, C. F., and T. H. Ho (1999), 'Experience-weighted attraction in games', *Econometrica* **67**(4): 827–74.

(2004), 'Learning in games', in C. R. Plott and V. L. Smith (eds.), *Handbook of Experimental Economics Results*, Amsterdam and New York: North-Holland.

Casti, J. L. (1992), *Reality Rules*, New York: Wiley.

Chiaromonte, F., and G. Dosi (1993), 'Heterogeneity, competition and macroeconomic dynamics', *Structural Change and Economic Dynamics* **4**: 39–63.

Chiaromonte, F., G. Dosi and L. Orsenigo (1993), 'Innovative learning and institutions in the process of development: on the microfoundations of growth regimes', in R. Thomson (ed.), *Learning and Technological Change*, London: Macmillan, 117–49.

Cohen, M. D., and P. Bacdayan (1994), 'Organizational routines are stored as procedural memory: evidence from a laboratory study', *Organizational Science* **5**: 554–68.

Cohen, M. D., R. Burkhart, G. Dosi, M. Egidi, L. Marengo, M. Warglien, S. G. Winter and B. Coriat (1996), 'Routines and other recurring action patterns of organisations: contemporary research issues', *Industrial and Corporate Change* **5**: 653–98.

Cohen, M. D., J. G. March and J. P. Olsen (1972), 'A garbage can model of organizational choice', *Administrative Sciences Quarterly* **17**: 1–25.

Conlisk, J. (1989), 'An aggregate model of technical change', *Quarterly Journal of Economics* **104**: 787–821.

Coriat, B., and G. Dosi (1995), *Learning How to Govern and Learning How to Solve Problems: On the Co-evolution of Competences, Conflicts and Organizational Routines*, Working Paper WP 95-06, International Institute of Applied Systems Analysis, Laxenburg, Austria.

(1998), 'The institutional embeddedness of economic change: An appraisal of the "evolutionary" and "regulationist" research programmes', in K. Nielsen and E. J. Johnson (eds.), *Institutions and Economic Change*, Cheltenham: Edward Elgar, 3–32.

Cosmides, L., and J. Tooby (1994), 'Better than rational: evolutionary psychology and the invisible hand', *American Economic Review* **84**(2): 327–32.

(1996), 'Are humans good intuitive statisticians after all? Rethinking some conclusions from the literature on judgment and uncertainty', *Cognition* **58**: 187–276.

Cyert, R. M., and J. G. March (1992), *A Behavioral Theory of the Firm*, 2nd edn., Cambridge: Basil Blackwell.

Dalle, J. M. (1993), *Dynamiques d'Adoption, Coordination et Diversité: Le Cas des Standards Technologiques*, Strasbourg: Beta.

(1994a), *Decisions Autonomes et Coexistence des Technologies*, Working Paper 9401, Institut d'Economie et de Politique de l'Energie, Grenoble, France.

(1994b), *Technological Competition, Micro-decisions and Diversity*, paper presented at the EUNETIC conference on evolutionary economics of technological change: assessment of results and new frontiers, 6–8 October, Strasbourg.

David, P. A. (1975), *Technical Choice, Innovation and Economic Growth: Essays on American and British Experience in the Nineteenth Century*, Cambridge: Cambridge University Press.

(1985), 'Clio and the economics of QWERTY', *American Economic Review* 75(2): 332–37.

(1992), 'Path dependence and predictability in dynamic systems with local externalities: a paradigm for historical economics', in D. Foray and C. Freeman (eds.), *Technology and the Wealth of Nations*, London: Pinter, 208–31.

Davidson, P. (1996), 'Reality and economic theory', *Journal of Post-Keynesian Economics*, **18**: 479–508.

Dawkins, R. (1986), *The Blind Watchmaker: Why the Evidence of Evolution Reveals a Universe Without Design*, New York: Norton.

Devetag, M. G. (1999), 'From utilities to mental models: a critical survey on decision rules and cognition in consumer choice', *Industrial and Corporate Change* 8: 289–351.

Dosi, G. (1984), *Technical Change and Industrial Transformation: The Theory and an Application to the Semiconductor Industry*, London: Macmillan.

(1988), 'Sources, procedures and microeconomic effects of innovation', *Journal of Economic Literature* **26**: 1120–71.

(1995a), 'Hierarchies, markets and power: some foundational issues on the nature of contemporary economic organisations', *Industrial and Corporate Change* 4: 1–19.

(1995b), *The Contribution of Economic Theory to the Understanding of a Knowledge-based Economy*, Working Paper WP 95-56, International Institute of Applied Systems Analysis, Laxenburg, Austria.

Dosi, G., and M. Egidi (1991), 'Substantive and procedural uncertainty: an exploration of economic behaviours in changing environments', *Journal of Evolutionary Economics* 1(2): 145–68.

Dosi, G., Y. M. Ermoliev and Y. M. Kaniovski (1994), 'Generalized urn schemes and technological dynamics', *Journal of Mathematical Economics* 23: 1–19.

Dosi, G., S. Fabiani, R. Aversi and M. Meacci (1994), 'The dynamics of international differentiation: a multi-country evolutionary model', *Industrial and Corporate Change* 3: 225–41.

Dosi, G., C. Freeman, R. R. Nelson, G. Silverberg and L. Soete (eds.) (1988), *Technical Change and Economic Theory*, London: Pinter.

Dosi, G., and Y. M. Kaniovski (1994), 'On "badly behaved" dynamics', *Journal of Evolutionary Economics* 4(2): 93–123.

Dosi, G., and D. Lovallo (1997), 'Rational entrepreneurs or optimistic martyrs? Some considerations on technological regimes, corporate entries, and the evolutionary role of decision biases', in R. Garud, P. R. Nayyar and Z. B. Shapira (eds.), *Technological Innovation: Oversights and Foresights*, Cambridge: Cambridge University Press, 41–70.

Dosi, G., and L. Marengo (1994), 'Toward a theory of organizational competencies', in R. W. England (ed.), *Evolutionary Concepts in Contemporary Economics*, Ann Arbor, MI: University of Michigan Press, 157–78.

Dosi, G., L. Marengo, A. Bassanini and M. Valente (1999), 'Norms as emergent properties of adaptive learning: the case of economic routines', *Journal of Evolutionary Economics* 9: 5–26.

Dosi, G., O. Marsili, L. Orsenigo and R. Salvatore (1995), 'Learning, market selection and the evolution of industrial structure', *Small Business Economics* 7: 411–36.

Dosi, G., and J. S. Metcalfe (1991), 'On some notions of irreversibility in economics', in P. Saviotti and J. S. Metcalfe (eds.), *Evolutionary Theories of Economic and Technological Change: Present Status and Future Prospects*, Chur, Switzerland: Harwood Academic, 133–59.

Dosi, G., and R. R. Nelson (1994), 'An introduction to evolutionary theories in economics', *Journal of Evolutionary Economics* 4(3): 153–72.

Dosi, G., R. R. Nelson and S. G. Winter (eds.) (2000), *The Nature and Dynamics of Organizational Capabilities*, Oxford: Oxford University Press.

Dosi, G., and S. G. Winter (2002), 'Interpreting economic change: evolution, structures and games', in M. Augier and J. G. March (eds.), *The Economics of Choice, Change, and Organizations*, Cheltenham/Northampton: Edward Elgar, 337–53.

Dubois, D., and H. Prade (1988), 'Modelling uncertainty and inductive inference: a survey of recent non-additive probability systems', *Acta Psychologica* 68: 53–78.

Durlauf, S. N. (1994), 'Path dependence in aggregate output', *Industrial and Corporate Change* 3: 149–71.

Easley, D., and A. Rustichini (1995), *Choice without Beliefs*, working paper, Center for Operations Research and Economics, Catholic University of Louvain, Louvain-la-Neuve, Belgium.

Edgerton, R. B. (1985), *Rules, Exceptions and Social Order*, Berkeley and Los Angeles: University of California Press.

Egidi, M. (1996), 'Routines, hierarchies of problems, procedural behaviour: some evidence from experiments', in K. J. Arrow, E. Colombatto, M. Perlman and C. Schmidt (eds.), *The Rational Foundations of Economic Behaviour*, London: Macmillan, 303–33.

Einhorn, H. J., and R. M. Hogarth (1985), 'Ambiguity and uncertainty in probabilistic inference', *Psychological Review* 86: 433–61.

Eliasson, G. (1985), *The Firm and Financial Markets in the Swedish Micro-to-Macro Model*, working paper, Research Unit of Industrial Economics (IUI), Stockholm.

Elster, J. (1998), 'Emotions and economic theory', *Journal of Economic Literature* 36: 47–74.

Epstein, J. M., and R. Axtell (1996), *Growing Artificial Societies: Social Science from the Bottom Up*, Washington, DC: Brookings Institution.

Erev, I., and A. E. Roth (1998), 'Predicting how people play games: reinforcement learning in experimental games with unique, mixed strategy equilibria', *American Economic Review* 88(4): 848–81.

(1999), 'On the role of reinforcement learning in experimental games: the cognitive game theory approach', in D. Bodescu, I. Erev and R. Zwick (eds.), *Games and Human Behavior: Essays in Honor of Amnon Rapoport*, Mahwah, NJ: Lawrence Erlbaum Associates, 53–77.

Ericsson, K. A., and J. Smith (eds.) (1991), *Toward a General Theory of Expertise*, Cambridge: Cambridge University Press.

Estes, W. K. (1950), 'Toward a statistical theory of learning', *Psychological Review* 57: 94–107.

Feldman, M. (1991), 'On the generic nonconvergence of Bayesian actions and beliefs', *Economic Theory* 1: 301–21.

Festinger, L. (1957), *A Theory of Cognitive Dissonance*, Stanford, CA: Stanford University Press.

Fisher, R. A. (1930), *The Genetical Theory of Natural Selection*, Oxford: Clarendon Press.

Föllmer, H. (1974), 'Random economies with many interacting agents', *Journal of Mathematical Economics* 24: 51–62.

Fontana, W., and L. W. Buss (1994), 'What would be conserved if "the tape were played twice"?', *Proceedings of the National Academy of Sciences USA* 91: 757–61.

(1996), *The Barrier of Objects: From Dynamical Systems to Bounded Organizations*, Working Paper WP 96-27, International Institute for Applied Systems Analysis, Laxenburg, Austria.

Foray, D., and B.-Å. Lundvall (1996), *The Knowledge-based Economy*, Paris: Organisation for Economic Co-operation and Development.

Foster, D., and P. Young (1990), 'Stochastic evolutionary game dynamics', *Theoretical Population Biology* 38: 219–32.

Freeman, C. (1982), *The Economics of Industrial Innovation*, London: Pinter.

(1994), 'The economics of technical change', *Cambridge Journal of Economics* 18: 463–514.

Friedman, D. (1991), 'Evolutionary games in economics', *Econometrica* 59(3): 637–66.

Friedman, M. (1953), *Essays in Positive Economics*, Chicago: University of Chicago Press.

Fudenberg, D., and C. Harris (1992), 'Evolutionary dynamics with aggregate shocks', *Journal of Economic Theory* 57: 420–41.

Fudenberg, D., and D. M. Kreps (1993), 'Learning mixed equilibria', *Games and Economic Behaviour* 5: 320–67.

Fudenberg, D., and D. K. Levine (1995), 'Consistency and cautious fictitious play', *Journal of Economic Dynamics and Control* 19: 1065–89.

Geertz, C. (1963), *Peddlers and Princes*, Chicago: University of Chicago Press.

Gigerenzer, G. (2000), *Adaptive Thinking: Rationality in the Real World*, Oxford: Oxford University Press.

Gigerenzer, G., and R. Selten (eds.) (2001), *Bounded Rationality: The Adaptive Toolbox*, Cambridge, MA: MIT Press.

Gigerenzer, G., P. M. Todd and the ABC Research Group (1999), *Simple Heuristics that Make us Smart*, Oxford: Oxford University Press.

Girotto, V., P. N. Johnson-Laird, P. Legrenzi and M. Sonino (2000), 'Reasoning to consistency: how people resolve logical inconsistencies', in L. Garcia-Madruga, M. Carriedo and M. J. Gonzalez-Labra (eds.), *Mental Models in Reasoning*, Madrid: Universidad Nacional de Educación a Distancia, 83–97.

Glaziev, S. Y., and Y. M. Kaniovski (1991), 'Diffusion of innovations under conditions of uncertainty: a stochastic approach', in N. Nakicenovic and

A. Grubler (eds.), *Diffusion of Technologies and Social Behaviour*, Berlin: Springer-Verlag, 231–46.

Goffman, E. (1974), *Frame Analysis: An Essay on the Organisation of Experience*, Harmondsworth: Penguin.

Goldvarg, Y., and P. N. Johnson-Laird (2000), 'Illusions in modal reasoning', *Memory & Cognition* 28: 282–94.

Granovetter, M. S. (1985), 'Economic action and social structure: the problem of embeddedness', *American Journal of Sociology* 51: 481–510.

Granstrand, O. (ed.) (1994), *The Economics of Technology*, Amsterdam: North-Holland.

Griffin, D., and A. Tversky (1992), 'The weight of evidence and the determinants of confidence', *Cognitive Psychology* 24: 411–35.

Grimmett, G. (1989), *Percolation*, New York: Springer-Verlag.

Grossman, G. M., and E. Helpman (1991), *Innovation and Growth in the Global Economy*, Cambridge, MA: MIT Press.

Hammersley, J. M., and D. J. A. Welsh (1980), 'Percolation theory and its ramifications', *Contemporary Physics* 21: 593–605.

Heiner, R. A. (1983), 'The origin of predictable behavior', *American Economic Review* 73(4): 560–95.

Herrnstein, R. J., and D. Prelec (1991), 'Melioration: a theory of distributed choice', *Journal of Economic Perspectives*, 5: 137–56.

Herz, A. V. M. (1994), 'Collective phenomena in spatially extended evolutionary games', *Journal of Theoretical Biology* 169: 65–87.

Hicks, J. R. (1936), *Value and Capital*, Oxford: Oxford University Press.

Hirschman, A. (1965), 'Obstacles to development: a classification and a quasi-vanishing act', *Economic Development and Cultural Change*, 13: 385–93.

Hodgson, G. M. (1988), *Economics and Institutions: A Manifesto for a Modern Institutional Economics*, Cambridge: Polity Press.

(1993), *Economics and Evolution: Bringing Life Back into Economics*, Cambridge: Polity Press.

Hoffmeister, F., and M. Bäck (1991), *Genetic Algorithms and Evolution Strategies – Similarities and Differences*, Paper on Economics and Evolution no. 9103, European Study Group for Evolutionary Economics.

Holland, J. H., K. J. Holyoak, R. E. Nisbett and P. R. Thagard (eds.) (1986), *Induction: Processes of Inference, Learning and Discovery*, Cambridge, MA: MIT Press.

Hors, I., and F. Lordon (1997), 'About some formalisms of interaction: phase transition models in economics?', *Journal of Evolutionary Economics* 7(4): 355–73.

Huberman, B., and T. Hogg (1995), 'Distributed computation as an economic system', *Journal of Economic Perspectives* 9: 141–52.

Ioannides, Y. M. (1990), 'Trading uncertainty and market form', *International Economic Review* 31: 619–38.

Johnson-Laird, P. N. (1983), *Mental Models*, Cambridge, MA: Harvard University Press.

(1993), *The Computer and the Mind*, London: Fontana Press.

(2000), 'The current state of the mental model theory', in J. Garcia-Madruga, M.Carriedo and M. J. Gonzalez-Labra (eds.), *Mental Models in Reasoning*, Madrid: Universidad Nacional de Educación a Distancia, 17–40.

Johnson-Laird, P. N., and R. M. J. Byrne (2000), 'Mental models and pragmatics', *Behavioral and Brain Sciences* **23**: 284–86.

Kahneman, D., J. L. Knetsch and R. H. Thaler (1990), 'Experiment tests of the endowment effect and the Coase theorem', *Journal of Political Economy* **98**(6): 1325–48.

Kahneman, D., and D. Lovallo (1993), 'Timid choice and bold forecast: a cognitive perspective on risktaking', *Management Science* **39**: 17–31.

Kahneman, D., P. Slovic, and A. Tversky (eds.) (1982), *Judgment under Uncertainty: Heuristics and Biases*, Cambridge: Cambridge University Press.

Kahneman, D., and A. Tversky (1986), 'Rational choice and the framing of decision', *Journal of Business* **59**: 251–78.

Kalai, E., and E. Lehrer (1994), 'Weak and strong merging of opinions', *Journal of Mathematical Economics* **23**: 73–86.

Kandori, M., G. J. Mailath and R. Rob (1993), 'Learning, mutations, and long-run equilibrium in games', *Econometrica* **61**(1): 29–56.

Kaniovski, Y. M., A. V. Kryazhimskii and H. P. Young (1996), *On the Robustness of Stochastic Best-Reply Dynamics in Repeated Games*, Working Paper WP 96-45, International Institute of Applied Systems Analysis, Laxenburg, Austria.

Kaniovski, Y. M., and H. P. Young (1994), 'Learning dynamics in games with stochastic perturbations', *Games and Economic Behavior* **11**: 330–63.

Katona, G. (1951), *Psychological Analysis of Economic Behavior*, New York: McGraw-Hill.

(1968), 'Behavioral and ecological economics, consumer behaviour: theory and findings on expectations and aspirations', *American Economic Review* **58**(2): 19–30.

Katzner, D. W. (1990), 'The firm under conditions of ignorance and historical time', *Journal of Post-Keynesian Economics* **13**: 124–56.

Kauffman, S. A. (1993), *The Origins of Order*, Oxford: Oxford University Press.

Kirman, A. P. (1992), 'Variety: the coexistence of techniques', *Revue d'Economie Industrielle* **59**: 62–74.

(1993), 'Ants, rationality and recruitment', *Quarterly Journal of Economics*, **108**: 137–56.

(1997), 'The economy as an interactive system', in W. B. Arthur, S. N. Durlauf and D. Lane (eds.), *The Economy as an Evolving Complex System II*, Santa Fe Institute Studies in the Sciences of Complexity, Reading, MA: Addison-Wesley, 491–531.

Kirman, A. P., C. Oddou and S. Weber (1986), 'Stochastic communication and coalition formation', *Econometrica* **54**(1): 129–38.

Kogut, B. (ed.) (1993), *Country Competitiveness: Technology and the Organizing of Work*, Oxford: Oxford University Press.

Koza, J. R. (1993), *Genetic Programming*, Cambridge, MA: MIT Press.

Kreps, D. M. (1996), 'Market, hierarchies and mathematical economic theory', *Industrial and Corporate Change* **5**: 561–95.

Kuran, T. (1987), 'Preference falsification, policy continuity and collective conservatism', *Economic Journal* **387**: 642–55.

(1991), 'Cognitive limitations and preference evolution', *Journal of Institutional and Theoretical Economics* **146**: 241–73.

Kwasnicki, W. (1996), *Knowledge, Innovation and Economy*, Cheltenham: Edward Elgar.

Lakoff, G. (1987), *Women, Fire and Dangerous Things: What Categories Reveal about the Mind*, Chicago: University of Chicago Press.

Lane, D. (1993a), 'Artificial worlds in economics: part 1', *Journal of Evolutionary Economics* **3**(2): 89–107.

(1993b), 'Artificial worlds in economics: part 2', *Journal of Evolutionary Economics* **3**(3): 177–97.

Lane, D., F. Malerba, R. Maxfield and L. Orsenigo (1996), 'Choice and action', *Journal of Evolutionary Economics* **6**(1): 43–75.

Lane, D., and R. Vescovini (1996), 'Decision rules and market share: aggregation in an information contagion model', *Industrial and Corporate Change* **5**: 127–46.

Langton, C. G. (ed.) (1989), *Artificial Life*, Reading, MA: Addison-Wesley.

Langton, C. G., C. Taylor, J. D. Farmer and S. Rasmussen (eds.) (1991), *Artificial Life II*, Reading, MA: Addison-Wesley.

Leibenstein, H. (1950), 'Bandwagon, snob and Veblen effects in the theory of consumer demand', *Quarterly Journal of Economics* **64**: 183–207.

Lesourne, J. (1991), *Economie de l'Ordre et du Désordre*, Paris: Economica.

Levinthal, D. (1996), 'Surviving in Schumpeterian environments', in G. Dosi and F. Malerba (eds.), *Organization and Strategy in the Evolution of the Enterprise*, London: Macmillan, 27–42.

Levinthal, D., and M. Warglien (1999), 'Landscape design: designing for local action in complex worlds', *Organizational Science* **10**: 342–57.

Lewis, A. (1985a), 'On effectively computable realization of choice functions', *Mathematical Social Sciences* **10**: 43–80.

(1985b), 'The minimum degree of recursively representable choice funtions', *Mathematical Social Sciences* **10**: 179–88.

(1986), *Structure and Complexity: The Use of Recursion Theory in the Foundations of Neoclassical Mathematical Economics and the Theory of Games*, mimeo, Department of Mathematics, Cornell University, Ithaca, NY.

Lindgren, K. (1991), 'Evolutionary phenomena in simple dynamics', in C. G. Langton, C. Taylor, J. D. Farmer and S. Rasmussen (eds.), *Artificial Life II*, Reading, MA: Addison-Wesley, 57–92.

Loewenstein, G., and J. Elster (eds.) (1992), *Choice Over Time*, New York: Russell Sage Foundation.

Lovallo, D. (1996), 'From individual biases to organizational errors', in G. Dosi and F. Malerba (eds.), *Organization and Strategy in the Evolution of Enterprise*, London: Macmillan, 103–24.

Lucas, R. E. (1986), 'Adaptive behavior and economic theory', *Journal of Business* **59**: S401–S426.

Lundvall, B. Å. (ed.) (1995), *National Systems of Innovation: Towards a Theory of Innovation and Interactive Learning*, London: Pinter.

(1996), *The Social Dimension of the Learning Economy*, Working Paper 96-01, Danish Research Unit for Industrial Dynamics, Aalborg, Denmark.

Luria, A. R. (1976), *Cognitive Development: Its Cultural and Social Foundations*, Cambridge, MA: Harvard University Press.

Malerba, F., and L. Orsenigo (1996), 'The dynamics and evolution of industries', *Industrial and Corporate Change* **5**: 51–87.

March, J. G. (1988a), 'Variable risk preference and adaptive aspirations', *Journal of Economic Behavior and Organization* **9**: 5–24.

(1988b), *Decision and Organizations*, Oxford: Basil Blackwell.

(1994), *A Primer on Decision Making: How Decisions Happen*, New York: Free Press.

March, J. G., and H. A. Simon (1958), *Organizations*, New York: Basil Blackwell.

March, J. G., L. S. Sproull and M. Tamuz (1991), 'Learning from samples of one or fewer', *Organization Science* **2**: 1–13.

Marengo, L. (1992), 'Coordination and organizational learning in the firm', *Journal of Evolutionary Economics* **2**: 313–26.

(1996), 'Structure, competences and learning in an adaptive model of the firm', in G. Dosi and F. Malerba (eds.), *Organization and Strategy in the Evolution of the Enterprise*, London: Macmillan, 199–216.

Marengo, L., and N. Lazaric (2000), 'Towards a characterization of assets and knowledge created in technological agreements: some evidence from the automobile-robotics sector', *Industrial and Corporate Change* **9**: 53–86.

Marengo, L., and H. Tordjman (1996), 'Speculation, heterogeneity and learning: a model of exchange rate dynamics', *Kyklos* **47**: 407–38.

Margolis, H. (1987), *Patterns, Thinking and Cognition*, Chicago: University of Chicago Press.

Marimon, R. (1997), 'Learning from learning in economics: towards a theory of the learnable in economics', in D. M. Kreps and K. F. Wallis (eds.), *Advances in Economics and Econometrics: Theory and Applications*, vol. 1, 278–315.

Marimon, R., E. McGrattan and T. J. Sargent (1990), 'Money as a medium of exchange in an economy with artificially intelligent agents', *Journal of Economic Dynamics and Control* **14**: 329–73.

Mayer, R. E. (1992), *Thinking, Problem Solving and Cognition*, New York: W. H. Freeman.

Maynard Smith, J. (1982), *Evolution and the Theory of Games*, Cambridge: Cambridge University Press.

Metcalfe, J. S. (1994), 'Evolutionary economics and technology policy', *Economic Journal* **425**: 931–44.

Milgram, S. (1974), *Obedience to Authority: An Experimental View*, London: Tavistock Institute.

Milgrom, P., and J. Roberts (1991), 'Adaptive and sophisticated learning in normal form games', *Games and Economic Behaviour* **3**: 82–100.

Montgomery, C. A. (ed.) (1995), *Resource-based and Evolutionary Theories of the Firm*, Dordrecht: Kluwer Academic.

Nelson, R. R. (1987), *Understanding Technical Change as an Evolutionary Process*, Professor Dr F. de Vries Lectures in Economics no. 8 – Theory, Institutions, Policy, Amsterdam: North-Holland.

336   *Giovanni Dosi, Luigi Marengo and Giorgio Fagiolo*

(ed.) (1993), *National Innovation Systems: A Comparative Study*, Oxford: Oxford University Press.

(1994), 'The coevolution of technology, industrial structure and supporting institutions', *Industrial and Corporate Change* 3: 47–63.

(1995), 'Recent evolutionary theorizing about economic change', *Journal of Economic Literature* 33: 48–90.

Nelson, R. R., and S. G. Winter (1982), *An Evolutionary Theory of Economic Change*, Cambridge, MA: Harvard University Press.

Newell, A., and H. A. Simon (1972), *Human Problem Solving*, Englewood Cliffs, NJ: Prentice Hall.

Nowak, M. A., and R. M. May (1992), 'Evolutionary games and spatial chaos', *Nature* 359: 826–29.

(1993), 'The spatial dilemmas of evolution', *International Journal of Bifurcation and Chaos* 3: 35–78.

Orléan, A. (1990), 'Le rôle des influences interpersonnelles dans la détermination des cours boursiers', *Revue Economiques*, 41: 839–68.

(1992), 'Contagion des opinions et fonctionnement des marchés financiers', *Revue Economiques* 43: 685–97.

Padgett, J. F. (1997), 'The emergence of simple ecologies of skills: a hypercycle approach to economic organization', in W. B. Arthur, S. N. Durlauf, and D. Lane (eds.), *The Economy as an Evolving Complex System II*, Santa Fe Institute Studies in the Science of Complexity, Reading, MA: Addison-Wesley, 199–216.

Palmer, R. G., W. B. Arthur, J. H. Holland, B. LeBaron and P. Tayler (1994), 'Artificial economic life: a simple model of a stockmarket', *Physica D* 75: 264–74.

Pavitt, K. (1984), 'Sectoral patterns of technical change: towards a taxonomy and a theory', *Research Policy* 13: 343–73.

Pearl, J. (1984), *Heuristics*, Reading, MA: Addison-Wesley.

Polanyi, K. (1944), *The Great Transformation*, Boston: Beacon Press.

(ed.) (1957), *Trade and Market in the Early Empires*, Glencoe, MN: Free Press.

Posch, M. (1994), *Cycling with a Generalized Urn Scheme and a Learning Algorithm for 2 X 2 Games*, Working Paper WP 94-76, International Institute of Applied Systems Analysis, Laxenburg, Austria.

Purkitt, H. E., and J. W. Dyson (1990), 'Decision making under varying situational constraints', in K. Borcherding, D. L. Larichev and D. M. Messick (eds.), *Contemporary Issues in Decision Making*, New York: North-Holland, 353–65.

Rabin, M. (1998), 'Psychology and economics', *Journal of Economic Literature* 36: 11–46.

Riolo, R. L. (1990), *Lookahead Planning and Latent Learning in a Classifier System*, mimeo, University of Michigan.

Rip, A., T. J. Misa and J. Schot (eds) (1995), *Managing Technology in Society*, London: Pinter.

Romer, P. M. (1990), 'Endogenous technological change', *Journal of Political Economy* 98(5, part 2): S71–S102.

Rosenberg, N. (1976), *Perspectives on Technology*, Cambridge: Cambridge University Press.

(1982), *Inside the Black Box*, Cambridge: Cambridge University Press.

(1994), *Exploring the Black Box: Technology, Economics and History*, Cambridge: Cambridge University Press.

Sargent, T. J. (1993), *Bounded Rationality in Economics*, Oxford: Clarendon Press.

Savage, L. (1954), *The Foundations of Statistics*, New York: Wiley.

Shackle, G. L. S. (1955), *Uncertainty in Economics*, Cambridge: Cambridge University Press.

(1969), *Decision, Order and Time in Human Affairs*, Cambridge: Cambridge University Press.

Shafir, E. B., and A. Tversky (1992), 'Thinking through uncertainty: inconsequential reasoning and choice', *Cognitive Psychology* **24**: 449–74.

Silverberg, G. (1988), 'Modelling economic dynamics and technical change', in G. Dosi, C. Freeman, R. R. Nelson, G. Silverberg and L. Soete (eds.), *Technical Change and Economic Theory*, London, Pinter, 531–59.

Silverberg, G., G. Dosi and L. Orsenigo (1988), 'Innovation, diversity and diffusion: a self-organisation model', *Economic Journal* **393**: 1032–54.

Silverberg, G., and D. Lehnert (1994), 'Growth fluctuations in an evolutionary model of creative destruction', in G. Silverberg and L. Soete (eds.), *The Economics of Growth and Technical Change*, Cheltenham: Edward Elgar, 74–108.

Silverberg, G., and B. Verspagen (1994), 'Learning, innovation and economic growth: a long-run model of industrial dynamics', *Industrial and Corporate Change* **3**: 199–223.

(1995a), *From the Artificial to the Endogenous: Modeling Evolutionary Adaptation and Economic Growth*, Working Paper WP 95-08, International Institute for Applied Systems Analysis, Laxenburg, Austria.

(1995b), *Evolutionary Theorizing on Economic Growth*, Working Paper WP 95-78, International Institute for Applied Systems Analysis, Laxenburg, Austria.

Simon, H. A. (1976), 'From substantive to procedural rationality', in S. J. Latsis (ed.), *Method and Appraisal in Economics*, Cambridge: Cambridge University Press, 129–48.

(1981), *The Sciences of the Artificial*, Cambridge, MA: MIT Press.

(1986), 'Rationality in psychology and economics', in R. M. Hogart and N. W. Reder (eds.), *Rational Choice*, Chicago: University of Chicago Press, 25–40.

(1988), *Models of Thought*, New Haven, CT: Yale University Press.

Slovic, P., S. Lichtenstein and B. Fischerhof (1989), 'Decision making', in R. J. Herrnstein, G. Lindrey and R. D. Luce (eds.), *Steven's Handbook of Experimental Psychology*, Chichester: Wiley, 673–738.

Smelser, N. J., and R. Swedberg (eds.) (1994), *The Handbook of Economic Sociology*, Princeton, NJ: Princeton University Press.

Sterman, J. D. (1989a), 'Deterministic chaos in an experimental economic system', *Journal of Economic Behavior and Organization* **12**: 1–28.

(1989b), 'Modeling managerial behavior: misperceptions of feedback in a dynamic decision making experiment', *Management Science* **35**: 321–38.

Stoneman, P. (ed.) (1995), *Handbook of the Economics of Innovation and Technological Change*, Oxford: Basil Blackwell.

Suppes, P. (1969), 'Stimulus-response theory of finite automata', *Journal of Mathematical Psychology* **6**: 327–55.

(1995a), *A Survey of Mathematical Learning Theory 1950–1995*, mimeo, Stanford University.

(1995b), *Learning by Doing, or Practice Makes Perfect*, mimeo, Stanford University.

Teece, D. J., and G. Pisano (1994), 'The dynamic capabilities of firms: an introduction', *Industrial and Corporate Change* **3**: 537–55.

Thaler, R. H. (1992), *The Winner's Curse: Paradoxes and Anomalies of Economic Life*, New York: Free Press.

Topol, R. (1991), 'Bubbles and volatility of stock prices: effects of mimetic contagion', *Economic Journal* **407**: 786–800.

Tordjman, H. (1996), *The Formation of Beliefs on Financial Markets: Representativeness and Prototypes*, Working Paper WP 96-87, International Institute of Applied Systems Analysis, Laxenburg, Austria.

Tversky, A., and D. Kahneman (1982), 'Judgments of and by representativeness', in D. Kahneman, P. Slovic and A. Tversky (eds.), *Judgment under Uncertainty: Heuristics and Biases*, Cambridge: Cambridge University Press, 84–98.

Vassilakis, S. (1995), *Accelerating New Product Development by Overcoming Complexity Constraints*, working paper, European University Institute.

Verspagen, B. (1993), *Uneven Growth between Interdependent Economies: An Evolutionary View on Technology Gaps, Trade and Growth*, Aldershot: Avebury.

Vickers, D. (1986), 'Time, ignorance, surprise, and economic decisions', *Journal of Post-Keynesian Economics* **9**: 48–57.

Vriend, N. J. (1995), 'Self-organization of markets: an example of a computational approach', *Computational Economics* **8**: 205–31.

Warglien, M. (1995), 'Hierarchical selection and organizational adaptation', *Industrial and Corporate Change* **4**: 161–85.

Weibull, J. W. (1995), *Evolutionary Game Theory*, Cambridge, MA: MIT Press.

Winter, S. G. (1971), 'Satisficing, selection and the innovative remnant', *Quarterly Journal of Economics* **85**: 237–61.

(1975), 'Optimization and evolution in the theory of the firm', in R. H. Day and T. Groves (eds.), *Adaptive Economic Models*, New York: Academic Press, 73–118.

(1987), 'Knowledge and competence of strategic assets', in D. J. Teece (ed.), *The Competitive Challenge*, Cambridge, MA: Ballinger, 159–84.

(1988), 'Economic natural selection and the theory of the firm', in P. E. Earl (ed.), *Behavioural Economics*, vol. 1, Aldershot: Edward Elgar.

Witt, U. (ed.) (1992), *Explaining Process and Change: Approaches to Evolutionary Economics*, Ann Arbor, MI: University of Michigan Press.

Young, H. P. (1993), 'The evolution of conventions', *Econometrica* **61**(1): 57–84.

10 The evolutionary perspective on organizational change and the theory of the firm[1]

Ulrich Witt

1 Introduction

From an abstract point of view, the organization of the firm is a prototype of a planned institution deliberately created to coordinate the division of labour. As such, it contrasts with the wide range of informal institutions – most prominently the markets – that emerge spontaneously to promote the coordination of specialization and exchange. Indeed, the contrast between firms and markets is a leitmotiv in the theory of the firm. It has inspired a huge number of arguments trying to explain why the two institutions coexist and which of them is used when. Somewhat fewer explanatory efforts have been undertaken to explain the genesis of firm organizations – i.e. how and when firms are created, and how and when their organizational form changes over time[2]. However, business history shows that changes in the organizational set-up of, and the internal interactions within, firms are the rule rather than the exception, and that these changes often have a crucial impact on the firms' performance (Chandler, 1992). Indeed, a firm's growth or decline often hinges on whether and when organizational metamorphoses occur and how they are managed. Once the level of abstract, functional comparisons between formal and informal institutions is left, the 'why?' and 'how?' of organizational change is therefore a major issue.

Organizational changes may be caused by exogenous shocks, such as shifts in demand, in the factor costs or in technology. However, although such shocks may affect the recurrent patterns of organizational change during the genesis of the firm, they do not generate them. Systematic

[1] I am grateful to Brian Loasby, Peter Murmann, Bart Nooteboom and Klaus Rathe for our continuing discussions over the years, in which the ideas expressed in this chapter took shape. The usual disclaimer, of course, applies.
[2] See Foss, 2001. In general, this question has been a stepchild in research on formal institutions, contrasting with the research on informal institutions, where the problem of evolution has gained more attention – at least at the level of abstract, game-theoretic approaches; see for example, Binmore, 1998.

patterns result instead from changes that are caused inside the organization through learning and experimentation by all the actors involved. These endogenous changes seem to be connected intimately to the growth that successful firms go through. To explore the patterns and regularities of organizational change, an approach is therefore needed that keeps track of a whole sequence of changes, which may extend over long periods of time (see Rathe and Witt, 2001). The comparative-static method of analysis (widely used in the theory of the firm), which focuses on a – hypothesized – transition between two organizational equilibria, does not fit this requirement well. For this reason, the question arises as to the way in which systematic, endogenously emerging organizational change should be conceptualized. In the literature, different routes have been suggested.

Perhaps because of the paradigmatic role that biology has gained in dealing with endogenously caused change (see Witt, 2003, chap. 1), the patterns of organizational adjustments and transformations are often conceptualized on the basis of biological analogies or metaphors. Biology deals with two radically differing forms of endogenous change in nature. One is evolution proper – i.e. the adaptations that occur in the species during their phylogeny. The other process is called 'development', and covers the organic changes that the individual exemplars of a species go through in the same way over their life cycle – i.e. during their ontogeny. Accordingly, the analogous constructions and metaphors may refer to quite different processes in the biological domain. Indeed, they do so either by drawing on the Darwinian concept of natural selection (see Winter, 1964, Nelson and Winter, 1982, Metcalfe, 1998, part 1, and Levinthal, 2000) or by borrowing the developmental life cycle metaphor (see for example, Alfred Marshall, 1890, book IV, chaps. 12 & 13, who referred to the life cycle of trees in the forest and, with his notion of the 'representative individual', transferred the typological method from developmental biology to economics)[3]. The fact that two fundamentally different routes have been suggested for conceptualizing organizational change invites some more general reflections about the methodological background of theories of endogenous change in economics.

Accordingly, this chapter proceeds as follows. The connection to the (static) theory of the firm is briefly summarized in section 2. Section 3 reviews the evolutionary interpretation that conceptualizes endogenous organizational change by means of analogies to the Darwinian theory of

---

[3] An ontogenetic metaphor is, of course, not necessary for a developmental approach to firms and industries, as the work of Edith Penrose (1959) has shown. Her work has, more recently, gained a renewed interest in the so-called 'competence perspective' on the firm; see Foss (1993, 1996) and Langlois and Robertson (1995).

natural selection. Section 4 goes on to discuss the conceptualization of intra-organizational change based on the organic life cycle metaphor – i.e. a developmental regularity occurring in a single firm. In view of the differences between these approaches, section 5 suggests some core issues that any theory of endogenous organizational change should address – independently of its possible metaphorical background. On the basis of the identified issues, section 6 then outlines how elements from both the population-based, selectionist interpretation and the typological, developmental view can be merged in a fruitful way. For illustrative purposes, section 7 briefly highlights some typical organizational transformations predicted by the hypotheses derived. Section 8 offers the conclusions.

2   The 'nature' of the firm – anything evolving?

The division of labour within (and by means of) firm organizations is based on employment contracts, which differ significantly from the market contracts used otherwise to safeguard specialization and exchange contractually. In its very abstract approach to production and exchange, contemporary economic theory has long neglected these differences and, hence, left out the institutional framework of production from its canon. It was only with the theory of the firm that the questions of why and when economic agents choose markets exchange contracts, and why and when they rely on firm organizations and the corresponding employment contracts, gained proper attention (see Williamson, 1985, and Coase, 1988). In trying to come to terms with these questions, the emerging 'new institutional economics' expanded the explanatory domain of the theory. However, with an unchanged commitment to equilibrium analysis it retained an essential part of the neoclassical abstraction strategy. This comes at a price: the focus on equilibrium states of institutions and their optimality makes it difficult to grasp conceptually the systematic changes going on inside firm organizations over time. Indeed, 'the' firm is often represented in theory as if there were no differences between, for example, a newly founded small entrepreneurial business and a large multi-division corporation. In such an approach there is little room for understanding that, for a firm to grow from the former state to the latter, critical organizational transformations have to be mastered (see the business history studies in Chandler, 1962, 1990, Fransman, 1995, and Murmann, 2003).

In its endeavour to determine the 'nature' of the firm (as opposed to markets), the new institutionalist approach has singled out three programmatic questions (see Holmström and Roberts, 1998, and Foss, 2000).

a) Why do firms exist? (This is the seminal question raised by Coase, 1937.)
b) What factors determine the firms' boundaries, or, conversely, what activities are left to the markets? (This is the question epitomized by the 'make or buy' decision problem.)
c) What determines the firms' internal organization? (This is the question of hierarchical control and incentive structures.)

The suggested answers referred to equilibrium states in the firm organization in which incentive problems were resolved, transaction costs were minimized and incomplete contractual relations were agreed upon (see Alchian and Demsetz, 1972, and Williamson, 1996). In this light, safeguards against contractual hazard appeared as the main determinant for the organizational form of the firm[4], and the attempt to safeguard specific investments against contractual holds-up appeared as the determinant of the boundary between firms and markets (see Williamson, 1985, and Hart and Moore, 1990).

These answers are, of course, not the only ones that can be given to the above three questions enquiring into the nature of the firm. Different ones have, for example, been suggested by the 'resource-based' or 'competence' theory of the firm. The firm organization is identified there as an efficient means of using and, most notably, accumulating specific knowledge on productive activities (see Foss, 1993, Teece et al., 1994, and Montgomery, 1995). Different from the often entirely discontinuous market interactions, the continuing intra-organizational interactions allow a firm to become a 'repository of productive knowledge' (Winter, 1988). This is, obviously, a different aspect of the internal operations of firms, but it seems complementary to the aspects highlighted by the new institutionalist approach[5]. Indeed, the efficiency considerations relating to the knowledge base of the firm often result in comparing (equilibrium) states that the organization can attain – an analysis akin to an inquiry into the abstract 'nature' of the firm.

As mentioned in the introduction, the question of systematic organizational change presupposes a process-oriented approach. Such an

[4] This problem can be interpreted as a special case of an agency problem; see Holmström and Milgrom (1994).
[5] Knowledge problems that can probably be solved better within a firm organization than by relying on market transactions also relate to the protection of specialized knowledge against uncontrolled diffusion and exploitation by third parties. Further reasons why the organizational form of the firm is chosen may be as follows. Without founding a firm it may also be difficult, or impossible, to contract the crucial entrepreneurial input of judging the judgement capacity of others (see Knight 1921, chap. 10, and Langlois and Cosgel, 1993). Alternatively, the creation of a firm may permit the solution of the problems of work motivation and cognitive identification with, and adherence to, entrepreneurial business conception in ways not feasible in ordinary market contracts (see Witt, 1998).

approach may offer few, if any, additional insights concerning the 'nature' of the firm[6]. For this reason, rather than continuing that debate, a shift of attention to organizational change means opening a new chapter in the theory of the firm. To arrive at a heuristic framework for the process-oriented enquiry into the emergence and change of firm organizations, several routes can be taken. As already mentioned, some of them rely on an analytical framework for dealing with endogenous change that is inspired by analogies to, and metaphors borrowed from, biology. In one approach, the key concept is a population-oriented analogy to natural selection. In the other approach, the metaphor of the ontogenetic development of the single organism figures prominently. As a source of inspiration both biological processes have some appealing features, as the discussion in the next two sections will show.

3   Selection and evolutionary change in firm populations

The level of analysis in the modern neo-Darwinian theory of phylogeny is the species, defined as a population of interbreeding organisms. The genetic endowment (the genotype) of the living population represents the current state of the gene pool of the species. It finds its phenotypic expression in the traits – e.g. body size, morphological features, etc. – of the living exemplars of the species. With respect to the entire population, the realizations of the various traits can be described by their corresponding frequency distributions. According to the theory of natural selection, differences in the genetically coded traits between individual exemplars of the species, which affect their chances of reproductive success, translate into systematic changes of the frequency distribution of traits within the population between successive generations.

The analogy to be constructed puts a population of firms making up an industry in place of the population of interbreeding organisms. The firm population also shows a variety of traits, particularly organizational traits, that may be described by their corresponding frequency distributions. Experience teaches that the variety of organizational traits in an industry and, hence, the frequency distributions change over time. The crucial point here is that the analogy suggests interpreting these changes as resulting from selective processes operating on the organizational traits. It is, of course, not differential success in the competition for reproduction

[6] Note, however, that, if the implications of future organizational changes can at least partially be anticipated, they are likely to influence the choice of the institutional form for organizing the division of labour as reflected, for example, in the 'make or buy' consideration (see Langlois, 1992, and Nooteboom, 1992).

that produces the selective effect here[7]. Rather, it is a) differences in the persistence (survival) and multiplication of an organizational trait within the organizations and b) a different ability to diffuse by imitation among the organizations. Furthermore, by the same analogy, random variations in an organization's traits are interpreted as organizational mutants that create new variety. Differences in persistence and imitation rates tend to erode variety over time in the case of organizational traits, as does differential reproductive success in the case of natural selection.

The analogy just outlined underlies the evolutionary approach to firms, industries and markets in Richard Nelson and Sidney Winter's seminal (1982) contribution to evolutionary economics. Basically, they identify 'traits' with the routines of interacting and communicating within a firm organization (to be distinguished from routinized individual behaviour, which may well be associated with organizational routines but does not by itself establish the latter type of routines). Nelson and Winter argue that organizations regularly have to rely on such routines to achieve coordination. They refer, *inter alia*, to production planning, calculation, price setting and even the allocation of R&D funds as examples where organizational routines are applied. These routines are interpreted as the 'genotypes' while the firm's specific decisions thus derived are interpreted as 'phenotypes'. The latter may be more or less favourable to the firm's overall performance in its market environment, as measured in terms of profitability and growth. Not only does it seem reasonable to assume that organizational routines that successfully contribute to growth will persist within the growing firm organization so that, by its mere expansion, the relative frequency of the corresponding 'routine-genes' already in the population increases; it also seems straightforward to assume that such organizational routines are more likely to be imitated by other firms in the industry. The opposite may be assumed to hold for routines that cause decisions that lead to poor performance by the firm.

The pool of organizational routines in a population of firms forming an industry is thus considered to develop much in the same way as the gene pool of a species, even though the actual replication mechanism is different. The idea has been shown to be a powerful tool for enquiring into the structural change that is produced in capitalist economies by the competitive market processes (see Metcalfe, 1994, 1998, part 1). However, keeping track of the changing composition of the routines in an industry is perhaps a more compelling device for analysing how firms

---

[7] Since there is no analogue to the biological reproduction process, some authors argue that the basis for the use of the concept of natural selection is a metaphor rather than a true analogy. For a discussion of this point, see Geoffrey Hodgson (2001).

and industries coevolve than for spotting the organizational change within the individual firm. Indeed, the population perspective underlying the analogy to natural selection is difficult to align with the notion of the individual firm as the basic unit of analysing change[8]. The difference in perspective seems to imply a diverging assessment also of the *agens movens* of organizational change. A case in point is the role attributed to insight and intentionality, and – more specifically – entrepreneurship, in the generation of organizational change[9].

In evolution in nature, the origin of genetic variation is considered a 'blind' random process. Moreover, the individual exemplars of a species are unable to manipulate their genetic fitness in order to escape from, or adjust to, selection pressure. Variation and selection operate in a strictly independent fashion. Natural selection cannot create new variants, and the existing variants cannot modify their behavioural repertoire. Obviously, the way in which organizational change is brought about in a firm is different from this. Entrepreneurs often try actively to invent a way out when the firm faces poor performance or is even threatened in its existence. In fact, an important part of observable endogenous changes in organizations may be attributed to deliberately created remedies for failures and weaknesses. This presupposes insight and intentionality and

[8] The population perspective on firm organizations is taken to the extreme in the approach of organizational ecology (see Aldrich and Mueller, 1982, Hannan and Freeman, 1989, and Hannan and Carroll, 1992). Rather than focusing on the pool of organizational routines in an industry, organizational ecology considers the population of firms as evolving. Hence, the unit of selection is not a routine applied in the firms, as in the case of Nelson and Winter's model, but the entire firm. The evolution of organizational forms is recorded by the variation of the relative size of entire populations of firms, such as the population of newspaper makers in Argentina, brewing firms in North America, banks in Manhattan, or American life insurance firms (see Hannan and Carroll, 1992). Each of these populations is supposed to represent a homogeneous and invariable organizational form. Therefore, differential success among the firms in one population is not considered, and selection effects matter only indirectly through the compound effects of founding rates, merger rates, disbanding rates, and rates of structural change. By the very assumption that there is no organizational change at the level of the firm, the organizational ecology approach is, of course, of limited relevance for the present considerations.

[9] A perfect definition of entrepreneurship has been given by Penrose (1959, pp. 31–32), who refers to 'individuals or groups within the firm providing entrepreneurial services, whatever their position or occupational classification may be. Entrepreneurial services are those contributions to the operations of a firm which relate to the introduction and acceptance on behalf of the firm of new ideas, particularly with respect to products, location, and significant changes in technology, to the acquisition of new managerial personnel, to fundamental changes in the administrative organization of the firm, to the raising of capital, and to the making of plans for expansion, including the choice of method of expansion. Entrepreneurial services are contrasted with managerial services, which relate to the execution of entrepreneurial ideas and proposals and to the supervision of existing operations. The same individuals may, and more often than not probably do, provide both types of services to the firm.'

room for entrepreneurial discretion (see Fransman, 1999, chap. 1.4.1). In response to what is perceived as a need to adapt, firms can therefore modify their organization and performance. Where they rely on organizational routines, they can replace or improve deficient ones in a kind of intentionally produced mutation of their 'genes'. In short, selection forces residing outside the firm may often only be the trigger for what would have to be labelled an 'internal' (cognitively based) selection phenomenon. In pursuing their intentions, conceptions and conjectures, people in a firm organization may cause regular and predictable features in business behaviour, as they do in their compliance with organizational routines. This is particularly true if, through informal communication, socially shared cognitive content and attitudes emerge that are significant and specific for the firm organization in which people work.

In the population-based selectionist approach, insight, intentionality and entrepreneurial discretion do not play much of a role. What is emphasized instead is the notion that improvements or replacements at a lower organizational level are made on the basis of organizational routines or aggregates of routines at a higher level of the firm hierarchy (see Nelson and Winter, 1982, chap. 5, Dosi et al., 2000, and Murmann et al., 2003). This is certainly often the case, particularly in large, hierarchical firm organizations. Nonetheless, the higher the level of the routines the less likely the changes guided by higher organizational routines are to be made independently of the insight and intention of the involved managers. In fact, the higher one gets in the organizational decision-making hierarchy, the more the individual problem-solving capability and the subjective understanding of the particular decision maker involved can be expected to be influential. This fact does not only imply an additional degree of freedom (if different people are involved in the same higher routines of change at different times, this can have an effect on the differential persistence of the routines), it also calls for an extension of the whole approach. The explanatory apparatus required to deal with 'internal selection' needs to account for the intentions, conceptions, decision-making attitudes (and, perhaps, individual routinized behaviour) of leading actors inside the firm organization[10].

A related point is the role played by incentive problems. While new institutional economics may be said to be preoccupied with these

---

[10] Their cognitive activities follow their own regularities (to which we will return below) that might be called individual cognitive routines. However, apart from semantically, cognitive routines have nothing in common with organizational routines. Moreover, there is no indication that the selection metaphor is of any use in explaining cognitive processes. Even though humans are forced to be selective in what they sense, learn and perceive, the dynamic patterns and constraints of their cognitive processes differ from those described by population dynamics.

problems, the population-based selectionist approach is much less concerned with them. It is rarely noticed that, for routines to operate in the sense of Nelson and Winter, reliable and mutually shared expectations about how to perform must be established among the firm members. Wherever routines allow room for individual discretion about the level of effort there is an incentive problem, and the mutually shared expectations are likely to depend on how it is solved. Because of 'free riding' and 'hold-up', the efficacy of organizational routines and, as a consequence, the firm's performance may suffer. Such cases are likely to elicit action to control and fight free riding and hold-up. As has been said, the way in which countermeasures are invoked may be a matter of higher intervention routines, and may partly result in the re-engineering of organizational routines. Even then, however, the organizational change thus induced is a response that presupposes the diagnosis of incentive problems and the intention to solve them. As will be submitted below, such problems depend on the size and age of an organization. Their systematically changing impact may give rise to an endogenously caused development of firm organizations.

4   Typology-based organic metaphors for the development of firms

Another way of framing the phenomenon of endogenous organizational change on the basis of a biological metaphor is the developmental, or ontogenetic, interpretation. In its heuristic source of inspiration such an approach clearly contrasts with the population-oriented selectionist approach (see Foss, 2001). The contrast has already been made clear in the work of Penrose. As an early critic of economic analogies to natural selection (Penrose, 1952, 1953) she worked out a theory of the growth of the firm that is intimately connected to a process of endogenous change (1959). The core notion of that theory is that the growth of firms is a process of endogenous change. However, unlike the selectionist approach, she tried to conceptualize the endogenous changes within the firm as 'a process of development . . . akin to natural biological processes in which an interactive series of internal changes leads to increases in size accompanied by changes in the characteristics of the growing object' (1959, p. 1)[11].

---

[11] Her theory is based on assumptions that have also been centre stage later in the evolutionary economic approach: bounded rationality and a limited but growing knowledge; and a process-oriented perspective rather than an equilibrium-oriented one. Nonetheless (perhaps this is an indication of the difference between the two approaches), Nelson and Winter refer to Penrose only once in their book (1982, p. 36) and do not mention the particular way in which she conceptualizes the endogenous process of change within the firm.

Perhaps because of her earlier rejection of analogies to natural selection, Penrose did not make explicit that, by those 'biological processes', she was alluding to the ontogenetic development of the individual exemplar of a species – i.e. the unfolding of an organism from its procreation to its ageing and eventual exit.

In biology, 'ontogenetic development' refers to the regular, systematic unfolding of the individual organism – an irreversible process that expresses the individual's genetic programme (subject to the particular environmental conditions). Its most easily observable realization is the successive changes of the organism's morphology from its birth to its death. Ontogenetic development repeats itself very regularly, even chronologically, in each organism of the same species. It results not only in a quantitative growth of an organism but also in qualitative changes in its structure – sometimes stunningly complex ones that go far beyond the simple scheme of growth, stagnation and decline on which the life cycle metaphor rests[12].

The contrast with phylogenetic evolution, which operates on the gene pool (i.e. on the level of the population), is obvious. From this ontological difference follow some methodological differences in dealing with ontogenetic and phylogenetic phenomena. The orderly nature of the successively occurring morphological features during ontogenetic development suggests the use of typological methods. Ontogenetic processes are therefore often described in terms of the various stages of development that a 'representative' exemplar of a species runs through. The explanation of the development is fairly involved. Besides physiological laws, phylogenetic hypotheses about the adaptive value of a species' particular ontogenetic development under the typical environmental conditions of its habitat usually also play a role. Phylogenetic processes, by contrast, deal with a potentially systematically changing frequency distribution of genetic traits in the population. Unlike thinking in terms of representative exemplars, the analysis of phylogenetic processes thus requires 'population thinking' – i.e. methods accounting for the existence of the genetic variety on which selection forces operate.

If there is an incidence of endogenous change in the economic domain that lends itself to an analogous developmental interpretation at all, then it

---

[12] A striking example is the butterfly, which undergoes a complete metamorphosis during its ontogeny, which comprises the four very different morphological stages of egg, larva, pupa and adult. In each of the stages the organism displays, in addition, a typical pattern of growth and maturing. Mammals do not undergo such metamorphoses during their lifetime, yet they do display a stereotypic development in their morphology related to their growth from the embryonic phase to that of the juvenile, the adult and – eventually – subsequent ageing and decay.

is perhaps the transformations that a single firm organization can undergo over its lifespan. Indeed, there is a whole literature on the firm's life cycle that relies on the analogy to the regularities of ontogenetic morphological development of single organisms in nature. Besides Marshall (1890), who has already been mentioned in the introduction, contributions have also been made by, for example Mueller (1972), Greiner (1972) and Quinn and Cameron (1983). But this analogy has its problems and limitations too. A first and very basic question that may be raised is why organizational change should be expected to give rise to stereotypic developmental patterns such as successions of organizational states. Since there is nothing comparable to a common causation like the genetic programme, which expresses itself, it is not clear where a stereotypical development corresponding to the life cycle metaphor should come from. A second question is what organizational features one should look for in seeking empirical evidence for analogies to the systematically changing morphological features of organisms. Development may be expressed by changes in the structure or quality of an organization (as they are indicative of morphological development). However, there is no eye-catching empirical evidence for stereotypic changes in organizational structure or quality as there is evidence for the development of organisms.

It is not surprising, therefore, that there is not much agreement as to what an adequate typology for characterizing any regularities in the development of firm organizations in general, and successions of regular states in particular, would be[13]. Whatever typology is chosen, a regularity comparable to the natural analogue in its stereotypic sequencing and timing of transitions can hardly be expected. There are simply too many internal factors on which the individual firm's development is contingent: the decision makers' capabilities and preferences, constraints resulting from earlier investments and performance, and – not least – good or bad luck. Accordingly, firms would not only have to be expected to differ significantly with respect to how far in the prototypic development they

---

[13] For any typology, the firm needs to be defined as a persistent unit of analysis in the first place. Already this condition is non-trivial (compare the extensive discussion of this point in Penrose, 1959, chap. 2) – not only, but in a particularly significant form, in a theory presupposing systematic changes in the firm. Continuity may be observed at the personal, legal or the ownership level. Usually, firms are identified with legal, administrative entities (Chandler, 1992). Unlike organisms (which may well represent a collection of distinguishable organs), which show very little change in their composition over their lifespan, the composition of legal, organizational entities can vary greatly over time through divisionalization, acquisition, merger, etc. This creates major difficulties for a developmental typology: should it refer to the changes of some components or to the entire composition? How long may a changing composition of legal, organizational entities be considered as continuing to exist as the developing unit? More generally speaking, how can the timespan of a life cycle be determined?

get, but also with respect to how long a time they remain in certain stages of that development.

Penrose seems to have been aware of these imponderables and, hence, the limited value of the metaphor. Throughout her book she did not return to it, but instead interpreted organizational development as an unfolding of the organizational changes required by a growing business. The regularities that she diagnosed can indeed be stated independently of any biological analogy or metaphor: the typical contingencies of the growth process; the regular sequences of organizational change; and the limitations, at any point in time, not of the ultimate size of the firm but of its rate of growth. All this is traced back by Penrose to learning and growing managerial experience on the one hand and the entrepreneurial figuring out of, and gaining experience with, the firm's 'set of productive opportunities' on the other hand.

In her interpretation, the major contingency of the organizational growth process is the availability of managerial capabilities covering the firm's requirements at the different stages of expansion (see Penrose, 1959, chaps. 3–5; incentive problems and motivational conflicts are assumed to be absent). The highly specific and partly tacit character of knowledge shared in a managerial team – not least the knowledge of the resources available to the firm – makes managerial services themselves a distinct resource. They cannot be contracted directly in the market, but need to be accumulated by experience gained in carrying out the daily business activities. Since the growth of the firm's business needs to be planned and coordinated, and since this absorbs management capacity, the availability of idle managerial capacity may become a bottleneck for further expansion. This availability thus determines when the firm's business can be expanded and which opportunities for further growth can be seized.

However, precisely because there is something like a learning curve for managerial services provided in-house, the managers need less attention and effort for the ongoing business the more experience they gain with it. As a consequence, idle managerial capacity re-emerges over time and invites engagement in new businesses. The growth of the firm sooner or later also requires reorganizations in management. Accounting, controlling, human resources, etc. become ever more complex and difficult to manage. From a certain point on, specialization in the internal management processes and a hierarchical coordination of that specialization become necessary. If the managerial resources required for that reorganization cannot be made available (or if the firm fails for other reasons to make the transition to specialized management), its expansion process comes to a halt or even declines, particularly in the case of fierce competitive pressure.

The regular sequence of stages the firm organization runs through in its process of expansion is strongly influenced by changing entrepreneurial perceptions (see Penrose, 1959, chaps. 7–9). At any point in time, the firm's management perceives a certain set of opportunities for investment and growth. With a cumulatively growing collective awareness of additional prospects that can be pursued with the productive resources and the knowledge the firm has previously accumulated, these perceptions change. The more competitive the environment and, thus, the less profitable the business becomes in the markets for its existing products and services, the more likely the firm is to be willing to engage in new projects. Among them are the processes of introducing new technologies, of entering new markets or of acquiring and merging with other organizations. All these innovations trigger organizational adaptations that, again, absorb managerial capacity and may, therefore, temporarily constrain the further growth of the firm. Even though they appear at different stages of the firm's development, organizational transformations therefore follow similar patterns.

5 Beyond analogies: key issues in organizational change

As the preceding discussions have shown, the proper conceptualization of endogenous organizational change is not without controversy. However, the very fact that such changes occur cannot be denied. In the theory of the firm, some way must therefore be found to account theoretically for the changes and to derive their implications where, in the new institutionalist approach, the changes are largely neglected. Before continuing to discuss the role of analogies, it may for this reason be useful to pause and reflect on what the issues at stake are. Is it possible to specify more precisely the problems that a theory of endogenous organizational change should address – independently of what the particular heuristic analogy may suggest? It is clear that there are very many phenomena and potentially relevant questions at the diverse layers at which organizational change materializes. To come to terms here one may, therefore, try to identify the questions that can substitute for the programmatic questions (a)–(c) of the static theory of the firm, if focus is shifted from the nature of the firm to the characteristics of organizational change (see Rathe and Witt, 2001).

Thus, in lieu of asking why firms exist, the question may now be posed: (i) How do firm organizations come into being?
Unlike the question of *why* a firm organization is founded (i.e. exists), the question of *how* a firm organization is created draws attention to the fact that a genuinely entrepreneurial input is required here. Without

entrepreneurial visions, conceptions and actions, it is not possible to found and run a firm organization. As an implication of the dynamic focus on organizational change it is, therefore, vital to reflect – as suggested by Penrose (1959) – on the entrepreneurial role within the firm organization and its transformations. We shall return to this point in the next section.

Once a firm organization has been created, its further course of development is, of course, not only contingent on how the entrepreneurial role is played. In its input and output markets the firm may face expansion or contraction and, hence, more or less competitive pressure. The firm's competencies may give it more or less of a technological or commercial advantage. Such influences are crucial contingencies for the firm's growth. But they are also likely to affect the boundary between the firm and the market. Accordingly, where it was asked above what factors determine the firm's boundaries, the question now is:

(ii) How do the firm organization and the market(s) in which it operates coevolve, and how does that coevolution shift the boundary between firm and market?

Some answers to this question have been offered by Richard Langlois (1992) and by Langlois and Paul Robertson (1995). The capabilities of a firm organization, including its production knowledge, usually over time face a change in demand, for example through technical progress in the industry. The effects on the boundaries of the firm then depend on how the improvement of capabilities is easier to achieve: inside the firm or through contracting capabilities in the markets. Innovations with 'systemic' character, which require the adaptation of many complementary activities, would be expensive to realize through market transactions, because of the high costs of instructing, persuading and coordinating the contracted firms (called 'dynamic transaction costs' by Langlois, 1992). Accordingly, vertical integration would be attractive. In the case of process innovations and innovations with 'modular' character, in contrast, lower dynamic transaction costs are likely to result in vertical specialization and producer networking.

A question of particular relevance for explaining organizational change is whether there are forces residing inside the firm that trigger change and, if so, what forces these are and when they occur. This may be considered the dynamic equivalent to the third programmatic question on the institutionalist agenda above – what determines the firm's internal organization – which can be formulated as follows:

(iii) What are the determinants of organizational change internal to the firm and what kind of organizational transformations do they trigger?

This question is implicitly addressed in Penrose (1959). As was argued in the previous section, for her the essential determinant is to be found in the growth of the firm. She interprets the firm as a collection of productive resources that can be put to different uses and can yield different services. Since the productive activities of the firm are seen as planned and coordinated by a central management, what a firm actually undertakes depends on the conceptions and capabilities of its entrepreneur and management. However, what Penrose actually elaborates on is not the role of the entrepreneur but the impact of the changing quality and availability of managerial services if the firm is expanding.

A different answer to question (iii) has been given by Nelson and Winter (1982). They emphasize the role of innovative activities that tend to modify both the organizational and technological routines applied by the firms in an industry. (Nelson and Winter, thus, simultaneously include questions (ii) and (iii) in their reflections.) Indeed, both the population-based selectionist interpretation and the typological developmental view implicitly or explicitly offer answers to the last question – though in remarkably differing ways. With the whole set of question (i)–(iii) in mind, it seems promising, therefore, to return to the conceptual debate of the previous sections. The aim is to figure out what, more precisely, an evolutionary theory of organizational change implies, and how – by observing the order of organizational transformations over time – it can merge insights from both approaches in a fruitful way.

6   Conceptions, routines and the entrepreneurial role in the organizational genesis

The questions raised in the preceding section provide some hints as to how the theory of the firm, and its focus on the individual firm as the basic unit of analysis, may be dynamically extended. In keeping track on what happens to the firm over time from its creation to its exit, the three questions (i)–(iii) complement each other nicely. The various organizational transformations are thus framed within an encompassing theory of the genesis and change of the firm – a basic perspective that has much in common with the developmental view. However, unlike from what the ontogenetic metaphor may suggest, no rigid, unconditional sequence of transformations has to be invoked, nor is it necessary to adopt a reductionist interpretation that ignores the fact that each single firm is embedded in the social context of a population of firms in which ideas, conceptions, business practices, organizational routines and techniques may diffuse. To the contrary, a fully-fledged evolutionary approach can hardly ignore the sources of organizational change that reside in the observation and imitation of what is practised in other firms, be they competitors, purveyors or customers.

Although the underlying motivations and mechanisms are different, imitation and selection have some formal similarity. Both imitative learning and selection processes can be represented, for example in terms of a model of replicator dynamics. Even without adopting a selectionist metaphor, the dynamics suggested by the above-discussed selectionist approach may, therefore, be relevant for understanding organizational change. What seems desirable, however, is to break down the processes to the level of the individual firm as the unit of analysis in the theory of the firm. Both the motivation for imitation, and its impact on organizational change, can usefully be analysed at the level of the individual firm. Hence, although neither of the two approaches to conceptualizing organizational change by analogy to processes of change in nature exactly fits the conditions prevailing in the domain of the theory of the firm, both approaches do offer valid insights. The reason is that, while in biology phylogenetic evolution and ontogenetic development are distinct (but not disconnected) processes operating on drastically differing timescales, there is no support for an analogous distinction in the case of the genesis and change of firm organizations. Adaptations in firm behaviour are basically due to learning processes going on simultaneously at the level of the individual firm and at the population level; 'evolution' and 'development' coincide.

To begin with question (i), the genesis of any firm organization starts with the particular conditions of its creation and early operations. The intra-organizational modes of coordinating interactions need to be established since the multi-person firm is, after all, a way of organizing the division of labour. Much as in the case of the division of labour via markets, a firm has to rely on knowledge dispersed among several agents. These agents must be motivated to undertake the physical and mental efforts by which they acquire, improve and apply their individual knowledge to contribute to the objectives of the firm and the particular ways in which they are pursued; in short, they must be motivated to contribute to the firm's 'mission'. Moreover, all the individual efforts must be coordinated. In the early stages of a firm's genesis – usually under the conditions of a small, or even very small, organization size – the agents who have to achieve all this are the entrepreneurial founders. Their performance is decisive for the shaping of the organization's procedures and performance alike. Much of what entrepreneurs do at this stage may be intuitive actions. An important facet of those actions – in fact, a prerequisite for establishing a firm organization – is the conceiving of new, potentially profitable opportunities for production and trade. As with the entrepreneurial role in general, this crucial entrepreneurial input is usually neglected in the theory of the firm.

As has been argued elsewhere, any endeavour of seeing through new opportunities by setting up and running a firm organization is guided by at least some rudimentary entrepreneurial 'business conception' (see Witt, 1998). In a world of bounded rationality, the imagining of what business to do, the available knowledge on how to do it, and the interpretation of newly gained experience are based on the cognitive cues that a business conception provides[14]. For organizing the division of labour within the firm, the problem then is: how can the entrepreneurial business conception be conveyed to the newly hired members of the firm organization? How can they be induced to adopt it as the basis for their own decision making on the job? This problem refers to social cognitive learning processes (see Bandura, 1986, and Levine et al., 1993). What is at stake here is the degree of cognitive coherence among firm members[15].

An entrepreneur may devise organizational routines, including the assignment of specific tasks to particular firm members. By monitoring compliance, he/she may, moreover, be able to ensure coherent forms of interacting within the organization (which may, indeed, be an important prerequisite for organizational coherence and efficiency). However, procedural routines leave interpretative room as to how the firm members frame newly arising non-routine problems. They also leave room with

---

[14] Cognitive cues channel selective information processing and control the access to memory on an associative basis (see Anderson, 2000, chaps. 6 & 7). Cognitive cues are usually organized into larger cognitive frames, on the basis of which decision problems are interpreted. Since the limited mental operating capacity allows only one cognitive frame to be used at any point in time, this also means that, while in use, such a frame cannot itself at the same time be made the object of cognitive reflection. Constrainedness and selectivity also apply to the capacity of imagining and reflecting on alternatives for action. Some particular courses of action, rather than others that could in principle be imagined, are conceived and thought through more or less carefully.

[15] This problem is usually neglected in economics, particularly in the research on incentive conflicts and in agency theory, even though it has a significant impact on individual motivation and receptivity for incentives (see Osterloh and Frey, 2000, for a related argument). Imagining and reflecting on alternatives for action under one cognitive frame precludes doing the same under a different, perhaps opportunistic, one. Moreover, it makes a great difference from the motivational point of view whether or not people see themselves as contributing to a common goal. If they do, their task perception tends to be framed in such a way that their attention is devoted more to solving problems in the interest of the common goals than to pursuing their private inclinations. In the opposite case, it may be concluded that the level of individual effort – which is particularly difficult to observe in problem-solving behaviour – may suffer. That case may occur when rival business conceptions are pursued within the firm or, even worse, if the firm members do not perceive anyone as contributing to a common goal.

respect to the level of effort taken to solve such problems. Independent of formally devised interaction routines, the task of concerting the knowledge, expectations and beliefs of the staff hired is therefore important for achieving intra-organizational coordination. But, unlike in the case of procedural routines, no firm member can be made to adopt a specific cognitive frame, such as the entrepreneurial business conception, simply by being given orders to do so. Similarly, unlike in the case of routines, monitoring the adoption of a particular cognitive frame by the firm members is extremely difficult, if not impossible. Indeed, the formation of individual cognitive frames follows its own regularities, in which social influences play an important role (see Bandura, 1986, chap. 2).

Communication with, and the observation of, other agents constitute a major factor in guiding individual attention processes. Accordingly, they are also a prominent source of learning. The more intense and lasting communication and observational learning are, the more likely the agents involved will tend to develop collectively shared interpretation patterns as well as common tacit knowledge of facts, hypotheses, practices and skills. (In part, these cognitive commonalities result from the fact that, in intensely communicating groups, the agents' selective information processing is occupied with much the same topics, which, in a sense, are processed in parallel – leaving less attention for other topics.) Observational learning is also behind the formation of social models of how to behave that are characteristic for a group. Certain patterns of behaviour tend to prevail within any group of regularly interacting individuals. Conformity to, as well as deviation from, these patterns can be observed by the group members. Since the members focus on much the same limited set of behavioural patterns, these tend to become socially shared models of behaviour.

Since a firm organization (or some of its divisions) usually forms an intensely interacting group, there may thus be commonalities in the conceptions adopted by the firm members and in the alternatives of action that they selectively recognize as being feasible – and, of course, those that they disregard. Moreover, as a consequence of intense and lasting communication, the firm members may share some common standards of conduct, exemplified by socially shared models of behaviour. For the entrepreneur, it would be desirable to be able to control the kind of behaviour that emerges as a social model. However, under observational learning this is difficult to achieve, because the agenda of informal communication is difficult to control. The entrepreneur's conceptions and social models may be contested by rival cognitive frames and social models. Failure to prevent these from tacitly taking the lead in the firm's informal communication can have far-reaching consequences for organizational coherence and, hence, for the firm's performance[16]. In the struggle to maintain 'cognitive leadership' (Witt, 1998), particular social skills – such as communicativeness, persuasiveness and persistence, as well as fairness, credibility and appreciativeness – are relevant. But the intrinsic features of business conceptions are also important. If a conception is too complex and sophisticated, or if it lacks soundness, not least in terms of career options, remuneration, qualification enhancement and working conditions for the employees, then it is difficult to imagine how employees can be made to adopt it.

When considering question (i) in the light of these considerations, a couple of alternative developments appear possible. The entrepreneur may indeed try to gain cognitive leadership. The problem then is whether his/her social skills suffice to exert cognitive leadership and whether the intrinsic features of the entrepreneurial business conception are sufficiently convincing for the firm members to be induced to adopt it. It may, of course, be the case that no attempt is made to gain cognitive leadership, perhaps because the entrepreneur does not expect to command the necessary skills. Or, alternatively, the entrepreneur may try, but fail, to exert cognitive leadership. In these cases there is another way of running the firm organization. The entrepreneur can try to counter the inevitable tendency of the employees towards incoherence, inefficiency and declining work effort by introducing a monitoring regime – that is, by the detailed supervision of all actions and their outcome. Such a development would probably result in a mode of running the firm that seems to have been perceived as the only one feasible in Armen Alchian and Harold Demsetz' (1972) monitoring approach to the theory of the firm.

However, running an organization on the basis of a monitoring regime exacts a high price. Monitoring curbs individual creativity and the intrinsic motivation for problem solving (see Williams and Yang, 1999). Furthermore, coordination using detailed directions, regulations, authorization and tight control causes friction and is slow and costly in terms of time resources. All this is likely to reduce the profitability of the firm

---

[16] Since, in small groups, the consequences of the other members' behaviour can easily be grasped by everyone without requiring the effort and costs of their own experimentation, any attempt to challenge an established social model acquires the status of a vicarious experiment (Bandura, 1986, chap. 7). If it is observed to be successful, deviating behaviour may pose a serious challenge to a prevailing social model of behaviour: the members of a firm organization may be induced to recognize previously unconsidered extensions of their choice set. Observational learning can thus lead to a weakening of a socially approved standard of conduct and may induce a reframing of action knowledge, with corresponding behaviour adjustments.

and to curb its growth prospects. Nonetheless, the firm may still be able to continue on this basis and may even be able to generate growth.

If, in contrast, the entrepreneur tries to gain cognitive leadership, he or she may succeed in doing so because of sufficient personal skills and the intrinsic attractiveness of the business conception. If so, an organizational culture of loose hierarchical ties, more informal than formal organizational routines and a significant extent of intrinsic work motivation may become feasible. All this should result in a significantly higher level of organizational achievements. Such success may fuel the expansion of the firm's operations. Sooner or later, the firm organization will then have to be expanded as well.

7   Organizational growth and transformation: a contingent feedback

With the expansion of the firm organization, a development will be triggered that leaves the early stage of the small entrepreneurial firm behind. The genesis of the firm organization thus leads over to questions (ii) and (iii) in a natural way. For reasons of space, only question (iii) will be addressed here. Thus, it will be asked what kinds of transformations the firm organization can be expected to go through in its further genesis, and what determines whether or not these changes occur. As argued elsewhere, the growing size of the organization results in typical organizational transitions (see Witt, 2000). Thus, as in Penrose's (1959) contribution, growth is considered a determinant of organizational change here too, albeit for reasons different from (but not incompatible with) those given by Penrose.

In an entrepreneurial start-up venture with, initially, a very small organization, all interactions between entrepreneur and employees take place on a face-to-face basis. Informal agenda-setting effects and social models can, in principle, be kept under the close scrutiny of the entrepreneur. At a certain point in time, the growing number of personnel will start to strain the entrepreneur's capacity to exert cognitive leadership, to dominate the social learning processes and to coordinate the firm members on his/her business conception. Even the most skilled entrepreneur must face an upper bound where, simply because of the declining frequency of personal interaction, his/her capacity to achieve all this is exceeded. (It is for this reason that the organization of the start-up firm cannot be expanded by simply multiplying business volume and the number of employees.) With the continued growth of a successful start-up firm a point will thus be reached at which the entrepreneur faces increasing difficulty in upholding his/her business conception and some supporting social models of behaviour as the prevailing cognitive regime among the members of the firm organization. It is a bifurcation point, where several alternative organizational changes can occur, which differ dramatically in their implications for the entrepreneur's role in intra-organizational coordination.

One possible development is, of course, that the entrepreneur indeed waits until his/her capacity to exert cognitive leadership fails. Conceptions other than his/her business conception may then spread in the organization. If the employees adopt cognitive frames and corresponding social models of behaviour that compete with the entrepreneurial business conception or invite opportunistic reflections, organizational incoherence and declining work effort are pre-programmed. As a consequence, the firm organization would perform in a significantly less coherent and efficient way than before. If no countermeasures are taken, profitability would be affected negatively, as would the potential for further growth. A critical stage like this is particularly likely to be reached by, and is often reported for, start-up firms with a founder-entrepreneur after the phase of soaring growth and maturation. Once such a situation prevails, it is difficult – if not impossible – for an entrepreneur to (re)gain cognitive leadership, even if, as a consequence, the size of the organization declines. The employees' cognitive frames have changed in an irreversible way.

However, the threat of stagnation or even decline in the firm's performance may induce the entrepreneur to react instead of clinging to the progressively declining regime of cognitive leadership. What had emerged as an organizational culture of loose hierarchical ties and a (now fading) intrinsic work motivation demands some kind of transformation. One possibility is to try to switch to the above-mentioned monitoring regime in running the firm organization. Because of the size already attained by the firm organization, this would now mean bureaucratization: the activities of the firm members would have to be controlled by a more or less elaborate hierarchy of hired managers. Most likely, such a transition would be accompanied by an explicit codification of many of the intra-organizational interactions and a corresponding increase of formal routines. The benefits of the earlier investments in tangible and intangible assets (firm-specific capabilities and accumulated reputation in the markets) may thus be safeguarded, as could, perhaps, the economies of scale that have already been attained. However, as just explained, the formalization of interactions and the implementation of tight hierarchical controls curbs flexibility and creativity within the organization. With an effective monitoring regime, both bureaucratization and a fading intrinsic motivation and cognitive coherence do not necessarily imply losses of (static) efficiency. But they are very likely to impede the organization's capacity to cope with a rapidly changing and innovative environment. Therefore, the further development of such firms hinges, essentially, on whether, and for how long, they can compensate for their lack of flexibility by economies of scale that they may be able to realize merely by their size.

Among the ways of attempting a transformation of the firm organization other than by transition to a monitoring regime, probably the most important one is what may be called an 'intra-organizational subdivision of entrepreneurship'[17]. Such a transformation would require the entrepreneurial role of cognitive leadership to be taken over by managers in separate divisions of the corporate organization. In the individual divisions a sufficient degree of cognitive coherence may then be maintained, provided these managers are familiar with the business conception underlying the firm's activities. This is likely to be the case if these managers have been socialized within the organization. However, as emphasized by Penrose (1959, chap. 9), the availability of such managerial resources within the firm may be a potential bottleneck. When managers are hired from outside (and when developments in the firm's environment require adaptations of the business conception), a new and superior entrepreneurial task arises. This is the task of coordinating a peer group of managers with entrepreneurial roles (rather than the entire organization) on an overarching business conception shared among them. To grant the entrepreneurial employees resources to use at their own discretion (for pursuing a business conception on their own within the divisions of the corporate organization) means that separate domains of responsibility and leadership are created. As discussed before, coordination can be achieved here too, through reliable, socially shared cognitive and motivational commonalities.

The coordination of the sub-entrepreneurs on the overarching business conception for the entire corporation is just a reprise on the problems of

---

[17] If the entrepreneur does not expect or experience the transition to a monitoring regime or to a subdivision of entrepreneurship within the firm organization to work, he/she still has another move available. Indeed, this move can often be observed: he/she can put the firm up for sale and takeover. The fact that resignation from the entrepreneurial role may occur at this point indicates that entrepreneurship itself can be subject to specialization – a kind of inter-firm subdivision of entrepreneurship. Some entrepreneurs specialize in founding and building up start-up businesses to notable size. When they resign and offer these businesses for sale, profit opportunities are provided for entrepreneurs of a different kind: specialists in reshaping the organizational set-up of the economy by implementing and carrying through their vision of the synergies to be achieved in the acquisitions and mergers market. The cognitive underpinnings of such a business are likely to be quite different from the type of entrepreneurship that specializes in founding and building up firms, and they deserve separate treatment.

cognitive coherence and intrinsic motivation at a higher level. And, again, it may be a serious problem, having to be resolved through superior cognitive leadership within the group of entrepreneurs. As in other groups, observational learning may give rise to socially shared cognitive frames and models of behaviour. In a non-hierarchical group of entrepreneurial peers, this process and its outcome may be entirely spontaneous. Where there is a superior entrepreneur who employs subordinate entrepreneurs, it is again important for him/her to succeed in shaping communications, now within the entrepreneurial group, in a way that is advantageous to the propagation of the overarching business conception. This means that 'cognitive leadership' has, once more, to be shown, this time among subentrepreneurs. And, here as well, the business conception and the desired social models are vulnerable to invasion by rival frames and models. Failure to prevent such an invasion in the interactions and communication in the entrepreneurial group is, again, likely to induce far-reaching consequences for organizational coherence and for the corporation's overall performance.

8   Conclusions

A fully-fledged evolutionary theory of the firm – or, perhaps better, of the genesis and change of firm organizations – does not yet exist. However, some desiderata of such a theory may already be identified. In this chapter they have been highlighted by formulating some programmatic questions that an evolutionary theory of the firm might reasonably be supposed to raise. The discussion has shown that the proper conceptualization of what evolution can mean in the context of firm organizations is neither unproblematic nor uncontroversial. Selectionist and ecological interpretations of organizational change have been opposed to developmental interpretations. Different from the phylogenetic, population-oriented perspective of the former, developmental interpretations focus on the ontogeny (life cycle) of individual firms. All these interpretations share a common source of inspiration: they rest on analogies to, and metaphors taken from, biology. It has been argued that organizational change follows regularities that neither of the two analogies can fully do justice to, but that elements from both approaches can usefully be integrated into an encompassing evolutionary theory of the firm. In order to explain the observable regularities in organizational change, that theory has to account for the strongly neglected entrepreneurial role in the genesis of firm organizations. Related to this, attention needs to be paid to the changing cognitive underpinnings of organizational interactions as an important source of growth-driven organizational change.

REFERENCES

Alchian, A. A., and H. Demsetz (1972), 'Production, information costs, and economic organization', *American Economic Review* **62**(5): 777–95.

Aldrich, H., and S. Mueller (1982), 'The evolution of organizational forms: technology, coordination and control', in B. M. Staw and L. L. Cummings (eds.), *Research in Organizational Behavior*, vol. IV, Greenwich: JAI Press, 33–88.

Anderson, J. P. (2000), *Cognitive Psychology and Its Implications*, 5th edn., New York: Worth Publishers.

Bandura, A. (1986), *Social Foundations of Thought and Action: A Social Cognitive Theory*, Englewood Cliffs, NJ: Prentice-Hall.

Binmore, K. (1998), *Just Playing*, Cambridge, MA: MIT Press.

Chandler, A. D. (1962), *Strategy and Structure: Chapters in the History of the Industrial Enterprise*, Cambridge, MA: MIT Press.

(1990), *Scale and Scope: The Dynamics of Industrial Capitalism*, Cambridge, MA: Harvard University Press.

(1992), 'Organizational capabilities and the economic history of the industrial enterprise', *Journal of Economic Perspectives* **6**: 79–100.

Coase, R. H. (1937), 'The nature of the firm', *Economica*, New Series 4: 386–405.

(1988), 'The nature of the firm: origin, meaning, influence', *Journal of Law, Economics and Organization* **4**: 3–47.

Dosi, G., R. R. Nelson and S. G. Winter (2000), 'Introduction: the nature and dynamics of organizational capabilities', in G. Dosi, R. R. Nelson and S. G. Winter (eds.), *The Nature and Dynamics of Organizational Capabilities*, Oxford: Oxford University Press, 1–22.

Foss, N. J. (1993), 'Theories of the firm: contractual and competence perspectives', *Journal of Evolutionary Economics* **3**(2): 127–44.

(1996) 'Capabilities and the theory of the firm', *Revue d'Économie Industrielle* 77: 7–28.

(2000), 'The theory of the firm: an introduction to themes and contributions', in N. J. Foss (ed.), *The Theory of the Firm: Critical Perspectives on Business and Management*, London: Routledge, xv–lxi.

(2001), 'Evolutionary theories of the firm: reconstruction and relations to contractual theories', in: K. Dopfer (ed.), *Evolutionary Economics – Program and Scope*, Boston: Kluwer Academic Publishers, 317–55.

Fransman, M. (1995), *Japan's Computer and Communications Industry: The Evolution of Industrial Giants and Global Competitiveness*, Oxford: Oxford University Press.

(1999), *Visions of Innovation: The Firm and Japan*, Oxford: Oxford University Press.

Greiner, L. (1972), 'Evolution and revolution as organizations grow', *Harvard Business Review* **50**: 37–46.

Hannan, M. T., and G. R. Carroll (1992), *Dynamics of Organizational Populations: Density, Legitimation, and Competition*, Oxford: Oxford University Press.

Hannan, M. T., and J. Freeman (1989), *Organizational Ecology*, Cambridge, MA: Harvard University Press.

Hart, O., and J. R. Moore (1990), 'Property rights and the nature of the firm', *Journal of Political Economy* **98**(6): 1119–58.

Hodgson, G. M. (2001), 'Is social evolution Lamarckian or Darwinian?', in J. Laurent and J. Nightingale (eds.), *Darwinism and Evolutionary Economics*, Cheltenham: Edward Elgar, 87–120.

Holmström, B., and P. Milgrom (1994), 'The firm as an incentive system', *American Economic Review* **84**(4): 972–91.

Holmström, B., and J. Roberts (1998), 'The boundaries of the firm revisited', *Journal of Economic Perspectives* **12**(4): 73–94.

Knight, F. H. (1921), *Risk, Uncertainty and Profit*, New York: Harper & Row.

Langlois, R. N. (1992), 'Transaction costs in real time', *Industrial and Corporate Change* **1**: 99–127.

Langlois, R. N., and M. M. Cosgel (1993), 'Frank Knight on risk, uncertainty, and the firm: a new interpretation', *Economic Inquiry* **31**: 456–65.

Langlois, R. N., and P. L. Robertson (1995), *Firms, Markets and Economic Change*, London: Routledge.

Levine, J. M., L. B. Resnick and E. T. Higgins (1993), 'Social foundations of cognition', *Annual Review of Psychology* **44**: 585–612.

Levinthal, D. (2000), 'Organizational capabilities in complex worlds', in G. Dosi, R. R. Nelson and S. G. Winter (eds.), *The Nature and Dynamics of Organizational Capabilities*, Oxford: Oxford University Press, 363–79.

Marshall, A. (1890), *Principles of Economics*, London: Macmillan (8th edn., 1920, London: Macmillan; 9th variorum edn., 1961, London: Macmillan).

Metcalfe, J. S. (1994), 'Competition, Fisher's principle and increasing returns in the selection process', *Journal of Evolutionary Economics* **4**(3): 327–46.

(1998), *Evolutionary Economics and Creative Destruction*, London: Routledge.

Montgomery, C. A. (ed.) (1995), *Resource-based and Evolutionary Theories of the Firm*, Dordrecht: Kluwer Academic Publishers.

Mueller, D. C. (1972) 'A life cycle theory of the firm', *Journal of Industrial Economics* **20**: 199–219.

Murmann, J. P. (2003), *Knowledge and Competitive Advantage: The Coevolution of Firms, Technology, and National Institutions*, Cambridge: Cambridge University Press.

Murmann, J. P., H. Aldrich, D. Levinthal and S. G. Winter (2003), 'Evolutionary thought in management and organization theory at the beginning of the new millennium', *Journal of Management Inquiry* **12**(1): 22–40.

Nelson, R. R., and S. G. Winter (1982), 'An evolutionary theory of economic change', Cambridge, MA: Harvard University Press.

Nooteboom, B. (1992), 'Towards a dynamic theory of transactions', *Journal of Evolutionary Economics* **2**(4): 281–99.

Osterloh, M., and B. S. Frey (2000), 'Motivation, knowledge transfer, and organizational forms', *Organization Science* **11**(5): 538–50.

Penrose, E. T. (1952), 'Biological analogies in the theory of the firm', *American Economic Review* **42**(5): 804–19.

(1953), 'Biological analogies in the theory of the firm: rejoinder', *American Economic Review* **43**(4): 603–9.

(1959), *The Theory of the Growth of the Firm*, Oxford: Basil Blackwell.

Quinn, R. E., and K. Cameron (1983), 'Organizational life cycles and shifting criteria of effectiveness: some preliminary evidence', *Management Science* **29**: 33–51.

Rathe, K., and U. Witt (2001), 'The nature of the firm – static vs. developmental interpretations', *Journal of Management and Governance* **5**: 331–51.

Teece, D. J., R. Rumelt, G. Dosi and S. G. Winter (1994), 'Understanding corporate coherence: theory and evidence', *Journal of Economic Behavior and Organization* **23**: 1–30.

Williams, W. M., and L. T. Yang (1999), 'Organizational creativity', in R. J. Sternberg (ed.), *Handbook of Creativity*, Cambridge: Cambridge University Press, 373–91.

Williamson, O. E. (1985), *The Economic Institutions of Capitalism*, New York: Free Press.

(1996), *The Mechanisms of Governance*, Oxford: Oxford University Press.

Winter, S. G. (1964), 'Economic "natural selection" and the theory of the firm', *Yale Economic Essays* **4**(1): 225–72.

(1988), 'On Coase, competence, and the corporation', *Journal of Law, Economics and Organization* **4**: 163–80.

Witt, U. (1998), 'Imagination and leadership: the neglected dimension of an evolutionary theory of the firm', *Journal of Economic Behavior and Organization* **35**: 161–77.

(2000), 'Changing cognitive frames – changing organizational forms: an entrepreneurial theory of organizational development', *Industrial and Corporate Change* **9**: 733–55.

(2003), *The Evolving Economy: Essays on the Evolutionary Approach to Economics*, Cheltenham: Edward Elgar.

B

Evolutionary mesoeconomics

11 The self-organizational perspective on economic evolution: a unifying paradigm[1]

John Foster

1 Introduction

Evolutionary economists have tended to build upon biological metaphors and analogies in constructing analytical representations of structural change in the economic domain. However, evolutionary biology, with its focus upon selection mechanisms, is limited in its applicability in socio-economic contexts. Because of this limitation, some evolutionary economists have begun to explore a more morphogenic perspective, namely the self-organization approach (see Foster, 1994a). Although this approach has its roots at a more fundamental physical level of enquiry, namely non-equilibrium thermodynamics, it is argued that it offers a more useful analytical representation of structuration for those interested in detecting evolutionary change in time series data. As such, it is not used as a metaphor or an analogy; the self-organization process is present at all levels of scientific enquiry. However, physio-chemical, biological, socio-political and economic self-organization all involve interconnected, but distinct, processes of structuration. For example, economic structuration cannot be understood properly using a physio-chemical self-organization approach, yet economic structures contain dissipative features that they share with chemical compounds.

Generally, as we move upwards from the chemical to the economic, energy/entropy aspects of self-organization have to be overlaid with knowledge/complexity considerations. Indeed, questions arise as to whether self-organization is best viewed as a thermodynamic phenomenon or as a more general process within which energy-entropy interplay

[1] This chapter constitutes part of the ongoing research of the Emergent Complexity and Organization in Economics research group at the University of Queensland. I would like to thank group members David Anthony, Bryan Morgan and Pradeep Phillip for their valuable comments. Thanks are also due to those who commented upon earlier versions of the chapter when it was presented as a paper at the European Association for Evolutionary Political Economy conference in Copenhagen and at the University of Versailles. Particular thanks are due to Robert Delorme and Martin O'Connor. The usual caveat applies.

is a special case. This question was raised recently in evolutionary biology by Daniel Brooks and Edward Wiley (1986), and their answers were met with fierce opposition from both neo-Darwinian evolutionary biologists, on the one hand, and strict thermodynamicists, on the other. The same question arose earlier in cybernetics (see, for example, Atlan, 1972), leading to views of systems that stress the priority of complexity over entropy considerations.

In economics, thermodynamical considerations, which provide the starting point for self-organizational thinking, have been neglected in the mainstream of the discipline because of their uncomfortable implications for neoclassical economics (see Georgescu-Roegen, 1971). Thus, the mainstream view of economic evolution tends to have been restricted to assertions that a Darwinian mechanism lurks behind static representations of the competitive system. Despite the fact that neoclassical economics can be viewed, at least in principle, as compatible with the first law of thermodynamics (the 'conservation principle'), which deals with closed systems, the second law of thermodynamics, which deals with open systems, has not been widely used to provide an alternative basis for understanding economic evolution. Typically, mainstream economists have been satisfied with the view that rational economic agents employ knowledge to negate entropy processes, through, for example, the timely provision of maintenance and the replacement of economic structures. In other words, very strong knowledge/informational presumptions have been employed that have no basis in real experience.

Outside the mainstream, this view has not been upheld. Institutionalists, such as Kenneth Boulding (1981) and John Gowdy (1992), have stressed that energy/entropy considerations are important in economic evolution, and Kurt Dopfer (1986) has stressed that economic self-organization centres upon knowledge/complexity considerations. Austrian economists have provided the most vigorous critique of the mainstream treatment of knowledge and complexity, stressing the subjective nature of knowledge, the complexity of the economic system and the evolutionary character of economic processes. Furthermore, Austrians and institutionalists alike have stressed the importance of cultural considerations in economic evolution. Culture is, clearly, not a thermodynamic phenomenon, but it constitutes a form of organized complexity in shared knowledge, absent at the chemical and biological level of enquiry.

Austrian and institutionalist characterizations of evolution suggest that Brooks and Wiley's view that self-organization is primarily an informational process in the biological domain applies with even more force in the economic system. However, with the exception of Dopfer (1986), on the institutionalist side, and Ulrich Witt (1991), on the Austrian side, relatively few members of these schools have set their arguments in a self-organizational context that can embrace knowledge as well as energy. Parallels have been drawn between the Austrian view of 'spontaneous order' and self-organization, but closer inspection reveals that such a view is conjectural rather than an abstraction that can provide a stylized representation of an evolutionary process in history. On the institutionalist side, the 'cumulative causation' representation of a historical process, stemming from the work of – for example – Allyn Young, Gunnar Myrdal and Nicholas Kaldor, also has properties that appear to be self-organizational in nature. However, we do not find any strong link between these ideas and the emergence of the self-organization approach in the post-war era.

The purpose of this chapter is to argue that many Austrian and institutionalist insights concerning economic evolution can be placed within a self-organizational approach, provided that it is uniquely economic in orientation. Furthermore, it is also argued that Marshallian neoclassical economics can be placed within such an approach, unlike post-Marshallian neoclassical economics, which is viewed as inadmissible in a self-organizational context. It is shown how a formal representation of the process of economic self-organization, suitable for empirical application using historical data, can be built upon existing neo-Schumpeterian depictions of the diffusion of technical change through innovation. Thus, it is argued that the self-organization approach is capable of offering a pluralist theoretical framework for the investigation of economic processes, set in an explicit historical context, in contrast to timeless post-Marshallian neoclassical economics.

2   Austrians, institutionalists and mathematics

Members of both the Austrian and institutionalist schools of thought founded their distinctive approaches to economics on the presumption that economic agents operate in the real domain of historical time. For the Austrians, this gave rise to true uncertainty concerning the future and the need to set economic analysis in the subjective domain of the individual. For the institutionalists, history implied time irreversibilities in economic structure, rendering institutions, which are viewed as sociopolitical/cultural in character, the appropriate subject of study in gaining a full understanding of human behaviour in the economic domain. The old debates between the German 'Historical' school, from which American institutionalism grew, and the Austrian school were not about the relevance of history but, rather, how economic analysis could accommodate the fact that economic processes are set in history.

The Austrians preferred to stress the impact of history on individual decision making, so that appropriate subjective abstractions could be constructed for economic application. The resultant complexity of interactions was seen as precluding a formalizable macroeconomic depiction of a historical process. Instead, spontaneous order was seen as emerging, endogenously, in custom, norms, regulations, laws and other institutions. The institutionalists, on the other hand, preferred to view institutions in collective terms, examining power relations between groups and documenting the history of institutional formation. Theorizing about individual behaviour was seen as unproductive, on account of the limited range of individual choices available beyond those dictated by cultural and habitual practices.

The concern with history, manifestly present in both these schools, led to methodological positions that were widely regarded as nihilist by mainstream economists. The refusal of the Austrians to recognize formal, objective representations of economic behaviour, either at the micro- or macro-level, led to their marginalization. The absence of mathematics, the conventional language of science, led them to be viewed as abstractionists concerned with ideology rather than science. The similar institutionalist refusal to recognize the validity of formal neoclassical economic theory, plus an insistence on extensive empirical description, led to the charge of undisciplined historicism, which was seen as constituting neither ideology nor science.

The marginal status of these two schools was not due to their lack of insight in understanding the key problems that economists face. On the contrary, acknowledgement of the problems faced in making decisions in historical time, leading to structural irreversibility and evolutionary conceptions of structural change, led to many outstanding contributions. The joint award of the Nobel Prize to Friedrich von Hayek and Myrdal is testimony to the importance of insights on both sides. Although it is tempting to ascribe the marginalization of minority schools of thought to ideological considerations, this can hardly be the case when one of these schools contained some of the most ardent supporters of the 'free market'. It seems logical that the problem should lie in an area where both of these schools are in agreement, in juxtaposition to the mainstream.

As has been noted, it is the insistence of members of both of these schools that economic analysis should take explicit account of historical time that is their distinguishing feature. However, why should eminently reasonable propositions concerning the existence of *time irreversibility*, *structural change* and *true uncertainty* in historical processes have been so unpalatable to the mainstream of the economics profession in the post-war era? Surely, an emerging science has a bleak future when its promoters deny the importance of fundamental features of the historical processes that they are attempting to explain. The answer does not lie in a widespread belief that the formal *Homo oeconomicus* representation of economic behaviour, which contains none of these three features, is more realistic. Many neoclassical economists have stressed that such economic theory cannot be applied to understand historical processes. Instead, the answer seems to lie in the chosen language of scientific discourse, namely mathematics. If it is believed that the correct level of economic enquiry is the individual and that the price mechanism is the primary context within which economic coordination takes place, a 'scientific' desire to use mathematics as formal medium for deduction leads, inevitably, to neoclassical economic theory. The problem does not lie in the chosen economics but, rather, in its limited expression in the chosen language of discourse. We can choose a different type of economics, say, stressing group behaviour and the distribution of income as the favoured coordinating mechanism, and precisely the same problem arises if formal mathematics is used to provide a basis for deduction.

Mathematics, as all institutionalists and Austrians clearly understand, is a very inadequate language for capturing all three 'evolutionary' aspects of historical processes alluded to. The use of mathematical logic *requires* structure to be fixed, as Alfred Marshall understood clearly when formalizing his 'mechanical analogy' for short-period and partial use (see Marshall, 1890, and Foster, 1993). For Marshall, in other words, the mathematically formal neoclassical model was an *approximation* that could not hold over long periods or across the economy in a general sense. Marshall realized that the economic system was evolutionary in character, and this is reflected in the many qualifications and warnings concerning the use of neoclassical economic theory that he offered throughout the several editions of his *Principles*. Unfortunately, he never wrote his promised 'volume II', which was intended to offer an explicitly evolutionary treatment of economic behaviour. Although there are several reasons for this, it is clear that an important one was his inability to devise a way of expressing economic evolution in formal mathematical terms. Economics had begun to be enslaved by the mathematical language that was deemed to be the centrepiece of respectable science.

From Paul Samuelson's *Foundations of Economic Analysis* (1947) on, mathematical logic became the cornerstone of economic dialogue. In his view (p. xvii)

It finally achieved for economics a synthesis of Cournot's Newtonian calculus method of maximising with Walras's equations of general equilibrium.

Moreover (p. xviii),

Debreu once commented to me – soberly – that the discipline which most fully uses in its daily work the frontier refinements of mathematical analysis is modern economic theory.

Gérard Debreu (1991) explains why this should be (p. 3).

Being denied a sufficiently secure experimental base, economic theory has to adhere to rules of logical discourse and must renounce the facility of internal inconsistency. A deductive structure that tolerates a contradiction does so under the penalty of being useless, since any statement can be derived flawlessly and immediately from that contradiction.

The ascendancy of mathematics as the favoured medium of economic discourse led, inevitably, to a preference for timeless, deductive theories that could easily be represented mathematically. Gradually, the warnings of Marshall were forgotten and propositions derived from timeless mathematical logic were 'tested' using historical data. Elsewhere, I have discussed the fundamental methodological problems that arise in such an enterprise, particularly in the context of modern 'new Keynesian' economic analysis (see Foster, 1994c). Debreu (1991, p. 5) offers a clear statement of the problem that widespread adoption of mathematical discourse has presented for economics.

In the past two decades, economic theory has been carried away further by a seemingly irresistible current that can be explained only partly by the intellectual successes of its mathematization. . . . The very choice of the questions to which (the theorist) tries to find answers is influenced by his mathematical background. Thus, the danger is ever present that the part of economics will become secondary, if not marginal, in that judgement.

This is a position that the Austrians and institutionalists have held for many decades. Furthermore, if we regard Marshall as the founding father of neoclassical economics, we can argue that modern mathematical economic theory *cannot be construed as neoclassical either*, in the Marshallian sense. What it constitutes is mathematical logic with economic labels appended. As time has elapsed, the illusion that mathematics is economics has become more difficult to ascertain, because the mathematics used has become more general, in the sense of allowing for discrete intervals, delay and non-linearities. The fixed structure equilibria to which variables tend have moved from fixed points to fixed curves (e.g. limit cycles), to predictable multiple equilibria (e.g. catastrophe theory) to unpredictable multiple equilibria regions (e.g. chaotic attractors). The illusion that such a generalization has led to better deductive representations of actual economic processes has arisen because movements between multiple equilibria appear to match the non-linear 'jumps' that we observe in the history of some economic variables, and because equilibrium regions appear to encapsulate the true uncertainty we experience in history.

However, no matter how complex a non-linear dynamical mathematical formulation is, it remains a representation of a deterministic, time-invariant structure, and, therefore, must be non-evolutionary in character. Thus, it *cannot* be used deductively to shed light upon the workings of a historical process. A mathematical formulation represents the closure of a system, and historical systems are open. It represents a reversible, structurally fixed and deterministic process, whereas a historical process involves irreversibility, structural change and true uncertainty. Despite these well-known properties of mathematical representations, non-linear dynamic mathematics has now become the deductive medium of mainstream economic analysis. This is no better illustrated than in the case of the advanced graduate textbook of Costas Azariadis (1993), which purports to be concerned with 'intertemporal macroeconomics'. Despite the seductive title, we find that our three evolutionary characteristics of historical processes (time irreversibility, true uncertainty and structural change) are almost entirely absent from the analysis presented. In the preface, it is even argued that the great achievement of modern economists is the mastery of a more general deductive mathematics (differential equations with discrete intervals) within which traditional discourse can be conducted. However, any institutionalist or Austrian would point out that what is offered remains only mathematics and that such mathematics remains deficient as a logical basis for economic analysis (see Boland, 1986). Whether the deductive mathematical framework offered represents a significant achievement in the field of logic is only for *mathematicians* to judge.

Mathematics cannot constitute science. This is made clear if one examines how mathematics is used in a natural science such as physics. The latter is an experimental science where mathematics is used as a tool for formalizing processes that have been identified through experimental closure. At all times, deductive mathematics is used as an *approximation* to assist in generating an orderly representation of an observed process subject to an array of experimental controls. In this regard, the physicist is interested in *specific* applications of mathematics. General aspects of mathematical systems, such as asymptotic properties, are of little interest, and, if no solution eventuates, numerical methods are applied that yield solutions with unknown mathematical properties.

Debreu and Samuelson were wrong in supposing that, in general, mathematical rigour could be a scientific substitute for experimentation in economics. Mathematical logic remains just that unless it is used within an empirically based scientific framework as a justifiable approximation. Furthermore, these two distinguished economists were also wrong in implying that there is no other scientific way to go. Marshall did not think so, and neither do modern institutionalists, such as Geoffrey Hodgson (1993), and modern Austrians, such as Witt (1991). Practising scientists do not begin in the domain of theory but, rather, in understanding – intimately – their data. From this understanding emerge hypotheses concerning processes. Economic theorists, such as the aforementioned distinguished two, have been singularly uninterested in data, despite the fascinating information that time series data can reveal. Thus they have been in no real position to assess possible alternatives to experimentation in the context of time series data. Indeed, like many other economic theorists, they have tended to distance themselves from the messy context of empirical economics.

This disconnection between theorizing and data has led to a lack of development of what can be called 'theories of historical processes' in economics that can be related, directly, to historical time series data. This serious deficiency has not been remedied to any significant extent in the theoretical work of unorthodox schools either. The Austrians' aversion to dealing with aggregative data and the institutionalists' dislike of formal abstraction has meant that these minority schools have not been inclined to develop process theory to any great extent. Yet often, in their insightful depictions of economic behaviour, lurk implicit theories of historical processes. In the institutionalist case we have, for example, much discussion of cumulative causation, and in the Austrian case conjectures concerning the emergence of spontaneous order. They tend not to be formalized but cast, instead, in discussions of the evolution of particular institutional structures.

3   The self-organization approach

Biological metaphor and analogy have been favoured in much of modern evolutionary economics (see Nelson, 1995). This has led to a focus upon the appropriate choice of selection mechanisms in different economic contexts. Illuminating as much of this literature is, it offers little in the way of a theory of process that can be used to address historical data. Although the presence of structural change is recognized, biological selection models offer no way of assessing the historical timescale of change or of discriminating between different evolutionary theories through the examination of historical data. As John Maynard Smith (1982) has stressed, evolutionary theories are timeless in construction.

In the light of this problem, Brooks and Wiley (1986) argue that the process of biological evolution should be analysed using a more general self-organization approach, building on the second law of thermodynamics, which encapsulates a time-dependent process that all living systems must transcend to survive in historical time. The entropy process is observable in historical time and, thus, theories of evolutionary processes that are capable of expression in historical data can be constructed upon the entropy law.

The self-organization approach came to the attention of natural scientists mainly through the work of Ilya Prigogine and his associates (see Prigogine and Stengers, 1984, for a history of the development of his work). He argued that a system far from thermodynamic equilibrium can achieve a degree of self-organization through the importation of free energy and the exportation of high-entropy waste, which, in turn, creates time irreversibility in structure and, as such, constitutes part of the boundary conditions that limit structural development. 'Dissipative structures' that form in this manner are macroscopic in character, since the exact initial conditions that give rise to them can never be known; therefore, a microscopic approach cannot be adopted to understand the process of structuration that eventuates. It is the macroscopic limit placed on development by time irreversibility and macroscopic boundaries that lead to the identification of the structuration process.

Brooks and Wiley (1986) point out that, although the Prigoginian account of self-organization works well as a theory of structuration in physio-chemical contexts, its energetic focus and its emphasis on exogenously determined boundary conditions are not adequate for understanding self-organization in biological contexts. They refer to the Prigoginian approach as dealing with 'energy entropy systems', which are a special case where energy is imposed rather than purposively acquired. The acquisition of energy requires stocks of knowledge from which flows of information can be drawn. They view the biological organism itself as a structure of information flows, controlling the importation of energy and the exportation of high-entropy waste. In such circumstances, history and the associated time irreversibility become much more important than they are in the Prigoginian account – structuration becomes not just a matter of an irreversible tendency towards an exogenous boundary but, rather, an endogenous historical process with no determinate final state.

Prigogine stressed that structuration is a time-irreversible process, with implications for the bifurcatory potential of the process once a defined boundary is attained. What Brooks and Wiley offer, through their move from energy/entropy considerations to those of information/complexity, is a theory of the process of structuration in history appropriate to systems that are at the biological, rather than the physio-chemical, level of evolutionary complexity. Historical initial conditions matter, and the history of the developmental process also matters. Over time, organisms accumulate knowledge imposed upon them by their environment, and, in so doing, they become consumers of particular forms of free energy and dispose of high-entropy waste in specialized ways. Internally, increased organization consists of an expansion of energetically driven webs of information flows, which permits an increase in structured complexity unavailable in the physio-chemical domain.

The process of evolution, from this self-organizational perspective, becomes one that still has, at its base, energy/entropy processes, but these are now controlled by information/complexity processes that not only thwart the entropy law temporarily but also, because of the diversity of historical experience, lead to a great diversity of species, organisms and individuals. Thus, evolution is not teleological, in the Lamarckian sense, but contingent upon history, with traditional Darwinian forms of selection confined to historical conditions where a boundary state is approached. Both biological evolution and ontogeny can be represented using a biological self-organization approach that is explicitly historical in character and, thus, amenable to investigation using historical data over appropriate time periods.

4   Economic self-organization

Prigogine conceived of self-organization in physio-chemical systems as a process where energy is imposed and irreversible structuration proceeds towards some exogenously defined limit. Brooks and Wiley argue that, in biological systems, energy is not imposed but acquired through the use of knowledge imposed by historical experience. In moving to the context of socio-economic behaviour of the non-biological type, another 'gear change' is necessary. In the economic system, in particular, knowledge is not only imposed by history but actively acquired by people. Particular types of knowledge are sought to design structures that embody both information/complexity and energy/entropy features. Resultant economic structures, such as the firm, are not simply a reflection of historical experience but are a product of acquired specialist knowledge and informed conjectures concerning the future. Boundaries to growth and development need no longer be determined only by history; some systems will be able to anticipate them and enact structural adaptations that transcend them. For example, firms can acquire new knowledge, which informs novel replacement investment strategies, product mix changes and changes in production techniques that can shift it smoothly from one evolutionary development phase to another. Equally, failure to seek out new knowledge exposes the firm to the vagaries of history, with associated struggles and crises of the biological type.

Applying the self-organization approach in economics involves an even greater emphasis on information/complexity, over energy/entropy considerations, than in biology. Thus, it is not surprising that many of the central debates in economics have been concerned with the question of how we deal with stocks of knowledge and flows of information. Before the widespread use of mathematical language forced concepts of knowledge and information into a form that cannot exist in history, except as an approximation in particular circumstances, the rudiments of an economic self-organization approach had already been presented informally. We have noted that these rudiments have persisted in Austrian and institutionalist thought. However, it is argued in Foster (1993) that such an approach was even present in the thinking of Marshall, an acknowledged founding father of modern neoclassical economics. He did not, however, move beyond an intuitive grasp of the principles of economic self-organization. Being unable to discover in evolutionary biology a formal representation of an evolutionary process that could constitute an analogy, or even a metaphor, he never produced the promised second volume of his *Principles of Economics* on evolutionary economics. Furthermore, there was little prospect of him using the entropy law as a starting point, since he saw it as embodying the opposite of economic progress, and, moreover, non-equilibrium thermodynamics had yet to be conceived of in the natural sciences. Thus, the possibility of translating his penetrating remarks concerning the role of information/complexity in economic evolution could not gain formal expression.

To associate economic self-organization with an economist who promoted mathematical deductivism appears, on the face of it, to contradict what has been said about mathematical formalism. However, what we must remember about neoclassical economics is that it was popularized by Marshall for a particular purpose, namely to understand price determination through the use of supply and demand constructs. He did not argue that price theory could be useful in understanding economic phenomena in a general sense, as has often been the case in post-Marshallian neoclassical economics. Marshall saw his analysis of price determination as an *approximation* for application in specific circumstances and over short time periods. Because of this, it is necessary to make a strict distinction between Marshallian neoclassical economics and post-Marshallian neoclassical economics, which deals with general equilibrium in markets over an illusory 'long run'.

Marshallian price theory has widespread uses as an approximation, and it was John Maynard Keynes (1936) who developed a comparable short-period income determination theory at the macroeconomic level, where Marshallian relative price effects cancelled out, leaving income/expenditure associations to determine effective demand. The resultant principle of effective demand remained mechanical and comparative static in construction. However, Keynes clearly understood that it constituted an approximation suitable only for short-period application. It did not, and could not, deal with the long period where evolutionary change dominated the historical dynamics of economic systems (see Foster, 1989). Keynes did not find it necessary or practical to develop Marshall's evolutionary insights, beyond a few informal remarks, to confront the long period in the *General Theory*, given its immediate policy objectives and its target audience in the community of economists.

Post-Marshallian neoclassical economists, by arguing that the long-run general equilibrium price mechanism determines the course of the economic process in the long period and that quantity adjustments are short-run disequilibrium movements appropriate to the short-period, destroyed the attempts of both Marshall and Keynes to use comparative static analysis as a reasonable short-period approximation. As we have noted, what we were left with was a timeless mathematical framework, convenient for deduction. In other words, mathematics, *not* economics.

It follows that there is no need to dismantle Marshall's price theory or Keynes' income theory in attempting to provide a coherent treatment of evolutionary economics. What *is* necessary is to revive Marshall's agenda to provide an alternative theoretical approach that can offer a suitable approximation for scientific inquiry concerning evolutionary change in the economic system. As has been pointed out, the self-organization approach offers such a framework, provided we allow for the fact that knowledge is acquired rather than imposed in the historical process of structuration. As such, knowledge itself constitutes structure that is complex and self-organized. It is precisely this point that Austrians and institutionalists have focused upon from their respective microscopic and macroscopic perspectives. It follows that the economic self-organization that we observe is the formation of informational complexity and organization. Energy/entropy flows must be present in the presence of any structure, but they are not the driving force of economic structures because they are controlled within informational webs, such as, for example, sophisticated accounting systems in firms.

The importance of acquired knowledge and information in economic self-organization means that it is not possible to understand fully economic processes from a quantitative input-output perspective. Of course, this has been recognized in mainstream 'new' growth theory both in the context of technological change and in the acquisition of human capital as factors that shift production functions. However, in the presence of endogenous self-organization, output growth depends on *organizational* development, rather than simply technological change or educational improvement. The latter two processes are necessary, but not sufficient, to explain economic self-organization. Although there is no doubt that shortages of skills and novel ideas will define the boundaries for a self-organizing system, it is the *simultaneous conjunction* of skill and knowledge – i.e. their organizational juxtaposition at a point in time – that is crucial.

In Foster (1987), the abstraction of *Homo creativus* was proposed to capture this two-dimensional (knowledge/skill) nature of economic self-organization in historical time. Such a construct stresses the fact that structuration requires increases in the stock of perceptual knowledge and the stock of interactive skills, which can yield parallel flows of information and activity necessary to produce a structure in historical time. In the economic domain, the resultant processes of structuration are viewed as tractable if a monetary valuation can be ascribed to creative activities and the structures they give rise to. These processes are limited by energy stocks, knowledge stocks and skill stocks, but are driven by something much less quantifiable and subject to volatility, namely the *aspiration*. Economists have often recognized the importance of this ultimate, forward-looking driver of economic self-organization: Keynes, drawing from a much older tradition, called it a product of 'animal spirits', and the Austrians have tended to call it 'imagination'. It results in endogenous structuration that is structurally unstable. Social, political and cultural influences can all play a role in forming aspirations, as the institutionalists have stressed. The aspiration is also a psychological state, and, as Tibor Scitovsky (1977) explains, it induces *tension*, which directs behaviour towards structuration and goal achievement.

In principle, this process is similar to that found in natural science examples of self-organization. The difference is one concerning the complexity of self-organization itself, which, in the economic sphere, involves neither the imposition of energy nor the imposition of knowledge; both are actively sought by the human agents of economic structure. Thus, aspiration does not involve simply avoiding entropy through the structuration of imposed energy into organized physical complexity, as in chemical systems, nor does it involve only the use of imposed knowledge to create structure, as in biological systems. Birds have aspirations to construct nests, and do so in line with imposed information. Economic aspirations can involve structures in the imagination, leading to the acquisition of new skills and new knowledge. Limits faced in the presence of imposed information can be transcended through imagination and creativity.

Economic self-organization is a more endogenously driven process than its biological counterpart. The boundary limit of a developmental process is still strongly influenced by history but it is also affected by forward-looking plans enacted through institutions entirely absent in the biological domain. Thus, we have largely exogenous limits in chemical systems, they become endogenized – in a historical sense – in biological systems, and in economic systems history gives way to conscious, forward-looking behaviour; we are not always prisoners of history in the economic domain. For example, Joel Mokyr (1990), using the Foster (1987) *Homo creativus* construct, discusses the manner in which both energy/entropy constraints and historical constraints, of the 'institutional inertia' type, have been circumvented in history through the acquisition and use of new knowledge and new skills. There are, of course, many examples in history where this was not the case; some phases of economic development ended in crisis and socio-economic collapse. However, such events are also consistent with a self-organizational perspective.

The question arises as to whether such endogenous processes of structuration can be represented by a theory of economic process that is formalizable and, thus, useful for modelling in the presence of time series data. When data are yielded from a chemical experiment, then it is possible to present a formal representation of self-organization. A tendency towards exogenous boundaries can be approximated by dynamic mathematics and the presence of time irreversibility can be employed to explain why structural transition occurs in stationary states. This is the 'science of synergetics' pioneered by, for example, Herman Haken and Friedrich Weidlich. However, it has been pointed out (Foster and Wild, 1996) that the endogenous nature of structuration and the limits to which it tends in the non-experimental domain of economic time series data precludes the deductive use of dynamic mathematics. It does not preclude, however, the use of mathematics to provide a non-deductive abstraction of a smooth process self-organizational structuration. It is this possibility that we shall now explore.

5   The logistic diffusion equation: a theory of an evolutionary historical process

An endogenous process of structuration cannot be one that is deterministic, converging on a stationary state that has stable, equilibrium properties. However, Prigogine and Stengers (1984) point out that endogenous structuration due to self-organization tends to assume a particular trajectory over time, if structuration is measured in terms of some homogenous measure of growth. The trajectory can be represented by the logistic diffusion equation, which assumes a sigmoid shape, tending towards a stationary state at a boundary. Thus, the self-organization approach contains a formal representation of smooth structuration over time, which, as an abstraction of a process that will not be smooth in actuality, offers a theory of an evolutionary historical process. However, as a deterministic mathematical equation, we know that the logistic diffusion equation cannot encapsulate the inherent tendency of self-organizational development to tend towards structural instability. This is because self-organization is a non-equilibrium endogenous process, and the logistic equation is a deterministic mathematical form. However, if we do not use such an equation deductively and make no judgement concerning its underlying stability properties (i.e. if we use the continuous form of the logistic equation), it can still provide an abstract representation of a smooth phase of structuration. It then becomes necessary to capture the fluctuation of the actual process around such a trajectory through the introduction of auxiliary hypotheses concerning quasi-exogenous effects and homeostatic mechanisms. Furthermore, the structural integrity of the system must be gauged from the behaviour of the unexplained residuals.

The logistic diffusion equation is well known in economics, at least since the famous paper of Zvi Griliches (1957), but it has received most attention in studies concerning the innovation process. Neo-Schumpeterians, employing strands of both Austrianism and institutionalism as well as the insights of Joseph Schumpeter, have viewed the equation as capturing the process of structuration in the presence of evolutionary change (see Andersen, 1994, chap. 3). A number of studies have been undertaken to discover particular cases of logistic trajectories, both individually and in cascades (see Dixon, 1994). As Witt (1993) stresses, such an approach to the process of innovation becomes a natural counterpart to the Austrian preoccupation with invention. But it is also true, following the comments of neo-Schumpeterians, such as Richard Nelson and Sidney Winter (1982), that the observation of such diffusion processes gives rise to more fundamental theoretical questions concerning the underlying evolutionary process. Correspondingly, neo-Schumpeterians have tended to view the logistic diffusion equation in descriptive, rather than theoretical, terms.

There have been explorations, through simulation, of the implications of structural transition assuming a non-linear logistic shape, as well as conjectures concerning the outcomes of competitive interaction in the presence of logistic diffusion equations between innovating firms (see

Metcalfe, 1994), in the ecological tradition of R. A. Fisher, but such interactions have, as yet, been difficult to represent in statistical studies. Theoretical considerations have tended to remain in the traditional context of identifying the forces at play in stationary states that give rise to transition processes to new stationary states. The tendency has been to offer qualified versions of existing economic theory, employing, for example, bounded rationality to explain why a diffusion process exists. Deterministic mathematical deduction is used to capture 'disequilibrium' between stable equilibrium states. Alternatively, the logistic equation has been viewed as a special mathematical case of general non-linear dynamics of the type specified by, for example, Richard Day in his many contributions. As such, the logistic equation is not a disequilibrium representation but rather a non-linear form with special bifurcatory properties, if specified in terms of discrete intervals.

These treatments of the logistic equation do not view the logistic diffusion equation as a theory of historical process in the presence of evolutionary change, even though it is logistic diffusion transitions that appear most clearly in the data. In contrast, the data tell us little about transient stationary states that, invariably, give way to structural discontinuities with no clear theoretical explanation. In the natural sciences, repeated observation of a particular tendency in the data usually gives rise to the formulation of a theoretical abstraction of such a tendency. Furthermore, repeated observation in a wide range of contexts permits the abstraction to have axiomatic status, enabling ancillary hypotheses to be introduced and tested.

It is a 'stylized fact' that, when structuration of a self-organizational type occurs, it tends to do so along a logistic curve. However, in economics, it may not always *look* like a logistic curve in the historical data, because the boundary to which structuration tends will vary and the diffusion rate, which determines the slope of the logistic, is also likely to vary over time. Observation of a fixed logistic is a special case in the economic domain. Typically, in economic self-organization, logistic trajectories will not look the same as those to be found in chemical reaction kinetics or population ecology. Once we accept that the logistic equation describes, in an abstract way, the underlying density dependence that is a feature of self-organization, then we are in a position to undertake some economics. It is through the boundary and diffusion coefficients that economic hypotheses, derived largely from a mix of induction and deduction, can be introduced and tested.

Following Foster (1994b) and Foster and Wild (1999a), consider the following commonly specified member of the logistic family (the

'Mansfield' variant), where X is a measure of structure, evolving continuously over time. In economic applications we can often measure X structure in terms of monetary valuation.

$$X_t = X_{t-1}[1 + b(1 - \{X_{t-1}/K\})] + u_t \tag{1}$$

where b is the diffusion or structuration coefficient, K is the carrying capacity and u_t is an error term.

The time differential of this curve determines the rate of structuration achieved per unit of time that can be determined from equation (1).

$$(X_t - X_{t-1})/X_{t-1} = b - bX_{t-1}/K + u_t/X_{t-1} \tag{2}$$

or, approximately,

$$\ln X_t - \ln X_{t-1} = b - bX_{t-1}/K + e_t \tag{3}$$

where $e_t = u_t/X_{t-1}$. Equation (3) now has the advantages that it can be estimated linearly and the error term is corrected for bias because of the upward drift of the mean of the X series.

Equation (1) can be seen as describing, in an abstract way, the structuration phase of a self-organizing economic system subject to time irreversibility, attendant structural change and true uncertainty. In order to describe, more completely, the historical process involved we must accept the following augmentation:

$$\ln X_t - \ln X_{t-1} = [b(\ldots)][1 - \{X_{t-1}/K(\ldots)\}] + e_t \tag{4}$$

Thus, b and K are now, themselves, functions of other variables. The function $b(\ldots)$ allows for factors that affect the diffusion coefficient, rendering it non-constant over time. The $K(\ldots)$ function takes into account factors that expand or contract the capacity limit faced by the system in question. Typically, the $b(\ldots)$ function will contain factors that are 'short-period' in influence and the $K(\ldots)$ function will contain 'long-period' factors that determine the capacity limit to which structuration will tend. In no sense is a capacity limit analogous to 'equilibrium'; the opposite is true: if a system moves into the saturation phase of the logistic, the likelihood of instability and discontinuous structural transformation will increase. Endogenizing the fundamental parameters of the logistic diffusion process can help it address a self-organization process that is economic in nature, but it still cannot address the structural uncertainty inherent in an evolutionary process. We can infer from the self-organization approach that the discovery that a process is in the 'saturation' phase of the logistic equation means that structural discontinuity is more likely. However, the crucial information must remain in the unexplained residuals of an estimated augmented logistic equation (see Foster and Wild, 1999b).

6   The economics of economic self-organization

The transcendence of externally imposed energy and knowledge limits to self-organization in the economic system results in structures that are not unlimited in their capacity to develop. Despite the human capacity to adapt and redefine economic structures through the application of knowledge and information, the basic logistic form of structuration will remain. Sometimes logistic curves will cascade into trajectories that look remarkably linear in terms of a general measure, such as monetary valuation. At other times structural inertia will set in and a non-linear discontinuity will eventuate. Economic structuration does not take place in a vacuum; political and social boundaries, inherited from history, will be decisive. Even though knowledge is not imposed in economic self-organization, many other dimensions of knowledge remain imposed in legal, cultural and religious form. It is because of this that no empirical investigation of economic self-organization can proceed before an exhaustive investigation of these and other institutional factors has been conducted.

Once this has been done, the economics of economic self-organization can be introduced to model the historical process of interest. To do this, we must build upon the extended logistic representation in equation (4). Economic thinking must address two issues. First, what economic factors will affect the diffusion rate? And, second, what economic factors will affect the boundary limit of structuration? The factors that enter $b(. . .)$ and $K(. . .)$ will be contingent upon the existence of monetary valuation, exchange and contracting – i.e. an infrastructure of economic knowledge collection/transmission and economic coordination channels, as evidenced in the preliminary investigation of the legal/institutional/cultural/religious background. In general, factors in $b(. . .)$ will be short-period in influence and those in $K(. . .)$ will relate to the long period.

Following Marshall, relative prices will be economic factors that will influence the diffusion rate in the short period. Following Keynes, we could also expect income flow to affect diffusion rates in the short period. If the period is short enough to argue that the infrastructure of knowledge and coordination is relatively unchanged, then approximate mechanical, comparative static models of price and income determination should shed some light upon variations in the diffusion rate.

Understanding K limits is, of course, much more difficult. Because, the economic system is hierarchically structured and componentized, the K of a subsystem will often be driven by the development of a higher system. However, we have argued that, within the various non-economic restrictions that exist, the economic K is largely aspirational in nature. Thus, macro-conscious aspirational movements will ripple down the hierarchy to conjoin with micro-conscious aspirations to affect micro-Ks. Keynes depicted this process vividly in his discussion of swings in investor confidence in the business sector and the hierarchical micro-/macro-interdependence that eventuates. Relative prices, which affect the diffusion rate, cannot correct for diffusion slowdowns that are due to temporary aspirational collapses that lower the K limit.

Since K is affected by so many factors that are non-economic and unmeasurable, there is no prospect of modelling such a variable accurately. It could be estimated as a parameter in the logistic equation but, unlike many chemical examples, K cannot be regarded as fixed. However, in many cases it may be possible to discover variables, both economic and non-economic (such as wealth measures and demographic data), that are related to systematic K movements. It would appear to be an empirical matter to discover variables of significance in $K(...)$. Shifts in non-measurable influences, such as regulation changes, often define the periods over which structuration will take place, and less important changes can be identified and dated through institutional study and expressed as various types of 'qualitative shift variables' and their statistical significance checked, when appropriate.

We have noted that the discovery of empirical representations of equation (4) enables a logistic relationship to be identified in data that need not appear to exhibit a logistic form. This, in turn, enables a researcher to isolate the underlying logistic form and to identify what stage structuration is in. This is vital to any assessment of the stability of the structure in question in the face of external shocks. Following R. Foster (1985), economic structures that progress into the saturation phase of the logistic face instability and structural discontinuity. Where the size of the data sample permits, the structural integrity of a system in saturation can be investigated in more detail through examination of the properties of regression residuals.

Estimating and diagnosing augmented logistic equations in this way provides a coherent way of assessing whether or not evolutionary change of a self-organizational type is present in time series data over appropriate periods. Auxiliary hypotheses can be tested concerning factors that influence the rate of structuration and its limit. Importantly, it is possible to assess the stage of structuration a system is in and, therefore, the likelihood that structural discontinuity will occur. Such information would appear to be of importance to both economic forecasters and regulators. More generally, the approach leads to a new 'process' perspective in economic analysis. In contrast, the heart of mainstream economics lies in production and utility functions that are static representations. A depiction of process is absent in such representations, both in terms of the operation of a system and in terms of the system's emergence. Beyond the short period, such timeless representations cannot constitute even special cases in economic self-organization.

A mathematical representation of economic self-organization has been offered that can be verified in statistical testing. The danger that lies in formalization is that it provides an opening for post-Marshallian neoclassical economists to reinterpret mathematics intended to offer abstract representations of smooth structuration in deductive terms. This has already happened before, when J. Black (1962) reinterpreted Kaldor's (1957) 'technical progress' function as a special case of a neoclassical growth theory. Only by making a firm distinction between Marshallian neoclassical approximation and post-Marshallian neoclassical mathematical logic can we avoid such a misinterpretation.

Marshall's marginalism was set in the context of time irreversibility, as his discussion of 'sunk costs' and fixity of capital in the short period emphasize. What he offered is a useful *approximation*, not a literal representation of an economic process. Neoclassical economics is focused upon price theory and, thus, upon substitution effects. If we view aspiration sets as exogenously given, much in the way that conventional neoclassical economists view preferences, then relative prices become determinants of which structure creating, repairing or maintaining activity will be chosen in any time period. In other words, relative prices have the power to affect the rate of structuration, or diffusion, towards an aspiration. The possibility that the aspiration set itself is affected by relative prices is not denied, only that such knowledge can only be impressionistic and that many other non-price factors, both economic and non-economic, will be more important.

The great weakness of post-Marshallian neoclassical economics is in its presumption that relative prices are the most important factors in long-period planning, set against exogenous preferences. This type of timeless theorizing yields a very poor approximation of historical process, and its adoption undermines, seriously, the value of price theory in economics. Long-period, general equilibrium neoclassicism has, in the post-war era, replaced the Marshallian neoclassicism practised in, for example, the Chicago tradition, as understood in Milton Friedman's *Price Theory* (1962). The power of neoclassical analysis in partial, short-period contexts is amply demonstrated in this tradition, and, indeed, it was this demonstrable power from which neoclassical economics originally drew its legitimacy. By setting such economics in a self-organization approach, to provide an evolutionary treatment of the long period instead of time-less general equilibrium, Marshallian neoclassical economics can regain much of its lost legitimacy in applied economics.

7   Concluding remarks

The self-organization approach can be quantified in economics because monetary valuation of structures and processes exists. Economic structures, thus, exhibit money flows that parallel energy/entropy and information/complexity processes. Economic structures pay for energy and knowledge, which, in turn, dissipates their stock of money-valued wealth. This is replenished through economic activities that generate goods and services of value to others. Internal information webs consist of accounting systems and external information flows are represented by prices. Just as the biological organism seeks out special forms of energy, so the economic structure seeks out special types of customer who provide money flows. This provides self-organizational possibilities absent in the biological domain. Correspondingly, the standard interactive Lotka-Volterra logistic equations employed in population ecology to analyse states such as competition, mutualism and predator-prey have to be superseded by logistic equations where competition is not simply a 'power struggle' but can be represented by relative prices that provide information to facilitate adaptation before 'competitive exclusion' exerts its decisive and catastrophic effect. Economic coordination mechanisms are the enlightened alternative to power struggles. Subscription to such mechanisms, in itself, is a form of socially embedded mutualism that has self-organized in society to replace predator-prey-style power hierarchies as the means to achieve economic coordination.

Because of its distinctiveness at each level of enquiry, the self-organization approach offers a unifying paradigm that is pluralist in character. It can embrace Marshallian neoclassical approximations concerning the short-period operation of the price mechanism in certain market conditions. It can deal with Austrian considerations concerning the variety of subjective knowledge, aspiration and uncertainty, and it can give spontaneous order an explicit process meaning. Of course, a wide range of institutionalist concerns can also be translated into propositions concerning self-organization. It can accommodate situations where economic self-organization degenerates into its biological form, where knowledge is imposed and power structures engage in exploitative relations and struggle in the face of capacity limits. From a self-organizational perspective, there is no difficulty in accepting that the economic system can be dominated by feudal, Marxist or capitalist interactions in particular historical epochs. Economic self-organization can assume bio-logical, or even physio-chemical, characteristics at certain points in his-tory, and it is important for the economist to understand why such transi-tions take place. It has been argued that the identification and estimation of logistic diffusion models can assist greatly in this regard.

What we cannot incorporate into a self-organizational framework is post-Marshallian general equilibrium neoclassicism and associated dis-equilibrium or market failure analysis. Neither can we embrace new Keynesian propositions concerning asymmetric information or incom-plete markets. All applications of non-linear differential equations to make *deductions* concerning the general properties of economic processes in terms of multiple equilibrium, equilibrium curves and equilibrium regions are inadmissible in the context of economic self-organization. All of these approaches involve timeless deduction where no notion of a historical process is involved. Thus, they constitute mathematics, not economics. It is not denied, however, that the unattainable Utopias that such systems of deduction represent can have a profound impact on aspi-rations and, thus, on economic structuration. Imagined worlds, whether in the religious or secular domain, have, for better or worse, influenced the real world. It is the responsibility of the scientist to distinguish these worlds and to provide a way of understanding how they interact.

REFERENCES

Andersen, E. S. (1994), *Evolutionary Economics: Post-Schumpeterian Contributions*, London: Pinter.
Atlan, H. (1972), *L'organization biologique et la theorie de l'information*, Paris: Hermann.
Azariadis, C. (1993), *Intertemporal Macroeconomics*, Cambridge: Basil Blackwell.
Black, J. (1962), 'The technical progress function and the production function', *Economica* **29**: 166–70.
Boland, L. A. (1986), *Methodology for a New Microeconomics: The Critical Foundations*, London: Allen & Unwin.
Boulding, K. E. (1981), *Evolutionary Economics*, Beverly Hills and London: Sage.
Brooks, D. R., and E. O. Wiley (1986), *Evolution as Entropy: Toward a Unified Theory of Biology*, Chicago: University of Chicago Press.
Debreu, G. (1991), 'The mathematization of economics', *American Economic Review* **81**(1): 1–7.
Dixon, R. (1994), 'The logistic family of discrete dynamic models', in J. Creedy and V. Martin (eds.), *Chaos and Non-linear Models in Economics: Theory and Applications*, Aldershot: Edward Elgar, 81–105.
Dopfer, K. (1986), 'The histonomic approach to economics: beyond pure theory and pure experience', *Journal of Economic Issues* **20**(4): 989–1010.
Foster, J. (1987), *Evolutionary Macroeconomics*, London: Allen and Unwin.

(1989), 'The macroeconomics of Keynes; an evolutionary perspective', in J. Pheby (ed.), *New Directions in Post-Keynesian Economics*, Aldershot: Edward Elgar, 124–46.

(1993), 'Economics and the self-organization approach: Alfred Marshall revisited?', *Economic Journal* **419**: 975–91.

(1994a), 'The self-organization approach in economics', in S. P. Burley and J. Foster (eds.), *Economics and Thermodynamics: New Perspectives on Economic Analysis*, Boston: Kluwer Academic Publishers, 183–202.

(1994b), 'The evolutionary macroeconomic approach to econometric modelling: a comparison of sterling and Australian dollar M_3 determination', in R. Delorme and K. Dopfer (eds.), *The Political Economy of Complexity: Evolutionary Approaches to Economic Order and Disorder*, Aldershot: Edward Elgar, 282–301.

(1994c), *Economic Analysis with Time Irreversibilities: The Reintegration of Economics into the Social Sciences*, paper presented at the conference on pluralistic economics, 25–27 March, Bad Boll, Germany.

Foster, J., and P. Wild (1996), 'Economic evolution and the science of synergetics', *Journal of Evolutionary Economics* **6**(3): 239–60.

(1999a), 'Econometric modelling in the presence of evolutionary change', *Cambridge Journal of Economics* **23**(6): 749–70.

(1999b), 'Detecting self-organisational change in economic processes exhibiting logistic growth', *Journal of Evolutionary Economics* **9**(1): 109–33.

Foster, R. (1986), *Innovation: The Attacker's Advantage*, New York: Summit Books.

Friedman, M. (1962), *Price Theory: A Provisional Text*, Chicago: Aldine.

Georgescu-Roegen, N. (1971), *The Entropy Law and the Economic Process*, Cambridge, MA: Harvard University Press.

Gowdy, J. M. (1992), 'Higher selection processes in evolutionary economic change', *Journal of Evolutionary Economics* **2**(1): 1–16.

Griliches, Z. (1957), 'Hybrid corn: an exploration in the economics of technological change', *Econometrica* **25**(4): 501–22.

Hodgson, G. M. (1993), *Economics and Evolution: Bringing Life Back Into Economics*, Cambridge and Ann Arbor, MI: Polity Press and University of Michigan Press.

Kaldor, N. (1957), 'A model of economic growth', *Economic Journal* **268**: 591–624.

Keynes, J. M. (1936), *The General Theory of Employment, Interest and Money*, London: Macmillan.

Marshall, A. (1890), *Principles of Economics*, London: Macmillan (8th edn., 1920, London: Macmillan; 9th variorum edn., 1961, London: Macmillan).

Maynard Smith, J. (1982), *Evolution and the Theory of Games*, Cambridge: Cambridge University Press.

Metcalfe, J. S. (1994), 'Competition, Fisher's principle and increasing returns in the selection process', *Journal of Evolutionary Economics* **4**(3): 327–46.

Mokyr, J. (1990), *The Lever of Riches*, Oxford: Oxford University Press.

Nelson, R. R. (1995), 'Recent evolutionary theorizing about economic change', *Journal of Economic Literature* **33**: 48–90.

Nelson, R. R., and S. G. Winter (1982), *An Evolutionary Theory of Economic Change*, Cambridge, MA: Harvard University Press.

Prigogine, I., and I. Stengers (1984), *Order Out of Chaos: Man's New Dialogue with Nature*, Boulder, CO, and London: New Science Library and Heinemann.

Samuelson, P. A. (1947), *The Foundations of Economic Analysis*, New York: Atheneum.

Scitovsky, T. (1977), *The Joyless Economy*, London: Macmillan.

Witt, U. (1991), 'Reflections on the present state of evolutionary economic theory', in G. M. Hodgson and E. Screpanti (eds.), *Rethinking Economics*, Aldershot: Edward Elgar, 83–102.

(1993), 'Turning Austrian economics into an evolutionary theory', in B. J. Caldwell and S. Boehm (eds.), *Austrian Economics: Tensions and New Directions*, Boston: Kluwer Academic Publishers, 215–36.

12 Evolutionary concepts in relation to evolutionary economics

J. Stanley Metcalfe

1 Introduction

Evolutionary theory is enjoying a renaissance; in many disciplines, including economics, there has been a substantial flourishing of ideas that does much more than pay scholarly homage to one of the principal scientific developments of all time. For economists interested in innovation, competition, growth and development, an interest in the evolutionary idea is not difficult to establish; for the central empirical fact of the past two centuries, if not longer, has been sustained change and transformation in the patterns of activities that define modern economies. The evidence is pervasive and compelling. The creation of new activities, the demise of established ones and the constant shifts in the economic importance of surviving activities are ever-present symbols of the changes taking place in many different locations at different rates. The structural and qualitative transformations they produce in our economic world in comparatively short spaces of time are remarkable indeed – nothing less than a continuous remodelling and shifting around of the economic furniture.

Two principal approaches to evolutionary theory provide a powerful framework within which to order and comprehend these self-transforming events and make sense of the colourful tapestry of economic change. The two meanings of evolution I shall refer to are the traditional, developmentalist idea of the internal unfolding of entities, and the modern idea – post-Darwinian – of evolution as the adaptation of populations of entities under a guiding process of competitive selection. Together they provide us with a comprehensive understanding of economic change, from the local to the global. Within economics, major reviews and syntheses of evolutionary theory have appeared recently (such as Nelson, 1995, Andersen, 1994, Witt, 1993, Hodgson, 1993a, 1993b, Dosi, 2000, and Nelson and Winter, 2002), and I do not intend to go back over the ground they have already covered so well. Rather, in this chapter I propose to connect economic ideas with the nature of major evolutionary concepts: concepts that define any evolutionary dynamic, and which have nothing inherently to do with biology and related disciplines. The labels attached to these concepts do not matter at all; it is their substance that concerns me, and in the following I want to accomplish three interwoven tasks. The first is to show how major evolutionary concepts – such as development, selection, variation, fitness and adaptation – can be useful aids to the study of economic change. The second is to distinguish different modes of evolutionary change, selection, sorting and stochastic drift, and to privilege the former as evolutionary change par excellence because of its close links with the economics of innovation and the competitive processes. Thirdly, though less explicitly, to establish that evolution depends on the interaction between and coordination of rival behaviours, and thus upon the specifics of the institutions of a market economy. Change the institutional framework, and one can be certain to change the way economic life evolves.

To recapitulate, I shall suggest that economics provides a fruitful domain for evolutionary thinking because it is a natural framework for understanding the role of the diversity of 'individuals' – whether as people or organizations – in the economic process. Economic evolution resides in human diversity and in trial and error experimentation, and it contains an inherent unpredictability and open-ended character that is the direct consequence of individual creativity. But variety in behaviour is also constrained by personal knowledge and by norms, conventions and other institutions – those elements of shared understanding that put limits upon 'self-expression' such that what we have to comprehend is the role of guided variation in economic (and social) change. For variation in economic behaviour is constrained by a wide variety of instituted forms, which also evolve over time. The theory of economic evolution depends critically upon a theory of instituted coordination and order; it does not depend upon the often related notion of equilibrium, when the latter is interpreted as a rest point of the system under investigation. The implication of this is that patterns and rates of economic evolution are deeply conditioned by market institutions and the wider contexts in which these market institutions are embedded.

Throughout our discussion, the central point to cling to is that evolution provides a non-equilibrium account of why the world changes (Metcalfe, 2001). With its emphasis upon the structural dimensions of change, evolution provides the natural framework in which to analyse the ever-changing relative importance of firms, industries, regions and nations, as structural transformation is the central fact about economic growth. To analyse economic growth in capitalism as if all sectors and activities expand at the same proportionate rate is to miss the point entirely: economies grow as a consequence of their structures changing; growth is inseparable from transformation. Historians have indicated this with clarity (see Landes, 1968, Mokyr, 1990, and Freeman and Louçã, 2001); economic growth is the embodiment of microeconomic diversity translated into macroeconomic change. To call this endogenous growth is, of course, entirely appropriate, although it is not the endogenous growth that has recently been discussed widely in the literature. For any evolutionary economist innovation looms large in the set of issues to be treated, precisely because it provides the variation on which evolutionary processes depend.

I am deeply conscious in saying all this that evolutionary theory is itself developing apace as the implications of self-organization and complexity begin to be incorporated into modern thinking (Foster, 1993, and Depew and Weber, 1995). A decade from now evolutionary thinking may well be quite different in content from today, but my claim is that – whatever developments take place – the variation-selection-development mode of reasoning that I discuss will remain intact in its essentials. This is particularly so with respect to economic evolution, and must stay so as long as innovation-based competition remains the central principle of economic self-transformation.

The broad structure of this chapter is as follows. In section 2 I outline the main elements contained in evolutionary processes by joining together the idea of population thinking to the idea of a competitive process. In section 3 I consider a sequence of concepts that are key elements in the structure of any evolutionary argument. Finally, in section 4 I argue that the evolutionary approach provides a distinctively different way of conducting dynamic arguments in economics – one that frees dynamic analysis from the need to identify states of rest in the neighbourhood of which dynamic analysis is conducted. This leads, in conclusion, to some remarks on the relation between evolution and the nature of complex systems. It will soon become clear that there are many interesting aspects of economic evolution that I will not address. They are important topics in their own right, deserving of much future investigation, but let me list them and pass on. They are the welfare effects of economic evolution; the extent to which economic evolution can be said to be 'progressive'; the way in which patterns of consumer behaviour evolve (what disappears from consumption is as interesting as what is added); and the policy and regulatory dimensions of developmentalism and selection[1].

---

[1] On the progress theme, I have had my say in Metcalfe (2001), in an essay written in honour of Richard Nelson.

2   Populations and the competitive process

2.1   Evolutionary process

One of the enjoyable features of the evolutionary literature is that, like economics, it is full of contention: red ink is spilt with great regularity. As in all such cases, the issues often relate to matters of demarcation; is the debate to be around a narrow core of ideas or is it to enfold a wider discussion of concepts and facts[2]? Thus, in the past half-century, a strong body of consensus has emerged around the variation-selection model of evolutionary processes and its application at genotypic, phenotypic and higher levels of analysis. I shall take this as my starting point and sketch out the implications for evolutionary models of economic change.

We begin with an abstract statement of what I mean by evolution. An evolutionary argument explains changing patterns of coexistence between certain kinds of entities, the patterns being described in terms of frequency measures of the relative importance of those entities. More precisely, an evolutionary argument based upon selection processes is concerned with explaining how the relative importance of specified entities within a well-defined population changes over time: why some are eliminated and others continue to survive, and yet others enter the population. Thus, the concern is ultimately with two phenomena: viability, and the differential growth of entities between which meaningful comparisons can be made. What is the criterion for meaningful comparison? It is that the entities are elements in the same population and thus subjected to common selective pressures.

Before looking at this in more detail we should set down the three widely accepted ideas that, jointly, define an evolutionary process (see Lewontin, 1974, and Brandon, 1990). These are: the principle of variation, that members of a relevant population vary with respect to at least one characteristic with selective significance; the principle of heredity, that there exist copying mechanisms to ensure continuity over time in the form and behaviour of the entities in the population; and the principle of selection, that the characteristics of some entities are better adapted to prevailing evolutionary pressures and, consequently, these entities increase in numerical significance relative to less well-adapted entities. Essential to this view is the idea that the entities interact in a particular environment in a way that the differential growth advantage of any one entity depends on the characteristics of the rival entities and the specification

---

[2] The classic account of many of the controversies is to be found in Sober (1984). See Sober (1993) for a summary, and also Hull (1988) for a clear statement of contentious issues.

of the environment. Evolutionary change therefore involves the mutually supporting ideas of interaction and mutual coordination. Rather more precisely, John Endler and Tracey McLellan (1988) distinguish five distinct processes that define an evolutionary mechanism, as follows:

• processes that generate variation in the pool of characteristics in the population by adding or subtracting competing entities or by altering the characteristics of existing entities;
• processes that restrict and guide the possible patterns of variation in behaviours;
• processes that change the relative frequency of different entities within the population;
• processes that determine the rate at which the above three processes regulate change; and
• processes that determine the overall direction of evolutionary change.

In economic terms the first category covers the entire field of innovation, radical or incremental, carried out by existing firms or associated with the creation of new firms, together with the processes determining rates of entry and exit into and out of a population. In this category the elimination of 'old' patterns of behaviour is as significant as the creation of 'new' ones. The second category points to the guided nature of variations in behaviour, how it is focused within limited regions of the possible design space of technological and organizational innovations, and how behaviour is not infinitely adaptable. In any evolutionary argument there is always a place for inertia and constraint[3]. The third category leads us towards the dynamics of resource allocation in instituted market contexts, as it is through markets that the waves of evolutionary change are transmitted. Processes four and five in the list cover the overall framework of institutions and behavioural norms that shape innovation and the way in which markets transmit change. The economic historian P. K. O'Brien provides a fine example of a top-level evolutionary process in his comparative discussion of the different rates of structural change in British and French agriculture and the correspondingly different rates of urbanization (O'Brien, 1996). He expresses the central idea thus (p. 214):

[s]tructural change in France was in large measure 'predetermined' by a combination of geographical endowments and a system of property rights inherited from its feudal past. Both constraints, operating within the context of pre-chemical and pre-mechanical agricultural systems, so limited the scale and scope of French endeavours to follow the path taken by Britain between the sixteenth and nineteenth centuries that 'the British way', as Count Mirabeau told Arthur Young, became almost irrelevant to conditions in France.

---

[3] See the contributions in Ziman (2000) for elaboration of this theme.

Thus, innovative activities and market evolution fit within a wider context of beliefs and institutions that are rate and direction determining, and that also evolve so that patterns of evolution follow because of differential rates of change at multiple levels within and between the categories listed above.

The most significant feature of all this is that evolutionary arguments are concerned with patterns of change not only in the entities themselves, which could be treated as entirely fixed in nature, but in terms of the relative importance of these entities in the population. Mary Williams (1973) puts this well when she expresses the distinguishing feature of evolutionary processes as a matter of selection acting on individual entities to produce changes in the structure of the population. Change in the set of entities is not only reducible to changes in the characteristics of the entities themselves – a property that gives evolutionary thinking an inevitably holistic cast.

Richard Lewontin has usefully distinguished between two forms of evolutionary change: variational change in the composition of the population, and transformational change in the nature of the individual elements in the population (Levins and Lewontin, 1985). Of course, any proper evolutionary theory requires both. It is the variational change that is specifically evolutionary, but we cannot experience this mode of change if we do not have variety in behaviour across the members of the population; hence we need an explanation of how variety is generated by transformational or developmental processes. This is particularly so for our economic theory of evolution, which is premised upon the existence of differential innovation processes to account for novelty – the emergence of new activities – and the development of existing activities. From this it is easy to see how influential writers such as Ernst Mayr (1982) have categorized evolution as a two-step process; variety is generated by some mechanism, and variety is subsequently selected to produce a pattern of change within the relevant population. However, in the economic sphere this would be a mistake, because three logically separate steps are involved: initial variation, selection, and revised variation as a consequence of development induced by the pressures, incentives and opportunities arising out of the selection process[4].

2.2   *Population thinking*

Population thinking is the phrase, first coined by Mayr (1959), to distinguish the emerging pattern of thought in what has since come to be

---

[4] On the three-stage nature of economic evolution, see the introduction to Foster and Metcalfe (2001).

termed the 'modern evolutionary synthesis'. It is the central notion in any selection type theory in which there is interaction between entities to produce the effect of differential rates of growth and survival (Darden and Cain, 1989). Now, the fundamental point is that selection type theories are concerned with frequencies of behaviours that differ, not with uniform behaviours, and there is a considerable shift in emphasis by comparison with typological thinking. Typological thinking is concerned with ideal types, in which the entities are regarded as fixed and identifiable in terms of a limited number of defining characteristics – characteristics that constitute the essence of the entity. In this essentialist perspective, all variations around the ideal type are accidental, aberrations due to interfering forces, lacking in information content like the flickering shadows on the walls of Plato's cave.

By contrast, in population thinking the focus of attention is on the variety of characteristics within the population, and – *pace* typological thinking – variety is not a nuisance that hides the underlying reality but, rather, it is the distribution of variety that is the reality and is the prerequisite for evolutionary change. As Elliott Sober (1984) has expressed it, variety is a natural state in evolutionary theory, and it is the operation of interfering forces in the shape of selection dynamics that tends to produce uniformity. Typological thinking is turned on its head. Equally significant is the fact that the population perspective does not require a theory of how variety is generated. It is sufficient to take variety as given and work through the consequences. While it is enticing to subscribe to a theory of variety generation (mutation, imitation, innovation or whatever), this is not necessary to make the population perspective coherent. It is for this reason that evolutionary theory is often described as being a type of statistical theory (Horan, 1995), not in a probabilistic sense but rather in terms of dealing with the frequencies of entities with deterministic characteristics.

It follows that the statistical moments of the population distributions of characteristics – mean, variance and covariance to successively higher orders, and their rates of change over time – provide natural measures of the rate and direction of evolutionary change. Such statistical explanations are based only on abstract counting properties, derived from but not equated with the properties of the individual population members. The relevant population moments are *our* theoretical constructs, defined as appropriate functions of the characteristics of *all* the members in the population. Such statistical measures are convenient summaries based on the information contained in the population; they are convenient descriptive aggregates, and they are not representations of any individual. More fundamentally, however, they are the basis for understanding the dynamics of change and for incorporating many different kinds of populations within the same conceptual framework. Thus, the fundamental point about population thinking is that deterministic systems allow explanation in terms of statistical properties, and the case for such explanation rests on the foundation it provides for understanding the dynamics of change. Of course, none of this forbids the use of probabilistic reasoning to explain the selective characteristics that the entities possess or the selective forces that act upon them; indeed, the balance between selection and chance is a long-standing theme in evolutionary theory. But, if probabilistic reasoning is to be meaningful, one must have grounds for writing down the appropriate probability-generating function; if not, the probabilities are devoid of explanatory content.

One consequence of this approach is a shift in emphasis away from the adaptability of the individual entities making up the population. Selection is quite consistent with change in the entities, but what it does require is an element of inertia to hold the competing varieties in a stable form for long enough for selection to change *their* relative importance. If entities were perfectly adaptable in all relevant dimensions and so adapted their behaviours uniformly to the dictates of the environment, there would be no scope for selection. However, and especially in the economic and social sphere, there are multiple sources of inertia, preventing entities such as firms or consumers from responding instantaneously to market pressures.

A major issue that arises within the population perspective relates to the criteria by which an entity is to be assigned to a particular population. A population is an ensemble of entities, and it is in the nature of such a collection to have members assigned to it on the basis of specific principles of inclusion. Clearly, the members must have some attributes in common, but they must also be different enough for selection to be possible. Evolutionary populations cannot be based on identical entities. They could, for example, be defined as possessing a common qualitative set of characteristics while holding those characteristics in different quantitative degrees. But which characteristics? And is it absolutely essential that the entities have qualitatively identical character sets? The answer to these questions is, I think, 'no'. What matters in defining the members of the population is not their characteristics per se but that they be subjected to common environmental and selective pressure. They are in competition with one another; the entities become mutually interdependent by virtue of being subject to common selective pressures, and it is this that unifies the entities into the relevant population and, incidentally, identifies the characteristics that have selective significance. The consequence of this is that neither the relevant population nor the relevant characteristics can be identified unless the relevant selection environment is also specified. On this view, there is surely nothing amiss in seeing the same entity as being a member of more than one population if, with respect to one group of entities, it faces a common set of selection pressures while, with respect to another group, it faces a different set of pressures. Similarly, entities that appear to be radically different in their qualitative characteristics can still compete within the same population. All this means that the entities are classified not by their attributes but by the fact of their competing in common environments; they are members of the same population by virtue of being subject to the same selective forces. Indeed, this is what the biologists imply when they refer to populations as spatio-temporal aggregates (Brandon, 1990).

2.3   Competition, collaboration and selection

It has long been a part of the folklore of evolutionary theory that Darwin hit upon the idea of a 'struggle for survival' after reading Malthus' *Essay on Population*. To the extent that this is true, it may be a reflection of the deep similarity in structure between the idea of competition as a process and the idea of evolution by natural selection. At the outset we ought to repeat our claim that the concept of an evolutionary process is quite independent of its application to any particular set of phenomena. That evolution is a core concept in biology does not mean that it is an inherently biological concept. Evolution can happen in other domains provided that the conditions for an evolutionary process are in place. Thus, as economists applying evolutionary ideas to economic phenomena, we can learn from the debates on evolutionary biology in order to understand better the logical status of concepts such as fitness, adaptation and units of selection without in any sense needing to absorb the associated biological context. In particular, this does not mean that economic evolution is identical with Darwinian evolution, for it is not. Fortunately, there is no need to limit evolutionary concepts to the language of biology and genetics, even though their application to these disciplines has been a principal source of theoretical development. It is also comforting to note that controversy in biology is as fierce as controversy in economics. Terms such as 'adaptation' are as much contested as terms such as 'competition', which is all to the good. However, the meaning of 'competition' in evolutionary theory is quite different from the meaning given to the term in equilibrium economic theory. There the state of competition is a structural property defining a state of rest in a particular market context, usually characterized in terms of the number of identical competing firms. Contrast this with evolutionary competition, a process of change driven by rivalry between firms that actively seek to differentiate themselves one from another, searching for those product and process characteristics that yield competitive advantage (Metcalfe, 1998). It is self-evident that the process perspective fits well with the reality of everyday market phenomena, and it is a feature of evolutionary theory that links it to the Austrian notion of the open-ended historical development of market economies. Thus, from an evolutionary perspective a central feature of capitalism is its experimental nature – that it is a discovery process for the trial and error formulation and application of new economic conjectures (Eliasson, 1998).

Now, the consequence of this change in perspective is twofold. It replaces a concern with thinking in terms of representative, uniform behaviours with one focused around a population of different behaviours. Secondly, it emphasizes the role of market institutions as selection environments within which competitive interactions between consumers and suppliers take place. However, market institutions are not to be appraised in terms of the efficiency with which given resources are allocated to given ends but, rather, in terms of their facilitation of adaptation to the new use of resources and their responsiveness to changing ends. What is distinguishing about market institutions is their openness to new forms of activity and their capacity for eliminating obsolete activities. Market incentives provide the stimuli to development, and within markets every established position is open to challenge. Competition is a process of selection undertaken in a market environment, the outcome of which is economic change as new discoveries of better ways of satisfying needs progressively displace outmoded methods. Market institutions are primarily institutions to promote economic change, and should be appraised from this perspective rather than from the perspective of static efficiency in the allocation of given resources to given ends (Schumpeter, 1942).

Of course, in any economy there exists a wide spectrum of forms of market selection, ranging from bilateral transactions between buyers and sellers to far more anonymous arrangements in which intermediaries such as specialized merchants and retailers facilitate the coordination of transactions. The specific role of firms in these arrangements is to determine the nature of what is produced and the price at which it is offered for sale, within the constraints established by the behaviour of rival suppliers. In this regard, the perfect market in which identical products must be sold at the same price is very much the limiting case. How well, in general, market arrangements work depends upon how well informed producers and consumers are about their respective needs: the latter need to find out who makes the best offers of supply in relation to specific requirements; the former need to discover the customers who will value their capabilities the most. It is because the market problem is so much an information problem that the media available to diffuse knowledge of prices and qualities are crucial to effective market arrangements. In this regard, perhaps one of the more significant historical aspects of technical progress has been the development of new forms of media to transmit and store information. From the printed page to computer networks, the costs to firms and their customers of interacting in a knowledgeable fashion has been reduced by several orders of magnitude, thus facilitating the emergence of more efficient market selection processes (Loasby, 1996).

Now, what is important here is what I would call the central organizing paradox of capitalism. On the one hand, the generation of competing behaviours, primarily via innovation, is a development process that is almost entirely uncoordinated; 'individual' initiative remains the mainspring of the system. On the other hand, the consequences of these rivalrous, diverse behaviours are strongly coordinated by market interactions to impart a rate and direction of change to the economic process. In a suitably defined way, 'better' activities displace 'inferior' activities relatively and absolutely over time. The conditions under which this takes place form the core of economic models of competitive selection and economic development in the broad. Let me try to state this claim more precisely. In terms of a firm's competitive status we can identify three principal elements at work: the ability to earn profits from its existing products and methods of production; the ability to use those profits to expand its capacity to produce in line with market growth; and the ability to innovate to develop its product range and production methods and explore new markets. The relevant selective characteristics of firms are thus multidimensional and tied to its underlying patterns of decision making in ways that are difficult to untangle. However, we can gain a great deal in understanding by paying attention to only one dimension of firm variety, and for none other than traditional reasons let me take unit cost as the varying selection trait.

Consider, then, the following canonical world of evolutionary competition. There is a set of firms producing the same product using idiosyncratic production techniques, the origin of which need not concern us yet. Evaluated at the prevailing input prices, the firms have different unit costs and different unit profitability. Each firm invests all its profits in capacity expansion and sets a price that matches the growth of its capacity with the growth of its own particular market. Note that firms set prices and market institutions facilitate the dissemination of that information to potential buyers and rival suppliers. If that dissemination of information is complete and if consumers are sufficiently sensitive to any difference in prices on offer when choosing between the products of rival firms, we have a perfect market and a uniform price. More generally, if markets are less than perfect, each firm sets a different price that is lower than its rivals' prices to the extent that its unit costs are lower. It is a consequence of these assumptions that firms with lower unit costs grow more quickly than their higher-cost rivals and thus account for an increasing share of the total market. Ultimately, the firm or firms with the absolutely lowest costs dominate the market. As every businessman knows, firms compete for monopoly positions. At the other end of the cost spectrum, firms that no longer cover their costs are forced to exit the industry. In its core elements this is what selection processes are about: differential growth, market concentration and exit.

One fruitful way to think of this process is in terms of a population distribution of unit costs, each activity's cost level being assigned a 'frequency' equal to its share in the overall market. Economic evolution can then be measured by the rate at which this distribution of market shares changes over time. The central principle behind this process of change is what I shall call the replicator dynamic (see Hofbauer and Sigmund, 1988, Vega-Redondo, 1996, and Metcalfe, 1998): that market shares change at a proportionate rate equal to the difference between a firm's growth rate and the average growth rate in the population. In the canonical model the growth rate differences are proportional to the differences between a firm's unit costs and average unit costs in the population, the precise relationship depending on the details of market coordination. Consequentially, there is great diversity in the patterns of change of individual market positions, firms of above-average efficiency increasing market share and below-average firms losing market share. At the micro-level, the distance from mean dynamics produces complicated patterns of change as the frequency distribution is continually reshaped. It is sensible, then, to enquire if we may find useful summary measures for all this complex dynamic of change. We can, and the clearest way to do this is to understand how the statistical moments of this population distribution change over time. Thus, for example, we have the famous Fisher/Price principle, that the market-share-weighted average of the distribution of unit costs declines over time at a rate proportional to the variance in unit costs across the active firms[5]. Similarly, it can be shown that the median of the distribution declines over time at a rate proportional to the gap between the average unit cost in the more efficient half of the population and the average unit cost of the firms in the less efficient half of the population. But not all the measures of

---

[5] On the role of Price's equation, see the recent papers by Andersen (2003) and Knudsen (2004), as well as Metcalfe (1998).

evolution need focus on the moments. For example, take any given unit cost level and enquire what share of total output is accounted for by firms that are more efficient than that chosen value (Iwai, 1984). The answer is clear: this share grows asymptotically towards unity with time. Thus scholars are developing a formal understanding of evolutionary economic dynamics, building on the seminal work of Nelson and Winter (1982). All of these theorems embody the same general message. Selection is about economic change; it involves the continual resifting in the relative importance of different activities – something that the population perspective encompasses with ease. Behind all such changes lie the microdynamics contained in the distance from mean principles of the replicator process[6].

Let us step back, take stock and consolidate our thoughts. It is clear, first and foremost, that this kind of evolutionary theory is naturally growth theory; it is about relative and absolute rates of expansion and contraction. It is, thus, about how firms require the resources to grow and the effectiveness with which they use them. However, it cannot only be about firms. Consumers play an equivalent dynamic role in determining the growth and decline of the markets for particular firms in the way in which they respond to rival offers. Their behaviour is a central part of the story, and one that needs much more emphasis as we develop evolutionary theories of demand (Witt, 2001). Similarly, we must also pay attention to the market institutional context and how that develops over time, for it is this context that governs the prices that firms are able to set, and thus the rapidity with which the competition process operates. Is there a better framework to comprehend the deep connections between competition, growth and economic change? I doubt it.

That said, one must not leave the discussion imagining that competition is everything. Competition is possible only within a framework of collaboration. There must be broad agreement as to the framework of institutions, private property and contract, and the rules of the game that make competitive interactions possible. More specifically, firms often collaborate to establish standards in an industry, and smaller groups of firms, with or without the involvement of their customers, frequently collaborate to enhance the probabilities of innovating. Indeed, so frequent is collaboration as a corollary of competitive activity that it is a special concern of antitrust authorities seeking to regulate the competitive process. Moreover, the modern state plays a central role in determining the conditions of evolutionary competition and in preventing firms from entering into

---

[6] For further elaboration, see the extensive discussions contained in Saviotti (1996), Dosi (2000), Witt (2003) and Nelson and Winter (2002).

cartel type arrangements to suppress and distort the selection process. In banning restraints on trade or in removing barriers to entry, it seeks to prevent firms from biasing the selection process to their own advantage. Somewhat less transparently, the modern state, through its support for public institutions devoted to the development of knowledge, helps maintain open and competitive conditions and helps identify widespread opportunities to innovate and attack established market positions. From this viewpoint, the dangers of monopoly lie not in the setting of prices that give excess profits but in limiting the possible sources of innovative challenges to the status quo. Nothing would be worse for competition than the monopolization of the sources of knowledge in the hands of a single firm in an industry.

This opens up an interesting issue, namely a trade-off between the ferocity of the competitive environment and the conditions under which innovation will sustain competition over time. As Jack Downie (1958), G. B. Richardson (1960) and others have pointed out, a competitive environment that is too severe may generate the very conditions that inhibit capacity expansion and investment in innovation, and thus undermine the very developmental behaviours that make the competitive process possible. Thus, stabilizing contractual arrangements linking, albeit temporarily, specific firms and their customers and suppliers are very much part of the competitive process. As Richardson has so aptly expressed it (1972, p. 885), 'firms form partners for the dance but, when the music stops, they can change them'. In short, contracts become the instituted mode of operation of the competitive process. Nonetheless, the firm that adheres to inappropriate arrangements must jeopardize its own market position, and the most likely source of the inappropriateness of once satisfactory arrangements is likely to be the innovative activity of rivals.

Our simple canonical model provides a useful introduction to the rest of this chapter, for it hides within it a set of evolutionary concepts (the unit of selection, fitness, deterministic selection versus chance, selection versus sorting, development and adaptation) that are landmarks in the unfolding of evolutionary theory more generally. By examining these concepts more closely we can come to a keener understanding of the nature and contribution of evolutionary thinking in economics. Then we will be in a far stronger position to develop the canonical model in new directions. Competition is multidimensional and we need to reflect this if we are to have more useful evolutionary models, although adding more sources of variety will be meat and drink to any evolutionary-minded theorist. Let us turn to these evolutionary concepts.

3   Evolutionary concepts

3.1   *The unit of selection*

Consider first a matter that has been central to the development of evolutionary theory: that of the appropriate unit of selection. What is it that changes in frequency in a selection process? Whatever it is, it must be distinctively individual, be stable and possess the characteristics capable of being selected. There is, perhaps, a case for starting from the individual person, but within the current state of evolutionary economics a different choice has been made: either specific technologies or organization practices or specific firms are the units of selection[7].

If we remember that our central concern is with the changing relative importance of different economic activities, this suggests immediately that the appropriate unit of selection is a transformation process in which productive activity translates inputs in one form into outputs of another form. At first glance, the unit of selection is a technology, a method of production for some set of goods or services, and as such it denotes a particular pattern of behaviour. It may entail transformations in the state of matter and energy, transformations in the spatial location of matter and energy, and transformations in the temporal location of matter and energy – or production, transport and storage for short.

While appropriate, this emphasis on the transformation process alone is not enough. Under the capitalist rules of the game, transformation processes are activated for a purpose: to make the value of the output exceed the value of the input. Transformation cannot be a matter of technique alone; it must also depend upon matters of organization within the business unit, together with matters of intent. Thus the appropriate unit of selection is an organizational-cum-technological complex: a set of instructions for translating input into output for a purpose. This complex is constituted by a set of routines to guide behaviour – routines that collectively constitute the knowledge base of the particular activity. We shall call this complex a 'business unit' (Nelson and Winter, 1982). In some cases the business unit is coterminous with the idea of a firm, but not in general. The modern firm is a unit of ownership, not a unit of transformation. It is a convenient simplification, and nothing more, if we use the terms 'business unit' and 'firm' as if they are entirely interchangeable in the following exposition. More generally, though, it

---

[7] Compare the interesting argument in Fleck (2000), where the idea of the business unit as artefact-interactor is developed.

is clear that the evolution of populations of business activities is not the same as the evolution of populations of firms[8].

On what principle are different business units to be combined into a particular population? The answer will now be obvious: when they are subject to common market pressures. Selection environments mean market environments, product markets and factor markets. Two business units competing in the same product market belong to the same population. If they draw upon different factor markets for their inputs we could further say that the overall population consists of two interacting sub-populations[9]. However, to say that a market environment selects a business unit needs unpacking further. Take the case of product market selection. What are selected are the outputs of the competing transformation processes – outputs that have certain performance attributes in the perception of users and that have a price attached to the attributes bundle. Product markets define selection environments in a number of distinctive ways. They relate to particular groups of customers, whether individuals or organizations. They have a scale and an aggregate rate of growth or decline. They have an institutional context, which shapes how efficient they are and the degree to which the overall market is divided into partially competing segments. This institutional context is often reflected in the existence of specialized intermediaries – merchant, wholesale or retail traders linking suppliers to their customers. They are shaped by legal and regulatory frameworks and they are characterized by contractual arrangements of different kinds and durations. The frequency of selection varies considerably: in some markets selection decisions are made at infrequent intervals (e.g. in the markets contracting for defence equipment or civil aircraft); in others the selection process operates continuously (as it does in many commodity markets). They may be stable or they may suffer turbulence, in a way that is often used to describe markets for fads and fashion goods. Hence, market selection environments are complex institutions in their own right. Similarly with factor markets. In labour markets, we may imagine workers choosing which of rival business units offers the more favourable wage and employment conditions. So with capital markets and the flow of finance to firms; investors form views on which firms would provide the desired return on their capital, due allowance being made for perceptions of risk. Both kinds of factor market environment, like product market environments, are describable in

---

[8] See Hannah (1996) for an interesting discussion of the evolution and survival of firms over the period since 1900.
[9] A familiar model of international trade is one in which firms in different countries 'compete' in the same product market while drawing upon local factor markets for their inputs.

terms of instituted arrangements for exchange, scale, growth, efficiency, the role of intermediaries, the frequency of operation and turbulence.

Hence the business unit is selected by virtue of being located within multiple selection environments for products and factors. It competes for customers and it competes for inputs, and the outcome of this competition will be a change in the scale of its activity relative to that of its rivals. What makes it competitive is its intent and the comparative organizational and technological attributes that underpin the design of the product it produces and the method of production. It is these attributes that also underpin the variety we seek across the business units, and that determine the selective characteristics of the rival firms.

An appropriate framework for exploring this further is the notion of the business unit as a bundle of routines, or stable patterns, for conducting its activity. It is these routines that ultimately determine the competitive fate of the business unit. Market mechanisms do not, of course, select between these bundles of routines directly. Rather, it is the specific product attributes and the factor input utilization attributes derived from the operation of the routines bundle that determine the selective fate of the business, and it is these performance characteristics that are the direct consequence of the design of the business unit. No performance characteristic will be determined uniquely by a single routine, and any routine will impinge upon a number of characteristics. It is the ensemble of routines that matters, and it is the ensemble that gives the business unit its systemic properties, its distinctive signature (De Liso and Metcalfe, 1996)[10]. Consequently, it is to changes in routines that we must look to understand the development over time of the business unit in terms of its selective characteristics (Foss and Knudsen, 1996).

Closely related to the unit of selection problem in evolutionary theory is the species problem – the existence of real, higher-level aggregates in relation to which evolutionary forces can be identified. Economists confront a parallel problem when they attempt to define and identify industries for practical statistical purposes. Then the practice is to locate firms in the same industry if they have certain common characteristics, such as the material basis for production (the cotton industry) or the nature of the output (yarn for the cotton-spinning industry, cloth for the weaving industry). As a practical matter it is doubtful if one can do better, but there is a different evolutionary way of looking at the 'glue' that holds certain business units in the same industry. This recognizes the role of specialization and the division of labour in the accumulation of

[10] That organizations have to be designed for a purpose is emphasized in Bausor, 1994.

knowledge and skill, and the fact that, in the process of acquiring particular knowledge and skill, other possible avenues of knowledge and skill are closed off. In learning to perform some transformations one creates a trained incapacity to operate others. Thus, for example, a business unit in the steel industry can learn to do what another steel producer does, in that they carry out similar activities; it cannot expect to learn to do successfully what a textile firm does (see Downie, 1958, and Richardson, 1972). Firms are in an industry on this definition by virtue of certain things that they know in common, and thus industries are defined in terms of common understanding, not private knowledge. One consequence of this definition is that industries and economic populations are different concepts, even if in practical terms they may overlap at some levels of aggregation. Firms in the same industry as defined above may be competing in entirely different populations. Economic populations and species should not be confused.

3.2   *Differential growth and fitness*

We have suggested that an evolutionary process explains how population structures change over time, and how structure is an emergent property that arises from interaction and interdependence. Necessarily, therefore, it is concerned with the differential rates of expansion and changing relative frequencies of the competing, interacting members of the population. In answer to the question 'change in the relative frequency of what?' our response should now be clear. The relative frequencies are defined in terms of the contribution each transformation-process-cum-business-unit makes to total activity in the population; they are measures of differential economic importance, or, as I prefer to call it, of differential economic weight.

This topic takes us into potentially troublesome waters, as it involves the nature of fitness – a notion that has been enormously contentious in evolutionary biology, in part due to the tautology claim associated with the unfortunate phrase 'survival of the fittest'. Needless to say, when fitness is properly specified, no question of tautology arises at all. The rates of the expansion or decline of activity measure economic fitness, and since it applies to the business unit it is partly determined by the routines and intention of that unit. But the crucial property of economic fitness is that it is not a property of the business unit alone but arises from the interaction between rival business units in a given market environment. It follows that a change of environment will normally entail a redistribution of economic fitness across the population. Fitness is inherently an emergent dynamic feature arising from membership of that particular population, and it is caused by the interaction between the individual business units. Fitness does not cause anything: it is caused (which, incidentally, disposes of the tautology problem). Let us explore this a little more.

The conventional view of fitness, built around the concepts of variation and selection, has been expanded in recent years by the addition of two new concepts, and they have been used to expand the modern theory of evolution and to apply it to new domains. The new concepts define two distinct processes – replication and interaction – and different stylized entities – replicators and interactors (see Dawkins, 1986, Hull, 1988, and Harms, 1996). The new concepts bear directly on the issue of fitness and the unit of selection[11]. The fundamental ideas behind replication are copying and the repetition over time of the relevant activities. The philosopher David Hull has described a replicator as 'an entity that passes on its structure largely intact in successive replications' (1988, p. 408). At this point we need to be careful, for biological replication – essentially a birth process – is by no means the same as economic replication, which contains two correlates, the growth of knowledge and the growth of activity, to each of which we can apply a different kind of replication. What is replicated in an epistemic context is the capability to undertake the *activity* of the business unit in a repeated sequence of productive and other operations, while the structure that is passed on is the set of routines and practices – formal and informal, codified and tacit – that defines the cycle of operation of the business unit. Moreover, replicators are active entities; the knowledge structure they contain must be used for them to qualify as replicators. Broadly speaking, it is the unit of business organization, understanding and practice that is copied, over time, to generate the characteristic properties of continuity of operation and inertia in response to the possibilities for change. So, replication is a type of production process that maintains and extends the operation of the business unit. Kim Sterelny et al. (1996) provide a useful set of criteria for deciding when entity B is a copy of A, which bears directly on our definition of the activity of the business unit as a replicator unit. A and B stand in a replicator relationship if A plays a causal role in producing B, if B contains information similar to and performs a similar function to A, and if B participates in a repetition of the process leading to C and so on. On all these counts we are justified in taking the business unit as not only a unit of selection but as a unit of selection with replicator properties. In

---

[11] It is important to distinguish replication and interaction from the idea of replicating and interacting entities. I will require one entity, the business unit, both to replicate and interact. For discussion of the development of these concepts and their application to cultural evolution, consult Plotkin, 1994, chaps. 3 & 6. A recent paper by Hodgson and Knudsen (2004a) explores the distinction in detail.

this specific sense, business units engage in replication; they have built in copying mechanisms to ensure that production can take place tomorrow, the day after and so on in a way that preserves a particular pattern of activity. What is copied, transmitted over time and used is the firm's knowledge and skill, scientific, technological and managerial – a template to maintain its capability; in Nelson and Winter's terms (1982), the 'collectivity of routines'.

Notice that this does not mean rigidity over time in the capability of the business unit. Copying processes cannot be assumed to be perfect, and we might expect that favourable errors tend to be built into the routines in order to benefit future applications of the transformation process, while unfavourable errors are perhaps not repeated. Indeed, much managerial activity is associated with trial and error attempts to improve business performance. In this way the operation of the set of routines can itself evolve over time within an essentially resilient structure. Moreover, there is a natural Lamarckian tendency in all this incremental innovation. Not only random copying errors but intended experiments in the redesign of the business unit are tested by the environment, and the favourable ones are incorporated in the set of routines within the population. Learning is an integral part of the modern capabilities perspective on the firm (Montgomery, 1995, and Foss and Knudsen, 1996), and it is learning from experience – the incorporation and passing on of favourable practices as acquired behaviours – that is one characteristic of a Lamarckian process (Tuomi, 1992, and Laurent and Nightingale, 2001). Of course, this raises questions about the way in which errors are discovered and corrected and the stimuli for experiments to occur, but these important matters of the internal generation and selection of new ideas and routines are not our current concern[12].

How many changes can we allow and yet maintain that replication takes place within the same business unit? When does change cumulate to give a new business unit? Our approach to this is to recognize that the basis for replication is a bundle of ideas at different levels. At the topmost level is the particular theory of business that defines the unit, the conceptual framework that defines the transformation process and the markets it serves and draws upon. Below this are all the myriad operating routines that determine day-to-day activity. Maintaining the business unit intact means keeping the theory of business and the associated activity intact. In

---

[12] Lamarckian ideas present their own problems in evolutionary thinking; see Laurent and Nightingale (2001) and Hodgson and Knudsen (2004b) for further discussion. The difficulty with all Lamarckian arguments lies in clarifying the transmission mechanism that modifies behaviour over time. It is a topic where the attempt to treat the problem with reference to biological analogy is almost certainly mistaken.

this way change at lower levels can be accommodated, but presumably not too much change too quickly, otherwise day-to-day replication becomes impossible to articulate. Stability in the operating routines is usually a necessary condition for the firm to exist at all. Notice that these puzzles are not a problem for a theory of selection; rather, they are problems in making clear the practical criteria for establishing the continuity of a particular unit of selection. If at some point one kind of replicator becomes another kind of replicator, so be it.

This discussion, it may be noted, is not unrelated to the notion of heredity: that there is a sufficiently close correlation between parent and offspring generations, otherwise one cannot have evolution. The analogue is with the fidelity of the copying mechanism. In the same spirit, the behaviours of the business unit must be closely correlated across sequences of production activity. Capability today must correlate with capability yesterday, not identically but closely; as Winter (1964) pointed out many years ago, behaviours that vary randomly over time cannot be said to evolve[13].

Consider next the idea of interaction. Hull (1988) has defined interactors as a second fundamental evolutionary category. An interactor (p. 408; my emphasis) is 'an entity that interacts as a cohesive whole with its environment in such a way that this interaction *causes* replication to be differential'. If business units replicate, what interacts? The answer is that it is, again, the business unit associated with the particular activity, as expressed in terms of the products that are produced and the methods by which they are produced. This answer reflects the fact that competing to sell the product and competing to acquire the inputs are the two principal forms of economic interaction. Since it is activities that are copied over time, a natural measure of the rate of replication is the change in the rate of activity of the business unit, as measured by the rate of flow of outputs and inputs, and this provides the link with the concepts of interaction in markets and economic fitness. From this perspective, differential replication or fitness is the differential rate at which business units expend or contract their activity through interaction in market processes. Thus, to paraphrase Sober, there is selection of the products and production methods, and selection for the business units in which they are produced, and thus selection for the bundles of routines. Or, as originally stated, there is 'selection of objects and selection for properties'. 'Selection of' relates to the effects of selection, while 'selection for' relates to the causes

---

[13] In conducting evolutionary argument it is important to explain what does not change as well as what does; see Loasby, 1991. For further discussion of routines interpreted as recurring action patterns, see Cohen et al., 1996.

of selection (Sober, 1984, p. 100). In our case, the 'causes' are the differential behaviours – routines – of the business units, and the 'effects' are the differential rates of expansion of the different transformation activities.

Let us return to the discussion of fitness by making a distinction, first introduced by Elisabeth Vrba and Stephen Jay Gould (1986), between sorting and selection. The issue here is that selection is only one kind of sorting process. A sorting process is any process in which members of a population experience differential growth with the consequence that the weight of the population is attached increasingly to the fastest-growing entity. Market growth in the presence of different income elasticities of demand is a familiar basis for sorting in this sense (see Pasinetti, 1981, and Leon, 1967). Selection requires much more. In a selection process the growth rates of the different entities are mutually determined by the interaction between members of the population in a specific environment. Mutual determination is the key; the fitness of any one entity is a function not only of its own characteristics and behaviour but of the characteristics and behaviour of all of its rivals in that population (Byerly and Michod, 1991, and Brandon, 1990). Lindley Darden and Joseph Cain (1989) put this rather well when they distinguish the variant properties of the units of selection from the critical factors in the environment that evaluate those variant properties. It is the variant properties of the units of selection that play the causal role and the critical factors that translate the variant properties into the differential fitness of the units of selection. Fitness itself is not a variant property of anything. Thus fitness is what some philosophers call a 'dispositional variable', a conditional statement that, with a set of characteristics or variant properties 'a' and an environment E, the fitness of the entity in question will be g. Change 'a' or E and the theory will predict the change in g – and the rest, as they say, is evolution. To repeat, fitness and replication is not a determining attribute of anything; it is a determined, emergent consequence of variety and selection. This is why the market context is so important; markets coordinate the behaviour of the different business units, and it is in market contexts that interaction takes place and economic fitness is determined.

Finally, let us consider one further aspect of the fitness debate, centred around the so-called 'propensity interpretation' of fitness (see Mills and Beatty, 1979, Sober, 1984, and Brandon, 1990). In many ways economists will be familiar with the general theme of this debate, which is akin to the distinction between *ex post* and *ex ante* conditions. On this reading the economic fitness of the business unit is an *ex ante* concept; it relates to the expected rate of expansion or the propensity to expand. Realized expansion, the *ex post* consequence of interaction in product and factor markets can be quite different from what was expected due to the interference of forces outside the explanatory framework. Thus, recorded fitness is some blend of the expected and the unexpected – the combination of selection with interfering forces. Interference may come from changes in the environment or from fluctuations in the behaviour of the business units, and to the extent that it is unsystematic it gives rise to random drift in the population frequencies. This connects with environmental turbulence and the impossibility of predicting future states of the world with any degree of exactitude. Originally intended as an escape from the tautology claim, the distinction between systematic and unsystematic forces is, perhaps, not necessary to our present understanding of differential growth.

To summarize this brief survey of evolutionary concepts, the units of selection we have focused on are the transformation processes (bundles of technological and organizational routines) identified with individual business units. The behaviours of these business units are such that they involve replication and interaction. Thus, following Hull's account, we find that 'the differential extinction and proliferation of interactors *cause* the differential perpetuation of the relevant replicators' (1988, p. 409). Fitness is a caused attribute of a business unit; what it is depends on the environment and the different selection characteristics of all the business units in the population.

3.3   *Survival, adaptation and adaptability*

As we have developed the argument, the distinguishing feature of evolutionary theory is its concern with the dynamic consequences of the existence of variation of behaviour in a population. We need not ask where the variation comes from in order to explain the dynamics of selection, nor need we allow the units of selection to change during selection; a canonical evolutionary model can be one with stasis at the individual level. On the other hand, a deeper account must certainly encompass the sources of variety in behaviour in the population, the stimuli to and the constraints on changes in behaviour. Indeed, evolution is necessarily a three-stage process if it is to be sustained over time by ongoing innovation. In particular, this is because we have good grounds for believing that the variations arise from within the economic process; that they reflect the self-transformation of the relevant interactors and replicators. We turn to this below, but first we must deal briefly with the questions of adaptability and adaptation.

A consequence of selection is adaptation, and it is often said that being fit also means being adapted to the resulting environment. Good entities are well designed; they have attributes that fit the environment and they satisfy a test of fitness for purpose. An entity that is adapted has the property of aptness; relatively speaking it is a good design. By contrast, adaptability is about the potential to adjust to changing circumstances in an appropriate way; it is about the capacity to respond to changes in the selection environment; to maintain good design (Toulmin, 1981). A number of points need to be clarified here, not the least of which is the unfortunate tendency to use 'fitness' to mean quite different things: on the one hand, differential growth; on the other hand, differential survival.

To distinguish between fitness as differential growth and fitness as differential survival one is making a distinction between adaptation as process and adaptation as outcome (Burian, 1983). We have dealt with the former in terms of changing scales of activities in different business units, although it is clear that a survival test must be passed before differential growth is possible. However, survival of the business unit is a separate question, and involves considerations different from differential growth. It is a question of viability; business units making negative profits usually do not survive for long, because they are maladapted to their economic environment. Now, there is not necessarily a close link between economic viability and survival in the relevant population, at least in the short term. What are the rules for declaring a business unit non-viable and terminating its activity? Clearly, they are a vital aspect of the market institutional context in which business units operate. What if the business unit has amassed resources to fund its operations even though it is currently unprofitable, and what if it is part of a firm prepared to subsidize its activities from the profits of its other business units? What if a government finds failure unacceptable and injects subsidies to maintain the activity of loss-making business units? Over what time horizon is survival of a marginal business determined? Each of these questions raises relevant issues about adaptedness, by which I mean the survival of good business designs and the elimination of bad designs as a consequence of competitive selection. These issues are very much a part of the understanding of market processes. Just as many new businesses are created in any one month, so many others fail. Thus the criteria for being adapted play an important role in evolutionary economic arguments.

None of this is a problem for evolutionary theory so long as adaptability is differential. What would kill the evolutionary argument stone dead would be if all units of selection adapted their behaviour in identical fashion to the appropriate signals. Then we would have uniform responses, no variety and no evolution. Fortunately neither empirically nor conceptually are there grounds for believing that business units can adapt identically to perceived market pressures. They do not necessarily perceive the same pressures nor do their theories of business lead them to interpret the evidence in the same way. In part this relates to the limitation of Olympian rationality and the corresponding relevance of bounded capabilities (Langlois and Robertson, 1995). Business units live in the same world but see different worlds; they do the best they can to be rational in the intentional sense, but their optimizations are at best local, not global[14]. More fundamentally, it is inherent to modern capitalism that firms seek competitive advantage by trying to be different and by protecting the sources of differential advantage from rivals for as long as they possibly can. Being continually better than one's rivals is the only route to sustainably superior profitability, which in turn provides the link between competition and the stimulus towards improvements in transformation processes. Unfortunately for the business unit, what constitutes better behaviour is not always obvious a priori; rather, it is a matter of discovery through trial and error. This is particularly so for those developments that press beyond the current ways of operating, as Joseph Schumpeter (1934) emphasized. It is not only differential adaptability that is important to the evolutionary argument. One must also include limited adaptability, at least if selection is to play an important part in the process of structural change. Again we find that evidence and conceptual considerations lead us in this direction. Limitless adaptability is not a property of any specialized organization, such as a business unit[15].

3.4   Determinism and chance

In the discussion of fitness we have already alluded to the interest shown in giving this concept a probabilistic dimension. In so doing we are again in danger of treading in some deeply controversial areas in the history of evolutionary theory, namely the respective roles of determinism and chance in shaping population change over time. If selection is a deterministic process yet operating in a stochastic world, what does this imply for how we look at economic evolution (see Depew and Weber, 1995, chap. 11)? It matters greatly here as to what we mean by 'chance' and where it is allowed to interfere in the selection process. To illustrate, return to our canonical model and associate with each firm two unbiased 'coins'. In each play of the competitive process the 'coins' are tossed independently for each firm, and some fixed value – positive or negative – is attached to the outcome. One coin influences the value of the selective

---

[14] For a survey of concepts of 'local' technological progress, see Antonelli, 1995.
[15] See Mathews (1985) and Winter (1975) for a clear discussion of the role of inertia in economic models of evolution.

characteristic, so that unit cost has a deterministic and a random component. The other toss of a coin causes the change in market share for each firm to differ from its value as predicted by the replicator dynamics of the selection process. In principle these are quite different stochastic effects, so take the latter case first. Here, selection becomes noisy but nothing more, provided that the underlying selection dynamics is devoid of positive feedback from internal economies of scale or bandwagon effects in demand. With positive feedback the consequences are more fundamental: noisy selection becomes historical selection as the random events along the way also influence the selection characteristics, through the link between market shares and those characteristics. W. Brian Arthur (1989, 1994) has shown the profound changes this can have on simple selection processes.

Consider now the first case, where the selective characteristics themselves have a stochastic component. Clearly, this first kind of chance effect is important for competition. But, this is the important point, chance variations in the selective characteristics – unit costs in the canonical model – have their effects through the replicator process. Chance and determinism do not compete for influence; they enhance one another. Moreover, what matters for each business unit is not the individual shock but how the shock it experiences compares with the average shock experienced by the population as a whole. Random effects are exactly subject to the distance from the mean principle of the replicator dynamic. Furthermore, if the coins are unbiased, one might reasonably assume that the chance effects wash out over time, leaving selection in accordance with the distribution of deterministic characteristics. But here one ought to be careful, for we are dealing with finite, not infinite, samples. There is nothing to stop a firm from having a run of bad luck that cumulatively raises its unit costs sufficiently to drive it into bankruptcy, however good it may be in terms of the basic deterministic component of its efficiency. Such drift effects cannot be entirely ignored in economics, as in biology. Similarly, if the number of active competitors is small, the population mean sample shock may differ significantly from the zero expected value implicit in an unbiased coin, and may thus have a considerable effect on the selection process.

Notwithstanding these arguments, they must be kept in proportion. It is an essential attribute of any selection argument that there is stability of the selective characteristics and environment over time. This does not imply that they are rigidly fixed but that they change slowly, at least relative to the speed of selection. We can allow for random effects, although it seems that the variance of these effects must be small enough for determinism to dominate – otherwise selection shades into stochastic drift.

3.5   Development, innovation and good design

It is a well-known criticism of the theory of selection that it constitutes only half an evolutionary theory. Selection is contingent on variety in the characteristics of competing entities, but no account is provided of how that variety is generated or of the nature of the novelties that emerge. For the discussion of consequences selection is sufficient, but to be properly evolutionary we cannot ignore development processes (Foster and Metcalfe, 2001). There is a deep reason why this is so: evolution qua selection consumes its own fuel; the process of competition destroys, uses up, the very variety on which continual selection depends. As variety is diminished so the pace of selection declines, and when a single entity, or identical group of entities, account for all the activity in a population evolution stops. In a world of identical entities evolution of the kind we are discussing is impossible. As Alfred Marshall knew well, variation is the chief source of progress (Marshall, 1890). Students of innovation and technological change therefore have a double-sided interest in the evolutionary argument. On the one hand, such arguments mirror the manifest diversity of innovation that they uncover in their empirical and historical studies, while, on the other hand, their studies may illuminate the very processes that keep economic evolution alive.

I do not propose in any sense to review our understanding of innovation (the many different kinds of innovation, not by any means all technological) or the multiple contexts in which innovations occur. From an evolutionary viewpoint, innovation produces changes in the selective characteristics of existing products and processes, and introduces distinctively new products and processes into a population. It is typically active variation stimulated by the search for competitive advantage, the search to do things differently from and better than one's rivals, perceived or imaginary. Innovation in market institutions must also be given clear weight, while the changing nature of what is demanded is a major factor in the development of market environments. However, the central point I wish to draw attention to is the non-random nature of these processes in the economic and social sphere; that is, the development of activities, organizations and transformation processes constitutes guided variation. There are essentially three reasons underpinning this non-Darwinian perspective. The first is a practical matter: the combinatorial design space of possible technologies is so vast that we cannot hope to explain development in terms of random search. Random exploration is inefficient, it is too slow, it is not cumulative, it would be productive of an endless sequence of Heath Robinson devices (Dennett, 1995). To make progress we need to put bounds on progress and consider only limited regions of design space, so the search for new designs normally follows established paths, only occasionally jumping to new channels[16]. The second reason is the three-stage nature of economic evolution, which has already been alluded to. The accumulation of technological and organizational knowledge is very much dependent on the accumulation of experience gained in the selection process – and for very good reason. New designs are valued by economic and social criteria, not only by the criteria of engineering and scientific validity, and when first introduced they are characteristically imperfect, defining a potential to be improved and extended in application as experiences on both sides of the market evolve (Basalla, 1988). Nor should it be forgotten that intelligent consumers are as much part of the innovation process as intelligent suppliers. Consequently, the third stage of evolution, that of the feedback from selection to design development, reflects the endogenous trial and error nature of experience-based learning and the fact that the resources to cover the costs of design activity are distributed and redistributed as an outcome of the competitive process.

In this last regard there is a difficulty. Selection rewards the currently efficient; these are the firms that potentially grow in size more rapidly and account for an ever-increasing share of the profits in the relevant population. Such firms will gain a disproportionate share of the resources to innovate, but there is nothing to guarantee that they have the necessary imagination or capability to innovate in an above-average fashion. This is why evolutionists typically emphasize the crucial importance of many dispersed and independent sources of innovation trials; the fall of the favourite and the triumph of the unknown dark horse are not unusual aspects of the innovation process. As pointed out above, a particularly dangerous consequence of the concentration that comes from competition is the narrowing of the field of innovators; it is a dimension of competition that antitrust authorities and those responsible for public science and technology policy need to be aware of continually. The point to remember is that much innovation is induced innovation, and it is this dimension that makes economic evolution a necessarily three-stage process in which variation, selection and development are interdependent and reinforcing.

The final point to be raised relates to the role of non-economic and non-social constraints in the development of new, improved designs. These are the constraints over and above those that bind simply because designs must be both useful and profitable if they are to be capable of being adaptations. They arise out of the inner logic of the design process in relation to the materials used, the production methods employed and

---

[16] See Perkins (2000) and Stankiewicz (2000).

the very configuration of the component parts of the artefacts in question. Many authors (such as Dosi, 1982, Sahal, 1985, and De Liso and Metcalfe, 1996) have drawn the parallel between design constraints and paradigms in the Kuhnian sense: those frameworks of thought and experience that shape the questions that are more likely to be posed by practising designers. Design constraints also play an important role in modern evolutionary biology (see Gould and Lewontin, 1979, and Maynard Smith et al., 1985), and so they should in evolutionary economics too. From a positive viewpoint, constraints help the design process; they help indicate the possibly narrow paths forward. From a negative viewpoint, they limit what is possible; they create interdependencies, which are necessarily costly to overcome, and they help explain inertia and resistance to further innovation in the development of technologies and organizations. This may be particularly so for any activities that have a strong systemic component and in which the need to have the appropriate fit between constituent parts is a major design constraint (see Henderson and Clark, 1990, and Frankel, 1955). For all these reasons it is important to see innovation as guided variation, contextually dependent, proceeding along the normal lines for established transformation processes. At far less frequent intervals radically new design configurations make their appearance and expand the domain for economic evolution.

Having emphasized the constraints on variation one must not play down entirely the role of chance in the development process but, instead, emphasize that chance plays within the constraints too. Innovations are inherently unpredictable, in Campbell's (1960) very persuasive sense that they are blind variations, the full consequences of which cannot be known and can only reside in the imagination of the innovators. No damage is done by calling unpredictably 'chance', but to go further one should know the probability-generating function for the chance events. For innovation this is genuinely a tall order, given the individual uniqueness of non-trivial innovation events. Nor is there harm in introducing stochastic drift in the form of cumulative probabilistic processes to supplement the study of innovation. There is nothing to stop apparently equivalent firms enjoying innovative sequences of quite different characters; after all, that is also fuel for the selection process. The debit side of the blind variation argument is, of course, the necessarily 'wasteful' nature of innovative activities in the broad. Success for one often hides failure for many, and it cannot be otherwise given the trial and error nature of innovation experiments. Predictable innovation is a contradiction in terms. On the credit side, within market capitalism widespread experimentation is possible and is encouraged. This, ultimately, is the elemental fact that has underlain the great economic transformation since the mid-eighteenth century. To borrow from a famous phrase, 'the greatest innovation of all was the innovation of innovation'. Those who come to the study of technical progress from an efficient, rationalist perspective should mark this well. The optimality of design is discovered, not imposed; it is an adaptation in the proper sense. In a world of ambiguity and ignorance, the open-ended nature of market competition is the most distinctive evolutionary aspect of modern capitalism.

3.6   The domain of evolutionary logic

Before proceeding, one or two remarks are in order to assuage the reader tempted to think that the use of biological analogy is fundamentally inappropriate in economics, or any social science. Let him/her be assuaged. Let me emphasize again that nothing I have said is intrinsically a matter of biological analogy; it is a matter of evolutionary logic. Evolutionary theory is a manner of reasoning in its own right, quite independently of the use made of it by biologists. They simply got there first and, following Darwin's inspired lead, built arguments for dynamic change premised upon variety in behaviour in the natural world. What matter are variety, selection and development – not the natural world.

More to the point, in the economic world we are offered an immensely rich basis to which to apply evolutionary concepts. The fact that rates of economic evolution are extremely fast relative to many (but not all) natural processes, combined with the fact that economic behaviour is intentional, that it depends on anticipation and feeds off memory, creates a powerful basis for generating new varieties in behaviour. Indeed, it is the distinguishing feature of modern capitalism that what it capitalizes upon is this extended scope for the distributed and disaggregated generation of variety in personal knowledge. Two individuals faced with the same information may claim to know differently precisely because their different past experiences or different expectations lead them to interpret that information differently. Indeed, it is *essential* to the idea of individuality that we hold different theories and interpret information through different distorting mirrors. Thus, an evolutionary approach to economic behaviour encompasses mistakes and errors, the differential ignorance of individuals and their false hopes. All add to the source of variety, and, insofar as beliefs depend on past experience, they give rise to the possibility of a deep and lasting path dependence in economic processes. That individuals and organizational teams learn, possess memory and imagine is a major source of irreversibility in economic affairs and of creativity in behaviour.

Less clear-cut is the fact that the selection environment and unit of selection are not always so easily separated. Business units quite understandably wish to bias selection environments in their favour; influencing the regulation of markets, defining standards and lobbying for tariff or other privileges are all part of the political economy of business. These practices, honest or corrupt, must inevitably blur the distinction between environments and selective units; but they do not destroy the distinction. Such complications greatly expand the scope for evolutionary thinking in economics by drawing our attention to the wider social and cultural instituted contests in which evolution occurs.

In understanding evolution the fundamental point to grasp is that all behaviours are significant and merit attention, but not all behaviours are of equal standing. It follows that an evolutionary explanation is quite different in kind from an explanation based upon the concept of a representative, agent – that is, a class of agents with uniform behaviour. In such an essentialist world change can be defined only in terms of changes in the representative agent, and if they are to remain identical and representative then all must change in the same fashion identically. Hence, representative agent thinking precludes any consideration of structural change or innovation as it is normally understood[17]. Moreover, in evolutionary terms what is representative cannot be decided a priori; rather, it is an emergent consequence of the processes at work.

It may now be clear why evolutionary economists have found so much inspiration in Schumpeter's writing, for he was describing economic worlds of continual structural change, driven from within by entrepreneurs introducing new (different) combinations from those already in use. Acts of entrepreneurship meant differential behaviour in the form of localized technological change, the consequences of which spread throughout the economic system, and much of Schumpeterian theory is about the rate-determining processes that govern the speed with which innovations are absorbed into the system. Nothing to do with biology per se, but everything to do with evolution. In short, Schumpeter combined two kinds of change in his theory of the development of capitalism: transformational change, as entrepreneurs brought innovations into effect, and variational change, as market processes selected between the competing innovations.

4   Dynamic processes: a comparison

I conclude this discussion with some brief remarks comparing the evolutionary dynamic with the treatment of dynamic questions in economics

---

[17] This is not to deny the usefulness of representative agent theory in other contexts. On the non-evolutionary limits to the representative agent, see Kirman, 1992.

more generally. To claim very much in such a brief account would be foolish, but nonetheless some remarks are in order. We have built the evolutionary approach around the central assumption of the coordination of behaviours in the market: this we have in common with the economic theory of competitive equilibrium. If one wishes to define equilibrium as simply a state of coordination, that is fine, but economic theory goes further when it defines equilibria as rest points for the economic system under investigation. From an evolutionary perspective this is a step too far, as it begs the question of whether there is ever a state of rest in the sense intended. Evolutionary systems may always be far from such positions, in the sense that they should be considered to be open-ended in their development (Metcalfe, 2001).

To understand why the idea of equilibrium or state of rest is so important in modern economic theory, we must recognize its central role in economic dynamics. According to this line of thinking, equilibria are only interesting to the extent that they are stable and to the extent that out-of-equilibrium behaviour converges rapidly to the state of rest. Provided that adjustment is sufficiently rapid, they are the normal states in which the economy is to be found. Now, the central methods of stability analysis establish these properties by defining the dynamics of the system in the neighbourhood of its state of rest. In short, to investigate stability one must first know the equilibrium position and its immediate neighbourhood. As is well known, the procedure has a number of drawbacks. At a substantive level there is no way of judging whether an actual economy is in equilibrium or not. If the relevant variables are changing slowly, this may be due to strong inertia in a system that is yet far from equilibrium. On the other hand, very rapid change may be true of a system that is always in equilibrium but in which the states of rest are themselves changing rapidly due to changing fundamentals. We simply have no transparent way of deciding such cases, and, as Franklin Fisher (1983) has rightly insisted, we must confine ourselves as a consequence to the understanding of the dynamic properties of our models. Here the conventional difficulties are four in number. First, the processes of out-of-equilibrium adjustment are typically ad hoc in that they do not usually derive from the same behavioural principles that determine the states of rest[18]. Second, the presence of multiple equilibria means that we have no non-arbitrary procedure for deciding which of the alternative states of rest are appropriate. Thirdly, and more fundamentally, the method

---

[18] See Koopmans, 1957, and Hahn, 1987. This is most obvious in the case of the theory of price adjustment in general equilibrium. For excellent surveys, see Negishi, 1962, Fisher, 1985, chap. 2, and Arrow and Hahn, 1971, chap. 11.

fails whenever the equilibrium is changing more rapidly than the out-of-equilibrium adjustment processes can establish convergence; the moving target is always receding. Finally, and most fundamentally of all, if the states of rest depend on the past history of the endogenous variables then we have the possibility of path dependence, in which it is impossible to define the equilibria without specifying how those positions are approached[19].

How does our simple replicator dynamic compare with the general method of describing dynamics around the rest points? The most significant difference is that it is a distance from population mean dynamic, not a distance from equilibrium dynamic. The evolution of market shares and output levels depends upon how each firm's current behaviour differs from the current population average behaviour. It does not depend upon how those individual behaviours differ from those defined by any rest point, however the latter is defined. It is a quite different principle of dynamic adjustment, in which the replicator dynamics can be understood quite independently of there being a rest point (or, for that matter, a limit cycle) and independently of any changes in that rest point whether they are small or large, rapid or slow. This is particularly important in any system that deals with the dynamics of creative destruction. If, for example, unit costs in the 'best' firm were declining more rapidly than the population average, this would in no way affect the system dynamics, which would continue to be governed by the replicator equations. Equally important is the fact that the speed of adjustment is not ad hoc but is grounded in the behavioural routines followed by firms and their customers.

Of course, the fact that our canonical system will discover the least-cost producer within a *given* population of behaviours means that this producer can be called a 'centre of gravity' in the classical meaning of this term. It follows that the replicator method is perfectly compatible with the classical idea of centres of gravity; if the data remain constant, such an attractor is discovered by our replicator dynamic. However, our results are far stronger, and allow us to portray the competitive process as open-ended. For the central weakness of the centres of gravity argument is that it defines long-run positions independently of the path of approach towards them, effectively holding constant what no student of capitalism would want to hold constant, namely the state of knowledge. When innovations are changing the underlying economic data this in no way

---

[19] This is a point that Joan Robinson made a great deal of (1974). This is the strongest form of historical effect in dynamic models. A weaker form allows the rest points to be defined independently of the path but makes the choice between different rest points contingent upon historical accident; see Arthur, 1989.

undermines the replicator dynamic; quite the contrary – the innovations provide it with more fuel with which to work. Yet it does seriously undermine the idea of invariant centres of gravity. This is the great strength of the distance from mean principle. The dynamics of capitalism require coordination; they do not require equilibrium. They certainly do not depend on the existence of a long-run centre of gravity, and this, I claim, justifies the replicator dynamic as the appropriate model for analysing competition and structural change.

5   Concluding remarks

I am certainly not going to attempt a summary of the arguments presented in this chapter. In part, my purpose has been to convince the reader that there is much more to economic evolution than the rote transfer of ideas from biology in general and Darwinism in particular. Evolutionism is a distinct form of reasoning, of general applicability to problems of change and development, and I have tried to show when its application to an economy is appropriate.

At the moment there is in the air a sense of evolutionary imperialism as the concepts outlined above find application in an increasingly wide range of disciplines. No doubt part of this confidence lies in the connection between evolution and complex processes and between evolution and self-organization (see Foster, 1993, Burley and Foster, 1995, Louçã, 1997, Allen, 2001, and Potts, 2000). The fundamental issue here is the creative aspect of evolutionary systems, in terms of their internal capacity for quantitative and qualitative transformation. They are systems in which innovation and the entrepreneurial response are fundamental system properties, and I need hardly add that neither innovation nor the entrepreneur has any place in equilibrium theory. Such systems have the capacity to generate multiple responses to their current state – and this is exactly what characterizes modern capitalism. The system persists but its order is unstable. It is restless, and it is restless for the fundamental reason that knowledge is restless and things cannot be otherwise.

This is the fundamental reason why economies evolve; they do so because private knowledge and shared understanding also evolve and know no equilibrium states. Variation, selection and development apply to knowledge as well as to the economy, and the evolution of the one is inseparable from the evolution of the other. The manner in which they evolve is embedded deeply in an instituted structure of coordination processes, in which markets are of primary but not unique importance. How the diversity of coordination processes is to be represented in 'weakly' connected systems remains a central issue on the evolutionary research agenda (Potts, 2000). This is perhaps nothing more than a gentle reminder that evolution is a problem in hierarchy and connectedness; it is neither 'top down' nor 'bottom up', but rather the continuous interplay between emergence and constraint, between variation, selection and development at multiple levels of an economy.

Much remains to be done, not least the linking together of micro- and macro-evolutionary arguments – perhaps the most significant challenge we face if we are to make sense of the positive stimulus to evolutionary theory raised by concepts of complexity and self-organization (see Dopfer, Potts and Foster, 2004). Much also remains to be resolved in terms of the evolutionary approach to demand and preference formation, in terms of evolutionary concepts of economic well-being, and in relation to the close connection between non-Olympian concepts of rationality and economic evolution. However these arguments develop, I doubt very much if they will stray far from the theme of diversity as the progenitor of change – change as the progenitor of diversity.

Acknowledgement

Much of the material in this chapter appeared originally as a Centre for Research on Innovation and Competition (CRIC) discussion paper in 1997 and is a development of my Graz Schumpeter lectures, published as *Evolutionary Economics and Creative Destruction* by Routledge. The arguments were developed further during my tenure as S. W. Brookes Fellow in the Department of Economics at the University of Queensland in 1996, and I wish to record my appreciation of the generous hospitality received there during my stay. Many conversations with Clem Tisdell and John Foster at the University of Queensland, and with seminar participants at the University of New England and the Australian Defence Force Academy, helped refine my initial thinking. Kurt Dopfer provided the necessary stimulus to reconsider the original draft. Ronnie Ramlogan and colleagues in CRIC and the Economic and Social Research Council Nexsus network have helped further develop the ideas. I am grateful to them all, and to Sharon Dalton for putting together this chapter at a considerable distance. The draft was finalized in August 1997, and I have made only a limited attempt to incorporate the explosion of literature that has marked the field of evolutionary economics since then. Nonetheless, I believe that the main lines of the argument still hold true as originally drafted. I am particularly grateful to the ESRC for its financial support of CRIC, within the programme of research of which this chapter was written. The author may be contacted at stan.metcalfe@man.ac.uk.

REFERENCES

Allen, P. M. (2001), 'Knowledge, ignorance and the evolution of complex systems', in J. Foster and J. S. Metcalfe (eds.), *Frontiers of Evolutionary Economics*, Cheltenham: Edward Elgar.

Andersen, E. S (1994), *Evolutionary Economics: Post-Schumpeterian Contributions*, London: Pinter.

——— (2003), *Evolutionary Economics: From Joseph Schumpeter's Failed Econometrics and Beyond*, working paper, Danish Research Unit for Industrial Dynamics, University of Aalborg, Denmark.

Antonelli, C. (1995), *The Economics of Localized Technological Change and Industrial Dynamics*, Dordrecht: Kluwer Academic Publishers.

Arrow, K. J., and F. Hahn (1971), *General Competitive Analysis*, Edinburgh: Oliver & Boyd.

Arthur, W. B. (1989), 'Competing technologies, increasing returns and lock-in by historical events', *Economic Journal* **394**: 116–31.

——— (1994), *Increasing Returns and Path Dependence in the Economy*, Ann Arbor, MI: University of Michigan Press.

Basalla, G. (1988), *The Evolution of Technology*, Cambridge: Cambridge University Press.

Bausor, R. (1994), 'Entreprenuerial imagination, information and the evolution of the firm', in R. W. England (ed.), *Evolutionary Concepts in Contemporary Economics*, Ann Arbor, MI: University of Michigan Press.

Brandon, R. N. (1990), *Adaptation and Environment*, Princeton, NJ: Princeton University Press.

Burian, R. M. (1983), 'Adaptation', in M. Grene (ed.), *Dimensions of Darwinism*, Cambridge: Cambridge University Press.

Burley, P., and J. Foster (1995), *Economics and Thermodynamics: New Perspectives on Economic Analysis*, Dordrecht: Kluwer Academic Publishers.

Byerly, H. C., and R. E. Michod (1991), 'Fitness and evolutionary explanation', *Biology and Philosophy* **6**: 1–22.

Campbell, D. T. (1960), 'Blind variation and selective retention in creative thought as in other knowledge processes', *Psychological Review* **67**: 380–400. [Reprinted in G. Radnitzky and W. W. Bartley III (eds.) (1987), *Evolutionary Epistemology, Rationality, and the Sociology of Knowledge*, La Salle, IL: Open Court, 91–114.]

Cohen, M., R. Burkhart, G. Dosi, M. Egidi, L. Marengo, M. Warglien, S. G. Winter and B. Coriat (1996), 'Routines and other recurring action patterns of organisations: contemporary research issues', *Industrial and Corporate Change* **5**: 653–98.

Darden, L., and J. A. Cain (1989), 'Selection type theories', *Philosophy of Science* **56**: 106–29.

Dawkins, R. (1986), *The Blind Watchmaker: Why the Evidence of Evolution Reveals a Universe Without Design*, New York: Norton.

De Liso, N., and J. S. Metcalfe (1996), 'On technological systems and techno-logical paradigms: some recent developments in the understanding of tech-nological change', in E. Helmstädter and M. Perlman (eds.), *Behavioural Norms, Technical Progress, and Economic Dynamics*, Ann Arbor, MI: Univer-sity of Michigan Press.

Dennett, D. (1995), *Darwin's Dangerous Idea*, London: Allen Lane.

Depew, D. J., and B. H. Weber (1995), *Darwinism Evolving: Systems Dynamics and the Genealogy of Natural Selection*, Cambridge, MA: MIT Press.

Dopfer, K., J. Potts and J. Foster (2004), 'Micro-meso-macro', *Journal of Evolu-tionary Economics* 14: 263–80.

Dosi, G. (1982), 'Technological paradigms and technological trajectories', *Research Policy* 11: 147–62.

    (2000), *Innovation, Organisation and Economic Dynamics*, Cheltenham: Edward Elgar.

Downie, J. (1958), *The Competitive Process*, London: Duckworth.

Eliasson, G. (1998), 'On the micro foundations of economic growth', in J. Lesourne and A. Orléan (eds.), *Advances in Self-Organization and Evo-lutionary Economics*, London: Economica.

Endler, J. A., and T. McLellan (1988), 'The process of evolution: towards a new synthesis', *Annual Review of Ecological Systematics* 19: 395–421.

Fisher, F. M. (1983), *The Disequilibrium Foundations of Equilibrium Economics*, Cambridge: Cambridge University Press.

Fleek, J. (2000), 'Artefact-activity: the coevolution of artefacts, knowledge and organization in technological innovation', in J. Ziman (ed.), *Technological Innovation as an Evolutionary Process*, Cambridge: Cambridge University Press, 248–66.

Foss, N. J., and C. Knudsen (eds.) (1996), *Towards a Competence Theory of the Firm*, London: Routledge.

Foster, J. (1993), 'Economics and the self-organisation approach: Alfred Marshall revisited?', *Economic Journal* 419: 975–91.

Foster, J., and J. S. Metcalfe (2001), *Frontiers of Evolutionary Economics*, Cheltenham: Edward Elgar.

Frankel, M. (1955), 'Obsolescence and technological change in a maturing economy', *American Economic Review* 45(3): 296–319.

Freeman, C., and F. Louçã (2001), *As Time Goes By: From the Industrial Revolution to the Information Revolution*, Oxford: Oxford University Press.

Gould, S. J., and R. C. Lewontin (1979), 'The spandrels of San Marco and the Panglossian paradigm: a critique of the adaptionist programme', *Proceedings of the Royal Society* 205: 581–98.

Hahn, F. (1987), 'Information dynamics and equilibrium', *Scottish Journal of Political Economy* 34: 321–33.

Hannah, L. (1996), *Marshall's 'Trees' and the 'Global' Forest: Were 'Giant Redwoods' Different?*, mimeo, London School of Economics.

Harms, W. (1996), 'Cultural evolution and the variable phenotypes', *Biology and Philosophy* 11: 357–75.

Henderson, R., and K. Clark (1990), 'Architectural innovation: the reconfigu-ration of existing product technologies and the failure of established firms', *Administrative Quarterly Journal* 35: 9–30.

Hodgson, G. M. (1993a), 'Theories of economic evolution: a preliminary taxonomy', *Manchester School* **61**: 125–43.

(1993b), *Economics and Evolution: Bringing Life Back Into Economics*, Cambridge and Ann Arbor, MI: Polity Press and University of Michigan Press.

Hodgson, G. M., and T. Knudsen (2004a), 'The firm as an interactor: firms as vehicles for habits and routines', *Journal of Evolutionary Economics* **14**: 281–308.

(2004b), *The Limits of Lamarckism Revisited*, mimeo, University of Hertfordshire, Hatfield.

Hofbauer, J., and K. Sigmund (1988), *The Theory of Evolution and Dynamical Systems*, Cambridge: Cambridge University Press.

Horan, B. L. (1995), 'The statistical character of evolutionary theory', *Philosophy of Science* **61**: 76–95.

Hull, D. (1988), *Science as a Process*, Chicago: Chicago University Press.

Iwai, K. (1984), 'Schumpeterian dynamics II: technological progress, firm growth and "Economic Selection"', *Journal of Economic Behavior and Organization* **5**: 321–51.

Kirman, A. P. (1992), 'Whom or what does the representative individual represent?', *Journal of Economic Perspectives* **6**(2): 117–36.

Knudsen, T. (2004), 'General selection theory and economic evolution: the Price equation and the replicator/interactor distinction', *Journal of Economic Methodology* **11**: 147–73.

Koopmans, T. (1957), *Three Essays on the State of Economic Science*, New York: McGraw-Hill.

Landes, D. (1968), *The Unbound Prometheus*, Cambridge: Cambridge University Press.

Langlois, R. N., and P. L. Robertson (1995), *Firms, Markets and Economic Change*, London: Routledge.

Laurent, J., and J. Nightingale (eds.) (2001), *Darwinism and Evolutionary Economics*, Cheltenham: Edward Elgar.

Leon, P. (1967), *Structural Change and Growth in Capitalism*, Baltimore: Johns Hopkins University Press.

Levins, R., and R. Lewontin (1985), *The Dialectical Biologist*, Cambridge, MA: Harvard University Press.

Lewontin, R. C. (1974), *The Genetic Basis of Evolutionary Change*, New York: Columbia University Press.

Loasby, B. (1991), *Equilibrium and Evolution: An Exploration of Connecting Principles in Economics*, Manchester: Manchester University Press.

(1996), 'The organisation of industry', in N. J. Foss and C. Knudsen (eds.), *Towards a Competence Theory of the Firm*, London: Routledge.

Louçã, F. (1997), *Turbulence in Economics: An Evolutionary Appraisal of Cycles and Complexity in Historical Processes*, Cheltenham: Edward Elgar.

Marshall, A. (1890), *Principles of Economics*, London: Macmillan (8th edn., 1920, London: Macmillan; 9th variorum edn., 1961, London: Macmillan).

Mathews, R. C. O. (1985), 'Darwinism and economic change', in D. Collard and D. Helm (eds.), *Economic Theory and Hicksian Themes*, Oxford: Oxford University Press.

Maynard Smith, J., R. M. Burian, S. A. Kauffman, P. Alberch, J. Campbell, B. Goodwin, R. Lande, D. Raup and L. Wolpert (1985), 'Developmental constraints and evolution', *Quarterly Review of Biology* **60**: 265–87.

Mayr, E. (1959), 'Typological versus population thinking', reprinted in E. Mayr (1976), *Evolution and the Diversity of Life: Selected Essays*, Cambridge, MA: The Belknap Press.

(1982), *The Growth of Biological Thought*, Cambridge, MA: The Belknap Press.

Metcalfe, J. S. (1998), *Evolutionary Economics and Creative Destruction*, London: Routledge.

(2001), 'Institutions and progress', *Industrial and Corporate Change* **10**(3): 561–86.

Mills, S., and J. Beatty (1979), 'The propensity interpretation of fitness', *Philosophy of Science* **46**: 263–88.

Mokyr, J. (1990), *The Lever of Riches*, Oxford: Oxford University Press.

Montgomery, C. A. (ed.) (1995), *Resource-based and Evolutionary Theories of the Firm*, Dordrecht: Kluwer Academic Publishers.

Negishi, T. (1962), 'The stability of a competitive economy: a survey article', *Econometrica* **30**(4): 635–69.

Nelson, R. R. (1995), 'Recent evolutionary theorizing about economic change', *Journal of Economic Literature* **33**: 48–90.

Nelson, R. R., and S. G. Winter (1982), *An Evolutionary Theory of Economic Change*, Cambridge, MA: Harvard University Press.

(2002), 'Evolutionary theorizing in economics', *Journal of Economic Perspectives* **16**: 23–46.

O'Brien, P. K. (1996), 'Path dependency, or why Britain became an industrialised and urbanised economy long before France', *Economic History Review* **49**: 213–49.

Pasinetti, L. L. (1981), *Structural Change and Economic Growth*, Cambridge: Cambridge University Press.

Perkins, D. (2000), 'The evolution of adaptive form', in J. Ziman (ed.), *Technological Innovation as an Evolutionary Process*, Cambridge: Cambridge University Press, 159–73.

Plotkin, H. (1994), *The Nature of Knowledge*, London: Allen Lane.

Potts, J. (2000), *The New Evolutionary Microeconomics: Complexity, Competence and Adaptive Behaviour*, Cheltenham: Edward Elgar.

Richardson, G. B. (1960), *Information and Investment*, Oxford: Oxford University Press.

(1972), 'The organisation of industry', *Economic Journal* **327**: 883–93.

Robinson, J. V. (1974), *History Versus Equilibrium*, Thames Papers in Political Economy, London: Thames Polytechnic.

Sahal, D. (1985), 'Technological guideposts and innovation avenues', *Research Policy* **14**: 61–82.

Saviotti, P. P. (1996), *Technological Evolution and Economic Variety*, Cheltenham: Edward Elgar.

Schumpeter, J. A. (1934), *The Theory of Economic Development: An Inquiry into Profits, Capital, Credit, Interest, and the Business Cycle* (translated by R. Opie from the German edition of 1912), Cambridge, MA: Harvard

University Press. [Reprinted 1989 with a new introduction by J. E. Elliott, New Brunswick, NJ: Transaction.]

(1942), *Capitalism, Socialism and Democracy*, New York: Harper & Row.

Sober, E. (1984), *The Nature of Selection*, Cambridge, MA: MIT Press.

(1993), *Philosophy of Biology*, Oxford: Oxford University Press.

Stankiewicz, R. (2000), 'The concept of "design space"', in J. Ziman (ed.), *Technological Innovation as an Evolutionary Process*, Cambridge: Cambridge University Press, 234–47.

Sterelny, K., K. C. Smith and M. Dickison (1996), 'The extended replicator', *Biology and Philosophy* 11: 377–403.

Toulmin, S. (1981), 'Human adaptation', in U. F. Jenson and R. Harre (eds.), *The Philosophy of Evolution*, London: Hansta Press.

Tuomi, J. (1992), 'Evolutionary synthesis: a search for the strategy', *Philosophy of Science* 59: 429–38.

Vega-Redondo, F. (1996), *Evolution, Games and Economic Behavior*, Oxford: Oxford University Press.

Vrba, E. S., and S. J. Gould (1986), 'The hierarchical expansion of sorting and selection: sorting and selection cannot be equated', *Paleobiology* 12: 217–28.

Williams, M. B. (1973), 'The logical status of the theory of natural selection and other evolutionary controversies', in M. Bunge (ed.), *The Methodological Unity of Science*, Dordrecht: D. Reidel.

Winter, S. G. (1964), 'Economic "natural selection" and the theory of the firm', *Yale Economic Essays* 4(1): 225–72.

(1975), 'Optimization and evolution in the theory of the firm', in R. Day and T. Groves (eds.), *Adaptive Economic Models*, New York: Academic Press, 73–118.

Witt, U. (ed.) (1993), *Evolutionary Economics*, Aldershot: Edward Elgar.

(ed.) (2001), *Escaping Satiation: The Demand Side of Economic Growth*, Heidelberg: Springer.

(2003), *The Evolving Economy*, Cheltenham: Edward Elgar.

Ziman, J. (ed.) (2000), *Technological Innovation as an Evolutionary Process*, Cambridge: Cambridge University Press.

13 Understanding social and economic systems as evolutionary complex systems

Peter M. Allen

1 Introduction

This chapter sets out a view of social and economic systems as being a constituent part of a set of evolving, multi-scale spatio-temporal structures. The complexity of these structures means that the decisions taken by any particular actor or agent will necessarily be taken under considerable uncertainty, and this uncertainty will be further compounded for everyone by the interacting effects of whatever decisions the actors or agents take. Each individual, group, firm, corporation, shareholder and even observer experiences 'path-dependent learning', whereby learning in a given period is conditional on the decisions taken, and therefore in the next period the options considered and the problems posed are changed by what happened in the previous period. This gives rise, for the system of multiple agents and actors, to a divergent evolution of multiple behavioural 'conjectures' and 'experiments', some of which will turn out to be fruitful, and others fruitless. The spreading patterns of behaviour are narrowed by the differential selection of success and failure, and, broadly speaking, success goes to those evolutionary trajectories that find self-reinforcement in their environment, instead of either indifference or hostility.

A mathematical representation of these phenomena is presented, showing how human systems are characterized by the simultaneous operation at multiple levels of this combined exploratory and self-reinforcing behaviour. In economic systems, the actual products and services offered to customers are characterized by the trade-offs between the attributes that any technological concept can attain. The organizations that evolve to produce and deliver these goods and services are themselves the result of the exploratory additions of possible working practices and techniques, where each organization is a unique historical construction of the practices that proved to be synergetic. In this way, the internal structures and capabilities of an organization lead to an ability to supply goods and services with particular attributes. In turn, customers learn how to use new products and services in adapting their own lifestyles to the emerging opportunities and difficulties. So, we see how the multiple scales of non-linear interactions lie at the heart of the emerging structures of an evolving economic system, as exploratory changes tap into unexpected loops of positive feedback, leading to amplification and structural evolution. From this new view we can begin to set out the outlines of more successful strategies for surviving in such a world. These will accept uncertainty as certain, exploration as necessary and a perspective of constant change, in which success tends to lead to complacency and failure and failure either to extinction or to later success.

In the longer term, the sustainability of an organization is dependent on its ability to participate successfully in this evolutionary game involving the real existence of functional capabilities and the generation of new ones through the exercise of a freedom to explore and experiment with new ideas and novel behaviours. This ability to 'respond' with appropriate adaptive innovations over the longer term can be defined only as 'intelligent', but this is not the rational, logical form of intelligence that corresponds to IQ but is instead 'evolutionary intelligence', which reflects the ability to learn and change as well as to function in the immediate present. These ideas demonstrate the radical importance of complexity as a new basis for understanding and dealing with the evolutionary, adaptive systems that we both drive and are embedded in.

2   Social and economic systems as evolutionary complex systems

In previous essays (Allen, 1988, 1990, 1993, 2001) it was shown how systems of interacting multiple agents can be modelled and described as coevolutionary, complex systems models in which the agents, the structures that their interactions create and the products and services that they exchange all evolve qualitatively. This is, of course, broader than just 'economics', since it is a generic new paradigm that indeed suggests that 'disciplinary reduction' is as false as any other. The new ideas encompass evolutionary processes in general, and apply to the social, cultural, economic, technological, psychological and philosophical aspects of our realities. Of course, we can restrict our view to only the 'economic' aspects if we wish, but we should not forget that we may be looking at very 'lagged' indicators of other phenomena involving people, emotions, relationships and intuitions – to mention but a few. We may need to be careful in thinking that our views will be useful if they are based on observations and theories that refer only to a small sub-space of reality – the economic

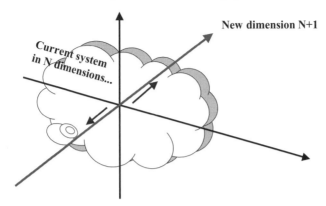

New dimension N+1

Complex systems are emergent 'synergies'...

Figure 13.1 The evolution of complex systems
Note: The evolution of complex systems, at different possible levels
within structures, is a 'dialogue' with the aspects and factors that are
not playing an active part within it at present.

zone. The underlying causes and explanations may involve other factors
entirely, and the economic 'effects' of these may be only delayed ripples,
or possibly tidal waves.

In Allen (2001) a model of competing firms has been described, showing how their strategies interact and why an ability to adapt, learn, respond
and 'make sense' of what is happening is a necessary strategy for survival.
In this chapter it is proposed to continue further with these ideas and
to show how the nested coevolution of a complex system is about its
'dialoguing' with the dimensions that it does *not* occupy at present.

This idea of evolution as a question of 'invadability', with respect to
what was not yet in the system, was the subject of an early paper by
the author (Allen, 1976). Essentially, then, systems are temporary, emergent structures that result from the self-reinforcing non-linear interactions that have been included. History is written by the dialogue of any
particular given system structure, with other possible internal behaviours
and other possible environmental factors that can 'take off' or modify the
system if they occur. Some things, even if they occur, cannot take off,
because there are competing processes that restore the previous state;
while others, if launched, encounter growing positive feedback and are
amplified until some other limiting factors restrain the growth. Such an
event is an 'evolutionary step', and in many economic systems may be
seen as an innovation.

3   A coevolutionary model

In the previous articles cited above the author established the assumptions that must be used in order to reduce a complex, real situation to its mechanical representation.

1. That we can define a boundary between the part of the world that we want to 'understand' and the rest. In other words, we assume first that there is a 'system' and an 'environment', and that we can understand the workings of the system on the basis of its components, working in the context of the environment. For this to be useful we would also assume either that the environment was fixed or how it would change.

2. That we have rules for the classification of objects that lead to a relevant taxonomy for the system components, enabling us to understand what is going on. This is often decided entirely intuitively. In fact, we should always begin by performing some qualitative research to try to establish the main features that are important, and then keep returning to the question following the comparison of our understanding of a system with what is seen to happen in reality. With these two assumptions we arrive at *complex adaptive systems* that evolve qualitatively over time; we shall be describing these further in this chapter.

3. The third assumption concerns the level of description below that which we are trying to understand, and assumes that the individual entities that underlie our 'populations' are either all identical to each other and to the average, or have a diversity that is at all times distributed 'normally' around the average. With this assumption, changes in micro-diversity are eliminated, as are the 'evolutionary' effects that this can have. We create a 'stereotype'-based simplification of reality, with a 'typology' of functioning that remains fixed and does not evolve. When we make this simplifying assumption, although we create a simpler representation we lose the capacity for our model to 'represent' evolution and learning within the system. With these three assumptions we arrive at *self-organizing dynamics*, capable of switching spontaneously between attractor basins, giving rise to different regimes of operation and causing surprise.

4. That the overall behaviour of the variables can be described by the smooth average rates of individual interaction events. So, for example, the output rate for a group of employees in a business would be characterized by their average output rate. This assumption (which will never be entirely true) eliminates the effects of 'luck', and of randomness and noise, that really are in the system. The mathematical

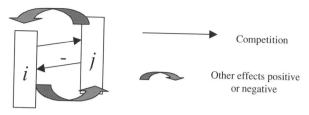

Competition

Other effects positive
or negative

Figure 13.2 Interactions between i and j
Note: Each pair of possible behaviours, types i and j, have several possible effects on each other. First they compete for resources. But,
secondly, each one may have effects that are antagonistic, neutral or
synergetic on the other.

representation that results from making all four of these assumptions
is that of a *mechanical system* that appears to 'predict' the future of the
system perfectly.

In order to explore the evolution and coevolution of possible populations of agents or of behaviours, let us consider twenty possible agent
types or behaviours. In the space of 'possibilities', numbered 1 to 20,
highly similar behaviours are considered to be most in competition with
each other, since they occupy a similar niche in the system. Any two particular types of agent i and j may have an effect on each other. This could
be positive, in that side effects of the activity of j might, in fact, provide
conditions or effects that help i. Of course, the effect might equally well
be antagonistic, or indeed neutral. Similarly, i may have a positive, negative or neutral effect on j. For our simple model, therefore, we shall choose
values randomly for all the possible interactions between all i's and j's. fr
describes the average strength of these, and $2 * (rnd - 0.5)$ is a random
number between -1 and $+1$.

This interaction is only 'potential' as the real effect of behaviour i on j
will be proportional to the amount of activity of agent i – the population of
type i. If agents of type i are absent then there will be no effect. Similarly,
if j is absent then there is no one to feel the effect of i. For each of twenty
possible types we choose the possible effect of i on j and j on i randomly.

$$\text{Interaction } (i, j) = fr * 2 * (rnd - 0.5) \qquad (1)$$

where random(j, i) is a random number between 0 and 1, and fr is the
average strength of the interaction. Clearly on average we shall have equal
numbers of positive and negative interactions.

Each agent type that is present will experience the net effect of all the
other active agents present. Similarly, it will affect those agents by its

presence.

$$\text{Net effect on } i = \sum_{j} x(j).\text{Interaction}(j, i) \tag{2}$$

The sum is over j including i, and so we are looking at behaviours that, in addition to interacting with each other, also feed back on themselves. There will also always be a competition for underlying resources, which we shall represent by

$$\text{Competition}(i) = \sum_{j} \frac{x(j)}{(1 + \rho \text{Distance}(i, j))} \tag{3}$$

where ρ is an inverse distance in character space, scaling the distance(i, j) in character space. In other words, if distance is « ρ then the competition is very strong, but if distance is » ρ the competition is weak and activities can easily coexist. At any time, then, we can draw the landscape of synergy and antagonism that is generated and experienced by the populations present in the system. We can, therefore, write down the equation for the change in the volume of the activity i – the population x_i. It will contain the positive and negative effects of the influence of the other populations present, as well as the competition for resources that will always be a factor, and also the error-making diffusion through which populations from i create small numbers of offspring in $i + 1$ and $i - 1$.

$$\frac{dx(i)}{dt} = b * (fx(i) + 0.5 * (1 - f) * x(i - 1) + 0.5 * (1 - f)$$
$$* x(i + 1)) * (1 + 0.04 * \text{Neteff}(i)) * (1 - \text{Competition}(i)/N)$$
$$- m * x(i) + \text{stochasticterm} \tag{4}$$

where f is the fidelity of reproduction – that is, the accuracy with which the behaviour is exactly passed on to new x's. It varies from 0 to 1, and $1 - f$ is a measure of the degree of 'exploration' of neighbouring behaviours. The term b reflects the value-added or pay-off of the activity $x(i)$. The terms with 0.5 in equation (4) take into account the fact that the exploration of behaviours is made equally to right or left, $i + 1$ and $i - 1$, since only the operation of the dynamics will reveal whether one of these offers a higher return than the other. The growth rate reflects the 'net effects' (synergy and antagonism) on $x(i)$ of the simultaneous presence of activities other than $x(i)$. There are limited resources (N) available for any given behaviour, so it cannot grow infinitely. The term $m * x(i)$ reflects the costs of the activity $x(i)$. The stochastic term concerns random jumps to explore new behaviours.

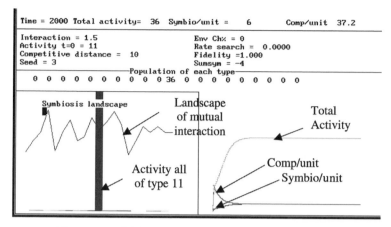

```
Time = 2000 Total activity=  36  Symbio/unit =    6        Comp/unit  37.2

Interaction = 1.5                  Env Ch% = 0
Activity t=0 = 11                  Rate search =   0.0000
Competitive distance =  10         Fidelity =1.000
Seed = 3                           Sumsym = -4
                    Population of each type
  0  0  0  0  0  0  0  0  0  0 36  0  0  0  0  0  0  0  0  0
```

Figure 13.3 With no exploration in character space, fidelity $f = 1$, the system remains homogeneous, but its performance will support total activity of only 36

Let us consider an initial simulation. If we start initially with a single activity present, for example $x(10) = 5$, all other $x(i)$'s are 0. If we plot the net effect of this activity on the pay-off of the nineteen other possible behaviours, it will provide a simple one-dimensional 'landscape' showing the potential synergy/antagonism that would affect the other activities *if they were present*. But they are not present, and so the whole system may be unaware of this landscape of potential mutual interaction.

Consider that we launch activity $i = 10$, so that $x(i) = 10$. What happens? If the pay-off is greater than the costs then it grows, and if there is no exploration of other behaviours the system rapidly reaches equilibrium. It grows until the activity is such a size that the pay-off is balanced by the costs. This is shown in figure 13.3. There is no knowledge that other activities were possible, or that an advantageous division of labour may have been arrived at, leading to a growth in the possible pay-offs and hence an equilibrium with much higher activity.

If the same simulation is repeated with the same hidden pair interactions and the same initial conditions, but this time there is a 1 per cent permitted diffusion (lack of fidelity) between neighbouring activities, then the result is shown in figure 13.4. We see that the performance of the system increases to support a population of 72, the competition experienced per individual falls to 19 and the symbiosis per individual rises to 26.

In these figures, the lower left-hand graph is a moving histogram of populations $x(i)$ along the ordinate, 1 to 20 for the possible populations.

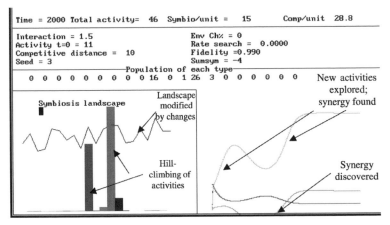

Figure 13.4 Here the exploration of neighbouring possibilities leads activity 11 to hill-climb into activities 10 and 13; these lead to an improved pay-off

Total activity is the sum of all populations. Symbio/unit is the amount of symbiosis (positive net effect) per individual. This is $(\sum_{ij} x(i) * x(j) * \text{Neteff}(i,j))/\text{Total Population}^2$. Comp/unit is the amount of competition per individual.

In this simulation the activity 11 grows initially and begins to 'diffuse' into the types 10 and 12. Then 12 diffuses into 13 and the activities 10 and 13 discover a strong synergy. This leads to a higher level of activity 46, and much higher synergy per unit. However, in both simulations 1 and 2, the system has come to equilibrium and nothing more will occur. The system is 'trapped' in its routines.

Let us consider next the effect of adding in a 'stochastic term' that allows the random exploration of new activities. Instead of being trapped on the 'hill' the initial activity happens to be on, we can see if these explorations allow a more successful ability to create new organizational forms of activity, leading to higher pay-offs and greater levels of activity (figure 13.5).

What happens if we allow very frequent explorations?

An intermediate value of 0.01 leads to different possible *structural attractors* for the time 5,000, as shown in the figure 13.7, where one started with activity 11 and the other with 18. This demonstrates the fact that the structural attractors discovered are 'history dependent'; instead of running deterministically to a predictable result, the future is changed by the action of chance in the present.

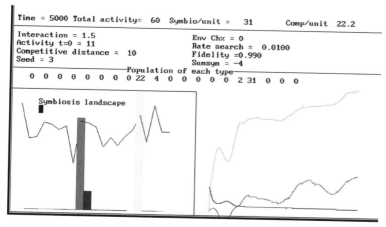

Figure 13.5 Here the occasional random explorations have allowed the system to find new hills to climb, and to climb them; total activity is 60, and synergy per unit is 31

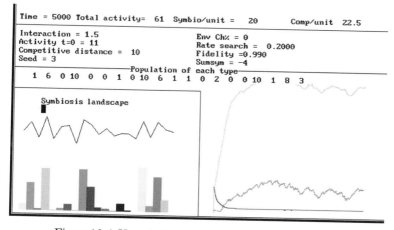

Figure 13.6 Here the frequent trials lead to some confusion, as the precise synergies and antagonisms are not clearly marked; total activity is high, nonetheless

Clearly, although the history that the simulation leads to is entirely dependent on initial conditions and the parameters chosen, the inclusion of exploratory mechanisms for learning does improve the performance. It allows our network to discover better organizational structures. We can test these results by using other random seeds for choosing the

440   *Peter M. Allen*

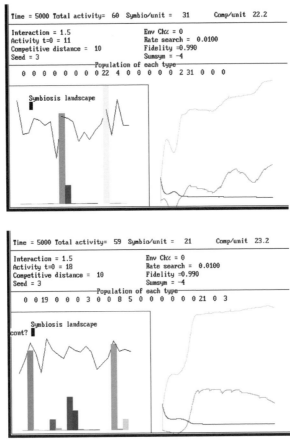

Figure 13.7 For the same parameters, different initial conditions lead to different structural attractors

mutual pair interactions, and we can explore other initial conditions in figure 13.8.

This shows us that the key element that allows learning is the internal heterogeneity of a system, and its capacity to explore the potential complementarities that may be found within it. This shows us that the capacity to try *only* neighbouring activities leads to hill-climbing for the system, improving its performance, but it still stays trapped on the hill it happens to be on. By adding an additional random exploration term the system can improve its behaviour considerably and, through structural reorganization, find new, more successful organizational forms. This

Different seed for
random sequence
choosing pair
interactions

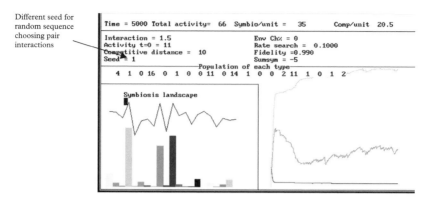

```
Time = 5000 Total activity= 66  Symbio/unit =   35      Comp/unit  20.5
Interaction = 1.5                Env Ch% = 0
Activity t=0 = 11                Rate search =  0.1000
Competitive distance =  10       Fidelity =0.990
Seed = 1                         Sumsym = -5
                      Population of each type
  4  1  0 16  0  1  0  0 11  0 14  1  0  0  2 11  1  0  1  2

    Symbiosis landscape
```

Figure 13.8 Here a different set of pair interactions is successfully explored by the system, leading to a high level of total activity

shows us how a system can learn what its internal possibilities are, and how to make good use of them in a particular environment.

4   Structural attractors

There are several important points about these results. The first is that the model above is very simple, and the results very generic. It shows us that, for a system in which we do not make the assumptions 3 and 4 that would take out the natural micro-diversity and idiosyncrasy of real-life agents, actors and objects, then we *automatically obtain the emergence of structural attractors* such as figures 13.7 and 13.8. The concept of structural attractors arose in some collaborative work with Mark Strathern and James McGlade (first written up in Nexsus Working Paper no. 3). These are complex systems of interdependent behaviours, the attributes of which are, on the whole, synergetic. They achieve a better performance than their homogeneous ancestors (initial states), but are less diverse than if all 'possible' behaviours are present. In other words, they show how an evolved entity will not have 'all possible characteristics', but will have some that fit together synergetically and allow it to succeed in the context that it inhabits. They correspond to the emergence of hypercycles in the work of Manfred Eigen and Peter Schuster (1979), but also recognize the importance of emergent collective attributes and dimensions. The structural attractor (or complex system) that emerges results from the particular history of search undertaken and from the patterns of potential synergy of the components that comprise it. In other words, a structural attractor is the emergence of a set of interacting factors that have mutually supportive, complementary attributes.

What are the implications of these structural attractors?

(i) Search carried out by the 'error-making' diffusion in character space leads to a vastly increased performance by the final object. Instead of a homogeneous system, characterized by intense internal competition and low symbiosis, the development of the system leads to a much higher performance, and one that decreases internal competition and increases synergy.

(ii) The whole process leads to the evolution of a complex, a 'community' of agents, whose activities – whatever they are – have effects that feed back positively on themselves and the others present. It is an emergent 'team' or 'community' in which the positive interactions are greater than the negative ones.

(iii) The diversity, dimensionality and attribute space occupied by the final complex is much greater than the initial homogeneous starting structure of a single population. However, it is much less than the diversity, dimensionality and attribute spaces that all possible populations would have brought to the system. The structural attractor therefore represents a reduced set of activities from all those possible in principle. It reflects the '*discovery*' of a subset of agents whose attributes and dimensions have properties that provide positive feedback. This is different from a classical dynamic attractor, which refers to the long-term trajectory traced by the given set of variables. Here, our structural attractor concerns the *emergence* of variables, dimensions and attribute sets that not only coexist but actually are synergetic.

(iv) A successful and sustainable evolutionary system will clearly be one in which there is freedom and encouragement for the exploratory search process in behaviour space. Sustainability, in other words, results from the existence of a capacity to explore and change. This process leads to a highly cooperative system, where the competition per individual is low, but where loops of positive feedback and synergy are high. In other words, the free evolution of the different populations, each seeking its own growth, leads to a system that is more cooperative than competitive. The vision of a modern, free-market economy leading to, and requiring, a cut-throat society where selfish competitivity dominates is shown to be false – at least in this simple case.

The most important point is the generality of the model presented above. Clearly, this situation characterizes almost any group of humans – families, companies, communities, etc. – but only if exploratory learning

	Heavy	Large volume	Elegant	Good for bouquet	Stable	Dishwasher-safe	Clear
Heavy	1	1	-1	0	1	0	-1
Large volume	1	1	-1	0	1	0	0
Elegant	-1	-1	1	1	-1	-1	1
Good for bouquet	0	0	1	1	-1	-1	1
Stable	1	1	-1	-1	1	1	-1
Dishwasher-safe	0	0	-1	-1	1	1	-1
Clear	-1	0	1	1	-1	-1	1

Figure 13.9 The pair-wise attribute interaction table for a possible 'glass' leads to at least two alternative 'structural attractors'

is permitted will the evolutionary emergence of structural attractors be possible. If we think of an artefact (some product resulting from a design process), then there is also a parallel with the emergent structural attractor. A product is created by bringing together different components in such a way as to generate some overall performance. But there are several dimensions to this performance, concerning different attributes. These, however, are correlated so that a change that is made in the design of one component will have consequences for the performance in different attribute spaces. Some may be made better, and some worse. Our emergent structural attractor is, therefore, relevant to understanding what successful products are and how they are obtained. Clearly, a successful product is one that has attributes that are in synergy and that lead to a high average performance. From all the possible designs and modifications we seek a structural attractor that has dimensions and attributes that work well together. This is arrived at by R&D that must imitate the exploratory search of possible modifications and concepts that is 'schematically represented' by our simple model above.

A successful design for an automobile, aircraft or even a simple wineglass will be a 'structural attractor' within the space of possible designs, techniques and choices that have emerged through a search process. This shows us that, although a 'wineglass' is not itself a complex system, it is produced by a complex system. The complex system searches and discovers what combinations of shape, thickness, glass composition, etc. lead to attributes that are mutually compatible and that are desired. Part of the complex system that produces the wineglass is about the technology and production processes that lead to the attributes of the emergent objects.

This is why the organizational forms, the technologies and the skill bases that underlie wineglasses over time will, in fact, evolve through successive stages – just like our simple model above.

One is a 'tumbler', which is heavy, large in volume, stable and dishwasher-safe, and the other is a 'wineglass' that is elegant, good

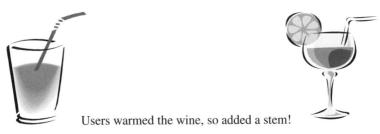

Users warmed the wine, so added a stem!

Figure 13.10 An example of an emergent structural attractor
Note: Maybe tumblers came first, but as they warmed the wine a genius
had the 'wineglass' concept and added a stem and a flat stand for some
stability.

for the bouquet and with crystal-clear glass, but not as stable and
not dishwasher-safe. This simple, slightly imaginary, example can illustrate many issues. First, it is likely that the idea of a glass drinking
vessel would initially simply take the 'easiest' route technologically and
make a tumbler. But users might have found that the warmth of their
hands warmed the wine too much, and so there was a search for a
solution to this problem. At some point, instead of suggesting that
wine drinkers should wear insulated gloves, someone had the intuition
that one could add a 'stem', but give it a flattened bottom to provide
some stability again. This shape, and the particular gestures and manner of holding it, led to the emergent property of 'elegance' that could
be ascribed to the new form. Further development found how to shape
the upper bowl in ways that enhanced the experience of the bouquet. The
existence of a design concept (bowl + stem + stand) that could provide
all these factors synergetically is an example of an emergent structural
attractor, as the trade-offs of the new concept proved to find a niche in
the world.

An important point is that, although our model shows us how exploration in character space will lead to emergent objects and systems with
improved performance, it is still true that we cannot predict what they will
be. The model above used random numbers to choose pair-wise interactions in an unbiased way, but in fact in a real problem these are not
'random' but reflect the underlying physical, psychological and
behavioural reality of the processes and components in question, as shown
in our wineglass 'story'. The structural evolution of complex systems is
about how explorations and perturbations lead to attempts to suggest
modifications, and these sometimes lead to new 'concepts' and structural attractors that have emergent properties. The history of any particular product sector can, then, be seen as an evolutionary tree, with new

types emerging and old types disappearing. But, in fact, the evolution of 'products' is merely an aspect of the larger system of organizations and of consumer lifestyles, which also follows a similar, linked pattern of multiple coevolution. Let us look next at organizational evolution.

5   Manufacturing evolution

The previous sections have demonstrated theoretically how microdiversity in character space, tentative trials of novel concepts and activities, will lead to emergent objects and systems. However, it is still true that we cannot predict what they will be. Mathematically, we can always solve a given set of equations to find the values of the variables for an optimal performance. But we do not know *which* variables will be present, just as we do not know what new 'concept' may lead to a new structural attractor, and therefore we do not know *which* equations to solve or optimize. The changing patterns of practices and routines that are observed in the evolution of firms and organizations can be looked at in exactly the same way as that of 'product' evolution above. We would see a 'cladistic diagram' (a diagram showing evolutionary history) showing the history of successive new practices and innovative ideas in an economic sector. It would generate an evolutionary history both of the artefacts and the organizational forms that underlie their production (see McKelvey, 1982, 1994, McCarthy, 1995, and McCarthy et al., 1997). Let us consider manufacturing organizations in the automobile sector.

The organizational forms that have been identified are:
- Ancient craft system
- Standardized craft system
- Modern craft system
- Neocraft system
- Flexible manufacturing
- Toyota production
- Lean producers
- Agile producers
- Just in time
- Intensive mass-producers
- European mass-producers
- Modern mass-producers
- Pseudo lean-producers
- Fordist mass-producers
- Large-scale producers
- Skilled large-scale producers

Table 13.1 *Fifty-three characteristics of manufacturing organizations*

Standardization of parts	1
Assembly time standards	2
Assembly line layout	3
Reduction of craft skills	4
Automation (machine-paced shops)	5
Pull production system	6
Reduction of lot size	7
Pull procurement planning	8
Operator-based machine maintenance	9
Quality circles	10
Employee innovation prizes	11
Job rotation	12
Large volume production	13
Mass subcontracting by sub-bidding	14
Exchange of workers with suppliers	15
Training through socialization	16
Proactive training programmes	17
Product range reduction	18
Automation (machine-paced shops)	19
Multiple subcontracting	20
Quality systems	21
Quality philosophy	22
Open-book policy with suppliers	23
Flexible multifunctional workforce	24
Set-up time reduction	25
Kaizen change management	26
Total quality management sourcing	27
100% inspection sampling	28
U-shape layout	29
Preventive maintenance	30
Individual error correction	31
Sequential dependency of workers	32
Line balancing	33
Team policy	34
Toyota verification of assembly line	35
Groups versus teams	36
Job enrichment	37
Manufacturing cells	38
Concurrent engineering	39
Activity-based costing	40
Excess capacity	41
Flexible automation of product versions	42
Agile automation for different products	43
In-sourcing	44
Immigrant workforce	45
Dedicated automation	46
Division of labour	47
Employees are system tools	48
Employees are system developers	49
Product focus	50
Parallel processing	51
Dependence on written rules	52
Further intensification of labour	53

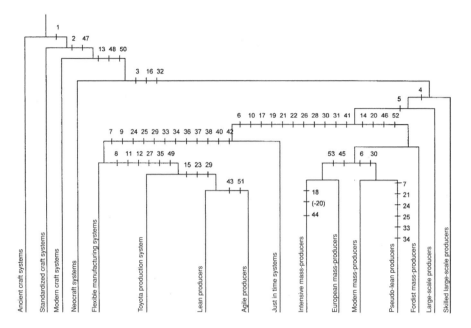

Figure 13.11 Cladistic diagram for automobile manufacturing organizational forms
Source: McCarthy et al., 1997.

If we consider the co-occurrences of particular features then we can begin to understand the probably synergy or conflict that different pairs of attributes actually have.

Figure 13.12 suggests the 'reasons' behind the emergent organizational forms as being the hidden pair interactions between attributes. In our network simulations, successful evolution is about the discovery and exploitation of emergent synergies, and the rejection of conflictual attributes. As an illustration of the ideas behind the models we can use the co-occurrence matrix of figure 13.11 to parametrize our 'pair interactions' instead of equation (1). If we do this and consider fifty-three possible characteristic behaviours instead of twenty as above, we can run an enlarged version of our model and see which organizational forms emerge.

The model starts off from a craft structure and is given characteristics 1, 2, 3 and 4. After that, the model tries to 'launch' new characteristics every 500 time units. These are chosen randomly and are launched as a small 'experimental' value of 1. Sometimes the behaviour declines and disappears, and sometimes it grows and becomes part of the 'formal' structure, which then conditions which innovative behaviour can invade

Characteristics	1	2	3	4	5	6	7	8	9	10	11	12
1	1	1	1	1	1	1	1	1	1	1	1	1
2	0.866667	1	1	1	1	1	1	1	1	1	1	1
3	0.6	0.714286	1	1	1	1	1	1	1	1	1	1
4	0.6	0.714286	1	1	1	1	1	1	1	1	1	1
5	0.333333	0.428571	0.666667	0.666667	1	1	1	1	1	1	1	1
6	-0.06667	0	0.166667	0.166667	0.4	1	1	1	1	1	1	1
7	-0.33333	-0.28571	-0.16667	-0.16667	0	0.428571	1	1	1	0.6	1	1
8	-0.6	-0.57143	-0.5	-0.5	-0.4	-0.14286	0.2	1	0.5	0.2	1	1
9	-0.46667	-0.42857	-0.33333	-0.33333	-0.2	0.142857	0.6	1	1	0.6	1	1
10	-0.33333	-0.28571	-0.16667	-0.16667	0	0.428571	0.6	1	1	1	1	1
11	-0.6	-0.57143	-0.5	-0.5	-0.4	-0.14286	0.2	1	0.5	0.2	1	1
12	-0.6	-0.57143	-0.5	-0.5	-0.4	-0.14286	0.2	1	0.5	0.2	1	1
13	0.733333	0.857143	1	1	1	1	1	1	1	1	1	1
14	-0.33333	-0.28571	-0.16667	-0.16667	0	-0.42857	-0.6	-1	-1	-1	-1	-1
15	-0.73333	-0.71429	-0.66667	-0.66667	-0.6	-0.42857	-0.2	0.333333	0	-0.2	0.333333	0.333333
16	0.6	0.714286	1	1	1	1	1	1	1	1	1	1
17	-0.33333	-0.28571	-0.16667	-0.16667	0	0.428571	0.6	1	1	1	1	1
18	-0.86667	-0.85714	-0.83333	-0.83333	-0.8	-1	-1	-1	-1	-1	-1	-1
19	-0.33333	-0.28571	-0.16667	-0.16667	0	0.428571	0.6	1	1	1	1	1
20	-0.46667	-0.42857	-0.33333	-0.33333	-0.2	-0.42857	-0.6	-1	-1	-1	-1	-1
21	-0.2	-0.14286	0	0	0.2	0.714286	1	1	1	1	1	1
22	-0.33333	-0.28571	-0.16667	-0.16667	0	0.428571	0.6	1	1	1	1	1
23	-0.73333	-0.71429	-0.66667	-0.66667	-0.6	-0.42857	-0.2	0.333333	0	-0.2	0.333333	0.333333
24	-0.33333	-0.28571	-0.16667	-0.16667	0	0.428571	1	1	1	0.6	1	1
25	-0.33333	-0.28571	-0.16667	-0.16667	0	0.428571	1	1	1	0.6	1	1
26	-0.33333	-0.28571	-0.16667	-0.16667	0	0.428571	0.6	1	1	1	1	1
27	-0.6	-0.57143	-0.5	-0.5	-0.4	-0.14286	0.2	1	0.5	0.2	1	1

Figure 13.12 The co-occurrences of fifty-three possible attributes in the sixteen different organizational forms

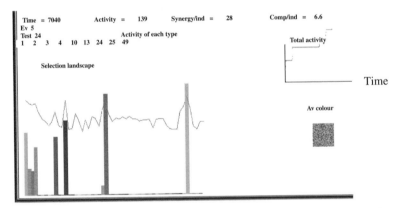

Figure 13.13 An evolutionary model tries to 'launch' possible innovative practices in a random order; if they invade, they change the 'invadability' of the new system

next. In the sequence shown, our model depicts a particular evolutionary story. The history presented in figure 13.13 is summarized in table 13.2. It shows how, from the initial situation where characteristics 1, 2, 3 and 4 are present, other innovations are tried out at intervals to see whether they will 'take off'. The condition for 'take-off' is not that the practice should necessarily improve overall performance in the long term, but

Table 13.2 *A particular sequence of evolutionary events describing the organizational changes that occurred over time*

Characteristic	Time	Result	Structure
1,2,3,4	0	Succeeds	1,2,3,4
43	T=500	Succeeds	1,2,3,4,43
42	T=1,000	Succeeds	1,2,3,4,43,42
9	T=1,500	Succeeds	1,2,3,4,43,42,9
48	T=2,000	Succeeds	1,2,3,4,43,42,9,48
17	T=2,500	Succeeds	1,2,3,4,43,42,9,48,17
20	T=3,000	Fails	1,2,3,4,43,42,9,48,17
28	T=3,500	Succeeds	1,2,3,4,43,42,9,48,17,28
14	T=4,000	Fails	1,2,3,4,43,42,9,48,17,28
15	T=4,500	Fails	1,2,3,4,43,42,9,48,17,28
34	T=5,000	Fails	1,2,3,4,43,42,9,48,17,28
45	T=5,500	Fails	1,2,3,4,43,42,9,48,17,28
45	T=6,000	Fails	1,2,3,4,43,42,9,48,17,28
19	T=6,500	Succeeds	1,2,3,4,43,42,9,48,17,28,19
13	T=7,000	Succeeds	1,2,3,4,43,42,9,48,17,28,19,13
15	T=7,500	Fails	1,2,3,4,43,42,9,48,17,28,19,13
38	T=8,000	Fails	1,2,3,4,43,42,9,48,17,28,19,13
5	T=8,500	Succeeds	1,2,3,4,43,42,9,48,17,28,19,13,5
16	T=9,000	Fails	1,2,3,4,43,42,9,48,17,28,19,13,5
10	T=9,500	Succeeds	1,2,3,4,43,42,9,48,17,28,19,13,5,10
20	T=10,000	Fails	1,2,3,4,43,42,9,48,17,28,19,13,5,10

merely that, for the activities with which it is in interaction (i.e. those it affects), there should be a perception that it has made things go better, faster, cheaper, etc. So, it is based on a local perception of advantage, since it is impossible in the short term to know whether there will be a long-term overall gain or not when all the loops and interactions have worked themselves through. This is important since, in reality, the full consequences will take a very long time to work through, and it will be impossible to know exactly which consequences have arisen from which action very much earlier, or from other intervening decisions.

So, local judgement is used to amplify an experimental activity if it appears to those involved to work, and this, once it has been integrated into the organization, changes the selection rules of compatibility or conflict for any new experiments that may follow.

The model is able to describe how particular characteristics are tried out in a random fashion, and either can or cannot invade the system. Those that can invade change the structure of the organization qualitatively and produce a particular pathway through possibility space.

Different simulations lead to different structures – and there are *fifty-three* (factorial 53 – a very large number) possible 'histories'! This demonstrates a key idea in complex systems thinking. The explorations/ innovations that are tried out next at a given time cannot be logically or rationally deduced because their overall effects cannot be known ahead of time. Therefore the system has 'choices' about which to try, and we mimic this by using a random number generator to make the actual choice in our simulation. In real life there would, no doubt, be debate and discussion by different people in favour of one choice or another, and each would cite his/her own projections about the trade-offs and the overall effect of his/her choice. However, depending on what choice is made, the selection criteria for further change is modified by the successful incorporation of a previous innovation. So, the pattern of what can then invade the system (if it were tried) has been changed by what occurred before. This is technically referred to as a 'path-dependent' process, since the future evolutionary pathways that are possible are affected by the path the system has taken previously.

If we compare the many different possible structures that the model can generate with those observed in reality, then obviously, since we calculated the 'interaction matrix' of figure 13.12 on the basis of the co-occurrences and non-co-occurrences, they will naturally tend to be at least the sixteen observed ones. However, what we must think about is how much people knew as the evolution was proceeding, and what initiatives failed, which succeeded and how much 'luck' was involved.

It also highlights a 'problem' with the acceptance of complex systems thinking for operational use. The theory of complex systems tells us that the future is not completely predictable because the system has some internal autonomy and will undergo path-dependent learning. However, this also means that the 'present' (existing data) cannot be proven to be a *necessary* outcome of the past, but only – hopefully – a *possible* outcome. So, there are, perhaps, so many possible structures for organizations to discover and render functional that the observed organizational structures may be sixteen out of several hundred that are possible. In traditional science the assumption was that 'only the optimal survive', and therefore that what we observe is an optimal structure with only a few temporary deviations from average. But selection is actioned through the competitive interactions of the other players, and if they are different – catering to a slightly different market, and also suboptimal at any particular moment – then there is no selection force capable of pruning the burgeoning possibilities to a single, optimal outcome. Complexity tells us that we are freer than we thought, and that the diversity that this freedom allows is the mechanism through which sustainability, adaptability and learning occur.

This picture shows us that evolution is about the discovery and emergence of structural attractors that express the natural synergies and conflicts (the non-linearities) of underlying components. Their properties and consequences are difficult to anticipate and therefore require real explorations and experiments to be going on, based, in turn, on the diversity of beliefs, views and experiences of freely acting individuals.

6   An integrated view of an economy

The ideas explored above show how organizations such as firms explore possible functional innovations, and evolve capabilities that lead either to survival or to failure. They describe a divergent evolutionary diffusion into 'possibility space', helping to provide a fuller explanation of the 'evolutionary economics' perspective (see Nelson and Winter, 1982, Foster and Metcalfe, 2001, and Dopfer, 2001). Each of these is then either amplified or diminished depending on the 'performance' of the products or services provided, which depends on the internal trade-offs within them and on the synergies and conflicts that it encounters or discovers in its supply networks, in its retail structures and in the lifestyles of final consumers.

Similarly, exploratory changes made in the supply network, in the retail structures or in the different elements of the lifestyles of different types of individual all lead to a divergent exploration of possibilities. These are amplified or diminished as a result of the dual selection processes operating, on the one hand, 'inside them' (in terms of the synergies and conflicts of their internal structures) and, on the other hand, 'outside them' (in their revealing of synergy or conflict with their surrounding features). So, a new practice can 'invade' a system if it is synergetic with the existing structure, and this will then either lead to the reinforcement or the decline of that system in its environment if the modified system is synergetic or in conflict with its environment. Because of the difficulty of predicting both the emergent internal and external behaviours of a new action, the pay-off that will result from any given new action can, therefore, generally not be anticipated. It is this very ignorance that is a key factor in allowing exploration at all. Either the fear of the unknown will stop innovation, or divergent innovations will occur even though the actors concerned do not necessarily intend this. Attempting to imitate another player can lead to quite different outcomes, if either the internal structure or the external context is found to be different.

Throughout the economy, and indeed the social/cultural system of interacting elements and structures, we see a generic picture at multiple temporal and spatial scales in which uncertainty about the future

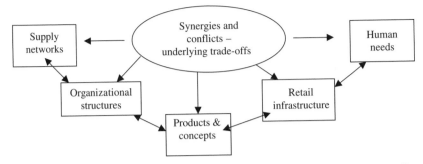

Figure 13.14 Throughout the economy, exploratory behaviour is amplified or suppressed as a result of both internal and external trade-offs

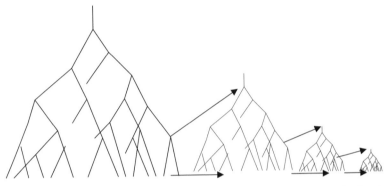

Figure 13.15 The evolutionary process of exploration and selection is nested in successive levels of the system; the 'innovation' arises within an individual system, and is 'judged' by its environment: the context

allows actions that are exploratory and divergent, which are then either amplified or suppressed by the way that this modifies the interaction with their environment. Essentially, this fulfils the early vision of dissipative structures, in that their existence and amplification depend on 'learning' how to access energy and matter in their environment. They can form a self-reinforcing loop of mutual advantage, in which entities and actors in the environment wish to supply the resources required for the growth and maintenance of the system in question. In this way, structures emerge as multi-scalar entities of cooperative, self-reinforcing processes.

What we see is a theoretical framework that encompasses both the evolutionary and the resource-based theory of the firm. Not only of the firm, either, but of the social and economic system as a whole. This is the complex systems dialogue, between explorations of possible futures at one level and the unpredictable effects of this at both the level below and the level above. There is a dialogue between the 'trade-offs' or 'non-linearities' affected inside and outside the particular level of exploration. But it is also true that all levels are exploring. Unless there is an imposition of rigid homogeneity up and down the levels of the system, there will necessarily be behavioural explorations due to internal diversity. And internal diversity can be suppressed only by an active selection strategy that *immediately* knows which entity will be effective and which will not. This is impossible, however, since the process is dynamic and takes time to register the relative performances. Because of this, diverse behaviours will invade the system and will coexist for considerable times, with selection operating only gradually. In this way, the multi-level systems are precisely the structures that can 'shield' the lower levels from instantaneous selection and allow an exploratory drift to occur, which can generate enough diversity to *discover* eventually a new behaviour that will grow. Without the multiple levels, selection would act instantly, and there would be no chance to build up significant deviations from the previous behaviour.

7   Sustainability and evolutionary intelligence

The key concept that emerges from our new understanding of complexity and the behaviour of socio-economic systems is that of coevolution – and as a consequence of 'evolutionary intelligence' (EvI). This measures the propensity of an organization to persist over time – to coevolve successfully. In essence, it is the idea of the evolutionary potential of a socio-economic system.

It reflects the current capacity that a system has to evolve and adapt, either in response to its changing environment or, perhaps, proactively. Obviously, an organization needs only to evolve as quickly as its environment, but, of course, in many cases this environment will consist of background resources (supply systems and human needs) as well as organizations like itself – capable of evolution and learning. Sustainability therefore requires an evolutionary capacity at least as great as that of competing organizations. As we know, the capacity to adapt depends on the system possessing sufficient 'non-average' parts and behaviours – internal diversity. Any particular system sits somewhere along a continuum that goes from a perfect 'machine', operating in the short term very efficiently, to a structureless entity in which no clear average can even be defined. The secret of adaptability lies, therefore, in the existence of a suitable balance between the average and the non-average entities and behaviours present in the system. The balance must be such that 'current' operations work sufficiently well so as not to compromise current survival, but such that the present structure is significantly tested fairly frequently, so that rapid adaptation can occur and new avenues be explored without delay. EvI is about having *the right balance between freedom and functional servitude!*

Evolutionary intelligence encompasses other ideas of 'what it takes to succeed'. First, we may say that traditional IQ measures the ability to solve immediate, rational problems. It probably does reflect the capability associated with rational, logical problems of importance in a clear and well-defined situation. The idea behind 'emotional intelligence' and the emotional quotient (EQ) is that of the ability to relate and interact successfully with other participants, and in this way to be able to form groups and teams with successful emergent properties. This has been recognized as being of great importance in the successful working of organizations and groups. An additional step was taken in the discussion of the spiritual quotient (SQ) by authors such as Dana Zohar (see Zohar and Marshall, 2001) suggesting the relevance of SQ referring to the ability of people to see 'meaning' in other people's activities and to feel that they were part of a 'greater project', thus enhancing and maintaining their motivation. Again, this is an important element in the survival of companies and firms, and each of these is a useful factor within the more fundamental one of survival. EvI contains these other forms of intelligence, since rational efficiency, successful relationships and communication, and motivation are all – necessarily – part of a sustainable system. However, it also reflects the internal diversity, confusion and misclassifications that characterize organizations in practice, as the 'structure' of any organization – or, indeed, of a market, a sector or a region – is always a matter of 'approximate' representation. Boundaries are never absolute, and interactions are always more or less than the formal structure would suggest. It is because of this that the system diverges from the 'perfect machine', focused and perfectly able to perform a fixed task, and in fact possesses an evolutionary potential allowing it to discover and adapt to doing some new tasks.

The measure of evolutionary intelligence will be that of the rate of 'exploration' compared to the dimensionality of the space to be explored. In essence, this could link the rate of experimentation to the rate at which new dimensions (new technologies, new markets, etc.) are arriving in the environment of the system. In an earlier essay (Allen and McGlade, 1987) the idea of 'evolutionary drive' was developed, and it showed how error-making exploration was required in order for evolution to occur. Furthermore, it related the amount of error making – the exploration rate – to the 'slope' of the hill to be climbed in the 'fitness landscape'. The more there is to gain, potentially, the more it is worth investing in exploration, and so in new areas of activity high levels of exploration will be rewarded. As the domain matures, however, the average 'pay-off' per unit of investment in exploration falls, and so it becomes less attractive, and investment is switched more into the efficient performance of the activity and less into exploring new terrain. In general, we may say that the essay showed that, as a domain matures, the ratio of successful to unsuccessful changes falls and it becomes harder and harder to discover radically new aspects. This ratio of successful to unsuccessful pay-offs associated with exploratory steps is the essential 'cost' of evolution. If 20 per cent of all trials are successful and lead to improvements, then this would be very positive. However, in a more mature domain this level may fall to 0.1 per cent, with the effect that only one exploration in a thousand leads to an improvement, or a new product, by which time evolutionary change would become a very costly exercise and efforts would switch to simple process improvements and making the existing system more efficient and lean.

The working of EvI will, therefore, *generate* naturally a 'life cycle' within the new domains that it opens up. Initially, it will be advantageous to invest strongly in exploration, and this will be limited simply by the viability of the enterprise or organization because of the diversion of production into exploration. However, as this field develops in sectors and subsectors, the return on exploration gradually falls off and the costs of exploration increase, and competing organizations switch over to increasing their efficiency and leanness and improving their internal processes. This, naturally, marks the end of any exceptional returns, and heralds a mature market place that will probably not change markedly before declining and disappearing with further technological and societal evolution. In this new vision of evolutionary intelligence we see that, instead of evolution hill-climbing a 'slope', we are concerned with a more general picture of dimensions with unknown rewards and dangers, and matching the rate of exploration with the rate of occurrence of new technologies, attributes, needs and dimensions.

8   Conclusions

This chapter sketches out an integrated theory of economic and social evolution. It suggests how the different types of people channel their needs into particular patterns of need for different products and services. These are delivered according to the non-linear interactions of synergy and conflict that lead to particular retailing structures, both expressing natural 'markets' and – within them – complementarities between product categories and lines.

Products themselves exist as embodiments of attributes that cluster synergetically, and different product markets emerge naturally as a result of inherent conflicts between attributes. For example, a palmtop computer cannot have a really easy-to-use keyboard (under existing design concepts), and so notebooks and laptops exist in a different market from palmtops. Similarly, toasters and telephones also occupy separate markets, because answering a call on a toaster/telephone can set your hair on fire. So, again, it is the 'complementarities and conflicts' of possible attributes that structures the space of possible product or service markets.

On the supply side, the capabilities of organizations, and the products and services that they create, are the result of a creative evolutionary process in which clusters of compatible practices and structures are built up, in the context of the others, and discover and occupy different niches. At each moment, it is difficult to know the consequences of adopting some new practice (such as 'best' practice), since the actual effect will depend on both the internal nature of the organization and its actual context and the relationships it had developed. For this reason, it is bound to be an exploratory, risky process to try new practices and new products. In the short term it will always be better simply to optimize what already exists, and not to risk engaging on some innovation. But, over time, without engaging in evolution extinction becomes not simply possible but, in fact, certain.

The synergies and conflicts of the supply network exhibit similar properties, as new technologies provide possible opportunities and threats, and it may be necessary for new technologies and new knowledge to be adopted if extinction is to be avoided later. It is necessary to couple the driving potentials of 'human needs' to the products and services that are consumed to satisfy them, and the technologies, the structures and the organizations that form and evolve to create new responses to their changing embodiments. The whole system is an (imperfect) evolutionary learning system, in which people learn of different ways that they can spend their time and income, and what this may mean to them. Companies attempt to understand what customers are seeking, and how they can adapt their products and services to capture these needs. They attempt to find new capabilities and practices to achieve this, and create new products and services as a result. These call on new technologies and materials and cause evolution in the supply networks. Technological innovation, cultural evolution and social pressures all change the opportunities and possibilities that can exist, as well as the desires and dreams of consumers and their patterns of choice and of consumption.

This seemingly utopic view of 'restless capitalism' is, of course, not the whole picture. This imperfect learning process means that decisions will tend to reflect the short-term positive performance of something with respect to the dimensions of which we are aware; obviously, though, in a complex system there will be all kinds of less obvious factors that are perhaps adversely affected, sometimes over the longer term, but even quite immediately. In other words, what we choose to do is dependent on 'what we are measuring', and so the system changes reflect our limited understanding of what will actually affect us. This is because our actions are based on our limited understanding and knowledge of the complex systems we inhabit; and their evolution, therefore, bears the imprints of our particular patterns of ignorance. So, we may grab economic gain, by pushing 'costs' into the 'externalities', or we may seek immediate satisfaction by consuming some product that actually harms us, or our community, or our region, or the ozone layer, etc. over the longer term.

Complex systems thinking is not simply telling us that we are forever doomed to evolve into an unknown future, with sometimes interesting, sometimes painful, consequences. It is also telling us that the alternative to innovation and change is decline and impoverishment. There are two basic messages here, which are slightly contradictory. One is that some models of particular situations can help you understand what it is you believe is going on, and therefore how you might behave in ways that are most advantageous to you – given what you think you know. The second is that, since this knowledge is extremely dubious, it is always better to have multiple options, hidden diversities, and multiple interpretations available to deal with what you cannot understand and cannot anticipate. The old adage is that it is better to travel than to arrive. We would say that complex systems tell us that nobody ever arrives, and so we'd better get to like travelling.

REFERENCES

Allen, P. M. (1976), 'Evolution, population dynamics and stability', *Proceedings of the National Academy of Sciences* 73(3): 665–68.
(1988), 'Evolution: why the whole is greater than the sum of its parts', in W. Wolff, C. J. Soeder and F. R. Drepper (eds.), *Ecodynamics*, Berlin: Springer-Verlag.
(1990), 'Why the future is not what it was', *Futures* 22(4): 555–69.
(1993), 'Evolution: persistent ignorance from continual learning', in R. H. Day and P. Chen (eds.), *Non-linear Dynamics and Evolutionary Economics*, Cambridge: Cambridge University Press, 101–12.
(2001), 'What is complexity science? Knowledge of the limits to knowledge', *Emergence* 3(1): 24–43.
Allen, P. M., and J. M. McGlade (1987), 'Evolutionary drive: the effect of microscopic diversity, error making and noise', *Foundations of Physics* 17(7): 723–28.

458   *Peter M. Allen*

Dopfer, K. (2001), 'History-friendly theories in economics: reconciling universality and context in evolutionary analysis', in J. Foster and J. S. Metcalfe (eds.), *Frontiers of Evolutionary Economics*, Cheltenham: Edward Elgar.

Eigen, M., and P. Schuster (1979), *The Hypercycle*, Berlin: Springer.

Foster, J., and J. S. Metcalfe (2001), 'Modern evolutionary economics perspectives: an overview', in J. Foster and J. S. Metcalfe (eds.), *Frontiers of Evolutionary Economics*, Cheltenham: Edward Elgar.

McCarthy, I. (1995), 'Manufacturing classifications: lessons from organisational systematics and biological taxonomy', *Journal of Manufacturing and Technology Management – Integrated Manufacturing Systems* **6**(6): 37–49.

McCarthy, I., M. Leseure, K. Ridgeway and N. Fieller (1997), 'Building a manufacturing cladogram', *International Journal of Technology Management* **13**(3): 2269–96.

McKelvey, B. (1982), *Organizational Systematics*, Berkeley and Los Angeles: University of California Press.

(1994), 'Evolution and organizational science', in J. Baum and J. Singh (eds.), *Evolutionary Dynamics of Organizations*, Oxford: Oxford University Press, 314–26.

Nelson, R. R., and S. G. Winter (1982), *An Evolutionary Theory of Economic Change*, Cambridge, MA: Harvard University Press.

Zohar, D., and I. Marshall (2001), *SQ: Spiritual Intelligence*, London: Bloomsbury.

C

Evolutionary macroeconomics

14 Perspectives on technological evolution

Richard R. Nelson

1 Introduction

Scholars of cultural change are explicitly putting forth the argument that the elements of culture they are analysing are subject to evolutionary processes. By 'culture', I mean to include both customary ways of doing things and ways of understanding and explaining what the right thing to do is, and why. In most of the arenas I have in mind these two aspects go together: that is, a body of practice is supported by a body of argument rationalizing that practice.

By an 'evolutionary process' I mean one in which the processes of change involve mechanisms that 'select on' an extant variety; there are forces that sustain the character of what is selected, but there also are mechanisms that introduce new departures to the evolutionary system in question. To argue that change occurs through an evolutionary process in the sense above does not deny or even play down the importance of human purposes, thinking – and even calculating – in guiding action. Indeed, later in this chapter I will stress the importance of human reasoning, understandings and rhetoric in determining what people do. However, the argument that change is evolutionary does deny the capability of humans to foresee fully the consequences of the actions they take, and does highlight that learning is, to a considerable extent, the result of processes that involve trials and feedback from the results of those trials.

In an article a few years ago (Nelson, 1995), I briefly surveyed bodies of evolutionary theorizing about science, law, business practice and organization, and technology. In this chapter I will focus on evolutionary theorizing about technological change. But, before I home in on that topic, I want to lay out some characteristics of this kind of cultural evolutionary theorizing more generally.

First of all, scholars theorizing that human culture evolves come from several different intellectual starting places. One is ethology and sociobiology – fields that see animal behavior, and human behavior by inclusion, as as much a product of Darwinian biological evolution as the structure of the human eye or the shape of the hand. At one end of the spectrum of scholars here are those that see patterns of human culture as closely constrained by human biology, and as being 'selected upon' by the contribution of those patterns to human survival – literally. Here the work of Charles Lumsden and Edward Wilson (1981) is perhaps the best-known example. On the other hand, Luigi Cavalli-Sforza and Marcus Feldman (1981), Robert Boyd and Peter Richerson (1985) and William Durham (1991) all see a much looser biological 'leash', and often back off from the notion that biological inclusive fitness considerations are what are driving the evolution of human culture.

A related, but somewhat different, intellectual base is evolutionary epistemology, which – in the eyes of some of its founders – views the growth of distinctly human knowledge as a natural, if very human, extension of biological evolution. Donald Campbell (1960, 1974) played a prominent role in developing this line of argument. As we shall see, this strand of theorizing has played a significant role in the evolutionary analysis of technological change.

Other explorers in this arena, while recognizing the basic biological equipment that humans need to have before culture can come into existence, have emphasized the role of shared understandings and symbols, and cross-individual and cross-generational cumulative learning, which in their view make the evolution of science, or technology, or the understanding of human history, or the law, a whole new ball game. More generally, historians, economists and other social scientists have long used evolutionary language to describe the processes of change they were studying, without proposing any connections with biological evolution. In recent years a number of social scientists have tightened their language and put forth a cleanly articulated evolutionary theory of cultural change. This certainly is so in the arena I focus on in this chapter (for a survey, see Nelson, 1995).

The notion that science evolves has a long tradition, with recent writing drawing somewhat conflicting themes from Karl Popper, 1968, on the one hand, and Thomas Kuhn, 1970, on the other (see, for example, Plotkin, 1982, and Hull, 1988). The argument that the law evolves also has a long tradition, but is less coherent (see, for example, Demsetz, 1967, and Landes and Posner, 1987). Alfred Chandler's great work on business history (1962, 1990) puts forward an evolutionary theory of business organization.

A significant body of evolutionary economics has grown up in recent years, much of it following along the lines mapped out in Nelson and Winter (1982), but with several alternative strands also being developed.

The Nelson and Winter strand is focused on the key role of technological advance in driving economic growth. The key actors in this theory are for-profit business firms, competing with each other for market dominance. However, in this theory there also is a technological community, among which technology is shared (see Nelson, 1995). Both of these themes will be discussed at greater length later in this chapter.

There are significant matters that divide scholars of cultural evolution into different camps, and these will be considered in the following section in the context of the discussion of evolutionary theorizing about technological advance. However, all of them share certain perspectives. The central one, of course, is that the processes of change moulding the aspect of human culture under consideration involve mechanisms that 'select on' an extant variety, and forces that sustain the character of what is selected, while at the same time there are also mechanisms that introduce new departures to the evolutionary system.

There also seems to be broad adherence to the position that cultural evolution often takes place at several different levels. Thus, the use of a new business practice, or the use of a new material to make parts of products, may be spreading at the same time within a particular business unit, across different business units belonging to the same firm, across the firms in the industry and across industries.

While there is less discussion of this matter, I would like to return to a theme I introduced earlier. I want to argue that an important feature of many aspects of human culture, and most certainly technology, is that what evolves is both a body of practice and a body of understanding. Some scholars proposing that technology evolves focus on one of these aspects, while other scholars focus on the other. Yet it can be argued that what makes the evolution of human practice, and especially technology, different from the evolution of animal behaviour as studied by ethologists is exactly that extant human practice is generally supported by a rather elaborate body of reasons, or rationalizations.

The above proposition – that extant human practice tends to be supported or rationalized by a body of understanding or belief – holds for many aspects of human culture, from religion, to business practice, to technology. However, it can be argued that a hallmark of technology that makes it different from, say, religion or certain areas of business policy is that actual practice often provides a sharp testing of prevailing understanding.

One striking feature of the evolution of technology compared with other aspects of human culture is the rapid pace of change. This obviously is not the case with all areas of technology. For example, much of what goes on today in the construction of residential housing would have been quite familiar to an architect and builder operating a century ago. But, on the other hand, compare the pace of change in semiconductor technology with that of accounting practice.

Behind the rapid advance of technology, compared with other areas of human culture, I would propose that there are two related major causes, which I have begun to bring out above. One is that the understanding part of technology often provides relatively strong guidance regarding how to improve practice. Put another way, the mechanism generating 'new departures' in technological evolution is more likely to come up with new variants that are significant improvements over what previously existed than is the case, say, with respect to new business practice.

The argument here certainly is not that technologists can clearly see the exact nature of the new departures that will solve a perceived problem, or make a desired improvement. Walter Vincenti's wonderful study (1994) of competition among various ideas as to how to reduce the drag on aircraft caused by fixed landing gears is a good antidote to that kind of thinking. Indeed, a hallmark of evolutionary theories of technological change is precisely that significant advances cannot be planned *ex ante*.

However, compare what we know about how new technology comes into existence with what is revealed by the literature on 'business fads'. Eric Abrahamson's (1996) discussion of the ideas that led to the rise, and – for a while – the fashionability, of 'quality circles' is a fine example. Or, along a somewhat different vein, reflect on the studies describing how American automobile companies have struggled to try to understand the factors behind Japanese prowess in that industry. Both of these examples reveal the companies shifting from one theory to another, from one tried reform to another, in a manner that highlights the weakness of human understanding in this practical arena.

The second feature of technological evolution that should be highlighted is that selection criteria and mechanisms are often sharp, steady and rapid. Studies such as those by Vincenti (1990, 1994) show that it often takes a considerable period of time before a consensus judgement is made regarding the merits of competing technologies. However, the sharpness and speed of the selection criteria and mechanisms revealed in the technological histories with which I am familiar are striking compared with the vague, shifting and slow processes of selection involved in many areas of business practice, or the law.

Clearly, however, I am on contentious grounds here. I turn next to differences among scholars of technological change regarding just these issues.

2   Differing views on selection criteria and mechanisms

One can identify basically three different intellectual camps of scholars working at present to develop and support the theory that 'technology evolves'. First, there are the historians of technology, such as Vincenti (1990), and George Basalla (1988). For this group, the proposition that technology evolves is basically a theory that seems to explain the phenomena they are observing. However, once that evolutionary theory is adopted there is a natural inclination to join intellectual forces with the evolutionary epistemologists, such as Campbell.

Contemporary sociologists studying technology strike me as comprising a quite different camp. While the interest of sociologists in technological advance goes back a considerable time, and so too the point of view that social structure influences the path of technological evolution, the last two decades have seen the sharp articulation of a 'social construction' theory of technological advance. Wiebe Bijker (1995) is a good spokesman for this group.

Economists studying technological advance, and who have come to see the process as an evolutionary one, tend to form a fourth camp. By and large (there are exceptions), the economists proposing that technology 'evolves' are operating somewhat at odds with the canons of mainline economics. Nonetheless, they tend to be thought of by members of the other three camps as 'thinking like economists'.

These differences show up strikingly in the treatment by the different camps of the processes involved in the selection or winnowing out of technological alternatives. This chapter will consider later how it matters which aspects of technology are seen as evolving: practice, understanding, or both together. It seems useful to note here, however, that the evolutionary epistemologists tend to have it in mind that the evolutionary process is mostly about getting a better fit between understanding and reality (which, however, cannot be completely experienced), while the economists tend to focus on how well a technology fits user needs, with the technological historians and the sociologists sometimes going back and forth between these aspects.

The discussion here also will repress the issue that selection would appear to proceed at several different levels. The following will focus largely on how the different camps see selection at the community or user level.

The hallmark of historians of technology who propose an evolutionary theory is, of course, the proposition that multiple possible solutions tend to exist for most important technological problems, and discovering that which works best can be determined only through actual competitive comparison. The adoption of the perspective of 'evolutionary epistemology' involves a commitment to the view that attempts to solve technological problems are, to some extent, 'blind'.

Theorists in this camp do not display – in my view, at least – any particular dogma regarding the precise nature of selection criteria, or even the selection mechanisms involved. However, in much of this writing the assumption would appear to be that there are (in some sense) natural 'technological' criteria of merit, and that a 'technological community' tends ultimately to converge on what the best alternative is. Partly this orientation reflects a focus on the understanding aspect of technology, and partly, perhaps, that the scholars in question are very interested in the technological communities involved in their own right. In any case, while often presented cautiously, the flavour of this kind of theorizing is that technology 'gets better' over time.

The sociologists of technological evolution tend, sometimes gleefully and scornfully, to attack this point of view. The first part of the theoretical argument – that selection is a key mechanism at work – is not in contention. What is is the nature of selection mechanisms. The sociologists tend to agree with the evolutionary epistemologists and historians of technology that some sort of 'community' is involved, but they see the community as much broader than simply that of 'technologists'. And the notion of natural compelling technological criteria is emphatically denied. Rather, the selection process is seen partly as the battling of competing interests, and partly as a matter of campaigns of varying effectiveness to capture hearts and minds. Criteria of merit are established in these processes, which is a very different matter from proposing that these processes assess competing alternatives against a pre-existing and 'natural' set of performance criteria.

Social constructionists take issue both with the historians who propose natural technological standards of merit and with the economists who propose that there is a market 'out there' that, ultimately, is doing the selecting. One way of thinking about the latter difference is that the economists, more than any of the other camps, have a set of users in their theory of technological evolution that is distinct from the community of technologists and other internal actors that is involved in advancing the technology.

Evolutionary theories of technological advance in economics represent the coming together of two strands. One of these stems from the writings of Joseph Schumpeter, and kindred contemporary economists, who see competition in many industries as largely involving the introduction to the market of new products by different firms, with the fate of the firms depending to a considerable degree on how well their new product sells in competition with the products of other firms. The other strand represents the growing awareness, on the part of at least some economists, that technological advance, in fact, does seem to proceed through a process in which there is variation, systematic selection on that variation, and then further introduction of new variety.

Together, these elements have led to a theory that is mostly concerned with the practice aspect of technology, and which presumes that users and the 'market' select on new technologies. Technologies that are better than others, given the criteria of the market, win out because customers buy the products embodying them, and the firms that employ them do well relative to firms that do not. The better technology expands in use, both because the firm or firms that employ it expand relative to other firms, and because these other firms are induced to adopt it themselves.

As noted earlier, this body of evolutionary economic theorizing has been part of attempts by evolutionary economists to make sense of the broad patterns of economic growth that have been experienced. It also has been part of a revival of 'Schumpeterian' notions about the nature of competition in high-tech industries, with competition focused on the introduction of better products, and not simply 'price'. These economic theories are 'evolutionary' theories in the sense that innovation and *ex post* selection are driving the dynamics. But the market, which is doing the selection, is, in a sense, 'out there' and determining which technological alternatives survive. It is distinct from the technological community, which is engaged in advancing the technology.

To sharpen the contrast, one could say that all scholars of the evolution of technology recognize that, ultimately, a new technology has to be accepted by those who will use it. The technological historians tend to see technologists making their judgements as agents for the users. The social constructionists see user needs as being defined by a political process, which often has some of the characteristics of a bandwagon. Economists, at least in their first cuts at an analysis, see the users as knowing what they want and ultimately enforcing their choices.

Where do I come out on all this? Clearly, there are quite different theories of selection here. If I were forced to come down strictly for one position or another, I would strongly lean towards the presumption that the selection environment is often reasonably sharp and steady, and that in most – if not all – arenas of technological change selection criteria reflect both technological effectiveness and user needs. However, I propose that the issue is not which of these theories is right, and which ones wrong, in general. Rather, my strong belief is that the different theories are applicable in different arenas. Bicycles differ from aircraft. Both differ from electric razors and pharmaceuticals. More-over, as the examples indicate, in many cases one can find elements of several selection criteria and mechanisms at work at one and the same time.

In addition, it makes a big difference whether the focus is on the practice or the understanding aspect of technology. I turn now to this issue.

3   Technology as both practice and understanding

A theory of technological change as an evolutionary process that focuses strictly on practice naturally points its analysis of selection towards how well technology meets user needs. Students of technolog-ical change may differ on how and by whom the criteria for superior-ity are determined in this dimension, but the nature of the debate is clear, I believe – as are the ways to resolve, or combine, the arguments empirically.

To the extent that technology is seen as not simply a body of prac-tice but also a body of understanding, the nature of the evaluation and selection processes becomes more complicated. While the criteria for selection on the former aspect may well 'fit' with user needs, the criteria for the latter would appear to be the 'ability to explain observed rele-vant facts and enable problems to be solved and progress made'. The selection processes and those who control them, as well as the crite-ria, may be very different. For practice, the process is ultimately under the control of users, or their agents; for understanding, control rests with the community of technologists. There may, or may not, be some overlap.

If the user community is diverse, or there are many different kinds of uses, selection may preserve a wide variety of artefacts and techniques. On the other hand, the body of understanding that is the result of selection may be quite unified.

If both aspects are recognized, it would seem that technological advance needs to be understood as a coevolutionary process. The man-ners in which the two aspects evolve, and how they relate to each other, all would seem essential aspects of the story. And these processes would appear to differ significantly from field to field.

One central variable is the strength of technological understanding at any time. Another is the knowledge of the technological community regarding user needs, or its ability to control or define them. If both are very strong, technological advance can almost be planned. This seems to be the presumption behind at least some aspects of technology pol-icy, public and private. However, empirical scholars of technological change can cite many examples of disaster when these conditions were, incorrectly, assumed to hold. In general, they do not. Attempts to develop new and better artefacts and practical techniques almost always involve significant elements of technological or user response uncertainty – usually both.

Another key set of variables relates to the sources of new understanding, the relationships between the processes through which these are won, and the processes that create new practice. Until recently, and even in many fields at the present time, the principal source of understanding is experience with practice. Thus, a hallmark of much 'inventing' until recently was that those who used or operated a technology were the most likely sources of improvements in that technology. Understanding was largely a body of lore shared by those who practised a trade.

Nowadays, of course, most technologies are understood, in part at least, 'scientifically'. In some fields of technology advances in relevant scientific understanding come largely from autonomous developments in science, but in most fields this is not the case. Most fields of technology nowadays are marked by the presence of applied sciences or engineering disciplines, the business of which is to advance understanding relevant to practice. These disciplines often draw on more basic sciences, but they are bodies of understanding in their own right.

And, while conventional wisdom often presumes that advances in understanding come before and enable advances in practice, scholars of technological advance know that often it is the other way around, or that the process is strongly interactive. The development of thermodynamics as a scientific field after the development of the steam engine, and with the purpose of understanding that technology, and the development by William Shockley of a theory of holes and electrons in semiconductors as a result of the successful invention of the transistor (see Nelson, 1962) are only two classic examples of the understanding following the practice.

In the engineering disciplines and applied sciences, the intimate relationship with practice suggests that one can sharpen up somewhat the selection criteria for developments that are advertised as new or improved understanding. Do they enable problems in prevailing practice to be solved, or advances to be made, that were not possible, or were more difficult, in the absence of that proposed contribution to understanding? This kind of operative selection criterion obviously provides a two-way linkage between the evolution of practice and understanding.

The writings that propose that technological change proceeds through an evolutionary process differ dramatically on how they treat the relationships between the evolution of practice and the evolution of understanding, if they recognize the difference and the relationships at all. Unlike the differences in the treatment of selection processes sketched in the preceding section, the differences here are not so much to do with the disciplinary background as with the fact that scholars of technological advance are only now beginning to struggle with these relationships.

REFERENCES

Abrahamson, E. (1996), 'Management fashion', *Academy of Management Review* 21(1): 254–85.
Basalla, G. (1988), *The Evolution of Technology*, Cambridge: Cambridge University Press.
Bijker, W. (1995), *Bicycles, Bakelites, and Bulbs: Towards a Theory of Sociotechnical Change*, Cambridge, MA: MIT Press.
Boyd, R., and P. J. Richerson (1985), *Culture and the Evolutionary Process*, Chicago: University of Chicago Press.
Campbell, D. T. (1960), 'Blind variation and selective retention in creative thought as in other knowledge processes', *Psychological Review* 67: 380–400. [Reprinted in G. Radnitzky and W. W. Bartley III (eds.) (1987), *Evolutionary Epistemology, Rationality, and the Sociology of Knowledge*, La Salle, IL: Open Court, 91–114.]
    (1974), '"Downward causation" in hierarchically organized biological systems', in F. J. Ayala and T. Dobzhansky (eds.), *Studies in the Philosophy of Biology*, Berkeley and Los Angeles: University of California Press, 179–86.
Cavalli-Sforza, L. L., and M. W. Feldman (1981), *Cultural Transmission and Evolution: A Quantitative Approach*, Princeton, NJ: Princeton University Press.
Chandler, A. D. (1962), *Strategy and Structure: Chapters in the History of the Industrial Enterprise*, Cambridge, MA: MIT Press.
    (1990), *Scale and Scope: The Dynamics of Industrial Capitalism*, Cambridge, MA: Harvard University Press.
Demsetz, H. (1967), 'Toward a theory of property rights', *American Economic Review* 57(2): 347–59.
Durham, W. H. (1991), *Coevolution: Genes, Culture, and Human Diversity*, Stanford, CA: Stanford University Press.
Hull, D. (1988), *Science as a Process*, Chicago: University of Chicago Press.
Kuhn, T. S. (1970), *The Structure of Scientific Revolutions*, Chicago: University of Chicago Press.
Landes, W. M., and R. A. Posner (1987), *The Economic Structure of Tort Law*, Cambridge, MA: Harvard University Press.
Lumsden, C. J., and E. O. Wilson (1981), *Genes, Mind, and Culture*, Cambridge, MA: Harvard University Press.
Nelson, R. R. (1962), 'The link between science and technology: the case of the transistor', in R. R. Nelson (ed.), *The Rate and Direction of Inventive Activity*, Princeton, NJ: Princeton University Press.

Nelson, R. R., and S. G. Winter (1982), *An Evolutionary Theory of Economic Change*, Cambridge, MA: Harvard University Press.

(1995), 'Recent evolutionary theorizing about economic change', *Journal of Economic Literature* **33**: 48–90.

Plotkin, H. C. (1982), *Learning, Development, and Culture: Essays in Evolutionary Epistemology*, New York: Wiley.

Popper, K. R. (1968), *Conjectures and Refutation: The Growth of Scientific Knowledge*, New York: Harper Torchbooks.

Vincenti, W. (1990), *What Engineers Know and How They Know It*, Baltimore: Johns Hopkins University Press.

(1994), 'The retractable airplane landing gear and the Northrop anomaly: variation-selection and the shaping of technology', *Technology and Culture* **35**: 1–33.

15 Evolutionary economic dynamics: persistent cycles, disruptive technology and the trade-off between stability and complexity

Ping Chen

1 Introduction: bridging the gap between economics and biology

Alfred Marshall once remarked that economics should be considered closer to biology than to mechanics (Marshall, 1890). Living systems have two essential features: life rhythms, and the birth/death process. However, the current economic framework is far from Marshall's dream: economic order is widely formulated by a steady-state solution plus random noise. Can we bridge the gap between equilibrium economics and evolutionary biology?

There are two fundamental problems in theoretical economics: the nature of persistent business cycles, and the diversity in developing the division of labour. To study these problems, there are two different perspectives in economic dynamics: the equilibrium-mechanical approach, and the evolution-biological approach.

The existence of persistent business cycles and chronic excess capacity is hard to explain by using equilibrium models in macroeconometrics. External noise cannot maintain persistent cycles in the Frisch model (see Chen, 1999); aggregate fluctuations in the Lucas micro-foundations model are too weak for generating large macro-fluctuations according to the principle of large numbers (Lucas, 1972, Chen, 2002); and random walk and Brownian motion are not capable of explaining persistent fluctuations in macro-indicators (Chen, 2001). Adam Smith once observed that the division of labour was limited by the extent of the market (Smith, 1776). George Stigler noted that the above Smith theorem was not compatible with the Smith theory of the 'invisible hand' (Stigler, 1951). Joseph Needham asked why capitalism and science originated in Western Europe, not in China or other civilizations (Needham, 1954). Diversified patterns in the division of labour and corporate strategies cannot be explained within the equilibrium framework.

In our analysis, the time scale plays a key role in understanding economic dynamics. The birth–death process is the first approximation of growth fluctuations. Business cycles can be further decomposed into a smooth trend, plus colour chaos and white noise. Persistent cycles and structural changes can be directly observed from a time-frequency representation. Market share competition and disruptive changes in technology can be described by the logistic model with resource constraint. Innovative corporate strategies can be studied from a behavioural model of risk culture and learning by trying. Logistic curves and product cycles can be inferred from marketing strategy and technological progress. The division of labour is limited by the market extent, resource variety and environmental uncertainty. The Smith dilemma can be solved by the trade-off between stability and complexity (see Chen, 1987). Resilient market and economic complexity can be understood from persistent business cycles and technological metabolism. Economic evolution and structural changes can be directly observed over a wide range of time scales, including product cycles, business cycles and Kondratiev long waves.

2   Endogenous fluctuations and statistical nature in macro-dynamics: from equilibrium noise to persistent cycles

The nature of business cycles is an unsolved issue in macroeconomics. There are two schools of thought in business cycle theory: the exogenous-shocks-equilibrium school and the endogenous-cycles-disequilibrium school.

The exogenous school is founded on four models: the Frisch model of a noise-driven damped oscillator; the Lucas micro-foundations model of rational expectations; the random walk; and the Brownian motion model in macro- and finance theory (see Frisch, 1933, Lucas, 1981, Nelson and Plosser, 1982, and Black and Scholes 1973). Endogenous cycles are represented by deterministic oscillators, including the harmonic cycle, limit cycle and colour chaos (see Samuelson, 1939, Goodwin, 1951, and Chen, 1988).

In this section, we will show that equilibrium models are not capable of explaining large fluctuations and persistent cycles in macro-movements. The thought experiments that argue against the existence of economic chaos have fundamental flaws in theoretical thinking. The birth–death process and the colour chaos model both provide a better picture of market resilience and the economic clock observed from business cycles.

2.1   The Copernicus problem in macroeconometrics: linear and non-linear trends in macroeconomic indexes

The non-stationary feature of economic growth imposes a great challenge to theoretical economics and economic physics: how to identify some stable patterns from an evolving economy? Can we simplify the observed complex movements into some simple patterns by means of mathematical mapping? This is the Copernicus problem in macroeconometrics. The time scale plays a critical role in observing business cycles.

Measurement and theory cannot be separated from each other. The dynamic patterns from competing observation references can be seen in figure 15.1. In econometrics, the linear filter of first differencing (FD) is widely applied to construct an equilibrium (short-term) picture of economic fluctuations. The resulting time series are erratic and short-correlated (figure 15.1b). The random walk model with a constant drift is also called the unit-root model in macroeconometrics (Nelson and Plosser, 1982). In neoclassical growth theory, the long-term equilibrium path is characterized by an exponential growth or a log-linear (LL) trend (Solow, 1956). The resulting cycles are long-correlated. The problem is that measurement is sensitive to the choice of time boundaries.

An intermediate trend between FD and LL is a non-linear smooth trend obtained by the HP (Hodrick-Prescott) filter, to be found in the real business cycle (RBC) literature (Hodrick and Prescott, 1981)[1]. Its correlation time is in the range that National Bureau of Economic Research business cycles have been in for several years (Chen, 1996a). We will show that the HP trend is better than the other two in giving a consistent picture of medium-term business cycles. This finding reveals the critical role of the time scale in choosing a preferred reference system.

From figure 15.1b we can see that the short correlations of FD series look random but that HP cycles have an image of damped cycles, which could be generated either by colour noise or by colour chaos. 'Colour' means a characteristic frequency from the observed fluctuations. The observed variances also depend on the choice of the observation reference trend: the longer the time window, the larger the variance. The LL indicates the largest time window of the entire observational period. The FD implies the shortest time window of one time unit, when macroeconomic trends are completely ignored. FD is the root of equilibrium illusion in macroeconometrics. The HP implies a medium time window in the range of business cycles.

[1] Edward Prescott told the author at the 2001 American Economic Association meeting that the HP filter was first used by John von Neumann; a more accurate name for it, therefore, would be the VHP filter.

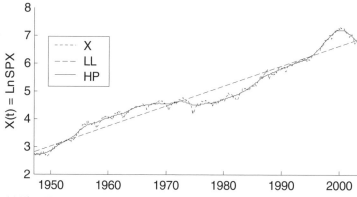

(a) The HP trend and LL trend of X(t), the logarithmic Standard and Poor's (S&P) time series

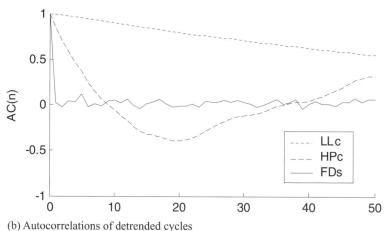

(b) Autocorrelations of detrended cycles

Figure 15.1 Three detrending references and their autocorrelations of detrended cycles from the logarithmic SPX, Standard and Poor's 500 Price Index monthly series (1947–2002), $N = 672$
Source: yahoo.finance.

2.2 Equilibrium illusion in business cycle theory: the challenge of large and persistent fluctuations

The four pillar models for the equilibrium theory of business cycles have analytical solutions, all of which contain fundamental difficulties in understanding persistent business cycles. The popular belief in an efficient market would be in trouble when economic complexity exists.

2.2.1   The Frisch fantasy of noise-driven cycles: a perpetual motion machine of the second kind?

Ragnar Frisch realized that the linear model has marginal stability in parameter changes (this issue will be discussed further in section 3.3.1). He speculated that persistent cycles could be maintained by a stream of random shocks, claiming this scenario in an informal conference paper (Frisch, 1933). Equilibrium economists quickly embraced the Frisch model because the stable nature of a market economy could be preserved by a damped harmonic oscillator with friction. However, the Frisch speculation was rejected by physicists in their study of the harmonic Brownian motion, which had been solved analytically before Frisch's paper (see Uhlenbeck and Ornstein, 1930).

The conclusion in physics is contrary to the Frisch fantasy: the harmonic oscillation under Brownian motion will be dampened in an exponential way. Persistent cycles cannot be maintained by random shocks. The relaxation time T_β and realized period T_r can be estimated from observed autocorrelations:

$$\rho(\tau) = \exp\left(-\frac{\tau}{T_\beta}\right)\left[\cos\left(\frac{2\pi\tau}{T_r}\right) + \frac{T_r}{2\pi T_\beta}\sin\left(\frac{2\pi\tau}{T_r}\right)\right] \tag{1}$$

For the Brownian oscillator model of the logarithmic US real GDP, the estimation of relaxation time depends on the choice of the observation reference system. American business cycles would cease within four years for FD series or ten years for HP cycles respectively (Chen, 1999). The FD reference is worse than the HP reference, since the FD cycles need a large source of external noise, the standard deviation of which should be 30 per cent larger than the standard deviation of the US real GDP. Since the US economy is the largest in the world, we could not identify an external source to drive American business cycles. Clearly, a linear oscillator is not capable of modelling persistent cycles.

Historically, Frisch quietly abandoned his model as early as 1934. Frisch's promised paper, 'Changing harmonics studied from the point of view of linear operators and erratic shocks', was advertised three times in the category 'papers to appear in early issues' in *Econometrica*, in issues nos. 2, 3 and 4 of volume 1 (April, July and October 1933). The promised paper was never published in *Econometrica*, which had Frisch himself as the editor of the newly established flagship journal for the Econometric Society. Surprisingly, Frisch never even mentioned a word about his prize-winning model in his Nobel speech in 1969 (Frisch, 1981).

If Frisch had been able to use random shocks to generate persistent cycles it would have implied a perpetual motion machine of the second kind, violating the second law of thermodynamics.

2.2.2   The Lucas issue of micro-foundations and the principle of large numbers

The new classical school called for micro-foundations of macroeconomic fluctuations. Lucas suggested that independent fluctuations at the level of the household (e.g. the intertemporal substitution between work and leisure) would generate large fluctuations at the aggregate level (see Lucas, 1972 and 1981). He simply ignored the essential differences between the one body and many body problems.

As a first approximation, we may consider a macro-economy as a static system with N identical agents. The macro-economy can be described by its total output. We assume that fluctuations in a firm's output or a household's working hours follow an identical independent distribution. The mean is μ, the standard deviation is σ. Based on the law of large numbers and the central limit theorem in probability theory, the mean of the aggregate positive output is $N\mu$, while its variance is $N\sigma^2$. Therefore, we can define the relative deviation (RD = Ψ) by the ratio of the standard deviation to the mean when the mean of positive variables is not zero.

$$\Psi = \frac{\sqrt{VAR[S_N]}}{mean[S_N]} = \frac{C}{\sqrt{N}} \quad \text{where } C = \frac{\rho}{\mu} \tag{2}$$

For a non-stationary process with internal fluctuations, a linear birth–death process for economic growth will generate similar results (Chen, 2002). We can define an implied number N^*, which can be estimated from the observed macro-series

$$N^* = \frac{1}{\Psi^2_{macro}} = \frac{\mu^2_{macro}}{\sigma^2_{macro}} \tag{3}$$

We can say that the relative deviation for aggregate fluctuations of N statistically independent positive elements is in the order of $\frac{1}{\sqrt{N}}$; we call this rule based on the law of large numbers and the central limit theorem the *principle of large numbers*. The RD is a very useful measure for a wide class of systems with a positive range of variables, such as population, output, working hours and price.

Empirical measurement of the RD depends on the reference system in observing business cycles. Here, the RD is measured by the ratio of the standard deviation of the HP cycles to the mean of the HP trends within a moving time window, since the HP reference produces the largest implied numbers that are compatible with empirical facts (table 15.1). Other references have even worse results. Here GDPC1 is US real GDP in 1996 dollars, PCECC96 real personal consumption, GPDIC1 real domestic investment and LBMNU the hours of non-farm business. The

Table 15.1 *The relative deviation and implied number of degrees of freedom for several macro-indexes by HP detrending (1947–2000)*

$\Psi(\%)$ [N^*]	GDPC1Ln	PCECC96Ln	GPDIC1Ln	LBMNULn
HP	0.21[200,000]	0.17[300,000]	1.3[6,000]	0.29[100,000]

estimates of relative deviations are averages over the period from 1947–2000 with logarithmic data series.

The magnitude of the RD of the macro-indexes is in the range of 0.2 to 1 per cent; its implied number is between 200,000 and 6,000. How can we associate these figures with the actual numbers in the US economy? According to the US Bureau of Census, there were 81 million households, 3 million corporations with more than $100,000 in assets and about 20,000 public companies in 1980. If we compare these numbers with the implied numbers under HP trends, we can see that the observed implied numbers of these macro-indexes are several hundred smaller than household or firm numbers. In other words, the observed relative fluctuations are at least twenty times larger than could be explained by the micro-foundations models in labour or producer markets.

There are several implications arising from comparisons of these numbers.

First, *the representative model in the real business cycle theory is not valid,* since the observed implied numbers are much larger than one.

Second, *fluctuations in households or firms are not capable of explaining large relative deviations in aggregate output, consumption, business hours or investment.*

Third, financial intermediaries and industrial organizations appear to play a critical role in generating large business fluctuations, since the number of large companies and large financial corporations matches the quantitative range required by the implied numbers in investment.

A further examination of the Lucas model of intertemporal substitution between goods and leisure reveals fundamental flaws in equilibrium thinking. In the Lucas island economy, identical agents believe and act in perfect correlation under rational expectations. If these agents have individual freedom of choice, arbitrage activity will eliminate correlations among individual fluctuations. Lucas claimed that government policy was effective only when it was unexpected. Similarly, rational expectations cannot last long if they mislead believers! Diversified choices are driven by conflicting interests rather than a common belief in a competitive but unequal society. *The rational expectations hypothesis suffers the same self-defeating syndrome of macroeconometrics under the Lucas critique.* Clearly, the efficient market, rational expectations and micro-foundations

Table 15.2 *The statistical properties of linear stochastic processes*

Order	Drifted diffusion	Birth–death	Random/walk
Mean	$\sim\exp(rt)$	$\sim\exp(rt)$	$\sim t$
Variance	$\sim\exp(2rt)\{e^{\sigma^2 t}-1\}$	$\sim e^{rt}(e^{rt}-1)$	$\sim t$
RD	$\sim e^{\frac{\sigma^2}{2}t}\sqrt{(1-e^{-t\sigma^2})}$	$\sim\dfrac{1}{\sqrt{N_0}}$	$\sim\dfrac{1}{\sqrt{t}}$

theories do not provide a consistent framework for business cycle theory. They are, in fact, contradictory in explaining large business fluctuations.

2.2.3   The endogenous mechanism and statistical property: the birth–death process against the Brownian motion and random walk

In modelling stochastic growth, the exogenous school is based on the drifted diffusion model, which is also called the geometric Brownian motion model in finance theory (see Black and Scholes, 1973). Two stochastic models of endogenous fluctuations are used in the economic theory of growth and fluctuations: the random walk model and the birth–death process (see Nelson and Plosser, 1982, and Chen, 2002). It is widely perceived that the three stochastic models exhibit similar behaviour. There is little doubt about the validity of geometric Brownian motion in economic dynamics.

In the previous section, we saw that the relative deviation plays a fundamental role in studying micro-foundations. RD is quite stable for observed macro-indicators. Here, we further compare the RDs for three popular stochastic models of growth and fluctuations. Their analytical results are shown in table 15.2 (see also Chen, 2001, and Li, 2002).

Here, N_0 is the size of the initial population of micro-agents in the birth–death process and $r > 0$ for economic growth.

From table 15.2 we can clearly see that neither the random walk nor Brownian motion model can generate sustained fluctuations; *the random walk is damping* and *the diffusion model is exploding in time*. It is interesting to note that these two models are representative agent models in nature. The persistent pattern in economic fluctuations can be explained only by the birth/death process, which is a population model of growth and an endogenous model of fluctuations. This result raises a fundamental challenge to equilibrium models in terms of the representative agent and exogenous fluctuations in macroeconomics and finance theory.

2.2.4   Monetary neutrality and coordination costs: the Ricardo device, the Loschmidt paradox and uneven distribution

The Ricardo device is a thought experiment to justify the neutrality of money (thought experiments are typically named after their authors). This device is the hypothetical operation of doubling overnight the cash holdings of all business enterprises and households without changing relative prices. It means that all supply and demand functions are a homogeneous function of zero degree, which is the basic argument against Keynesian economics (Leontief, 1936). David Ricardo ignored the redistribution problem in an unequal society. The Ricardo operation implies the levying either of a progressive subsidy or of regressive taxation – which has no chance of being passed into law in a parliamentary democracy. The Ricardo device can work only in a primitive economy with an even distribution of wealth.

The Ricardo device in economics is very similar to the Loschmidt reversibility paradox for challenging Boltzmann's H theorem of thermodynamic irreversibility. Josef Loschmidt argued that one should be able to return to any initial state merely by reversing all molecules' velocity under Newton's law. The trouble here is the huge coordination costs. As noted by Ludwig Boltzmann in 1877, the possibility of reversing all the initial conditions is very unlikely when dealing with a large system with many particles (Brush, 1983). The empirical and theoretical evidence for monetary chaos is a challenge to the neutrality of money (see Barnett and Chen, 1988, and Chen, 1988). Our finding may revitalize the Austrian theory of endogenous money.

2.2.5   The rational arbitrageur and non-replicate patterns: Friedman spirits, the Maxwell demon and information ambiguity

Friedman spirits are rational arbitrageurs who wipe out any destabilizing traders on a speculative market (Friedman, 1953). The implication is that no structures can exist in a competitive market, which is the main argument for the efficient market hypothesis.

Friedman spirits behave much like the Maxwell demon in equilibrium thermodynamics. The Maxwell demon is an imaginary gatekeeper trying to create a non-equilibrium order from an equilibrium state by operating a frictionless sliding door between two chambers that are filled with moving molecules. James Clerk Maxwell assumed that his demon had perfect information about the speed and position of all molecules, such that he could allow a fast molecule into a designated portion only by opening or closing the mass-less valve in perfect timing. Therefore, by utilizing information in a smart way, the Maxwell demon could create a temperature difference without doing work – an outcome that is contrary to the second law of thermodynamics. No information cost is essential for its operation.

Friedman spirits face a similar problem to the Maxwell demon, but in an opposite situation. To eliminate any market instability, Friedman spirits need perfect information and unlimited resources. However, informationally efficient markets are impossible because of the information cost (Grossman and Stiglitz, 1980). Under financial constraints, the Friedman spirits may give up negative feedback strategy by following the mass psychology to avoid arbitrage risk, which results in the creation of instability (DeLong et al., 1990).

There is an even greater problem with information ambiguity. Milton Friedman assumed that a winner's imitator could quickly replicate the winning pattern and drive down the profit margin to zero. This scenario would be true only if the destabilizing pattern were replicable. This is unlikely, because of imperfect information (having only finite data with significant noise and time delays), information ambivalence (in the face of conflicting news and misinformation), unpredictable events (such as a financial crisis and changing structure) and limited predictability (the existence of deterministic chaos or wavelets). The critical issue of information ambiguity is not only associated with bounded rationality but also rooted in dynamical complexity (see Simon, 1957, and Chen, 1993a).

2.3   Living rhythms and economic organisms: colour chaos versus white noise

The controversy of noise versus chaos reveals the limitations of numerical tests in parametric econometrics and non-linear dynamics (see Chen, 1988, 1993a, Brock and Sayers, 1988, and Benhabib, 1992). Testing deterministic chaos in a non-stationary economic time series is more difficult than testing stationary data in laboratory experiments. Conventional econometrics can detect non-linearity but not chaos. The critical issue here is finding a proper representation in dealing with a non-stationary economic time series.

In this section we will introduce the Wigner transform in Gabor space for separating noise and cycles. We found abundant evidence of colour chaos, which is similar to a biological clock.

2.3.1   The uncertainty principle and the Gabor wavelet

The uncertainty principle in time and frequency is the very foundation of signal processing.

$$\Delta f \Delta t \geq \frac{1}{4\pi} \tag{4}$$

Here, f is the frequency and t is time. Minimum uncertainty occurs for a harmonic wave modulated by a Gaussian envelope, which is called the Gabor wavelet in signal processing or a coherent state in quantum mechanics. This is the very foundation of time/frequency analysis in the two-dimensional time-frequency Gabor space.

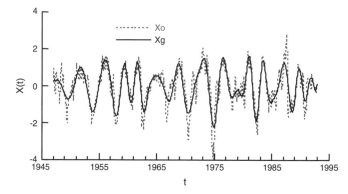

Figure 15.2 Filtered and original HP cycles (1947–1992)
Note: The filtered FSPCOM (S&P 500 Price Index) HP cyclic series Xg
closely resembles the original time series Xo. The correlation coefficient
between Xg and Xo is 0.85. The ratio of their variance is 69 per cent.
The correlation dimension of Xg is 2.5.
Data source: Citibase.

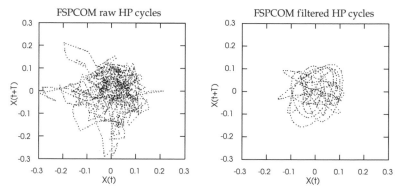

Figure 15.3 Phase portraits of the unfiltered (left-hand) and filtered
(right-hand) FSPCOM HP cycles; the time delay T is 60 months

2.3.2   Separating noise and cycles in time-frequency space

For analysing a time-dependent series we have introduced a new analytical
tool, the joint time-frequency analysis (see Qian and Chen, 1996, and
Chen, 1996a, 1996b). A time-varying filter in a two-dimensional time-
frequency lattice space can be applied for separating cycles and noise. Its
localized bases are the Gabor wavelets. The filtered and unfiltered HP
cycles are shown in figure 15.2. The deterministic pattern of filtered HP
cycles can be seen clearly from the phase portrait in figure 15.3.

The phase portrait of filtered FSPCOM HP cycles shows a clear pattern of deterministic spirals – a typical feature of colour chaos (colour chaos here refers to the non-linear oscillator in continuous time). Colour shows a strong peak in the Fourier spectrum, in addition to a noisy background (Chen, 1996b).

2.3.3 Natural experiments with an economic clock: intrinsic instabilities and external shocks in evolving economies

According to new classical economists, business cycles are all alike if they are generated by pure stochastic processes (Lucas, 1981). From new observations in time-frequency analysis, we find that business cycles are not all alike because of strong deterministic components. The time-frequency patterns of macroeconomic indicators resemble biological organisms with multiple rhythms. The frequency path can reveal valuable information in economic diagnostics and policy studies (Chen, 1996b).

Our picture of an economic clock makes a dramatic contrast with that of a random walk in equilibrium economics. Can we conduct some out-of-sample tests to distinguish these two approaches? Perhaps not, because non-stationarity is the main obstacle to the application of statistics. However, the 'natural experiments' of the oil price shock and the stock market crash demonstrate that time-frequency representation reveals more information than white noise representation (see figure 15.4).

Our finding of persistent cycles supports the biological view of business cycles (Schumpeter, 1939).

In addition to stock market indexes, persistent cycles are widely observed from HP detrended economic aggregate indicators, including real GDP, consumption, domestic investment, long-term interest rates, monetary supply indexes, the velocity of money, the consumer price index and the unemployment rate (Chen, 1996a). The range of their characteristic period is from two to ten years – a common feature of National Bureau for Economic Research business cycles. The noise component ranges from 20 to 50 per cent. Certainly, not all macroeconomic indicators behave like biological clocks: short-term interest rates and foreign exchange rates are very noisy. This information provides valuable guidance for macroeconomic study.

The frequency stability of economic indicators is remarkable. Surprisingly, market resilience is quite robust, as most characteristic frequencies are very stable under external shocks and internal instabilities. The stock market crash in October 1987 led to a 23.1 per cent drop in the level of the S&P 500 index in two months, but only a 6 per cent shift in its characteristic period.

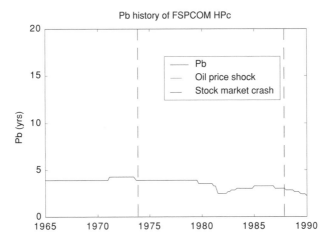

Figure 15.4 The time path of the basic period Pb of FSPCOMln (the S&P 500 Price Index) HP cycles stock market indicators
Note: The basic period Pb shifted after the oil price shock in October 1973, which signalled an external shock. In contrast, the frequency changes occurred before and after the stock market crash in October 1987, indicating an internal instability during the crash.

The existence of persistent cycles within business fluctuations is strong evidence of economic colour chaos. We should point out that the term 'chaos' has a negative image of disorder; therefore we use the term '*colour chaos*', which adds a *life rhythm* to a non-linear oscillator in continuous time. 'Colour' means a characteristic frequency, which is similar to a biological clock; this is in contrast to white noise, which has no characteristic frequency.

2.3.4   Structural instability and market resilience

The structural stability of a market economy is hard to explain within the framework of linear dynamics. This problem can be demonstrated by the Samuelson multiplier-accelerator model (see Samuelson, 1939). The structural instability of the periodic mode in the Samuelson model can be seen in parameter space (figure 15.5).

We can see that *the periodic regime PO has only a marginal stability* on the borderline between DO and EO. A small deviation from PO in parameter space will lead to damped or explosive oscillations. *The unit-root model in econometrics has similar marginal stability at the unit circle* (Nelson and Plosser, 1982). The problem of structural instability is common for linear

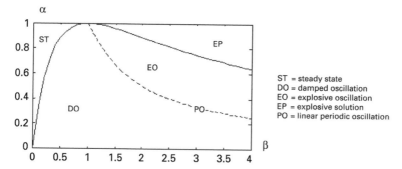

Figure 15.5 The stability pattern of the Samuelson model in parameter space

models. In the real world, a market economy is very resilient under various shocks.

The problem of structural instability in linear models can be solved by non-linear models. Consider the example of the soft-bouncing oscillator or 'freeway model', which is a mixed difference-differential equation with a targeted floor and ceiling (Chen, 1988). Overshooting is caused by time delay τ in feedback control.

$$\frac{dX(t)}{dt} = aX(t) - bX(t-\tau)\,e^{-\left[\frac{X(t-\tau)^2}{\sigma^2}\right]} \tag{5}$$

where X is the deviation from the target, τ the time delay and $\pm\sigma$ the targeted floor and ceiling. The soft nature of control targets is characterized by a non-polynomial control function.

We may consider the left side of equation (5) as the rate of change in excess supply, while the right side has a linear supply function but a non-linear demand function. Soft boundaries can be observed in many economic mechanisms, such as monetary control and the target zone of an exchange rate.

A colour chaos model of the soft-bouncing oscillator has a unified explanation of structural stability and pattern changes ('regime switch'; see figure 15.6). Pattern stability can be maintained under external shocks as long as a parameter shift does not cross a regime boundary, since periodic and chaotic regimes have finite measures. A regime switch occurs when an attractor moves into another regime in parameter space. During a regime switch, a small deviation in a parameter may induce a dramatic jump in dynamical patterns. In other words, a quantitative change leads to a qualitative change in such a situation, a so-called 'noise-induced phase transition'.

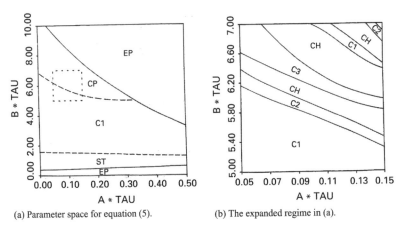

(a) Parameter space for equation (5).   (b) The expanded regime in (a).

Figure 15.6 The stability pattern in parameter space
Note: C1, C2 and C3 are limit cycles of period one, period two and period three respectively. CH is the chaos mode in continuous time. The complex regime CP is enlarged in (b), which includes alternative zones of limit cycles and chaos.

3   Market share competition, excess capacity and creative destruction: behavioural dynamics and the complexity puzzle in the division of labour

There is a visible chasm between microeconomic theory and macroeconomic dynamics. In the Arrow–Debreu model in microeconomics, economic order is characterized by a fixed point solution, while persistent fluctuations are observed in macro-dynamics. There is also a culture gap between armchair economics and the business community. There is no room in microeconomics for the product cycle, market share competition and entrepreneurship, which are core issues in business economics.

The social division of labour can be described by a biological model of species competition (see Houthakker, 1956). From the previous discussion on the nature of business cycles, we saw strong evidence of endogenous fluctuation and intermediate structure. In this section we will study the industrial foundation of business cycles, which is rooted in market share competition and economic metabolism. In dealing with macroeconomic fluctuations, both Keynesian and new classical economics focus on the demand side, but economic recessions and crises are rooted in excess capacity on the supply side. We will integrate Schumpeter's idea of 'creative construction' into Smith's original idea of market extent in the division of labour. The behavioural dynamics based on a generalized population dynamics will shed new light on market share competition, disruptive technology and the rise and fall of industries or organizations. We may gain a new understanding of the Smith dilemma from the perspective of complexity science.

3.1 Resource-limited growth and market share competition: disruptive technology and economic metabolism

Technological advancement is the driving force behind industrial economies. The birth and death of technologies and waves of product cycles are common features of a modern economy. Industrial competition to increase market share is driven more by technology than by price. The essence of industrial revolution is opening up new resources – not just the efficient utilization of existing resources. The problem is how to describe disruptive technology changes in economic dynamics. The production function in neoclassical mechanics and endogenous growth theory has a fixed parameter for a scale economy, and technology innovation is represented by small disturbances (in the form of random noise) in the RBC model; they cannot describe the rise and fall of an industrial technology.

In this section, we introduce the ecological model of market share competition. The economies of scale and scope are described by the market size in logistic growth and the number of resources available. Product cycles and excess capacity can be understood by the coexistence of old and new technologies. The continuous flow of technology wavelets is the ultimate root of uneven growth and business cycles in a macro-economy.

3.1.1 Logistic growth and dynamic return to scale

In business practice, marginal pricing cannot be a winning strategy. Two widely used pricing strategies are cost-plus pricing and strategic pricing (see Nagle and Holden, 1995). Generally speaking, the output and market share of a product will grow when the profit margin for a product is larger than zero.

$$\frac{dn}{dt} = nF(p, c) \tag{6a}$$

where n is the output, p the unit price and c the unit cost; the profit margin for a product $(p, c) = (p - c)$. If the market extent for the product is N^*, the profit margin must decline to zero when the growth space $(N^* - n)$ shrinks to zero (Zhang, 2003):

$$F(p, c) = (p - c) = k(N^* - n) \tag{6b}$$

Combining (6a) and (6b), we have

$$\frac{dn}{dt} = kn(N^* - n) \tag{6c}$$

This is the well-known logistic (Verhelst) equation in theoretical ecology (Pianka, 1983). Its solution is an S-curve, which is familiar in management science (Porter, 1980). The market extent N^* can be considered as a function of existing technology, population size, resource limitation and cost structure. Unlike neoclassic microeconomics, any realistic product or technology has its market extent. Technological advancements are characterized by a sequence of technology shifts. Therefore, technological advancement can be better described as a disruptive change in resource ceiling rather than a continuous accumulation (Christensen, 1997). The key point here is the growth space $(N^* - n)$. As long as there is a growth space, the profit margin will be more than zero, which is true for both monopolies and small firms. This is the essential difference between our approach and neoclassical economics.

For a more general case with birth (growth) rate k and death (exit) rate R, the logistic equation has the general form

$$\frac{dn}{dt} = f(n) = kn(N - n) - Rn = kn(N^* - n) \tag{6d}$$

$$N^* = N - \frac{R}{k} \tag{6e}$$

Clearly, economic competition for market share is similar to biological competition for living niches, where the market extent can be described as the population limit or carrying capacity N.

In a decentralized market, the logistic equation can be applied to technology diffusion or information dynamics (see Griliches, 1957, and Bartholomew, 1982). In learning dynamics, n is the number of adopters of new technology or the size of the occupied market, $(N - n)$ is the number of potential adopters or the size of an unoccupied market, k is the learning rate and R is the removal rate. This perspective will be very useful later for the study of culture orientation and corporate strategy.

The logistic curve has a varying degree of dynamic economies of scale. The model has a dynamic increasing return for $f'' > 0$ when $0 < n < 0.5N^*$ and dynamic diminishing return for $f'' < 0$ when $n > 0.5N^*$. For a model of asymmetric growth, the reflection point may not be the middle point. In contrast, the production function in neoclassical microeconomics has fixed returns to scale. Therefore, the neoclassical theory of the firm is not capable of describing economies of scale and market share competition.

3.1.2   Two-species competition and the source of excess capacity

When there are two competing technologies, their market shares are characterized by their resource ceilings N_1 and N_2. The Lotka–Volterra competition equation in population dynamics can be applied to market share competition under conditions of limited resources (Pianka, 1983).

$$\frac{dn_1}{dt} = k_1 n_1 (N_1 - n_1 - \beta n_2) - R_1 n_1 \tag{7}$$

$$\frac{dn_2}{dt} = k_2 n_2 (N_2 - n_2 - \beta n_1) - R_2 n_2$$

where n_1 and n_2 are the population (or output) of species (technology or product) 1 and species 2; N_1 and N_2 their carrying capacity (or resource limit); k_1 and k_2 their growth (or learning) rate; and R_1 and R_2 their removal (or exit) rate; β is the overlapping (or competition) coefficient in resource competition ($0 \le \beta \le 1$). The equations can be simplified by introducing effective carrying capacities $C_i = N_i - \frac{R_i}{k_i}$. In this model, the essence of price competition is still in the form of market share competition, since either better quality or a lower price implies a larger market extent N_i.

When $\beta = 0$ there is no competition between the two species; both of them can grow to their market limit. A firm or industry without competition could realize its full capacity to occupy the designated market share C. Species 2 will replace species 1 under the following conditions. The winner may have a higher resource capacity, a faster learning rate or a lower death rate:

$$\beta \left(N_2 - \frac{R_2}{k_2} \right) = \beta C_2 > C_1 = \left(N_1 - \frac{R_1}{k_1} \right) \tag{8}$$

When $0 < \beta < 1$ the two species can coexist. However, the realized market share would decline for both species.

$$\beta < \frac{C_2}{C_1} < \frac{1}{\beta} \tag{9a}$$

$$n_1^* = \frac{C_1 - \beta C_2}{1 - \beta^2} < C_1 \tag{9b}$$

$$n_2^* = \frac{C_2 - \beta C_1}{1 - \beta^2} < C_2$$

$$\frac{1}{2}(C_1 + C_2) \le n_1^* + n_2^* = \frac{(C_1 + C)_2}{1 + \beta} \le (C_1 + C_2) \tag{9c}$$

From equation (9c) we find that excess capacity may increase by up to 50 per cent under symmetric technology competition. Excess

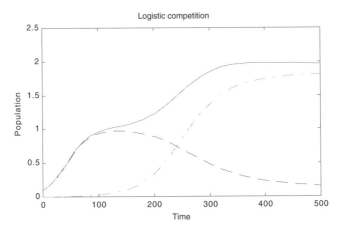

Figure 15.7 The staged economic growth characterized by the dynamic path of equation (7).
Note: The output envelope is the sum of the competing species; here, $\beta = 0.4$ and $C_2/C_1 = 2$ (the units here are arbitrary).

capacity could be even higher under asymmetric competition. Now we may solve the puzzle observed in section 2.2.2: why is the fluctuation in investment much larger than that in GDP and consumption? *The excess capacity is caused by the coexistence of old and new technology*, and is not just speculators' psychology (called the 'animal spirit' by John Maynard Keynes).

A striking fact is that the chronic excess capacity in US industry persists at a level of about 18 per cent, which is hard to understand through optimization theory (Hall, 1986). We may calculate β for two empirical cases. β is 0.22 for the 18 per cent excess capacity in the United States, and 0.52 for the 36 per cent excess capacity that China recorded in 1995. The excess capacity can be a measure of Schumpeter's 'creative destruction'.

3.1.3   The Lotka–Volterra wavelet and the stages of economic growth
A numerical solution to equation (7) is shown in figure 15.7. Without competition, the growth path of species 1 would be an S-curve. However, the realized output of technology 1 looks like an asymmetric bell curve. This feature represents a product cycle in marketing and management literature (see Moore, 1995). We call it the Lotka–Volterra (LV) wavelet, which is a result from the competition provided by technology 2. The envelope of the aggregate output has growth trends and cycles that

both mimic the pattern of a macroeconomic index. Now we can understand why persistent business cycles are well portrayed by time-frequency representation, since the asymmetric bell curve is close to the shape of a bell curve.

We may characterize industrial revolution as a higher resource ceiling or a larger market extent. Seemingly continuous growth can be decomposed into a sequence of staged growth or disruptive changes in technology advancement (see Rostow, 1990, and Christensen, 1997). The time scale of an LV wavelet varies from a product cycle of several months to a Kondratiev long wave of several decades, depending on the questions asked in history. Financial crises are often triggered by emerging technology and a subsequent bifurcation in investment choice.

3.2   The risk attitude and corporate culture in behavioural dynamics

In equilibrium finance theory, financial risk is characterized by the variance around the mean of returns; rational agents are defined by risk aversion behaviour. In our competition model, we introduce another kind of risk: the risk facing an unknown market or technology. This concept of learning by trying is inspired by Schumpeter's thinking on entrepreneurial spirit. Competing corporate cultures are characterized by their risk attitude in facing a challenge or opportunity.

3.2.1   Learning by trying: risk aversion versus risk-taking behaviour
The culture factor plays an important role in decision making and corporate strategy; there is great variety in the degree of 'individualism' or risk taking among different cultures. Both risk aversion and risk-taking strategies are observed when competing for an emerging market or new technology (figure 15.8). From this perspective, knowledge in old technology does come from learning by doing, which is an accumulation process in endogenous growth theory (Arrow, 1962). In a new market, knowledge comes from learning by trying, which is a trial and error process in evolutionary economics (Chen, 1987, 1993b).

When facing an unknown market or unproved technology, risk-averting investors often follow the crowd to minimize the risk, while risk-taking investors take the lead to maximize the opportunity. A critical question is: which corporate culture or market strategy can win or survive in conditions where technology is changing rapidly or in an evolving market?

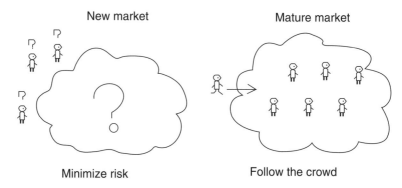

(a). Risk aversion behaviour.

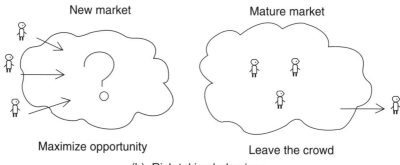

(b). Risk-taking behaviour.

Figure 15.8 Risk aversion and risk-taking behaviour in the competition for market share and technology advancement

The original logistic equation describes risk-neutral behaviour by assuming a constant removal rate. We introduce a non-linear removal rate as a function of the learner's population ratio and the behavioural parameter a (Chen, 1987).

$$R\left(r, a, \frac{n}{N}\right) = r\left(1 - a\frac{n}{N}\right) \qquad (10)$$

where $-1 < a < 1$.

We may consider the constant r as a measure of the learning ability, or degree of difficulty in studying a new technology.

The factor a is a measure of risk orientation. If $a > 0$ it is a measure of risk aversion or collectivism. When few people enter the new market, the exit rate is large. When more and more people accept the new technology, the exit rate declines. On the contrary, if $a < 0$ it is a measure of risk taking or individualism. When varying a from -1 to $+1$, we have a full spectrum of varying behaviour, from an extreme conservatist to an extreme adventurer.

3.2.2 Resource-saving and resource-consuming cultures

The equilibrium rate of resource utilization is

$$\frac{n^*}{N} = \frac{\left(1 - \dfrac{r}{Nk}\right)}{\left(1 - \dfrac{ra}{Nk}\right)} \tag{11a}$$

$$n^*_{a<0} < n^*_{a=0} < n^*_{a>0} \tag{11b}$$

The resource utilization rate of the conservative species $(n^*_{a>0})$ is higher than that of the individualist species $(n^*_{a<0})$. The individualist species needs a larger subsistence space than a conservative one in order to maintain the same equilibrium size n^*. Therefore, individualism is a resource-consuming culture, while collectivism is a resource-saving culture (Chen, 1991, 1993b).

This difference is clearly visible between Western individualism and the Oriental tradition. Cultural differences are rooted in economic structures and ecological constraints. Resource expansion is a key to understanding the origin of a capitalist economy and the Industrial Revolution (Pomeranz, 2000).

3.2.3 Market extent, resource variety and economies of scale and scope

In an ecological system with L species, resource capacities are N_1, $N_2, \ldots, N_L$. The economies of scope and scale can be described by a system of coupling logistic-type equations. Here, the market extent is represented by the resource capacity N, while the scope of economies is described by the number of species L. The division of labour can be characterized by the coexistence of competing technologies.

Let's start from the simplest case, with only two species with competing technologies and cultures (Chen, 1987).

$$\frac{dn_1}{dt} = k_1 n_1 (N_1 - n_1 - \beta n_2) - r_1 n_1 \left(1 - \frac{a_1 n_1}{N_1}\right) \tag{12}$$

$$\frac{dn_2}{dt} = k_2 n_2 (N_2 - n_2 - \beta n_1) - r_2 n_2 \left(1 - \frac{a_2 n_2}{N_2}\right)$$

Here, n_1 and n_2 are the new technology adopters in species 1 and species 2 respectively. We also take $\beta = 1$ for simplicity.

3.2.4   *The latecomer's opportunity and the entrepreneur's advantage*

We may solve equation (12) in the same way as in section 3.1.2. The replacement condition is

$$C_2 > \frac{\left(1 - \dfrac{a_2 r_2}{k_2 N_2}\right)}{\beta} C_1 \tag{13}$$

(for species 2 replace species 1). What will happen when an individualist species competes with a conservative one? If two species have equal resources ($N_1 = N_2$), then the conservative species will replace the individualist one. If we compare (13) with (8), a latecomer from a conservative culture has a better chance of beating on individualistic leader even if $C_2 \le C_1$ when $\beta \approx 1$ and $0 < a_2 \approx 1$. This is the story of how the Soviet Union and Japan caught up with the West in the 1950s and 1970s respectively. Conservative cultures can concentrate their resources in a 'catching up' game.

Therefore, the only survival strategy for an individualist species in competing with a conservative one is to explore a larger resource or learn more quickly. If we consider entrepreneurship as a risk-taking culture, then we may reach a similar conclusion to Schumpeter's: that creative destruction is vital for capitalism in the competition between socialism (collectivism) and capitalism (individualism). Once innovations fail to discover new and larger resources, the individualist species will lose the game to the conservative in the existing markets.

3.2.5   *Progressive culture and a pluralistic society*

Now, we examine the coexistence condition

$$\frac{\beta}{\left(1 - \dfrac{a_1 r_1}{k_1 N_1}\right)} < \frac{N_2 - \dfrac{r_2}{k_2}}{N_1 - \dfrac{r_1}{k_1}} < \frac{1}{\beta}\left(1 - \dfrac{a_2 r_2}{k_2 N_2}\right) \tag{14}$$

From this equation, it can be seen that two individualist species may coexist. Individualism is the root of diversity and democracy in the division of labour and capitalism. However, two conservative species cannot coexist; the only result is that one replaces the other.

This is the story of the peasant wars and dynastic cycles in Chinese history. Therefore, the division of labour cannot emerge in a conservative society – which is a theoretical answer to Needham's question (Chen, 1987, 1991).

3.2.6   *The culture dimension and the thermodynamics of evolution*

Max Weber identified the accumulation of capital as the essence of the Protestant and the capitalist culture; he also considered Confucianism to be the main barrier to the development of a market economy (Weber, 1930). I disagree. The rise of the 'Asian tigers' and the success of China's reform programme provide strong evidence that the Confucian culture, emphasizing family values, equal education and the encouragement of saving, may be a positive factor in developing a market economy. The key difference with China before and after 1979 is its open door policy, and the resultant access to the world market. This is the most important lesson the author learned from Ilya Prigogine's thermodynamics of evolution (Prigogine et al., 1972).

According to Prigogine, there are three types of order. Maximum entropy (disorder) in an isolated system is dictated by the second law of thermodynamics, where no structure exists; equilibrium structure (such as a crystal) can exist in a closed system, where energy is exchanged with the surroundings; non-equilibrium order can emerge only in open systems, where a dissipative structure is maintained by continuous energy flow, matter flow and information flow. Certainly, any living or economic system is an open system by nature. However, the essential pattern in social evolution depends on the degree of openness. The rise of the West is a clear history of resource expansion, first by geographic discovery of the New World, then by revolutions in science and technology. In contrast, China's involution was caused mainly by land limitation and technological stagnation (see Huang, 1985, and Chen, 1991, 1993b). China was able to reverse its involution after achieving access to modern technology and the world market.

3.2.7   The number of resources and the competition exclusion principle
From equation (9) we have the well-known 'competition exclusion principle' in theoretical biology, since complete competitors cannot coexist. It implies that the number of species should equal the number of resources.

However, the definition of species and division of resources is arbitrary (Pianka, 1983). There are similar problems with the theory of complete markets. In other words, the number of prices should be equal to the number of assets in market equilibrium models. Equilibrium in the asset market is defined by the absence of arbitrage opportunity, which implies linear pricing (Ross, 1976). In fact, non-linear pricing is widely observed in the form of volume discount, credit rationing and discriminative pricing, all of which are shaped by market uncertainty, information asymmetry and scale economy.

Our model overcomes this difficulty. According to equation (14), the outcomes of competition also depend on the behavioural factor a_i. Therefore, *the number of species may not be equal to the number of resources*. This may shed light on the mechanism of price differentiation.

3.3   The complexity puzzle and the Smith dilemma

There are conflicting perspectives on the convergence or divergence issues in the division of labour. The neoclassical school believes in market convergence, based on optimization and rationality (see Yang and Borland, 1991, and Becker and Murphy, 1992). The division of labour could be a divergent process with bifurcation and uncertainty, where multi-humped distributions and path dependence are rooted in non-linear interactions (see Chen, 1987, 1992, and Arthur, 1994).

Interestingly, the Smith dilemma in classical economics is related to the complexity puzzle in theoretical ecology and the science of complexity. The question is whether or not increasing complexity is associated with increasing stability. Some biologists believe the correlation is positive. The doctrine of 'the survival of the fittest' seems to imply that the fittest must be stable. However, mathematical simulations produced negative correlations. We call this a complexity puzzle (see May, 1974, and Chen, 1987).

Contrary to the belief of some biologists and many economists, I suggest that evolution from simplicity to complexity does decrease a system's stability, but that it also increases the potential for further development. We call the negative correlation the *trade-off theory between stability and complexity*, or *the trade-off between security and opportunity*. This trade-off provides a clue to solving the Smith dilemma. We shall now discuss system stability under environmental shocks.

3.3.1   Monolithic society and stability under environmental shocks
Let us start from a single species. By means of the Langevin equation and the Fokker–Planck equation, we may consider a stream of random shocks adding to the carrying capacity (market extent) N. The realized equilibrium size X_m is reduced by a fluctuating environment, which is described by the variance of shocks:

$$X_m = N\frac{\left(1 - \dfrac{r}{kN} - \dfrac{k\sigma^2}{2N}\right)}{\left(1 - \dfrac{ra}{kN}\right)} \quad \text{when } \sigma < \sigma_c = \sqrt{\frac{2N}{k}\left(1 - \frac{r}{kN}\right)} \tag{15a}$$

$$X_m = 0 \quad \text{when } \sigma > \sigma_c = \sqrt{\frac{2N}{k}\left(1 - \frac{r}{kN}\right)} \tag{15b}$$

If there exists some survival threshold in population size, then the conservative species has a better chance of surviving under external shocks because of its larger population size. Obviously, the World Trade

Center in New York was intrinsically more vulnerable to being bombed than a village in Vietnam.

3.3.2   The trade-off between stability and complexity and a two-way evolution of the division of labour

The Fokker–Planck equation corresponding to (12) can be solved numerically. Let us consider an environmental fluctuation imposed to the carrying capacity, and study its stability condition (May, 1974). The main results are the following.

First, environmental fluctuations will further reduce the size of the equilibrium state. Second, the system's stability will decrease as competition between species increases.

Third, if we compare two systems, one is the mixed system with one conservative species and one individualist species, while the other is the liberal system with two individualistic species; then the stability of the mixed system will be greater than that of the liberal system (Chen, 1987). This result is seen in practice when we compare the two-party system in the Anglo-Saxon countries with the multi-party system in Continental Europe.

Finally, we can see that the division of labour is a two-way evolutionary process. When environmental fluctuation is within the boundary of the stability condition, the system with more species can survive; when fluctuation is beyond the stability threshold, a complex system may break down into a simpler system with fewer elements. This conclusion is dramatically different from the optimization model of the division of labour (Yang and Borland, 1991).

3.3.3   The generalized Smith theorem: the division of labour is limited by the market extent, resource variety and environmental fluctuations

From the above discussions, we gain a new understanding of corporate structure and comparative advantage in a changing environment. The Smith dilemma indicates a problem since small competitive firms and large monopoly corporations cannot coexist within the framework of equilibrium economics (see Stigler, 1951). This is not a problem in evolutionary economics because of the trade-off between stability and complexity.

I propose *a generalized Smith theorem* in order to integrate the new findings from evolutionary dynamics: *the division of labour is limited by the market extent, resource variety and environmental fluctuations*. Its applications are discussed below.

Based on the generalized Smith theorem, we can easily explain the rise and fall of great civilizations. Imperial China lasted for more than two thousand years, which was much longer than either the Roman Empire or the Byzantine Empire. Its structural stability was rooted in self-sufficient grain-based agriculture, with an underdeveloped division of labour. This system was influenced by severe ecological constraints, cyclic disasters and large-scale peasant wars. On the other hand, the origin of the division of labour and capitalism lay in the resource expansion and moderate fluctuations in the natural and social environment in Western Europe. China's involution towards self-sufficiency was shaped by intensive agriculture under resource limits and a severe environment. For example, from the third century BC to the nineteenth century there were thirteen periods of large-scale warfare resulting in a population reduction of more than one-third of the Chinese population, but Western Europe faced this type of turbulence only once, in the Black Death. The frequency and intensity of ecological crises in China were also much higher than those in Western Europe. The bifurcation point occurred sometime between the thirteenth and fifteenth centuries, when the Black Death acted as a catalyst for labour-saving innovations and the spice trade stimulated geographical discovery and the emergence of a global market. This scenario is a historical answer to Needham's question (Chen, 1991).

Some puzzles characterizing transition economies can also be understood from the perspective of complex systems. The collapse of the Soviet economy and success in China's reform are two polar cases in transition economies. An extreme international division of labour characterized the Soviet economy, with little redundancy or competition. Once a single link in the economic chain was damaged, the entire system in Eastern Europe broke down. In contrast, China's self-sufficiency policy in the era of Mao Zedong created many potential competitors in regional economies. When China's open door policy broke the regional protectionism, local firms had to compete in a national and global market. The existence of competing firms is the precondition for a successful programme of market liberalization. Sufficient redundancy in a complex system is necessary for its structural stability – a valuable lesson for Eastern Europe.

Based on the trade-off between stability and complexity, we have also gained a new understanding regarding the causes of mergers and break-ups. Increasing efficiency and market power are often considered to be the two main reasons for merger activities in the theory of industrial organization (Carlton and Perloff, 1994). A third cause of merger or sell-off waves can now be offered, based on the trade-off between opportunity and stability. Merger waves generally appear during an economic upturn and end when confronted with a downturn; conversely, corporate restructuring and sell-offs often arise during an economic downturn because large firms are rigid and slow in adapting to technological changes (Weston et al., 1998).

4   Conclusion: understanding market resilience and economic complexity

Equilibrium economics has not developed a consistent framework of economic dynamics. Microeconomics is a static theory, where there is no room for the product cycle, market share competition, strategic innovation and over-investment. Macroeconomic modelling is dominated by a linear stationary model of the representative agent, which cannot explain the persistent nature of business cycles. The critical issues of non-integrable systems and continuous time are ignored by the regression approach in econometrics.

Based on non-linear dynamic models of business cycles and the division of labour, I am developing a biological framework of evolutionary economic dynamics. Starting from the empirical analysis of macroeconomic time series, there is abundant evidence about the endogenous nature of macroeconomic fluctuations. Based on this theoretical study, the birth–death process is a better alternative than Brownian motion in the first approximation of stochastic growth (Zeng, 2004). Persistent cycles around the HP trend can be further refined by the deterministic model of colour chaos in the soft-bouncing oscillator. Product cycles and excess capacity result from market share competition.

From the biological perspective, business cycles are living rhythms with structural stability and dynamic resilience. Product cycles and business cycles fall in the same time scale, ranging from several months or several years to decades; examples are short cycles in computer software and long cycles in railway construction. Disruptive technology changes are the driving force behind persistent business cycles. This perspective will fundamentally change our views on economic systems and government policies. Compared to the Fourier (plane wave) transform and pulse (noise) representation, the Gabor wavelet representation (or coherent state in quantum mechanics) provides a better mathematical representation of evolutionary ecology and economic dynamics. (The development of economic physics will be discussed elsewhere.) The differences between the equilibrium-mechanical approach and the evolution-biological approach are summarized in table 15.3.

From the above discussion, we can see that these two approaches are complementary to each other to some degree. However, the mechanical approach can be considered a special situation within the more general framework of a biological approach, since a conservative system is a special case of an open system.

In macro-issues, the evolutionary approach can be a synthesis of conflicting linear theories. For example, the new classical school and the Keynesian school can be integrated into a general macro-dynamics

Table 15.3 *Concepts and representations in the mechanical and biological approaches*

Subject	Mechanical	Biological
Micro	Factor cost, marginal pricing	Product cycle, market share competition
Macro	Stability and convergence	Uneven growth and persistent cycles
Mathematics	Static optimization	Non-linear dynamics
Micro-foundations	One body (representative)	Many body problem
Test	Regression, forecasting	Natural & laboratory experiments
History	Ergotic (no memory)	Path dependence
Information	Perfect/imperfect information	Complexity, ambiguity
Decisions	Individual rationality	Social learning
Risk	Risk aversion	Risk taking/risk aversion
Strategy	Maximizing profit	Balancing opportunity/risk
Variable	Relative price	Market share
Order	Balancing demand/supply	Technology competition
Technology	Fixed parameter	S-curve
Innovation	Random shocks	Disruptive stages
Pricing	Price taker (perfect market) Price setter (monopolistic)	Strategic pricing Profit margin and growth space
Division of labour	Different commodities	Coexistence of technologies
Business cycles	External shocks	Endogenous cycles
Growth	Brownian motion	Birth–death and wavelets
Trend reference	FD, LL, HP	HP
Fluctuations	Linear cycles + white noise	Non-linear colour chaos + white/fractal noise

Prediction	Mechanical	Biological
Prices	Convergence	Differentiation
Development	Convergence (Solow) Learning by doing	Rise and fall of organizations Learning by trying
Macro-fluctuations	Labour choice (Lucas) Technology shocks (RBC) Money shocks (Friedman) Labor rigidity (Keynes)	Industrial competition Birth and death of technologies Excess capacity and overinvestment Structural and financial changes
Institution	Transaction costs, coordination costs	Trade-off between stability and complexity
Socio-evolution	Convergence	Bifurcations in evolutionary tree
Policies	Laissez-faire (classical)	Regulations and standards
Governments	Demand-side policies	Supply-side policies
Institutions	Property rights	Rule of innovations

including different time scales: the new classical school mainly on the long run, Keynesians on the medium term, and financial economists on the short run. In our decomposition of macro-indexes, the long run is the non-linear (HP) smooth trend, the medium run is persistent cycles around the trend, and the short run is residual noise imposed on persistent cycles.

In micro-issues, the evolutionary approach may establish a link between cost analysis on the demand side and market share analysis on the supply side. Empirical observations of product cycles and marketing strategies in business research may provide a solid foundation for microdynamics.

In these discussions, 'dissipative structure' and 'self-organization' mean a higher kind of order in living systems, such as living rhythms, metabolism and complex systems. The classical concepts of equilibrium and entropy describe only the orderless state without differentiated structure. If we compare self-organization in complexity science with the equilibrium order shaped by 'friction' or 'rigidity' in equilibrium economics (Coase, 1960), you may appreciate our new concepts of *market resilience* and *persistent cycles*. The central concept in cybernetics and economic science is 'stability' under 'negative feedback' (see Wiener, 1953). We propose the terms '*complexity*' and '*resilience*' to combine the two aspects within living systems and social systems: *stability* under small external shocks and *viability* under large environmental changes. Both features can be observed from parametric space in complex dynamics and stable regimes of time rhythms in Wigner–Gabor–Qian representation.

The proposed trade-off theory between stability and complexity and the generalized Smith theorem may address a wide range of phenomena in living and social systems. I believe that economic science is facing a great transition from equilibrium thinking to an evolutionary paradigm. The efficacy of this approach to economic dynamics is open to future research and experiments.

Finally, I would like to quote James Buchanan regarding his prediction on the future of economics (1991).

The shift toward emergent order as a central perspective will be paralleled by a corollary, even if not necessary, reduction of emphasis on equilibrium models. The properties of systems in dynamic disequilibrium will come to centre stage, and especially as economics incorporates influences of the post-Prigogine developments in the theory of self-organizing systems of spontaneous order, developments that can be integrated much more easily into the catallactic than into the maximizing perspective . . .

Acknowledgements

I would like to thank William Barnett, Siwei Cheng, Alex Chien, Gregory Chow, Partha Dasgupta, Richard Day, John Doggett, Kurt Dopfer, Fukang Fang, Martin Feldstein, Duncan Foley, James Galbraith, Liutang Gong, Philip Huang, Tehming Huo, David Kendrick, Finn Kydland, Justin Lin, Leigh McAlister, Douglass North, Qi Ouyang, Xinqino Ping, Shie Qian, Andrew Reati, Linda Reichl, J. Barkley Rosser, Jr., Willi Semmler, Charlotte Shelton, Jianhuai Shi, George Soros, Binghong Wang, Duo Wang, John Warfield, Ulrich Witt, Michael Woodford and Victor Zarnowitz for their stimulating discussions. Financial support from the National Science Foundation of China under the grant of 79970118 and the George Soros Foundation is also acknowledged.

REFERENCES

Arrow, K. J. (1962), 'The economic implications of learning by doing', *Review of Economic Studies* 29: 155–73.

Arthur, W. B. (1994), *Increasing Returns and Path Dependence in the Economy,* Ann Arbor, MI: University of Michigan Press.

Barnett, W. A., and P. Chen (1988), 'The aggregation-theoretic monetary aggregates are chaotic and have strange attractors: an econometric application of mathematical chaos', in W. A. Barnett, E. Berndt and H. White (eds.), *Dynamic Economic Modeling*, Cambridge: Cambridge University Press, 199–246.

Bartholomew, D. J. (1982), *Stochastic Models for Social Processes*, 3rd edn., New York: Wiley.

Becker, G. S., and K. M. Murphy (1992), 'The division of labor, coordination costs, and knowledge', *Quarterly Journal of Economics* 107(4): 1137–60.

Benhabib, J. (1992), *Cycle and Chaos in Economic Equilibrium*, Princeton, NJ: Princeton University Press.

Black, F., and M. Scholes (1973), 'The pricing of options and corporate liabilities', *Journal of Political Economy* 81(3): 637–54.

Brock, W. A., and C. Sayers (1988), 'Is the business cycle characterized by deterministic chaos?', *Journal of Monetary Economics* 22: 71–80.

Brush, S. G. (1983), *Statistical Physics and the Atomic Theory of Matter from Boyle and Newton to Landau and Onsager*, Princeton, NJ: Princeton University Press.

Buchanan, J. M. (1991), 'Economics in the post-socialist century', *Economic Journal* 404: 15–21.

Carlton, D. W., and J. M. Perloff (1994), *Industrial Organization*, 2nd edn., New York: HarperCollins.

Chen, P. (1987), 'Origin of division of labour and a stochastic mechanism of differentiability', *European Journal of Operation Research* 30: 246–50.

(1988), 'Empirical and theoretical evidence of monetary chaos', *System Dynamics Review* 4: 81–108.

(1991), 'Needham's question and China's evolution: cases of nonequilibrium social transition', in G. P. Scott (ed.), *Time, Rhythms, and Chaos in the New Dialogue with Nature*, Ames, IA: Iowa State University Press, 177–98.

(1992), 'Imitation, learning, and communication: central or polarized patterns in collective actions', in A. Babloyantz (ed.), *Self-Organization, Emerging Properties and Learning*, New York: Plenum, 279–86.

(1993a), 'Searching for economic chaos: a challenge to econometric practice and nonlinear tests', in R. H. Day and P. Chen (eds.), *Nonlinear Dynamics and Evolutionary Economics*, Cambridge: Cambridge University Press, 217–53.

(1993b), 'China's challenge to economic orthodoxy: Asian reform as an evolutionary, self-organizing process', *China Economic Review* **4**: 137–42.

(1996a), 'Trends, shocks, persistent cycles in evolving economy: business cycle measurement in time-frequency representation', in W. A. Barnett, A. P. Kirman and M. Salmon (eds.), *Nonlinear Dynamics and Economics*, Cambridge: Cambridge University Press, 307–31.

(1996b), 'Random walk or color chaos on the stock market? Time-frequency analysis of S&P indexes', *Nonlinear Dynamics & Econometrics* **1**(2): 87–103.

(1999), *The Frisch Model of Business Cycles – A Spurious Doctrine, but a Mysterious Success*, Working Paper no. E1999–007, China Center for Economic Research, Peking University, Beijing.

(2001), *The Nature of Persistent Business Cycles: Random Shocks, Microfoundations, or Color Chaos?*, paper presented at the American Economic Association meeting's session on economic complexity, New Orleans, 7 January.

(2002), 'Microfoundations of macroeconomic fluctuations and the laws of probability theory: the principle of large numbers vs. rational expectations arbitrage', *Journal of Economic Behavior & Organization* **49**: 327–44.

Christensen, C. M. (1997), *The Innovator's Dilemma: When New Technologies Cause Great Firms to Fail*, Boston: Harvard Business School Press.

Coase, R. H. (1960), 'The problem of social cost', *Journal of Law and Economics* **3**(1): 1–44.

DeLong, J. B., A. Shleifer, L. H. Summers and R. J. Waldmann (1990), 'Positive feedback investment strategies and destabilizing rational speculation', *Journal of Finance* **45**(2): 379–95.

Friedman, M. (1953), 'The case of flexible exchange rates', in M. Friedman, *Essays in Positive Economics*, Chicago: University of Chicago Press, 157–203.

Frisch, R. (1933), 'Propagation problems and impulse problems in dynamic economics', in K. Koch (ed.), *Economic Essays in Honour of Gustav Cassel*, London: Cass, 171–206.

(1981), 'From Utopian theory to practical applications: the case of econometrics', *American Economic Review* **71**(6): 1–16.

Goodwin, R. M. (1951), 'The non-linear accelerator and the persistence of business cycles', *Econometrica* **19**: 1–17.

Griliches, Z. (1957), 'Hybrid corn: an exploration in the economics of technological change', *Econometrica* **25**(4): 501–22.

Grossman, S., and J. Stiglitz (1980), 'On the impossibility of informationally efficient markets', *American Economic Review* **70**(3): 393–408.

Hall, R. E. (1986), *Chronic Excess Capacity in U.S. Industry*, Working Paper Series no. 1973, National Bureau of Economic Research, Cambridge, MA.

Hodrick, R. J., and E. C. Prescott (1981), *Post-War US Business Cycles: An Empirical Investigation*, Discussion Paper no. 451, Carnegie Mellon University, Pittsburgh.

Houthakker, H. S. (1956), 'Economics and biology: specialization and speciation', *Kyklos* **9**(2): 181–89.

Huang, P. C. C. (1985), *The Peasent Economy and Social Change in North China*, Stanford, CA: Stanford University Press.

Leontief, W. W. (1936), 'The fundamental assumption of Mr Keynes' monetary theory of unemployment', *Quarterly Journal of Economics* **51**: 192–97.

Li, H. J. (2002), *Which Stochastic Process Has Better Description of Micro-foundations of Macroeconomic Fluctuations?*, thesis, Department of Mathematical Finance, Peking University, Beijing.

Lucas, R. E. (1972), 'Expectations and the neutrality of money', *Journal of Economic Theory* **4**: 103–24.

(1981), *Studies in Business-Cycle Theory*, Cambridge, MA: MIT Press.

Marshall, A. (1890), *Principles of Economics*, London: Macmillan (8th edn., 1920, London: Macmillan; 9th variorum edn., 1961, London: Macmillan).

May, R. M. (1974), *Stability and Complexity in Model Ecosystems*, Princeton, NJ: Princeton University Press.

Moore, G. A. (1995), *Inside the Tornado: Marketing Strategies from Silicon Valley's Cutting Edge*, New York: HarperBusiness.

Nagle, T. T., and R. K. Holden (1995), *The Strategy and Tactics of Pricing: A Guide to Profitable Decision Making*, Englewood Cliffs, NJ: Prentice-Hall.

Needham, J. (1954), *Science and Civilization in China*, vol. I, Cambridge: Cambridge University Press.

Nelson, C. R., and C. I. Plosser (1982), 'Trends and random walks in macroeconomic time series: some evidence and implications', *Journal of Monetary Economics* **1**: 139–62.

Pianka, E. R. (1983), *Evolutionary Ecology*, 3rd edn., New York: Harper & Row.

Pomeranz, K. (2000), *The Great Divergence: Europe, China, and the Making of the Modern World Economy*, Princeton, NJ: Princeton University Press.

Porter, M. E. (1980), *Competitive Strategy, Techniques for Analyzing Industries and Competitors*, New York: Free Press.

Prigogine, I., G. Nicolis and A. Babloyantz (1972), 'Thermodynamics of evolution', *Physics Today* **25**(11): 23–28; **25**(12): 38–44.

Qian, S., and D. Chen (1996), *Introduction to Joint Time-Frequency Analysis*, Englewood Cliffs, NJ: Prentice-Hall.

Ross, S. (1976), 'Return, risk, and arbitrage', in I. Friend and J. Bicksler (eds.), *Risk and Return in Finance*, Cambridge, MA: Ballinger, 189–218.

Rostow, W. W. (1990), *The Stages of Economic Growth*, 3rd edn., Oxford: Oxford University Press.

Samuelson, P. A. (1939), 'Interactions between the multiplier analysis and the principle of acceleration', *Review of Economic Statistics* **21**: 75–78.

Schumpeter, J. A. (1939), *Business Cycles: A Theoretical, Historical, and Statistical Analysis of the Capitalist Process*, New York: McGraw-Hill.

Simon, H. (1957), *Models of Man*, New York: Wiley.

Smith, A. (1776), *The Wealth of Nations*, reprinted 1981, Indianapolis: Liberty Classics.

Solow, R. (1956), 'A contribution to the theory of economic growth', *Quarterly Journal of Economics* **70**(1): 65–94.

Stigler, G. J. (1951), 'The division of labor is limited by the extent of the market', *Journal of Political Economy* **59**(3): 185–93.

Uhlenbeck, G. E., and L. S. Ornstein (1930), 'On the theory of Brownian motion', *Physical Review* **36**(3): 823–41.

Weber, M. (1930), *The Protestant Ethic and the Spirit of Capitalism*, London: Allen & Unwin.

Weston, J. F., K. S. Chung and J. A. Siu (1998), *Takeovers, Restructuring, and Corporate Governance*, Englewood Cliffs, NJ: Prentice-Hall.

Wiener, N. (1953), *Cybernetics*, New York: The Technology Press of MIT and Wiley.

Yang, X., and J. Borland (1991), 'A microeconomic mechanism for economic growth', *Journal of Political Economy* **99**(3): 460–82.

Zeng, W. (2004), *Stock Price Fluctuations are Characterized by the Geometric Brownian Motion or the Birth-Death Process?*, thesis, Department of Financial Mathematics, Peking University, Beijing.

Zhang, H. (2003), *Biological Behavior in Firm Competition*, student research note, China Center for Economic Reasearch, Peking University, Beijng.

16   Evolutionary theorizing on economic growth

Gerald Silverberg
Bart Verspagen

1   Introduction

While an evolutionary perspective has been urged upon economists since
at least the time of Alfred Marshall (1890; see Hodgson, 1993, for a contemporary reiteration), what has been lacking until recently, at least for
a large portion of the economics profession, has been a body of formal
theory and quantitative analysis on an explicitly evolutionary basis. This
has changed since the work of Richard Nelson and Sidney Winter in
the 1960s and 1970s (summarized in Nelson and Winter, 1982), which
operationalized and extended many of the concepts going back to Joseph
Schumpeter (1934, 1942), Armen Alchian (1950), Jack Downie (1955),
Josef Steindl (1952) and others. Since then a number of authors have
been enlarging on this foundation and systematically extending the evolutionary economics paradigm in a number of directions. A survey of
some of these can be found in Nelson, 1995.

In this chapter we intend to deal with the basics of a formal evolutionary approach to technical change, economic dynamics and growth.
In so doing we will leave out for the most part the burgeoning new areas
of application of evolutionary ideas to game theory, learning dynamics
and bounded rationality, organization theory, financial markets, industrial organization and the interface between economics, law and culture –
most of which are dealt with elsewhere in this volume. Instead, we will
concentrate on a restricted class of interrelated models of growth and
dynamics to see whether a viable alternative paradigm to the mainstream,
neoclassical approach, as well as a new class of insights, is emerging.

There are essentially two reasons for believing that an evolutionary
approach is applicable to economics. One is based on analogy and an
appeal to the type of explanation common in biology: that forms of competition, innovation, variation and selection have analogues in the two
subjects, and thus that similar reasoning can profitably be applied in the
non-biological domain. Here most authors stress that the analogy should
not be taken too seriously, and that it is useless to search for whatever

corresponds exactly to genes, sexual reproduction, crossover or mutation in the economic sphere. Moreover, discredited forms of evolution such as Lamarckianism (the inheritance of acquired characteristics) may be perfectly conceivable in the socio-economic realm.

The second reason takes a more universalistic perspective. It argues that, just as biological evolution has passed through distinct stages (prokaryotic and eukaryotic life, asexual and sexual reproduction, as well as a prebiotic stage), so modern industrial society is just a distinct stage of this single process, subject to the same underlying laws even if constrained by specific features of its current realization. Thus economic evolution would be an intrinsic component of a larger evolutionary process, and not merely something accidentally amenable to certain forms of reasoning by analogy.

What reasons might we have to believe this? Alfred Lotka (1924) proposed the concept of 'energy transformers' to capture the common thermodynamic features of all life forms. This is quite similar to what were later termed 'dissipative systems' (see Nicolis and Prigogine, 1977) – i.e. thermodynamically open systems, far from equilibrium, that maintain a high state of internal organization by importing free energy from their environment, consuming it for the purposes of self-repair and self-reproduction, and exporting the resulting waste as high entropy back to the environment. Thus the apparent paradox of life, already pointed out by Henry Adams (1919), of complex structure emergence in the face of the second law of thermodynamics (that in thermodynamically closed systems entropy – i.e. disorder – must increase) is transcended.[1] Life (or, at least, carbon-based life as we have known it until the Industrial Revolution) can be seen as a sea of such 'converters' living off the waterfall of free energy flowing between the sun and the low-value infrared radiation reflected by the earth into deep space.[2]

---

[1] The observation that open systems (in particular, organisms) can seemingly circumvent the second law of thermodynamics by exporting entropy to the environment (or, equivalently, importing 'negentropy' or free energy – i.e. energy of a higher 'quality' than the ambient heat, which can be converted to mechanical work) goes back at least to Ludwig von Bertalanffy (1932) and Erwin Schrödinger (1945).

[2] Thus Rainer Feistel and Werner Ebeling (1989, p. 91) observe: 'Summarizing we may say that self-organization is necessarily connected with the possibility to export entropy to the external world. In other words, self-organizing systems need an input of high-valued energy and at the same time an output of low-valued energy. In the interior of self-organizing systems a depot of high-valued energy of another form is observed. The evolution processes on our planet are mainly pumped by the "photon mill" with the three levels sun-earth-background radiation (let us mention, however, that the geological processes are pumped by the temperature gradients between the centre of the earth and the surface). On the cosmic scale the general strategy of evolution is the formation of islands of order on a sea of disorder represented by the background radiation.'

From this perspective human civilization is distinguished from earlier forms of biological evolution by the fact that the information carriers of the self-organizing structures, rather than being encoded in a form such as DNA that is internal to the organism, have now attained an *exosomatic*[3] (Lotka, 1945) form. Information is encoded both in an intangible sphere existing between human minds, known as culture, and a more tangible sphere consisting of writing and other forms of representation, and cultural and industrial artefacts. But the fact remains that, within the constraints imposed by the various physical substrates of information storage and transmission, evolution must still proceed along the basic Darwinian lines of (random) variation and selection. The complication associated with modern socio-economic evolution is that we now have to deal with a mosaic of simultaneous biological (DNA), culturally tacit (existing in the human pyschomotoric systems of individuals and groups) and culturally codifiable (existing in exosomatic artefacts) information transmission and variation mechanisms, the latter category being increasingly machine based.

The task of an evolutionary theory of economic growth, then, might be to formulate a population dynamics of this multi-level evolutionary process, taking account both of the human components and of the increasingly sophisticated forms of artefactual energy and information transformers collectively referred to by economists in a rather undifferentiated manner as 'capital'[4]. But, even, if we agree that this more fundamental perspective on economics as an integral part of the evolutionary process has a certain validity, the 'genetic code' of the various non-DNA-based levels remains to be discovered. Even in biology, in fact, where a firm understanding of the molecular basis of genetics has emerged since the 1950s, many extreme simplifications of a phenomenological sort still have to be made in formal models of population genetics and evolution[5]. Thus, from a practical point of view, it may not make much difference whether we apply evolutionary thinking to economics as an exercise in restrained analogizing or regard the economics of human societies as a specific stage

---

[3] There is, of course, another level of *endosomatic* information processing based on the neuronal system of animals, which Gerald Edelman (1987) hypothesizes to function according to neuronal group selection. This allows organisms to learn from experience during their lifetimes; i.e. it is a type of acquired characteristic with clear survival value. However, until the advent of language and culture, which permit *intergenerational* transmission, the neuronal system in itself cannot serve as a basis for long-term evolution but must still rely on the DNA substrate to generate further development.

[4] This is the theme of Kenneth Boulding (1978) – without the author proceeding very far down the road of formal modelling, however.

[5] Thus one often assumes asexual rather than sexual reproduction so as to simplify the mathematics.

in a universal evolutionary process, until such time as canonical descriptions of the 'genetic deep structure' of socio-industrial processes can be agreed upon[6]. For the time being we will have to make do with more or less plausible and heroic assumptions about the entities and the variation and transmission mechanisms implicated in economic evolution, and judge them on the basis of a limited range of micro- and macroeconomic 'stylized facts'.

2   Behavioural foundations and formal evolutionary modelling in the economics of growth and Schumpeterian competition: selection

The formalization of evolutionary thinking in biology began with R. A. Fisher (1930), who introduced what are now called '*replicator equations*'[7] to capture Darwin's notion of the survival of the fittest. If we consider a population to be composed of n distinct competing 'species' with associated, possibly frequency-dependent, fitnesses $f_i(x)$, where x is the vector of relative frequencies of the species $(x_1, x_2, \ldots, x_n)$, then their evolution might be described by the following.

$$\dot{x}_i = x_i(f_i(x) - \overline{f}(x)), i = 1, n, \quad \text{with } \overline{f}(x) = \sum_{i=1}^{n} x_i \, f_i(x)$$

The intuition is simple: species with above-average fitness will expand in relative importance, those with below-average fitness will contract, while the average fitness $\overline{f}(x)$ in turn changes with the relative population weights. If the fitness functions f_i are simple constants, then it can be shown that the species with the highest fitness will displace all the others and that average fitness will increase monotonically until uniformity is achieved according to

$$\frac{d\overline{f}}{dt} = \text{var}(f) \geq O$$

where $\text{var}(f)$ is the frequency-weighted variance of population fitness. Thus, average fitness is dynamically maximized by the evolutionary process (mathematically, it is referred to as a Lyapunov function). This is known as Fisher's fundamental theorem of natural selection, but it should

---

[6] One difference, however, is the central importance placed upon energetic and environmental constraints associated with the latter perspective. These, for better or worse, will not play any explicit role in the following discussion.
[7] See Sigmund (1986) and Hofbauer and Sigmund (1988, pp. 145–46) for a discussion of their basic form and various applications.

be noted that it is valid only for *constant* fitness functions. In the event of frequency-dependent selection, where fitness depends on population shares, including a species' own share, and increasing and decreasing 'returns' may intermingle, multiple equilibria are possible and no quantity is a priori necessarily being maximized (see Ebeling and Feistel, 1982, for an extensive discussion of maximal principles). The replicator equation describes only the relative share dynamics and thus takes place on the unit simplex S^n (where $\sum_{i=1}^{n} x_i = 1$), an $n - 1$ dimensional space. To derive the absolute populations it is necessary to introduce an additional equation for the total population level. An alternative description due to Lotka and Vito Volterra is based on growth equations for the population levels y_i (with the frequently used log-linear version on the right-hand side):

$$\dot{y}_i = g_i(y) = r_i y_i + \sum_{j=1}^{n} a_{ij} y_i y_j$$

A theorem due to Josef Hofbauer asserts that Lotka–Volterra and replicator systems are equivalent (see Hofbauer and Sigmund, 1988, p. 135).

Most evolutionary economics models to a considerable extent consist of giving the functions f_i or g_i economic meaning in terms of market competition or differential profit-rate-driven selection mechanisms. The former usually defines a variable representing *product competitiveness*, which may be a combination of price, quality, delivery delays, advertising and other variables (for examples, see Silverberg et al., 1988, or Kwasnicki and Kwasnicka, 1992). The latter assumes that product quality and price are homogeneous between producers (or subject to fast-equilibriating dynamics compared to the evolutionary processes of interest) but that unit costs of production differ, so firms realize differential profit rates. If their growth rates are related to profits, as seems reasonable, then their market shares or production levels (corresponding to x_i and y_i in the biological models) can be described by replicator or Lotka–Volterra equations, respectively.

All the models we will discuss in this chapter focus primarily on technical change as the central driving element of the evolutionary processes with which they are concerned. They differ considerably, however, in their representations of technology and how it interfaces with firm strategies and the market. A major distinguishing characteristic is whether technology is *capital-embodied* or *-disembodied* – i.e. whether changes in technological performance are primarily (though not necessarily exclusively) related to investment in new equipment or not. In the former case technical change is highly constrained by investment in physical capital (as well as possible complementary factors); in the latter case it is not, and can be almost costless. Yet, even on the assumption of embodied technical change, there can be important differences in formal treatments. The classical approach to embodied technical change uses the *vintage* concept going back to Wilfred Salter (1960), Robert Solow (1960) and Nicholas Kaldor and James Mirrlees (1962), as in essence do national statistical offices with the perpetual inventory approach to the measurement of the capital stock. One assumes that at any given time there is a single best-practice technology, in which investment is made. The capital stock then consists of the vintages of past investment going back in time until the scrapping margin – i.e. that oldest vintage on the verge of being discarded due to technological obsolescence and/or wear and tear. This defines the technological lifetime of capital equipment[8]. The aggregate capital stock is a sum or integral (in the discrete- and continuous-time cases respectively) over the vintages during this lifetime, and average technical coefficients (labour productivity and capital/output ratios) are the corresponding vintage-weighted sums or integrals.

Vintage capital stock levels may be easy to compute from data but they have two disadvantages, which detract from their realism and tractability. First is the assumption of a single best-practice technology, which rules out multiple competing technologies at the investment frontier – a topic dear to the hearts of most evolutionary economists and students of innovation diffusion. This can be overcome to some extent by assuming multiple, parallel vintage structures of distinct technologies, as in Silverberg et al., 1988. The second is that, although particularly discrete-time vintage capital stocks can be easily calculated from data, when they are embedded in a dynamic framework with endogenous scrapping they can lead to awkward mathematical complications. Delay difference or differential equations and even age-structured population dynamics become involved, the mathematical properties of which, except under extremely simple assumptions, are still poorly understood compared to systems of ordinary difference or differential equations.

An alternative implicitly exploited in the models of J. Stanley Metcalfe (1988), Katsuhito Iwai (1984a, 1984b), Gennadi Henkin and Victor Polterovich (1991), Gerald Silverberg and Doris Lehnert (1993, 1996) and Silverberg and Bart Verspagen (1994a, 1994b, 1995, 1996) might be termed a '*quasi-vintage*' framework. Capital 'vintages' are labelled by their type instead of their date of acquisition, so the service age no

---

[8] Except for the case in which capital is assumed to decay exponentially according to some presumed depreciation rate, in which case its lifetime is infinite, although older vintages rapidly become insignificant.

longer plays any role, only the technical characteristics (although decay by type independently of age is still possible). Thus several qualitatively distinct technologies can diffuse simultaneously into and out of the capital stock. Furthermore, only ordinary differential (or difference) equations are needed to handle the quasi-vintage structure – a considerable mathematical simplification. This gain in realism and tractability is compensated for by an inability to track the vintages by chronological age, however. But quasi-vintages lend themselves more naturally to the kind of multiple replacement dynamics investigated by Cesare Marchetti and Nebojsa Nakicenovic (1979), Nakicenovic (1987) and Arnulf Grübler (1990). And one view on evolution holds that its essence resides exactly in the sequence of such replacements (Montroll, 1978), whether related to technologies, behavioural patterns or social structures.

The disembodied side of technical change (disembodied at least in the sense that it is not representable by tangible equipment) is still even more of a black box than the embodied side. It can reside in (tacit) human skills or organizational and societal capabilities, but little of a very fundamental nature is known about how it is accumulated, stored and refreshed. *Learning by doing* (Arrow, 1962) is a standard phenomenological approach, finding expression in power laws for the relationship between productivity and cumulative investment or production. Recently, it has also become central to much of the neoclassical endogenous growth literature. The effects of *technological spillovers* between competitors have also received considerable attention. One possible way of combining learning by doing and spillovers in an industrial dynamics framework is given by Silverberg, Giovanni Dosi and Luigi Orsenigo (1988), while Giorgio Fagiolo and Dosi (2003) provide an interesting endogenous growth model incorporating these factors involving locally interacting agents. The net effect of both of these phenomena is usually one form or another of increasing returns, such as increasing returns to adoption or agglomeration, network externalities, etc. (see Arthur, 1988, 1994). Within the replicator framework this means that the fitness functions $f_i(x)$ truly depend on the frequencies x, resulting in multiple equilibria, threshold phenomena, lock-in, etc.[9].

---

[9] The increasing returns phenomenon was studied by W. Brian Arthur, Yuri Ermoliev and Yuri Kaniovski using the Polya urn stochastic tool, which assumes an indefinitely increasing population to establish asymptotic results. The alternative case of a fixed population size with stochastic effects can be studied using Master or Markov equation methods (see Feistel and Ebeling, 1989, Bruckner et al., 1994, and especially Jiménez Montaño and Ebeling, 1980, for stochastic formulations of the Nelson and Winter model). We will make only limited use of stochastic tools in the following, so the deterministic replicator equation will serve our purposes.

3 Behavioural foundations and formal evolutionary modelling in the economics of growth and Schumpeterian competition: innovation and learning

Evolution would soon come to an end were it not for the continual creation of new variety on which selection (as well as drift) can act. This is especially crucial for growth models, where the ongoing nature of the technical change process is at the fore, although other aspects may well converge to stable stationary patterns. Thus considerable attention has to be devoted to how innovation is realized by firms, individually and collectively. In principle, most scholars agree that innovation should be modelled stochastically, to reflect the uncertainty in the link between effort and outcome. The details on how this is done may very considerably, however. The classical formulation is due to Nelson and Winter, described in more detail later in this chapter. Nelson and Winter lump technologies and behavioural rules/strategies together under the concept of *routines*. Since technical change is disembodied in their model, this equivalence is perhaps admissible, since a change in technique for a firm's entire capital stock requires only the expenditure necessary to undertake innovative or imitative search – not investment or training per se. While there is technological learning at the economy-wide level, firms themselves are completely unintelligent, as they operate according to given search and investment rules that cannot be modified as a result of experience. Instead, the firm is subject to selection as a consequence of the technologies it has stumbled upon. A somewhat peculiar aspect is the very literal application of Herbert Simon's notion of satisficing to mean that firms undertake innovative search only if their performance is unsatisfactory[10].

An interesting elaboration of search activity and entry in the original Nelson and Winter model is presented in Winter (1984)[11], where firms are broken down into two types: primarily innovative or imitative. Further, the notion of technological *regime* is introduced (going back to the early or later Schumpeter), depending on whether the source of technical progress is external to the firm (e.g. from publicly available scientific knowledge bases) or from its own accumulated technological capabilities. These regimes are referred to as the *entrepreneurial* and the *routinized*,

---

[10] This should be contrasted with the Silverberg and Verspagen models, where firms undertake behavioural *imitation* with increasing probability the more unsatisfactory their performance is.

[11] The discussion of the model is couched in terms of *industry* dynamics, not economy-wide growth, although there is nothing in the basic assumptions to preclude analysis of the latter.

and are exogenously imposed by means of specific parameter settings. Although firms can be of two types, neither type is capable of learning. Instead, the market is shown to select between the two depending on the technological regime. The entry of new firms also assumes a greater importance than the mere supporting role to which it is relegated in most evolutionary models, being stimulated in the entrepreneurial regime.

While learning based on selection/mutation dynamics has begun to play a major role in the evolutionary games literature (see, for example, Kandori et al., 1993, and Young, 1993), very little has found entrance into evolutionary models of a general economic orientation. A first stab at changing this state of affairs for the theory of growth was undertaken by Silverberg and Verspagen (1994a, 1994b, 1995, 1996), drawing on the evolution strategy literature (see Schwefel, 1995). Here mutations are local around the current strategy, and the probability of imitation is an increasing function of dissatisfaction with current performance and the size of the imitated firm. In contrast to the Nelson and Winter tradition, strategies and technologies are treated separately. The learning algorithm applies only to the firms' R&D expenditure strategies; their technological performance then follows in a somewhat complex manner from these decisions and market feedbacks. In this way it is possible to implement simple boundedly rational decision rules gleaned from actual business practice, such as targeted R&D/total investment or R&D/sales ratios, or a combination of the two.

Genetic algorithms and classifier systems have also been gaining favour in recent years as mechanisms for operationalizing learning with artificial agents[12]. Although these appeal even more directly to a discrete genetic mechanism of inheritance *à la* biological DNA than social scientists may feel comfortable with, they may also be employed agnostically simply as algorithmic tools to allow learning to happen, if not as models of how learning actually happens. The goal of an *artificial economics* modelling philosophy as espoused by David Lane (1993a 1993b) is to put together a basic web of economic interactions between artificial agents endowed with a *tabula rasa* knowledge of their environment but fairly sophisticated abilities to learn, and see what sorts of markets, institutions and technologies develop, with the modeller prejudicing the developmental possibilities as little as possible. Something along these lines has already been implemented to a certain extent in the 'sugarscape' model of Robert Axtell and Joshua Epstein (see Axtell and Epstein, 1995, and Epstein and Axtell, 1996), paralleling the artificial worlds movement in the biology

---

[12] See Booker et al. (1989) and Goldberg (1989) for basic theory and methodology, and Dawid (1999), Holland and Miller (1991), Kwasnicki and Kwasnicka (1992) and Lane (1993a, 1993b) for some economic applications.

domain (see Langton, 1989, and Langton et al., 1992). It has led to a new form of economic modelling known as agent-based computation economics (ACE; see Tesfatsion, 2002). While this direction of research has generated much excitement under the general umbrella of complexity theory, it has not avoided the fate of many overhyped scientific trends in the form of a sceptical backlash (see Horgan, 1995). Be that as it may, in the following we shall limit ourselves to those models rooted in the economics tradition that promise to address issues of long-standing empirical interest.

4   An overview of evolutionary growth models

In this section we discuss the similarities and differences between several growth models that have been developed over the last decades, and which were based upon the evolutionary principles that we have outlined so far[13]. The first model that will be discussed is the one presented in Nelson and Winter (1982). This model can be seen as the first evolutionary growth model, and, as will be shown in the rest of the discussion, can be regarded as the pioneering effort in the field. The Nelson and Winter model is a model with an explicit microeconomic foundation, which consists of modelling the behaviour of firms in their search for more advanced techniques. Basically, because of the complexity arising from the simultaneous existence of multiple firms with different search behaviour and, hence, different technological levels, the Nelson and Winter model is analysed by means of computer simulations.

One class of more recent growth models in the evolutionary tradition follows the Nelson and Winter perspective of adopting a microeconomic foundation. Consequently, these models also resort to computer simulations for analysis. In this group of models, the main contributions are to extend the original Nelson and Winter set-up by introducing more realistic representations of technology, to extend the analysis to a multicountry framework, or to extend evolutionary principles to the issues of behavioural strategies instead of just technological change.

A second broad group of evolutionary growth models does not take the explicit microeconomic perspective proposed by Nelson and Winter, at least not in the sense of modelling the individual firm. Consequently, the similarities to the original Nelson and Winter model are less pronounced in this group of papers. The main reason for not taking into account the microeconomic foundations explicitly seems to be the desire either

---

[13] The papers that we discuss by no means form an exhaustive list of 'evolutionary growth theories'. However, in limiting ourselves explicitly to papers in which mathematical models with a clear 'population perspective' are the core of the analysis we hope that the present list covers at least the most prominent contributions.

516 *Gerald Silverberg and Bart Verspagen*

to keep the models analytically tractable or to keep the complexity of a simulation model within bounds, so that extensions to – for example – a multi-country context, or more systematic analysis of the closed economy case, become easier.

Because this second group of papers does not have clear roots in any specific approach, these contributions are necessarily more heterogeneous than those of the first group. It is possible, all the same, to find two broad approaches here. The borderline between the two sub-groups is the distinction between analytical solutions and computer simulations.

The guidelines for our discussion of these different approaches within the field of evolutionary growth theory will be four different points. The first three of these points correspond to the three basic principles of the evolutionary process that we have discussed: the heterogeneity of the population (usually firms, or alternatively countries, or techniques); the mechanism for generating novelty in the population (mutation, usually in the form of technical innovations); and, finally, selection (related to the economic environment in which the population operates). The last point we shall discuss is the economic interpretation, or outcomes, of the models.

One particular type of model that does not fit easily into the categories of our scheme consists of those aimed at simulating actual empirical economies. Examples of this are the Swedish MOSES model and the model for the Dutch economy developed by Verspagen (2001). The latter presents a model rooted in input-output economics, but with replicator dynamics for foreign and domestic goods markets added to it. The Swedish MOSES model is a micro- to macro-model, in which the behaviour of individual firms is modelled along similar lines to the Nelson and Winter model. The outcome of this micro-behaviour is then added up to the macro-accounts, using data both for existing firms and for artificial firms. The basic form of the MOSES model is described in Eliasson (1977, 1991). More recently, Ballot and Taymaz (2001) have added human capital to the model, and analysed the impact of various type of training policies on growth.

4.1   The Nelson and Winter model

We start our discussion with a brief summary of the model presented in Nelson and Winter (1982, part IV), which can be regarded as the pioneering effort in the field of evolutionary growth models[14]. This model

---

[14] The discussion in Nelson and Winter (1982) largely focuses around an earlier article by Nelson et al. (1976).

(the NWM for short) will be used as a benchmark case in the rest of this chapter.

In the NWM, heterogeneity is defined in terms of firms. Firms use production techniques that are characterized by fixed labour and capital coefficients (a_L and a_K respectively). Output is homogeneous, so we have a pure model of process innovation[15]. Thus, firms produce using a Leontief production function, which does not allow for substitution between labour and capital. Over time technical change may be biased (i.e. changes in a_L and a_K are not proportional), so a phenomenon that resembles substitution between labour and capital may result (this is a key result in the outcomes of the model; we shall come back to this below).

The generation of novelty occurs as a result of search activities by firms. Search is undertaken in a (given and finite) pool of existing techniques (i.e. combinations of a_K and a_L). At any point in time some of the techniques available in the pool are known, while others remain to be found in the future. Search activities are determined by satisficing behaviour – i.e. firms engage in search only if their rate of return falls below an arbitrarily set value of 16 per cent. The mutation or search process may take two different forms: local search, or imitation. In the first case, firms search for new, yet-undiscovered techniques. Each undiscovered technique has a probability of being discovered that declines linearly with a suitably defined technological distance from the current technology (hence the term 'local search'). By varying the skewness of this distance function, either labour or capital bias can be introduced into the search process. In the second search process, imitation, a firm searches for techniques currently employed by other firms but not yet used in its own production process. Thus, this aspect of the search process does not generate novelty in the strict, aggregate sense; rather, it produces novelty at the micro-economic level. The probability of success in imitation is proportional to the share in output of each technique.

Given that a firm engages in search (i.e. that its rate of return is smaller than 16 per cent), it can engage in only one type of search. The type of search that is undertaken is a random event, with a fixed probability for each type. If the search process is successful (i.e. if the firm finds a new technique), it adopts this new technique only if the expected rate of return is higher than its present rate of return. Expectations are subject to error with regard to the true values of the capital and labour coefficients.

An additional source of novelty in the economy is entry by firms that were not engaged in production previously. This is conceptualized by 'empty' firms, with a capital stock equal to zero, but which are active

---

[15] Alexander Gerybadze (1982) has extended the NWM to the case of product innovation.

in the search process. If such an 'empty' firm discovers a production technique that promises a rate of return over 16 per cent, there is a 25 per cent probability that it will actually enter the market. If entry does occur, a value for its capital stock is drawn randomly.

The selection process is thus largely driven by the rate of return on techniques. This rate of return depends on the (real) wage rate, which is a function of exogenous labour supply and endogenous labour demand. The latter is a function of output, which, in its turn, depends on the capital stocks and the techniques currently employed. Net investment in capital is equal to firm profits (minus a fixed fraction that it must pay as dividends) minus depreciation (at a fixed rate). Insufficient profits lead to negative investment – i.e. firms that make losses see their capital stock shrink. Thus selection takes place simultaneously on firms and production techniques; one may think of firms as the phenotype and techniques as the genotype.

Like most models we discuss here, the NWM has to be simulated on a computer to obtain an impression of its implications. The model, which is calibrated for the case of the Solow (1957) data on total factor productivity for the United States in the first half of the twentieth century, yields an aggregate time path for the variables: capital, labour input, output (GDP) and wages (or labour share in output). The analysis in Nelson and Winter (1982) is confined to sixteen runs, in which four main parameters (the localness of innovation, the emphasis on imitation search, dividends and the labour-saving bias of local search) are varied between a high and a low state.

Nelson and Winter primarily address the question whether these time series correspond in a broad qualitative sense to the ones actually observed by Solow. Given the affirmative answer to this question, they argue at length that 'it is not reasonable to dismiss an evolutionary theory on the grounds that it fails to provide a coherent explanation of . . . macro phenomena' (1982, p. 226). More specifically, it is argued that, although both the neoclassical explanation of economic growth offered by Solow (as well as later work in this tradition) and the NWM seem to explain the same empirical trends, the underlying causal mechanisms between the two perspectives differ greatly (p. 227):

[T]he neoclassical interpretation of long-run productivity change . . . is based upon a clean distinction between 'moving along' an existing production function and shifting to a new one. In the evolutionary theory . . . there was no production function. . . . We argue . . . that the sharp 'growth accounting' split made within the neoclassical paradigm is bothersome empirically and conceptually.

Looking below the surface of the broad qualitative resemblance between the simulation and the actual empirical data, Nelson and Winter arrive at some interesting conclusions with regard to the effects of varia-tions in their four parameters. They find that decreasing the localness of search leads to higher values of technical change, a higher capital/labour ratio and lower market concentration. Search biased towards the imita-tion of other firms (rather than local search for new techniques) leads to a higher capital/labour ratio and lower concentration. Higher capital costs (dividends) lead to lower technical change and a lower capital/labour ratio. Finally, labour-saving technical change leads to a higher capital/labour ratio. All these effects (which were established by regressions on the simulation results) have some plausible explanation from the point of view of the evolutionary theory provided by Nelson and Winter.

Thus, the NWM seems to provide two sorts of outcomes. First, there is the 'mimimalistic' point of view, that an evolutionary model may explain the macro-facts about economic growth on the basis of a 'plausible' microeconomic theory (i.e. a theory that can account for the observed heterogeneity between firms at the micro-level)[16]. While this a useful result, there are at least two reasons why one should not be satisfied with it as the sole basis for further development of evolutionary growth models. First, a more 'positive' approach to scientific development would require an evolutionary theory to provide fresh results of its own and not only benchmark itself against neoclassical results, even if the latter have dom-inated economic discourse until now. Second, the empirical validation of the NWM is highly specific to a single data set – i.e. the one used by Solow. After the events of the 1970s (such as the productivity slowdown, or productivity paradox) the stylized facts about economic growth that were predominant in the period when Nelson and Winter formulated their model are no longer uncontested.

The second type of result from the NWM – i.e. the relations between the four main parameters in the model and the macroeconomic predic-tions – can be seen as a first attempt at a more 'positive' approach. But perhaps more important than these results, which only play a minor role in the exposition, is the paradigmatic function of the model as such. As we shall see below, the NWM has set the stage for a number of more elab-orate evolutionary models capable of analysing economic growth as an evolutionary process, using much more refined assumptions and model set-ups, and arriving at conclusions that go beyond broad similarity to the

---

[16] See also Nelson (1995) for an extensive argument along this line. The fact that growth accounting with an aggregate production function can lead to a deceptively high goodness of fit even with a micro-economy of heterogeneous firms inconsistent with aggregation or even absurd underlying production functions has been pointed out repeatedly in the literature. See Houthakker (1956), Phelps-Brown (1957), McCombie (1987), Shaikh (1974, 1980, 1990), Simon and Levy (1963) and Simon (1979).

'stylized facts' developed in the 1950s. Some of the ways in which these newer models refine the NWM concern the endogenization of the mutation and imitation process, and the extension of the model to one in which firms in different countries interact, or in which there are input-output relations between firms. The common roots of most of these models in the NWM is evident, however.

4.2   *Evolutionary 'macro-models'*

Perhaps the most important aspect of the NWM is its explicit microeconomic foundation. As was argued above, this seems to be the basis for the most important conclusion regarding the outcomes. Among the evolutionary growth models inspired by the NWM, there are models with an explicit micro-foundation, but also models formulated only at the macroeconomic level. The discussion here will start by outlining the latter category. The microeconomically founded models will be discussed in the following subsection. The models considered in this subsection are by John Conlisk (1989: CON), Metcalfe (1988: MET), Verspagen (1993: VER) and Silverberg and Lehnert (1993, 1996: SL).

The first two of these models can be solved analytically, whereas the last two follow Nelson and Winter in using computer simulations for analysis. The analytically solvable models necessarily have to make extensive simplifications relative to the rich picture of the NWM, which has become something of a standard for the second group of evolutionary growth models discussed below. In the case of the Conlisk model, these simplifications go so far that it is arguable as to whether the model is still a truly evolutionary one. As will be shown below, however, some of the most important assumptions and results of evolutionary theory remain in the Conlisk model, so that we have no hesitation discussing it here alongside the other models. The abstractions necessary to yield analytical solutions should not be regarded in a dogmatic way leading to the exclusion of these models from the evolutionary category. It is in the interests of the discipline to explore the boundaries of what is analytically possible while at the same time exploring more complex models by means of simulation techniques.

The assumptions on the role of heterogeneity in the CON, MET and SL models are quite similar. In all three models production techniques are the most basic entities. These techniques differ with respect to their technological levels, for which labour productivity is the sole indicator. This is the main source of the heterogeneity on which selection operates. In the VER model, heterogeneity occurs between sectors within countries – i.e. the sector is the smallest unit of analysis. Sectors differ with regard to the product they produce, which might have different income elasticities in different countries, and also with regard to labour productivity, as an indicator for technology.

The way in which novelty is generated varies the most in the models in this group. The simplest approach is found in the MET model, where novelty is assumed to be absent. To keep the model tractable, the analysis is confined to the selection process operating upon a given set of techniques. Only a little more advanced is the assumption in VER, where technical progress is purely deterministic, and specified in the form of a 'Kaldor–Verdoorn' type of process, which stresses learning by doing and dynamic scale economies. Basically, a higher output growth rate leads to faster productivity growth, although the 'returns' to output growth in this process are diminishing.

More squarely in the evolutionary tradition are the novelty-generating processes in CON and SL. In these models a stochastic mechanism is at work in which new techniques are generated from a random distribution. In CON this is a normal distribution of labour productivity increments with a positive mean, whereas in the SL model innovations arrive according to a time-homogeneous or inhomogeneous Poisson process. In the SL case, whenever an innovation occurs the new production technique is assigned a labour productivity equal to $(1 + a)$ times the prevailing best-practice technique, where a is an endogenously fixed constant.

Selection is crucial in all models in this group. In this case, the simplest representation is provided by the CON model; here there is a ranking of techniques according to their productivities[17]. At any point in time the search process is based upon the first n techniques in this ranking; the mean of the distribution from which new techniques are drawn is a weighted mean of these first n techniques. This means that '[s]ince new plant technology will build on the innovative plants from the past rather than on the average plants of the past, productivity will grow. In the absence of randomness, all plants would be alike; hence there would be no innovative plants to induce growth. Thus, randomness is essential' (Conlisk, 1989, p. 794).

In the VER model the selection mechanism is represented by a replicator equation in which sectors from different countries compete with each other on the basis of production costs (profits are assumed to be zero). Production costs are a function of the technological level of the sector,

---

[17] Conlisk's techniques can be ranked in two different ways. The first is by means of their actual productivities at any point in time. Because labour productivity depends partly on capital depreciation in this model the labour productivity of a technique varies over its lifetime. Techniques can also be ranked on the basis of their productivities at the time of invention. This is the relevant way of ranking in the rest of the discussion here.

the wage rate and the exchange rate. Wages depend upon productivity growth and the unemployment rate, and exchange rates adjust slowly to achieve purchasing power parity between nations in the long run. There is no explicit economic basis for the replicator equations other than a short reference to the idea that consumers (in the absence of quality differences between producers) prefer those products with the lowest price, and that adjustment to these long-run preferences is slow. At the aggregate level, selection in the VER model is a function of sectoral shares in total consumption, which evolve according to different real income elasticities in different countries.

Finally, the selection mechanisms in the SL and MET models are quite similar. In these models the replicator mechanisms result from explicit economic theorizing. In both of them profits are the driving force for selection. Confronted with economy-wide wage and output price levels, techniques with different levels of labour productivity will yield different profit rates. The assumption is that profits are reinvested in the same technique[18], so that the share in productive capacity of techniques with above-average productivity increases.

In the SL model real wages are a function of the unemployment rate, and effective demand does not play a role (production is always equal to productive capacity). This leads to a model that is essentially a multi-technique version of Richard Goodwin (1967). In the MET model nominal wages are given, while the price of output is found by confronting demand and supply. The demand curve is given exogenously, whereas the supply curve is found by aggregating over the different production techniques, which are assumed to supply all their output at the cost level determined by the wage rate and labour productivity. The price of output is found at the intersection of the demand and supply schedules. All techniques with cost levels higher than the current output price are assumed to be scrapped from the market. New techniques enter at the lower end of the supply schedule, and thus achieve high profit rates.

Despite the similarities in model set-up in this broad group of 'aggregate' evolutionary models, there is not much similarity between the outcomes of the different models. Under the assumption that technology advances are indeed random (see above), Conlisk shows that the growth rate of the aggregate CON economy is a function of three variables: the standard error of the productivity distribution of new plants (which can be interpreted as the average innovation size); the savings rate (which is

---

[18] In fact, in the SL model a certain fraction of profits is redistributed towards the more efficient techniques. Hence, more advanced techniques attract a more than proportional share of total profits. This is not essential, however, to the working of the selection process, although it tends to speed up selection.

defined somewhat unconventionally); and the speed of diffusion of new knowledge. Moreover, by changing some of the assumptions about the specification of technical change, the CON model emulates three standard specifications of technical change found in growth models in the neoclassical tradition. In this case, the first and third factors no longer have an impact on growth (they are specific to the 'evolutionary' technical change specification of the model). However, the impact of the savings rate can be compared between the various model set-ups. Conlisk finds that using purely exogenous technical change (as in the Solow model), or learning by doing specifications as in the models by Kenneth Arrow (1962) or Paul Romer (1986), the savings rate does not have an impact upon (long-run) economic growth. This result, which is, in fact, also well known from standard neoclassical growth theory, marks an important difference between these models and his more evolutionarily inspired specification.

The other analytical model discussed in this section, the MET model, does not aim at deriving such specific results. Instead, the aim seems to be to provide an exposition of the workings of a possible selection mechanism on the growth pattern of an open economy. Due to the many simplifying assumptions that are necessary to arrive at an analytical solution (such as the constancy of countries' shares in world demand, and fixed nominal wages and exchange rates), it is not easy to link the results to actual empirical trends. Nevertheless, the model clearly shows how a country's share in world demand and its technological level shape the interaction between the trade balance and the growth rate of the economy. The model is thus clearly one in which growth depends on the openness and competitiveness of the economy. The long-run outcome of these forces is that the share in world production of the technologically more advanced country tends to one, although production in the more backward country may still be positive. Moreover, applying comparative statics, the model predicts the effects of events such as currency devaluations or protective tariffs.

The VER model can be seen as an attempt to analyse the same issues as in the MET model, but here the emphasis is more on the long-run dynamics of technical change, wages and the exchange rate than on the adjustment process. Verspagen uses simulations to analyse the effects of differences in technological competence between countries, or differences in demand patterns between countries. Because the model is multisectoral, endogenous specialization patterns arise, and countries' technical performances depend upon their specialization. These differences in technological competitiveness in turn have an effect upon unemployment and the wage rate, which again feeds back upon competitiveness. In essence, this model highlights the interaction between specialization and growth, and the outcomes show that, in a world in which there are differences between the technological potentials of sectors and countries, growth rate differentials between countries may be persistent though not exactly predictable (due to the non-linear nature of the model).

The SL model predicts a complex pattern for the rate of technical change in which long-run fluctuations of a $1/f^\alpha$ noise character dominate, although the stochastic input is simple white (Poissonian) noise. The time series for technical change and growth generated by their simulations are analysed by means of spectral analysis, in order to decompose them into harmonic oscillations of various frequencies. The result is a downward sloping linear curve in a plot of the log of spectral density versus the log of the frequency of the oscillations, known as $1/f^\alpha$ noise, and is interpreted by Silverberg and Lehnert to be a form of long or Kondratiev waves, which are neither strictly periodic nor a random walk. In fact, they show that these series have characteristics of deterministic chaos, allowing more precise short-term prediction than a random series would warrant. They term this finding 'evolutionary chaos'. Moreover, technological replacement shows the same robust pattern of successive logistic diffusion into and out of the economy as has been repeatedly revealed in the empirical literature.

Summarizing, perhaps the most important common factor in these models is the role of technological differences between sectors, technologies or countries. These differences are continually modified by a selection process that, no matter how specified, is the driving force behind economic growth in all four approaches. It is clear that, although these models share a number of general evolutionary principles in their approach to the issue of economic growth, there is no standard set of assumptions; nor does a common set of results emerge.

4.3   *Evolutionary 'micro-models': in the footsteps of the NWM*

We continue our discussion of recent evolutionary models of economic growth by considering a number of models resembling the original NWM in the sense that they are rooted in an explicit microeconomic theory of firm behaviour. Once again, the discussion will be organized around four themes: heterogeneity, the generation of novelty (mutation), selection and the economic outcomes of the analysis. We shall discuss models by Francesca Chiaromonte and Dosi (1993: CD), Dosi et al. (1994: DEA), Fagiolo and Dosi (2002: FD) and Silverberg and Verspagen (1994a, 1994b, 1996: SV).

All four models follow the NWM in assuming that technological differences are the prime source of heterogeneity between firms. They also follow the NWM in adopting process innovation as the sole form of technological progress, and thus use the labour and capital coefficients to characterize technology. The SV model adopts the formalism for dealing with capital-embodied technical change (which we termed the *quasi-vintage* structure above) from SL and assumes that each firm may apply a number of production technologies at any point in time. In the CD, DEA and FD models a firm is characterized by a single labour coefficient. DEA explicitly takes an open economy perspective with firms operating in different sectors and different countries (characterized primarily by different labour markets and exchange rates). The firms are located in a home country, and when they serve a market in a different country the flow of goods is counted as exports.

All four models potentially allow for a second source of heterogeneity in the form of behavioural differences between firms. In FD and SV these behavioural differences are the R&D strategies, whereas in DEA and CD the firm strategies may also extend to decisions on price setting (mark-ups), although no systematic study of the effects of heterogeneity or of selection on these strategies is undertaken. In CD the pricing strategy is based upon demand expectations, which may also vary between firms. The firms in these models are thus characterized by their technological capabilities (in the form of input coefficients) and by economic strategies, which determine how much resources they invest in the search for new technologies or how they price their products.

In the NWM local search and imitation were the two means by which firms could generate novelty. This is where the newer models discussed here start expanding on the original NWM approach. In CD the search process takes place in a complicated two-dimensional space. One dimension in this space corresponds to 'typologies', or 'technological paradigms', and is formally defined as the labour coefficient of producing a unit of productive capacity of a certain type. Within each of these typologies the labour coefficient for producing a homogeneous consumption good by means of the unit of productive capacity defines the other dimension in the two-dimensional space. In CD firms either produce 'machines' (each of which is characterized by a set of coordinates in the two-dimensional plane) or they produce consumption goods (i.e. they use machines as inputs). The evolution of the plane itself, as well as the specific trajectories realized by individual firms in the plane, is a complex stochastic process depending on a number of assumptions with regard to the cumulativeness of technology as well as the realized history of the model.

In DEA the search space is more similar to the one in the NWM, with the probability of an innovation depending on R&D employment, and the productivity improvement in the event of an innovation also being a random event. In CD the innovation process differs between the two sectors in the economy. In the first sector, which produces capital goods, the success of innovation is determined by a similar stochastic procedure to DEA – i.e. success depends on the number of R&D workers. When successful, the new capital good's productivity is drawn randomly. In the consumption goods sector, firms possess a skill level for each available capital good type. This skill level evolves by a learning process, which has both public and private features (i.e. a firm using a certain type of capital good improves its own as well as the publicly available skill of working with this machine). Firms are not able to predict their skill level precisely but, rather, under- or overestimate this level by some systematic value. Actual labour productivity is a function of the capital good's characteristics and the firm's skill level. Firms in the consumption goods sector maximize a function involving labour productivity, prices and the order backlog, and thereby choose which capital good they want to use.

In FD search takes place on a two-dimensional lattice with only some sites occupied by viable technologies with a given exogenous probability, and with underlying productivities increasing with the site's distance from the origin. Should a firm decide to explore the space instead of to continue to exploit the site it is already on (which is determined by a per-period probability that may be specific to the firm), it begins to sail through the lattice at random from site to site until it discovers a better one, incurring a cost of search each period and forgoing any production. The model is enriched by a number of competing influences. First, realized productivities increase with the number of agents exploiting a site, reflecting increasing returns to the scale of adoption. Second, firms send and receive signals communicating their current productivities. If a firm decides to imitate an existing technology, it has a higher probability of receiving a signal from a more intensely exploited site nearby than a less intensely exploited one far away. Thus the model incorporates the exploration/exploitation dilemma and information diffusion.

In SV firms may also invest in R&D, and the probability of innovation depends on their R&D effort. When an innovation is made, it is introduced as in SL. Firms that are behind the economy-wide best-practice frontier have a higher probability of making an innovation (i.e. adopting the next technology, which brings them closer to the frontier but does not advance the latter itself) than would be the case if they were currently on the frontier. This reflects the diffusion of technological knowledge between firms – i.e. technological spillovers. However, they still assume that this form of technological catch-up requires R&D investment of the backward firms, and is thus not costless. The main difference between

SV, on the one hand, and DEA and CD, on the other hand, is that the former allows for the evolution of the R&D strategies themselves – in other words, behavioural learning. In CD and DEA a firm's R&D and price strategies remain fixed for its entire lifetime. In SV there are actually selection, mutation and imitation processes with regard to these strategies, so evolution takes place at two levels[19]. It is assumed that firms have a (small) probability of changing their R&D strategies every period (mutation of strategies). If this occurs, the firm adds a random increment to its present strategy, where the increment is drawn from a normal distribution with mean zero. Thus, mutation of strategies is a local process, with a low probability for the firm to make large jumps in parameter space. There is also a variable probability that a firm imitates the R&D strategy of another firm. This probability decreases with a measure of firm success, the firm's growth rate, with the result that laggard firms are more likely to imitate than successful ones (to reflect satisficing behaviour). Which firm is imitated is also a random process, with the probability of being imitated equal to market share. In DEA the probability of innovation depends on the number of past and present R&D workers. A successful innovation increases firm-wide productivity by a random step.

Selection takes place according to a replicator process in all models except FD, where agents are infinitely long-lived and differ only in productivity. In SV the process is essentially the same as in SL (discussed above), which means that there is a Phillips curve determining the real wage rate, and firms expand their productive capacity at a rate equal to their overall (averaged over technologies) profit rate. Thus, there is a predator-prey process in which more efficient technologies tend to extend their market share, and thus firms applying these technologies will grow more rapidly. The exit of firms occurs whenever their market share falls below a threshold, and a new firm with random characteristics takes the place of the old firm.

In CD and DEA the selection process is represented by a replicator equation that is not specifically founded in any theory, as in the VER model discussed in the previous section. Prices and exchange rates (in DEA) are the variables determining competitiveness in these models. Thus, technological competences (labour productivity), aggregate characteristics of the economy such as wages, as well as other behavioural variables (pricing rules) enter directly into competitiveness. In CD the competitiveness of a firm also depends on the backlog of orders (i.e. unfulfilled

---

[19] In Silverberg and Verspagen (1996) firms are characterized by a combination of two different R&D strategies: one targeting the R&D/total investment ratio, and one targeting the R&D/sales ratio.

demand in the previous period). The market shares following from the replicator equation are translated into actual production levels by considering the size of the aggregate market, which is endogenous to the model. The total size of the market is the minimum of aggregate demand and supply[20]. Aggregate demand is found from the total wage bill (the consumer goods sector in DEA and CD), or total firm demand for machines (the capital good sector in CD).

Silverberg and Verspagen provide a relatively systematic, although by no means complete, search of the parameter space of their model. They arrive at three different types of results. First, they find that, for sufficiently high values of technological opportunity (which links the R&D/capital ratio of the firm to the probability of innovative success), firms tend to converge after a considerable adjustment period to a common R&D strategy[21]. In this long-run evolutionary equilibrium of the system, R&D strategies converge to well-defined values (around which the system fluctuates randomly) quite comparable to values observed in high-tech industries in advanced countries. The growth rate of the economy in this state is characterized by the same $1/f^{\alpha}$ noise pattern found in SL. Second, SV find that, after initializing the economy with zero R&D strategies, convergence to the equilibrium strategy takes the economy through different growth phases. These phases are characterized by different R&D levels, growth rates and market concentration patterns in the following sequence. The economy starts out in a low-R&D, low-technical-progress, and near-monopoly regime (with the monopoly firm being replaced by a different firm at more or less regular intervals). After passing through a state of intermediate values for all variables, the long-run R&D equilibrium is characterized by low concentration (a nearly even size distribution of firms) and a high rate of technical change. Finally, SV find that, by varying such parameters as technological opportunity, R&D spillovers, and the mutation and imitation rates of the R&D strategies, there are systematic variations in the level of technical progress and market concentration consistent with economic intuition.

The discussion in DEA and CD is less systematic, and does not arrive at clear-cut relations between the parameter values and the outcomes of the model. In fact, Chiaromonte and Dosi do not provide results for more than one particular run, and Dosi et al. provide very little information about alternative runs. Neither of the two papers provides systematic summary statistics for multiple runs, whether for different parameter sets

---

[20] Neither CD nor DEA discuss very extensively what happens when supply falls short of demand.

[21] This should be compared with the analogous results from neoclassical endogenous growth theory, such as in Aghion and Howitt (1992).

or for identical parameter sets with different random seeds[22]. Keeping the 'preliminary' nature of the results in mind, the following seems to be the main outcome of the CD model. In the Nelson and Winter tradition, they put much emphasis on the interpretation of their results as empirically plausible, yet rooted in a more sophisticated microeconomic foundation (compared to mainstream theory) (p. 56):

[o]ne can only say that the generated series of income and average productivity seem 'plausible' (. . .): we conjecture that the aggregate dynamics might show econometric properties similar to those empirically observed. As with 'real business cycle models', one cannot distinguish between transitory (cyclical) and permanent (trend) components in the generated time series. However, unlike the former models, innovations do not take the form of exogenous stochastic shocks but, rather, are generated endogenously by agents themselves.

Thus, it seems as though the evolutionary model has evolved (from NWM to CD), as has the 'adversary mainstream' model (from the Solow model to the real business cycles and endogenous growth models), but that nothing else has changed.

While DEA put some emphasis on this property of their outcomes, their main interest relates to growth rate differentials between countries. They find that, for the fifty-five countries in the particular runs for which results are presented, there is a significant trend for GDP per capita levels to diverge. This is tested by using a linear functional form that relates the growth rates of GDP per capita to the initial level of this variable. A significantly positive slope is found. Applying a 'post-selection bias' and testing only for those countries that at the end of the period turn out to be developed, they obtain a negative coefficient (pointing to convergence), that is, however, not statistically significant[23]. Given the available empirical evidence for long time periods and large cross-country data sets, it is not clear whether this property of the simulated data is in close correspondence with reality. Most authors in the field of empirical 'convergence' have found significant convergence for a group of relatively advanced economies in the 1950–73 period. Divergence seems to prevail in a larger sample of countries (including, for example, the African countries). It is also clear that convergence in the relatively rich group of

---

[22] DEA state that 'the results that we shall present appear to be robust to rather wide parameter variations' (p. 235), without presenting statistics to support this statement, or specifying how 'wide' the variations actually were. CD, discussing one particular outcome, state that it 'holds across most of the simulations that we tried' (p. 58).

[23] This experiment seems to be derived from J. Bradford DeLong's (1988) critique of William Baumol (1986), who, as have many other authors before and after him, estimated the convergence equation tested by DEA.

countries was much weaker, if present at all, in earlier periods[24]. Thus, it seems as if the DEA results are (at least partly) compatible with a particular period in time (before the Second World War), but not necessarily so with the strong post-war convergence period observed in the OECD countries.

Fagiolo and Dosi present a very extensive analysis of growth behaviour as a function of parameter constellations, which are, admittedly, rather complex given the number of significant and competing factors entering into their model. Their main results concern the robustness of self-sustained growth for intermediate values of the search and diffusion parameters, the independence of growth rates from population size (in contrast to many neoclassical endogenous growth models), and the time series properties of the sample paths generated. FD show that a balance between exploration and exploitation must be achieved, and thresholds in parameter space surpassed, for long-term growth to be viable.

5   Evolution, history and contingency as the driving forces of economic growth: an attempt at a synthesis

Having outlined the assumptions and results of a number of contributions to 'evolutionary growth theory', it is time to ask whether this discipline has added to our understanding of the phenomenon of economic growth. We have already seen that the results of many evolutionary growth models are not very specific, in the sense that they do not provide insight into exactly which factors play which role in the growth process. Compared to other approaches in growth theory, such as the neoclassical model with its highly practical 'toolbox' of growth accounting, it may seem at first glance as though not much will be learned from their evolutionary alternatives.

As has already been stressed by Nelson and Winter (1982), it is indeed one aim of evolutionary models to demonstrate that the sense of precision offered by the mainstream models is to some extent illusory. The causal relationships between the main variables in these models, Nelson and Winter argue, are not so clear once one adopts a microeconomic framework in which heterogeneous firms, disequilibrium and bounded rationality are the key ingredients. The implications of this point of view may certainly be far-reaching. The importance of this argument resides perhaps not so much in the critical attitude towards mainstream theory as in the proposition that models of economic growth are simply not able to

---

[24] See, for example, Verspagen (1995) for further characterizations of the convergence debate.

make precise predictions on the basis of exact causal relations. This idea is quite well illustrated by a quotation from Nelson (1995, pp. 85–86):

> There is no question that, in taking aboard this complexity, one often ends up with a theory in which precise predictions are impossible or highly dependent on particular contingencies, as is the case if the theory implies multiple or rapidly shifting equilibria, or if under the theory the system is likely to be far away from any equilibrium, except under very special circumstances. Thus an evolutionary theory may not only be more complex than an equilibrium theory. It may be less decisive in its predictions and explanations. To such a complaint, the advocate of an evolutionary theory might reply that the apparent power of the simpler theory in fact is an illusion. . . . Such a framework would help us see and understand better the complexity of the economic reality. . . . But it will not make the complexity go away.

Nelson thus seems to argue that we must simply accept as a fact of life the inability to predict and explain precisely that characterizes many of the evolutionary growth models outlined above. Although we sympathize with this line of reasoning in general, we wish to argue that there are indeed ways in which evolutionary growth theory can take up Nelson's gauntlet of 'complexity' in a more positive way. We suggest going back to an old discussion in evolutionary biology, which focuses on the interaction of 'chance and necessity'.

This debate, which was stimulated by Jacques Monod (1970), enquires into the consequences of adopting a view of evolution in which random events, such as genetic mutations, or random changes in the selection environment (such as the now famous meteorite that supposedly led to the extinction of dinosaurs on the earth) have an impact on the general characteristics of 'life as we know it'. In the words of Stephen Jay Gould, the question is whether the biological diversity on earth would be different if 'the tape were played twice'[25]. As far as chance and contingency are concerned, the answer to this question would be a firm 'yes': if evolution completely depended on random events, a literally infinite number of natural histories would be possible, and there is no reason why any of them would turn up more often than others in imaginary experiments.

Applying the analogy to economics and the history of technology, the question is, if the tape were played twice, would textile innovations and mechanical power be the technological stimulus for an Industrial Revolution, and, if so, would England again be the place of origin of such a revolution? Taking this reasoning a step farther, would a Great Depression always occur, and would the equivalent of the United States always surge

---

[25] See Fontana and Buss (1994) for a discussion of Gould's question in the context of an abstract evolutionary model of self-organization.

to economic and technological dominance, inducing a period of sustained catch-up and convergence in part of the world after the Second World War?

The economic historian's explanation for such events rests on specific historical circumstances not obviously connected to a more general causal mechanism extending across time periods. For example, Angus Maddison (1991) points to specific institutional and policy factors that led to a succession of growth phases in the modern world since 1820. Although Maddison does not discuss the causal mechanisms underlying these factors at great length, it is obvious that there is a considerable degree of contingency associated with these factors, making them hard to explain from an economic point of view.

However, the biological discussion also highlights the role of more systematic factors in the evolutionary process, suggesting the hypothesis that some 'histories' are more likely than others. Taking this argument even further, Walter Fontana and Leo Buss (1994), on the basis of simulation experiments, have argued that there are certain characteristics of biological life that seem to be generic and robust to different randomizations of the model. They argue that 'these features . . . might be expected to reappear if the tape were played twice' (p. 757). Hence, the dual relationship between 'chance' and 'necessity' leads to a world-view in which there is considerable uncertainty with regard to exact outcomes and causal mechanisms, but in which there is also some limit to the randomness of history. Thus, the basic SV model and its derivatives point to a definite value of R&D, and distinct preferences for particular strategic routines over others, as an emergent outcome of this process of chance and necessity. In fact, the stochastic component of learning models can actually reduce the number of possible outcomes as compared to the equivalent deterministic one (see Foster and Young, 1990, and Young, 1993).

The evolutionary growth models we have discussed almost all rely upon stochastic technical change as the driving force behind economic growth. In many of the models one outcome of this stochastic process after a selection process has acted upon it is that a wide range of 'economic histories' are possible, some of which seem to be compatible with the 'stylized facts' of actual empirical observations. While these results are often used to argue the 'minimalist' position, that an evolutionary theory can explain the phenomena explained by mainstream theory but with a more realistic (Nelson, 1995, p. 67) microeconomic foundation, we wish to argue that this approach should be extended along the lines suggested by the debate on 'chance and necessity' in biology.

Viewed in this way, evolutionary growth models would have to become more precise on the possible range of outcomes they predict, by outlining the general features of the histories generated in the simulation experiments. For example, in a model of international growth rate differentials as suggested by DEA, the main question would be under what circumstances a fairly 'narrow' bandwidth of outcomes would exist – for example, in the sense of a small range of values for the coefficient of variation of per capita GDP in the different countries. Such an approach would, admittedly, not help us much in understanding specific events in economic history. It would not give us an answer as to why the Industrial Revolution took place in England, or why the productivity slowdown occurred in the mid-1970s. However, given the inability of evolutionary theory to identify clear-cut causal mechanisms explaining these facts, it would certainly provide a powerful tool of analysis, which would take the field a step ahead of the currently available results.

In an extension of the SV model to the international economy, we have taken a first step in trying to establish results along these lines (Silverberg and Verspagen, 1995). There we showed that one needs only a fairly simple set of assumptions in order to generate robust artificial time series of international economic and technological leadership similar to those observed empirically. We argued that this exercise, although still of a preliminary nature, shows that historical events such as the post-war catch-up boom can be seen as broadly compatible with an evolutionary model of international growth rate differentials. What is robust is not any particular sequence of events but the $1/f^{\alpha}$ noise pattern of the time series, which will always generate such patterns if one waits long enough. In other words, we are arguing that, despite the impact of 'random' events, such as US leadership over much of the twentieth century, we would expect that similar patterns would have arisen had we been able to 'play the tape twice'. In order to stimulate other contributors to the evolutionary debate to take a similar perspective in the future, further work on methodological issues – such as the status of simulation experiments relative to analytical results, or the statistical evaluation of results generated by computer simulations – is obviously required.

Finally, there remains the issue of the relationship between evolutionary growth models and the view on economic growth from different theoretical perspectives, such as the neoclassical theory or (post-)Keynesian approaches. We have already seen that evolutionary theorists, whether old or new, tend to benchmark their results against those of neoclassical growth theorists. Following the logic of the above debate on 'chance and necessity', we would argue that the usefulness of comparing the two perspectives is not very high. The possible directions for evolutionary theory we have emphasized imply that the results of evolutionary simulation models would be of a different class from those derived from conventional models. Just as Newtonian mechanics remained useful after the development of the theory of relativity, the sort of evolutionary results we have in mind would definitely have something to say about the circumstances in which neoclassical predictions are useful, but they would also paint a broader picture in which the role of historical contingencies in the process of economic growth on the one hand, and specifically evolutionary invariant features on the other, would be highlighted.

A more fruitful synthesis may arise from the incorporation of the classic Keynesian theme – the role of demand – into evolutionary growth models. This is a topic that remains largely unexplored in evolutionary growth models. Recent attempts to analyse demand from an evolutionary perspective have been made in a series of papers published as a special issue of the *Journal of Evolutionary Economics* (see for example, Andersen, 2001, Saviotti, 2001, Metcalfe, 2001, and Witt, 2001). While these papers all illuminate important aspects of the demand problem, a comprehensive model of the role of demand in economic growth from an evolutionary perspective is still lacking.

REFERENCES

Adams, H. (1919), *The Degradation of the Democratic Dogma*, reprinted 1969, New York: Harper & Row.
Aghion, P., and P. Howitt (1992), 'A model of growth through creative destruction', *Econometrica* **60**(2): 323–51.
Alchian, A. A. (1950), 'Uncertainty, evolution and economic theory', *Journal of Political Economy* **58**(3): 211–21. [Reprinted in U. Witt (ed.) (1993), *Evolutionary Economics*, Aldershot: Edward Elgar.]
Andersen, E. S. (2001), 'Satiation in an evolutionary model of structural economic dynamics', *Journal of Evolutionary Economics* **11**(1): 134–64.
Arrow, K. J. (1962), 'The economic implications of learning by doing', *Review of Economic Studies* **29**: 155–73.
Arthur, W. B. (1988), 'Self-reinforcing mechanisms in economics', in P. W. Anderson, K. J. Arrow and D. Pines (eds.), *The Economy as an Evolving Complex System*, Reading, MA: Addison-Wesley, 9–33.
——— (1994), *Increasing Returns and Path Dependence in the Economy*, Ann Arbor, MI: University of Michigan Press.
Axtell, R., and J. M. Epstein (1995), 'Agent-based modeling: understanding our creations', *Bulletin of the Santa Fe Institute* (winter): 28–32.
Ballot, G., and E. Taymaz (2001), 'Training policies and economic growth in an evolutionary world', *Structural Change and Economic Dynamics* **12**: 311–29.
Baumol, W. J. (1986), 'Productivity growth, convergence, and welfare: what the long-run data show', *American Economic Review* **76**(5): 1072–85.
Bertalanffy, L. von (1932), *Theoretische Biologie*, vol. I, Berlin: Borntraeger.
Booker, L., D. Goldberg and J. Holland (1989), 'Classifier systems and genetic algorithms', in J. Carbonell (ed.), *Machine Learning: Paradigms and Methods*, Cambridge, MA: MIT Press.

Boulding, K. E. (1978), *Ecodynamics: A New Theory of Societal Evolution*, Beverly Hills and London: Sage.

—— (1981), *Evolutionary Economics*, Beverly Hills and London: Sage.

Bruckner, E., W. Ebeling, M. A. Jiménez Montaño and A. Scharnhorst (1994), 'Hyperselection and innovation described by a stochastic model of technological evolution', in L. Leydesdorff and P. van den Besselaar (eds.), *Evolutionary Economics and Chaos Theory*, London: Pinter, 79–90.

Chiaromonte, F., and G. Dosi (1993), 'Heterogeneity, competition and macro-economic dynamics', *Structural Change and Economic Dynamics* 4: 39–63.

Conlisk, J. (1989), 'An aggregate model of technical change', *Quarterly Journal of Economics* 104: 787–821.

Dawid, H. (1999), *Adaptive Learning by Genetic Algorithms: Analytical Results and Applications to Economic Models*, revised 2nd edn., Berlin: Springer-Verlag.

DeLong, J. B. (1988), 'Productivity growth, convergence and welfare: comment', *American Economic Review* 78(5): 1138–54.

Dosi, G., S. Fabiani, R. Aversi and M. Meacci (1994), 'The dynamics of international differentiation: a multi-country evolutionary model', *Industrial and Corporate Change* 3: 225–41.

Downie, J. (1955), *The Competitve Process*, London: Duckworth.

Ebeling, W., and R. Feistel (1982), *Physik der Selbstorganisation und Evolution*, Berlin: Akademie-Verlag.

Edelman, G. M. (1987), *Neural Darwinism: The Theory of Neuronal Group Selection*, New York: Basic Books.

Eliasson, G. (1977), 'Competition and market processes in a simulation model of the Swedish economy', *American Economic Review* 67(1): 277–81.

—— (1991), 'Modelling the experimentally organized economy', *Journal of Economic Behavior and Organization* 16: 163–82.

Epstein, J. M., and R. Axtell (1996), *Growing Artificial Societies: Social Science from the Bottom up*, Washington, DC: Brookings Institution.

Fagiolo, G., and G. Dosi (2003), 'Exploitation, exploration and innovation in a model of endogenous growth with locally interacting agents', *Structural Change and Economic Dynamics*, 14(3): 237–73.

Feistel, R., and W. Ebeling (1989), *Evolution of Complex Systems*, Berlin: VEB Deutscher Verlag der Wissenschaften.

Fisher, R. A. (1930), *The Genetical Theory of Natural Selection*, Oxford: Clarendon Press.

Fontana, W., and L. W. Buss (1994), 'What would be conserved if "the tape were played twice"', *Proceedings of the National Academy of Sciences, USA* 91: 757–61.

Foster, D., and H. P. Young (1990), 'Stochastic evolutionary game dynamics', *Theoretical Population Biology* 38: 219–32.

Gerybadze, A. (1982), *Innovation, Wettbewerb und Evolution*, Tübingen, Germany: Mohr.

Goldberg, D. (1989), *Genetic Algorithms in Search, Optimization, and Machine Learning*, Reading, MA: Addison-Wesley.

Goodwin, R. M. (1967), 'A growth cycle', in C. H. Feinstein (ed.), *Socialism, Capitalism and Economic Growth*, London: Macmillan, 54–58.

Grübler, A. (1990), *The Rise and Decline of Infrastructures: Dynamics of Evolution and Technological Change in Transport*, Heidelberg: Physica-Verlag.

Henkin, G. M., and V. M. Polterovich (1991), 'Schumpeterian dynamics as a non-linear wave theory', *Journal of Mathematical Economics* **20**: 551–90.

Hodgson, G. M. (1993), *Economics and Evolution: Bringing Life Back into Economics*, Cambridge: Polity Press.

Hofbauer, J., and K. Sigmund (1988), *The Theory of Evolution and Dynamical Systems*, Cambridge: Cambridge University Press.

Holland, J. H., and J. H. Miller (1991), 'Artificial adaptive agents in economic theory', *American Economic Review* **81**(2): 363–70.

Horgan, J. (1995), 'From complexity to perplexity', *Scientific American* (June): 74–79.

Houthakker, H. S. (1956), 'The Pareto distribution and the Cobb-Douglas production function in activity analysis', *Review of Economic Studies* **23**: 27–31.

Iwai, K. (1984a), 'Schumpeterian dynamics I: an evolutionary model of innovation and imitation', *Journal of Economic Behavior and Organization* **5**: 159–90.

(1984b), 'Schumpeterian dynamics II: technological progress, firm growth and "Economic Selection"', *Journal of Economic Behavior and Organization* **5**: 321–51.

Jiménez Montaño, M. A., and W. Ebeling (1980), 'A stochastic evolutionary model of technological change', *Collective Phenomena* **3**: 107–14.

Kaldor, N., and J. A. Mirrlees (1962), 'A new model of economic growth', *Review of Economic Studies* **29**: 174–92.

Kandori, M., G. J. Mailath and R. Rob (1993), 'Learning, mutations, and long-run equilibrium in games', *Econometrica* **61**(1): 29–56.

Kwasnicki, W., and H. Kwasnicka (1992), 'Market, innovation, competition: an evolutionary model of industrial dynamics', *Journal of Economic Behavior and Organization* **19**: 343–68.

Lane, D. (1993a), 'Artificial worlds in economics: part I', *Journal of Evolutionary Economics* **3**(2): 89–107.

(1993b), 'Artificial worlds in economics: part II', *Journal of Evolutionary Economics* **3**(3): 177–97.

Langton, C. G. (ed.) (1989), *Artificial Life*, Reading, MA: Addison-Wesley.

Langton, C. G., C. Taylor, J. D. Farmer and S. Rasmussen (eds.) (1992), *Artificial Life II*, Reading, MA: Addison-Wesley.

Lotka, A. J. (1924), *Elements of Mathematical Biology*, reprinted 1956, New York: Dover.

(1945), 'The law of evolution as a maximal principle', *Human Biology* **17**: 167–94.

Maddison, A. (1991), *Dynamic Forces in Capitalist Development: A Long-Run Comparative View*, Oxford: Oxford University Press.

Marchetti, C., and N. Nakicenovic (1979), *The Dynamics of Energy Systems and the Logistic Substitution Model*, Research Report 79–13, International Institute for Applied Systems Analysis, Laxenburg, Austria.

Marshall, A. (1890), *Principles of Economics*, London: Macmillan (8th edn., 1920, London: Macmillan; 9th variorum edn., 1961, London: Macmillan).

McCombie, J. S. L. (1987), 'Does the aggregate production function imply anything about the laws of production? A note on the Simon and Shaikh critiques', *Applied Economics* 19: 1121–36.

Metcalfe, J. S. (1988), *Trade Technology and Evolutionary Change*, mimeo, University of Manchester.

(2001), 'Consumption, preferences and the evolutionary agenda', *Journal of Evolutionary Economics* 11(1): 37–58.

Monod, J. L. (1970), *Le Hasard et la Nécessité*, Paris: Seuil.

Montroll, E. W. (1978), 'Social dynamics and the quantifying of social forces', *Proceedings of the National Academy of Sciences, USA* 75: 4633–37.

Nakicenovic, N. (1987), 'Technological substitution and long waves in the USA', in T. Vasko (ed.), *The Long-Wave Debate*, Berlin: Springer-Verlag, 76–103.

Nelson, R. R. (1995), 'Recent evolutionary theorizing about economic change', *Journal of Economic Literature* 33: 48–90.

Nelson, R. R., and S. G. Winter (1982), *An Evolutionary Theory of Economic Change*, Cambridge, MA: Harvard University Press.

Nelson, R. R., S. G. Winter and H. L. Schuette (1976), 'Technical change in an evolutionary model', *Quarterly Journal of Economics* 90: 90–118.

Nicolis, G., and I. Prigogine (1977), *Self-Organization in Non-Equilibrium Systems*, New York: Wiley-Interscience.

Phelps-Brown, E. H. (1957), 'The meaning of the fitted Cobb-Douglas function', *Quarterly Journal of Economics* 71: 546–60.

Romer, P. M. (1986), 'Increasing returns and long-run growth', *Journal of Political Economy*, 94(5): 1002–37.

Salter, W. E. G. (1960), *Productivity and Technical Change*, Cambridge: Cambridge University Press.

Saviotti, P. P. (2001), 'Variety, growth and demand', *Journal of Evolutionary Economics* 11(1): 119–42.

Schrödinger, E., 1945, *What is Life? The Physical Aspect of the Living Cell*, Cambridge: Cambridge University Press.

Schumpeter, J. A. (1934), *The Theory of Economic Development: An Inquiry into Profits, Capital, Credit, Interest, and the Business Cycle* (translated by R. Opie from the German edition of 1912), Cambridge, MA: Harvard University Press. [Reprinted in 1989 with a new introduction by J. E. Elliott, New Brunswick, NJ: Transaction.]

(1942), *Capitalism, Socialism and Democracy*, New York: Harper & Row.

Schwefel, H. P. (1995), *Evolution and Optimum Seeking*, New York: Wiley.

Shaikh, A. (1974), 'Laws of production and laws of algebra. The humbug production function: a comment', *Review of Economics and Statistics* 56: 115–20.

(1980), 'Laws of production and laws of algebra: humbug II', in E. J. Nell (ed.), *Growth, Profits, and Property: Essays on the Revival of Political Economy*, Cambridge: Cambridge University Press, 80–95.

(1990), 'Humbug production function', in J. Eatwell, M. Milgate and P. Newman (eds.), *The New Palgrave: Capital Theory*, London: Macmillan, 191–94.

Sigmund, K. (1986), 'A survey of replicator equations', in J. L. Casti and A. Karlqvist (eds.), *Complexity, Language and Life: Mathematical Approaches*, Berlin: Springer-Verlag.

Silverberg, G., G. Dosi and L. Orsenigo (1988), 'Innovation, diversity and diffusion: a self-organisation model', *Economic Journal* **393**: 1032–54.

Silverberg, G., and D. Lehnert (1993), 'Long waves and "evolutionary chaos" in a simple Schumpeterian model of embodied technical change', *Structural Change and Economic Dynamics* **4**: 9–37.

(1996), 'Evolutionary chaos: growth fluctuations in a Schumpeterian model of creative destruction', in W. A. Barnett, A. Kirman and M. Salmon (eds.), *Nonlinear Dynamics in Economics*, Cambridge: Cambridge University Press, 45–74.

Silverberg, G., and B. Verspagen (1994a), 'Learning, innovation and economic growth: a long-run model of industrial dynamics', *Industrial and Corporate Change* **3**: 199–223.

(1994b), 'Collective learning, innovation and growth in a boundedly rational, evolutionary world', *Journal of Evolutionary Economics* **4**(3): 207–26.

(1995), 'An evolutionary model of long-term cyclical variations of catching up and falling behind', *Journal of Evolutionary Economics* **5**(3): 209–27.

(1996), 'From the artificial to the endogenous: modelling evolutionary adaptation and economic growth', in E. Helmstädter and M. Perlman (eds.), *Behavorial Norms, Technological Progress and Economic Dynamics: Studies in Schumpeterian Economics*, Ann Arbor, MI: University of Michigan Press, 331–71.

Simon, H. A. (1979), 'On parsimonious explanations of production relations', *Scandinavian Journal of Economics* **81**: 459–74.

Simon, H. A., and F. K. Levy (1963), 'A note on the Cobb–Douglas production function', *Review of Economic Studies* **30**: 93–94.

Solow, R. M. (1957), 'Technical change and the aggregate production function', *Review of Economics and Statistics* **39**: 312–20.

(1960), 'Investment and technical progress', in K. J. Arrow, S. Karlin and P. Suppes (eds.), *Mathematical Methods in the Social Sciences*, Stanford, CA: Stanford University Press, 89–104.

Steindl, J. (1952), *Maturity and Stagnation in American Capitalism*, New York: Monthly Review Press.

Tesfatsion, L. (2002), 'Agent-based computational economics: growing economics from the bottom up', *Artificial Life* **8**: 55–82.

Verspagen, B. (1993), *Uneven Growth between Interdependent Economies: An Evolutionary View on Technology Gaps, Trade and Growth*, Aldershot: Avebury.

(1995), 'Convergence in the world economy: a broad historical overview', *Structural Change and Economic Dynamics* **6**: 143–66.

(2001), 'Evolutionary macroeconomics: a synthesis between neo-Schumpeterian and post-Keynesian lines of thought', *Electronic Journal of Evolutionary Modeling and Economic Dynamics*, http://www.e-jemed.org/1007/index.php.

Winter, S. G. (1984), 'Schumpeterian competition in alternative technological regimes', *Journal of Economic Behavior and Organization* 5: 137–58.

Witt, U. (2001), 'Learning to consume – a theory of wants and the growth of demand', *Journal of Evolutionary Economics* 11(1): 23–36.

Young, H. P. (1993), 'The evolution of conventions', *Econometrica* 61(1): 57–84.

Index of topics

Adaptability
384, 395, 398, 413–15, 450, 453
See also Adaptation. Artificially Adaptive
Agent (AAA). Learning, Adaptive.

Adaptation
13–18, 20, 21, 25, 26, 29, 30, 31, 36, 38,
42, 46, 50, 65, 111, 123, 157, 161, 186,
187, 188, 203, 205, 212, 233, 245, 248,
256–57, 258, 259–84, 290, 291, 294, 298,
299–302, 309, 314, 316, 319, 320, 322,
323, 324, 325, 340, 351, 352, 354, 360,
376, 387, 391–92, 394, 398, 399–400,
404, 413–15, 418, 420, 432, 433, 434,
453–54, 456, 477, 498
See also Adaptability. Artificially Adaptive
Agent (AAA). Imitation. Learning,
Adaptive. Rules, Adaptation of.

Additivity
34, 242, 243, 244, 251
See also Aggregation. Production
Theory.

Adoption
4, 11, 20, 29, 31, 32, 33, 36, 37, 41,
42, 43, 48, 49, 50, 107, 113, 120,
125, 134, 136, 154, 160, 161, 163,
169, 174, 175–83, 187, 197–98, 202,
206, 207, 209, 212, 263, 265, 293,
294, 296–97, 372, 375, 386, 456, 465,
466, 467, 488, 493, 515, 517, 525, 526,
530, 531
• Frequency 44–46, 47–49, 51
• Macroscopic 43–47, 50
• Microscopic 45–46
• Primacy of 43, 47, 50
• Processes 31, 37, 44–47, 176
  See also Processes. Increasing Returns, to
  Adoption. Rules. Technology.

Adverse Selection
247
See also Information. Selection.

Agency
34–40, 121, 122, 256, 257–73, 278, 308,
317, 322, 323, 326
See also Carrier. Entrepreneur. Firm.
Household.

Agent
29–33, 35, 38, 41, 46, 47, 52, 53, 63, 98,
112, 114, 121, 129, 156, 157, 160, 162,
165, 166, 167, 169, 173, 174, 176, 178,
184, 185, 186, 187, 188, 198, 205, 323,
341, 354, 356, 368, 369, 379, 414, 431,
432–33, 435–41, 442, 467, 477, 478, 479,
491, 498, 499, 512, 526, 527, 529
• Representative 28, 41, 314, 421, 479,
  491, 499
  See also Neoclassical Economics.
  Artificially Adaptive Agent (AAA).
  Carrier. Cognition. Entrepreneur.
  Heterogeneity, of Agents.

Aggregation
40, 47, 243, 374, 397, 408, 420, 511,
519
See also Additivity.

Allocation
35, 151, 153, 168, 175, 180, 182, 186,
188, 200, 224, 225, 236, 315, 344, 395,
400
See also Coordination.

Altruism
33, 89–103, 201, 211–12
• (Non-)Reciprocal 33, 35, 91, 92
• Religious 91
See also Behaviour, Altruistic. Biotic
Foundations. Coordination. Docility.
Trust.

Analogy
20, 42, 54, 77, 107, 115, 137, 165, 320,
340, 343, 344, 345, 349, 351, 354, 361,
367, 377, 383, 507, 508, 531

Index of names